‘Reading these diaries brought many wonderful memories flooding back, as well as telling me loads I never knew about the inside workings of *Blue Peter*. A heartfelt, humorous, belter of a read!’
Simon Thomas (1999-2005)

‘This book transported me back to the studio floor, the buzz of live TV and all the behind the scenes gossip. I raced through the diaries in a couple of days and just couldn't put them down. With hilarious honesty Richard made me laugh so much and, in the end, cry too.’
Stuart Miles (1994-1999)

‘After all these years, it’s amazing – and a bit surreal – to get the chance to read chunks from Richard’s diaries. I found it fascinating. It takes you right behind the scenes. Sometimes it’s hilariously funny, sometimes really sad. If you’ve ever wanted to know more about life in TV, the highs and the lows, this is the book for you.’
Gethin Jones (2005-2008)

‘I love the way Rich writes, it’s so compelling and addictive, just makes you want to keep on reading...’
Konnie Huq (1997-2008)

‘Reading the diaries has been enlightening, understanding the trials and tribulations faced when you’re in charge of such a huge brand. Thought provoking as well as funny.’
Ayo (Andy) Akinwolere (2006-2011)

The Blue Peter Diaries

Richard Marson

miwk

The Blue Peter Diaries

First published November 2017 by Miwk Publishing Ltd

Miwk Publishing, 45a Bell Street, Reigate, Surrey RH2 7AQ

ISBN 978-1-908630-30-8

A CIP catalogue record for this book is available from the British Library.

Book design and layout by Robert Hammond
Cover by Colin Brockhurst

Typeset in Utopia and Papercute.

www.miwkpublishing.com
This product was lovingly Miwk made.

CONTENTS

DEDICATION

To Rosy, Kieran and Martha Alice

ACKNOWLEDGEMENTS

It is often said that *Blue Peter* is like a family. Certainly, that is how I feel about many of my former colleagues, a number of whom were aware that I kept a diary during the years we worked together. I hope that publishing them brings back some of the sometimes challenging but frequently wonderful times we shared.

First, I'd like to thank the presenters who spanned my era: Stuart Miles, Katy Hill, Richard Bacon, Konnie Huq, Matt Baker, Simon Thomas, Liz Barker, Zöe Salmon, Gethin Jones and Andy Akinwolere. From earlier years, I also enjoyed working with Mark Curry, Romana d'Annunzio, Peter Duncan, Janet Ellis, Yvette Fielding, Sarah Greene, Diane-Louise Jordan, Tina Heath, Peter Purves, Valerie Singleton and Anita West.

I'd like to record my particular gratitude to Gethin Jones. He has been a true and loyal friend through some dark and challenging times, revealing a loyalty and kindness of which I was only partly aware when we were actually on the programme together.

Biddy Baxter and Edward Barnes have always been hugely supportive, and I'm appreciative, too, of the kindness and comradeship of my other predecessors, Lewis Bronze, Oliver Macfarlane, and Steve Hocking.

Many of our talented and interesting production team became good friends, including Bridget Caldwell, Clemmie Chamberlain, John Comerford, Sarah Courtice, Annie Dixon, Karen Dorling, Amanda Gabbitas, Anne Gilchrist, Melissa Hardinge, Alex Leger, Gilly Longton, Jack Lundie, Kez Margrie, Caroline Morgan-Fletcher, Lucy Morris, Audrey Neil, Gill Shearing, Julian Smith, and Richard Turley.

From the wider BBC and freelance world, I'd like to record my lasting gratitude to some very special and gifted people, among them Nigel Bradley, Hilary Briegel, Bob Broomfield, Duncan Bragg, Chris Capstick, Karen Cohen, Dave Cooke, Sam Diamond, Paul Dobson, Adrian Gooch, Priscilla Hoadley, Adrian Homeshaw, Valery Katsuba, Carmella Milne, Juergen Moors.

From my publishers, Miwk, I'd like to thank Matt West and Robert Hammond, as well as Colin Brockhurst, who designed the cover.

My own family continues to mean most to me; my parents Norma and Peter, my siblings Deb and Geoff, my children Rosy and Rupert, and my wonderful wife Mandy, who deserves her own special badge for all she's done to support me ever since we first met.

A Note On The Text:

The original diaries were all written longhand, often in special books which I bought for the purpose, but sometimes on stray pieces of script or hotel notepaper, during long journeys by plane, train and automobile. Transcribing all this scrawl was a challenge. I'm indebted to those who agreed to read the diaries in draft form and helped to spot any of the howlers which crept in during the editing process. Throughout, I've tried to make it clear who is who, and to provide necessary context or explanation where I think it essential, but otherwise the body of the text is as it was written, usually each evening, frequently at the expense of some much-needed sleep.

WHO'S WHO AT A GLANCE

Akinwolere, Andy
Blue Peter presenter 2006-2011

Bacon, Richard
Blue Peter presenter 1997-1998

Baker, Matt
Blue Peter presenter 1999-2006

Barker, Liz
Blue Peter presenter 2000-2006

Barnes, Edward
Blue Peter producer 1962-1969
Deputy Head of Children's Programmes 1970-1978
Head of Children's Programmes 1978-1986

Baxter, Biddy
Blue Peter producer 1962-1965
Blue Peter Editor 1965-1988

Bradley, Clare
Blue Peter gardener 1991-2000

Bronze, Lewis
Blue Peter producer 1982-1983
Blue Peter Assistant Editor 1983-1988
Blue Peter Editor 1988-1996

Caldwell, Bridget
Blue Peter Assistant Producer 1991-1996
Blue Peter producer 1996-1999
Blue Peter series producer 1999-2001
Blue Peter producer/director 2004-2007

Cohen, Karen
Blue Peter make-up designer 1995-2007

Collins, Chris
Blue Peter gardener 2003-2013

Comerford, John
Blue Peter assistant producer 1987-1989
Blue Peter producer 1989-1994
Blue Peter Deputy Editor 1996-1999

Cooke, Dave
Blue Peter musical director 1980-2007

Cragg, Marina
Blue Peter animal handler 1999-2011

Curry, Mark
Blue Peter presenter 1986-1989

D'Annunzio, Romana
Blue Peter presenter 1996-1998

Deverell, Richard
Controller of CBBC 2006-2009

Dixon, Anne
Blue Peter secretary 1975-1985

Blue Peter researcher 1985-1988
Blue Peter assistant producer 1988-2000
Blue Peter producer 2000-2007

Duncan, Peter
Blue Peter presenter 1980-1984, 1985-1986

Ellis, Janet
Blue Peter presenter 1983-1987

Fielding, Yvette
Blue Peter presenter 1987-1992

Gabbitas, Amanda (Gabby)
Blue Peter producer 1998-2000
Head of CBBC Creates (development) 2000-2005
Channel Executive, CBBC and CBeebies 2005-2006
Head of Creativity and Audiences 2006-2008

Gilchrist, Anne
Blue Peter producer 1998
Head of CBBC Entertainment 2004-2005
Executive Editor of Independents and Events, CBBC 2005-2006
Creative Director, CBBC 2006-2009

Goodchild, Marc
Blue Peter assistant producer 1994-1997
Blue Peter producer 1997-1998

Greene, Sarah
Blue Peter presenter 1980-1983

Harwood, Barney
CBBC presenter 2002-2010
Blue Peter presenter 2011-2017

Heath, Tina
Blue Peter presenter 1979-1980

Heggessy, Lorraine
Head of Children's Programmes 1997-1999

Hill, Katy
Blue Peter presenter 1995-2000

Hocking, Steve
Blue Peter Editor 1999-2003

Home, Anna
Head of Children's Programmes 1986-1997

Huq, Konnie
Blue Peter presenter 1997-2008

Inglis, Joe
Blue Peter vet 1998-2002

Jones, Gethin
Blue Peter presenter 2005-2008

Jordan, Diane-Louise
Blue Peter presenter 1990-1996

Judd, Lesley
Blue Peter presenter 1972-1979

Leger, Alex
Blue Peter assistant producer 1975-1980
Blue Peter producer 1980-2011

Leslie, John
Blue Peter presenter 1989-1994

Macfarlane, Oliver
Blue Peter producer 1987-1995
Blue Peter Assistant Editor 1995-1996
Blue Peter Editor 1996-1999

Miles, Stuart
Blue Peter presenter 1994-1999

Noakes, John
Blue Peter presenter 1965-1978

Pickard, Nigel
Controller of CBBC 2000-2002

Pocock, Leonie
Blue Peter animal handler 1986-2011

Prior, Dorothy (Dot)
Controller of CBBC 2003-2005

Purves, Peter
Blue Peter presenter 1967-1978

Sharman, Alison
Controller of CBBC 2005

Shearing, Gill
Blue Peter correspondence unit and makes creator 1986-2008, 2010-2011

Singleton, Valerie
Blue Peter presenter 1962-1972

Thomas, Simon
Blue Peter presenter 1999-2005

West, Anita
Blue Peter presenter 1962

PREFACE

I was born into a *Blue Peter* family. That is to say that I, my brother and sister, were all part of the generation that watched the programme religiously during what is often called its 'golden' era.

In some respects, this reflects the fact that there were then only three channels, so not much in the way of competition. But it goes deeper than this. *Blue Peter*'s values were *our* values, too, and quite familiar to us from our own upbringing; reflecting an interest in getting your hands dirty and making things, in exploration, new inventions, a love of history and stories, the urge to do good works and to try new hobbies and past times. Like most children, we were definitely 'square' rather than cool, and we were certainly not streetwise.

In 1972, when I was six, there was a family outing to the National Cat Club show in Olympia, where we hoped to enter our handsome moggy Tiger in the *Blue Peter* classes. It wasn't to be (my mother hadn't filled in the right forms) but I did get the chance to meet Lesley Judd at the *Blue Peter* stand, and obtain an autographed photo (years later, I put this on display in my office).

My brother, sister and I also jointly entered one of the programme's competitions and were all awarded badges (I still have that thrilling letter in its utility brown BBC envelope). Mine, alas, was unwisely taken to school, to be shown off, against parental advice, where it was quickly lost or stolen.

I never tried to win another, but I did continue to watch fairly regularly most

Mondays and Thursdays. On June 30th, my 1977 diary contains the following entry: "Last programme of *Blue Peter*. Petra is retiring after appearing in 1,192 programmes."

My interest finally dwindled about the time I went away to school in 1979, when it was no longer possible to watch much in the way of television. And that might have been that. But then, in the spring of 1983, when I should have been revising for my mock A-levels, I found a cosy displacement activity, idling in front of children's TV again, armed with a bowl of cereal. Comfort eating and comfort viewing, I suppose.

One day I happened to see a *Blue Peter* which went into loving behind-the-scenes detail about Janet Ellis, the foxy new presenter's first day. I was captivated by this film, and the way it distilled the obvious thrill of working on a live programme which also filmed all over the world; it was a genuine epiphany. I decided pretty much there and then that I wanted to join the show and be its Editor. Such a cool title, too; more like a newspaper or magazine, and fitting given that my previous ambition had been journalism.

Several times over the next few years I was able to visit Television Centre, and actually watch *Blue Peter* rehearse and transmit from the studio. This only stoked my excitement and determination to work on the programme.

I eventually joined the BBC in 1987, and this marked my first professional encounter with the show, in the humblest of positions, a floor assistant (or, as they are these days known, runner). *Blue Peter* was just one of the many shows on which one might be allocated, and, sad to say, it was not a hugely popular booking among my colleagues; the production team were generally too grumpy and full of themselves. I was once roundly scolded for having been seen at lunch in the BBC canteen with Yvette Fielding, one of the presenters. I was more or less told that this wasn't my place. Certainly, any hope that I nurtured that this most junior of positions might prove a gateway into achieving my ultimate dream was soon shattered. They didn't want to know.

But I persevered and finally, in 1992, I was sent to the children's department on attachment as a Trainee Assistant Producer. Despite the title, this meant that you worked chiefly as a director, both on location and in the studio. It was a perfectly wonderful and utterly immersive training. I loved it and didn't look back, continuing to work as a director, both within the BBC and, as a freelance, beyond it.

Towards the end of 1994, there was a vacancy for a studio producer on *Blue Peter*. I applied, even though by now it would mean a sizeable drop in salary. I was invited for a 'board' in the recently refurbished office of the Head of Children's Programmes, the formidable Anna Home. I wasn't daunted by the toughness of the questions, indeed I was overflowing with enthusiasm and passion. As I got into my stride, I felt it must be going well. Unfortunately in my enthusiastic gesticulations, I sent a tall pot of coffee flying. Evil-smelling black liquid sprayed all over Anna's brand-new carpet. I looked at the devastation in horror. "Shall I just go now?", I said, in a weak attempt at relieving the tension. Anna's eyes bored into me.

"Not yet" was her curt response.

Meanwhile the *Blue Peter* Editor Lewis Bronze dashed out to the nearby kitchen to get tissues for an impromptu clear-up. But the coffee cataclysm had ruined the moment and the rest of the interview was stilted. I wasn't surprised to hear that I hadn't been successful, "on this occasion", to use the BBC's parlance.

It wasn't until 1997, when I returned to the children's department to direct a series of *Record Breakers,* that another opportunity presented itself.

And that's where this book begins.

1997

14th May 1997

Blue Peter have advertised a short-term contract or, for staff only, an attachment, as a studio producer. John Comerford, my old chum from children's entertainment, who is now the Deputy Editor on *Blue Peter,* calls and encourages me to apply. But I know how these things so often work and I'm not so sure. The department have to be *seen* to go through a supposedly 'open' process but very often the outcome is predetermined. In this case, the obvious stand-out candidate is Marc Goodchild, who has been working on the show as an assistant producer for the past couple of years, occasionally directing films and studios. He's been very successful and is popular in the team. I know all this because Marc is a mate. In fact, I employed him as an assistant producer myself when I was producing at Disney – so I know how good he is.

I share my misgivings with John who agrees that Marc is a strong contender but he is adamant that I must put myself forward and give Oliver, the Editor, a chance to see what I can offer. He adds that he has already put in a good word as he knows how much I'd like to do it and thinks that I'd be ideal. So after all that, I am going to apply and give it everything I possibly can.

Who am I kidding? I would have done this anyway, of course.

5th June 1997

The day of my interview board for the producer job on *Blue Peter*. I'm faced with Anna Home, the head of department, Oliver Macfarlane, the Editor of the show, and Jennifer Hardwick, the personnel manager for children's. They are all pretty relaxed and, on the surface at any rate, friendly, but the process is just as thorough and searching as I expected. There was a lot of written 'homework' to complete beforehand and this is all put forensically to the test. I had to furnish them with a detailed running order or breakdown for a special programme to commemorate the forthcoming Enid Blyton centenary. Also, a running order for a complete studio programme. Then a written report on a suggested item about a drugs awareness campaign. It is well-known within the department that Anna is no great fan of *Blue Peter* – she grudgingly admits its value in the schedules – but such was the mutual distaste between her and Biddy that it is always said that she made her return to the department as its head conditional on being able to, as it was related to me, "get rid of that woman."

Oliver is courteous, friendly, and relaxed; much less aggressive than his predecessor, Lewis Bronze (I shudder to recall the board I endured with him three years ago), with a soothing voice in the manner of a Radio 4 announcer and a chuckle rather than a laugh. As I talk through my written work, I can feel myself warming up and shedding doubt. I reject the idea that the drugs awareness item was a good fit for *Blue Peter* ("that's what you've got *Newsround* for") and talking about my core principles for the show; that it was presenter-led for a reason. "For every generation of kids, these people should be their heroes – we need to fuel that, give the presenters every possible opportunity to shine." I've watched the show avidly, so I'm able to back up my prejudices and views with plenty of specific examples. I could see that all this was going down well. The board seemed to fly past and then, when I felt there was still plenty left to say, there were the usual mutual courtesies and I was out of the room. I knew I had done my best and been on form. I went back to the *Record Breakers* office, took off my tie and tried to get on with my day.

I was still in the office when Jennifer Hardwick called me a few hours later. She came straight to the point. "We were all very impressed with the amount of work that you obviously put into your application, and by the passion you showed for the job, but I'm sorry to say that you haven't been successful. We decided it was only fair to give the opportunity to someone already on the programme, who, probably, we otherwise would lose. I know Oliver would like to talk to you, too, but I hope you understand."

No, I bloody didn't. I was absolutely raging. I realised I should have been quietly dignified and followed the usual protocol for these rejections, but my irritation and disappointment got the better of me and I just went into a full on rant.

"Everybody said this is *exactly* what would happen. Of course I understand that you want to promote a deserving candidate from within but then why not just do that? Why do you always feel as if you have to have some sort of process? I know you think it makes it look fairer and more open but everybody *knows*. As soon as it was announced, people told me, 'Don't bother applying, Marc is going to get it.' Do you know how dispiriting that is? Especially when you are asking for us to do so much work beforehand? If it had just been a chat, fair enough – but you hold up all the hoops and it's just a farce. Totally wrong. And I feel really angry and stupid that I fell for it."

There was a pause at the other end of the line. Then Jennifer said, "Actually, I do understand all of that and I wanted to tell you that you have been found 'also suitable.'"

"What does that mean?," I countered, already feeling embarrassed about my outburst.

"Exactly what it says. It means we all felt you could do the job and would be just as equipped as the other candidate. And if another opportunity occurs within the next six months, we can offer you the job without further interview. As I say, Oliver would really like to talk to you...."

When I track him down, Oliver is charm itself – very complimentary and honest about the difficult situation in which he found himself. "You know Marc," he said. "He really has earned his moment. But you did very well indeed. I know it's not a definite promise and that, in any case, you may not be free, but I wanted you to know that should we need another producer in the next few months, I'd like to give you first refusal."

After I hang up, I consider the prospects glumly. Producers on *Blue Peter* don't tend to move around that often. And I'd have to be in the department to be eligible. I am only on *Record Breakers* until October. What they'd said was better than nothing but in the words of my grandmother, "fine words butter no parsnips..."

2nd December 1997

A typical day at Teddington, directing *Tomorrow's World*. First the crack of dawn nightmare of actually getting there. Then the sheer amount of stuff to get through (we record two shows in one day). A big plus are the presenters. Peter Snow, impossibly charming, a true eccentric, and a genuine enthusiast – and the beautiful and highly intelligent Philippa Forrester, whom I know so well from our time on Disney (or Mouse-shwitz, as it was known to almost everyone working there).

The Editor, Saul Nassé, draws me to one side for a quiet word. He's a bit concerned about what Philippa is wearing and asks if I might tactfully address this. I look over to where Philippa is toying with a styrofoam cup of coffee and passing the time with Peter. She is wearing a very short leather skirt and a pair of black suede over-the-knee thigh boots. She looks fabulous, and I say as much to Saul.

"Yes, yes," he sighs, "but I'm worried it distracts rather from the seriousness of the content."

Back in the first stages of planning for this series, Saul had told me that he had cast Peter and Philippa as a riff on *Doctor Who*, of which he is a big fan, with Peter as a kind of Doctor figure and Philippa as his clever and foxy companion. Philippa and I had had great fun discussing how she might dress to impress a BBC1 audience with a higher than average quota of males. This was the catalyst for exactly the kind of clothes she was now wearing. She had started slightly more conservatively and, each week, pushed her luck a little more. "Here comes the science slut", I'd tease, as she emerged from her dressing-room in the latest slinky number.

It is never an easy conversation asking a female presenter to change and, although she understands and complies, Philippa clearly isn't overjoyed. The other tension in the air is generated by the jittery presence of the Deputy Editor who, judging by her manic contributions to the planning meetings, is a bit of a fruit cake. She now turns out to be a lot of a fruit cake.

We have just started to rehearse a complicated set up using a steadicam when she screeches that we must stop right now.

"What is it?" I demand, rather irritably.

"The anglepoises on the desks," she splutters.

"What about them?" I ask her.

"Do you think the colours are right? Won't they be a distraction?"

Adopting a soothing but hopefully authoritative tone, I say, "Absolutely not. They are fine. If the audience are looking at the colour of the anglepoises in the back of this very lovely shot, then something is very wrong with the content, don't you agree?"

My apparent certainty seems to help and, after a piercing look, she nods and we continue. But she is like this all day, throwing up tiresome and irrelevant objections for which we can ill afford the time.

We just about finish on schedule and then I discover my car won't start. Gloomily, I face the prospect of waiting in a freezing Teddington car park until the AA turn up – but then Peter Snow bounds to the rescue, arms waving.

"I'm sure it won't be anything serious," he exclaims and, taking off his coat and jacket, and rolling up his sleeves, he gets stuck into the engine. Twenty minutes later I'm on the road, feeling slightly guilty that Peter is now covered in oil, though he seems perfectly cheerful about it.

As soon as I arrive home, my wife tells me that Oliver Macfarlane has called and left a message – could I call him back please? On the spot, my stomach performs a series of flip-flops. I snatch the scribbled number and call. After the necessary pleasantries ("come on, come on," I'm thinking) Oliver begins.
"Do you remember our conversation back in the summer? Well, now we are looking for another producer and I wonder if you might still be free and interested?"
It takes less than ten seconds to say "Yes" and "when do I start?"
I ring off and race upstairs three steps at a time, to find Mandy trying to put the kids to bed. She better than anyone knows what this news means to me, and our joy and excitement transmits to the kids too, so that in seconds we are all whooping and jumping up and down in the sheer euphoria of the moment.

3rd December 1997

Have to tell Saul that I'm declining his kind offer of a year's contract on *Tomorrow's World* (including a lengthy foreign filming trip) to join *Blue Peter* for six months instead. He is not so much annoyed as utterly baffled. "But why would you do that? I'm offering you a much longer contract and we are a BBC1 prime time show, whereas *Blue Peter* is, well, it's a great show, but it's for children...."
I explain that it's been my dream job for years and that I have to take this chance now that it has arisen. He is nice about it, but I don't think he can begin to understand what it means to me.

10th December 1997

My first contract arrives. It is to run from 19th December to 30th June 1998. I'm to do a bit of trailing before Christmas and start proper in the New Year. My excitement is now accompanied by a sudden onrush of nerves. Will I be up to it? Will it be what I'm expecting? One way or the other, I'm impatient to start and find out.

21st December 1997

The pre-record for the Christmas programme. I'm here to watch how it all comes together and meet as many of the team as possible. As it is pretty much all hands on deck, it's a good day to start. The whole experience is completely weird, especially as this particular show – running order and script more or less unchanged from year to year – is like a distillation of the magic of *Blue Peter*. Everyone (other than the coolly appraising PA, who makes it clear that she thinks I'm surplus to requirements on this busy day) greets me with apparent enthusiasm and Stuart Miles, the most senior of the presenters, even gives me a (no doubt hastily scrawled) Christmas card of welcome. This is the team's last day before the Christmas break so there is a sense of holiday and fun, as well as the hard work and adrenalin of actually getting such a big and demanding show recorded. I am excited but overwhelmingly daunted too.

1998

5th January 1998

My first official day in the office. Such is my state of nervous anticipation, I arrive far too early and have to kill time in one of the tea bars, though I can't face anything to eat or drink. About half 8, I make my way up to the 5th floor of the East Tower and, peering through the porthole in the office door, notice that Annie Dixon is the only person there, bustling about a bank of desks in the middle of the room, watering the plants. Annie has been on *Blue Peter* since the mid-70s, and spent years as Biddy Baxter's secretary before eventually becoming a researcher, and now a senior assistant producer. Back in the days when I was regularly floor assisting *Blue Peter*, she took a fairly dim view of me; she'd wink and smile but her manner was frosty. This morning she is polite but brisk. I like that. No fake bonhomie. If I'm going to be accepted by her, or by any of the others who have been on the show for years, I'm going to have to earn my place at the table.

I'm allocated my predecessor's desk. I investigate the drawers and among the usual detritus of discarded pens and gummed up rolls of sellotape, find a heap of condom packets shoved right to the back. These make sense when my assistant producer tells me in hushed tones that this predecessor is currently locked in the throes of a passionate affair with his PA – and shock! horror! – she happens to be married with a small child. News of my discovery of the condom haul is quickly spread (not by me) and in this very female-dominated environment, I note much disapproval expressed about the PA who has left her child to move in with the producer. The producer is largely regarded as blameless, being younger, boyish and charming. The inference is that she seduced him; the Mata Hari of the 5th floor.

I have a brief meeting with Oliver, who tells me that he wants me to produce the next run of garden items with Clare Bradley, who has been the resident gardener since 1992. Around me, I notice a few barely suppressed smirks as Oliver suggests a minimum of six slots between now and June; the garden, it transpires, is seen as a poisoned chalice. A lot of hard work for items which are popular with almost no one; production team or audience. Still, I like a challenge.

As a studio producer, I am one of a team of four; as well as myself, there is an experienced assistant producer who doubles as studio director (Sarah), and two slightly less experienced APs (Tanya and Nadia) who will work up the items we need to fill every week's running order. We have a dedicated production assistant (indeed, we've got the one locked in her torrid affair with my predecessor) and access to the services of a small Forward Planning team. Films are provided by the film team and scheduled by their overall producer (Bridget) and the Deputy Editor, John. I am slightly crestfallen to discover that studio producers have no say in this process; you just have to work with what is allocated to you. I have a look at the draft schedules for Wednesdays over the weeks to come and I'm not inspired by the sound of films on the subject of Sunday school and an Oxfam fashion challenge (whatever that might be).

6th January 1998

Spent the day 'trailing' my predecessor in the studio pre-recording tomorrow's transmission. The pattern at the moment is that Monday and Friday's programmes are live and the Wednesday show (which, from next week, I take over) is pre-recorded on the Tuesday, as live. This saves a bit of money but, as a result, the Wednesday shows are regarded as the runt of the litter; Mondays being the prestige start of the week slot, in which all the major new competitions and long-running items launch, with Fridays as 'feel good' entertainment-heavy shows, all froth and fun. The holy grail for most of the team, as they all want to be in on the 'cool' stuff.

I have quickly noticed what a divide there is in the production team, between the old guard – producers who have been here for years and who are quite happy churning out the worthy stuff everyone expects from *Blue Peter*, and the younger set, who all aspire to lead a revolution from within, to make the show modern and 'cool'. This is apparent in everything from the way they dress (baggy cargo or combat pants for both sexes, T-shirts with 'ironic' logos or messages, and fleeces) their grumbles about anything 'trad' and their attempts to 'funk up' the style of the programme. This approach has the wholesale approval of the presenters, who would all like *Blue Peter* to be as cool and street cred as *Live and Kicking*. Leader of the pack is undoubtedly Katy, and as Queen Bee, she is vocal with her opinions. Anything which seems to her old-fashioned or twee is loudly denounced as "Very jolly!" If she feels an item might compromise the presenters' image, she declares that it is "eggy" or "oogie" and will leave her with "oeuf sur la visage!" Another of her favourite catchphrases is "Jambon!" or 'ham' (usually a reference to someone's performance) and if she thinks anything is a little bit near the knuckle or OTT, she'll exclaim, "Easy Tiger!" Stuart is a total pro and needs minimal direction, Richard has huge likeability and puppyish enthusiasm, Konnie is bright-eyed and keen to make her mark, but Katy is the star – and she knows it. Perhaps because he was there first and no one could fail to respect his professionalism, Katy is thick as thieves with Stuart. She treats Richard (whom she refers to as "Bacon") just as she might a slightly annoying younger brother, slapping him down when he becomes a bit too familiar (which is often). Konnie is largely ignored or slightly patronised. Like me, she is yet to prove herself. To me, they are all very friendly and I take it as a compliment that Katy is already calling me "Marson" or sometimes "Marsupial".

There's too much to do to stand around on the sidelines and, throughout the day, I make various editorial contributions so that the decision is taken to credit me as today's co-producer. John, the Deputy Editor, leans over to me in the gallery and whispers, "Well done! From floor assistant to producer in one leap – not bad!" Countering this is the remark that Annie Dixon has reportedly made to one of the producers, which naturally they have taken great delight in quoting back to me: "He's just a jumped-up fucking floor assistant!"

8th January 1998

I want to do an item in next week's programme (my first in sole charge) tied in with an exhibition about the work of the famous jeweller Cartier. I take this to Oliver, who says, "If you can get them to bring anything worth seeing into the studio, fine...." though he quite plainly doubts that they'll agree to co-operate. I contact Cartier and an hour or so later, with one of the APs in tow, take a black cab to meet their PR, who is so posh as to be beyond parody. I mimic her plumminess in the hope that the PR princess will be fooled into thinking we are kindred spirits. The knack is scarcely to open your mouth as you speak. I sounded like an impressionist attempting Prince Charles. No matter – we come away in triumph as agreement is reached for Cartier to bring a priceless selection of fabulous gems to the studio. We agree to arrange security and to pre-record the item in the morning so that the precious items need only be on the premises for the briefest possible spell. Return to the office and can't wait to show off my mini-coup to Oliver, who seems relatively impressed.

13th January 1998

Katy and Konnie both have an early make-up and costume call for this morning's Cartier item. The joy of this show is that it has so many resources; and I plan to make full use of them. I'd briefed the costume and make-up designer that I wanted Katy to appear in the guise of Lillie Langtry, Edward VII's famously beautiful mistress, so that we can smother her with an array of Cartier's most extravagant Edwardian jewels, including a magnificently OTT tiara. Konnie, meanwhile, will be styled on the lines of another royal mistress, Wallis Simpson, as mannequin for a display of priceless art deco gems. I, too, arrive in make-up early, expecting both girls to be over the moon at the chance to model so much extravagant finery. 'Diamonds are a girl's best friend', right? Not a bit of it. As I walk through the door, I am greeted with an accusing cry from Katy; "Is that you, Marson! What is going on?! A ginger wig and a fat suit? Is there any need? I am NOT impressed; hardly the best way to start!"

I have to admit that the result is not quite what I anticipated. In true BBC style, both designers have done their research and what was considered fetching at the turn of the century sadly doesn't suit Katy. The offending wig is indeed a shade of ginger (though not luridly so), heavily curled, its bouffant shape less than complimentary as a crown to Katy's round face. She has been corseted into an ornate silk evening gown of the period, but Katy's own look, a kind of chic contemporary 'Amazon', cannot be said to suit a dress with a huge bustle and which makes her shoulders seem so American football-broad. To rub salt in the wound, by contrast, Konnie appears slight and svelte in her shimmery 30s cocktail gown, her hair sleek on her head, the geometric jewels she is modelling much less fussy and ornate than Katy's sparklers. She doesn't let me forget my offence, and it's an object lesson in making sure that if you're going to dress up your star, it pays to be sure that it's going to make them look and feel good.

Richard finds my fashion *faux-pas* hilarious, whispering bitchily: "You could fit me *and* Konnie in that tent that Katy's wearing..."

20th January 1998

An exhausting but brilliant day in the studio. A couple of weeks ago, I went to the press preview of James Cameron's new *Titanic* film. Word on the street was that it was going to be an almighty disaster and the mood in the preview theatre was accordingly hostile. I was next to a miserable cow from the *Daily Mail* who told me cheerfully how she was looking forward to tearing it to pieces. But a couple of hours later she was crying her eyes out and the mood around us was very different indeed.

Ever since I was a child, I've been deeply fascinated by the Titanic tragedy and I'm determined to go to town on it, using the film as a tie-in. The first problem is persuading Oliver that we should feature a certificate 12 film. I get round him by stressing how we will be focused on the real-life story and that, even if some of our audience won't be allowed to see the film itself, they will scarcely miss the media hype, on which we can provide some relevant context. He buys this argument and the full *Blue Peter* machine swings into action. We are able to source some items which were actually rescued from the wreck or brought off the sinking ship by survivors. We have booked a string quartet to play 'Nearer My God to Thee', reputedly the last tune played by the Titanic's band before the great liner sank.

Carefully, I script a detailed dramatic recreation of the story, to be pre-recorded in the morning, with Stuart, Richard and Konnie all in costume. Best of all, we manage to trace one of the last British survivors of the tragedy; an old lady called Millvina Dean, living in Southampton. When I speak to her on the phone, she seems frail and uncertain about whether she can face the journey to London to appear on the programme. Without stopping to check with anyone, I offer to hire a car to fetch her and take her back, putting her up overnight in London so that the whole trip won't have to be done in a day. She agrees to this impromptu plan and then I have to face the wrath of Leah, the programme's production exec, in charge of the budget. This show is already soaring over budget, she tells me, as if I didn't know, with the set and costume costs, the hire of the band, transport and insurance for the artefacts and now these additional expenses for our guest of honour. I make suitably apologetic noises, but, having had her say, she now supports my ambition, merely warning me that I'll have to do some cheap shows in the next few weeks to balance the books.

As the show comes together, I'm bothered that, on the same date, Forward Planning have scheduled a pop performance. The etiquette is that I'm supposed to feel pleased – everyone generally wants pop in their shows – and as a rule they are strictly rationed and kept for Fridays. But I suspect this one has only come my way because it's so obviously a lame duck which isn't going to go anywhere. The group are called Pure Gossip, their song, *Pride.*

"You gotta have pride, pride...don't be ashamed, our love is the same...," drones the chorus.

It's obviously intended to be some kind of stomping gay anthem but it sounds like a weak disco parody. I try to get it dropped, arguing that it is utterly out of kilter with the rest of the show but this outrages the Forward Planning producer, whom Oliver backs. He says that I've got to remember that *Blue Peter* is a magazine programme and that it's my job to navigate the light and shade between very different items. No, really?

The morning is fraught, the recording over-runs, which means that the edit is also up against it to try to have the insert ready for our 'run-through' at around 4. But when we finally reach this point, I can see that Oliver is impressed with the scale of the show, and the performances of the presenters. On the run-through, Richard handles the interview with Millvina Dean brilliantly. It is genuinely moving, especially when she confesses that she won't watch the film. Even though she knows that it is fiction, she can't rid herself of the thought that her father went down on the ship. For her, it isn't just a story.

From this supremely poignant interview, we have to segue into the ghastly unwanted pop act and, to make matters worse, the vocals are live and the lead singer can't sing. As a real musician himself, Oliver looks pained and I again press him to drop the band. But it turns out they have been booked in one of those 'you scratch our back, we scratch your back' deals with a record company – a kind of horse-trading arrangement – and I'm told we can't.

The 'as live' recording doesn't go quite as well as the run-through – Richard is less in control of the interview – but it's still a programme of which I feel proud.

22nd January 1998

Team meeting. This is a bit like a *Blue Peter* version of a school assembly, with notices and points of information – though, thankfully, no hymn. It also offers a chance to review the last week's output. I've quickly noticed how it is here that the competition between the three programme teams plays out – as well as certain personal rivalries – and so the atmosphere is rather mean-spirited and begrudging. However, the Titanic show – with the exception of the pop disaster – is extravagantly praised by one and all and now I can sense that people in the office are treating me for the first time both as one of them, and, more importantly, as a producer.

3rd February 1998

My only studio with Romana (known as Roma to the other presenters) and I really enjoy the experience. There is a long and complicated item about the suffragettes. I've given her the bulk of this and she does it very well indeed. She's sweet and obviously intelligent but somewhat reserved. I'm curious as to why it hasn't worked out for her. If they are free, all the producers attend each other's run-throughs (as the programme dress rehearsal is called) – the idea being we all help to pitch in with supposedly helpful notes and suggestions before the

Editor gives his final notes, cuts and changes. Romana has been off over Christmas appearing in panto (a ruse to get her out of the way, so I gather, to cover the awkwardness after she was told that her contract wasn't to be renewed) and since she has returned, I've noticed a real hostility to her. Any item in which she is involved is inevitably followed by a flurry of critical comments.
"Silly cow can't even hold the card straight..."
There is an unpleasant bitchiness about her appearance too. "Fuck me sideways – what *is* she wearing this time? Jesus Christ!"
The other presenters seem to like her though. "No threat, that's why," says one of my fellow producers, cynically.
Casting Romana was the final act of Oliver's predecessor, Lewis Bronze. Apparently, Oliver (and most of the production team) favoured the other contender, Gail Porter. So I suppose that, from the off, Romana was on a hiding to nothing. She leaves next week.

10th March 1998
This morning we record the second of the garden items I've been told to champion. They are bloody hard work. The *Blue Peter* garden genuinely seems to have its own weather system – several degrees colder than anywhere else. For this reason alone, the presenters moan. Also the recording takes most of the morning, leaving us short on rehearsal for the rest of the show, while the editing runs right up to transmission (or recording) which is another stress.
Today's item was worth the aggro. I had seen an article about a snow-making machine and invited the company to demonstrate its prowess in the garden; the effects were magnificent and there's something about the audaciousness of a winter white-out on an otherwise balmy March day that lifts everyone's spirits.
Oliver is pleased. He can sometimes give the feeling of going through the motions, booking items because they are standard parts of the *Blue Peter* mix, rather than because he truly believes in them. For instance, he's told me I've got to do a 'religious round-up' in the show nearest Easter.
"A religious round-up? What's that?," I query. He spells it out.
"Tick all the boxes, mention what all the faiths get up to at this time of year, so none of the buggers can complain."
If you make the effort and go to town (as with the Titanic show, or today, with the snow-covered garden), Oliver is clearly a little surprised but generally appreciative.

16th March 1998
Take a hire car and, in the early afternoon, leave Television Centre and drive to

the Luton Hoo estate in Bedfordshire, to select some artefacts which once belonged to the last Tsar of Russia and his family. These were smuggled out of Russia during the revolution by the tutor to the Tsar's children. They ended up here as one of the Luton Hoo chatelaines was a Romanov relative. I'm planning another lavish historical recreation (if at first you succeed...), this time as a tie-in to a major new kids' animation, *Anastasia*.

We'll tell the gruesome story of the imprisonment and murder of the Tsar and his family and, as with the Titanic, I'm keen to have some actual objects closely connected to the real-life drama in the studio. There's something about these talismans of history that really helps convey the story's significance and poignancy, hopefully firing the imagination of the audience. I can vividly remember visiting Luton Hoo as a child, when it was still open to the public. It has had a sad history of late. Oppressed by the responsibility of running such a vast pile, and beset with mounting debts, the last owner took his own life. Ever since, the house has been shut and shrouded, awaiting sale.

But *Blue Peter* is an extraordinary 'door opener'; as soon as I contacted the Trustees, and explained what I was after, they were keen to help. An appointment was made for me to present myself at the house to inspect which items I might like to borrow.

It is a bitterly cold, wet and foggy day, and the whole place has a forlorn atmosphere. Even from a distance, it is obvious that the stucco of the buildings has seen better days and work is urgently needed if it isn't to deteriorate further. I park and make my way to a side entrance, where I ring the bell. There is a distant clanging sound, reminiscent of a bad 1970s horror film. Eventually, the door opens and a neatly dressed middle-aged lady ushers me inside. She is some kind of housekeeper, I suppose, and she leads me slowly through a maze of dim corridors and shuttered and dust-sheeted rooms until we reach a vast chamber. This is empty except for a Louis Quinze chair, what looks like a battered kitchen table on which is a stack of cardboard boxes and carrier bags. In these are the items I seek.

"Just have a look through, take your time, and choose which ones you'd like to borrow," says my hostess, before leaving me to my task. There are watercolours by the Tsar's children, and some of their school exercise books. They spoke and wrote English and in one of them I register an essay about Mary, Queen of Scots and the tragedy of her execution. Such irony. I am most taken with a little brass bell, which belonged to the Tsar's son and heir, Tsarevich Alexei. Alexei had haemophilia and when confined to bed with an attack, he used the bell to summon help or company. I make my selection and wait to discuss the arrangements for transporting them to and from the studio. But the housekeeper shrugs this off, producing a couple of large carrier bags, and saying

that I should just take them now, myself, so long as I sign for them and return them the day after the recording.
Carefully, I take my historic haul back to the car and place them gently on the passenger seat. I drive home in a state of some tension, only too aware that the contents of these bags are all priceless and irreplaceable. Arriving home, I show them to my wife, who pronounces them all "creepy", and then put them safely away in a high cupboard out of reach of the kids. I can just see Rupert loving that little bell and I'm tempted to show it to him, and let him play with it a while, linking him to another boy in another time.

19th March 1998
Start of a two-day shoot for my very first BP film, telling the story of the 'Flying Duchess' of Woburn Abbey. When I joined, as well as produce studios, I asked if I might make a film or two, and it was made clear that this was entirely possible, so long as I fit the work in around my existing commitments. After I'd submitted the script, Oliver had summoned me and said, "This is a bit of an epic – reminds me of the old *Blue Peter Special Assignments.*"
I basked in what I thought was a compliment and then he continued, "What I mean is that it's very long!"
Now here I am actually making it and only slightly put out by the fact that Konnie, with whom I am sharing a car, and who is on full-beam charm, clearly hasn't read a word of the 15-page script, never mind made any attempt to memorise her sizeable number of pieces to camera. This is a worry.
At Woburn, we are supervised by a very pleasant and easy-going woman called Cheryl, but not before we have received a lecture on the correct etiquette for filming in the great house from its curator, a lantern-jawed martinet called Lavinia, who truly resembles a live-action Cruella de Vil. Only the fur coat and cigarette holder are missing. Lavinia and Cruella seem to share a manner too.
"If it were up to me, there would be NO film crews on the premises," she barks. "Film crews cause disruption. They are a RISK. In my considered opinion, film crews are More Trouble Than They Are Worth."
As the leader of my small team, I bow and scrape and make oleaginous noises until the old tartar nods grimly and leaves us to get on with it.
"She's a funny one, Lavinia, but she means well," said Cheryl, attempting to restore the previous harmony.
Everything goes well until we reach the sequences to be shot in the Flying Duchess room itself, which is small by the standards of this stately place. In high Victorian style, it is crowded with a mountain of clutter and souvenirs pertinent to the great aviatrix. The proximity of all this irreplaceable tat makes me nervous, especially as our camera assistant is 6 ft 4 tall and doesn't exactly have

the grace of a ballet dancer. Good for hefting the heavy camera and lighting equipment but a fish out of water inside a place like this. I suggest to John, the cameraman, that the assistant stay outside while we complete this section. But it is too late. There is an ear-splitting crash. We both spin round to see the camera assistant, his face a mask of horror, standing in the middle of a small pile of porcelain shards. I feel violently sick. For a few moments, nobody says anything.

Then Cheryl speaks, in a voice of utter resignation. "I'll have to fetch Lavinia."

A kind of awful limbo follows while we wait, not daring to move, frozen wherever we had been standing when catastrophe had struck. "I'm really, really sorry," whispers the camera assistant. "Do you want me to leave?"

"I think we're all going to be leaving any minute now," I tell him.

With one sweeping glance, Lavinia takes in the devastation and her contempt is undisguised and triumphant, too. We have so comprehensively proved the dim view she takes of all film crews.

"Her Grace will have to be informed," she tells us, and there is another torturous wait until the Duchess of Bedford herself appears, Lavinia at her elbow like a sergeant-major. The Duchess, wearing pearls and a padded gilet, coolly appraises the damage and demands to know "Who's in charge?"

Meekly, I step forward, expecting to be told that it's all over and she wants us to leave. Instead, she is curt and to the point.

"You're in luck. It's insured."

We are allowed to continue the filming, on condition that, for the rest of the shoot, the culprit is banished to the crew van. I think he is relieved. I am euphoric, Konnie amused. Only Lavinia has the face of a hunter deprived of its kill.

31st March 1998

Pre-record. One aspect of the show I'm finding rather tiresome is the insistence on what's a called a 'peg' (i.e. something from which to hang an item) – very often an anniversary or a new exhibition. It's supposed to impart a sense of topicality, but some of the 'pegs' are so artificial and random, it rarely feels genuinely newsy or relevant.

It also means that sometimes, when you just want to do an item for the sheer fun of it, you have a fight on your hands. Today, however, I've got my peg – it is 40 years since Paddington was first published – and I've invited his creator, Michael Bond, to the studio. He doesn't know that we intend to award him a gold badge for all the enjoyment he's given children over the years. He's a lovely man, now rather frail and seemingly a little shy. He started writing his stories while still working as a studio cameraman for the BBC. This was how the series of

Paddington stories he wrote for the *Blue Peter* annuals came about; Biddy knew him as one of the regular crew and asked him to contribute.
"You didn't say no to Biddy," he remarks.

8th April 1998
Filming the story of Elizabeth I at Hatfield House. Konnie is playing Elizabeth I but I've given her far fewer lines, having learnt my lesson from the agony of watching her fluff take after take during the two-day Flying Duchess shoot. She is lazy, but bright, so the best approach is to keep the scripted stuff short and let her improvise as much as you can. She loves this and comes alive.
I've given myself a cameo as Elizabeth's tutor which means having my face gummed up with a fake beard and moustache.
It is not a good look.

19th April 1998
I'm spending my Sunday in a freezing cold waiting room at King's Cross and I've only myself to blame.
It didn't take long for Oliver to realise that I'm a *Blue Peter* anorak. He's blatantly amazed that anyone adult should be so interested in the programme but agrees to my suggestion – for which I am to be paid an additional fee – that now we live in an era of computers, we (or rather I) should create a searchable database of all past editions, detailing dates, people involved and whether or not the edition survives in the BBC film library (very many do, thanks to Biddy insisting on keeping a comprehensive archive when all around her were happily signing wiping and junking orders).
He has also offered my services as a consultant to the BBC2 *Blue Peter* theme night proposed to celebrate the 40th anniversary later this year. Naturally, I'm enthusiastic, and have made a start compiling lists of possible clips. And now this. Oliver has asked if I'll give up my Sunday to look after two old presenters – John Noakes and Valerie Singleton – who have been booked to greet the arrival of the locomotive 532 Blue Peter at King's Cross. The current team have been accompanying the loco on a special 40th anniversary journey from Edinburgh.
"Should be right up your street," he smiles. "All you have to do is keep them amused until the train shows up."
This being TV, the call times are on the safe side, which means that I have at least a couple of hours in a cheerless little waiting room, valiantly trying to keep these two BP legends fed, watered and passably entertained. Val is no problem – she hasn't forgotten that I once went to the trouble of compiling a tape of all her favourite dressing-up items and she waxes lyrical about these. "I remember being at Versailles, dressed up as Queen Marie Antoinette. During the lunch

break, I wandered off by myself."
"Typical of you," observes Noakes.
Val ignores this and continues. "I was in the gardens of the Petit Trianon, which is supposed to be haunted by the Queen. A group of tourists spotted me and were convinced that they'd seen a ghost."
Noakes is polite enough but essentially morose. He has only been here a few minutes before he starts to tell me what a nightmare Biddy was and how much he hated her guts.
"Bloody awful woman," he says. "Should have been drowned at birth."

21st April 1998
An item for today's show falls through at the last minute. But Oliver isn't too concerned.
"If in doubt, wash the dogs," he tells me.
Apparently, this is one of the classic, never-fail, stand-by *Blue Peter* items. And he's right, it works an absolute treat. Who would have thought you could extract six minutes of highly entertaining telly from dunking a pair of dozy mongrels in a couple of tin baths, and watching them get inexpertly laundered by a trio of presenters all pretending they are having a great time while secretly hating every minute (water and stray soapsuds playing havoc with dress, hair and dignity)?

23rd April 1998
Recce to the Royal Military Academy, Sandhurst. It's an austerely beautiful place, rather like a cross between a stately home and a boarding school, set in acres of parkland. Mindful of the formality of the place, I'm wearing my best suit and tie and nicely shiny shoes. In consequence, from the moment I park my hire car on some vast parade ground, everywhere I go, I am smartly saluted by any passing cadet. Have to fight the impulse to demonstrate good manners by saluting back.
My guide and host is a semi-retired Major so blimpish in manner as to be beyond parody. He wears a suit, with a cavalry tie, a 'British warm' overcoat, and a bowler hat. His shoes, bulled to guardsman standards, put my efforts to shame. The Major holds 'traditional' views. As we tour the training ground, he confides, "Course we'd like more coloured chaps but the problem is as soon as there's a nip in the air, they simply keel over. Just can't take cold temperatures, you see."
He is equally forthright on the subject of women in the army. "You'll always get a few; daughters of army men in the main, making up for their fathers' natural disappointment at not having a boy. Then there are the lesbians, of course."
He looks at me as if to say everyone knows there is nothing to be done about

them. It dawns on him that perhaps that I might not be entirely sympathetic to his views, and he briskly demands. "You're not one of those pinko *Guardian* types, are you? Had one of them last week, making a dreadful fuss about so-called bullying."
I ask him whether recent press reports on this subject are therefore not to be believed.
"This is the army," he says, exasperated, as though to a fool. "If you can't take mental and physical pressure, you're in the wrong job. In my day, an officer cadet who made a nuisance of himself was woken up in the night, frogmarched outside and tied naked over one of those cannons with a feather up his arse. Nowadays, there'd be a terrible fuss. But it was only horseplay. A little rough justice."
We walk a terrific distance, taking in accommodation blocks, class rooms, gymnasiums, parade grounds, and a beautiful high Victorian chapel. Outside I am shown various training areas and while negotiating a muddy slope in one of these, the Major suddenly loses his footing, and slides all the way down. He brushes off my attempts to help him up.
"Bloody nuisance," he grumbles. "Will have to change for luncheon."
I suggest I have seen everything I need to and could just leave, but he is insistent that I stay. While he disappears to sort himself out, I am deposited in the officers' mess, where I'm served a gin and tonic of eye-watering strength. Everyone is courteous to a fault but the formality and etiquette only reinforce what a closed community this is, and that I am very much an outsider. My host rejoins me, in a fresh suit of identical cut and colour. The decor and atmosphere is that of an old-school gentleman's club. We sit at a long, highly polished mahogany table, and are served a proper three-course lunch with wine. Pudding is fresh strawberries, which the officers sitting around me all liberally coat with pepper. This habit is new to me, and I wonder if it's not a wind-up for the chap from the BBC, but I try it and find the result not unpleasant.

28th April 1998
Elizabethan-themed programme which includes my Hatfield House epic. Design have built some impressive Tudor sets in the studio, and we have a 'consort' of musicians to play the music which would have been popular at the court of Elizabeth I.
Throughout the day, constant cries of "Very jolly!" from Katy who is unimpressed to be laced into an elaborate Elizabethan gown and faced with the challenge of cooking 'apple snow' (a 16th-century treat you can supposedly still enjoy today) without trailing the long sleeves of her dress in the meringue mix. It's quite a skill.

5th May 1998

Pleasing postcard from ex-Editor Lewis Bronze, which says: "Congratulations on your Elizabeth programme which I thought was a *tour de force* in the best traditions of BP. It inspired us to visit Hatfield on the Bank Holiday (with our badges, of course!)"

Have also had a hilariously offensive letter from a viewer about the same programme, objecting to Konnie playing the young Queen.

"It may have escaped your notice, but when I last checked, Elizabeth I wasn't black."

I compose a reply, pointing out that the audience will have been well aware that it is a *Blue Peter* tradition for the presenters to dress up as famous figures from history and that perhaps it is just as well this viewer missed the show a few years back when Diane-Louise Jordan – a black woman – played King Henry VIII.

13th May 1998

Back at Sandhurst, filming with Richard. He's doing brilliantly and he's got the officers and NCOs eating out of his hands. From my point of view, he has a natural ability to extract the humour from the essentially ludicrous situations in which I've placed him. This elevates the sequences from standard *Blue Peter* action heroics to something even more entertaining. My particular favourites so far; having accomplished a quick-change task, Richard is looking childishly pleased with himself, when the NCO barks at him:

"Don't smile at me, I'm not your best mate!"

Cut to Richard looking crestfallen.

And, later, his studiously courteous response when ordered to shave off his sideburns.

"Colour sergeant, with the greatest possible respect...."

"GET THEM OFF, MR BACON!"

Comedy gold.

14th May 1998

Oliver has offered me a year-long contract to pick up from my current one, which expires at the end of next month. He wants me to take over this year's summer expedition to Mexico, which was originally to have been produced by my predecessor. However, office unrest (i.e. epic bitching) about this man's torrid affair with his PA (also scheduled to do the trip) means that Oliver has decided to intervene. My predecessor has been moved sideways, but the love-struck PA is to stay on the project. This isn't very helpful as, although it obviously isn't my fault, she seems to think that I am somehow implicated in her and her beloved's rather public humiliation. Every task (and when setting up a foreign filming trip of this scale, there are many) is accompanied by pointed silences or heavy sighs, and only haphazard results. I speak at length about this to the Assistant Producer who is on the trip with me and will be directing some of the films. She is concerned too.

18th May 1998

Have to deal with a virtual mutiny from the presenters who have all taken violently against today's studio director. It's true that he's been knocking around the department for years and that, while he can certainly do the job from a technical point of view, he can't be bothered to schmooze the talent. They find themselves infuriated by the more than slightly patronising instructions he issues in his dry Scots tones. I do my best to mediate – urging more charm from the gallery, more tolerance from the turns.

"They're such a bunch of children," says the director. "Why is such a battle to get them out of make-up to do their job and rehearse?"

"He's a total cunt," Richard tells me, vehemently, unbending. I remind him that he has worked for a "cunt" before – he often uses this word to describe his former boss at Live TV, the outspoken Kelvin Mackenzie.

"Yeah," counters Richard, "but Kelvin is a *talented* cunt," and he jabs his finger in the direction of the gallery, "whereas he's just a cunt..."

19th May 1998

Lorraine Heggessy, the head of department, saw yesterday's show and, ever since, has been raving about the Sandhurst film.

Oliver tells me that as her attempts to get a children's docu-soap off the ground have so far failed, her latest idea is that *Blue Peter* should make one for her. No presenters involved. Literally just bolting our titles onto the front of whatever docu-soap she wants to make. This, perhaps, to replace the frothy Friday edition for a few weeks. I ask Oliver what he thinks of this and he looks exasperated.

"She can fuck off," he says. "I didn't tell her that, of course. I've said we'll think about it and look into it. Then hopefully she'll fixate on something else and forget about it."

Inertia. A classic BBC initiative.

26th May 1998

Final day of Sandhurst filming; various leadership tests and a raft-building exercise. Richard gets stuck in. When we come to film him sliding down a vertiginous zip wire over a lake, I want a 'POV' (point of view) shot. A camera is rigged onto his helmet. Trouble is that this will look ugly in the wide shot, so the answer is for me to follow Richard, wearing the helmet cam myself. Much better than your average theme park ride, and no queuing.

3rd June 1998

Fly to Mexico with Linda Ross, the AP, for a two week recce to sort everything we need for the month it's going to take to filming the expedition. Linda is bright, funny and great company. We land in Mexico City and are met by our fixer, Sean, a 40-something hippy type, who has somehow fetched up here and whose job, as the title implies, is to smooth our path at every turn. He has shaggy hair, a beard and huge sweat patches under each arm. Despite his unpromising appearance, he's very friendly.

Mexico City is a dump. The pollution is so bad that my eyes stream as though I've been chopping onions, and everywhere there are hordes of little kids begging. I see be-suited Mexican businessmen literally kicking them out of the way. Their callousness disgusts me.

4th June 1998

We are on the hunt for a story about horses (major industry here) so we set off early in the minibus hired to ferry us about and are on the road for a couple of hours until we finally arrive at a hacienda/ranch in what seems to be the middle of nowhere. It reminds me of the fort in *Beau Geste.*

As we approach along a bumpy dirt track, Sean chooses this moment to tell us that our host is the area's biggest drug dealer (as if that's no big deal at all) – that he lavishes some of his wealth on horses, and has a young son who is an insanely talented rider. Which is why we are here. Our eyes take in the armed guards and the assortment of savage-looking dogs growling in cages by the main gates.

Inside, it is an utterly bizarre place. The hacienda is bigger than it looks; and we are escorted through room after room, each crammed with a series of bizarre collections – clapped-out old cookers are piled up in one room, gramophone players and records in another, ancient TV's and radios, pianos (the type that play themselves via a punched paper roller) and all manner of incongruous bric-à-brac.

Our host is friendly but intimidating – he wants us to admire everything and oh how we do. He is dressed from top to toe like the genuine cowboy I suppose he is (when not dealing drugs) from the Stetson to the spurs, in a dazzling white suit with huge wraparound shades cutting off any glimpse of his eyes. He has the most enormous drooping 'gringo' moustache. If I had to guess I'd say he was at least 60. The girl introduced as his wife, on the other hand, was disturbingly young – she had braces and spots and a manner that's pathetically keen to please.

A small retinue of staff – all equally young women dolled up like hostesses from a 1970s edition of *Sale of the Century* – troop around with us until we reach an ornate saloon bar, just like a set from a period Western. The staff scurry around offering us tequila or beer but we insist we are just fine with Coke (the legal variety, that is). The bar stools are high up and the seats are actually old saddles. Clambering onto these is slightly undignified. We sit around on our creaking perches, sipping our soft drinks while our host (and Sean the fixer) knock back a quick succession of tequilas. I'm beginning to wonder where the hell the horses are.

Refreshment at an end, we continue the tour – more piles of junk – and then a room that we smell before we enter. From floor to ceiling, it is full of tiny birds in what looked like incubators. Lining the walls above and around these are macabre displays of a variety of stuffed birds. It has a kind of Salvador Dali chic, but it is gruesome. Around the walls are tubs of feed which, when you look closely, are a writhing mass of beetles and worms. We fight our gag reflexes, and finally emerge outside in kind of miniature zoo, with a collection of exotic but lethargic caged animals. They are mangy and miserable in the stultifying heat. I enquire about the horses and I'm told that we should come back on Saturday to see them. We've been here for what seems like hours but by now I am past caring and only want to get out of this disturbing place. But instead we are ushered into an ornately mirrored dining-room, where, to my horror, I see that an enormous feast has been laid out. There is nothing for it but to sit down, grin and swallow it.

We are offered a "local speciality" to drink – cactus juice. I don't ask if the dead flies swimming in the bottom of the cloudy liquid are part of the recipe. The *Sale of the Century* girls begin to uncover a series of silver dishes, revealing a cornucopia of edible horrors; whitebait in an evil-smelling sauce, deep-fried beetles, cubes of some potent sweaty white cheese, and a large dish of ants' eggs in syrup.

As we sit down, and speaking from the side of his mouth like a ventriloquist, Sean hisses, "you must try a little of everything or you will cause great offence." I'm furious to be so hijacked but we do as we are told. I feel something hot and heavy land on my sandalled feet. I look under the table to find an enormous dog staring back up at me. Gently, I try to free my feet from his furry bulk, but the animal bares his teeth and issues a low warning growl so I think better of it and give up.

5th June 1998

The reward for taking part in yesterday's feast is my first violent attack of Montezuma's revenge. By the time I crawl into the bus, I feel like living death and when we arrive at our destination, the site of some extraordinary ancient Aztec monuments, it is all I can do to stagger about a bit, indicate a temple or two, mutter, "Yes, this'll do," before the next wave of intense nausea rolls in and I have to rush off to deal with it as best I can.

8th June 1998

Recce cardboard city, a few miles out of Mexico City itself. You smell it before you see it and we have to bring an armed guard with us because apparently we would last about five minutes here without. We are accompanied by a rep from a British charity which tries to engage with the endemic problem of street children, many of them abandoned or orphaned. To say the conditions are Dickensian is a cliché and, also, an understatement. It is a foul place, teeming with humanity, livestock and flies. It stinks worse than anywhere I've ever been in my life.

We visit a mother living in one room with her 11 children, sharing an inadequate water pump with about a dozen other families in the same jerry-built hovel. Despite the appalling circumstances in which she is forced to live, she has great dignity and welcomes us warmly – but her situation and prospects are hopeless. The children are beautiful, bright-eyed – shy but curious. The stories we hear from the charity woman are designed to shock, and they do so – but nothing can match the impact of being surrounded by all this concentrated poverty and deprivation. We leave for a six-hour journey to the jungle and, after this morning, none of us utters a word of complaint about the uncomfortable conditions. After what we have just witnessed, the baking hot breeze from the open car windows feels like heaven.

10th June 1998

Explore the Mayan site at Chichen Itza. The place is swarming with morbidly obese Americans. You have to admire them, though. Despite the heat and their excess baggage, they are absolutely determined to stagger their way to the top of the temple and take in the view (nothing to see, actually, just miles of monotonous lush green jungle). It is the getting down again which seems to present the bigger problem. I hear one woman bellowing to her mountainous friend, "Ahm just gonna do what everyone else is doin' and slide right down on my fanny!"

She lowers herself onto her monumental backside and begins to descend, one arse cheek at a time, and I wonder how long these ancient monuments will withstand the daily assault from the collective butts of tourist America.

13th June 1998

I'm battling unexpectedly severe homesickness. The days are OK – there is so much to do and there is relentless travelling between locations – but when we finally stop and I'm able to call home, it hits me hard right in the solar plexus. Today I get to the end of my chat with the children and then Rupert (who is only 4) says, "Don't go yet, Daddy." I am floored with misery and blinded by tears. But I have to get off the line as ahead we have another four-hour bus drive. In this country, it's a case of safety last – the bus has no seatbelts of any kind and every Mexican we encounter drives like a total lunatic. No wonder everyone crosses themselves all the time.

15th June 1998

Some of the meals served in hotels here defy description. The breakfast we are offered this morning resembles an autopsy from *Prime Suspect.*

"I know visual effects designers who'd charge £500 to come up with that," I mutter to Linda.

We both do without.

17th June 1998

Return flight to the UK. We are both exhausted – in fact, Linda is ill and I'm worried about her and whether she will be able to do the trip at all. I haven't taken to Mexico at all; but there is more than enough to make the range of films we need.

21st June 1998

Go through the Mexico plan with Oliver and John, the deputy. They are happy with everything except my insistence on a change of PA – I point out that in places the recce was thoroughly chaotic because she simply hadn't done her job properly. Mentally, she checked out when my predecessor was shifted sideways. But she is a strong personality, always ready to speak her mind and clearly neither Oliver nor John relishes the prospect of breaking the news. But, in the end, they agree that she is no longer a safe pair of hands and she is given the boot. To my delight, the programme's most experienced PA, Lucy, agrees to replace her. Nothing gets past Lucy. Sometimes she can be a little schoolmarmy but she cares deeply about the work and you know you're in absolutely safe hands. She is the queen of detail. Her 'at a glance' schedules are thicker than the latest Jackie Collins, and full of essential information. Lucy is precisely who we need.

Meanwhile, in my absence, my old friend Marc Goodchild has created ructions by taking Konnie to one side and suggesting that her voice is too harsh and mono-tonal, and that perhaps she might benefit from some kind of elocution lessons? She is furious, told him that was a bit rich "coming from someone who can't pronounce his Rs properly" and went straight to Oliver, who has now reprimanded Marc for his tactlessness. The office are hugely enjoying the general fall-out and drama. Those who don't think much of Konnie side with Marc, saying that he's only put into words what many feel and Oliver should have addressed ages ago. Those who think Marc is a bumptious upstart (and, last year, he committed the cardinal sin of petitioning Oliver to audition as a *presenter*) are enjoying his (relative) humiliation. Marc, who is leaving anyway, is unrepentant. Katy, meanwhile, remarks that Konnie can clearly wind Oliver round her little finger, so watch out world.

The PA whom we were forced to replace proved the office gossips wrong by making a lasting go of her relationship with my predecessor.

29th June 1998

Appraisal with Oliver, a business-like affair as he has a stack of these to wade through before he can enjoy his summer break. "It was clear from the beginning," he has written on the form, "that Richard understood the task in hand. He is very good at nurturing his team and pushing the envelope of what can be achieved in a studio."

Try to look suitably humble. The form contains a grid listing various key qualities producers are supposed to demonstrate ("decision making", "resilience", "creativity" and so on) and, rather like a teacher, Oliver has to mark these with a tick next to the letter he feels is appropriate ("E = exceptional performance", "G = good performance/performs well", A = attention needs to be given to this" and "P = progressing appropriately"). I come a cropper only in the section marked 'business awareness', for which I am given a P. I am not unduly heartbroken.

Oliver scribbles down a set of objectives, muttering, "go on a course or two, that's never a bad thing," looks up, smiles, asks me if I'm happy to sign the form, and we are done.

30th June 1998

To White City for the 'series debrief'. Some interesting facts emerge. During the last series, the programme has continued to feature regularly in the children's top ten, and to achieve figures of around 4.5 million. But there is fear for the future as competition increases, and budgets are squeezed.

For me, the most interesting part of the debate is about the audience; to whom we are aiming the show. *Blue Peter* is seen very much as a family programme. John says that the remit is to keep the figures high; Anne Gilchrist (one of the producers) says that Controllers are only interested in the overall viewing figure and don't care about the child audience. But Oliver is clear; our primary function

is to look after the 5-15 year olds. I float the idea for a 'badge squad'; a strand featuring kids reporting on the attractions they have visited free using the badges they have won.
Oliver raises Lorraine's point about whether the fact that *Blue Peter* started in 1958 is a good selling-point in the year 2000. However, this doesn't set much of a cat among the pigeons because he also informs us that we are the only children's programme so far re-commissioned for 1999/2000 "so we must be doing something right".

6th July 1998
Fly to Mexico for the summer expedition. The trip is divided so that we start with Stuart and Konnie, with Katy and Richard joining half way through, so that there is a brief overlap with all four presenters, and then the final fortnight is just Katy and Richard.
The schedule is brutal; we have 13 internal flights over the course of the month as well as countless hours of driving. On the way out, Stuart manages to get himself and Konnie upgraded to first class, and keeps bringing the plebs, i.e. myself and the crew, little 'care packages' in the form of glasses of Bucks fizz or a plate of scones and cream.
"I know economy sucks," he purrs, "but perhaps these will take the taste away!"
When we finally arrive in Mexico City, all is steamy chaos. We have 36 bags between us and inevitably some go AWOL. This is predictable but wearisome and it is a couple of hours before we can escape the seedy airport.

7th July 1998
Driving through Chihuahua (like the dogs), actually in the middle of nowhere, when the chorus of demands for the loo begins. Eventually, Sean, our fixer, spies a kind of roadside ranch house on the horizon and we stop. The toilet facilities have to be seen to be believed. We are directed to the back of this wooden shanty and there, lurking beneath a thick black cloud formed of thousands of flies, is a vast open pit, full almost to the brim with human excrement. The stench is beyond description.
Stretching across this vat of sewage is a wide wooden plank. Through the medium of mime, it is made clear that those needing to relieve themselves should 'walk the plank', squat and get on with it. I decline; but others are too desperate for relief to follow my squeamish example.
I return to the car to wait and, when everyone reconvenes, they inform me that the shack housed just one washbasin but this was without soap or running water. Fortunately, we have some wet wipes.
Steve, our Geordie sound recordist, seems quite unaffected by the experience.

He actually announces that "having made some room", he is hungry and buys a beef and cheese taco from the little stall at the front of the shack. When he clambers back inside the vehicle, everyone protests as the smell seeping from the taco is almost as pungent as the open-air toilet.
"You'll be in trouble later," I warn him.
But he is undeterred and quickly wolfs it down.
"I'm from Newcastle," he grins. "Stomach of steel, me."

8th July 1998
I nearly died today. No, seriously. We'd hired a local helicopter company so that we could shoot all the aerials I wanted for the film I'm making about the Copper Canyon. This is very similar to the North America's Grand Canyon and back in London I argued (successfully) that expensive helicopter coverage was essential to capture its scale and majesty.
The pilot is a middle-aged man with skin baked mahogany by the sun, a lurid Vegas baseball cap and plenty of gold jewellery. He boasts that he's done lots of filming and generally seems very full of himself; "Guys, I'm gonna give ya the ride of ya lives...so come on, let's do this thing, people!"
Paul, our cameraman, is going to sit on one side of the copter, actually hanging out of the gap, though secured with a special harness. My job, in the passenger seat, is simply to act as a counterweight. Paul is a natural worrier and just as we are ready to get started, I see him standing off to one side, dragging hard one of his endless tabs. I walk over and ask if he was OK.
"I'm fucking bricking it," he replies. "I don't want to fucking die chasing some pretties in the middle of the Mexican desert."
I do my best to reassure him, though I have my own butterflies to contend with. To allow for the weight of the camera equipment, the helicopter has been stripped of any extraneous weight and so is completely see-through. I'm not exactly scared of heights but I have a healthy respect for them and, as we take off, sitting perched on a tiny plastic seat with just a thin transparent layer between myself and the yawning chasms below, I experience revolutions in the pit of my stomach.
We are wearing head sets which, when the pilot isn't talking, he switches to a tape of 1950s rock 'n' roll classics – just the type of music that sets my teeth on edge. We have a perfect day for flying, or so he tells us, with a hard blue sky against mountainous scenery in every shade of green. We work our way through the sequences on my shot list and I begin to relax and think that this aerial photography was no great hardship, and actually rather glamorous. Eventually, we reach a fabulously beautiful waterfall, cascading right down the Canyon, and the pilot interrupts a chorus of "Peggy Sue" to suggest that he can attempt a 360

degree shot flying round the back of the waterfall, and then position the helicopter in a static hover for a final dramatic wide-shot. Sensing a BAFTA at my fingertips, I immediately agree. Paul, however, is reluctant. We hadn't discussed this. It isn't on the list. But, in the end, he says we should give it a go if we want to. We rehearse a first pass, which is OK, but rather too wobbly.
"OK guys, here we go again," says the pilot – and this time everything seemed to work perfectly, until the very last moment, when we arrive in the static hover which is Paul's cue to capture his final magnificent wide-shot. We remain static for just a few seconds and then the helicopter begins to shake and judder, listing to one side, with an appalling whining noise from the rotors above us. I can hear Paul swearing at the top of his voice and the pilot comes over comms to announce, somewhat unnecessarily, "Guys, we got a problem here."
I can see his hands wrestling with the controls, his face twisted in concentration. At that moment, I think "This is the end."
I wonder if it will hurt and feel fury at my own stupidity, which led to this disaster, and I think how the tune now playing through our headsets is suddenly grimly appropriate. "That'll Be The Day...that I die..."
Then, all of a sudden, the helicopter seems to right itself, drop sharply by several metres, and instead of juddering and pitching around, we are again flying away on a smooth straight course. "Sorry, guys, that was a close one..."
When we reach our landing area, there is brief, tense post-mortem. The pilot explains that we hit some thermals, caused by the different temperatures running through the extreme depth of the canyon. It was flying between these which so nearly made him lose control. Paul had a rant but I was just quietly grateful to be alive and back on solid ground, with the sweet prospect of seeing my family restored to me again.

9th July 1998
Everyone laughed at me for packing tea bags and Marmite; now they all want some, so supplies are going to run out fast. Send fax to London to instruct Katy and Richard to bring fresh supplies when they join us.

10th July 1998
An entire day mule trekking into the Canyon, with vertiginous drops just centimetres from the track on which we are plodding. When I finally clamber off my mule after about 8 hours, my thighs are red raw and I can scarcely walk. I've forgotten my own hat, and Stuart saves me from sun stroke by lending me his spare.
All day the heat has been ferocious and Paul has become increasingly testy as I keep insisting that we stop to get the passing shots and GV's (general views) that

I know we will need in the edit. He grumbles under his breath and relieves his feelings by slapping the kit about. In fact, we all get a bit peaky under the sun – except Konnie, whose laid-back temperament and general indolence is well suited to the 'manana' attitude of the Mexicans. I tell her that if we can harness her 'kooky' sense of humour, she could be *Blue Peter*'s version of Mary Tyler Moore. She has, of course, no idea to whom I'm referring.

11th July 1998

Today we take a steam train through the Canyon. We've hired our own carriage, which is just as well as the rest of the train is heaving with peasants, who come laden with baskets of live chickens and other produce. Their part of the train consequently stinks to high heaven. Stuart much amused whenever I whip out my lavender travel gel, which, on this trip, is often. He has his own cosmetic essentials, notably a tube of some potent lotion which he regularly applies underneath each eye. This obviously works, as he never seems to have any visible bags or dark shadows. I enquire what it is.

"Pile cream," he reveals, with a knowing wink.

As the day wears on, there are long intervals between sporadic filming. We eat, sleep, listen to music and gossip. On a trip like this everyone bonds and shares confidences, although Stuart says that in his experience (this is his fifth), the summer expedition usually feels like a mobile prison sentence. Konnie goes for a wander and 'rescues' the only other English passenger on the train, a very good-looking 19-year-old Etonian called Will. He stays with us for the rest of the trip and both Stuart and Konnie flirt outrageously with him.

As night falls it is still stiflingly hot and so we all clamber to the engine car right at front of the train (this is like something from a Hitchcock film, as it involves negotiating a series of metal platforms and ladders alongside and between each moving carriage), clinging on to the inadequate guard rail and relishing the sensation of the cool wind in our hair and, above us, the sight of the incredible starlight sky.

13th July 1998

Linda, who is supposed to be sharing the directing, arrives from the UK. But she hasn't been well since the recce (hence her delayed arrival) and all her bags have been lost in transit. So that's a good start for her.

14th July 1998

Three hour drive to film in a ghost town called Real de Catorce. At one point en route, our bus is speeding along at over 100 mph when suddenly there is a ear-shattering explosion and it veers out of control. Everyone is shrieking with fear.

By skill or miracle, our driver just avoids pitching us off the road and into the desert either side, and manages to slow down and stop. We emerge, shaking, from the vehicle. Turns out the rear tyre has blown – there isn't a shred of it left. Given the speed at which we were being driven, aware of what a lucky escape we have had, everyone is slightly hysterical. Linda, who is still unwell, is also nursing a wound picked up when she brushed into a vicious cactus earlier.

15th July 1998

We turn up to film in an abandoned silver mine. It is very big and very dark. We have three small lights in our kit, plus one that plugs into the front of the camera (and drains the battery fast). Paul lights up his customary fag and growls, "How the fuck do you expect me to light this?"

Annoyed by his attitude, I tell him to stop behaving like an overgrown kid, sulking and stamping his feet at every obstacle and problem, and to do the best job he can like the pro that he is. He calms down, apologises and surprises himself (and me) with the results, which are excellent and highly effective.

17th July 1998

Stuart and I stay up late in the hotel bar, drinking Baileys like a pair of teenage girls, talking our heads off. He is reading a book about the myth of romantic love. He keeps asking me what everyone on the production team thinks of him. I've hedged until now but tonight I admit that many of them are confused by his routinely euphemistic attitude to his sexuality. Nobody sees the problem in him being openly gay. But the sad truth is that when he was auditioning for *Blue Peter*, the Editor at the time kept asking in loaded tones whether he had a girlfriend. This understandably gave Stuart the impression that it wasn't acceptable to be a gay presenter on *Blue Peter* (though he would hardly have been the first). It didn't help that Stuart auditioned at the same time as Tim Vincent – who was given the job first. Stuart was only offered his place on the team six months later. He says that, for the first few months, he felt that the show was crushing his personality. It was only when Katy arrived that he found someone he could bond with.

When Richard joined the show, there was an instant connection. Richard naturally looks up to Stuart, admiring his professionalism and effervescent personality (Richard often refers to Stuart as 'L.E.D.', short for 'light emitting diode', because, as he puts it, "Stuart lights up a room"). But Stuart's feelings for Richard go deeper still. As he talks, it seems both difficult, and yet also a relief, for Stuart to give voice to his emotions.

"I've never told anyone," he admits, his voice dropping almost to a whisper. "You can imagine why."

I can. It's clear that what he's talking about is much more than physical attraction, though that, of course, is part of it. Richard has beguiled him completely. And, like anyone in love, at first Stuart sought any sign that Richard might reciprocate his feelings. Such was the mutual affection and admiration between them that, for a long time, he sustained these hopes.
"It must make things really difficult for you," I suggest, somewhat inadequately.
"It's complicated," he admits.
I ask him what he loves most about Richard. He thinks about this for a long time and then he says, simply.
"When he's around, he just makes everything better."

19th July 1998
Konnie has spent the last two days filming a report on the street children of Mexico, with Linda directing. Tonight I've arranged to meet Konnie in her hotel room, as I want to go through the script for tomorrow's shoot at the temples of Teotihuacan. We are being allowed to film there from sunrise until opening time which gives us a couple of hours without hordes of Oompa Loompa tourists spoiling the shots and slowing things down. I've been burnt by Konnie's lack of preparation before so the meeting is my attempt to maximise my chances of filming something better than a hesitant memory test of her various pieces-to-camera.
We go through the pages, though what Konnie really wants to do is bitch Linda; criticising her script for being too worthy and wordy, and her direction for being too rigid and unimaginative. "She just kept shooting interviews with kids, most of which will be cut, and that meant there was no time for much real interaction with them."
Later, I catch up with Linda, who is equally critical of Konnie. "She was only interested in bonding with the really cute kids. If they were over six, she just glazed over. She's got the attention span of a small child herself...."

20th July 1998
Trying morning at the temples of Teotihuacan. It all looked great but Konnie did not deliver. In fact, she really wound me up. She requires so much direction and, at times, you simply can't devote all your attention to the presenter – you have to think about shots and the schedule and so on – and they need to take some responsibility for their own performance. Not Konnie. She learns each piece just before we are ready to shoot it, so that the first few takes are really on-camera line rehearsals. Then, if you're lucky, some sort of performance will begin to emerge. If you're not, you're left with a piece which has been delivered, in so far as the words are there, but meaning and expression are not. It is deeply

frustrating, especially as I know that she is more than capable.
She struggles to deal with notes, too, always interpreting them as personal ("It's not my fault...") rather than professional. Linda spoke to me later and said that she watched me using every trick in the book to coax a performance out of Konnie, only for her to fail to deliver, take after take.
"At this rate," she remarks, "she's going to be doing lots of beach clean-ups and garden festivals..."
Flight to Acapulco, where we met up with Katy, Richard and Deputy Editor John, who wanted to pop over for the jolly. I told him if he was coming he'd have to bloody well direct something and give me a day off!
We all have dinner by the beach. Richard is being very serious; told me earnestly that, on the flight over, he had read and liked all the scripts. He is a puzzle at times. Quite insecure, I think. He can be very charming and sweet, and then bolshie and quite irrationally argumentative. When you argue back, he gets hurt and resentful. But he told us a funny story about a good friend of his who always keeps his eyes closed when he masturbates. One day, this friend left his mum making a pot of tea in the kitchen. He went upstairs to his room, sat at his desk, and decided to have a nice long wank. When he'd finished and opened his eyes, there on the desk in front of him was a steaming hot cup of tea.

21st July 1998
It's supposedly my day off but I've not been able to resist getting involved in today's shoot, which is located mainly on the beach and poolside at our hotel. At my behest, John is directing a music sequence, with the presenters dancing along to the Four Tops' *Loco in Acapulco*. I've devised a (sort of) dance routine for them to follow, and, as well as indulging my choreographer fantasies, I'm in charge of playback, walking beside the camera with an enormous ghetto blaster borrowed from the hotel blaring out the tune for the presenters to gyrate to. This doesn't impress some of the tourists dotted around us, but they don't say anything as they are plainly intrigued by the presence of a camera crew, and the buoyant behaviour of the giddy presenters. It's all a right laugh, and can scarcely be called hard work, which makes a welcome change on this trip.

23rd July 1998
Frantic day of filming in Mexico City, culminating in a 'money' shot of all four presenters watching the ceremonial flag-lowering in Zocolo Square.
Dinner afterwards on a terrace overlooking the square. Laughing very hard at our various attempts to speak Spanish. This morning Katy greeted us all with a breezy cry of "Buenos Aires" (which is the capital of Argentina) rather than "Buenos Dias" (good morning). At every meal, Richard, meanwhile, requests

"Una water, thanks, gracias" with the latter pronounced so that it sounds more like "grassy arse".

I start trying to soften up John to my idea of a special Christmas panto to mark the 40th anniversary, a time-travel fantasy I've called *Back in Time for Christmas.* I capture his interest (never easy, as he is frequently distracted) but he is wary as, in the past, the Christmas pantos have all gone way over budget. Aha, say I, but that was when they were just ten-minute inserts. This would be a complete programme so that the costs would be spread more efficiently. I need John on side because that's half the battle when it comes to persuading Oliver, especially if it's about anything vaguely showbiz. He in turn wants to know if I'd be happy to commit to next year's summer trip. He's delighted with what he's heard about this one. I prevaricate as, although I'm enjoying it, it is brutally hard work and I'm really missing my family.

24th July 1998

Pissed off when John asks me to reshoot a piece about the appalling pollution in Mexico City to tone down any implied criticism of the country. I have a real go about editorial weediness (the note has come from Oliver in London; John is merely the messenger) and Katy pats me on the shoulder and says, "Calm down, love, or you'll not reach 60..."

Later, we are due to film with a Mariachi band. The musicians all wear white suits embroidered with sequins and enormous hats. Stuart gets me to tease Richard by saying I want him to wear one of these heinous costumes. Usually this would be the cue for adamant refusals and passionate protests. But the joke backfires because Richard turns out to be surprisingly enthusiastic and so eventually I decide "why not?" and shoot the sequence with him in full Mariachi drag as one of the band, with the others joining in as amused onlookers.

25th July 1998

Film in the teeming street markets, accompanied by the necessary armed police, which makes me tense. Can't say I will ever want to return to this ugly, hostile city. During a break in filming, Richard is obsessing about his teeth, which someone has helpfully told him are too prominent and are bound to affect his career. I say that he'll go very mad, very fast in this business if he listens to crap like this. "People are always looking to have a sly dig at anyone on the telly; you can do without 'advice' like that."

We finish the day filming the presenters taking a ride on the enormous wooden rollercoaster in the city's standing funfair. We have the ride to ourselves and are offered the front seat in which to place the camera looking back at the presenters.

"We can fix it in position, set up the shot and leave it running," say I. "No fucking way," counters Paul. "Do you know how much this camera is worth? I'm not risking it on that thing."
Next I suggest that he shoots it using one of our small DVC cameras. Again he refuses. So, stupidly, I suggest I could do this myself. I clamber in and sit in the cab backwards. Paul and Steve use duct tape to carefully seal me in place and they securely tape the camera to my wrist, too. The presenters are all hugely amused and off we set, laughing and joking up the first long drag before the ride kicks in and then its everyone for themselves. The presenters are all screaming and waving their hands in the air. I suppress the panic and nausea I'm experiencing and try to focus on the all-important shot. But at the speed we are hurtling round the track, up and down, up and down, there is no way of telling whether I am recording anything remotely useable.
Just as the ride nears its end, on slam the brakes and I feel the web of tape around me ripping apart. I'm terrified I'm going to be sent flying to my doom. This doesn't happen but the impact of the breaking mechanism is exactly like being involved in a car crash. The minute we come to a stop, it's obvious I've sustained some kind of whiplash as my neck is now in total agony. I hobble off the ride and Lucy the PA offers me painkillers and sympathy. Paul doesn't say, "I told you so", which is good of him.

The injury I sustained on the rollercoaster turned out to be a serious neck trauma, for which I have had years of treatment without real success. It remains an unwelcome but lifelong souvenir of that trip, the rest of which was blighted with pain.

27th July 1998

Richard pisses me off at dinner by confidently telling everyone at the table that he happens to know "for a fact" that TV and radio presenter Toby Anstis is gay. "Oh, really? Is that so?," say I, and then put him straight (literally). I've known Toby for years – in fact, I shot his very first show-reels and got him the initial audition for CBBC, which kick-started his career. Toby may be more than a little camp – most male TV presenters are, especially on children's TV, but that doesn't mean he is actually gay. And, in any case, so what if he is? This kind of inaccurate, unfair, bitchy gossip may be inevitable within the industry that we work, but I tell Richard that he should be aware that some people spout exactly the same kind of crap about him – and that it's equally untrue and unfair. He back-pedals rapidly.

29th July 1998

Richard on top form today, as we film in trying circumstances in the ancient Mayan site at Chichen Itza. There are just so many wobbly Americans everywhere, pointing, clapping, shouting and shovelling junk food into their gobs. At one point we manage to get public access to one of the temples closed off so that we can shoot what we need. A group of tourists stand and wave at Richard from a distance and, being a friendly boy, he waves back – only to realise that they are actually trying to wave him (and the rest of us) off the temple so that they can take snapshots.

Back at the hotel, we all relax by the pool. I shove a T-shirt on my head as the best defence against the searing sun, and fish out my Evelyn Waugh.

"Looks like the kind of book they used to make us read at school," remarks Katy.

In the evening, it is still so hot that we agree to dine al fresco, under the pleasant shade of some heavily scented trees. We all gas away nineteen to the dozen and Katy claims that she doesn't think that girls can be camp.

"Purrlease," say I. "You're a camp icon yourself. There are little gays growing up, just loving you and your sassy ways and foxy boots."

I can tell that this thought doesn't entirely displease madam. I have given her the nickname "HRH" as she is *Blue Peter* royalty and announce what a pity it is that she has grown just a little too big for the special pair of jewelled boots I've had made for her.

As all this nonsense is going on, I feel something heavy land on my shoulder. Instinctively, I brush it off, assuming it is a branch from one of the overhanging trees. The next thing I know there is uproar. Everyone is pushing back their chairs and screaming and yelling while one of the waiters lunges forward, snatches up a serving knife and hacks away at the object which fell on me – not a branch at all, but an enormous, fat, writhing snake. Once he is sure that it is dead, the waiter delights in telling me that it is of an especially deadly variety. I remain strangely calm, while the others in our party are still gibbering and casting doubtful looks at the nearby foliage.

"You call me HRH," says Katy, "But, from now on, I'm going to call *you* Indiana Marson..."

30th July 1998

In his absence, everyone discusses how much they'd have to be paid to shag our fixer (who, it cannot be said, is a looker). All the girls say that they couldn't do so for any amount of money. All the boys could name a price.

What does that tell you?

31st July 1998

The crew and Linda are all hacked off with Richard and his general immaturity. When he argues the toss that people who like a cup of coffee after dinner are "middle-class" and "pompous", Paul goes for him. "I'm bloody working-class," he says, "And I like a coffee after dinner because that's what I like. What's pompous about that, you gibbon?"

Between shots, I find a moment to chat with Richard about these ridiculous outbursts that so put people's backs up. There is so much about him that's lovely and fresh and funny; but then he will get a bee in his bonnet, often about something entirely superfluous and spoil the good impression he otherwise makes. Earlier, he annoyed Katy by being unrepentantly late for his call because "I needed to send a fax". He is bright but, I think, rather spoilt though he takes the mild bollocking I give him in good part and thankfully it is back to charming Richard for the rest of the day.

3rd August 1998

Our last day. It has been an epic trip. Sometimes I've felt as if it would never end and have been truly wretchedly homesick, but there have also been moments of true wonder and exhilaration, laughter and joy. Lucy, who was the PA on last year's trip, warns me that it took her about two weeks to feel normal again after she got back. This is a problem with filming away. You can hardly come back to your loved ones, full of tales of extraordinary days, while they have been stuck in their usual routine, dealing with kids, loading the dishwasher and emptying bins.

After some time off, it was back to Television Centre and straight into edits for the six films and two half-hour specials which would make up the Mexico summer expedition. I was now the Films Producer, which meant that until Christmas I would be in charge of organising all the films made for the programme, as well as shooting quite a few myself. I was also acting as archive consultant for BBC2's Blue Peter Night, *to celebrate the 40th anniversary of the show and, to my great delight, it had also been agreed that I would write and produce a half-hour Christmas special,* Back in Time for Christmas. *As well as starring parts for the current team of presenters, this would offer plenty of opportunities for cameo roles for past presenters too. I was going to be very busy.*

6th October 1998

Filming a behind-the-scenes on *The Generation Game* with Stuart and Katy. I'd been warned about Jim Davidson, who dominates proceedings with a kind of lewd running commentary which generates sycophantic sniggers from some of the crew (well, the male ones, anyway) and a kind of awkward 'It's only Jim being Jim' response from others (especially the women, who are clearly long-suffering).

When we arrive, his producer tells me that we are in luck because "Jim's having a good day". When he spots us, he starts with the *Blue Peter* 'jokes', which continue all the time we are filming. "Oh, fuck me, *Blue Peter* are here. No more swearing, boys. *Blue* fucking *Peter* are recording everything. It's about fucking time they grew up!"

Katy is nervous around him ("you're a big girl..."), while Stuart gets a bit manic. When we wrap, it is with relief; think there is a decent film there, once we can cut round the swearing and endless puerile sex references.

9th October 1998

Filming with Katy in what remains of the battlefields of Northern France, for my First World War story. I'm pleased with her performance; I was worried she would be switched off by the 'heavy' nature of the script, but instead, she invests the lines with real sensitivity and understanding. I set up an enormous bleak wide shot with Katy walking across the battle field towards us, almost a silhouette, in her long black coat. I call "Action!" and she starts slowly to move towards us, her voice sonorously delivering the words. And then, in a trice, she completely vanishes from view, like a Paul Daniels illusion.

"Katy?" I shout.

Muffled sounds of swearing come from her mic, and then she slowly emerges, clambering up on the horizon ahead of us.

"I fell in a hole," she yells.

I make a mental note to send the clip in to *Auntie's Bloomers.*

16th October 1998

The 40th birthday programme and the studio is a chaos of past presenters. So noisy and chaotic that Bridget, who is producing, actually tries to use a megaphone to get everyone's attention. This, however, goes down like a cup of cold sick and the look of hauteur on Valerie Singleton's face as Bridget bellows for quiet is something to behold. I wander around with a DV camera, officially so I can capture behind-the-scenes material for possible use in the *Review of the Year.* But really it's just my way of ensuring an access-all-areas pass to everything that's going on. Wily Annie Dixon isn't fooled.

"Is that for your personal collection?" she comments archly.

It's especially good to catch up with Diane-Louise Jordan. During her first few months, I was often the floor assistant and I well remember her early struggles on the show. Every studio day would start fine; she'd be happy, bubbly, confident. Then, as the run-through and transmission drew ever closer, she would become increasingly nervous and unsure of herself, and start to squint at the camera and fluff her words. It was painful. And I wasn't impressed with how Diane was treated by production during this time. There seemed to be little patience or understanding. I vividly remember one show in particular, in which Di was down to make the famous advent crown, her nerves not helped by the fact that first there was going to be a VT clip of past presenters making the thing, as if to remind viewers just what she had to live up to. The item before this was a live call from Yvette, who was in Romania, reporting for that year's appeal. As rehearsed, the bulk of the questions were handled by John. But, during transmission, the show was running under, and editor Lewis Bronze suddenly instructed Diane to ask Yvette an additional question. Di, lost in thought going over what she had to do next, asked precisely the same question that John had just asked and Yvette had answered, in some detail. Over talkback, and down the presenters' ear-pieces, Lewis exploded, "Stupid fucking cow!"

Diane now had to move over to the make, of which, understandably, she proceeded to make a total dog's dinner.

It took some time for Di to turn a corner, and for her qualities to be showcased and appreciated by the programme, but she eventually blossomed into a hugely successful and intuitive presenter. Today, she is on full beam and there is not a trace of that nervous young actress whose hands used to shake with fear as the countdown began to another live ordeal.

There are so many familiar faces. Among them, I'm especially pleased to see Anita West. A few months back, I went to Oliver and explained that Anita was the 'lost' presenter; she auditioned at the same time as Val in 1962 and actually got the job. Sadly, at the time, her marriage was in trouble and so, fearing scandal, after just three months, she resigned. Runner-up Val replaced her and Anita was forgotten about. When it came to the 20th anniversary, Biddy decided that three months didn't count as a 'proper' presenter, so, in Stalin-esque fashion, Anita's name was expunged from that celebration and all official histories. I discovered her existence only by chance, when looking through bound copies of the *Radio Times* in the reference library in the basement of TV Centre.

I suggested to Oliver that her 'rediscovery' might make a good press story. It helped that I had found that by some miracle (or more likely, oversight) the BBC archive had retained the film recording of her (and Val's) audition, the film can labelled as 'experimental programme'. When we had this transferred, I could see why Anita had been chosen – she was radiantly beautiful and, on camera, had real poise and presence.

After the live show (which, perhaps inevitably, was a bit of a bear garden), the big

event for all of us on the programme is a lavish party held at the Natural History Museum. As well as everyone on the current team, and all the living presenters, the guest list also includes quite a few notable member of past production teams as well, inevitably, as a few of the current senior management. It is rather like a wedding reception, with everyone seated at round tables, with 'oldies' mixed up among 'currents'. This suits me but I do wonder if the 'oldies' wouldn't sooner have been with their own friends and contemporaries. I am sitting next to Anita on one side and Gillian Reilly on the other. Gilly (pronounced with a hard 'g') goes right back to the very beginning of the programme; she was creator John Hunter Blair's secretary. She can't get over the size of the current team.
"What do they all do?" she asks. "For ages, it was only the two of us. John would amble about the office and decide what he felt like including and I would get on the phone and organise everything."
Gilly remained on *Blue Peter* through to the latter half of the '60s, by which time she was running the correspondence unit, dealing with all the thousands of pictures, letters and cards which came in every week from an eager audience.
"But I got very fed up with Queen B," she says, indicating Biddy Baxter, who is sitting at a nearby table and smiling seraphically. "Always having to have the last word and never signing any of the viewers' letters, so that I had to perfect my forgery of her signature. I was offered the chance to escape to Bristol and work on *Vision On*, and that was that, I never looked back."
After dinner, everyone gravitates to those they knew best, until it is chucking-out time around midnight. I leave with John Comerford, Anthea Turner and several other presenters, including Richard. Outside there is a huddle of paparazzi and as our group walk down the steps, they start to click away like crazy. At first I think they are after Anthea, who is the most newsworthy of the 'turns'. But, no, they are aiming their lenses at Richard. Which is odd. In the taxi back to TV Centre, I try to puzzle this out and I'm left with an uneasy feeling that something is not right.

17th October 1998
Phone call from Oliver. He sounds calm but grave. "There's going to be a story in the Sunday newspapers," he explains. "It's about Richard."
Apparently, Richard has been secretly recorded by a friend, admitting to having taken cocaine in a night club. This 'friend' has sold the story to the *News of the World*, who deliberately held on to their story for this anniversary weekend. I ask Oliver what is going to happen next. He seems unsure, says there are going to be series of meetings. I'm scheduled to be making a film with Richard on Monday (ironically with him finding out what it takes to be a journalist) and Oliver suggests that, whatever happens, I should replace Richard with one of

the others and look at the forthcoming film schedules, in case Richard "has to keep a low profile" for a while. I ask if he is likely to be sacked and Oliver admits it is a possibility but that he is yet to meet with Lorraine, the head of the department.

I am absolutely stunned; just a few hours ago we were all celebrating like mad, and now a genuine crisis has exploded around us. Not long after Oliver has rung off, John calls. He doesn't think that Richard can survive this. He wants to know how many films we will have to reshoot or write off if the worst comes to the worst. I rattle through the list, and make suggestions of what can be salvaged.

"Is sacking him really the right message?" I ask John. "It sends a pretty bleak message – one mistake and you're out..."

John agrees; but points out that we are talking about a Class A drug, not a bit of weed, which might just be explained away as youthful folly. Later, I call Oliver back and suggest that perhaps Richard could serve a period of suspension and, during that time, we could make a special programme about the dangers of drugs. Oliver hears me out but it's obvious that since we last spoke the situation has shifted and the attitude hardened.

"How could we make a programme about a presenter and drugs for our audience?" he asks me. I am reminded of my own instinctive rejection of a drugs item on *Blue Peter* during my interview for this job.

"Maybe it could be a *Newsround* special, then?"

But I can sense that Oliver doesn't really want to waste time debating my bleeding heart suggestions and needs to get off the phone. "See you tomorrow," he says, wearily.

Tomorrow afternoon, Oliver, John, the producers and presenters are all scheduled to appear at the children's BAFTA awards, where the programme is to be given a lifetime achievement award. In the circumstances, it's all going to be very odd.

18th October 1998

The *News of the World* has gone to town. "*Blue Peter* Goody Goody is Cocaine Snorting Sneak" shrieks the headline.

The coverage is savage. Oliver calls to say that it has been decided that there is no alternative but to sack Richard and that I will need to work round the impact on the film team. He sounds shell-shocked, as well he might. Fortunately, there is no live show scheduled for tomorrow – it is a special programme with Stuart on the trail of mountain gorillas in Uganda. This buys us a little time to think and make plans.

Later, I drive to the BAFTAS and congregate with our party. We all feel conspicuous and funereal, and, in the circumstances, the idea of standing up to collect an award seems utterly surreal. What a total waste – for Richard and for us. None of us are exactly surprised that he could be capable of doing something reckless and stupid. We all know him to be immature. But we also know how bright and talented, funny and natural he can be – and we were just beginning to see his talent emerge from the months spent finding his own style and confidence, a process in which we all worked hard, as partners.

19th October 1998

Film the story with Stuart, substituted for Richard, as a young journalist. Stuart is struggling to put a brave face on the weekend's drama. It doesn't help that as we attempt to shoot the first piece to camera in Oxford Street, passers-by cheerfully call out things like, "Got any white powder, mate?" and "Here's one I snorted earlier", while black cabs toot their horns and give us the thumbs up. Stuart is quietly furious with Richard, who he says is some kind of strange denial about the furore, perversely enjoying being in the centre of a media whirlwind. "I don't think he gives a shit about the mess he's left us in," he fumes.

I can see all this from his point of view. Stuart is planning this to be his final season, and Richard's actions have spectacularly upstaged any possible impact he could hope to make with his own departure. But, like the pro he is, he gets on with our film and deals charmingly with the minor irritation of interviewing the pop group Steps. Naturally enough, they are agog to hear the goss, though, to be fair, they are sympathetic too.

The head of department, Lorraine Heggessy, has tacked an introduction onto the start of tonight's transmission in which, dressed in a formal black suit, she gives a Queen's Christmas broadcast-style address on why she felt Richard had let everyone down and wouldn't be on *Blue Peter* any more. Reaction in the office, and from the presenters, is uniformly scathing.

"Silly cow," sniffs Annie Dixon. "Why is she dressed as though she's going to a funeral?"

The general impression is that it's a monstrous act of part-building, so that senior management will sit up and take notice. The presenters feel that they should have been allowed to deliver a message of their own; that the audience will have expected this and will be completely confused by the appearance of this mysterious stern lady in black. Now that Richard has been abruptly excommunicated, they are all going to have to shoulder the burden. Spend the evening going through and revising their schedules. I'm also going to have to completely rewrite *Back in Time for Christmas*, in which Richard had the starring part. When I mentioned this dilemma to Stuart earlier, he pulled a face and said, "Why don't you offer it to Lorraine? I'm sure she'd jump at the chance."

21st October 1998

Karen, our make-up designer, has called to say that Stuart is extremely reluctant to shave off his goatee, which he's been cultivating for the last few days. Unfortunately we are due to return to the Imperial War Museum tomorrow to re-shoot sequences in this First World War story which had previously involved Richard. Karen points out that if she is to achieve the necessary continuity with what we have already recorded, the goatee will need to go. I come down to the studio, where I find Stuart and Katy in the make-up room. Carefully, and as tactfully as possible, I explain the problem. Stuart listens, then suddenly picks up his bag from a corner, yells, "Everyone wants a piece of me!" and storms out. I hadn't expected such a melodramatic reaction.

"Don't stress," counsels Katy, from her corner, "he'll be back. He's just feeling it today, poor love."

So I stay put until, sure enough, a little later, Stuart returns, somewhat sheepishly. He apologises for his outburst, and explains how he's just feeling really exhausted and pissed off with the way it's just being taken for granted that the presenters will carry all the extra work-load caused by Richard's removal, with no thanks and no extra money. He says that of course he will shave off the goatee.

Stuart later told me that he'd sought refuge in some nearby toilets, where he had a good cry. Although it was true that he was having to cope with the extra pressure of the work, his actual emotions about the sudden loss of Richard went deeper and were more complex; as Stuart had confided in me during the Mexico trip, he had intense feelings for Richard. Although these weren't fully reciprocated, their friendship meant a huge amount to him. Richard's abrupt removal understandably left Stuart sad, isolated and depressed, none of which he could share with anyone at the time.

6th November 1998

On location in Beamish open air museum, shooting the story of C.S. Lewis. This is an amazing place, a complete miniature town constructed from various houses, shops and buildings rescued from demolition and brought here brick by brick. It is the perfect location in which to shoot a period drama and so frequently in demand for this purpose. *Blue Peter* cannot offer much, if anything, in the way of location fees, but we can offer to plug a place in return for them allowing free access to badge winners. This is the deal at Beamish. I also arrange to copy the 1977 film the programme made here when the whole site was just starting to be developed.

For one sequence, we are shooting Lewis's nanny reading him a bedtime story.

Everything I select as suitable involves some expensive copyright trauma, so, in the end, I scribble the opening lines of a faux-fairy tale myself. As it says in the paperwork, SNF ('Staff – no fee').

8th November 1998

First day of filming on *Back in Time for Christmas.* I've managed a rapid rewrite and created a new central character to replace Richard. This is the 'Keeper of the Memory Machine', and Mark Curry has agreed to play him. Mark has been acting since childhood and this slice of campery is right up his street. We've agreed that he will play the part rather like his old mate Colin Baker as Doctor Who (though not quite as grumpy) and so the costume designer has given him a frock which echoes the multi-coloured clashes of the Sixth Doctor. We've only just begun but we are already over budget; Leah, our production executive, confides that the entire series is heavily in the red and she shares her frustration with Oliver and John, neither of whom, she feels, are taking the problem seriously.

12th November 1998

To Elstree to make a film going behind-the-scenes on *Top of the Pops.* The producer, a shaggy-haired Geordie called Chris Cowey, himself an ex-presenter, has agreed to Katy presenting tonight's edition. When I first put it to him, he "ummed" and "ahed" a bit, and then said, "Nah, she's cool enough, I reckon. Fuck it, why not?"

It all has an interesting effect on Katy, for whom this is a big deal. She's properly ambitious and would love to make the leap into entertainment and music.

"It's actually brilliant seeing you this nervous," I tell her at one point.

"What do you mean?" she asks.

"You're showing some vulnerability," I explain. "That's really appealing. You are so confident and so 'on it' most of the time, sometimes it's hard to believe there's anything genuinely at stake."

Ultimately it is a film about a presenter being a presenter, so I have to package it as a behind-the-scenes as well. I'm fascinated by how, hidden away up here at Elstree, miles from the scrutiny of Television Centre, the show has become its own court, with Cowey its amiable Emperor. What he says goes. Everywhere it's a chorus of, "Chris likes this.." or, "Chris wants that...." or, "I'll just have to check with Chris..."

As well as producing, he is also the nominal director of the show. He sprawls in the gallery with his feet on the desk, yelling encouraging remarks like, "Go camera one!" or "Love it, four!" rather than following any kind of script. The actual craft is down to a brilliant vision mixer and tip-top camera supervisor, who basically work out the shots between them, and a PA with nerves of steel who drives things from the gallery. It's not conventional but it clearly works. Chatting to Katy afterwards, my remarks that, from her point of view, despite the showbiz veneer, the show is basically just a series of links, and nothing like as demanding as *Blue Peter*, fall on deaf ears. I can see she is intoxicated with the 'jouzz' of the experience. *Blue Peter* may be the university of telly, but Katy is clearly keen to graduate.

13th November 1998

The 'junior journalist' film goes out. Oliver sees it for the first time during the run-through.

"Mmm," he says. "Perfectly enjoyable but rather lightweight. Let's not make a habit of having too many films like that, eh?"

18th November 1998

A whole day in a studio on an industrial estate just off the M40 shooting the *Last Christmas* disco routine for the Christmas special. It's supposed to look like a 1980s Stock/Aitken/Waterman video and so Katy and Konnie are dressed like the girls from Bananarama with tutus and cycling shorts, and Stuart (and the male backing dancers) are in lycra shorts and sleeveless vests. When I arrive, I discover that Stuart has slathered his arms in baby oil.

"One of the dancers told me it makes your arms look bigger," he confides.

19th November 1998

To Oxford, to shoot sequences for my forthcoming special about C. S. Lewis. The programme's financial crisis is now common knowledge and all the producers have been asked to come up with cost-saving suggestions. One of mine has been to turn what had been planned as a standard ten-minute film about Lewis into a complete programme. Today, we are at Magdalen (pronounced '*Moor-d'len*') College, where Lewis taught, and then filming at the bungalow he shared with his brother. Things don't get off to the best start when Katy, who has travelled here solo, reports to the college and asks, "Is this Magdalen?" only to have her literal pronunciation haughtily corrected by a snooty receptionist. This puts Katy in a mood ("Stupid snobs") and only slowly does she regain her composure.

We had been given special permission to film in the Lewis bungalow, which is not open to the public, despite being something of a shrine for his followers. The young man who acts as live-in curator is somewhat eccentric and it is quickly apparent that for him, we are treading on hallowed ground. He guides us round, speaking in hushed and reverential tones, and I put on my best

Sunday school manner, until I catch Katy's eye and have to fight my first urge to laugh.
We set up a piece to camera in the living room, in which Katy has to pick up a photo of Lewis as a child and say, "When he was a little boy, he pointed to himself and announced, 'He is Jacksy', and he was known as Jacksy or Jack for the rest of his life."
Earlier, in the car, Katy had mentioned this particular line to me and the cameraman; "What a ponce! Jacksy?! What was he thinking of? Any child of mine who said that would be given a slap and told to shut up!" and we had all had a good laugh.
Now we come to shoot it, with the eagle eye of the acolyte curator upon us, we all begin to get the giggles. First it is Katy who loses it, sniggering every time she has to say 'Jacksy'.
I do my best to be patient and professional, though inside I am equally desperate to laugh. We take a pause. A bottle of water for Katy. We try again. This time both Katy and I spot the cameraman's shoulders silently shaking with mirth and we lose it altogether. I begin to feel hysterical in every sense and when, several takes later, I burst out laughing the second after I call "Action!", I know that drastic measures are called for.
I clear the room of everyone except the cameraman and Katy and instruct them to get on with it without us. I wait in the corridor outside, still doubled up with suppressed laughter, as I hear Katy's efforts to deliver the line through the door. At long last, she manages a perfect take – but I can scarcely look the curator in the eye as I'm ashamed of my lapse of manners. I mumble something suitably apologetic. It is a relief to wrap and get the hell out of there.

23rd November 1998
Everyone is reeling from another unexpected bombshell. Oliver is leaving!
No one saw it coming – although he has been on the programme since 1987, he's only been Editor since 1996. He has been offered what he says is his "dream job" as an Executive Producer in classical music (he is himself a highly skilled organist), the result, so he tells us, of working closely with that department to produce the recent *Blue Peter* prom. The rumour mill tells a slightly different story; that he is being moved sideways because of management dissatisfaction with the whole Richard saga, and disquiet about the programme's out-of-control budget. There have been mutterings that there had been clear warning signs about Richard's behaviour for several months; well before the scandal broke, the tabloids had reported his enthusiastic partying at various nightclubs. *The Sun* even ran a *Blue Peter* 'lig-o-meter' in the pages of their gossip column, listing the running total of times presenters were spotted at various freebie

openings in town. Oliver has been criticised for doing nothing to warn a young and impressionable presenter about the temptations of London's showbiz life. But hindsight is all very well – and, anyway, Oliver is just not that kind of person. He's a democrat, not an autocrat. I don't suppose it occurred to him that Richard would ever be quite so reckless.

Within the programme, news of Oliver's departure – he goes early next year – has not been well received. Not quite that he's a rat leaving a sinking ship, but a slight sense of 'I'm all right, Jack' and 'good luck everyone'. There is going to be the usual 'board' process to interview for his replacement. The obvious candidate would be John, the deputy, and he's making no secret of the fact that he certainly wants it.

25th-26th November 1998

In deepest Norfolk, freezing cold, on a night shoot for a story about the life of a gamekeeper. The idea for this came from an article I'd seen in *Country Life* profiling actor Joseph Fiennes's twin brother, Jake, who is the only one of his siblings (the others being Ralph, also an actor, and Martha, a composer) not involved in showbusiness. I've never liked the way we sentimentalise animals in this country, especially for children, and I think *Blue Peter* should do its bit in explaining that there is actually a complex relationship between animals and man. The focus of the film will be on the unpalatable fact that a key part of a gamekeeper's job is to control certain species in order that others thrive. We film various fairly challenging sequences, including the 'gibbet', a kind of clothes-line on which Jake hangs the corpses of various vermin, like weasels and stoats, in order to discourage others (I'm unclear how this works and doubt this sequence will make the cut, as it really is pretty gruesome). Katy expresses a certain nervousness about being associated with the film. "I don't want to get hate mail," she says.

In the middle of the night, we go 'lamping', shining a torch to attract the eyes of wild animals like rabbits, which are then an easy target for Jake's gun. It's quite some way from *The Animals of Farthing Wood.*

30th November 1998

Studio recording for *Back in Time for Christmas*. There is so much to get done and we have to finish by 10 – there is absolutely no chance of an overrun. The tension is awful. We just about manage it, though the final scene is more rehearsal-on-tape than genuine take and I hope we have enough to cut round some shaky close-ups.

Sarah Greene, here to record her cameo as Futura, a presenter of the far distant future (when *Blue Peter* is no longer just a programme, but an entire channel),

keeps me at least partially distracted, by her stream of gossip and innuendo, and with the costume we have given her.
"Do you like where I've put the badge, darling?," she asks, flirtatiously, as she saunters out of make-up. The badge, a silver one, is nestling slap bang in the middle of her plunging cleavage.
"You know what they always say," she purrs. "*Blue Peter* badge winners get in free..."
Cripes.

2nd December 1998
I've persuaded Oliver and John that I should be allowed to make a film about the exhaustive audition process undergone whenever *Blue Peter* looks for a new presenter. They have laid down one main condition; that in the finished film, each of the four wannabes are given precisely the same amount of airtime. This makes it scrupulously fair and won't telegraph which of them is going to get the job. The idea is that the film will transmit just before the big reveal, and naturally they don't want to compromise that by giving the game away.
The four candidates are Jake Humphrey, hot favourite among a lot of the production team, who think he will bring a touch of the elusive 'cool' to the show, Jonas Hurst, who has been recommended by Alex, one of the other producers, Simon Thomas, John's protégé, and Michael Underwood, the only black candidate, whom I think Oliver favours. All four have to give their consent to having the audition process filmed, but they are hardly in a position to say no. It is fascinating to follow them through the process, which is famously tough. They are all grilled by Oliver and John. But the main event is the studio audition, a complete mini-programme recorded in the evening after today's live show.
They have to make a Christmas card, talk about the appeal, demonstrate a toy and have a go on the trampoline (the idea being that as you bounce about, some of your real personality is bound to come out). All the boys are competent and could do the job. Jake is very reminiscent of Richard, however, and might be seen as a bit of an 'identikit' replacement. Michael is sweet-natured and naturally warm, but his gentle, boyish manner might be more suited to young children's programmes. Simon has the necessary edge, and is obviously bright and keen, but he is somewhat closed and cold – Konnie finds him very stand-offish, she says – though she agrees this may just be nerves. At one point, waiting for me to say 'Action!', I see that his hands are shaking. I find this curiously touching. Jonas, the fourth contender, is the weakest, I'd say – a little bit dead behind the eyes on camera, though much more charming and animated when you talk to him one-to-one. He's also a really talented musician.
It is a very demanding process, but then the job is one of the most sought after

in British television. John asks me who I think should get the job and I tell him Simon or Michael, though I think Simon would be a better contrast with the existing team. John is determined that it will be Simon.

4th December 1998

The rules which govern the famous *Blue Peter* Totaliser amuse me. This giant-sized studio prop is the means by which progress on the Appeal is always tracked, with a series of stages that light up as the money (or whatever it is we are recycling) pours in. These days, when the summit is reached, there is an explosion of glitter to mark the achievement. Annie tells me that the original idea for this prop came from a former Deputy Editor, Rosemary Gill, who had childhood memories of similar 'totalisers' being used to chart the success of the 'Spitfire Fund' during the Second World War.

What I didn't know is that it is left up to the Editor to decide precisely when the Totaliser goes up and when it remains stuck where it is; the whole device is a piece of theatre designed either to reward the audience or to encourage them to greater efforts. I've learnt that it sometimes goes up on a Monday, frequently on a Friday (especially when we have celebrity guests bringing in donations), but rarely on a Wednesday. And when we carefully give out the exact figure (this year, measured by how many tonnes of aluminium we can recycle from donations of cans etc), this, too, is just a figment of the Editor's imagination. In the end, of course, it makes no difference – the money raised usually far exceeds the target set, but the whole elaborate process, pacing it out, is all part of the magic, harmless make-believe to stimulate a child's imagination and involvement.

7th December 1998

Final studio recording for *Back in Time for Christmas,* covering all the scenes in Stuart's flat, including two music numbers. There is far too much to do, which means that we are forced to accept takes with which I'm less than happy, including a whole section of the final song in which Katy is merrily miming to the wrong camera.

19th December 1998

Shooting Simon's first film (not counting the one about his audition) – taking a new year dip in the Serpentine, with Konnie there for added support and comedy chit-chat. He does well but there is a technical disaster – the camera in the water, which is pretty crucial for conveying the experience, fails to record – and so the coverage is not going to be as good as it should.

Konnie still has her doubts ("he's a bit of a cold fish") and it's true that Simon isn't on a charm offensive to win round her, me, or anyone else. But I suspect that this is principally because he can't quite believe he's got the job, and such is the effort and concentration which is going into the work, there just isn't room for chit-chat and laughter. This is understandable but unnerving, especially for someone like Konnie for whom the interpersonal connection is most important of all.

1999

5th January 1999

Joss Ackland comes in to the dubbing suite at TV Centre to record the C.S.Lewis voice-overs, in the special I'm calling *The World Beyond The Wardrobe.*

My interest in the Lewis story was first sparked one Christmas when I saw the BBC's film *Shadowlands*, coincidentally written by a former *Blue Peter* director, William Nicholson. Ackland is a fine actor and this was one of his most subtle and effective roles, his performance as the bereaved Lewis moving me to tears. I never thought there was any way such a grand actor would consider doing our bitesize version, especially given the fee was only going to be a few hundred quid, but I thought I might as well ask. Within an hour, the agent called me back to say that Mr Ackland would love to do it. It's thrilling to hear his unmistakable voice bring Lewis to life once more and he is thoroughly charming throughout, and, in breaks, chats to me engagingly about his great love for his wife and how important she is to him.

11th January 1999

Arriving first thing, just outside the East Tower (where children's programmes are based), I bump into Steven Eker, the film team secretary.

"Bit of a shock, eh?" he says, conspiratorially.

I have no idea what he's referring to, but it is obvious he is delighted to be the

one to break the big news.
"The new Editor is Steve Hocking. Bet you didn't see that one coming. That's going to upset a few people...."
It certainly will, not least John, who had been so confident of his chances. The other candidate had been Joe Godwin, who had produced on *Blue Peter*, leaving last summer (creating the vacancy for which I first applied) to join Nickelodeon. Joe is a very likeable man, with a dry sense of humour, a graduate of Saturday morning TV; his fondness for *Blue Peter* wouldn't have prevented him from pushing it into a more light-hearted, entertainment mode. He created the format for the Friday programme, much less content-driven than Mondays and Wednesdays, with pop groups and lighter, shorter items with an emphasis on playing for laughs. This fun Friday mix had worked with both the audience, the presenters and production team, who still see Fridays as the 'coolest' show on which to work. Some time ago, I worked for Joe as his AFM on *Take Two*, and I would have been happy to do so again if he'd got the job.
Steve Hocking I know too, from my time on *Going Live!*, where he was one of the producer/directors. I remember that he was once a teacher, that he comes from Bristol, is mad about football and, although keen to be 'one of the gang', was set apart by the fact that he didn't seem to have much of a sense of humour. Certainly, there was no lightness of touch to his directing. He took that very seriously indeed, which could be wearisome for everyone. We were chalk and cheese; I was loving every minute of being on the show, albeit in a junior role, into all the pop and showbiz stuff and dressing as fashionably as I could. Steve's only nod to fashion was a Bristol Football club T-shirt and he preferred items about books to style tips from Betty Boo.
The presenters, Phillip Schofield and Sarah Greene, didn't seem to take to him much. I remembered hovering in TC7 make-up with Steve asking repeatedly from the gallery, "Phillip and Sarah, Phillip and Sarah – can we rehearse this please? As soon as possible?"
The more he had to ask, the more stressed he became and the more pronounced his Bristolian accent. As both Phillip and Sarah wore 'open' talkback, they could hear all this for themselves and didn't need me to chivvy them. But, all the same, they both took great delight in taking their time to obey his frantic instruction. It was almost as if they were doing a link on air, but just for me.
"Can you hear that, Sarah?"
"What, Phil?"
"That annoying buzzing sound."
"You mean the director? I think he's called Steve."
"That's the one."
"Does he want to rehearse?"

"I think so. Fancy a cup of tea?"
"Sounds delightful."
"Tea first, then rehearse?"
"You read my mind..."
On another occasion, when we had left the studio for a *Going Live!* OB (outside broadcast) from the Isle of Wight, I'd also cleaned up his sick. This show had been extremely ambitious and technically complex. After transmission, there had been a kind of lunch/reception for the team, thrown by the grateful tourist board. Steve had enjoyed rather too much of their hospitality and by the time we all clambered onto the coach which was to take us all back to Television Centre, he was in a noticeably fragile state. He found a seat to himself and did the only sensible thing; fell fast asleep. Unfortunately, about half way home, he woke and immediately began to vomit all over himself.
"I never knew one man could have so much sick in him," whispered Gabby, one of the producers. She, like everyone else, watched in grim fascination as Steve was copiously sick over and over again. Finally, the choking and hurling seemed to subside and he was left, caked in his own waste, a miserable, abject specimen. I felt sorry for him and found a bottle of water and some kitchen roll and set to work to try to clean him up. He was pathetically grateful. No one else went near him.
All this flashed into my mind when Steven told me the news that Hocking is going to be our new boss. Note to self: probably best not to remind him of his unhappy experience on the *Going Live!* bus.
The office is soon buzzing with the announcement. Nobody had paid enough attention to the fact that Steve, who, like Joe, had been a producer on *Blue Peter* until last year, has, for the last few months, been working alongside Lorraine, our head of department, helping her with her overall strategy. Steve may be somewhat humourless, but he is highly intelligent and openly ambitious. These are qualities that someone like Lorraine values and it is no secret that she frequently found Oliver's laidback, don't-rock-the-boat, been-through-it-all-before approach, frustrating.
Steve Hocking may never have been very popular with the crew and some of the production team on *Going Live!*, but he always made quite sure he was well in with the Editor and the senior team who actually ran the show. He didn't bother much with me back then as I was too low down the food chain. If he had been asked back then, the word I suspect he would have applied to describe me was 'trivial'.
Mid-morning there is an impromptu meeting in the office, called by John, who, far from putting a brave face on it, seems intent on sharing his pain with the entire production team.

"Nobody really knows the reason why the decision has been taken," he says, solemnly. "It is a shock to us all. I can't say what will happen next...I don't know when Steve will start.....or what I will do. I'm due to see Lorraine tomorrow...."
As he talks, you can sense a slight shift in mood, from broad sympathy to a palpable awkwardness. He is over-sharing and I wish he would stop. When I get the chance to speak to him later, he is even less guarded – livid, in fact – feeling betrayed by Lorraine and maddened that the job he coveted has gone to a man for whom he has absolutely no affection or respect. He says he is going to leave as soon as they'll let him.

12th January 1999

Spend the morning pre-recording an item about famous diarists from history. Simon is to play Samuel Pepys, in full 17th-century clobber and curly wig. I happen to be in costume, inspecting the frocks, when I overhear an interesting exchange between the presenters, who are in the adjoining make-up room. Katy is offering Simon some 'advice'. "Whatever you do, don't be any good this morning, or you'll be wearing costumes for the rest of your time here."
She goes on in this vein for some time and there is a pause before Simon thanks her but says that he doesn't intend to start by being crap with any item he is given. He's going to do his best with everything that comes his way. I am so pleased with this response that I want to burst in and sing his praises, but I restrain myself as I shouldn't really have been listening.

15th January 1999

The news is out about Steve taking over. I bump into him having his photo taken in the studio. He is affable, if a little smug. Tells me that he would never have agreed to the making of the behind-the-scenes about the auditions, as it was "too cruel" to make the process public. He also tells me that, though he is a fan of history items, he doesn't like my use of specially drawn captions to illustrate points in the story. I ask him if there is anything of mine he *has* liked and he says that he enjoyed the Sandhurst films and the Mexico expedition. But I feel a bit depressed after this exchange.
I've heard what the presenters have to say too. Stuart and Katy are dismayed. From what they say, it is clear that neither of them have much time for Steve. Katy, in particular, thinks he is dull, worthy and out of touch. "You could give Steve the jouzziest film in the world, and he'd find a way of making it boring," she says.
"Do you remember the dinosaur dig?" Stuart asks Katy.
She nods and shudders. "The dinosaur dig?" I query.
"A film he directed," explains Stuart. "12 minutes of tedium looking for dinosaur

remains. We were losing the will, but Steve loved it. He told me that every little boy wants to be a paleontologist."

Konnie is more open-minded, as she has never worked with Steve, but there is the understandable apprehension that Oliver, the man who gave her the job, and offers protection from most forms of criticism (some of which she deserves), is leaving.

Simon, the new boy, is slightly bemused. "The two men who gave me the job are both going almost immediately," he says. "I hope it was nothing to do with me...."

25th January 1999

Spend a freezing morning in the Horseshoe Car Park at the front of Television Centre filming an item about a new kind of collapsible commuter bike called a City Bug. We've booked Carl Fogarty, Britain's most successful superbike racer, ostensibly to demo the bikes, but, really, the whole item is a smokescreen for us to award him a gold badge. Fogarty is a thoroughly down-to-earth Northerner, and he turns up as requested wearing his full competition leathers, ready to do whatever we ask of him. He's gratifyingly surprised when Stuart produces the gold. We wrap and, having said my thanks and goodbyes, I dash back to the office. Having swapped the bitter cold outside for the warmth within, the inevitable happens and I need to wee. The East Tower loos alternate floor by floor between male and female. This means the boys' toilets are the floor below the BP office. As I enter them, my nostrils are assailed with the most appalling stench coming from the only cubicle, from behind whose door primeval noises of effort can be heard. I know I won't make it to the nearest alternative gents so I'm forced to hold my nose and carry on regardless.

I'm just washing my hands when, to my amazement, the cubicle door swings open and there is Carl Fogarty, zipping up his leathers, still with the gold badge pinned in place. "Alright mate!," he says, cheerfully, as he shoves his hands under the basin next to mine, and I am forced to smile and ignore the choking effect of the foetid smell swirling around us. That, I reflect later, is a man with supreme confidence – deserving of a gold badge for sheer swagger.

Later, I pop over to the studio for this afternoon's run-through. For some reason, there is a feline theme, and one of the items features Konnie dressed and made-up as one of the characters from the musical *Cats*. The show has been structured in such a way that she is virtually segregated from the others in her own urban street set. Katy and Stuart, not slow to sense her self-consciousness about all this, have apparently been mercilessly taking the piss all day, and by the time I see her, Konnie is thoroughly hacked-off.

"I hate this stupid item," she hisses. "I look horrible and I've basically been

dumped by a load of bins and left to get on with it. It's my worst day ever."
Actually, she looks rather charming, but I realise that it would be pointless to say so. I commiserate and, when I bump into Stuart, chide him for his meanness.
"Konnie says it's her worst day ever," I tell him.
"Really?" he laughs, mischievously. "I think it's Katy's best day ever!"

1st February 1999
Recording the first of a series of Wednesday shows between 7 and 10pm, after the Monday programme. This is one of the more radical cost-saving measures which have been forced on us by the overspend; and muggins here has been 'volunteered' to produce the evening recordings. Oliver buttered me up by saying what a good job he knows I'll do. But it's a horrible process. Everyone has been working all day, building up to live transmission at five. Then, after a supper break, they've all got to concentrate like mad to get another whole show done in less than half the usual time.
The original plan was that we would be helped by having more VT than the other shows – maybe a couple of films – but this no longer seems like it is going to happen. Tonight we break the news that Bonnie the dog is being retired after 13 years on the programme. I'm in charge of marking this momentous occasion with a special half-hour tribute programme (also a way of saving some money – lots of old clips!) I've come up with the idea of giving Bonnie a parting gift of a special dog collar, mounted with a gold *Blue Peter* badge, the programme's highest award. This sentimental notion has been well received by everyone except Katy who is in high dudgeon.
"So typical!" she rants. "We give a gold badge to a bloody dog, but spend five years on the show working your socks off as a presenter and you don't get a light!"

5th February 1999
Oliver's last day. I imagine that, whatever his feelings about leaving, relief is prominent in the mix. As well as all the woes of the Richard fiasco, and the worry of the overspend, this year's appeal has been a real struggle. Usually, it is done and dusted by the first week of the New Year, but here we still are, desperately trying to think of fresh ways to get kids to collect aluminium cans. The general feeling is that this whole device has lost the excitement it held back before the days when recycling became routine. We've also been unlucky because, just before Christmas, the firm processing the aluminium nearly went bust. This would have been another very public disaster for the programme, and although it has narrowly been avoided, the amount of cans collected is making our progress up the famous Totaliser somewhat arthritic.

8th February 1999

Today is Steve's first official day in the job – and several of the papers are carrying the news that Stuart has quit the programme. *The Guardian*, in particular, is running a major interview with Stuart (with moodily brooding cover image) in which he is openly critical, not only of how the Richard Bacon fall-out was handled, but also of how the programme itself is run, its content and approach. He has warned nobody that this interview is imminent and consequently everyone is mightily pissed off with him. His candid words are seen as an act of huge disloyalty. But I know that Stuart will have been persuaded into this course of action; the only way that he can salvage some attention for his own departure from the show. It is a gamble, but I understand his reasons.

Steve seems to take this baptism of fire in his stride. I almost think he is enjoying himself, being calm, reasonable and saying nothing untoward about Stuart – just that they obviously need to talk and work out an exit strategy.

I later discovered the full story behind Stuart's Guardian *outpourings. In its original form, the interview, set up by his agent at the time, was deemed too bland and inoffensive. Rather than see it spiked, a confidential document which Stuart had sent to Lorraine Heggessy, was leaked to the paper. This detailed his frank views on the programme and offered some deliberately provocative ideas for ways it could be modernised and updated.* The Guardian *filleted this piece, presenting key extracts as quotes, creating the impression that Stuart was breaking ranks and letting rip. In one respect, the article did its job; immediately afterwards, Stuart was offered a role on a new ITV holiday programme. But it also left him compromised, as, at the time, he wasn't able to explain to anyone on* Blue Peter *why he had apparently given such an uncharacteristically outspoken and critical interview.*

16th February 1999

Today we turned the studio into a *Blue Peter* health spa, so that the presenters can try out various kinds of treatments. I confidently expected them all to love all this on-the-job pampering but as soon as I arrive in the studio, I am confronted with a deeply unhappy Katy. Turns out she has some kind of phobia about her feet – and hates the idea of them being seen in close-up on camera. She is supposed to be undergoing a seaweed body wrap, so I suggest that her feet are already covered by the time we reach her. She is mollified, just.

18th February 1999

Filming the story of King Charles I at the Banqueting Hall in Whitehall. Stuart is to play the doomed monarch and, as I leave the office this morning, Annie looks up from vigorously spritzing a rubber plant and says, “Do us all a favour and use a real sword...”

22nd February 1999

Along with a few other members of the team, I’m roped in to appear in an item on today’s show. Some bright spark has created a load of costumes based on famous buildings around the world. I get to model the Taj Mahal. It’s an impressive costume, but only covers my head (with a hole through which my face peeps out) and torso. So costume thoughtfully provide me with some exotic embroidered velvet trousers and a pair of brocade slippers to complete the ‘look’. When we get to transmission, I prance down the catwalk moving in what I fondly imagine to be a vaguely Bollywood fashion. Afterwards, my ‘performance’ is the subject of much mockery in the office.

“What on Earth were you doing with your hands?” snorts Annie. “You looked *ridiculous...*”

Query. Is it is possible to look anything other than ridiculous whilst casually dressed as an ancient monument?

23rd February 1999

Filming the story of the St. Paul’s Night Watch, the brave men who volunteered to stay inside the cathedral during the Blitz, extinguishing the sudden fires from incendiaries to try to ensure the survival of Wren’s great masterpiece. We are given permission to film in all the hidden passages and little rooms tucked away within the vast roof space. It is deeply fascinating to see graffiti from the time of the cathedral’s construction, as well as the traces the Night Watch themselves left behind them. The main problem is one we bring with us; Simon. He is thoroughly prepared, knows his script backwards, and is keen to take direction, but he has genuine trouble just walking and talking. This sounds ridiculous – I mean, we can all walk and talk, right? But doing so while delivering a piece to camera is a surprisingly difficult skill to master and Simon is struggling.

He tries walking with his hands clenched in front of him. “You look like you need the loo,” I say.

Then with his hands behind him. “Nope. Like a vicar showing Prince Charles round the place.”

When he leaves them either side, they lose all animation and just sort of hang there, as though they are artificial and not really connected to his body. It is all wrapped up with nerves and self-confidence, of course, and Simon badly wants to prove himself. He confesses that before his audition he had made up his mind that this was his last chance at becoming a presenter; if he had been rejected, he would have given up and tried a different career. He is 27, which is in our favour

– more life experience and judgement. It is a vast contrast to working with Richard who, when on form, was more natural and charming, but who was also frustratingly immature in so many ways. In the wake of Richard's dismissal, Simon wonders whether he had the edge over his competition because he is a vicar's son. I tell him, truthfully, that I don't think this signified in the decision-making. But Simon did endure journalists contacting old friends and visiting his home town, to see if they could dig up any dirt. These days there is nothing cosy about the shark-infested waters of children's TV.

26th February 1999
The Totaliser finally explodes, which means we can put this benighted appeal to bed. Nobody on the team ever wants to see another aluminium can.

1st March 1999
Katy is having some time off to get married and tonight we recorded the show where we announce the news. Before he left, I got Oliver to agree that we should give her a wedding present at the end of the show, but this impulse has not proved popular with the other producers. Bridget, in particular, is outraged. "Who's paying for this present? The public? IF the other presenters want to give her a present, fine. But I don't see why we should organise it or pay for it."
I stick to my guns – it's just a bit of theatre, and I think the audience will appreciate it.
Stuart tells me that, having initially invited Richard to her big day, Katy has now thought better of it, and has withdrawn the invitation. She's inviting Simon instead, who naturally feels a little awkward, because as yet he scarcely knows Katy. This, I tell him, is Showbiz.

10th March 1999
Filming the story of Nelson on board *HMS Victory*. We have been given special permission to film in the evening, after the ship is closed to the public, and to recreate the moment of Nelson's death on the actual spot where it occurred. This is a big deal as the Navy regard the ship, and this spot in particular, as nothing less than sacred. An Admiral is detailed to attend the shoot to ensure the correct gravity of approach, so we are all on our best behaviour. When the Admiral shows up, his manner is gruff and monosyllabic – no doubt he has better things to be doing than spending an evening babysitting a BBC film crew. Mandie, the PA, must be a shock to his system – or maybe she just confirms his suspicions about film crews. Very tall (even without the platform boots she is wearing), with cropped peroxide hair, very tight jeans which showcase her pneumatic figure and a broad Brummie accent, she is new to the show and keen

to impress. For the Admiral's benefit, she adopts a special "posh" voice, which sends Stuart into paroxysms of laughter.

All proceeds smoothly until the cameraman calls for another roll of tape. It is the PA's job to make sure we have plenty of these to hand, but turns out that Mandie has left the spares in the van. Everywhere inside the *Victory* is cramped and the decks have very low ceilings, so throughout the shoot the poor girl has been forced to stoop. She sets off on her mission virtually bent double.

Meanwhile, the rest of us set up for the *coup de grâce*, the climactic scene in which Stuart, as Nelson, mutters, "Thank God I have done my duty", before breathing his last. Karen, the make-up designer, checks that he sports a deathly pallor and adds a sheen of fake sweat. Stuart gets himself 'in the zone' and, by the time we have rehearsed, the Admiral unbends enough to lean over in my direction and whisper, "Jolly good this..."

We are ready to go for a take and the cameraman confirms that we have just enough tape before we need to change rolls. You could hear a proverbial pin drop as, softly, I give the command, "Action!", and, on cue, Stuart begins to shiver, seeming to fight for breath and letting his eyes assume the distant glaze of the mortally wounded. Just as he opens his mouth to deliver his final poignant line, from just above us, there is a sudden heavy pounding, a huge crash, and a loud Brummie voice shatters the atmosphere.

"Aw, shit, I've gone and given me bonce a right bloody bash..."

12th March 1999

The series producer board seems to go pretty well. I am one of three shortlisted candidates. The others are Bridget, who is talented and experienced, and has been a producer on the show for years, and Gillie Scothern, whom I first knew when she was a trainee camera operator. I'd be surprised if she gets it because she has never worked on the show before and isn't that experienced. I'd be surprised if I get it too, because I think Steve is intrinsically wary both of me and my personality. I'd say he is an introvert by nature, diffident, inscrutable, a plotter and schemer, who enjoys the secrecy of masterminding a strategy that works on a strictly 'need to know' basis. To him, the job is all about the 'big picture' and how you can position yourself to be a player among the movers and shakers, whereas I'm much more motivated by people and the actual process of programme-making. Politics and manoeuvring leave me cold. If I'd wanted them, I'd have gone into the city or the law, or somewhere the financial rewards are much greater for all that perpetual plotting and positioning.

During my board, there is a fair amount of focus on how it is possible to save money whilst keeping the show looking confident and ambitious. Steve kept stressing that, should I be appointed, I won't be able to go filming much any more. Ironically, I'm off again today, to recce the Guernsey special. As my brother and his family live there, I'm taking Rupert (my son) too and we are staying with them over the weekend, saving the BBC some hotel costs. It will be fun to have Rupert with me, and he is thoroughly excited at the prospect of the adventure ahead.

At the end of the day, we are on the way to the airport when my mobile phone rings. It is Steve, telling me that Bridget has got the job. Gillie, meanwhile, will join the show as the new films producer. He is complimentary about my "talent and dedication" to the show and says that he would be disappointed if I decide to leave. He would like me to produce the regular live OBs he wants us to stage from all over the UK – a chance to use the new lightweight technology (developed for sport) and to tick the regional diversity box. I'm disappointed but unsurprised. Bridget is a good choice, too, with excellent credentials, though she can be very bossy. Last year when she was the films producer, we locked horns on a few occasions. Not sure she has forgiven me for the time when I saw her, frown-faced, bearing down on my desk one day and I said, cheerily, "Here she comes – Hitler in knickers..." – a remark which got a bit too much of a laugh from the various bystanders.

17th March 1999

John Comerford's last show goes out today, and he is off, to take up some rapidly arranged attachment in another department. I shall miss him and his love of scurrilous gossip and fun. He is very scathing about Steve's decision to change the job title of the show's 'second-in-command' from 'Deputy Editor' to 'series producer'. Steve claims that this is simply to make the job title in line with the industry standard but nobody really buys this. As John puts it, "He just can't bear the thought of sharing the 'Editor' part of his job with anyone else...."

It isn't just the title of the job that Steve has altered. During John's time as Deputy Editor, his main responsibility was the programme's filming, especially the overseas jaunts (many of which John bagged for himself). Instead Bridget, the new series producer, will mainly be in charge of the studios, as Steve has decided that this isn't his strong point. He wants the freedom and flexibility to 'press the flesh' as Editor around the BBC and beyond, unencumbered by the detail needed to supervise three weekly shows. I actually think that this makes the job more attractive; there is far more scope for influence over the show's content and direction.

25th March 1999

Filming Simon taking part in a Royal Navy escape exercise on *HMS Hazard*. This is an incredible piece of engineering – from the outside, it is like some enormous fairground ride – a huge metal container resting on a massive gimble, which can swing the container up and down and side to side. Inside is a complete replica warship, over two levels, which, on command, can be flooded with water through a range of different-sized holes drilled in the walls and floor. It is here that naval crews train to cope with disaster scenarios in which their ship has been struck by a missile. It is an incredibly realistic, literally immersive experience. Happily for us there is a viewing platform where the main camera can be positioned without getting deluged with water. But to get the key action shots, I've volunteered to put on a wet suit and operate a mini-DV camera in a special waterproof housing. We've all been thoroughly briefed, but once the exercise begins, it feels frighteningly real, from the sound of the missile strike (and the simulation of impact) to the command over the tannoy system, "Brace, brace, brace..."

Seconds later, the water comes flooding in and Simon, along with the crew, must work as hard as he can, using pieces of wood and mallets (yes, really, that hi-tech) to try to fill the myriad leaks. It is incredibly dark, noisy, wet (obviously) and confusing, with everyone shouting and jostling for position. Team work is vital and so is staying calm. There are multiple minor injuries from people banging their heads or missing with a mallet (Simon hurts his hand), but the exercise is carefully supervised and controlled. It just doesn't feel that way. All morning during the briefing everyone has been quiet, focused, tense. None of the easy laughter and jokey comments that are usual when you work with the services. But afterwards, when it is all over, and everyone clambers outside, there is a sudden sense of jubilation from everyone, the air filled with laughter and relief. It is quite an experience.

7th April 1999

Spend the morning recording the bizarre story of a giraffe called Zarafa which became the toast of Paris in the 19th century. Accordingly, Stuart and Katy are both in period costume and both have severe wig angst. They complain to me forcefully. I ask Stuart to show me what he means. The wig he has been given is a frizz of tight blonde curls.

"I look like Vera Duckworth from *Coronation Street*," he wails.

He has a good point. They could be sisters. I agree that, in his case, the wig doesn't much matter and he can do the item without. Katy's, on the other hand, is a crucial part of the plot. During the Zarafa craze, fashionable ladies wore their hair piled as high on their heads as they could possibly make it, a style known as "a là Zarafa". Katy is supposed to demonstrate this with a vertiginous syrup that would be the envy of Marge Simpson. It is heavy and uncomfortable but, worse, from Katy's perspective, she looks ridiculous. I tell her that it is not *her* that people will be laughing at, but the hairstyle – and that is the whole point. Very reluctantly, she agrees to wear it but when I try to take photos for the annual, this is a step too far and most of the shots feature her giving me the finger; hardly what the annual is looking for.

It is a fraught day. The morning is eaten up by the Zarafa pre-record, and the rest of the show is devoted to a celebration of *Doctor Who*. When I pitched this to Steve, he couldn't see the point – the show is surely dead and buried as far as our audience is concerned. But there's a thing called the *Blue Peter* 'cyber café', a supposedly regular strand designed to reflect the growth of the internet, which is engaging children as never before. The problem is that websites and most related activities don't make very engaging or exciting television, so the 'cyber café' has become an intermittent slot, regarded by producers with the same 'enthusiasm' reserved for the garden.

I've discovered that there are some thriving *Doctor Who* internet groups involving children (most of them, it has to be said, indoctrinated by their parents) and this is the angle by which I get the go-ahead to do the item.

We have some kids in the studio to enthuse about how the internet helps them to share their interest, a parade of famous monsters (with clips from the original shows), a visit from a former star of *Doctor Who*, Louise Jameson, newly relevant again as she is known to kids from her *EastEnders* role, and the presenters, in costume as assorted Doctors, arriving in the TARDIS. No cliché left unturned. It has been a huge amount of work just to clear the clips, which are turning out to be expensive, as we have to pay every actor a repeat fee, as well as writers and composers.

Louise Jameson turns up and is delightful, very good with the kids, and utterly focused on what we are trying to do. I mention that she was the very first person I interviewed for *Doctor Who Magazine*, and it is great to have the chance to tell her how much that interview started for me.

The run-through, however, is tricky. Broadly speaking, Steve likes the show, but he hates some of the clips and thinks that they are far too violent – especially one in which Louise Jameson's character, Leela, throws a knife. He has a real go at me about it, "How on earth did you ever think that would be suitable for a children's programme going out at teatime?"

I point out that it *is*, in fact, a clip from a children's programme which went out at teatime, and he subsides a little. But he's not happy.

It's been an exhausting day and it's not over yet. The BBC have launched a digital TV service called BBC Choice which has a daily magazine programme called *Backstage*. This has approximately five viewers but, we are told, is the face of the future. The premise is that every evening from 6 to 7, *Backstage* transmits live from the set of a different BBC show or location. Today it's our turn. The

Backstage producer has told me that she isn't bothered that the set will be de-rigged around us during their show.
"It'll add to the atmosphere," she says, brightly, with all the optimism I suspect she needs to get this minutely budgeted show on the road. Unfortunately, it also adds to the noise as the scene crews don't bother to hold back with their hammering and banging and shouts of, "To you, Bill" and, "Easy, mate, you nearly had me eye out."
Very naughtily, Stuart and Konnie, who are supposed to be taking part, instead hide in the TARDIS prop, until we haul them both out. A slightly bewildered Louise Jameson is roped in, too, as am I and the director, Dominic. The 'big' item is a challenge to see which of us can assemble some flat pack furniture the fastest. Riveting telly eh? During all this pointless commotion, the hard-worked presenter, Julia Bradbury, throws in a few random questions. At one point, she says to me: "Is it true what I've heard about *Blue Peter*? That it's one big family?"
"Yes," I reply unguardedly, "just like the Borgias."

8th April 1999
Steve asks me into his office to discuss yesterday's show. He is complimentary about how rich it was, how we made *Doctor Who* relevant to our audience, and the ambition of the content and the visual style throughout. "You always get very good performances from the presenters," he adds.
But all this is a softening up for what he really wants to say. Leah has shown him the costs of the clips, and he starts to scold – "I don't want to spend thousands of pounds where I just don't see that money adding value to the programme," he explains.
I argue that, without the clips, there would have been no context and that the show simply wouldn't have worked. "You didn't need the clip of each monster," he says, adamantly. I admit that I didn't realise until too late just how expensive the clips were turning out to be. He then returns to the subject of what he considers the inappropriate levels of violence in some of them. "I *know* that's what they were able to get away with then, but times have changed and I think our judgement has got better. I really worry that we crossed a line with some of that stuff."
Fortunately for me, there have been no formal complaints, so we leave it at that, but I feel disgruntled, partly because I can see he has a point in both cases and I feel stupid that I didn't better anticipate the pitfalls.

13th April 1999
Arrive in Guernsey to shoot the special. Picked up from the hotel by this bod from the tourist board. He is very tiresome indeed, banging on and on about

how lucky we are that he is able to make himself free to accompany us ("my sec-a-terry Jackie had to clear my diary, no easy task...") and, from his talk about possible venues for lunch ("they have a very acceptable grouse") clearly imagining this is going to be one expense trip jolly. I soon disabuse him, explaining that, when we are filming, we generally grab a sandwich lunch 'on the go', and that, in any case, the BBC has a strict cap on what we can spend for meals. He shuts up for a bit but then I put my foot right in it.
"It's such a lovely island," I remark. "But what a pity they allowed the building of all these awful, ugly little bungalows. They are such an eyesore."
"I live in one of them," says the man from the tourist board.

17th April 1999
Filming the presenters taking a dip in the open sea swimming pool at La Valette. But the idiot from the Tourist Board has spread the word that we will be here so we are absolutely besieged by hordes of excited kids. This makes it very difficult for Katy, in particular, who, at one point, and despite our best efforts at crowd control, is trapped by her adoring public in a corner of the public changing rooms. She has to get out of her swimming costume while simultaneously signing autographs and fending off pushy parents brandishing cameras without a care for Katy's modesty.

4th May 1999
Filming on a *Blue Peter* RNLI lifeboat at Beaumaris, location for the first of these new-style cheap-and-cheerful OBs, which transmits live tomorrow. As soon as we wrap, the rushes go back to our unit hotel where we have set up a temporary edit suite in one of the rooms. The film will be cut overnight. It is a tough deadline and a key factor in this major new experiment, so we are working with extra adrenalin.
The crew of the boat are all local lads, thrilled to be on the telly, and very friendly. Katy is on a full charm offensive and she's soon got them all under her spell. Unfortunately, filming on these boats is undeniably sick-making. Katy, myself and the crew are all wearing RNLI dry suits, which are hot, heavy, and claustrophobic. When we are out at sea, we cut the engines to film various sequences, but looking down the viewfinder while bobbing up and down in the water has a disastrous effect on Nigel, our cameraman, who very soon admits defeat and starts to chunder over the side. He is too sick to take charge of the subsequent filming; just about all he can manage to do is to check the shots which the sound recordist and myself set up. We are feeling none too great ourselves and Katy asks one of the RNLI men if any of them ever get seasick like this. He shakes his head.

"We're all so used to it, see? But we know a cure, don't we boys?"
And so saying he gives Katy a firm push and the next thing I know our presenter is flailing about in the water. The suit and life jacket means that she is perfectly safe there, but I can tell she is not very happy about her sudden immersion.
"I wouldn't mind," she tells me later, "but I wasn't actually feeling ill..."

12th May 1999
Devoted most of today's show to a loose theme of TV past, present and future. We also have a brilliant interview with Nancy Cartwright, the voice of Bart Simpson. It is so odd to hear *that* voice coming from the mouth of a mature woman.
Straight after transmission, an email arrives from Lorraine: "Today's BP looked great," she writes. "Lots of strong, visual ideas and good use of the studio. It was a highly engaging show that kept making me turn the TV up, despite the meeting I was in!"

17th May 1999
Auditions for Stuart's replacement tonight. There are three contenders. Ben Thursby, who seems bright and fairly camp in a standard kids' show presenter way. He doesn't have any champions within the show so he seems unlikely to get it. Rhodri Owen is, I think, Steve's preferred candidate. Certainly, he is the one about whom Steve talks most enthusiastically, praising Rhodri's gravitas (he's been presenting on Welsh TV for some time), and useful experience and the fact that he is Welsh (another box ticked). He also thinks that Rhodri would be able to hold his own against Katy, while being a contrast to the other two.
The rank outsider is Matt Baker, who is only 21 and still at university. His only professional experience is a disco-dancing show which he and some mates perform in pubs for a few pounds here and there. He sent in a tape, shot by his girlfriend, on his family farm near Durham. He has that sing-song accent, an engaging face, a great smile and, for all his gaucheness, seems like a natural on camera. He was also a champion gymnast as a boy, so the trampoline part of the audition is not going to be his nemesis. From the first time I saw his tape, I am firmly in favour, and so is Bridget, the series producer, and Gabby, the forward planning producer.
If we were just applying our heads, the sensible choice would be Rhodri; but our hearts lead us all back to Matt. Steve, however, is definitely more of a head than a heart-type and Bridget, Gabby and I meet like conspirators and agree that he needs careful canvassing. If we push too hard, Steve will shut down and become stubborn and intractable. Whenever I see him, I pretend to be deeply conflicted about the choice, while (I hope) subtly underlining all the positives

that would result in casting Matt.
"Rhodri would obviously be such a safe pair of hands," say I, "but is that what we really need? Matt has so much potential..." followed by a quick recap of all those potentially useful skills – good with animals, former gymnast, excellent dancer, studying acting, instantly likeable. Then the play to Steve's ego and ambition. "From your point of view, you could be making a star instead of just booking a jobbing presenter."
Gabby, for her part, always plays Steve like a musical instrument, flattering, cajoling and advising him. He trusts her judgement, partly as they go back to his *Going Live!* days, when Gabby was kinder to him than most. Bridget is more direct. She puts it this way: "If we get Rhodri, I'll be OK with it. If we get Matt, I'll feel really excited."
On the night, Ben's audition, as expected, is a sideshow. Rhodri's is slick, polished and dull as ditchwater. In technical terms, Matt is much rougher round the edges but he has so much charm and charisma. You really want to watch him and when he goes wrong, there is no embarrassment – you are rooting for him to pull it back on track, and then he does.
Up in the gallery, Steve is loving every moment of having the casting vote. He is all smiles but giving nothing away. "There's certainly a lot to think about..."

18th May 1999
Matt Baker is going to be our new presenter. I am so delighted. As Bridget said, the prospect of working with him, helping to showcase all that natural talent, is exciting. He'll also be great alongside Simon, I reckon, a real contrast.

9th June 1999
Second of these experimental OBs, this time from Cornwall. We have a spectacular location, Trevaunance Point, and glorious weather. One of my team, Sarah, is directing. This is a cop-out on my part. It's supposed to be me, but I can't face the prospect of directing a live multi-camera show without the support of a vision-mixer. That's one of the ways these OBs come in cheaper; everyone is multi-skilling, and so the director not only cuts the show themselves, they also have to run the various VTs. I'm too scared I'll make a mess of it, so I've managed an exemption citing my heavy workload and the opportunity to give someone else a go. Sarah seems grateful. But so far I don't feel I'm missing anything.
After the show, we take the London-bound train, and Steve moves us all to the restaurant car where, over a riotously enjoyable dinner, we slowly come down from the high of such a skin-of-our-teeth live show.

15th June 1999

Long drive into the countryside with Anne Gilchrist, a fellow producer and old mate from my days in children's entertainment. It's good that we get on because we're on a bit of a wild goose chase. Our mission is to meet with Peter Purves and talk to him about an idea he cooked up last year with John Noakes and Val Singleton during the 40th birthday celebrations. The concept is for a kind of *Grey Peter* or *Old Presenters Behaving Badly,* in which they demonstrate that "age is just a number" by again trying all the kind of action and travel stuff for which they used to be famous back in the day.

It was first pitched to the head of department, Lorraine Heggessy, who passed it on to Steve, who passed it onto me. As the old saying goes, "shit rolls downwards". Steve is only too aware that we are just a few months away from digging up the box for the year 2000, and he wants a full turn out for that special occasion.

"Go and talk to him, use your charm, keep them sweet."

Actually, I think it's a pity that there is no will to take the idea seriously. It's not bad. This trio still have a certain currency and it could be very entertaining. It might also serve a purpose, given that the BBC don't have a very admirable record when it comes to programmes which empower older people. Or for employing older presenters, especially female ones, for whom the shelf-life is staggeringly short.

Peter and his wife live in a large and imposing Georgian rectory. It's rather like a scene from *Pride and Prejudice.* The house is all handsome antiques, ticking clocks and a general impression of elegant comfort. It is a warm day, so we have the meeting sitting in the beautiful garden. Pete is expansive and enthusiastic but only too aware that, in television, hyperbole rules and there is a long road between an idea, no matter how sound, and an actual commission. I'm glad for this cynicism. Given the cosmetic nature of our assignment, and the fact that we can offer and promise nothing, it helps that he clearly hasn't built his hopes too high. He makes some very disparaging comments about the management of *Blue Peter* back in his day, and about how poorly they were all paid.

"Well, you haven't done too badly," I suggest, indicating our surroundings. But Peter is dismissive; all this has nothing to do with *Blue Peter.* Surely, I argue, it was the foundation stone, what gave him his name and reputation. This he concedes.

He enjoyed the 40th anniversary, despite the sour ending of Richard's departure, about whom he asks with genuine concern. It was being reunited with Val and John on the BBC2 theme night which led to this idea. He waxes lyrical about how it could all work ("we're much funnier than we were ever allowed to be on *Blue Peter*") and suggests a pilot. We assure him that the BBC are broadly interested and will discuss further. I can sense that he is disappointed by our vagueness and I don't blame him. I wish we could level with him. It feels mean to sit in his garden, accept his hospitality, and waste his time.

16th June 1999

In the *Blue Peter* garden filming the links for Stuart's special half-hour goodbye compilation. For the closing sequence, I've decided to rip off the Peter Davison/Colin Baker regeneration from *Doctor Who* and, as we see Stuart walking out of the garden for the last time, I plan to add little clips and soundbites from his five-year stint, and make them spin round him, building up until they explode in a collage of memories, taking us into the closing credits.
I explain the concept to Stuart.
"Won't that seem a bit like an obituary?" he queries.

21st June 1999

Stuart's last show. As is customary on these occasions, while, as the departing presenter, the whole show is about him, it is all planned as a surprise for him, so that he doesn't actually rehearse anything, only taking part in live transmission. But someone is needed to stand in for him during rehearsals and Bridget asks me to do it. It's fun but also a salutary lesson in how difficult it is to present a multi-camera show. The other presenters take every opportunity to take the piss out of my efforts. It doesn't help that for some reason I've dressed all in black, which makes me look distinctly pale and interesting.
"Stuart, you're looking a little bit rough today..." says a beaming Katy.
"He's talking rather funny, too," adds Konnie.
Later, Karen, our make-up designer, insists on covering me with some slap. "Let me cover up that shaving rash," she murmurs, as I sit there while she dabs away at me feeling like The Ugliest Man on the Planet.
Hovering around the sidelines all day is Matt Baker, who is "trailing" the other presenters to get a flavour of what is imminently in store for him. I'm not sure it's the best idea. The poor lad is plainly terrified, his face fixed in a rictus grin. When I first greet him, he's talking nonsense, speaking so fast that he's falling over his words. His palms are so damp with terror sweat that I have to nip into make-up and wash my hands.
For the uninitiated, a studio day is an impressive sight; the sheer size of the place, the lights above, the camera gliding about, the floor manager bossing everyone through relentless rehearsals, the precise notes from the gallery above, and always the ever-present sense of the inevitable, point of no return live transmission. But I can only imagine what this is doing to Matt's psyche right now.

As part of the show, they are making Stuart a 'chocolate ring' friendship cake. Obviously someone's idea of a joke. During run-through, another wag amends the display of Smarties decorating the finished 'set piece' so that instead of reading 'Bye Stuart', they say, 'Die Stuart'.

25th June 1999

Matt's first live programme. Bridget has decided on a theme in which he constantly crops up throughout the show demonstrating his many talents, until we finally reveal that this multi-talented mystery man is the new presenter. I don't think the device works, because it makes Matt, wide-eyed and nervous, seem like an unwelcome intruder, as well as a total show-off.

28th June 1999

Last live show of the series, and I am in the director's chair. I've been incredibly nervous about this, as it is getting on for 18 months since I last directed a studio, and that wasn't live. But all the old clichés about riding bicycles apply and I am soon enjoying myself. The actual 'high' of transmission is brilliant, exhilarating and over far too soon. After the show, the traditional end of season *Blue Peter* garden party, with trestle tables of pinwheel sandwiches and finest BBC plonk, and a guest list of important contributors from the past year, as well as some of the general great and the good. At this week's production meeting, the team has been sternly reminded that this is not our party, but one for the friends and wider 'family' of *Blue Peter*. As we mill about waiting for people to arrive, one of our directors announces her intention of using tonight to pull a man. "It's been far too long since I had a decent shag," she tells everyone in earshot. She works the garden, focusing on pockets of potential males, from the assorted RNLI blokes, to a party of RAF Flying Falcons, and then a geekier contingent of museum types, getting steadily drunker and drunker. Eventually, she disappears behind the greenhouse where she can be heard throwing up and then wailing, much too loudly, "Why won't anyone fuck me?"
A small posse of friends and colleagues take charge and gently manoeuvre her off into the night, to find a cab to take her safely home.

30th June 1999

Blue Peter away day, to the faded glamour of the Passford House Hotel deep in the Hampshire countryside. I actually holidayed here as a child, so it's odd to have discovered that the programme has been coming here for years. The 'garden party' is for contributors and people we want to thank or impress. But the 'away day' is for us; a chance to swim, relax, gossip, plot, have a big lunch and tea, and then slump in the coach for the long journey home. With the connivance of Clive, our longest-serving editor, over the last few days I've covertly put together an end-of-series tape. We play this after lunch and it causes both mirth and consternation. Bridget is horrified to see that I've obtained her 1992 audition to be a presenter and included her clambering onto the trampoline. There is a sequence about Stuart's departure, cut to Divine's *You Think You're a Man, But You're Only a Boy*, and various fruity out-takes. But Steve is most concerned that I've obtained a copy of Lorraine's leaden piece-to-camera about Richard's dismissal. Prefacing it with a short link saying "And now from Buckingham Palace, Her Majesty the Queen..." I've dubbed Lorraine's words with one of our PAs who can do a passable imitation of HMQ addressing the masses.

"Whatever you do," he counsels, "don't ever let Lorraine get hold of that. She would not be amused."

"See what you did there," I say, but Steve isn't joking.

5th July 1999

We have been given permission from the high-ups to include Richard in the Mexico compilations. I've taken the opportunity to include a chunk of one film, about Mexican food, which we had to jettison when he was sacked. I have no idea why this small gesture is so pleasing to me. I suppose I just hate waste.

15th July 1999

Appraisal with Steve, for what he calls "a year of challenge and achievement." I get the impression that, over the last few months, he has revised his opinion of me somewhat. Certainly, when he first arrived I felt sure that this was going to signal the end of my own time on the programme. It hasn't quite worked out that way. He writes that I've "without complaint, taken a high degree of responsibility for the projects in which he has been involved (and) embraced change with enthusiasm."

It is true that there has been plenty of change recently and, on reflection, I can see that in the main it has been to my advantage. He sets me various objectives for the season ahead, including to produce 10 OBs from around the UK (and direct at least two – groans) and to raise the profile of Konnie. He doesn't actually ask me if I am happy to stick around for another year, but I'm not going to ruin a beautiful moment by being precious or playing hard to get.

18th August 1999

Postcard from John Noakes, who is travelling across North America, thanking me for sending him the comprehensive list of his films which he'd requested. The postcard shows a singular-looking bull moose. Noakes writes: "Put straw hair on antlers of pic and doesn't it look like BB!"

26th August 1999

To Elstree for 11am meeting with the Executive Producer of *EastEnders*, Matthew Robinson. All the usual tiresome trappings of telly power; the PA saying that "Matthew is running late" (though he can be seen just over her shoulder, pottering around his desk) and then, when I am finally admitted to the hallowed ground, "Can I get you a tea or a coffee?"

I'm here because I am planning an 'East End' special for Christmas and I want to discuss some kind of behind-the-scenes film on the BBC's number one soap. These days, we are always being told to 'cross fertilise' with other parts of the organisation and, as *EastEnders* is very popular with children, this feels like it could be good opportunity. During our email exchanges which led to this meeting, Matthew had been brief, but courteous and apparently enthusiastic. In the flesh, he seems much more suspicious, as though I've been caught in the act of pulling a fast one.

"I'm not sure how we can help you," he says, slowly. "We don't give away any secrets. That's absolutely non-negotiable."

I do my best to reassure him, offering him a chance to see the first cut of any film we make, and to transmit only after the relevant episodes of the soap have been shown.

We discuss what Simon might usefully do, once I've got him to understand that in *Blue Peter* films, the presenters are never merely onlookers, but always participate in some way. I suggest that Simon might be a floor assistant for a day. A floor assistant is the most junior member of the production team, chiefly responsible for making sure that the artists have been through make-up and costume and are ready on set, on time. It was how I started my career at the BBC, and, assuming one of the regular floor assistants is there to hold his hand, it shouldn't be beyond Simon's capabilities.

"Has he ever actually been a floor assistant?" says Matthew.

"Er...no. He's one of our presenters."

"But how will he know what to do then?"

"He'd have the real floor assistant there to show him."

"Hmm. I don't think the cast would like having your cameras around. They get very funny about things like that."

I suggest that, if we agree a date for the filming, he could make sure everyone on call that day is aware in advance and that we can shoot round anyone who isn't happy to be on camera.

"It's quite a difficult job being a floor assistant."

And so it goes on, this frustrating verbal skirmish, as Matthew puts up objections and problems, and I come up with solutions. This isn't unusual in itself, except that generally the people we meet to talk about plans for filming have broadly already made up their mind to say yes, and just want to work through the details. Robinson stares at me like an off-duty hypnotist, seemingly without blinking, and his attitude is as if I've somehow managed to sneak past his secretary and am now trying to cheat him out of his life insurance. It's a frustrating, drawn-out process and soon we start to go round in circles.

"Do you think he would be up to it, never having been a floor assistant before? We can't give away any secrets, you know."

Eventually, the secretary tells Robinson that he has to be somewhere and I am dismissed, with slightly more courtesy than I've been shown during our awkward interview, but still none the wiser as to whether we are likely to be welcome here or not, and feeling as if I've wasted my morning.

27th August 1999

Matthew Robinson has said yes, he'd be delighted for Simon to spend a day or two as a runner on *EastEnders*. Not a wasted morning after all.

31st August 1999

Arrive in St Petersburg for a week's filming, only to discover that all our bags have gone missing – not just our personal luggage, but all the crew's kit, without which, no film. It is a major crisis. We meet our fixer, Valery, and trudge about the airport, via him, pleading with various uninterested officials, trying to convey that we are not tourists, but here to make a film glorifying this great city. Forms are filled out, notes taken and promises extracted that this will all be looked into and our stuff will be traced. But Valery is obviously used to this kind of mishap. He has been making calls and announces that he has found a place where we might be able to hire kit until (and if) our own turns up. It's not going to be cheap – "you must pay in dollars," says Valery, calmly – and the other downside is that we are supposed to be shooting on the new digital widescreen cameras, which are not available here.

Before we leave the airport, I suggest we buy some essentials – a change of clothes and some toiletries – as it is getting late and the few shops are showing signs of closing. There is very little choice. I've decided that Matt should wear continuity clothing throughout the film, and, with this in mind, he had packed two of everything so that he could wear the outfit, and have the other in the wash. Now he settles on a cheap pair of trousers and the only fleece we can find that fits him and isn't covered in offensive logos.

When we are done shopping, Valery takes us to the van hired to transport us round the city and we meet Yuri, the driver, who is like some enormous Cossack and who speaks very little English. It is a wet night and Yuri drives us through the rain-soaked streets, until we reach a seedy-looking apartment block. The van swings into a turning which takes us to a vast and inadequately-lit underground car park. Everything about this *rendez-vous* is making me nervous. We are somewhere in the outskirts of St Petersburg, in a van driven by a pair of Russians we have just met, about to hand over hundreds of dollars to strangers. Maybe all this is a set-up and we are about to be robbed or worse.

"Come, we meet now," says Valery, smiling encouragingly.

When I step out of the van, I see that there is a kind of lock-up in the corner of the car park and this is where we head. Inside, two tough-looking men are lounging against the walls, both holding machine guns. My stomach somersaults. In a corner, behind a desk, sits another man with an equally uncompromising demeanour. He starts a quick-fire conversation with Valery, who seems to be saying "Da" (yes) rather a lot. Eventually, the man unlocks a metal cupboard and produces an antique-looking Beta camera, a battered sound kit and a small box of batteries. I suggest to Valery that we get Paul, the cameraman, to inspect the kit, to make sure we can use it. Valery nods and I fetch Paul, who takes a quick look and says, "Is this all they've got?"

The camera is not in great condition and, as well as being analogue, it is NTSC rather than PAL. But there is nothing else on offer and I decide that we have no choice but to pay the obviously inflated fee and hope that our kit turns up before we have to use this heap of junk. I am heartily relieved to get out of this spooky dive and finally, hours later than planned, we reach our hotel in time to grab a few hours rest before our early call in the morning. I bid everyone goodnight.

"Welcome to Russia!" says Valery, inscrutably.

1st September 1999

We are spending our first day at the Vaganova ballet school, in the heart of this beautiful city. The Russians are immensely proud of their ballet and this is where some of their top stars are trained. Parents invest everything to get their children an audition and the lucky ones often come from thousands of miles away. They lodge with strangers, seeing their own families only very rarely over the years of intense training which follow. We are here to film the start of a new term. It is an extraordinary spectacle as the chosen boys and girls queue up to be inducted into a school which, if they are lucky, may utterly transform their lives and fortunes. Paul isn't very happy with the lash-up we hired last night. It eats batteries, which we are having to change about every 15 minutes, so we have to be very sparing with what we decide to shoot. The picture quality is horrible, too. But it is better than nothing.

It has been agreed that Matt can join a class, but first we are sent to get him changed into suitable dance apparel. An unsmiling old dragon, her shapeless figure draped in black, sizes him up and mutters something to herself. I ask

Valery what she has said.
"He looks as if he has a hard body," he translates, "and perhaps the right physique for ballet."
She disappears for a moment and when she returns in one hand she is holding a pair of ballet shoes, some tights and a vest, and in the other hand, what looks like a small piece of black elastic.
"What's *that*?," asks Matt.
Valery asks and for the first time the woman cracks a slight smile.
"It is to deal with your private parts. Tuck them away between your legs. Every boy dancer must do this. She will show you how."
And Matt is led off, giggling nervously. He reappears, looking, to my eyes, like a young Nureyev, and I ask him if he's OK.
"There was no time to be embarrassed," he says, "I just got on with it, like."
This might just be Matt's mantra. He throws himself into the class, maximum effort, and I can see the instructors and other students warming to this pale and skinny foreigner, because of his attitude and a work ethic they all understand.
The main difficulty of the day is working round the deficiencies of the camera, so it is with huge relief that we hear that our kit has been found and so we can start shooting digital from tomorrow. A pity there will be a day of material which doesn't match, but it was that or nothing and totally out of our control.

2nd September 1999
Matt sees the humour in everything, and gets the giggles easily, which isn't great, as so do I and between us, once we've lost it, it can be a struggle to get back on track. Today was a good example. He had to do a piece-to-camera about Peter the Great which said, "Peter never cared for luxury and grandeur". After the first take, I gave him the note that he was making Peter sound like one of his mates down the pub. Well, that did it. He got the giggles and, inevitably, so did I.
Poor lad is really regretting his choice of clothing. When we arrived, it was cold and wet, so the fluffy brown fleece seemed like a sensible option. Since then, the weather has completely changed, the skies sunny and bright, the temperatures rising steadily. He really suffered today, boiling under the hated fleece, his face red and blotchy, his hair damp with sweat. Finally, when I call the wrap, Matt pulls off the garment in one swift movement and sits there, panting like a dog, looking wiped out and woebegone.
Saddest sight of the day was a hapless 'dancing' bear, chained to a post outside the Winter Palace.
"Fucking disgustin'," says Matt, speaking for all of us.
For dinner, Valery takes us to a hilariously pretentious 'movie' themed restaurant, where the choices include 'Liza Minnelli's heart' and 'Brigitte

Bardot's Tits' (actually deep-fried mozzarella balls).
Matt says he fancies some tits and promptly orders some.

3rd September 1999

We were filming in the city when I feel the sudden urge to go to the loo. Valery points me in the direction of some nearby public toilets. Sitting in a kiosk by the door is an elderly *babooshka,* grim-faced. Valery had told me I would have to pay so I offer her some coins, which she takes, unsmiling. In return, she hands over precisely four sheets of shiny hard toilet paper. Round the corner from the entrance is a row of cubicles, but the walls and doors are only high enough to cover your middle section. Once seated, your head sticks out over the top in full view of anyone else using the facilities. Worse, it is obviously a unisex toilet, as two elderly women in head scarves are sitting side by side in two of the other cubicles, having a good old gossip, quite unconcerned by my proximity.

This experience, however, is nothing to the horror that awaits Matt at the naval dockyards, where we are filming the replica of Peter the Great's ship, the Schtandart. The ship has been lovingly brought back to life thanks to the combined efforts of a team of sailors (mostly conscripts) and young volunteers from the city. On Saturday, we are going to film the grand re-launching ceremony.

Today is all about Matt joining the crew and getting his hands dirty. It has been agreed that Matt will join a working party of sailors, and that a uniform will be provided for him so that he looks the part.

"I tell you what," he said to me over breakfast, "I'm looking forward to having a day off from that fucking fleece."

But when we arrive, although everyone is very friendly, there is no spare uniform after all. Valery gabbles into action.

"It is not a problem. For five dollars, this man will give Matt his uniform."

'This man' is one of the sailors standing in a group nearby, waiting for orders.

"Good lad," said Matt, and encouraged by our nods and smiles, the sailor pulls off his top and strips down to his pants. Matt glances around but there is nowhere nearby to change, so he follows suit and the two of them swap clothes.

We start to set up the first shot. Matt ambles over to me and whispers in my ear.

"I don't know if you can smell it, but this uniform is absolutely steaming. It's obviously not ever been washed, like..."

The aroma of stale sailor's B.O. is indeed intense.

"But tell you what," says Matt cheerfully, "it's still better than that fucking fleece..."

He's in his element as one of the working party, getting stuck in and making everyone laugh. Other presenters would quickly have been asking whether I'd

Disc

1 GET ANGRY...
Dirty Money
Netflix
Hated hedge-fund manager M
features in a tough but meas
series about dangerous co
emissions and payday loa
investigated. Sh
pric
bu

g in the bare minimum needed to make the film
nothing wrong with this approach, it prevents any
esenter and the contributors. Matt's attitude gets
aderie is genuine and will show on screen.
Matt asks if there is a toilet anywhere.
Iatt that it is just a minute or so's walk away.
m starting to wonder what has happened to him,

e just seen," he mutters.
im and points at a small wooden cabin a few metres

e Worst Toilet In The World."
n he opened the door, he was nearly sick on the spot. He
s that I took a quick look for myself. Gingerly, I open the door. He isn't
exaggerating. The odour is atrocious. Inside the cramped space, the once-white cistern is now almost entirely black; black from layers of caked-on, hardened poo. Matt indicates an additional and horrifying detail. At some point, the seat has been covered with a *fur lining* – presumably because the winters here are so brutal. But what had once been fluffy and inviting is now the stuff of nightmares, indescribably matted, a still-life formed of little spikes of crusty, blackened, dried-hard shit.

I reel backwards to where Matt is laughing in disbelief.

"So did you find somewhere else?" I ask him.

"There *was* nowhere else," he says, his voice fluting upwards with the horror of it all. "I had no choice. I was desperate. And there was no paper and nowhere to wash your hands either.."

5th September 1999

We've hired a coach and horses to shoot some supposedly picturesque pieces-to-camera and, as we are paying by the hour, there is pressure to get the sequences shot as quickly as possible. The location doesn't help; there are noisy road works not far off, overhead planes are roaring intermittently, and passers-by are talking too loudly or wandering into the back of shot. Matt knows the words all right; he really does his homework – but his performance is wooden. One of the problems is that he is a natural mimic so, when you go through the delivery of a line with him, he picks up the cadence of your voice and then delivers a sort of impersonation of how you say the line. The effect is all wrong, and very off-putting. He has so much natural talent, but no experience or technique yet, and when things aren't quite working, he gets stressed and starts beating himself up.

"I'm a fucking idiot," I hear him mutter to himself over my cans, as he fluffs for the umpteenth time. "What's *wrong* with me?"

During the recce back in July, Valery, our fixer, suggested that we follow the ballet story with a short sequence of Matt visiting a traditional bath-house.

"It will look good, I think," he says. "Very Russian."

I'd thought, 'Why not?' and so it was added to our schedule. What Valery had omitted to tell me was that the bath-house he had selected as suitable for filming is not, in fact, anywhere in the city, but a lengthy drive away, deep in the middle of some impenetrable woodland. It is a trip we could all do without at the end of a long day, but one of Matt's characteristics is that he never moans.

"Give him time," observes Paul, our cameraman, cynically. "This is the honeymoon period."

Be that as it may, Matt keeps us laughing as the van drives on and on, over increasingly bumpy roads, until at last we are negotiating a rough woodland track cut into the forest. We are at least two hours later than planned. Our destination turns out to be a low-ceilinged pine shack, nestling among the trees. As Paul starts to unpack the camera kit, Valery goes in search of our hosts. A few moments later, he is back. There is no one there.

"Probably they have gone home, as we are late in coming. But there is no problem, because they have left the door unlocked."

Valery explains that in Russia, men go to the sauna to steam and sweat and then lie face down while a bath-house attendant beats them lightly with a bunch of wet birch twigs to stimulate the circulation. Yes, really. In the absence of the real bath-house attendant, Valery suggests that Boris, our driver, will be happy to play the part.

Paul and I go to take a look. Inside the bath-house, there are rows of individual sauna boxes, which resemble a human battery farm. Nearby are pine benches and tables for the punters to lie on. It is pitch black and we are going to struggle with lighting. Matt, meanwhile, has been exploring the rest of the building, and has found a pine-clad kitchen, with a kind of man-sized slatted shelf running along one side. We come up with a plan. Matt sits in one of the real saunas, getting good and sweaty, while Paul sets up a shot in the kitchen. On the action, Matt dashes from the real sauna into the kitchen and lies face down on the slatted shelf while Boris gets going with the birch twigs.

Behind the camera, we could hardly stand for laughing, and even on the final take, you can see that Matt, stark naked but sensitively framed, is borderline hysterical. Only a poker-faced Boris takes his 'role' deadly seriously and doesn't crack a glimmer of a smile until I shouted, "Cut!" when he starts to giggle with the rest of us.

7th September 1999

Our last day in St Petersburg, filming in the Winter Palace, where we are accompanied by a woman with the worst wig I have ever seen. She leads us to a life-sized waxwork of Peter the Great, which I gather we are greatly privileged to be allowed to film. It is distinctly creepy.

It has been a wonderful trip; both personally and professionally. I think of my own highlights; the day at the Vaganova, a night in the imperial box watching the ballet at the Marinsky Theatre, stepping 'over the red ropes' to film behind-the-scenes in the Tsar's various palaces, and the chance to make Matt the centre of attention and to watch him really blossom. He really is a remarkable find. Sitting in the airport waiting for our flight to be called and turning these poetic thoughts over in my head, I ask the boys what they have most enjoyed.

"Getting my own camera back," says Paul, the cameraman, without hesitation. "And trying their version of McDonalds."

"The fact that the lasses here dress like they used to back home in Newcastle," smiles Steve, the sound recordist. "Stilettos and tight white minis."

Matt's turn. He thinks for a moment and says, "I'll never forget the Worst Toilet in the World."

13th September 1999

Steve has told me that he wants me to produce the special programme, our first in Millennium year, in which we dig up the boxes for the year 2000. The anorak inside me is dancing a delighted jig and I think of when I was a child and read about the box in that year's annual; what I would have thought if someone had told me that, all these years later, I'd be in charge of disinterring it and delivering on decades' worth of viewer expectations.

Today I sent off the letter to John Noakes, Valerie Singleton and Peter Purves, inviting them to be involved and I start it with the line, "I suppose you could say that this letter has been in the post for 29 years....."

Swing by the studio, where Matt produces a brand new pair of Timberlands, of which he is clearly very proud.

"I'm going to keep them just for studios, like, then they won't get messed up."

"So they'll be your studio boots?" I suggest.

He nods.

"Your *Studio Boots....*?"

I start singing, adapting the jingle for Studio Line hair gel.

"S,S, Studio Boots....Studio Boots....wear your boots, any way you want them!"

Everyone in make-up is laughing now. Simon joins in the piss-take, talking loudly like a bossy floor manager.

"Please be VERY careful everyone, Matt is wearing his Studio Boots, and they

simply mustn't get a speck on them....."
I think it will be a while before Matt hears the end of his 'Studio Boots'.

14th September 1999
Major studio item celebrating 80 years of *Just William*. I've given Matt the lion's share to do and he is struggling, finding the sheer number of words on the autocue bewildering, and stumbling over them again and again as he tries to master the technique of reading from the screens mounted just below each camera. It doesn't help that, as well as reading the words as they scroll up and away, he has learnt the script too, creating conflict in his brain. The more he struggles, the more his frustration mounts and he rapidly loses confidence. It is painful to watch. The run-through is disastrous and, during the notes which follow, we redistribute the lines so that Katy takes over some of the wordier and more complex passages. Katy is glad to do so; she has been worried about Matt's faltering performance all day. Like the rest of us, she rates him, not only for his potential, but because she can see what this job means to him and she recognises in him a drive similar to her own, that ambition to be the best presenter possible. After the reallocation of lines, we go for the recording and, although there are still some shaky moments, we get away with it. I am annoyed at myself for yet again pushing Matt forward faster than he is ready to go.

22nd September 1999
Live OB from the Wildfowl and Wetlands Trust at Slimbridge. This is the notable as the first day on the programme so far in which I can truly say I was bored rigid throughout. I'm just not interested in birds or in the extended launch of this survey to which Steve has committed us, enlisting kids across the UK to help chart the nation's wildlife. Unlike me, Steve is a born twitcher, as well as being excited by the gathering of data, and so he is in his element here, chatting up (he thinks) our guest expert Michaela Strachan, and waxing lyrical to one and all that this is exactly the kind of programme *Blue Peter* does best.

28th September 1999
Take the train with Matt to the Commando Training Centre, Royal Marines, in Lympestone, Devon, where he is going to undertake the three-day potential recruits' course. The CTC has its own station platform, and here we disembark, along with a group of other young men, most with giveaway short haircuts and cheap suits. Matt is nervous. With my encouragement, he has agreed to immerse himself fully in the whole experience. In other words, he will live, eat, sleep and go through every stage of the tests with the other potential recruits, whether or not we are there to film. As well as making both his personal experience and the

end result as authentic as possible, by being "one of the boys" rather than "that wanker off the telly", my theory is that this way Matt will engender far more support and respect.

During the recce, I could see the Marines' eyes light up at the prospect of such a 'no holds barred' approach. I have booked two crews, so that we can 'leapfrog' most of the action we do film, to avoid any interruptions in what is naturally unfolding. I'll also have a DV camera myself.

Myself and the crew are staying in the officers' mess. Soon after we arrive, Matt is marched off with the rest of the potential recruits. I wonder how he is getting on and, just before we all go to bed, I nip down to the accommodation block where Matt is staying. I can see him through the windows of his dormitory, chatting in a small group of other lads, all of them cleaning boots. We have a quick chat in the corridor. The nerves have got worse and he is wide-eyed as he tells me, "Rich, it's a nightmare. They all want to know if I've fucked Katy or Konnie. They've taken my phone. And they've said they're going to shave off my eyebrows in the night."

I tell him that this will not happen, that they are just joking. I hope I'm right.

29th September 1999

Up at 4. We have arranged to film the 'wake up' drill at 5am and so we are lying in wait, cameras running, when the NCOs burst into Matt's dormitory, smashing on the lights and yelling their heads off, shouting for everyone to get out of bed and into the showers right now. Dazed, shocked, half-asleep, the lads stumble from their 'pits', many with the co-ordination of a newborn foal. Unfortunately, there is a problem. As the Marines only allow recruits to sleep in their underwear, wherever the camera trains its lens there are early morning erections, some hanging half out of their owners' pants.

There is nothing for it but to restage the whole thing. I'm annoyed as I really want the process of filming to stay firmly in the background, but what we've shot so far would not be useable after the watershed, never mind at teatime on BBC1. The NCOs order everyone back into bed, one of them screaming. "Sort your dick out NOW!" to the owner of a particularly rampant specimen. Another spotty and red-faced young man asks me in anguished tones, "you won't be using that, will you? Only my mum will be watching this, see."

Later this morning, we regroup to film the gym tests. Before these begin, there is a ferocious warm-up. Matt hurls himself into every exercise. A PTI (physical training instructor) pulls me to one side. "Your man needs to pace himself or he won't survive the morning."

But Matt is coursing with adrenalin and, despite a warning, barely slows down his frenetic pace. Sure enough, once the tests begin, one after the other, relentless, gruelling, he begins to flag. He's not the only one – others are reeling around, all co-ordination lost, and some have given up already and walked through the open fire doors where they can be heard groaning and being sick. I'm really worried about Matt. He is pouring with sweat and his face, contorted with pain, has gone a very strange colour. We pull him out into the fresh air.

"How are you feeling?" I ask, somewhat inadequately.

"I feel so bad, Rich," he replies. "Everything's just going round and round. I can see two of you."

It is a scary moment but, after a few minutes, he rallies and insists on going back inside.

"Does this mean he's failed?" I ask the PTI.

"If he'd given up, he would have," he tells me. "But he's worked through it, gone back and got stuck in. That's exactly what we are looking for. The right mental attitude to dig in and crack on."

30th September 1999

Matt has hit his stride now. The days are ridiculously demanding and the original group has thinned out considerably.

"But you'll find the pass rate is about 30% higher than normal," one of the officers tells me. "That's because these lads know they are being filmed and won't want to fail in front of their mums and girlfriends."

The main test of the day is an assault course, with a high-wire walk and literal leap of faith into a commando net, designed to test a recruits' head for heights and sheer nerve. Matt's background as a gymnast serves him well and he completes the course like a natural, though his eyes are blurred with sweat and he's clearly in a lot of pain.

Later, I ask him how he is finding it, and I'm surprised to discover he is loving every minute.

"I actually think I wouldn't mind being a marine," he says.

When I ask what the worst aspect has been, he doesn't hesitate. "The nights. The beds have a really thin plastic mattress. Sleeping on that is just horrific, and anyway you can't sleep because there's so much snoring and farting, and, you're so nervous about what's coming when you next wake up. You're just knackered *all* the time."

1st October 1999

The final day and the ultimate test; the endurance course. This is several miles of hell over the rough ground of Woodbury Common near the Commando Training Centre. The course is timed and, as well as the challenging terrain, there is a freezing pond for the potential recruits to wade through, as well as a 'sheep dip' tunnel, where, working in a trio, each man must allow himself to be pushed and pulled through a narrow underwater pipe and out the other side. Further 'smartie tubes', as they call them, are dotted around the course. Some of these are half filled with sludge and, as you crawl through them, get steadily narrower (I know this as I was made to try one during the recce).

Filming this exercise is going to be difficult as we cannot stop or restage anything, and covering all the key moments relies on the crews themselves moving very fast over the course, carrying all their heavy equipment. With this in mind, I've been allocated a Marine just to help carry kit and make sure we take the shortest cuts. Like all the Marines we have dealt with, he is unfailingly cheerful and uncomplaining, even when we nickname him "Marine PA".

Because of the marshy conditions, and so that none of our own stuff will be ruined, the Marines have also kindly agreed to equip us all from top to toe, boots included. We line up, collect our kit and change. None of us look very authentic.

"Budget bootnecks," says Marine PA.

"Yeah, we're not *Royal* Marines," agrees Adrian, our lead cameraman, "We're *Aqua* Marines!"

But it's a good thing we have the protection because when we get back to the Commando Training Centre a few hours later, we are all caked in mud from head to foot.

At the end of the day, we film Matt getting his result: "Congratulations," he's told. "You have passed the PRMC and can now proceed into recruit training."

Such has been the reality and intensity of the experience, Matt is almost reluctant to leave and catch the train back to civilian life. He has loved the camaraderie, the physical discipline and sense of achievement. We spend the long journey back to London laughing and reminiscing, and it's a good feeling to know this pair of films are going to be ones of which we are both proud.

12th October 1999

Extraordinary scene in the edit for tomorrow's programme. Steve has come for a viewing and takes issue with something in the story of Scott of the Antarctic, which we recorded this morning. I start to defend it, and before I've got very far, he loses it completely, the first time I have seen him have a tantrum of any kind.

"Oh well then," he shouts, "have it your own way, you'll never be told."

And he flounces out of the room. The editor raises an eyebrow, more amused than alarmed.

"Well, that was....odd," he says.

13th October 1999

After transmission, Steve calls me into his office and apologises for his loss of temper yesterday. "The programme was really strong," he tells me. "*Really* strong. It's just that you are so confident that you know where you want to go with a programme, it can be very frustrating trying to give you any kind of feedback. Sometimes I get the impression you don't want to listen to anything I have to say..."

He may have a point.

18th October 1999

Something of a new experiment in today's show; which is entirely devoted to Matt's video 'diary' supposedly recounting his own perspective of what it was like to take part in his first summer expedition (to Australia).

I say supposedly because he is far from happy with the results. The decision has been taken to use mostly material shot by the director, as a back-up in case Matt's self-shot footage wasn't up to scratch. Matt is deeply unhappy with the finished programme; in fact, when I see him, he is raging. He put his all into the exercise (which goes without saying as he always does), carrying his little camera everywhere, thinking up different sequences to shoot, staying up late and getting up early to work on it. But very little of this has been used. It's plain he thinks that the director has been on an ego trip and prioritised her own stuff over his. I wonder whether there were technical issues with the quality of what he shot, but he is adamant that he has looked at the material and there is nothing at fault with it. He feels strongly that it shouldn't be labelled as his video diary at all, when "I had nothing to do with most of it. It's her bloody programme, not mine."

Later, I catch up with the film editor and ask for his view. I always say that film editors are like butlers; vital in the running of things, they see and hear all, but are required to be discreet and uncomplaining, to keep secrets. But, without exactly saying so, it is clear this editor sides with Matt and shares his frustration at what he thinks could have been so much better had they been allowed to follow the original brief.

22nd October 1999

Arrive in Israel to shoot both a special and a film for the Christmas show about the baby Jesus. Despite torturous visa applications, and a lengthy meeting at the Israeli Embassy in London, actually getting into the country is far from straightforward. We are all split up and, after an interminable wait, are taken into separate interview rooms where we are grilled about our reasons for coming to Israel, our family backgrounds, our professional past and so on; with many of the questions repeated. Then the interviewer changes tack and starts to ask me all about Katy, and her reasons for coming to Israel, and what I know

about her background. When I am asked for the umpteenth time what I am planning to do while I am in Israel, I snap, "I thought I was coming here to make a special programme celebrating your country for Britain's most successful children's TV show. But I'm beginning to feel we are not welcome here."
This does not go down well with my interviewer, who gives me a stern lecture on the vital working of national security, before continuing his circuitous interrogation.
Seven hours later, we are finally released and able to meet our charming fixer, Amir, and clamber, exhausted, onto our minibus.

23rd October 1999
Making the film about baby Jesus for the Christmas show. Nazareth is a shit-hole, like a vast, filthy-dirty building site. We turn up at the church to film as planned, but the Father in charge dismisses our permit and says, "You must come back on Tuesday."
"We won't be here on Tuesday," I explain.
"That's your problem," he snaps back.
So we do what we can outside and move on. Journey to Bethlehem. Another shit-hole. Talk about no room at the inn – no room for anyone, more like – a heaving mass of traffic and people, many of them vacant, rotund tourists. We arrive at the shrine built over the sacred place where Jesus is said to have been born, and there is another tussle before we can film. We are told that the ceaseless flow of pilgrims shuffling through the tiny space can only be halted for a maximum of five minutes.
Paul the cameraman and I are allowed to cut into the endless queue to take a look and decide how we will light and shoot with such a serious limitation. Simon, meanwhile, frantically goes over and over his lines. When we are ready, officials hold back the queue and the clock begins to tick as we crowd into the cramped space. It is unpleasantly hot, airless and reeking from the never-ending procession of humanity. Yet there is still something undeniably magical about being on our own in this special place, which carries so much meaning for so many millions of people – among them Simon himself, as he is a practising Christian. He is word-perfect and we finish our shots with seconds to spare. The officials are pleased with us. As we are escorted out, one of them confides in me: "Yesterday we have to remove a Japanese crew, who took too long and showed no respect. But you are the BBC, yes? The best in the world, I think."
There is a lot of traffic in and out of Bethlehem, and, as we leave, there are hostile stares and gesticulation from groups of young men loitering by the roadside. They seem angered by us in some way. "Guys, I think you better lie down," says our fixer, Amir.

We do as he suggests, just as the first stone hits the side of the van. Others follow. It's a fairly half-hearted bombardment, and it doesn't last, but none the less, it is a reminder of the constant tensions in the area. During filming, we usually bring tapes to play on these long journeys and, by strange coincidence, just at the moment that the stones begin to hit the side of the van, the track playing is The Human League's *Lebanon*.

24th October 1999

Filming at the Dead Sea. This is a fairly amazing place but I am equally staggered by our hotel. Usually, given the rates the BBC are willing to pay, we are somewhere cheap and not always very cheerful. But the accommodation here is like something from a Jackie Collins novel. My bathroom alone is more than twice the size of my bedroom back home, with steps leading up to a sunken tub, garnished with hideous gold taps in the shape of swans' necks. The bed in the adjoining room is vast; I can stretch out at any angle I choose. Floor-to-ceiling windows offer spectacular views of the sea outside. Unfortunately, typically, we are here for one night only and, wallowing in the novelty of such overt and vulgar luxury, I find I'm strangely reluctant to leave my suite and join the others for dinner.

25th October 1999

There was no time to enjoy a hedonistic morning in my fabulous suite. In fact, this morning's call was one of the earliest I can remember – we have to check out and be on the road by 4am. This is so that we can travel to the legendary hilltop fort of Masada, whose Jewish community martyred itself rather than surrender to the invading Romans. The plan is to capture sunrise breaking over the ancient site. We reach the summit via an impressive chair lift and, as the whole place will not open for a few hours yet, we are the only people here. We find a position we like and set up the shot. No one is saying very much, which is unusual and nothing to do, I think, with the early start. I don't feel tired in the slightest, rather, I am exhilarated – the effect of the place is definitely spiritual. Slowly, the sun creeps out and light begins to spill over the golden stone of the city's remains.

9th November 1999

Another clash with Steve. He feels strongly that I've made a mistake in booking an item about a new fitness craze called 'Flexi-ball'. Basically, the premise is that you perform an aerobic circuit whilst attempting to stay balanced on these inflatable balloons. As *Blue Peter*'s ultra experienced AP, Annie Dixon, is fond of saying, "It's just a bit of fun, three minutes..." but Steve tells me, in a way that doesn't invite a debate, "children aren't interested in fitness gimmicks. It's just

vanity, and a purely adult pre-occupation."
When he sees the run-through, with all the presenters, and our vet, Joe Inglis, having a go, he changes his tune. It plays like one of the 'have-a-go' items in *The Generation Game*, and it's very funny, with Katy, Simon, Matt and Joe all making the most of their comedy efforts to keep up and not slide off the ball.
"OK, OK," he says, "I was wrong. It works."
I try not to look smug.

18th November 1999
To the jewellers Wartski, to film various priceless objects to cut into my Fabergé film. When Matt has completed a couple of pieces to camera, it is time for the close-ups. But I'm not happy. There is something clumsy and off-putting about the way Matt is handling these exquisite creations.
"Get those big fat farmer's hands out of there," I tell him. "That's a wrap for you."
I take over and do all the close-ups myself, loving every minute of the chance to handle such precious artefacts myself. Matt looks on, highly amused.
"You're such a ponce," he laughs.

25th November 1999
Filming at Longleat House for this year's Christmas special, *A Country House Christmas*. Spend much of the morning filming Konnie as a servant, slaving her way round the house. I've given her very few words so we rattle through the sequences in no time. One of the more complicated sequences requires Konnie to be receiving instruction from the housekeeper. I've roped one of our assistant producers, Gilly, into playing the part and the problem is that she's too good. Her face, set in stern lines, just makes us all want to crease up, and when she begins her ad-libbed diatribe, roundly reprimanding Konnie, this, together with Konnie's *faux* humble expression, results in me lying horizontal on the floor, paralysed with repressed laughter.
It's one of those days. The other AP, Sarah, is also dressed up for her part as the 'grey lady', one of the ghosts supposed to haunt Longleat's stately corridors.
Later, we are down in the great kitchens, filming the 'cook' – or how to make your own Longleat Log, which is basically a chocolate cake with icing 'snow' on top. The problem is that the kitchens are so cold that none of the ingredients will melt or mix properly. This is Sarah's item and, as she hasn't had time to change out of her elaborate 'grey lady' costume, once again we all get hysterical, as Sarah flaps about in her finery trying to make the margarine melt and the chocolate runny.
We pretty much have the run of the place, as the house is closed to the public, and, each evening we film till late. The staff are all terrified of Lady Bath, whose

imminent arrival nearly derails filming tonight.
"She can't see you here," says Ken, the man in charge. "It might make her really angry. We mustn't risk that."
"We're making a programme, not stealing the silver," I mutter.
Ken wants us to solve his problem by wrapping early. Apparently, her ladyship will have left by the time we return in the morning. But I'm part-way through a complicated sequence which has taken ages to light, with Simon and Konnie both in costume. Buggering off now will put us seriously behind and we only have three days (albeit with two crews) to shoot the whole show.
But, unusually for *Blue Peter*, we have paid a location fee and signed a contract, so I fight our corner and refuse to budge. Ken huffs and puffs but has to acquiesce and there is only a slightly awkward moment when Lady Bath finally makes her appearance, festooned with carrier bags, and stalks past, ignoring us and saying not a word.

26th November 1999
I've managed to persuade Steve to let me include some singing and dancing in this Longleat special and one of the numbers features Matt performing *Burlington Bertie from Bow*. All the vocals have been pre-recorded, but he is struggling to get the words right. One line in particular is proving a stumbling block.
"I'm Bert, perhaps you've heard of me? Bert! You'll have word of me..."
Except that Matt keeps miming, "You'll of had a the word of me..." which doesn't even make sense.
We are filming this part of the sequence outside in a corner of the formal gardens, and are fast losing the light. But now that awful familiar hysteria sets in, triggered by the pressure, and the basic ridiculousness of the situation, and, as he gets it wrong over and over again, we are pissing ourselves laughing as well as getting increasingly panicked. The cameraman gets cross and Matt finally just about manages it, so we can move inside to shoot the rest of the song. For this, Matt changes costume. But now he looks the spitting image of Kenny Everett's OTT character Marcel Wave.
"I'm Bert..."
More uncontrolled hilarity.

29th November 1999
Can't resist nipping down to make-up to show Matt a viewer's letter which has arrived in the wake of last week's St Petersburg special. Written in ink, by an elegant hand, and signed, "from a fan of yours", it reads: "I think your programme from St Petersburg was one of the best I have seen, so please let's

have more like it. I thought you joining the ballet in their training was great, you suited the black tights, and I was more than surprised to see how well you are endowed, you've nothing to be ashamed of in that area. Let's see some more of you in tight jeans, with your shirt tucked in, and let us see more of the outline of your lunch box..."
Matt is mortified. "Do you think there are people out there, you know, like actually having a wank over us and that?"
I suggest that it is not unlikely.

7th December 1999
Following my detailed instructions, and script, design have done a superb job recreating a typical suburban house of 1971 in the studio. A pre-record for the 'opening the boxes' special, it's a backdrop for Katy and Simon, in hot pants, flares and flowery shirt, to run through the popular toys, TV, sweets and snacks of the era. The item attracts a lot of attention from within TV Centre (rehearsals have obviously been on the 'ring main', the internal monitoring system which feeds to every TV screen in the building) and there are a lot of spectators.

16th December 1999
Freezing afternoon in the garden, filming Clare, the gardener, and the presenters, checking out the tree for the year 2000, and hunting for the boxes. The hunt is genuine as no one seems to have made a note of exactly where the boxes were interred, just a vague, "somewhere in that corner". So I've hired a high-tech metal detector and we go to work. It takes much longer than we expect, as the presenters do most of the digging themselves. There is a slightly awkward tussle when we are ready to film the actual moment of locating the treasure as Konnie clearly wants to be the one who owns the "Eureka!" moment, whereas Katy, always aware of her position as the senior presenter, is equally determined that it will be hers. This little power struggle amuses Simon, who suggests, "you should film them fighting for it, that would make good telly".
But in fact there is no contest. Katy gets her way.

19th December 1999
Pre-recording for the Christmas show. I've brought Rupert along to be in the audience. He loves every minute but there is an unfortunate altercation between him and a little girl over which of them gets to carry a lantern into the studio.
"My dad knows where you live," Rupert threatens.
The little girl turns out to be Steve's daughter.

2000

4th January 2000

A big day. Filming the opening of the boxes for the year 2000. We have one major problem. In 1984, the first box had to be moved to the *Blue Peter* garden from its original position at the front of Television Centre, where it was joined by a new box. Obviously, on that occasion, someone must have opened the 1971 model to check the state of the contents, and discovered that water had got in. Before the box was reburied, everything inside had been wrapped in plastic and sealed with tape. Unfortunately, this wasn't done on camera and so it means that the archive clip doesn't match what we are actually unveiling. Thank God I insisted that it wasn't live.

As Val, John and Peter prise open the box, the first thing we see is a wave of green sludge seeping out from inside.

"It smells like rotten cheese," exclaims Noakes, happily. "What a pong!"

Gingerly, Val fishes out some of the items and unhelpfully states the obvious, "*We* didn't put any of this packing on. Someone's obviously sneaked in there and wrapped everything up to protect it."

"Didn't work, did it?" adds Noakes, gleefully.

I stop the recording and intercede. I ask everyone to pick up in a more positive vein and soon everyone is laughing and reminiscing. I hope we will get away without too much emphasis on the discrepancy between what was buried and what we have just unearthed. The climax of proceedings is a moment to which I have given much thought. When Steve first asked me to produce this programme, he told me that 'upstairs' had offered to pay for a celebratory lunch afterwards. Working out the seating plan for this has been more complicated than producing the actual programme. The big issue is the continuing feud between John Noakes and Biddy Baxter and Edward Barnes, both of whom are guests here today, and are naturally invited to attend the lunch too.

First I spoke to all three first to check that there had been no thaw in the stand-off. There hadn't. So I suggest two separate tables, mixing up the current presenters with the oldies, and putting as much physical distance as I can between Noakes and his former employers. But I don't leave it at this. I also suggest that, at the end of the show, we award Noakes and Purves gold badges (Val was awarded hers years before) Not only does this give us a feel-good ending, it might make Noakes and Purves – both vocal in their bitterness about *Blue Peter* over the years – feel rather better disposed towards the programme. Perhaps it will help to avoid any unfortunate confrontations over lunch too. Thankfully, it pays off. Val turns up wearing her gold, and I hear both men commenting on this and complaining how yet again they have been overlooked and snubbed. Neither are expecting their big moment when it comes and Noakes, in particular, seems genuinely touched.

After this, the lunch goes like a bomb.

Footnote: The feud between Noakes and his then employers erupted in 1978 when he was in the process of leaving the programme. Noakes was offered the chance to keep Shep, his Border Collie co-star, who, like all the pets on the show, was the property of the BBC. The only condition was that Noakes sign an agreement not to use Shep in commercials. He refused to do so, and Shep remained in the care of Blue Peter*'s long-term animal handler, Edith Menezes. Noakes never forgave Edward or Biddy and made a series of adverts with a 'lookalike' dog called Skip.*

8th January 2000

Letters of thanks from Val Singleton and Peter Purves. Old-school manners. "Tuesday was great fun," writes Val. "We must seem <u>very</u> old to the present presenters but they never make us feel like that and it is always fun to come back."

To his letter, Pete adds a slightly paranoid postscript: "I shall stay in touch regarding the possibilities arising from our conversations last year. I'm not holding my breath, but I think someone has missed a trick somewhere along the line. Could the shade of the dreaded BB be penetrating and subverting our plans?"

Above: 10th March 1998 - Making it snow in the garden

Above: 26th May 1998 - Officer Cadet Bacon at Sandhurst

Left: 19th March 1998 - Directing Konnie as The Flying Duchess

Above: 20th July 1998 - Konnie at the temples of Teotihuacan

Above: 15th July 1998 - Mexican moments with Stuart

Right: 21st July 1998 - Going loco in Acapulco

Above: 18th November 1998 - *Last Christmas* 80s style

Above: 30th November 1998 Sarah Greene - fabulous as Futura. Note placing of badge

Left: Meanwhile, thanks to the plot, Katy feels her age

Above: 16th October 1998 - Celebrating the 40th anniversary with Leila Williams, Anita West and Gillian Reilly

Above: 5th May 1999 - Having fun rehearsing the live OB from Beaumaris

Above: 7th April 1999 - The return of *Doctor Who.* We were on to something!

Above: 22nd February 1999 - Bollywood modelling - the Taj Mah-Marson

Above: 26th November 1999 - Matt Baker, mover and shaker - as Burlington Bertie

Above: 26th September 1999 - Matt the Marine

Above: 3rd September 1999 - St Petersburg - just metres from the worst toilet in the world

Above: 13th April 2000 - Kippers with everything

Above: 25th November 1999 - Crisis in the kitchen - Konnie's Longleat log

Above: 26th November 1999 - Lighting the Advent Crown - Christmas at Longleat

Above: 29th November 2000 - *I Enjoy Being a Girl* - spot the odd one out

Above: 9th June 2000 - the "ladies from hell" *(L to R)* Moray London, Simon Thomas, RM, Julian Smith

Above: 31st August 2000 - No health and safety on the Golden Gate bridge

Above: 10th June 2000 - Braving the rain at the Highland Games

Above: 22nd December 2000 - Suit and tie to direct the Christmas show - *(L to R)* Vision Mixer Hilary Briegel, RM, PA Lucy Morris, producer Sarah Colclough

Above: 4th January 2000 - about to open the 80s time capsule with Janet Ellis and Simon Groom

Above: 21st June 2000 - Katy's last show and her ill-fated painting

Biddy herself writes that the event was "so thoughtfully and intelligently planned" and notes that I "must have put in a great deal of work to have got such superb performances out of all the presenters. Not a whiff of send-up."

14th January 2000

Everyone in a state of high excitement because Britney Spears has agreed to appear performing her new single. The only condition is that the item is pre-recorded (This is American record company control freakery at work – they don't want to risk 'live').

Matt is given the task of handling the brief interview which follows and he suggests it might be a nice idea to throw a question to one of Britney's dancers. This is agreed and he asks, "So, what's Britney like on tour?"

The dancer chosen is effusive and very camp.

"Oh, Britney – well, she loses EVERYTHING. She's like *totally* disorganised."

At which point the man from the record company intervenes. Muttering goes on between him and the dancer, who nods vigorously. Take two. Same question. This time the dancer is a little more reserved.

"Britney can be a little bit scatty, but mostly she's not..."

This sounded a bit odd, so another take is called for. More mutterings from the record company man.

"So, what's Britney like on tour?"

"She's great."

End of interview.

2nd February 2000

Producers' away day. All of us confined to a small conference room to discuss strategy and future plans. Steve absolutely loves this kind of occasion – he is never happier than when setting off for some kind of training programme or corporate navel-gazing exercise. It strikes me that we are a pretty dysfunctional bunch, each of us pulling in the direction we feel is right for the programme. There isn't much fellow feeling. So when the trainer announces brightly that we are going to start today by turning to the colleague on our left and say first, "One thing you celebrate about this person", followed by "One thing you'd like this person to do more of", there is a Mexican wave of awkwardness.

To my left is a producer who has been on *Blue Peter* some years. She is rather like an earnest primary school teacher, with a thin, pinched face, mousy-brown waist-length hair, and a hippyish Oxfam wardrobe. She is famous for having breast-fed her son until he was 4 (As one wag in the office put it, "It's not nice when they have teeth and can come in from the garden to ask for it every time they're thirsty...")

Her programmes reflect her invariably cautious approach; I am not alone in finding them dull, muddled and self-consciously worthy. It is no secret that Steve would like to see the back of her and having some sense of this has made her even jumpier of late. She regards me with thinly veiled distrust; I am too loud, too opinionated, and, as I seem to have Steve's favour, I'm a threat. What can I say out loud to "celebrate" her?

All too soon it will be my turn. Now it's Bridget, sitting on my right, who is doing the talking. She says, shortly: "One thing I would like Richard to do more of is listen."

There's some disconcerting nodding from round the table. Bridget smiles sweetly, having scored a bullseye. Then I'm on. I look at my colleague who flicks back her hair and manages a watery smile.

"One thing I celebrate about you is that you obviously love the programme," I offer, half-heartedly. "One thing I'd like you to do more of is....to be braver with the items you commission."

The trainer is nodding sagely, as though we are all sharing great wisdom and insight, rather than uttering empty compliments and subtly settling scores. This exercise complete, we are set up for a day of combative idea-sharing and jostling for position.

17th February 2000

Filming the story of Freddy, a brave horse of the Household Cavalry back in Edwardian times, who was sent out to the Boer War, which, by some miracle, he survived, becoming such an emblem for the regiment that they shipped him back to London. Here Queen Alexandra awarded him with a special medal. We're doing the usual mix of storytelling and reconstructions. The Household Cavalry have agreed to let Matt ride one of their horses in Rotten Row, and I've arranged to have him correctly costumed as a Boer War soldier. But health and safety shows no regard for historical accuracy and I've been told that he has to wear a modern riding hat, or the sequence is off. Various fraught meetings ensue with our costume designer. She spends hours camouflaging the modern hat with a period cover. It is a sterling piece of work but not altogether successful. The proportions are odd, and when he is wearing it, it gives Matt's head a curiously domed look, so that he looks more alien than Edwardian. As usual, we are both helpless with laughter over this minor debacle, but we press on and finally shoot something which might just work, so long as I stay on the wide shot.

More hysteria follows when Matt attempts to get through a piece-to-camera with the horse in a loose box just behind him. During rehearsals and in the intervals between takes, the horse is as good as gold, and could be auditioning for equine Hollywood. The instant I call "Action!", he rears his head and bares his teeth, gurning grotesquely over Matt's shoulder. It really is bizarre and hilariously funny.

"Have you got any apple?" says Matt, desperately, his eyes streaming with tears of mirth. "If we give him a piece of apple he might settle down."

An apple is found and quickly devoured by the horse. It makes absolutely no difference. I can no longer say "Action" because I can't trust my voice not to shake with laughter and so set Matt off once more. But even without a verbal cue the horse still seems to know whenever we are about to record. We eventually manage to sneak a useable take and when we stop to check, we find we've used an entire roll of tape on this one short piece.

29th February 2000

Arrive for our crack of dawn call at the Cutty Sark to find Katy huddled in the back of her cab, in floods of tears. She has decided to leave *Blue Peter* at the end of this series, and she is shocked to discover how much the prospect upsets her. "I suppose it's because there's no going back now, and it didn't feel real until now," she sobs.

Katy is ambitious and wants to move on to what she hopes will be bigger and better things, but, ever since she was a little girl, *Blue Peter* was her dream job, and she worked so hard, against all the odds, to achieve it. She's been a brilliant success at it, too; every year, presenter popularity is measured by the device known as 'AIs' (appreciation index). Katy is currently nudging 90, far ahead of the competition. She can be a real diva, and isn't always very generous to her colleagues, beadily mindful of the limelight and hungry for all the best films and items. But she brings real energy and sparkle to whatever material she is given, and she is fun to work with, too – bright, challenging and hard-working. I've called her Dame Katy, HRH Katy, but these days I've settled on 'Queen Mum'. This nickname definitely does not displease her.

She pulls herself together while we set up the first shot, dries her tears and touches up her make-up. Before we begin, she swears me to secrecy about her news as so far she has only officially told Steve.

1st March 2000

A wearisome and wet morning filming Simon prancing around the Greenwich Observatory dressed as the 18th-century clockmaker John Harrison. His stockings keep sagging and, from a few of the acid remarks he makes, I think he is getting a little pissed off with invariably being my first choice for films with period costume. It is with undisguised relief that he changes and we reconvene inside the National Maritime Museum, where we are due to film at their *Story of Time* exhibition. But when we arrive and start to set up, the woman from their press office is so snooty, rude, and obstructive ("you can't put your camera there. Or there.") that I lose my temper and let rip, much to Simon and the crew's embarrassment.

"Actually, do you know what? I've had enough of your shitty attitude *and* your shitty exhibition. You clearly don't realise how lucky you are to get a mention on *Blue Peter*, never mind us making the effort to film here. Looking at it, I really don't think it's of a high enough standard for the programme and so I think we had better leave and you can kiss goodbye to your plug."

I snarl at the crew to pack up. Unfortunately, in the murk of the exhibition, as I turn to storm off, I misjudge my step, crash into our camera, and kick a box of batteries halfway across the floor. Leaving my dignity behind me, I stomp off to the crew van. A few moments later, Simon joins me there, vastly entertained by my clumsiness. "You should have seen her face," he says. "She couldn't believe it. You were right though. It was a poor show on her part."

As my temper cools, however, I reflect that I might just have ended a long and fruitful relationship between the programme and the National Maritime Museum. This could be big trouble. When I get back to the office, I'm not surprised when Steve asks for a word. Sure enough, he has heard from the director of the museum. I expect the worst but, although Steve wants to know what happened, in fact, the director had been calling to apologise profusely for the behaviour of his press officer and to ask us to reconsider featuring the maligned exhibition. This is the power of the badge.

10th March 2000

Live OB from Crufts. A fair amount of chaos because this is first and foremost a public event, rather than a TV show, and everywhere we go both presenters and dogs are mobbed. Matt is having problems with Lucy, the programme's sweet-natured, but undeniably gormless, golden retriever. Lucy only has eyes for Leonie Pocock, *Blue Peter*'s resident 'dog lady', who has been looking after our four-legged friends since the mid-80s. Originally, Lucy was teamed with Simon Thomas, but he quickly lost interest when he realised that the dog wasn't ever going to obey him. During one of the films which a reluctant Simon made with Lucy, our vet, Joe, was also involved. Between them, Simon and Joe attempted to coax some kind of 'performance' from their four-legged co-star. At one point, they threw a ball for her to fetch. Lucy raced off in pursuit, seemed to forget what she was supposed to be doing, and disappeared into the distance, failing to respond to all calls for her to return. Eventually even Joe was moved to offer the damning comment, "She really is a shit dog, isn't she?"

15th March 2000

Filming through the night in the London Underground. It is an extraordinary, surreal, unnerving experience. We all squeeze into the driver's carriage of the night's last tube and this drops us off in a tunnel where we pick our way along the track and round a corner which suddenly reveals an entirely lost station, unused since Edwardian times. It's called Brompton Road, and was bricked up to keep it from the curious view of passengers in the trains which roar past just on the other side.

We've also filmed in Down Street (used as an intelligence base during the Second World War and still full of rusty equipment and peeling maps), Aldwych, a station used these days specifically for filming, and a whole section of King's Cross, which still has all the posters left there from the day it closed in the mid-60s. We are all fascinated and a bit spooked.

At Warren Street, some of the vast network of tube tunnels have been turned into a massive deep level archive, full of old films, TV shows and record masters. Adrian, the cameraman, suggests an ambitious shot in which he walks very slowly through hundreds of metres of these tunnels to find Simon, ready with his piece-to-camera, at the end. In the edit, we will speed up the shot and this will give some sense of the sheer scale of this subterranean world. This all takes some time to set up and, realistically, it has to be done in one take, so the tension is palpable as the camera creeps slowly through each tunnel, edging closer and closer to a waiting Simon, hiding away just behind a shelf of old film cans, ready to pop out and say his piece when I give the cue.

Simon, as usual, is word-perfect, and it works like a dream.

11th April 2000

Recording tomorrow's show. To accompany my film about Fabergé, the jeweller to the Russian Imperial family, I've asked Gill Shearing, who comes up with some of our 'make' ideas, if she can somehow devise a way that kids could create a Fabergé egg of their own. Her solution – using a couple of large yoghurt pots, enamel paints and stick on gems – is truly inspired. Gill's day job is as one of the 'correspondence unit' – a team of (almost exclusively) ladies who deal with the post and the emails – but she gets an extra £500 for any make idea we take up, so she's only too happy to have delivered.

12th April 2000

Three days in the Isle of Man with Konnie and Matt. We don't get off to the best start. We are picked up by a very friendly lady from the tourist board and she drives us through winding roads and picturesque scenery. At one point, she slows down the van and explains that we are about to approach the 'fairy'

bridge. Apparently, many islanders still believe in the 'little people' or fairy folk, and, she explains, it is the custom to say hello to them as you cross the bridge. As we do so, I hear Matt and myself dutifully chime in unison, "Hello little people!" but Konnie drowns us out, exclaiming, with uncharacteristic volume, "Fuck the little people!"
Awkward does not cover the pause which follows.

13th April 2000
Film in the Manx cat sanctuary. Turns out that Nigel, our cameraman, is severely allergic to cats, and, as well as the allergy, he's fairly afraid of them too. Bravely, he agrees to set up his camera inside one of the huge pens containing dozens of the creatures and, eyes streaming, shoots Konnie's crucial piece-to-camera. As she is talking, I notice that one of the cats, a particularly evil-looking specimen, is climbing stealthily up one side of the wire mesh cage. When it reaches the top, I am amazed to see it continue its progress, using its claws to hang upside down from the roof.
Konnie has very nearly reached the end of her speech, so I am loath to interrupt the take. Out of the corner of my eye, I can see the cat is stationary, dangling right above Nigel. Precisely as I shout, "Cut!", the animal leaps from its perch and manages a kind of *Mission Impossible* mid-air twist, landing, claws extended, on the hapless Nigel's shoulder. Admirably, he doesn't panic though it is only with some difficulty that we pull the cat from him.
"They always know, you see," says one of the ladies who run the place. "They can sense who's afraid of them."
Before we leave, we are offered tea and cake. But as the kitchen reeks of cat shit and all the surfaces are filthy and caked in matted cat hairs, we politely decline and beat a hasty retreat.
Kippers are one of the specialities of the island, and this afternoon we film in the factory where the fish are smoked. This is actually the second half of this story; the first, in which Matt goes out on a fishing boat, to help catch the fish, we shoot tomorrow morning. The man in charge is what they call 'a character'; dressed from top to toe in oilskins, he doesn't so much talk as boom enthusiastically, non-stop, at the top of his voice. Literally the only thing he ever wants to talk about are kippers.
"I've been in kippers all my life," he beams, "And there's nothing like 'em. If it were up to me, I'd have kippers for breakfast, kippers for lunch and kippers for tea. Kippers are king!"
I hardly dare look at Matt and, when I do sneak a look, I clock the corners of his mouth twitching, and know that he's struggling not to laugh. He fights it by becoming super-earnest about every stage of the smoking process, and all his

nodding and over-intent listening makes me want to lose it too. When we get to the end of the sequence it's with relief that I offer our thanks and say that we look forward to seeing him in the morning.

"No problem, sir!" he booms. "Now I don't need to ask what you're going to have for your dinner, do I? Because there's nothing like a kipper is there? Kippers! You just can't beat them!"

We bundle into our hire car and, as we make our way back to our hotel, we can finally give in to our collective hysteria. It is our PA Debbie's job to ring each contributor and make sure they have their call time for the next day and she asks us to shut up while she quickly works through them. Once she has done, we are straight back to laughing about the antics of Kipper Man. We all have a go but the natural mimic in Matt soon takes over and, hands waving and voice sing-song-ing up and down, he nails his uncanny impersonation and goes ever more over-the-top.

"Want a sun hat? You can't go wrong with a pair of kippers on your head. I use kippers for gloves and kippers for slippers. My wife has kippers for earrings...Kippers for goalposts!...Kippers for Prime Minister!"

A ringing interrupts his reverie. Debbie shouts for quiet again. We can tell from her voice that it's something serious.

"Hello? Yes....yes, I see. Yes, I understand. I'm so sorry...no, I do understand. Good night."

Mortified, she explains that when she called earlier, our contributor's answer machine had been switched on. She had left the message confirming tomorrow's call time but, without realising it, hadn't actually disconnected. He has just been on the line to tell her that his machine had carried on recording, that he had heard Matt doing his kipper impressions, with everyone laughing.

No one is laughing now. Matt is beside himself with shame; the last thing he or any of us wanted was to hurt someone's feelings. As soon as we get back to the hotel, I phone the man. It isn't an easy conversation. I apologise profusely and explain that we were all just letting off steam and being daft, that there was no malice in Matt's impression or mine; that, in fact, we had all been bowled over by his passion and dedication and so on. All of which is true. In the end, he seems mollified and agrees that we can go ahead and film in the morning as planned.

14th April 2000

At 7am we report to the jetty to film the fishing sequence, feeling distinctly sheepish and self-conscious. When 'Kipper Man' appears, there is no more fishy banter. At first, he is somewhat cool and businesslike. I offer fresh apologies. He warms up a bit, but it's awkward for Matt, who has to accompany the contributor on his boat and summon up a cheery performance, while the crew and I film from another boat alongside.

8th May 2000

My film about the Nazi occupation of the Channel Islands is transmitted. It does not go down well with one of my fellow producers who is married to a German and who uses the run-through to strongly express her view that she feels films like this are unhelpful in a "modern Europe". According to her husband, the British have an unhealthy obsession with the Second World War and need to get over it and move on. I accept that there is definitely some truth in this but the film isn't just focused on the tragedy which engulfed the islanders. It explains that by the end of the war, many of the German occupying force were themselves starving and desperate. It contains a sequence in which Simon visits the graveyard where many of the young German soldiers who died on the island are buried. She does not seem mollified and so I then cheapen my argument by sniping, "Anyway, we don't make the programme for your husband. We make it for the children of the UK, who, I think, are entitled to hear stories about their own history and people."

24th May 2000

An unexpected brouhaha erupts around our heads today, thanks to one of my assistant producers, Moray. One of the drearier chores for every team is the writing of Ceefax notes to accompany each programme. This week it is Moray's turn and, as a joke, he has annotated them with rude and outrageous asides, just for the amusement of his colleagues. The worst of these was a reference to Jet, the *Blue Peter* pony, bought through viewers' efforts, for the Riding for the Disabled Association. Jet had featured on the show and Moray had written this up, only with a postscript: "He may look like an old git but this walking glue factory's days are numbered." Unfortunately, he then forgot to delete this or his other embellishments and sent the document onto Ceefax, who normally trustingly publish whatever we supply, without taking much interest in the detail. On this occasion, and luckily for Moray, someone did take a look, spotted the dodgy reference to Jet and queried it with Steve. Once Steve realised what had happened, he hit the roof. He is all for making an example of Moray and turfing him off the show forthwith. I tell him that Moray is truly sorry, that, in fact, he's absolutely ashen about it, and that he is a good guy, with real ability. Fortunately, Steve likes Moray too, so he doesn't need much encouragement for a stay of execution, but he does write a strongly worded email to the team, warning that "self-inflicted wounds are the last thing we need" and that anyone taking such an attitude in future will obviously be happier working elsewhere, on a more cynical programme.

26th May 2000
Auditions tonight for Katy's replacement. It's a formality because Steve has pretty much made up his mind to give the job to a girl called Liz Barker. She is tall and unassuming, with a sweet smile and what I think is a somewhat unflattering hairstyle – the fringe cut straight across, pudding-basin style. When I comment on this, my studio director, Julian, ever the barometer of what's chic and what's shit, takes me to task and says I've got it all wrong.
"That girl is really stylish, trust me," he says. "That look is totally now."
It's a bit of a mystery as to how Liz ended up being auditioned. She's been working on the crummy *Backstage* programme on BBC Choice. She didn't send in her tape directly, by all accounts, but via a friend, who thought she might be in with a shout. She is certainly going to be a total contrast to our 'Queen Mother', Katy.
Steve tells me that his acid test for a good *Blue Peter* presenter is not someone with Katy's natural razzle dazzle but more of a friend "kids would like to invite round to tea after school."
He thinks Liz fits the bill exactly.

7th June 2000
Live OB from Whitby. Blazing sun all day, and everything seems to be going perfectly, until, just minutes before transmission, when we are all holed up in the scanner, getting ready for the 'live', Andy, our stoic technical manager, pokes his head round the door and calmly announces, "The scanner seems to be on fire."
I hop out to take a look, and sure enough, plumes of black smoke are pouring from the roof. I get straight on the phone to presentation in London to warn them that they may have to run a standby programme, but Andy and his team are bustling about with fire extinguishers and a series of rapid technical tests, and we are suddenly back in business. We're able to go on air as planned, albeit with collectively raised heart rates.

9th June 2000
Filming the history of kilts. All three boys on my team; myself, Julian (studio director) and Moray (AP) are having to act as extras to Simon (who is the star of the story). One of the sequences has us all dressed up as "ladies from hell", as kilted Scots soldiers from the First World War were nicknamed. There is a delay as Simon has been too enthusiastic with the cam cream.
"You look as if you're blacked up," I tell him.
Unfortunately, the stuff is a bugger to get off. When we are finally ready, I've set up a shot where the three of us will appear in silhouette over the brow of a trench

before advancing forward. I plan to treat this in the edit so that it looks like an authentic piece of film from the period. We all crouch down and, as I am 'acting', it is the cameraman, Adrian, who shouts, "Action!"
Up we clamber, giving it our all.
"Cuuuut!" Adrian yells. "That was bloody awful; you look like the campest Scottish soldiers ever, more like you're off shopping than out fighting. Richard – why were you holding onto the edge of your tin hat?"
"I dunno," I reply, sheepishly. "Just felt right."
"You look as if you're mincing around Ascot."
We crouch down for take two and I whisper to the others, so that when Adrian next shouts action, we all jump up holding our kilts above our knees and run towards the camera, screaming, "We've seen a German!"
Once we've got that out of our system, we scramble back into position, ready to try acting more convincingly like the warriors we are supposed to be.

10th June 2000
OB from the Kilmore and Kilbride Highland Games. This starts well enough but the weather soon turns nasty, with the threat of worse to come, and so we decide we will have to pre-record the whole show, rather than risk a live washout. This is just as well, because scarcely have we got the main sequences recorded when the skies blacken and truly open, and the crowds evaporate under the force of the downpour. We are left to shoot the remaining links as best we can, cheating any angle we can with the few hardy spectators still willing to stick around and fill out the background. We depart with the sobering thought that had we risked it and waited to tape the show in one go, viewers would have had nothing to watch but three kilted presenters soaked to the skin in a muddy, forlorn and deserted field.

15th June 2000
In the garden to film the links for Katy's farewell special, which I can't resist calling *What Katy Did*. Cue for one last accusation of being "very jolly!"
To begin with, Katy seems perfectly cheerful and she rattles through the various links without a stumble or a hesitation until we get to the final two pieces and the point of no return. Now her smile fades, her eyes well up and her lips start to tremble. She literally cannot get the words out without being choked by a torrent of tears. Several times she tries and every time it is the same. A painful stalemate. I suggest that we leave the tape running so that it is just Katy on her own with the camera. She agrees that this is worth a go, and so myself and the crew retreat and leave her to it. A few minutes later, she appears, restored to her usual full-beam smile, saying "I think you've got a couple you can use there."

We check and the ruse has worked. Word and pitch perfect, one last time. Katy sometimes gets a bad press for being a bit of a diva, but I'm reminded how much this job has meant to her, and I find it touching that her imminent departure can trigger such intense emotion. *Blue Peter* is so emphatically not just another job. I feel exactly the same way.

21st June 2000

Katy's last day in the studio. A scenic artist has produced a huge painting of Katy to hang in the back of some of the shots. It isn't a terribly flattering likeness and reminds me of the creepy portraits you see on some family graves in Mexico. Stuart has come back to act as MC for the day, and it is good to have him around again, relaxed, mischievous and on form. I ask him what he thinks about the likeness of Katy.

"She won't be happy," he remarks. "I bet it doesn't survive run-through."

Sure enough, in the interval before transmission, I see the portrait languishing ignominiously in the ring road, waiting its turn to be chucked in a skip.

29th August 2000

Flight to San Francisco, where we are to make a special show, plus a couple of standalone films with Simon and Matt. Matt is a last-minute substitution for Konnie, who may or may not be leaving the programme. She's discovered that she is currently paid less than either of the boys, and she is demanding an immediate increase to address this, or she'll leave. Steve, I know, is tempted to use the fracas as leverage to pitch her out and start again with someone else. But the situation is potentially explosive – Konnie is on strong ground with her claim that the situation is sexist and wrong. It reflects a wider truth about the BBC's unfair treatment of its female employees, who are routinely less well paid than the men. The one skill which Steve possesses in abundance is an acute sensitivity for corporate politics. There is nothing impulsive in his decision-making and he rarely makes up his mind without considering the potential (and therefore personal) ramifications. He would rather compromise and close down the situation than stick to his guns and risk a public row and potential embarrassment.

The boys have coined a fitting new nickname for their co-presenter; Kon-tract. As the flight wears on, I develop a headache and feel increasingly nauseous. Eventually, I stagger to the loo and vomit, furious because we are so nearly there. Back in my seat, I close my eyes and try to zone out. Then, without warning, I'm sick again (half-digested wine gums everywhere, one lodged painfully up my nose) and find I'm seeing double and struggling to breathe. The air stewards swing into action and I'm given oxygen via a mask until we touch down.

Everyone files off the plane but, despite my feeble protests, I'm told I must leave the flight by wheelchair. Some time later, this appears, with a cheerful young man to push me to arrivals. He talks to me loudly, as if I am deaf and simple. It takes a long while, and, when he finally wheels me through to be reunited with our group, they are all waving and laughing, taking the piss, and Simon is calling me "Dr Evil".

30th August 2000

Long day filming on the prison island of Alcatraz. We are shown some areas off limits to tourists, include a terrifying sensory deprivation cell. Anyone confined in here was plunged into absolute darkness. Our guide pointed out the concealed openings in the walls, where, at random intervals, the inmate could be hosed down with freezing cold water.

This evening, Simon orders a beer with his dinner and is absolutely delighted to be asked for his ID.

31st August 2000

Hit a major problem today when we arrive to film at the Golden Gate bridge. Back in London, we arranged, or thought we arranged, permission to shoot right at the top of one of the towers which loom halfway across the bridge. But now we are actually here, it's a different story. Some kind of supervisor in a hard hat and hi-vis jacket is sent to explain the situation. He introduces himself as Merv. At a guess, Merv is sixtysomething and, from the dead expression in his eyes, I'd say he doesn't give a flying fuck about our filming. But, boy can he talk, albeit in the most boring monotone I've ever heard. He drones on and on about insurance issues, culpability and missing bits of paperwork and then, without pausing or drawing breath, switches his lecture to wind speeds and altitude issues. So much for employing a fixer and a researcher back in London to set everything up well in advance.

Frantically, our PA, Karina, tries to reach someone in the BBC's New York office to help us negotiate. Eventually, she succeeds and Merv disappears to talk with them. There is a lengthy stand-off. I'm beginning to despair when he returns and, from the grim look on his poker face, I just know it is bad news. Except I'm mistaken. Without cracking a smile, or warming up one degree above zero, Merv informs us that we can go ahead after all. But, he explains, there is only room for director, cameraman and presenter. He leads us to a curious little vehicle, rather like a golfing buggy, in which he drives us to the base of one of the towers. Built into the centre of the tower is a tiny service lift, so small that for us all to fit we each have to hold a piece of the camera kit above our head. It is both intensely claustrophobic and uncomfortably close.

"I've been in less intimate positions with my wife," says Adrian, the cameraman. With some difficulty, Merv presses a button and the lift slowly judders into action. Progress is not swift.

"We're over the weight load," he informs us, impassively. "So there's a chance we might break down." A heavy pause. "Dunno what we do if that happens."

After about five minutes, the stuttering lift starts to slow down and I feel a stab of panic. I really don't want to be trapped in here. All our arms are aching (though, being boys, we are all trying to seem nonchalant about it) from the effort of keeping the heavy kit above our heads. It is very hot and airless now. The door inches open and we find ourselves in a tiny enclosed space, dimly lit by emergency lights, with a metal ladder reaching up to a trapdoor high above us. Merv goes first and we follow more slowly, hampered by the kit.

When we emerge through the trapdoor, it's quite literally breathtaking. The wind whips the words from your mouth. We are so high that there are clouds around us. Alarmingly, the metal platform is perforated so that wherever you walk, you look right down to the model cars zooming back and forth 289 metres way below us. That's not all – the guard rail only goes up to waist height. The wind batters us from all sides and I comment that the whole platform seems to be swaying.

"That's because it is," explains Merv, laconically. "It's designed that way to cope with the wind speeds. This is mild."

Having acclimatised, I consult with Adrian. We have no safety harnesses or equipment, not even a hard hat and a hi-vis jacket to match Merv's. On the plus side, this focuses your mind and we are all being ultra-cautious. When we have to move it is with tiny shuffling steps, one hand always gripping the guide rail.

"What do you think?" I ask him.

"We're here now," says Adrian. "Let's shoot the fuck out of it."

1st September 2000

Filming a story about Monterey Bay Aquarium. This illustrates the perils of going anywhere without a decent recce, as you are essentially making it up as you go along. We film Matt doing an impromptu interview with one of the animal experts and it doesn't go very well. It's not just Matt's lack of experience that's to blame, it's the absence of any proper background or research notes. The weather doesn't help – it is more like Dungeness in October than California in summer. There are, thankfully, some lighter moments. Matt and Simon have perfected a wickedly accurate impression of Liz's full-beam smile and round-shouldered stance, which they produce on cue as soon as anyone says "Liz".

They don't spare our PA, Karina, either. We've all noticed that she has been carting round a bulky silver flight case wherever we go and, eventually, curiosity gets the better of me and I ask what's in there. Turns out that it contains her

liberal supplies of make-up and other beauty products, and that she won't travel anywhere without it. Simon instantly christens it 'Karina's vanity hamper...'
I've exported one of my 6-year-old son Rupert's current sayings – "you said it, you do it". At home, this applies to any dreary task you ask him to do (clean his teeth, tidy his room etc). Out here on location it covers stuff like a request to carry kit, be ready for an early call, or learn an additional piece-to-camera.
Meanwhile, I've got a new nickname for Simon, who I think can be rather too quick to be cynical and dismissive. He's Doubting Thomas and he's not liking it very much. He cheers up when we tag tease Matt about this morning's less than successful interview, which I know I'll never use.
"Oh Linda, is the water in that tank very wet?"
"Do fish swim?"
Etc etc.

3rd September 2000
Film the boys touring the city in a bright red convertible. One sequence is shot in Lombard Street, otherwise known as 'the crookedest street in the world' – thinks: they've obviously never been to Harlesden. I rename it 'the dullest street in the world'. I mean, so what?
We were supposed to have a half-day but all the driving sequences take much longer than planned, and both Simon and Matt start to sulk as they see their time off evaporating. I put up with this until a take is ruined because it is so obvious they are in a huff – their lips are sticking out so much, you could arrange ornaments on them. I have a word – on the lines of "Oh poor you, being paid to drive around a beautiful city in a fabulous car. My heart bleeds. Now get on with it and, for fuck's sake, look like you're enjoying yourselves."

5th September 2000
Coaching session at the San Francisco Giants baseball stadium. We are out on the pitch under a boiling sun, and I'm gasping. Water is supposed to be on the way. As well as the dehydration, I don't know anything about baseball and, frankly, I'm not very curious about it, either. The result is that I'm uncharacteristically indecisive and I dither about until Adrian takes me to one side and gives me a well-deserved bollocking.
"I know this isn't your bag, but you are the director and it's not fair to leave it all to me and the boys. Get a grip and think about what you want from the story. Oh and have some gum – your breath stinks."
That evening we return to film an actual game and the PR team have arranged to flash a message up on the giant electronic screens, "San Francisco Giants Welcome *Blue Peter*".

When this appears, there is a collective gasp from the enormous (in all senses of the word) crowd.
"That's weird, it's like *Blue Peter* is a big deal or something," says Matt.
The fixer puts us right, and explains that a 'peter' is an American slang term for 'willy' – and that's why the name got such a reaction.

6th September 2000
Matt asks me to join him for breakfast and we have a long chat. He would like a closer relationship with Simon, who he feels keeps him at arm's length. I explain that this is in Simon's nature; he is the classic reserved Englishman. Actually, he feels things deeply but, unlike Matt, he is not naturally spontaneous, open and gregarious.
"What's gregarious mean?" asks Matt.
Matt tells me that during the summer trip he overheard Bridget, who was in charge, telling Simon that Matt would have to realise that he's a TV personality now, and not just a boy from the farm. Matt let rip at both of them, saying that they were "full of shit" and had "all the wrong priorities", and that if they thought the world of TV and celebrity was real and meant anything, they were wrong and could keep it. He says this aspect of the job makes him really unhappy. He doesn't understand why people can't just say what they think and mean.

7th September 2000
Our last day, and before we head to the airport, a scenic detour to film a story about the giant redwood trees in Muir Woods. Unfortunately, Simon isn't feeling very well. Last night our plush hotel gave us dinner on the house in their rooftop restaurant, which has wonderful views all over the city. We all drank a fair bit, but Simon was really knocking them back and the result is that all the way here we have to keep stopping the van so that he can stagger to the roadside and heave a little more. When we finally arrive, we are met by a ranger called Dolores. She's a sturdily built black woman with an impassive expression and a neat line in irony.
"I see you guys are from something called *Blue Peter*. I wasn't sure about that so I just put 'BBC' on the board..."
It doesn't take her long to clock the parlous state of poor Simon. When I am ready for a take, he is somehow able to summon his inner professional, and on camera, you'd truly have no idea that there was anything wrong. As soon as I call "Cut!", however, the mask slips and a woebegone wretch takes the place of the clean-cut TV pro.
Dolores says nothing until we set up a shot by one of the most impressive of these magnificent trees. I turn to look for Simon but there is no sign.

"Simon?" I call.
"He's in the bushes over there," says Dolores, wryly. "Er...Coughing..."
I follow her gaze to where Simon is doubled up, vomiting copiously into the undergrowth.
"Terrible case of food poisoning," I suggest, weakly.

28th September 2000
Arrive at Pompeii but, despite our fistful of paperwork, and the voluble entreaties of our fixer, we are told that we do not, in fact, have the correct permissions to film, only to photograph – i.e. with a stills camera. The fixer takes me to one side and says this is probably a ruse to extort some money. I become very stern and public service broadcasting and say that we have already paid a filming fee, and that there is no possibility of more. He looks depressed at this puritan stance but gamely returns to the argument, supported by our PA, Karen, who herself speaks passable Italian.
Even without understanding what's being said, I can quickly tell that they are locked in stalemate and going round in circles. After what feels like hours of this tiresome pantomime, James and Karen are invited to step inside the administrative offices to meet some higher authority. Karen quickly whispers that myself, Simon and the crew should go into the site and start filming. If challenged, we should say that our team are in the office and give out Karen's mobile number. This is exactly what we do, and all seems to be going well. We are just about to film a piece to camera by the amphitheatre when I spy a hatchet-faced man stalking towards us. Here comes trouble, I think, composing my face into what I hope is a pleasant and reasonable expression. But the man is neither an official, nor even an Italian. Instead, in a loud Cockney accent, he exclaims. "I thought it was – and it is. *Blue Peter.* Would you fucking believe it? You can't escape it."
The man introduces himself as Alan Russell, and, thanks to my anorak knowledge, I know who he is – a towering figure from the programme's early days. For several years, he was the main studio director, churning out two shows a week, and making films, too. Russell eventually left to produce *Record Breakers,* which he ran for years. An ex-cameraman, he is far from being the well-spoken University-educated BBC-type and indeed was well-known for being a tough cookie, who invariably spoke his mind. I remember being told how he'd returned to direct a few shows in the 80s when Peter Duncan was presenting.
"What's my motivation?" Pete had asked during rehearsals for one item.
"Your fucking pay cheque, lad," Russell had growled back.
Today he is all smiles and firm handshakes. He'd spotted the badge stuck to the

side of our camera and explains that he is on holiday in the area with his wife, a former PA, whom he had met while working on the programme. It is pleasing moment of symmetry.
A couple of hours later, Karen and James finally appear with everything sorted. Now we are free to step off the paths open to the public and to actually enter some of the staggeringly well-preserved buildings. I'll never forget the privilege of this; no fellow tourists jostling for position and getting in your way, we are free to stand inside Roman rooms, to explore as we please, and contemplate the romance and tragedy of this extraordinary place.

1st October 2000
Woke in Rome to torrential rain and slate grey skies. Unpromising breakfast – a choice from slices of a dry lemon cake, or an unappetising pile of bruised fruit. This followed by a three-hour drive through lashing storms to Assisi, where we are to make a story about St. Francis for the Christmas show. As the afternoon goes on, the weather slowly clears up but, just like Pompeii, bureaucracy and corruption present an obstacle to our plans. The monk in charge is curt and explains that to film in the Basilica, built on the site of St. Francis's tomb, will cost us $180 per minute. Not per minute of *finished* film (which would still be out of the question) but per minute we are in the building. I try to cajole, persuade, plead, anything it would take. After what seems like hours, the brother grudgingly concedes that we might film "at a special media rate" – $100 a minute, minimum of one hour's filming.
"They must want a new roof," I mutter at the fixer. When we explain that such a figure was out of the question, the monk shakes his head. He will negotiate no more.
"I didn't think the Church would be like this," I say to James.
"The Church are the worst," he replies, simply.
So much for the legacy of St Francis, the saint who rejected all worldly goods. We give up Father Sour-face as a bad job and James promises to keep trying on our behalf, and find some other way round the problem. I am not hopeful.
In the evening, we shoot some of the dramatic reconstructions for the story, with Simon dressed as St Francis. He's never self-conscious about stripping off to change in the van or round the corner of a street. "The Muscular Christian" I call him. "Worshipping at the gym, lifting weights for Jesus."
After we wrap, a late dinner and an interesting chat with Simon about his faith and beliefs. His father is a vicar, but he doesn't think that he has simply inherited his parents' beliefs. And it is perfectly true that children frequently reject these, in search of their own standards. By definition, faith must be felt, it is an instinct, beyond reason and science. Simon is 'moral' to a point which sometimes

bothers me; it can make him seem judgemental and sometimes unkind. But he is open to debate, and I know he is capable of real loyalty and comradeship, too. I think he is lonely and needs someone in his life to help him fully engage his emotions.

2nd October 2000

James has managed to fix a meeting between us and the Father in charge of deciding whether or not the church will waive the outrageous fee for filming at the tomb. James translates as I make one last plea. We are not here to make a commercial, or a holiday programme. I explain all about *Blue Peter* and how this is a rare opportunity to share with millions of children in Britain one of the great faith stories, and how we hope to screen it in our special Christmas programme. I explain that most Catholic children in Britain will never have the privilege of seeing the basilica for themselves and that this was a wonderful opportunity to experience the powerful and lasting message of this most famous saint. In the circumstances, could the Franciscans really turn us away?

The Father listens gravely and patiently and then disappears for ten minutes. When he returns, he is smiling. "You may film with our blessing."

There is one last problem. During the day, the Basilica is invariably heaving with people. It is simply not safe to film amid such a crowd, and, in any case, the noise would make unusable whatever we did shoot. The Father says he can allow us to film once the Basilica is closed, from 9pm, but he expects that this will not be possible for us. On the contrary, I assure him, this would be perfect. We are all smiles and mutual understanding. It is a complete about-turn. From being obdurate and uninterested, now the Franciscan brothers of Assisi couldn't be more friendly and helpful.

We are assigned a sweet-faced young monk to look after us and he never stops smiling and nodding, and is very attentive to Simon in particular. Every time we go for a take, he taps Simon on the shoulder, smiles and says, in his careful English, "Very good....luck....Simon."

A little later, when we have finished the various pieces to camera and are taking shots of the vivid medieval frescoes on the walls, a small choir of monks start to sing nearby and the air is filled with the pure sound of their devotion. I am not religious but I find I'm moved by the beauty of their voices, by our surroundings, and by the thought that this place has been the focus of so much intense worship for many hundreds of years.

18th October 2000

Spent last night at a crummy Blackpool hotel before today's OB. Breakfast is a grim affair. I bite into a piece of toast and am nearly sick on the spot. When I

take a closer look, I can see that it is riddled with a spider-web of blue mould. I summon the only waitress, a spotty and slack-jawed teenager squeezed into an ill-fitting maid's uniform. I show her the toast and explain that it is mouldy – not just this piece, but every slice in the rack. She takes it from me and holds it close for inspection.
"Do you want me to scrape it off then?"

24th-25th October 2000
In the Isle of Wight filming the story of Queen Victoria at Osborne House, with Liz as Her Maj and Matt as Prince Albert. To play the royal children, I've roped in my own two – Rosy and Rupert, and some of their friends. They are all as good as gold, though Rupert initially kicked off when he first felt how itchy the sailor suit costume is. He also gets a bit over-enthusiastic when he's asked to have a play sword fight with the other boy, Joe. Karen, our make-up designer, is just brilliant with all the kids, calm, kind and patient, as is Matt, who swings the boys round with unfeigned enthusiasm and generally romps about with them all between takes.
One of Liz's most likeable characteristics is her sense of humour. She laughs readily and pretty much constantly. At breakfast this morning, Rupert asked her, very politely, "Is laughter your life?" – which I thought was astute coming from a six-year-old.

8th November 2000
Stuck for an item, at the last minute I reluctantly schedule an old *Blue Peter* standby, how to make a 'winter warmer soup'.
"It's hard to get excited about soup, isn't it?" remarks Konnie, dolefully.
What with this, a bunch of gymnasts and an eight-minute history film, today's show might kindly be labelled 'classic' or 'retro'. Those of a more critical disposition will be more inclined to call it 'stale' or even 'fossilised'. I give my team a severe talking to about the calibre of ideas needed to feed the show and keep it fresh.

28th November 2000
First of three days filming for my *East End Christmas* special. After the success of last year's *Country House Christmas*, in which I managed to sneak in a few music numbers past the terminally unshowbiz Steve, this time he's let me go a little further. Which means that today we have taken over a pub just off the Caledonian Road to record that Cockney 'classic' *Knees Up Mother Brown*. Most of the extras are 'volunteers' from the *Blue Peter* office (I've bagged myself a part, too, playing a guardsman alongside AJ, one of our studio directors) while Matt's

Dad has travelled down from Durham to play Father Christmas. The only genuine Cockneys are a group of hired Pearly Kings and Queens, all of whom smell abominably (or rather their costumes do – I imagine they are almost impossible to clean) and none of whom appear to know the words to this supposedly East End standard. At first, this is hilarious, as they just kind of open and shut their mouths along with the music, but the joke soon wears thin as I realise how shit it looks on camera and that we are running out of time.

29th November 2000

All day spent filming two numbers at the Brick Lane Music Hall. The first has both of the boys in Carmen Miranda drag, singing *I Enjoy Being a Girl.* With his fine cheekbones, once clad in a frock and fully made up, Simon makes a convincingly beautiful woman, whereas Matt looks like a right old slapper. They make a great contrast, reminiscent of Jack Lemmon and Tony Curtis in my favourite film *Some Like It Hot*, and both thoroughly embrace their feminine side. I've asked costume to make them long dangly earrings out of *Blue Peter* badges, and these look great but have a habit of falling apart when the boys move too energetically – which is often. As I can't afford a choreographer, we are making up the moves between us, and Matt is so inventive with the next number, *Maybe It's Because I'm a Londoner*, that I agree to give him a choreography credit, if he can think of a suitable pseudonym. Eventually, he settles on 'Brandon Ash'.

30th November 2000

Filming with all four presenters in the Second World War house at the Imperial War Museum. This is the backdrop for an extended sketch which is basically a rip-off of *The Royle Family*. This being *Blue Peter*, however, we can't allow Matt, as the Jim Royle father figure, his usual catchphrase of "My arse". We have to substitute it with "My eye", which doesn't have quite the same impact.

4th December 2000

Lunch for the departing Clare Bradley. She's been the *Blue Peter* gardener for the best part of a decade, and I've enjoyed working with her, not just in the freezing wastes of the garden gulag, but on films like the Norfolk lavender harvest and the gardens of Versailles. She's very bright, sharp and funny, as well as really knowing her stuff, but, in the time I've been on the programme, I seem to be one of the few who rate her or see her worth. It's slightly reminiscent of the Romana scenario – a kind of group mindset prevails, which can feel uncomfortably bitchy and unkind. Often it is women being mean to other women. A while back there were lots of catty remarks about Clare's decision to

have her eyes done. The ageism is rampant. Comments like, "Who cares what this old bag is going on about?" and "We need someone young, who kids can relate to."
Ignoring the fact that pre-pubescent children often have their best and closest relationships with parents and grandparents.
Clare is well aware of this undercurrent of nastiness and negativity, but she's tougher and more worldly-wise than the more vulnerable Romana. Even so, it's never pleasant to know that the knives (or secateurs) are out and it's certainly been a factor in her decision to throw in the trowel (!).
The considerable consolation is that she's about to marry a super-wealthy man, and wants the freedom to work on her own huge garden, rather than dragging up to West London to tend our barren soil. I'll miss her.

7th December 2000
Filming Matt on stage at the Nottingham Arena as one of Steps' backing dancers. He's had precisely one day's rehearsal, yet you would never be able spot him as the amateur in the line-up. Pile the pressure on Matt, stake up the odds, and he responds and delivers, at least if there is any kind of performance or physicality involved. This is going to be a major film – and therefore a major plug – for Steps, but their record company have been a total pain throughout. The band clearly can't stand each other and are now at the point where they can't even be bothered to act the part when cameras are around. Individually, they are fine and sweet enough, but collectively they are a nightmare of sulks and tension.
As we wait, one of the dancers, at least, offers to run through the routine with Matt, who is gibbering with nerves, his lips sticking to his teeth whenever he talks. I'm feeling the pressure too. We are spending a lot of money on this shoot, with cameras dotted around the arena to capture the scale and drama of Matt's task. I've based myself backstage with our main crew and here we have constant obstruction from a total wanker of a stage manager, a spiteful little queen who is determined to build his part and fuck things up for us. We nearly come to blows as he tries to prevent us filming Matt in the moments before he goes on stage to perform. We get just enough to be useable but it is all so unnecessary. I storm off and rage about this fucker to the record company plugger, who is supposed to be here to help, but as usual is a total off-the-ball airhead. The music industry really is vile.

10th December 2000
At the BBC's film and videotape library at Windmill Road, Brentford, where I am filming all four presenters doing the links for the two *Review of the Year* programmes, responsibility for which has been handed to me. They are dressed

from head to toe in black, the idea being that they have to 'break in', *Mission Impossible*-style, to the film library, to 'liberate' the clips. This, of course, is a metaphor for my own relationship with the place, which through a combination of perseverance and persuasion has, over the years, yielded so many treasures. *Blue Peter* is virtually unique in having such a peerless archive. A librarian here tells me that Biddy was begged, on a regular basis, to release films and tapes for junking, but always steadfastly refused. Biddy herself claims this was for practical reasons – that the material could be repeated or reused. But I think it was just as much about her delight in having the power to say 'no', and frustrate the bureaucrats who have always populated the BBC.

22nd December 2000

Directing the last live show of the year, our traditional Christmas edition, which has followed pretty much the same script for several decades. This is not to say that you can feel relaxed about the work. Far from it. The last thing I want is to be the first director in all that time to screw up a magical moment in the BP calendar. The organisation of this show involves everyone on the team, and, as it is also our last working day of the year, there is a celebratory undercurrent to it all. The biggest pitfall remains the trickier words in the carol, *O Come All Ye Faithful*, ("Lo! Ye abhor not the virgin's womb.." etc) which frequently elude the kids in our studio audience. It is a bit like the dreaded Pearly Kings and Queens all over again; a sea of mouths opening and shutting vaguely and we spend a fair bit of time during rehearsals trying to position the kids who know what they're singing to favour the cameras, and tactfully exclude those for whom the lyrics are a lost cause.

2001

22nd January 2001

One of the over-used clichés of working on this programme is the phrase, "Only on *Blue Peter*!"

Today, however, it couldn't have been more apt.

When I get to the studio first thing, I hear hysterical giggling coming from wardrobe. Here I discover Simon and Matt practically paralysed with laughter. They are both squeezed into lederhosen of obscene tightness, Simon's riding right up his arse crack and cut so high at the front that they threaten to reveal a stray bollock.

At this moment, our long-suffering costume designer Debbie appears.

"I think they might be a bit on the small side," I suggest, unnecessarily.

Further collapse of both boys.

Debbie raises her eyebrows. "Yes, I've got some more on the way," she says, in tones which make it clear that *obviously* she has.

The reason for the fancy dress is that last week, Jeanette, my studio AP, went ferreting in the files of viewer letters in search of what we can never have too much of – "a short, lively item". She found a letter from a teacher in the midlands who explained that he ran a 'schuplattler' German dance group for the boys at his school, and that this had proved surprisingly popular. There was a video with the letter and it did indeed look as if the boys were having a high old time, jumping about and slapping each other's arses in true traditional German folk dancing style. They were all wearing home-made lederhosen to add to the authenticity, and, it must be said, strangeness. I booked them on the spot. This being *Blue Peter*, naturally I decided that when the group came to the studio to strut their stuff, Simon and Matt should also get dressed up and join in.

By the time we are ready to rehearse, Debbie has them both clad in less indecent lederhosen. But it's not long before they are giggling uncontrollably again, as they have spotted that, for some reason, all the boys have arrived wearing lipstick. This is somewhat disturbing. I have a discreet word with the accompanying teacher. He says that, this being television, he thought that the boys would be bound to have to wear make-up and that, as there were so many of them and this might take some time, they should arrive with some on already. I explain that we very rarely put make-up on children as these days both cameras and lighting are more sensitive than they once were.

It is a mad day. As well as the lederhosen malarkey, we have booked top chef Nancy Lam to show Simon how to cook something delicious to celebrate Chinese New Year. The actual recipe, however, is a sideshow. I'd spotted Nancy on another show and she was hilariously outspoken. Just watching her in action was an entertainment. Now I tell her, "Treat Simon as you would the most junior trainee in your kitchen" and she needs no second bidding, bossing him about and berating all his best efforts to do her bidding. I have to intervene a few times, as her comments are sometimes less than politically correct.

"Simon, what you doing? You waving your arms like a blinkin' spastic..."

The show is the very definition of the mission statement I've coined for what I consider the perfect *Blue Peter* – "trad with a twist". So, as well as the bonkers lederhosen kids and the comedy Chinese cooking, this edition also contains my film about Queen Victoria at Osborne House, and culminates in a performance from the band of the Royal Scots Dragoon Guards, who have flown from their base in Germany to help us mark Burns Night. They've brought a guest with them, a very tall, very skinny blonde violinist, dressed in a tartan ballgown. The plan is for Simon and Matt (still in lederhosen), to walk over and swing open the huge studio doors, revealing the whole regiment in all their kilted majesty, piping and drumming into the studio. Rehearsals are fine but between the run-through and transmission, some busy body in the scene crew must have spotted that the doors had been left with their opening mechanism ajar and reset them. When we are 'live' and Simon and Matt skip over to do their link and reveal the band, they find the doors stubbornly shut fast. It is a classic moment of live TV, with the boys in hysterics while up in the gallery, I'm screaming to the floor manager to send in someone to help. Meanwhile, a cacophonous drumming can be heard from outside in the ring road. The scene boys dash in, do their stuff and the doors finally swing apart, allowing the band to surge in and march to their positions. I don't know what has happened to the band's violinist in the gap between rehearsals and the actual performance, but this is the worst sound I have ever heard coming from any musical instrument, never mind a violin. The programme plays out to the baleful screech of what sound like several dying cats. The gallery is in an uproar of hysteria, and then we are off air and gasping for breath after a surreal 25 minutes of live TV.

12th February 2001

Ever on the look out for fun studio items in which the presenters can participate, I suggest we get them to try belly dancing. Jeanette goes off to research this and becomes very enthused by the idea of booking a group which are much more authentic than the typical Western take of a few foxy girls gyrating in diaphanous robes. I don't see any issue with this, until, that is, we get to the studio today and I realise that the more "authentic" approach involves generously-built ladies of a certain age wobbling their bits. The light-hearted fun item I had in mind is compromised because I'm worried that it will look as if we are being disrespectful to these women. Matt doesn't help, because it sounds as if he is taking the piss and the women get huffy.

"Only *Blue Peter* could take a serious *cultural* approach to belly dancing," says Simon, unhelpfully.

19th February 2001

Spend all morning rehearse/recording an ambitious item about Dan Dare. The AP, Steve, wants to do the whole thing like a television version of a cartoon strip and he has carefully story-boarded the whole thing. But it takes forever to achieve each painstaking set-up, and, by the time we go on air, not only have the edit had to make several major compromises simply in order to be ready for transmission (and then only just), the rest of the show is also seriously under-rehearsed. Luckily, most of this focuses on Matt's new puppy, who we are introducing to the studio, and so a degree of mayhem and shooting off into the sidelines doesn't worry anyone unduly.

5th March 2001

We actually have two studios today – TC3 for the normal live show, and TC2 next door, to record our Roman Banquet item, which I'll be using in my Rome special. Originally, I'd intended to shoot the banquet in the same studio, but after the fiasco of the Dan Dare item, and talking to our designer, I get the go-ahead to shift the whole thing into the studio next door.

Just as well, because it is a complex item, with all four presenters in costume –

Simon and Konnie as rich Roman citizens, Liz as their dizzy high society guest, Lady Barkonius (!) with Matt typecast as the hapless slave who has to wait on them all. The lavish display of food has cost a fortune.
I've roped in the series producer, Bridget, to direct, partly as she is far and away the best studio director in the department (in my opinion), and also because it means less attention will be drawn to my usual crime of over-spending in the pursuit of vintage *Blue Peter.*
Later I receive an email of mock outrage from Simon. Someone has pointed him in the direction of a dubious website called 'Famous Males', which, as the name suggests, specialises in screen grabs of TV, sporting and film celebrities generally wearing very little clothing. Simon doesn't seem entirely displeased to discover that both he and Matt have their own bespoke sections, but that Simon's is easily the biggest – or as I put it "positively bulging".
This includes key semi-naked Simon moments from various of our collaborations, including him getting measured in his pants for a pair of Levi's during the San Francisco trip, smothering himself in Dead Sea mud in Israel, and flashing the shorts he wore under his kilt during our Scottish filming trip. "Something for everyone," as I put it.

9th March 2001

I'm in make-up, talking to Karen, our designer, and loudly bemoaning the impact that this outbreak of foot and mouth is going to have on some of the films I have lined up, especially those about the Brontës and Beatrix Potter. Both of whose stories are closely associated with the landscape in which they lived and worked. Access may now be denied. Matt is glowering in a nearby chair, and what I'm saying clearly infuriates him, because presently he starts shouting at me that I haven't got a fucking clue what foot and mouth really means, that he can't believe that I'm bothered about the effect on a couple of crappy films for *Blue Peter,* that southerners are all a bunch of out of touch wankers and that this is typical of the thoughtless attitude you get down here.
Stung by his aggression, I lose my temper too.
"I wasn't actually talking to you," I snap. "But you've waded in, as usual, the oracle of all the fucking farmers. I'm *not* out of touch about foot and mouth, there's just nothing I can do about it. And I won't apologise for worrying about the impact on my job. That's what professionals do. Since you're a TV presenter, and not the Chiswick rep for the NUF, I think you should be capable of understanding that."
Matt is standing inches away from me now, his eyes ablaze, rigid with fury.
"I'm gonna give a few seconds' start but you better start running now," he snarls, "because if you don't I'm going to smash your fucking face in."

For a moment, I think about standing my ground. I'm even mildly curious about what will happen if he does hit me. But something in Matt's expression tells me it is probably a good idea to get out of there fast. Ducking past him, I dash out of the make-up room, through the studio, and into the ring road outside, where I hide behind one of the brightly coloured wooden 'eggs on wheels', one of the features of our set. Seconds later, I hear him following fast on my trail. It's like one of those childhood games of hide and seek, where your breathing seems unnaturally loud in your ears, and you are so terrified of being caught that you are almost tempted to give yourself up. I fight the urge and stay put.

When I see Matt again, just before run-through, I tell him where I was hiding, and he says, "It's just as well you did. I really wanted to give you a good punch, like."

We hug it out and laugh. It was a necessary release of tension, for both of us.

This minor spat sparked a catchphrase that in future I often used to describe Matt's various fluffs; 'foot in mouth'.

7th March 2001

Second day of filming the story of the Brontës at Haworth. Liz has got thoroughly immersed in the whole tragic saga, and, during a break, I find her sitting on a wall, peering intently at a book.

"What's that?" I ask.

"It's called Withering Heights," she replies.

"*Wuthering* Heights."

She bursts out laughing. I've given her a new nickname – Valerie Simpleton.

12th March 2001

Konnie has been sent to the Isle of Wight to make a couple of films for the forthcoming OB. The director is Julian, who is talented, effusively camp, sweet-natured, and popular with the turns. Lately, Konnie has had trouble with a stalker, some sad act who keeps writing her unpleasant and threatening letters. It's an occupational hazard for female presenters; Katy had a similar experience a year or so ago. But, as Konnie isn't slow to point out, "when Katy had a stalker, the BBC arranged a safe house and round-the-clock personal security. When it happens to me, I'm sent on a ferry to the Isle of Wight with Julian as my bodyguard!"

She also adds, mischievously, "And it took me ages to cut up all those letters from newspapers and turn them into messages for Katy..."

21st March 2001

Over the next few months, Steve has asked me to take charge of filming a series of stories with the Royal Collection. This is right up my street – I love nothing more than a ponce about a palace ("chintz" as Simon refers dismissively to these kind of films) but the point of the exercise is to make sure that *Blue Peter* is well in with Buckingham Palace before next year's Golden Jubilee.

"Of course what we *really* want is a film with William and Harry," I spout at the latest producers' meeting, but, in the meantime, these royal films will have to do. Today I take Liz to explore Queen Mary's Dolls' House at Windsor Castle. It's a startlingly realistic work of art, everything in perfect scale. There is a sweaty moment when I ask to demonstrate the way in which the gardens fold out from enormous drawers under the structure. This is only permitted on very rare occasions, but we are given the go-ahead and, despite the alarming creaking and groaning, all goes well. Liz is entranced and such is her natural awe that I have to keep reminding her, "you're not in church, love," to stop her whispering every piece to camera.

26th March 2001

Spend the morning in the garden, recording a party for over 100 pugs.

Why?

Why not?

We had been struggling for an item to involve the programme's vet, Joe Inglis, and I just suddenly thought, "Let's have a party for as many pugs as we can fit in the *Blue Peter* garden."

The design team set up marquees and a long, low table covered with doggy treats and the production team found the contributors. Everyone was more than happy to attend and it was a kind of joyous mayhem. By the time we finished, the table was a ruin and the whole place was covered in pug poo. But it is worth it, a great item.

27th March 2001

We arrived in Rome late last night for a three day whistle-stop shoot. The schedule is ridiculously crammed because we are attempting to cover in half the time what we would normally film over five or six days. The issue isn't budget, rather availability – principally mine and Simon's, who is presenting.

Not a good start either. Open the curtains to stair-rod rain and spend much of the morning miserably confined in a steamed-up van, while outside the rain continues to hammer down pitilessly. By some miracle, it does eventually pass, but then we are racing to catch up and shooting faster than I can remember in a long time. It's like some commando exercise. We are in and out of the first location – the Forum – in about an hour – rattling through the pieces to camera and the cutaways. It's in situations like this that Simon is absolutely in his element. Every line committed to memory, never a stumble nor a hesitation. I actually think he enjoys working like this, with the pressure on, and the chance to demonstrate his ability.

"Good skills," as he puts it.

At the Colosseum, there is a hiccup. We have hired a centurion's costume for Simon to wear, but the inevitable Italian bureaucracy rears its ugly head, and our written permissions prove worthless. While we argue the toss, Simon is wriggling out of his jeans and T-shirt and, with the PA's help, into the cumbersome garment we have lugged all the way from London. As soon as he has finished changing, Japanese tourists start to hover, anxious to have their photographs taken with him. But it is made clear that unless we can find a few hundred spare dollars (always the currency of choice when filming), Simon will not be allowed to film in his macho frock. Infuriated, I tell him to change back into his own clothes and he does so, disentangling himself from his newly acquired fan-club, who step back and snap him wrestling his way out of the thing, so that we can finally get started.

Finished at the Colosseum, we race to the Pantheon and then the Piazza Navona. There is no time to break, so we eat as we drive and take the Queen Mother approach to toilet breaks (i.e. hold it in till later). By early evening, we have shot sequences at the Capuchin Cemetery and arrived at our final destination – a pizza restaurant, to shoot Simon having a go at making his own pizza, Italian-style. It may be a combination of tiredness and hunger that means that Simon finds it impossible to master the art of transferring his pizza from the shovel into the oven; on three successive takes, he gives the shovel a jerk and propels the pizza onto the floor. It is hilarious and excruciating at the same time. We finally wrap well after ten and eat on the premises, exhausted but happy.

28th March 2001

Start the day filming an item about Italian fashion, with Simon modelling sharp suits and leisure wear in a high-end boutique. We borrow a £3000 suit for him to wear throughout our next sequence, a tour of the city with Simon riding a Vespa, which we've hired for the day. There isn't much time to practise, though Simon has ridden similar vehicles before. We complete several set-ups and then arrive in a square where the idea is that Simon will take the Vespa round the corner, then, on cue, drive into shot and past the camera.

When everyone is ready and the camera is running, I shout, "Action!" and a few seconds later, Simon appears on the Vespa. But there is something badly wrong as he is swaying from side to side. Seconds later, he loses control altogether, tumbling off the back, while the driverless Vespa careers off to one side. Luckily, there is no one in its path. I race over to where Simon is lying, dazed, in the road. Thank God he is not seriously hurt, though he is obviously shocked and has a few grazes. The £3000 suit is ripped and ruined.

I call a break while we regroup and decide what to do next. It is a truly nasty, frightening moment, and brings home how easily disaster can strike when you are filming. But we haven't been careless and neither is anyone too tired to be working safely. After a while, we all agree to carry on with our schedule, though the Vespa sequence is abandoned.

29th March 2001

Our final day, and the race against the clock to complete this insane schedule. We drive around to get some of the necessary high angles and wide shots of the city. I always prefer to shoot these myself, rather than relying on stock shots, but they invariably take time as you have to drive to the known vantage points and parking is often a fair distance from the actual spot from where you shoot.

We spend the afternoon in an ice-cream factory, with Simon learning how to make the stuff, before we can pack up and head for the airport and this evening's flight home. As we all wait, slightly brain-dead, for our flight to be called, Adrian, the cameraman, turns to me and says, with considerable feeling, "Rome wasn't built in a day, and it shouldn't be shot in one, either...."

2nd April 2001

In the never-ending search for items to feed the programme machine, I've stumbled across a winner from the pages of my local paper, the *Herts Advertiser*. This features a story about a group of junior cooks from the all-boys St Columba's College. It is so rare to find boys enthusiastic or capable in the cooking department that I contact the College and book them to appear on today's show to demonstrate their skills by taking part in a live cooking challenge throughout transmission. The boys are confident, well-mannered and charming and the item is a great success.

I was so impressed with the boys that my wife and I took a look round the school and decided it would be a good choice for our son, Rupert. A case of a coincidence changing our lives.

9th April 2001

Marooned on the Isle of Wight for the latest in our OBs. The main booking for the show is the celebrated yachtswoman, Ellen MacArthur. Matt is doing the interview. The only problem is that he has no idea who she is, and keeps calling

her Ellen McCarthy, which, understandably, pisses her off. He gets away with it because he is so charming, but, during a break in rehearsals I take him to task about his lack of general knowledge, and suggest he should at least show some interest in the news. He argues back pugnaciously, on the lines that he has better things to do than read. He is forever boasting that he has never read a book. I suggest that this is something to be ashamed of, rather than to shout about.
Actually, in some respects, I feel very sympathetic. All his bluster doesn't conceal the fact that he frequently feels at a disadvantage with scripts and some of the conversations in which he finds himself. Like so many boys, Matt would always rather have been active than struggling to get his head round pages of words. The problem is that he had no one to inspire or guide him to the kind of books which might have given him some pleasure and satisfaction. He was so hyper as a child that his mother took him to gymnastics to get rid of some of his excess energy. He soon revealed a natural talent and trained and competed every spare moment for years. We reap the benefits of his athleticism but also have to cope with the many telling gaps in his education. We discuss all this and conclude by agreeing a deal; he will read a book of my choice, or research and write a history script for the programme, as soon as I successfully build a dry-stone wall on his dad's farm.

14th April 2001

Today's big studio guest is one of my all-time heroes, Quentin Blake, who has agreed to take part in a master-class (questions from viewers) and demonstrate his skills by sketching the presenters live on air. This isn't exactly an original approach – I did the same when we had Shirley Hughes on a while back, except that she painted the dogs. Quentin's agent is rather grand and spends a long time explaining that Quentin mustn't be bothered by people asking him for sketches for themselves or for autographs. Apparently, he is expected to start doodling away at will – and for nothing – wherever he goes. I give the necessary reassurances. The sketch he completes of Simon, Matt and Liz is brilliant, catching their distinct personalities in a few decisive strokes. With her slight stoop and ear-to-ear smile, Liz, in particular, might have stepped straight from the pages of one of his picture books.
After we go off-air, I'm thrilled when Quentin gives me the drawing and fend off less than subtle suggestions from the presenters that they have a prior claim.
"I'll have you framed and put you in the downstairs loo," I tell them.

3rd May 2001

First day of shooting in the Lake District for my film about Beatrix Potter (played by Liz). Foot and mouth is still causing restrictions on free movement in the countryside so compromises have had to be made on access to her farm, now owned by the National Trust. I don an Edwardian suit for a cameo as Beatrix's boyfriend and the cameraman sets up various picturesque shots of us mooning about the grounds of the Potter family home. I quickly lose all integrity as director by quietly whispering a stream of obscenities to Liz as we walk arm in arm round the garden, repeatedly making her corpse and so spoiling several takes.

4th May 2001

Filming at what was once Beatrix Potter's home, near Hatfield. More recently, Dame Barbara Cartland owned the place, and indeed, I filmed her here for an unlikely item in *Record Breakers* (world's best-selling romantic novelist, I think). Cheryl Baker, as presenter, came with me, but Dame Babs took one look and refused to let her do the interview.

"Gels are no use," she trilled, insistently, "Their voices are pitched far too high and I simply can't hear a word they are saying. You must talk to me instead, young man."

There was no point arguing. I filmed Cheryl asking the questions and reacting, while actually conducting the interview myself. The Dame had several dogs of the small, snuffly variety and, to begin with, these were just out of shot on her lap. But no sooner had we turned over than the sound recordist held up his hand to stop and leant over to offer me his cans. I took a listen and, with the noise the dogs were making, it sounded just as if Dame Barbara was repeatedly and shamelessly farting. I found a way of explaining that the dogs would have to leave the room.

"Oh couldn't you just let Dickie stay?" asked Dame Barbara, plaintively. I had to insist, but seeing poor relegated Cheryl sitting in a sulk nearby, I couldn't resist adding. "Is Dickie named after Lord Mountbatten, by any chance?"

"Oh, did you know him?" enthused Dame B at once. "Such a darling man!"

I had to admit that I hadn't had that pleasure but continued to suck up in such an outrageous manner so that, when we had finished filming and were about to drive away in the hire car, Cheryl hissed at me from the passenger seat, "You! You had your tongue so far up her octogenarian arse, it was waggling out her ear-hole!"

I regale Liz with this and a few other choice memories from that shoot which, amazingly, was only four years ago. I say amazingly because, since the great lady's death, the whole place seems to have entered a rapid decline. Both inside and out, the house clearly requires much in the way of expensive repairs, and, although the eldest son is living here, the whole place smells slightly damp and musty and feels empty and neglected. This doesn't affect the filming, as the

sequences are all outside in the still-lovely grounds.
After their success in the Queen Victoria film, I've roped both my children back into acting again, with Rosy as the young Beatrix (in another curly wig, about which she is not impressed) and Rupert as her brother. He has a high old time pestering the cameraman for goes on the dolly (the tracking part of the camera rig) and looking down the lens to check the shot.

14th May 2001

Bridget is leaving; she will finish at the end of this summer. I'm not entirely surprised, as I think she has become thoroughly fed up with being always the bridesmaid and never the bride on this show. When I first joined, I found her suspicious, hostile (not an exceptional stance from the old guard on the programme, it must be said) and competitive. I gave as good as I got, and we frequently clashed. But, over time, I began to see her in an altogether different light, to appreciate her sheer ability, her creativity, and especially her sense of humour and fun, which too often had been suppressed by the demands of the programme. We began to trust each other. She has given so much to *Blue Peter*, probably too much. A couple of years ago, I wanted her job. This is still true but the difference is that, if I do get it, I'll miss her very much. We gossip while standing in for Steps during camera rehearsals. She seems to think that the process will be a formality and that I'm the obvious next-in-line. But I remember the spectre of poor, disappointed John Comerford, denied his chance to be Editor. You cannot take these things for granted.
Later, another of the producers tells me: "Do you really think that Steve will risk losing both Bridget and you? It's fine and dandy swanning around as the Editor of *Blue Peter*, but he still needs someone to actually make the programme for him....!"
This is true, and reassuring.
The top of today's show is supposed to be funny. It starts with Steps saying "Hello!" and trailing what's coming up, before they link to 'Steps' – actually, Simon, Matt and Liz, dressed as clones of the band, performing the chorus of *5,6,7,8,* the band's debut hit. Despite lengthy rehearsals and very accurate wigs and costumes, on transmission, it has to be said that Steps are rather more convincing as *Blue Peter* presenters than the presenters are as pop stars.

25th May 2001

In Vienna, filming a special to go out later this year. Today we are at the Vienna Boys' Choir. Being at the school is like leaving the 21st century. It is located in a kind of minor stately home, surrounded by ornate formal gardens. The boys themselves all wear sailor suits, exactly like Edwardian children, and they have

extremely good manners, to the extent that they seem almost unnatural in their politeness, the neatness of their dress, and even the decorous way they move about the place.
We spend considerable time setting up and lighting a special performance which they have agreed to give for us, and it looks magnificent on camera. Alas, after we have finished, and too late to do anything about it, the sound recordist admits that there is a major problem with the sound. I can only hope we can do something remedial in the dub. This technical disaster casts a considerable downer over the start of the shoot.

26th May 2001
Filming the permanent fun-fair in the heart of Vienna. I'd anticipated that this would be straightforward and fairly good fun; no lengthy pieces-to-camera, or tricky contributors, beautiful weather, and a reasonable amount of time in which to shoot everything. But I had reckoned without Liz's vertigo. She can only go round the first ride with her eyes tightly closed and when I look at the shots, I have to tell her gently that they are unusable.
"You look like you're shitting a brick," Simon tells her, unhelpfully.
"Don't look at me," she tells him, sharply. "Don't talk to me."
He is just like an annoying older brother. Holding her hand one minute but taking the piss the next. Liz summons all her courage to manage a take with her eyes open at least some of the time.
"It'll be better on the Riesenrad," I tell her, trying to impart a confidence I don't feel.
"Riesen-what?" she says, sounding hunted.
I point to the centre piece of the park – a giant wooden ferris wheel, dotted with compartments rather like little sheds. These are enclosed so I'm hoping this will help Liz to feel safer and more confident. We all crowd in and set off. Liz is OK if she doesn't look out of the window or think too hard about the fact that the room she is in is dangling high above the crowds. When she does, she sinks to the floor, moaning.
For Liz, our 'fun' afternoon has turned into a considerable ordeal.
For Simon, none of the rides hold any terrors. We film him trying out a kind of supersized sling, in which the participant lies face down, before the contraption is winched up high to one size and then suddenly released, so that the occupant plunges downwards and swings from side to side at cheek-wobbling speed. As Simon plummets towards us, he bellows, "Christopher Columbus!"
Afterwards, I ask him the reason for this curious cry.
"Well, I knew I was going to want to shout something. And I can hardly shout 'Fucking hell!' can I? So I thought I'd better come up with an alternative."

For the same reason, Simon frequently exclaims "Oh my days!" whereas Matt prefers "Dear me!"
These are the kind of problems which *Blue Peter* presenters have to think about.

28th May 2001
Our fixer, Juergen, is a singular character. He is ebullient, opinionated and volatile. Everything he says is accompanied by a gallery of exaggerated facial expressions. If I want to change the schedule, he is outraged and will protest violently, until succumbing and getting on with it. He keeps forgetting to schedule a lunch break.
"OK I get it, you are all close to fainting and I suppose you must eat. Maybe you can do it fast, yes?"
He and I bicker constantly, but I like him enormously and I think he likes us too. He has done a lot of fixing for international film and TV companies and is scathing about some of them; especially the Japanese ("they are fucking idiots, those people") and the Americans ("rude and obnoxious"). He is constantly asking me to explain what kind of programme *Blue Peter* is.
"We have no such programme in Europe, and in Austria TV for kids is just junk. Total shit."
Today Juergen has arranged for us to film at Schonbrunn Palace. One of the key locations is the room where the young Mozart was reputed to have played for Marie Antoinette, before she became Queen of France. The room is at the end of a long gallery, through a pair of ornate gilded doors.
We are setting up and not far from being ready for a take when I spot a trickle of Japanese tourists wandering into the gallery and staring in our direction. A pair of them instantly fire up their ubiquitous video cameras. A few more appear through the doorway. They are obviously the advance party from one of the large tours which swarm the place. I alert Juergen. He takes one look and his face is transformed into a sneering mask of contempt. Marching into the gallery, waving his arms like Air Traffic Control, he shouts at the hapless tourists, "No, no, this gallery is closed. Fuck off now. You fuck off. *We* are the BBC and *you* fuck off."
Utterly cowed, they immediately do as they are told and withdraw without a word of protest. Juergen stands guard by the entrance, his expression fierce, until we have wrapped. Later, I feel I must take him to task about his language and explain that he could get us into a lot of trouble by swearing like that while representing the BBC. He is utterly unrepentant.
"These people are fucking sheep," he shrugs his shoulders. "You cannot reason or ask, you must command. You have paid to be there. And it is my job to protect you from these fucking sheep-idiots."
You can't fault his passion.

29th May 2001

An idyllic summer day. Long drive into the countryside, to a place called Piber, home to the fabulous white Lipizzaner horses of Vienna's Spanish Riding School. Juergen has been through some tough negotiations to get us access, not least because the Riding School do not permit female riders and so it has been a major problem to get them to allow us to film Liz on horseback. The compromise is that she can be filmed under instruction in the school, but only once she has passed a strict riding assessment. This takes place behind closed doors, with none of the rest of us allowed to be present. Liz is understandably intimidated by this condition but we leave her mic on, so that we can listen in and monitor from outside.

"I feel like I'm going for my driving test," says Liz, as she is led off.

The instructor is tough and unsmiling, and, despite speaking good English, wastes none of it on small talk or charm. Amusingly, over our cans it all sounds extremely dodgy.

"That is good, yes, Liz, oh you are good. You are talented. Careful with your hands, that's better, harder now, keep going, keep going...."

And so on.

Liz is tested thoroughly but she keeps her cool and passes muster. We have the thumbs up and the meat of our story.

The 'money' shot of the film is Liz, strolling in a luscious meadow, delivering her opening piece-to-camera, when, on cue, a herd of the magnificent Lipizzaners charge over the brow of the hill behind her. The shot has been suggested by Alfred, the stables' genial director, and naturally, I'm enthusiastic. Juergen and one of the grooms are stationed just out of shot to chivvy the herd on cue. But it is a one-take situation, as once the horses have galloped down the slope, there will be no easy way of getting them back up there for a second go. Liz assures me she can cope and she takes up her position. I shout action and enjoy one of those all-too rare Hollywood moments as Liz finishes her words perfectly and, right on cue, the horses appear behind her and thunder towards the camera.

30th May 2001

We've done so well that our last day, originally planned as a fail safe to shoot anything we hadn't got round to, is free. It is another idyllic summer morning and Juergen suggests that we drive into the mountains and try tandem paragliding. Given Liz's chronic vertigo, she is ruled out, but Sam, the sound recordist, and I both agree to give it a go, and Adrian, the cameraman, films it anyway. It is interesting to have the chance to have a go at what the presenters have to accomplish day in, day out. I'm issued with a walkie talkie so that I can deliver a running commentary. I'm glad there's an expert in charge. All I have to do is concentrate on adopting the right position for take off and landing. It is very odd to literally run off the side of a mountain. The sensation of being suddenly lifted skywards is peculiar and elating. Then, airborne, there is a wonderful stillness and tranquillity. I love every minute of it. The others meet us at the landing site, and Liz is amused by my waxing lyrical about the experience. "You always know what to say, don't you?" she laughs.

A few months later, Juergen was involved in a terrible accident while paragliding from this same spot, breaking several bones and spending months afterwards in slow and painful recovery.

4th June 2001

Ever enthusiastic, my director, Julian, has finally sold me the idea of an item based around a fancy shop he's spied in Brighton called Choccy Woccy Doo Dah. I admit that my initial reluctance was about the name, which I find twee and annoying. Anyway, this outfit specialises in sumptuously over-the-top chocolate cakes for people with, as my mother would put it, "more money than sense". No matter how lukewarm I am, Julian won't let go of the idea.

"Baby, they'll look amazing in the studio – and the presenters can have a go at decorating one."

Having had days of listening to hyperbole like "they are edible works of art" and "more like installations in the Tate than something you slice up to eat", finally I cave in and agree to the booking.

They arrive this morning and time is spent carefully arranging the various ornate creations for the benefit of the cameras. Unfortunately, it is a hot day and the air-con in the studio is of the antique variety and has, in any case, to be switched off when we are recording or live. Within a couple of hours, the first display has melted and collapsed and there are puddles of high-end chocolate on the floor. The dogs are only too eager to take care of these. Reinforcements are sent for, but the same rapid deterioration sets in, and we only just get away with the item, a ruin of over-priced confectionery, a shadow of poor Julian's hopes, about which the presenters are derisive.

12th-13th June 2001

A lightning return to Austria to complete my film about Mozart. This time we are based in Salzburg, which is extremely pretty and, like everywhere I have visited in Austria, extraordinarily clean. Juergen has arranged for a local young actor to play the boy Mozart, for scenes we will shoot in Mozart's house, once it has closed to the public. The little boy, who is called Nicholas, cannot speak English, but takes direction well, via Juergen, who reveals a hitherto well-screened gentle aspect to his nature, explaining and coaxing the child into delivering a decent performance.

15th June 2001

Tales out of school from last week's Eden Project OB. Apparently, in the hotel the night before the show, both Simon and Matt drank themselves into a stupor. It was a bit like San Francisco all over again. They both took advantage of the plentiful foliage on offer to duck out of rehearsals and chunder, hoping that none of the tourists milling around would sneak a photo. But one of the items involved Simon being winched up to the roof. The height, the humidity and the swaying motion of the winch all combined to result in the inevitable and Simon was terrified that he was going to spray vomit all over the heads of both the crew and the mass of holidaymakers below him. "This is the kind of thing you'll have to manage if you get the job, my love," says Bridget, who has been busy scolding them both. Neither of the boys, however, take her very seriously, as she's not without form herself in the heavy drinking department.

18th June 2001

Entire show from the garden. I trialled this last year, as an alternative to having to cram a show into one of those hateful three-hour evening recordings. We use a studio gallery but, because the garden is our location, we are not charged for the studio floor space.

The centrepiece of today's show is an elaborate spoof of *This Is Your Life*, devoted to Francis, a hundred-year-old tortoise. We've invited various guests along to celebrate his centenary, with video clips of the momentous world events through which he has lived. I've asked Peter Purves to make a guest appearance, relating Francis to *Blue Peter* and the programme's long relationship with tortoises. I like Peter very much. He's always affable and supremely professional, and he has a dry cynicism that I find extremely entertaining. He has, of course, a tremendous and lasting chip on his shoulder about the way that he feels that he was treated, especially by Biddy. He seems by nature such a frank speaker, I wonder that he never had it out with her.

"I used to shave in the morning and rehearse all the things I wanted to say to her," he tells me. "By the time I arrived, I'd usually have thought better of them."

He had a better, though still occasionally combative, relationship with Edward Barnes, who produced *Blue Peter* for the first few years Pete was there, and then became first the deputy and then the head of children's programmes.

"I remember when Lesley joined," chuckles Peter, "Edward came to see me and Noakes and said, 'I'm putting a 'No Fucking Lesley Judd' clause in your contracts'. Well, that didn't last long. Our first summer trip together was in Tonga and that's when Lesley and I had a serious fling. Lovely girl. But it never got in the way of the job."

I listen to these revelations half-agog and half wanting to jam my fingers in my ears and go "lalalalala" as you do if your parents ever start talking about their sex lives. When I was a small boy, Lesley was my favourite, like a very pretty big sister on the telly.

Rehearsals continue. Konnie is carrying the long-lived super tortoise Francis on a special cushion which design have provided. The only snag is that Konnie stumbles slightly, pitching the aged tortoise from its luxury perch. Disaster is only averted by the lightning-quick reactions of Simon, who catches Francis before his 100th birthday turns out to be his last and we face a lawsuit for wrongful termination.

22nd June 2001

Back to Lympestone, for a follow-up to the films I made here with Matt a couple of years ago. Having passed his potential recruits' qualification back then, the idea is that he now tries aspects of life (well, some of the interesting and filmable ones, at any rate) as a Royal Marine. The other twist is that Simon is going to join him for part of the filming. It is much more focused and less 'fly on the wall' than last time, which means I can actually craft the sequences and produce them to ensure they are entertaining as well as factual.

Today is devoted to filming the 'domestic' stuff in one of the accommodation blocks. The NCO assigned to us is central casting in that off-camera he is a thoroughly friendly and easy-going bloke, but when I need him to play the fierce bootneck, he can turn it on like a tap. It's very funny. We film Matt undergoing a 'changing parade', used as a punishment here. This basically requires a Marine to get in and out of the various different orders of dress as quickly as possible, against the clock. It also has the side effect of fucking up all their kit, to remedy which represents hours of work. Matt is brilliant with all this, really throwing himself into the exercise.

The Marines pride themselves on their exemplary hygiene (they call anyone from the army "pongo") and we illustrate this by having our NCO give Matt the introductory lesson all new recruits receive on the standards they will be required to reach and maintain. It is very funny watching one grown man solemnly instructing another on the right way to clean his teeth, shave and then shower his armpits and groin. It's also a challenge because we obviously have to film round the nakedness without being too coy about it. But although we all have a good laugh, it's the NCO who really struggles, cracking up again and again as he tries to maintain his poker face and severe commanding tone.

We end the afternoon in the centre's barber shop and, surrendering to the moment, Matt agrees to having a proper Marine haircut. It's only when we wrap that he starts to worry about what his mum will say. I tell him to shove his beret on top and not to worry about it.
Simon, meanwhile, has reported to the guard room, and I go to fetch him. He's got a face like thunder as he's been given a proper bollocking for being late, even though he has tried to explain he was delayed filming elsewhere. It seems obvious that the bored Marines on duty are just taking the piss, but it has riled Simon and it takes him a while to calm down.
"Fucking muppets," he grumbles. "I nearly turned round and walked right out again."
I take him down to one of the lower fields to where I left Matt with a troop preparing to camp over night. I leave the boys here equipped with their own mini-DV camera to film some video diary pieces during the night. As I bid them farewell, Simon is cracking jokes though he is demonstrably less enthusiastic than Matt about the night ahead. But then Matt is one of nature's born boy scouts.

23rd June 2001

The crew and I are back early to film the camp wake-up call, and the whole meticulous morning routine of a Marine in the field. Safe to say that neither Simon nor Matt have had the best night's sleep. Under the guidance of the other men, they wash, shave and dress, boil up their breakfast and then pack up their camp, all at speed, the end goal being to leave not a trace that they have ever been here. This they accomplish but it isn't long before Matt and Simon are regretting the greasy breakfast they have wolfed down, as a brutal morning in the gym awaits them. This was nearly Matt's undoing the last time we were here, so he advises Simon to pace himself and to not burn out early.
The instructors are loving every minute of swaggering around in front of our cameras, bullying the boys off the telly as they drive them round a relentless assault course. At one point, Simon has to carry Matt on his shoulders, and vice versa, and they are both close to collapse. Simon manages to hurt his ankle making a heavy landing from a rope climb, but is determined not to be beaten. "Pain is weakness leaving the body" is a favourite phrase round here. I'm not convinced by that but I am impressed by how far both presenters are willing to push themselves for the sake of a piece of TV. Although the natural competition between them is perhaps the greater factor.

24th June 2001

The climax of our final day – and the final film – is what the Marines call the mud run. The Commando Training Centre is right next to the River Exe, and when the tide goes out, the banks of the river are revealed, a great expanse of thick, sticky, wet mud. It's common practice to 'beast' recruits by marching them down here and getting them to exercise hard in the mud. The mud weighs them down and makes the already intense exercise much more challenging.

As usual with the Marines, first there is a warm up. One of these exercises is called "cocks and hens" – and, as the smirking PTI explains, the idea of the game is for one line of men to act as the "hens" – walking around on their ankles and making loud "clucking" noises, while the other are the "cocks" who have to fight and subdue the hens. It's rather a peculiar game, to say the least, but everyone seems to be enjoying themselves.

The main event follows. It is the perfect day for it, the sun glinting off the swaths of mud facing the troop. The cameraman has pissed me off by refusing to take either of our cameras into the mud bank, despite the fact that the nature of the shoot had been carefully explained to him beforehand and wet weather housings provided.

"I'm just not happy about it," he says for the hundredth time. "I think they'll get carried away and I'm not prepared to risk a 40 grand camera being tackled by a bunch of mad Marines."

As a compromise, I agree to shoot what I can from the thick of things, using the mini-DV. The Marines offer to kit me out, as they did when I was last here, so I'm relatively happy, though it is a struggle to move once your boots sink into the mud.

The session starts with a series of gruelling drills and circuits, making sure that every man is thickly coated before a game of no-holds-barred rugby. Now everyone is covered, it becomes a real challenge to spot Simon and Matt in the melee of gunge. But the shots I am getting seem great. After a time, I wade over to the side and confer with the cameraman to check that he agrees we have shot enough, and then wade back to tell the PTI we are done. We might be finished but it turns out he isn't.

"Let me take your camera, sir," he says. "And I'd better have your glasses too."

I don't like the sound of this.

"No, no, you're all right, I can manage fine."

"It's up to you, sir, but I really would advise it. These lads were all supposed to be on leave this weekend. That leave was cancelled so that you could have the men for filming. It's time for a bit of payback."

He is grinning broadly. I realise I have no option but to comply. Carefully, he takes the camera and my glasses, turns to the troop and addresses them.

"Gentlemen, this is the man from the BBC. The man who is the reason why you have spent the entire weekend being beasted for the cameras. I'm sure you'd like to show him how grateful you are....standby, GO!"

It's a very odd experience to be on your own, facing a herd of men, covered from head to toe in thick mud, rampaging towards you and yelling their heads off with assorted death cries. I didn't have much time to contemplate the view, however. Despite the impediment of the mud, the first wave of men reached me in seconds. Tackled hard, I was sent flying into the ground, and there I found myself rapidly crushed under the weight of a steadily increasing pile of bodies. Those closest to me shovelled up handfuls of mire, which they stuffed down my neck, in my mouth and ears, and generally made it clear exactly how 'grateful' they were.

I hear the PTI, his voice severely muffled by the combined weight of bodies and mud, shouting that the fun is over and then I am helped to my feet. I am so caked, it is incredibly difficult to lift up one leg in front of another, never mind to move in any direction but eventually I make my way to the bank where I am dragged clear. Simon and Matt are looking on, royally amused by my predicament. The whites of their eyes and teeth are all that penetrates their matching coating of mud.

"Where can I change?" I ask, spitting out some of the muck in my mouth.

"First things first," said the PTI. "You need to get yourself squared away. Follow me."

He leads me towards a corner of the camp where a massive hose is being brandished in my direction. Much to the entertainment of a rowdy crowd of bootnecks, I am now the target of a jet of water so powerful that it is a struggle to breathe and to remain standing. When the deluge ceases, I feel as if I've been given a good all-over kicking. "*Now* you can go and shower," I'm told, and, when I hobble off to do so, I keep finding pockets of mud which have escaped my public bath. Finally restored to some semblance of normality, I join Simon and Matt to catch the train home.

"Hoofing good drills, Rich," says Simon, hijacking Marine slang. They are both in thoroughly good spirits, bonded by the experience, and by witnessing the unusual sight of a director for once getting some long overdue payback.

25th June 2001

Hand in my application for the Series Producer job. I conclude my case for the job; "The next five years will be difficult and demanding but exhilarating too. As never before we need to prove ourselves and get out there to our audience, listen to what they want, and work like hell to make them want to watch. As series producer, my guiding principle would be a combination of editorial vigour and financial dexterity so we can adapt, prosper and survive to hand on one of the BBC's crown jewels to future generations."

I mean every word and I feel ready to prove it.

26th June 2001

The *Blue Peter* garden party. Before the evening began, Dermot, one of our bright new directors, tells me that he is determined to introduce himself to Biddy.

I am in a small group to whom she is holding court when I see Dermot approach her, and hover tentatively to one side, out of her line of sight. He is just about to open his mouth and make his move when Biddy takes a sudden step back, stumbles slightly in her high heels, and collides into him. She turns and looks him sharply up and down.

"Oh," she remarks, "I thought you were a dog...."

16th July 2001

Filming the story of James Herriot, with our vet, Joe Inglis (or "Jingles" as the presenters have nicknamed him) playing James, and Matt presenting. Much of the story takes the form of careful period reconstructions, and we start with a whole series of driving shots, in the iconic Yorkshire countryside, using a specially hired 1930s car. This is a bugger to control and temperamental too, breaking down more than once, leaving us stuck until we can summon help to get the thing restarted.

I've persuaded Matt's girlfriend, Nicola, to play the part of Herriot's wife. She is radiantly pretty in a thoroughly English way, and turns out not to be a bad actress, which is just as well as I didn't audition her. She proves self-conscious only when I want her to kiss Joe, though in the end she manages this convincingly enough so I don't have to prolong the 'agony'.

17th July 2001

I felt that any self-respecting James Herriot story had to have a sequence in which we see the vet with his arm up a cow's backside, if only to pay homage to the TV series which so brilliantly brought the books to life. This is all accomplished with great good humour, but the mood is underpinned by the continuing spectre of foot and mouth. When we arrive, and again when we leave, we all have to walk through some kind of disinfectant bath though the farmer says that these are almost entirely cosmetic precautions. He stands to lose everything if the disease reaches his animals. As he talks to us about the dire implications for his business and his family, the lines between fiction and fact blurred and I'm reminded that for stories which have a "cosy" reputation, there is an awful lot that in them that is dark and dispiriting.

I heard later that, sadly, the farmer's stock was found to be infected and had to be entirely destroyed. It was a brutal time for so many farmers, and the compensation they were offered for the loss of their livestock was pitiful.

28th August 2001

Today is my first day as series producer. I'm clearly going to earn the modest pay rise. As well as being in charge of all the studios and OBs, I have the overview on the film team, too. The workload on *Blue Peter* is never light; whatever you are prepared to give, it will take and then demand some more. But who is complaining when the work is this satisfying?

11th September 2001

I'm sitting in Steve's office, in the process of having my annual appraisal, when there is a knock on the door. It is Clare, his secretary. "I think you should turn on the TV," she says, immediately alarming us with her ashen face and sombre tone. A shot of the Twin Towers in New York. Black smoke is pouring from the structure. Extraordinary, terrifying scenes follow, which look like they've been lifted from a disaster movie, and yet are not. My brain struggles to adjust and accept that this is reality, and that it is happening now. Suddenly, we feel that it isn't right for us to be behind closed doors, cut off from our colleagues, so we walk into the office outside where the film team sit. All the televisions are blaring out the coverage, and the babble of panic-stricken voices can be heard giving eyewitness accounts from every speaker in the room. Everyone around me is frozen where they sit or stand, a living tableau, faces transfixed with the unfolding horror. It is the same when I walk round to the other side of the office where the studio teams sit.

The day is no more, at least in the sense that it is about anything other than what we are witnessing and trying to process. We tell everyone that they can go home early. People need to be with whoever they love, not marooned in a tower block in Television Centre.

12th September 2001

We are in studio all day, and it is a struggle for everyone to concentrate. There is a long debate about the song which Steps are performing – a cover of *Chain Reaction.* Quite a few people feel that the lyrics may be seen, in the circumstances, as inappropriate. We take advice and are given the go-ahead. It's a minor point but indicative of how nobody wants to misjudge the mood. The presenters remain uneasy, not so much about the song, but the overall tone of the show, which is customarily bright and optimistic. I make a case for the validity of this, however odd it may feel to us as adults. Children will have been bombarded with images and words, many of which will seem frightening and hard to understand. They have *Newsround* to unpick some of that, whereas our job is to give them stability, normality and the reassurance that there is still plenty that's good and positive about the world in which they live.

15th October 2001

It's the 3500th programme, and we are celebrating with *Brain of Blue Peter*, a cheesy play-along-at-home quiz. I've chosen our studio contestants to represent the different eras of the programme; Val Singleton (60s and 70s), Peter Duncan (80s) and John Leslie (90s). They are all on good form, throwing themselves into the fun and games. It is especially enjoyable to catch up with John, who was always very friendly to me when I used to floor-assist the programme during his time on the show. The only problem was getting him to come out of make-up, where he was almost permanently glued to the phone, and onto the studio floor to rehearse. His girlfriend at the time was the very beautiful Catherine Zeta-Jones, and I remind him of the end of series party where she could be seen gyrating sexily amid a slow shuffling circle of old dears from the correspondence unit. John laughs hugely at this; like Liz, he laughs constantly, and so often that it forms a kind of punctuation in his conversation.

The show goes well. The only disaster is a misconceived item with James Breeze, an expert from *Antiques Roadshow*, looking at the value of assorted *Blue Peter* memorabilia. Breeze is very amiable but seems rather over-awed to actually be on the programme, and during transmission he loses it a bit, which affects Liz, so that the item feels awkward and uncomfortable. Afterwards there is sniping in the office, not only about this, but also about whether the material was of any real interest or relevance to the audience. I think this criticism is spot on and I'm annoyed with myself for agreeing to the item in the first place.

17th October 2001

Nothing to celebrate about today's programme, a bloody awful OB from a construction college. These OBs need such careful planning to avoid looking cheap and thrown-together, and this one is guilty of both crimes. It culminates with a 'performance' from some bloke dressed up as Bob the Builder, miming to a hyped-up version of the highly irritating theme tune, *Can You Fix It?*

On this occasion, no one can. The show is a total dud.

30th October 2001

On location at Harvington Hall, a beautiful old manor house which happens to be riddled with priest-holes. The film, recounting the Elizabethan cat-and-mouse pursuit of Catholic priests, is to go into our Christmas programme. It's a beautiful autumn day, perfect for filming, and I'm working with my favourite crew, but I'm also absolutely teeming with cold and finding it hard to function. I was supposed to be adding to my gallery of cameos, playing the man who built many of these ingenious hiding places in the dead of night, but as I can barely move, let alone face getting into an itchy and uncomfortable costume, I manage to persuade Sam, our sound recordist, to step in for me. He proves a natural. Later, when we have finished outside and are in the process of filming in one of the warren of low-ceilinged rooms here, I stand up without thinking and smash my head into the stone roof. The pain brings tears to me eyes and I have to lie down, stunned. Adrian, the cameraman, fusses and suggests taking me to A and E, in case I am concussed. But dazed though I am, I just can't face the prospect. I only want to finish the film and then drive onto to Eastnor, the location for tomorrow's OB. Reluctantly, the crew do as I say and complete the shoot, and, as a compromise, after we wrap, I agree to slump in the passenger seat and let Liz drive the hire car in my place. This turns out to be something of a mistake. Liz is an interesting driver. She is full of laughter and chat, which is very diverting. But once I realise that she is looking at me more than she is looking at the road, and after a few narrow escapes in the winding country lanes, I beg her to keep her eyes ahead and death off the roads.

31st October 2001

Eastnor Castle OB, a suitably gothic setting for our Halloween programme. Feel miraculously better, though I've got a big lump on my head as a souvenir from yesterday. Amazed to discover that the Eastnor's Estate Manager is none other than Simon Foster, once an AFM in studio management when I was a floor assistant in the same department. Back then, Simon was unfailingly kind to me (indeed, to everyone he encountered) and also happened to be very good at his job. I worked with him on *Going Live!* where he was forever being dragged into sketches as a slightly awkward stooge by the in-house comedy team, Trevor and Simon. I asked him how he had found himself here and he explained that about seven years ago he had been Location Manager on a kids' drama, *Little Lord Fauntleroy*, which was shot at Eastnor. He'd got on so well with the owners that they had asked him to stay on, and, as well as the job, they offered him a lovely cottage on the estate. He seems very happy, though he admits that seeing the crew in action today gives him a slight pang. This afternoon, he accompanied me on a local radio programme and we told the story of our surprise reunion while the DJ feigned interest.

23rd November 2001

Geri Halliwell is in the studio to mime her severely underwhelming new single. I've insisted that she does something else to validate her inclusion and so she's also demonstrating yoga. She is friendly, but manic, with very 'starey' eyes. She asks for a bottle of water and insists that it comes with the lid still sealed, as she explains she's terrified of what people might slip into anything that she drinks.

26th November 2001

Candlelight in a lavish set, with Liz looking gorgeous in full 17th-century costume, about to record a script on which I have lavished much time and research. I should be in my element but we are waiting for Simon, who is in a grump. When he finally stomps on the floor, in thigh-boots and curly wig, he wastes no time in venting his spleen.

"Honestly, Rich, I just can't see how you can do so many brilliant programmes and then come up with something as shit as this."

"This" is the, I think, engaging story of Lord Minimus, a dwarf at the court of King Charles and his various colourful adventures.

Simon rechristens it "Lord Mini-penis", much to the amusement of the camera crew, who'd rather be training their lenses on Atomic Kitten than framing up on a load of guttering candles and period frocks.

27th November 2001

First day of filming on this year's panto, *A Rock 'n' Roll Christmas*. After the Longleat *Country House Christmas*, and last year's *East End Christmas*, I've managed to get the go-ahead for another complete half-hour special. The whole thing is a none-too subtle spoof of *Grease* but rather than having to endure the presenters attempting cod American accents, I've placed it 'Wood Lane High', a somewhat unlikely 1950s school in West London.

I've incorporated all kinds of in-jokes, including a cameo role for ex-presenter Tina Heath as Miss Dripping, the head teacher. As some of the audience will know, Tina joined the programme having made her name in the whimsical children's drama *Lizzie Dripping*. Tina also happens to be married to our musical director, Dave Cooke, and their daughter Gemma, was the first *Blue Peter* baby. Gem has grown up to be a brilliant singer and Dave invariably ropes her in to provide 'BVs' as he calls them (backing vocals) for all the tracks. Today, as well as filming Tina's first scenes, we are shooting in a spit-and-sawdust boxing gym. I've roped in my personal trainer, Sam, to play's Matt's fierce instructor, though he will keep spoiling takes by smiling and laughing at Matt's very funny performance.

"You're supposed to be a mean bastard," I tell him. "Try to look like you hate him."

"I'm Australian, mate," says Sam. "We're the good guys."

For some of the time, we are watched by a small crowd of junior boxers and, during a break, I have a quick chat with them. Turns out that they are quite critical. One boy in particular tells me: "You come here and film boxing like it's all a comedy, but you'd never do it for real, show what it takes, and what it means to us."

I have to accept he has a point. I doubt I would be able to pitch a *Blue Peter* film about kids boxing. The BBC, so very middle-class, would recoil. And yet these kids are our audience, too. Who are we to judge, providing we include both sides of the argument for and against the sport? I promise to look into it and I will. Sometimes it is good to be challenged like this.

28th November 2001

Today is the culmination of several weeks' hard labour on the part of yours truly, as HMQ pays her much vaunted visit to the *Blue Peter* studio. This was first mooted back in the summer, and initially kept shrouded in great secrecy (Steve loves this kind of 'knowledge is power' scenario – which is why Simon has nicknamed him 'Secret Squirrel'!).

On the day, Steve would act as host and guide, but my job was to make sure all the mechanics were in place – liaising with the team from Buckingham Palace and planning a suitable line-up of guests, as well as a programme which would work for the audience and not just our VIP visitor. I asked Annie Dixon, ultra-experienced and always discreet, to produce, and she and I discussed the elements we felt would work. She suggested booking some young synchro-trampolining champions so that as HMQ entered the studio something dynamic could be happening. There will be a chance to meet the pets, of course, and to check out our latest make, a nativity scene made from toilet rolls, the idea of Margaret Parnell (the woman who has been dreaming up most of our makes since the early 60s).

From the first, it was clear that the Queen wasn't going to appear 'live', but, from our point of view, we wanted her visit to form part of that afternoon's show. The problem was that we had no say over the timing of the visit; it was happening mid-afternoon, as one part of her day exploring British media; take it or leave it. We were going to need to turn round the editing of her tour in super quick time, and that led us to the other principal item; a demonstration of the very latest fast turnaround editing facilities. All the current presenters would be on hand, and briefed to say something relevant and interesting when the royal person was introduced. I also thought that we should acknowledge the programme's heritage by inviting a select group of the best-known past presenters to be there too.

To represent the 1960s and 70s, I invited Valerie Singleton and Peter Purves, and, for the 1980s and 90s, I chose Peter Duncan and John Leslie. Buckingham Palace requested a half-page biography for everyone the Queen was going to meet, and I found these harder than I'd anticipated. It was a struggle to think of something sufficiently interesting but to the point for everyone who was going to be there. About a week beforehand, I was working late in the office when the phone rang.

It was my contact at the Palace, very politely but equally firmly asking for the biographies, "as Her Majesty will want to read through them well in advance". I made some comment to the effect that surely she doesn't actually read this kind of bumph and was put firmly in my place. Not only does she do her homework, she often asks questions based on her first class recall of the notes provided. As well as the planning of the programme and guest list, there were some wearisomely painstaking security meetings, as well as a long debate about toilet facilities (almost never used, I'm told, but required to be handy and in tip-top condition). For all these reasons, and because we wanted to showcase the largest studio at Television Centre, we requested studio one. Quite often this can be a palaver and a source of competition between programmes, but HMQ trumps all other considerations, and TC1 is ours.

So this morning all is in place. I'm in my best (well, my only) suit and standing near the stairs which lead to the gallery. The plan is for the Queen to enter the studio via the gallery, allowing her to get a sense of 'behind-the-scenes', and then process down the stairs and across the studio, with Steve introducing and explaining each guest as they go. I am used to studios feeling charged with an atmosphere of nervous tension, but this is unusual because you can tell that absolutely *everyone* is feeling it. Next to me is our films producer, Kez, who is a staunch republican and very 'right on'. I'd offered her the chance to duck out of the line-up, but she said, "Oh no, it's going to be fascinating."

Now, as the Queen emerges onto the gantry outside the gallery, and makes her way carefully down the stairs, I whisper to Kez out of the side of my mouth, "You're such a fucking hypocrite. What's it worth for me not to out you as a revolutionary? Get security to evict you."

We're still smiling when she reaches us. Steve introduces me as his "second-in-command" which is wonderfully archaic and I blether boringly, but as scripted, about my role making films to celebrate the Golden Jubilee. The Queen smiles beautifully and her eyes are very blue. Then she moves on, inexorably, sailing past the toilet roll nativity with little more than a nod, pausing to fuss the dogs and ask a few questions about them, and to exchange words with the trampolinists.

Peter Purves arrived for rehearsals having worked out exactly what he was going to say; sharing his memory of the day the young Prince Edward visited the *Blue Peter* studio and played with some lion cubs. So it is with surprise that I hear Valerie, first in the group of past presenters, trotting out this story instead. I figure they must have compared notes and agreed to swap.

When it is her turn, poor Liz loses the plot. She is supposed to explain that she has been doing some filming for Holocaust Memorial Day. Instead, she just stares glassy-eyed at her monarch and blurts out, "I've been to Auschwitz". But the Queen must have witnessed the strange effect of nerves times without number and she remains graceful and unperturbed.

The highlight of the visit is when Simon awards her with a gold badge, smiling as he tells her, "you may be interested to know that this lets you visit the Tower of London free..." and is rewarded with a royal chuckle.

Then it is over. The Queen and her entourage leave the studio and we are left with an odd mix of anti-climax and pre-transmission adrenalin, as Kez and our editor sit in one corner frantically cutting the pictures which have just been recorded, and our floor manager marshals the presenters into make-up for notes. I quickly do the rounds to thank our guests. Margaret Parnell, in her best Sunday hat, is deeply disappointed that the Queen showed so little interest in her nativity scene. I sympathise and tell her, "You can't expect her to be too excited by a load of toilet rolls and tissue paper when back home she's probably got a Fabergé version."

As I walk over to say goodbye to Val and Peter Purves, I see that they are involved in what looks like a pretty intense conversation. As I get closer, I realise that it's not a conversation at all, but a full-blown row. Pete is absolutely furious that Val stole his Prince Edward anecdote, leaving him fishing for something to say.

"It's always the fucking same," he growls. "You and your bloody selfish behaviour."

I leave them with Val still adamantly protesting her innocence.

Curiously, I think the actual transmission is rather flat – somehow we have failed to capture the excitement or adrenalin of the royal visit and the content, traditional, safe, seems a little like going through the motions. There's no time to dwell on this, however, as Steve and I are guests at this evening's gathering at Buckingham Palace to celebrate British media.

The golden halls are crammed with the great and the good (and a few others besides) from several decades of radio and TV, and various minor royals are there to supplement the big guns of HMQ and Prince Philip. At one point, I'm jammed in a corner with Cilla Black, who, seen close-up, is almost grotesque, with her thinning hair dyed a tawdry red and her sharp beady features. She seems to be pissed too. I'm amused to see Esther Rantzen working the room, nodding this way and that, ablaze with diamonds and looking more royal than the real thing.

All of us in the business could learn something from the expert stage management of the occasion. Every room is policed by a handful of equerries, generally distinguished-looking men from the services, who engage you with a little conversation, checking out your ability to string two words together and form an acceptable anecdote. It's a form of rehearsal, because, if you pass the test, they then ask you, "Would you mind if I introduced you to Her Royal

Highness, the Duchess of Gloucester?" as if you're going to say, "Actually, I'd rather you didn't. I've heard she's a dreadful bore."
We've all been carefully briefed on the form; whatever you do, don't introduce yourself, or ask any questions, and, if you meet the Queen, you refer to her as "Your Majesty" the first time, and "Ma'am" thereafter.
This presupposes that you will abide by the rules, of course. Among the party from the BBC is the head of children's drama, Elaine Sperber. She is certainly not one of the many content to mill around, drink in the surroundings and avoid attention. She announces loudly to anyone who's listening, "I'm American, so those rules don't apply to me" and proceeds to use her not inconsiderable weight to barge into a group congregated near to the Queen. Having made herself conspicuous, she gushes, "I'm the Executive Producer of a programme called *I Was a Rat*, which I think your grandchildren would just love..."
The Queen nods vaguely and moves on. No doubt she's seen it all before, just one more *de trop* loudmouth amid a crowd of the starstruck.
What will remain with me about today is the bizarre and mesmeric effect of the presence of royalty. All day long, I've heard people trotting out the usual clichés – "She's just another human being, when all is said and done..." and "I think their time really has been and gone" and yet the very same sceptics turn to mush when actually close to the real thing. The machinery which today in some small way I helped to function is extraordinary; practised, confident, charming and plainly, extremely successful. It is a continuing piece of theatre in which the Queen plays her part to absolute perfection.

29th November 2001

From the golden halls of Buckingham Palace yesterday, to the freezing grime of the disused Dimco Warehouse today. This is just over the road from TV Centre and the location for our big and expensive showcase number in *Rock 'n' Roll Christmas*, a version of *Uptown Girl*. Alison, our designer, has used the warehouse to create the perfect industrial garage background, and I've got Matt (on lead vocal), Simon, Joe (the programme's vet) and Anton (the programme's astronomy expert) in boiler suits and boots, ready to perform. Konnie is the 'uptown girl', preening in a red silk dress.
For the opening shot, I ask Simon to strip to the waist (torso suitably oiled), and walk towards the camera carrying a tyre under each arm, in homage to the famous Athena poster. He doesn't need much persuading. I also rip off *American Beauty* and take a high-angled cutaway shot of Konnie, being sprinkled with rose petals to match the colour of her dress.
We are using a crane for a lot of key shots, and this, plus the need to light everything, the use of a bubble machine, and the various costume changes, slow

everything down. There are a lot of set-ups to get through and I'm stressed. But I'm also loving every minute.

4th December 2001

Spend the morning in TC8 recording scenes for the panto; Konnie and her girl gang in her bedroom, and Konnie's big music number, *All I Want for Christmas*. As I can't afford a choreographer, I've had to devise the moves for this myself, which is all very well, but there has been minimal time to rehearse. We grab an hour in a basement dressing room to bash through it as best we can before the girls need to go to make-up and costume and I need to switch my attention to directing the cameras. The result, inevitably, doesn't look as good as I want and I'm pissed off. No use telling myself I should have insisted on a choreographer, because I know we are already over-budget and I've got to show willing, otherwise everyone will think it's one rule for the series producer and another for them. Even if this happens to be true, it doesn't do to be too overt about it.

5th December 2001

It is Matt's dog, Meg's first birthday, which we are celebrating with a reunion of her siblings. The usual mayhem ensues. We've had a few complaints from the crew about Meg being unruly and even dangerous. But this isn't really her fault. People want to play with her while it suits them and often they wind her up and she doesn't understand when to stop. She is a working dog, too, so she has a lot of excess energy. I love walking into the studio and seeing her dashing round and round the seat unit – according to Matt, she's under the impression that she's 'rounding-up' the presenters.

A handy skill, round these parts and I think Meg is better at it than some of our floor managers.

7th December 2001

I've booked Sophie Ellis-Bextor to perform her current single, *Murder on the Dance Floor*. She's happy to sing live, which is just as well as I've taken advice and I'm told that we need to ask her to remove the words "God damn" from the lyric, or else risk an uprising from middle England, citing unacceptable blasphemy on the nation's number one children's programme.

Sophie, of course, is Janet Ellis's daughter and so part of the extended *Blue Peter* family. As well as her performance, we have invited her mum to make a surprise reappearance in the studio to award her daughter a silver badge.

"Why a silver?" Janet asks me when I call her to suggest the plan.

"Because she appeared when she was a little girl, modelling bin-liner dresses..."

"Yes, not a fashion which caught on, that."

"....and you win your silver for doing something different from whatever it was that won you your blue."
"Ah, I was forgetting."
Everything goes according to plan, although the 'surprise' is a bit of a damp squib and I strongly suspect that Janet spilled the beans. Or perhaps we are just a bit predictable.

8th-9th December 2001
Spend all weekend shooting the school scenes for *Rock 'n' Roll Christmas* at Spencer School, in St Albans, where my own kids go. It was built in the 1950s so it's perfect from that point of view. It's a very happy business. The closing number, *We Go Together*, which involves the entire cast, feels really joyous and heartfelt. I reflect on the strange workings of showbiz, bringing such a disparate group of people together, dressing them up to sing and dance, when only one or two of them ever intended to perform for a living.

21st December 2001
Pre-recording the Christmas show, which I'm again directing. I'm not complaining, because in many ways, not least for its magical associations, this remains my favourite show of the year. Afterwards, it is our Christmas party and we have hired a giant screen to show everyone *A Rock 'n' Roll Christmas* which went out this afternoon. It is brilliant to watch it with the whole gang, and to hear them laugh themselves silly over all the in-jokes (the villain, never seen, is called Big Richard. At one point, Simon has the line: "Don't worry about him – he's got his Bacon").
The party goes on late and I am staggered by how much Matt and Simon manage to drink. Simon gets through something like 18 pints, which would kill me, yet he is still standing (albeit swaying slightly from side to side) and able to hold a conversation of sorts. Like most rather reserved people, alcohol liberates him and lets him voice some of the things he might otherwise leave unsaid. He tells me how much he loves working with me, how he thinks it is a total disgrace that Steve has basically abdicated and is letting me do his job for him, how brilliant he thinks I am but that I must never again do another item as "truly horrendous" as Lord Minipenis!

2002

2nd January 2002

Return to find a card from children's presenter Timmy Mallett (whom I've never met) on my desk, raving about the panto: "It was a delight to watch," he writes, "with some very funny lines, great songs well sung, lovely production values and brilliant performances. It's one of *Blue Peter*'s great skills to develop its talents like this and I want to congratulate you on a top show. Hope you get to make some more..."

Later, bump into Nigel Pickard, our boss, in the tea bar. He is also very complimentary about the panto, singling out Liz's performance for especial praise. He asks me some practical questions about the issues around making it. This is not idle curiosity. He's thinking of commissioning an hour-long CBBC Christmas comedy special, a kind of throwback, he explains, to the Morecambe and Wise Christmas show tradition in which they featured lots of cameos from the big stars of the BBC. He's been talking to CBBC entertainment, but confesses that he is underwhelmed with their ideas. He asks me if I'd be interested in coming up with a proposal, using *Blue Peter* as the framework and its presenters as the main stars, but finding a way of weaving in cameos from the rest of the department's talent. I try not to give way to the Vesuvius of excitement the prospect immediately unleashes in me. I return to the office, already turning over various possibilities.

8th January 2002

Splendidly rude letter in response to the Lord Minimus story. A Robert Smith writes that he was "appalled at the sloppy way the presenters spoke – a terrible example to children. They spoke 'Estuary' – it was all glottal stops. Can't you find educated voices any more? No wonder spoken English has declined to such a low ebb when children's role models speak so badly – or perhaps this is a deliberate 'dumbing down'. I would not be surprised."

"We take a lot of care with the scripting and delivery of *Blue Peter*," I reply, "but we don't feel it is appropriate to alter the way our presenters naturally speak. I'm glad you were interested in our story, however, and hope you agree that while we still feature items like this we can be spared the accusation of 'dumbing down'."

This is me on my high horse.

23-24th January 2002

A couple of hilarious days filming the story of Mary, Queen of Scots in and around Edinburgh. We spend a lot of the time at Holyrood House, with Liz playing the tragic Queen (we all agree there are a couple of people on the production team who could vie with Mary for that title) and Simon as the sinister Lord Darnley.

Liz struggles with the costume, which is very tight under the arms.

"It's chafing," she moans, pronouncing it "chaffing".

I've got my own problems. I've been over-enthusiastic in the gym and now have a bad case of DOMS (delayed onset muscle soreness) so that I can scarcely move my arms without pain. Inevitably, Simon finds this hilarious and occasionally gives me a sudden hard prod, asking, "Any better yet?", knowing I'll yelp. Happily for me, I've brought Karen, our make-up designer, and once the wigs and slap are safely on the presenters, I commandeer her attentions and she spends much of the rest of the shoot massaging my aching arms and shoulders – to the general derision of the presenters and crew.

25th January 2002

OB from Fettes College, whose current claim to fame is that Tony Blair is one of their old boys. It is very posh indeed, and a fitting backdrop for our Burns Night programme. But, as so often with these OBs, although the day goes well, with everyone in a good humour and each individual item looking good, it kind of falls apart on transmission. I think there are various reasons for this; there is no room for a vision mixer in the tiny scanner, so the director must cut their own pictures, and, really, these are two quite distinct jobs. One slip of the fingers or a slight distraction, and there is a fuck up. The OB crew are keen but their background is in sport, very different from a tightly scripted 25-minute magazine programme which demands a wide range of very specific shots, rather than just to follow the action in a horse race, or football game. Plus the presenters don't have autocue, which means they must be really on top of their game. With all these factors, there are almost always flaws in transmission, and today is no exception. Share a cab after the show with Matt and he is equally frustrated, ranting about people on the production team that he thinks are altogether too laid back and whose attitude is one of "it'll do".

28th January 2002

I get a call from one of the edits, asking me to come down and take a look at something. This turns out to be a compilation of out-takes from a film about sheepdog training. In every one, Matt can be heard complaining loudly about the director. "For fuck's sake, what do you think you're doing, man? You don't want to do that..."

From time to time, the director's soft voice can be heard, placating Matt or trying to retain some semblance of control, but Matt doesn't give him an inch. I take a copy to show Matt. A long chat follows. At first, he is truculent and dogmatic, adamantly refusing to accept that he has done anything wrong, and accusing the editor of stirring the shit, probably with the director's encouragement.

"He knows nothing about it," I assure him.

"That doesn't surprise me," says Matt. "He knows nothing about directing either. He's bloody useless, Rich, and you know it."

I agree that he was obviously out of his depth. But this is a man with a first from Oxford. True, he was probably not the best choice to make a film about sheepdogs, but he is a trainee, and the film was, in theory, relatively straightforward. Part of the reason I put him on it was because I knew that Matt was an expert on the subject.

"I thought you would help him," I suggest. "You have to remember that you never forget the people who are kind to you, or not, on your way up. This guy might end up as Controller of BBC1, or someone important, and then you'd be fucked. Besides which, it's daft to behave like this when you know it's all going on tape. What if it leaked? Who would come off worse – him or you?"

Matt sees the logic and says that he will have a word with the director. Now that he has thought it over, I can see that he genuinely feels bad. I have considerable sympathy with him too. It is the presenter who looks stupid on screen if the director isn't up to the job. Many are the horror stories I've heard from presenters who have had to make a film work in the absence of a director who knows what they are doing. *Blue Peter* always has its share of novices. Some are naturals, brilliant and innovative. Many are just OK – workmanlike and passing through. A handful are disasters and we weed them out as fast as we can, because poor films do great damage. Matt cares more deeply than most about the programme, and his work ethic is extraordinary. He is instinctively suspicious of the laid-back posh-voiced Oxbridge BBC type this director represents, and he hates any form of entitlement.

30th January 2002

I'm pottering around the office when my attention is drawn to an A4 home-made poster on the wall, in the style of a missing persons ad. It shows a photo of Steve and is accompanied with the text.

Has anyone seen this man? Steve Hocking (Alias 'Secret Squirrel')
Age: Getting on
Position: Children's ambassador and general flesh presser
Missing since: early 2002

I immediately recognise the writing to be Simon's and I can't help but laugh, but as I don't think it is a joke which Steve will share, I pull the poster down.

"That's not the only one," says a colleague, nearby.

Simon has been busy. There are posters dotted throughout the office and down in the studio too, where I catch up with him.

He is vastly amused to see me clutching my little bundle. I roll my eyes and say he's playing with fire, but Simon is unrepentant and now he is more indignant than amused.

"Rich, he's never, ever here, any more. When was the last time he came to the studio? He doesn't call us, or show any interest. He's too busy 'building the brand' and all that guff."

I think about what he says and wonder why I don't feel as disgruntled. I suppose because Steve has so completely abdicated from the day-to-day running of the show, that it's left me clear to do whatever I like with it. He seems to trust me completely with the content, and that is what I care about and why I'm here. Most of the ventures with which he is embroiled, the cross-BBC fertilisation, the 'flesh-pressing', as Simon puts it, with venerable outside bodies, would bore me to tears. I'm so happy to be doing a job I truly love, with minimal interference. That's got to be pretty rare in TV these days.

5th February 2002

Spend the morning in the studio, directing inserts for the Mary, Queen of Scots story. Given that much of her fate was driven by her stormy love life, I'm determined to include a kissing scene. When I tell Liz that she is going to be the first presenter in *Blue Peter* history to snog on the show, her eyes widen and she is convinced I'm just winding her up. Not a bit of it.

I've persuaded Liz's other half, Toddy, to play Mary's lover, Lord Bothwell, with the view that the kissing scene will be easier to achieve and more convincing if it's between a real couple. Not sure where I got this notion from. They are, of course, hideously embarrassed and shuffle awkwardly onto the studio floor in their period finery. I place them on the floor of the set, surrounded by scores of candles, which take forever to light. More time for tension to build. I direct Toddy to slightly delay his kiss, so that, when their lips finally connect, it seems more deliberate and passionate. But, though he tries to do what I've asked, on the first take, it actually looks as if he is moving in for the kill, smelling something disagreeable and thinking better of it. There are gales of laughter in the gallery, and on the studio floor. Poor Toddy blushes such a fierce red that I have to send in make-up to tone down his scarlet cheeks. Liz, inevitably, is having the devil's own job not to piss herself laughing with every take. She can scarcely look at her so-called paramour without the corners of her mouth twitching with humour. After a series of takes, they manage a kiss that looks reasonably passionate.
"I wanted Liz Taylor and Richard Burton," I tell the giggling 'lovers', "but you're more Joan Sims and Kenneth Williams!"

11th February 2002
Big brouhaha today throughout the department as it is the launch of the CBBC channel. I have mixed feelings about this. It is an inexorable development of the surge towards digital viewing, and children are, as always with any new technology, at the forefront of this, so from these points of view it makes sense. But it has inevitably meant an enormous and rapid expansion of output and staff, and I think in both cases we are in serious danger of diluting quality and standards. There are some dubious ideas getting the green light and, sad to say, a whiff of the mediocre about a lot of new recruits. One of the problems is that there have been so many rounds of redundancies in the last decade or so that an entire swathe of highly experienced producers and directors – people in their late-30s to 50s – have been dispensed with. The hordes of keen-but-green twentysomethings now filling up the place can't hope to have the same skills and experience.
There has always been a tension around the fact that *Blue Peter* is such an established and well-loved brand. I've already been told by more than one management apparatchik that this will have to change, as though we are guilty of some kind of innate disloyalty. As one of them lectures me, "we can't have a single programme being better known than the channel."
I'm not sure what we are expected to do about this; fuck up the show and run it into the ground? Surely it is the channel's job to use *Blue Peter*, along with the small core of other hit shows, to build its own brand. And do viewers have

channel loyalty in any case? I mean, you might watch the BBC, but who really cares what channel their favourite series is on? It's the programme you are bothered about. I also worry that, based on current schedules, CBBC will be spreading the jam dangerously thin. Certainly, they are starting with a whole load of eminently forgettable new stuff which won't hold the audience's attention once the novelty of the launch has worn off.

15th February 2002

The ghastly S Club 7 are cluttering up the studio with their latest dirge-fest. They have entirely lost their freshness and (albeit manufactured) enthusiasm. During rehearsals, I get a call from the gallery to come over to the studio because the 'band' are refusing to rehearse properly and, as a result, the director is struggling to get decent coverage. I talk to the record company plugger, a hard-faced uninterested blonde chewing gum, and explain the problem. "They're just really tired," she drones. "Can't they just mark it?"

"Not unless you want it to look bloody awful on transmission," I retort.

Later, just before the run-through, the floor manager takes me to one side with another problem. There are a couple of children in the studio who, it has been agreed, can meet the group in their dressing room. But the floor manager has been alerted by the floor assistant that there is a very strong smell of dope in the room and the corridor outside it. Again, I seek out the plugger and we agree that perhaps it isn't the best idea to send a posse of parents and their starstruck offspring into such an atmosphere. Sudden illness, that old reliable excuse, will be trotted out and I get the record company to agree that the kids will be offered all-expenses paid VIP trips to see their heroes in concert, at the earliest possible opportunity.

I'm sick of the seediness of the record industry. I don't blame the artists. They are almost always worked to death, clapped-out and disillusioned. But equally, I don't think we will invite this particular bunch back again.

26th February 2002

To Yorkshire with Simon and Matt for three days' filming which I may just regret. The idea is for them to experience authentic life in a First World War trench – authentic, that is, without the lice and the mortal fear – to shake up our usual approach to history and make it more immersive, which, if all goes well, should enable the presenters to actually convey a physical and emotional reaction to the experience. We are working with a re-enactment group called the Khaki Chums who specialise in making exact replicas of uniform and kit, and putting it all to the test by experiments in 'living history'.

"You'll spend the whole time exactly as though you are in the trenches for real,"

I enthuse to Simon and Matt. "Eating, sleeping, being inspected, on guard duty. It will follow a precisely researched pattern. All your uniform will be exact right down to your underwear. It'll be an incredible experience."

The boys listen and agree to go for it on one condition. That I take part alongside them.

"Isn't that what officers are supposed to do?" says Simon, cheekily. "Never ask their men to do anything which they aren't prepared to do themselves?"

Back in the warm, bright make-up room, where we were chatting it through, it didn't feel like such a big deal. Actually, it seemed like it could be great fun, and I'm never shy of a bit of dressing up.

Now I'm actually here, wearing the kit, which is itchy, heavy and uncomfortable, I'm aware I may be about to repent at leisure. The attention to detail certainly can't be faulted. We've even been issued with regimental identity discs, which are precise replicas of the real thing. The trench, which the Khaki Chums have built on a desolate stretch of exposed farm land, is similarly authentic. It is cold, muddy and wet. There are no toilets – if you want a shit, you are issued with a spade.

It starts all right. The 'chums' are a friendly bunch and interesting to talk to. We film Simon and Matt undertaking various jobs and taking part in a gas attack practice. But as the sun dips and the weather, already bitterly cold, turns much sharper, the laughter and chat dwindle to miserable silence, as we face the prospect of getting through a long, hard night out in the elements.

Matt remains the most cheerful in the group, organising sing-songs and digging out the trench to keep warm. Simon, by contrast, becomes steadily more morose and monosyllabic. He is hating every minute and withdraws into himself. Taff, the resident historical expert, is fascinated. He explains that Matt's personality means that he would be more likely to survive trench life, whereas Simon would be much more vulnerable. The experience is demonstrating with alarming clarity the overwhelming and immediate effect the trench experience must have had on newcomers to the line. I'm feeling it myself. My feet and hands are numb and the equipment I'm carrying is a serious encumbrance.

Paul, the cameraman, has a word. He is concerned to hear that I'm proposing to stay here overnight with the boys.

"I understand what you're trying to do," he says, "but don't. We need a director who is on top of what he's doing, not stumbling about, exhausted and good for nothing."

I can't fault the logic and I discuss it with Simon and Matt, who inevitably take the piss a bit, but agree I should stay in the hotel with the crew after all.

We leave them with a camera to record their experiences overnight. I feel guilty as fuck but also deeply relieved.

27th February 2002

A sorry sight greets us on our return to the trench this morning. In just a few hours, Simon and Matt have assumed the look of the genuine First World War soldier, grey with tiredness, grime in their pores. They remained at their posts overnight, but only one of the 'chums' stayed with them. The rest confess to having "cheated" during the small hours. As it was several degrees below freezing and there was clearly no prospect of getting any sleep, they had bedded down in one of the farmer's nearby chicken sheds. This wasn't unusual behaviour for squaddies at the time, albeit not those in the front line, so reality was scarcely sacrificed. It had been a bit warmer but they hadn't got much in the way of sleep, and the place was full of rats. Simon and Matt are huddled by a makeshift fire.

We film the men shaving, cleaning their teeth and having their feet inspected by an officer. Capturing these kind of routines becomes the highlight in the day, as it is apparent that much of the trench experience was terrible, stifling monotony and tedium. God only knows, it is actually unimaginable to consider how horribly scared most of them must have been, not to mention how much grimmer these surroundings would have been when teeming with rats, lice and mortal remains. I think particularly of my great-grandfather, Reginald Hann, who was promoted to being an officer and survived Gallipoli (where he contracted dysentery). My father told me that before the war Reg had been an outgoing fellow with a sunny and engaging personality. Once he returned he was transformed into a frequently moody and difficult man, who never spoke of what he witnessed and survived.

I decide that the boys have suffered enough. Tonight they too can stay in the hotel. We have more than enough to make a vivid and visceral film, and tomorrow the plan is to shoot a scripted story – the poignant tale of the 1914 Christmas Truce, when for both sides there was a brief pause in the bloodshed, with soldiers meeting in No Man's Land, exchanging gifts and playing football.

28th February 2002

Our final day and we rattle through the sequences, relieved to have a schedule to follow and on which to focus. It is even colder than before, and, talking to the cameraman, I realise that the colour palette around us is adding to the depression; a smeary succession of brown and grey. Not even the Khaki Chums, who choose to spend much of their spare time immersed in this brutal and unforgiving period, are sorry when I call the wrap and we can finally trudge away from the little glimpse we've shared into the hell our ancestors endured.

24th March 2002
Filming in Venice with Simon. Spend the morning making masks in a little shop tucked away in one of the myriad alleys which make up this city. I am amused to see a hitherto unseen creative side emerge from both Simon, and our cameraman, Adrian, neither of whom usually exhibits the kind of patience this activity demands. We borrow a few of the masks and aim to pick up shots around the city with Simon modelling them against assorted picturesque backgrounds.

25th March 2002
We've been given permission to film in the bell chamber right at the top of Venice's landmark Campanile. It is a privilege to have the place to ourselves, but also a pressure, as it is a classic one-take situation. We make a careful plan about how it is going to work – Simon's PTC, timed precisely before the huge bell begins to chime and the cutaways to follow. It all works like a dream and we troop out past the first queue of gawping tourists to have an overpriced coffee in St Mark's Square.
Later, we set up at an al fresco restaurant to film Simon trying one of the speciality dishes of Venice; black ink squid pasta. It smells atrociously fishy and, during the take, Simon just manages to take a bite without gagging. But it is a generous helping and it has hardly been touched. I don't want to cause offence as the restaurateur is standing by, like a proud father, urging, "You eat!"
Simon is pretending to study his script. The cameraman is very busy packing up the kit. I'm going to have to take one for the team, until, to my relief, our pescatarian sound recordist, Sam, leans in and says: "I wouldn't mind a taste", sits down and finishes the whole slimy plateful in a matter of moments, and with apparent relish.
"Fee justified," I remark.

28th-29th March 2002
We are in Turin, filming the story of the mysterious shroud, which some believe to be the burial cloth which wrapped the corpse of Jesus, and which bears the impression of his body seared into the cloth. More recent scientific opinion is that the shroud is an extremely clever medieval fake, but, whatever the truth, it makes a good story. Simon – or "chief faith correspondent" as I've taken to calling him – is scornful of the Catholic obsession with relics and the huge church souvenir industry – "toot" as he calls it.
Turin is a bit of a dump, the first Italian location about which I've felt unenthusiastic. We are setting up a shot outside the church where the shroud is kept when I notice that Simon is wearing a pair of jeans with a curious pale

pattern embedded in the denim. I point this out to the crew.
"It's the Turin jeans," I cry, and compliment Simon on his dressing to match the theme of the script.

6th April 2002
To the London Palladium with the family to watch Matt perform for one show only in *Chitty Chitty Bang Bang.* The other presenters are looking on from one of the ornately decorated boxes up to one side of the main stage. Konnie had to curtail her holiday to be here, and she wasn't best pleased about it, but I insisted.
"Why can't it just be Simon and Liz?" she wails. "It's like one shot in the whole show."
"You have to be there," I tell her. "The audience just won't understand why you haven't turned up to support your best friend."
"You can't force me," she threatens. "I could just not show up."
This is true enough, but somehow I never doubted that she would show. I totally understood her frustration, and didn't mind her venting at me, but Konnie basically 'gets' it, and so here she is, and no one would guess she wasn't delighted to be so.
Matt's big moment is as one of the dancers in the frenetic routine for *Me Old Bamboo* (hence I'm calling the programme *Baker's Bamboo Bang Bang*) and this is the culmination of several weeks' work. During the overture, have an interesting chat with Matt's mum, who says that his 'hyperactivity' used really to worry her; unless he is really busy and active, he gets very angry and frustrated. In this respect, *Blue Peter* is the perfect job for him.
The performance is another triumph. Nobody could possibly have spotted Matt as the outsider, and, when we see him afterwards, he is literally flushed with success, unable to keep still, his eyes dancing with excitement, revelling in the compliments coming at him from every direction.

24th April 2002
The latest Australian pop star Holly Valance has been booked to perform her new single, *Kiss Kiss.* I was a bit dubious about this, judging by the video and the lyrics, but have been assured that Holly will "tone it down" for a teatime audience.
Pop is very polarising. Production teams are always keen to include it, because they have a spurious feeling that it lends a coolness to a show. In fact, all the research shows that, with the exception of a very few key acts, most pre-pubescent children are utterly bored by chart music. Holly is the latest 'pop' graduate from *Neighbours,* so, slightly against my better judgement, I've been persuaded that she's more relevant to kids than most.

I see her in action for the first time during the run-through. From start to finish, it is jaw-droppingly inappropriate.
Miss Valance, who is not wearing very many clothes, appears to be masturbating on a fur rug. For once, I am more annoyed with the director and producer than the record company, because they must know that we could never put this out. There are hurried counsels, shots are changed and promises extracted, and the final version is marginally less pornographic. But it's hardly public service broadcasting at its finest.

26th April 2002
Email from Katy Hill. "Marson!!!! (said clearly with an accent Française)," she begins. "Keep seeing you on the clip of Queenie visiting the studio and every time I see you grinning like a gibbon, it makes me laugh. You must have been beside yourself that day – meeting HRH. I miss the BP game like you wouldn't believe but life goes on..."
Katy has popped into the studio a couple of times recently. She shared her thoughts with the current team on what a tough world it is out there; so, when you decide to leave, be careful what you wish for. I can see that this has had some impact on their thinking.
"I'm gonna beat Noakes's record," Matt tells me, in all seriousness.
"So am I," says Konnie. "Let's stay forever!"
For old times' sake, Katy signs off her email as "QM" concluding "clearly the name is now rather unfortunate! Or maybe it's good that the memory of bad teeth, blue hats and weak waves can live on through me!"

30th April 2002
Filming at Buckingham Palace and Windsor, for the first half of my George IV story. At Windsor we are allowed to sneak a look in the Queen and Prince Philip's private quarters. The rooms are handsomely proportioned but surprisingly shabby; rather like a slightly down at heel English country hotel.
Adrian, the cameraman, is unamused when I ask him to shoot some close-ups of various statues outside.
"You're always asking me to do this," he grumbles.
"What's the problem?" I ask, surprised. There is nothing technically testing about the request.
"There's no problem," he replies. "I mean, I can get you the shots. But the statues at these places are *always* covered in pigeon shit. Looks bloody awful when you get in tight."

7th May 2002

Filming yet more royal toot for the George IV story, this time at the Royal Pavilion, Brighton. The cameraman is again Adrian, these days always my number one choice. He and I are contemporaries, starting our careers at Television Centre at about the same time, Adrian as a junior cameraman in studios, while I was a floor assistant in studio management. I liked him from the first; though we are very different in lots of ways, he and I share a sense of humour. In the early days, when I frequently moonlit as a camera helper (or cable basher, as they were less elegantly known) on *Top of the Pops*, this sense of humour was tested to its limits. I was, it must be allowed, not the most gifted of camera helpers. Too easily distracted and apt to get myself (and the cameraman I was supposed to be 'helping') tangled up. On one ignominious occasion during a live *Top of the Pops*, I could be seen all too clearly, holding cable aloft, as I sailed through the frame during Timmy Mallett's rendering of *Itsy Witsy Teeny Weeny Polka Dot Bikini*. Adrian put up with me because I could make him laugh. Like so many at the BBC, he has long since turned freelance. He is very good at his job, and all the presenters like and respect him too. He is also responsible for one of my all-time favourite sayings.

"Nice guy. Bit of a cunt."

When you think about it, this applies to almost anyone you meet for the first time and most of those that you've known for years. Though it *sounds* rude, in its way, it's actually a term of endearment.

13th May 2002

Enrique Iglesias is in the studio today, and he tries everybody's patience with his sulky wraparound-shade-wearing, look-at-me-posturing and his insistence, via the ubiquitous record company plugger, that he should only be shot from one side. This is because on the other he has a prominent, though entirely inoffensive mole. It's a pain in the arse for the director, who has to re-script various shots, and the rampant vanity on display is repellent, even by the low standards of such a self-regarding industry.

15th May 2002

It's wheels-within-wheels today, as Simon is directing the show, and we are making a film about him doing so. I'd cooked up this idea because Simon is, in technical terms, far and away our most proficient presenter, with a genuine interest in the process and craft of making TV. He'll be the first of the turns ever to have been in charge of a live show. These days, Steve very rarely, if ever, makes an appearance in the studio, so when I suggest the idea to Simon, his first comment is: "What's the betting Hocking will be back for notes that day?"

In fact, Steve keeps a wide berth, Simon takes to the director's chair with aplomb and I have only to deliver minimal notes, which makes a pleasant change.

21st May 2002

Spend the morning recording the story of the famous 18th century actor, David Garrick. I've given the item to Matt, on the basis that when he joined the programme, he was midway through training to become an actor. He says he wants to query something in the script.

"It's this bit here, Rich," he frowns. "You've put, 'When I was training to be an actor, I was always taught that the most important thing about any performance was to find the truth in the part.'"

"Yeah? What's wrong with that?"

"Well, nothing, except that I wasn't ever taught that."

"OK. So do you want to change it?"

He frowns and thinks for a minute.

"Nah, fuck it. Leave it as it is."

And for the rest of the day, whenever we see each other, we launch into a chorus of, "When I was training to be an actor..."

3rd June 2002

Today we wrestle with our longest-ever programme, the *Blue Peter Jubilee Party*, a two-hour extravaganza live from Birmingham's Centenary Square. It's been a huge amount of work to organise, and to shoot the additional films which are peppered through the running order. There's a crowd of some 20,000 massed round the main stage. Simon and Matt are stoked by the adrenalin but, in the wings, Liz is a woebegone sight. She seems almost paralysed with fear. "I can't do it," she mutters. When it comes to transmission, she almost has to be pushed on stage and then, by some miracle of showbusiness, she is instantly transformed, working the crowd as if she's been on stage every day of her life – "Hello Birmingham!". She waves her arms and gives the impression of loving every minute. Either side of her, Simon and Matt are visibly amused, but also vastly relieved.

It's a typical British summer day – cold and wet – but the crowd don't seem to care. They are here to enjoy themselves. None of us are fooling ourselves that they are here for *Blue Peter*, though; it's the line up of pop stars who have drawn them in; S Club Juniors, Liberty X, and especially *Pop Idol* runner-up Gareth Gates. This creates a bit of drama around one of the other acts, Sophie Ellis-Bextor, who has apparently made some faintly critical comments in the music press about manufactured pop stars, singling out Gareth as a good example. His fans are not happy and a sizeable group of them are here today. When Sophie goes on stage, there is a huge surge of boos and shouts of "Fuck off, bitch!" and "We hate you!" Sound have a frantic few moments trying to adjust the mix so that viewers at home won't be aware of just what a terrible reception she is getting.

"It's murder on the dance floor," remarks Simon, "and no bed of roses in Birmingham, either."

For the grand finale, the presenters and all our guests gather on stage for a rousing chorus of *God Save the Queen*. Unfortunately, in her still-manic state, Liz grabs one of the pop stars' mics and, despite further frantic efforts from sound to rapidly adjust the mix, her enthusiastic but tuneless tones drown out the competition from the pop professionals.

7th June 2002

Fly to Munich, for an epic three-day shoot for the story of Ludwig of Bavaria. We are met by the trusty Juergen, who drives us from the airport to our first location – the fairy tale castle of Neuschwanstein. Liz, the crew, and my mate Jan, whom I've roped in to play Ludwig, thanks to his uncanny likeness to the mad monarch, all doze in the van. I'm far too excited to sleep. I was fascinated by Ludwig as a child, and I've wanted to visit Neuschwanstein ever since.

When we arrive, the first disappointment is discovering that one side of the edifice is covered with scaffolding. This is a blow as tomorrow I've hired a helicopter to shoot aerials of the castle. The bigger issue is the curator of the place, a Mr Scheck, who Juergen has already warned me is hostile to film crews and ready to pick a fight. As we set up our first pieces inside, from across the room I see that Scheck already appears to be sounding off at Juergen, who has a face like thunder himself. Knowing how volatile he can be, and not wanting to be chucked out before we begin, I move over in the guise of offering support.

"You film crews are all a crazy bunch of motherfuckin pigs," sneers Mr Scheck, before pointing at Adrian, our cameraman. "Always there is one guy doing the work, while all the rest are lazy snails, only watching at the sides. BBC, ZDF, ORF, all are the same bunch of idiots. I don't need them at all."

This is all very alarming, but he doesn't actually seem to have any specific complaint about us or the way we are working, and he isn't suggesting that we down tools and leave. It is more that he seems to want to get off his chest a few home truths about the way film crews function. So I humour him and nod and he eventually seems to run out of steam, which is just as well as Adrian now indicates he is ready for me to check the first shot.

Later, I discuss the angry Mr Scheck with Juergen. "Do you think he might be a little unhinged?"

"Nope," says Juergen, firmly. "He is merely German."

9th June 2002

Helicopter day. I've not been in one since my near-death experience in Mexico, and I'm nervous. But this machine is larger and feels more stable, and the pilot less of a wide boy show-off. Other than a range of standard aerials, I've planned one key 'money' shot. This will be a direct cut from Liz's final piece-to-camera, which will take place on a graceful metal bridge some distance from the castle, which offers a magnificent vista of the place.

The plan is that as Liz turns from the camera on the bridge, we will cut to the helicopter shot and zoom up, up and away until she is a tiny figure with the majestic Neuschwanstein towering behind her. The stumbling block is Liz's fear of heights. The bridge is perched high in the mountains and, to her mind, doesn't feel too substantial. We have got permission to close it off so that the shot will feature her alone, without the distraction of numpty tourists, but that's not an advantage for Liz herself. She will also have to withstand the not inconsiderable downdraft from the helicopter, which makes it feel as if you are being blown off your feet. Jan offers to stay on the bridge with her till the last possible moment, offering reassurance, until I give the signal, via walkie talkie, for him to clear. Liz is determined that she won't crumble under the pressure but fear is never rational. I prepare for the worst. But I needn't worry. She nails it in one magnificent take.

Trying to bring history to life for children is rarely straightforward. You want to inspire their imaginations and prompt their curiosity, not bore them to tears. If you get it right, these items can be a gateway to further exploration and discovery. But the inevitable process of simplification can be challenging. I remember after the Nelson film went out receiving a letter from a professor at a leading university accusing me of glorifying a war criminal. Whatever line you take, there are many necessary omissions and short cuts. This afternoon, when we are filming in the exotic Moorish grotto in the pleasure grounds. Juergen tells me luridly that this is where Ludwig frequently enjoyed orgies with young boys. "Not in this script, he doesn't," say I, firmly.

10th June 2002

I'm back in costume for my now inevitable cameo, playing the great German composer Wagner, who was something of a mentor to Ludwig. We are filmed strolling the flower-filled meadows, and then rowing a boat on the vast lake here. Years ago, when I was trying to think of what I wanted to be when I grew up, the main condition was that it shouldn't be something boring, where every day was the same. This thought returns to me now and I'm grateful that I cannot remember the last dull day in this job.

11th June 2002

I'm summoned to the edit for Wednesday's film. There is a problem. The story is about the 'cow parade', these life-sized cow statues which have been dotted around London's major landmarks, each of them vividly decorated with eye-catching designs. When the parade was being planned, we were offered the chance for a presenter to design the cow to be positioned by Marble Arch in Hyde Park. I thought that this would be right up Konnie's street as, like her, it is both creative and quirky. Shooting apparently went well but the editor now shows me the climax of the film in which the expert asks Konnie to name her cow.

"Hmmm," she says. "How about Katy? I think that's a perfect name for a cow! Katy the cow..."

There is clearly no way we can transmit this ending. I stomp off to vent at Konnie, but she is unrepentant and as I try to scold her, she just laughs her head off.

12th June 2002

Today we say goodbye to the *Blue Peter* vet, Joe Inglis. This was my decision, but one I felt forced into. Very soon after I first joined the show, I had brought Joe in as a regular contributor, having spotted his likeable personality in the BBC docu-soap, *Vets in Practice.* He was obviously keen to extend his five minutes of fame and the audience liked him too, so I gave him a regular slot in the studio. But, perhaps inevitably, as time went on, he seemed less and less motivated by the actual business of being a working vet and his motivation became focused more on being 'on the telly'. He acquired an agent and made personal appearances. I had no problem with any of this but when I asked a researcher to contact him for ideas about items and they came back with nothing useable, we began to set up items for which we would do all the work and into which Joe was merely grafted at the last minute. He was excellent at bluffing through, but I was increasingly uneasy with what felt more lazy than laid-back. I tried to engage him with my doubts, but he was resistant to change. I canvassed opinion across the team and was surprised to discover how strongly some felt about his "coasting".

"We don't need a vet, the presenters can do it."

"Matt knows more than he does anyway."

When I told him we had decided to dispense with the role, he wasn't happy, but agreed to a proper send-off. It is a pity, as I always liked him, and found him easy to work with, but perhaps he never fully understood what a good thing he had going and what he needed to invest to keep it that way.

8th July 2002

My annual appraisal with Steve. Other than the fact that I have managed to dodge any management training for the second year running, this is all very amiable and positive.

"He has proved to be an impressive diplomat," writes Steve, "handling contributors, staff and presenters with a skill greatly admired by both his Editor and Production Executive. He is an unusually good bearer of bad tidings..."

Perhaps I should transfer to a job in A & E?

29th July 2002

A sunny day in Skegness, location for the first of our six summer road shows from seaside resorts around the UK. It's a big operation to take the programme on tour like this, and we are not alone because some bright spark has had the idea of CBBC's daily magazine programme *Xchange* tagging along with us. As soon as we are off air, they use the same facilities to transmit their own show, with their own presenters and guests. It's an efficient use of resources, I suppose, but the shows are strange bedfellows. If we are the flagship, the gold standard, *Xchange* is the Cinderella of the department. Many of those who work on it cherish a barely concealed grudge against *Blue Peter*. They are understandably jealous of its greater resources for fewer slots and, perhaps most of all, the fact that we have an audience and, try as they might, they don't. I don't think they are helped by a pervasive team culture of wannabe cool, which means that the house style is frenetic and try hard, while the actual content is wafer-thin. A typical quiz is 'Name that Poo', in which photos of animal dung are flashed up on screen for the audience to identify. Be still my aching sides. Interactivity, the constant mantra of the department, is supposed to be at the heart of the programme, but so few are actually watching, never mind taking part, that it is not uncommon for the gallery PA to have to go on the phone lines and pretend to be a child calling in, as there is quite literally no one there. The presenters are not bad, but they have very little rehearsal time and they compensate by shouting and laughing like hyenas at every opportunity, as if this will somehow fill the gaps in the running order.

31st July 2002

Dreadful day in Manchester, trying to salvage a show. It poured with rain all day. Tense conversations with the police and the local authority, who seemed anxious to cancel the whole thing. These situations always bring out in full force the health and safety bores, and there are several hi-vis windbags in the huddle outside the scanner as we discuss options. I'm irritated to find that our producer seems to be more on the side of these bureaucrats, and I rapidly get thoroughly pissed off with him bleating about the problems and offering no constructive suggestions.

"It's just the British weather," I say. "It's not fucking Armageddon."

"We must be guided by the experts."

"That would be nice but they haven't actually come to any conclusions yet, have they? Seems to me they're just waffling on, trying to cover their backs."

He follows me back into the scanner, still bleating away and arguing the toss.

"We need to get on and rehearse," I insist. "Do what we can."

On and on he moans. Goaded beyond endurance, I push him out of the scanner and point to the hi-vis brigade.

"Why don't you go and have a good bitch with your new friends? You're no use to me here. Come back when you want to work on *Blue Peter*."

He goldfishes in disbelief, as firmly I close the door on him.

The rain continues drumming on the scanner roof and there is no question that it is exceptionally miserable out there. The design crew, swathed in waterproofs, gamely mop and swab the sodden stage, to try to reduce the ice-rink slipperiness and make it safe to block through the shots. Rain spots the lens of every camera and equipment keeps failing as water finds its way into sensitive workings. It is all utterly joyless and this is supposed to be a fun summer roadshow. I call CBBC back in London, to suggest that we might be better off pulling the programme and running a standby repeat instead. Unfortunately, most of the top brass are on holiday and the stand-in is too weedy to make such a radical decision. I'm told in no uncertain terms that we must proceed "unless you are absolutely forbidden to go ahead by the authorities."

So on we totter, staggering through some desultory rehearsals until the police and the local authority can make a decision. Finally, they do so – we can go ahead with the television transmission but the site is too dangerous for the thousands expected, and so this will be fenced off and closed. We arrange to speak to local radio to spread the message.

Our star guests for the day are the boy band Blue, who have remained safely cocooned in their stretch limo since they arrived. Their 'plugger' now asks for a word. She is tight-lipped. "Sorry but if there's gonna be no crowd, the boys aren't going to perform. They don't want to let down their fans."

Don't want to get their hair wet, more like.

"What about the millions of fans who'll be watching on TV?" I retort.

It is now only a couple of hours till transmission. The band are meant to be performing two numbers. If they pull out, we will have a big hole in our already damp squib of a show. So I nod and smile, and then reply slowly and clearly.

"If you pull out, I will *never* book your band again. Neither will anyone else in CBBC. And we will go on air and explain to all the disappointed kids in the

audience who have been looking forward to seeing Blue that their heroes aren't coming because they are afraid of a bit of rain."
The plugger tells me she will have to call the record company in London. A little while later, I get the message that Blue will do the show after all. The bluff has worked but I have never been so glad to leave a location in my life.

5th August 2002
Blackpool is our next venue. It is baking hot, which is just what we wanted. Everything looks and feels better in the sun. It's a great day until just before transmission when the police ask to have a word and let me know they have apprehended some creep who has infiltrated the crowd with a concealed camera, with which he has been taking inappropriate photos of young girls. It makes me think again about some of the content; throughout the road shows we have been running a very popular dance competition, and I have already had to intervene more than once to insist on a change of outfits for some of the young competitors. This is always tricky, as inevitably the child is upset and it is impossible to explain that we are only trying to protect them from a part of the audience about which they are hopefully innocent. For the same reason, I monitor the shots of their dancing very carefully – naturally some of them mimic moves they have seen being used by their favourite pop stars, and these are often overtly sexual. I'm not OK with transmitting these but rather than upset a child by asking them to completely change their routine at the last minute, I get the director to alter the shots. Liberty X are today's band, and the girls are channelling hardcore hooker chic in skin-tight rubber cat-suits. Very sweaty on a hot day like this and another taste and decency headache.

6th August 2002
As it's the summer holidays, Rosy and Rupert have joined me for this leg of the road shows. It's a long journey from Blackpool to Rhyl, our next venue, and, to keep him entertained, the coach driver has kindly allowed Rupert to have a go on the sound system normally used by tour operators. He has got the patter down just right, and everyone is laughing. As we arrive in Rhyl, he brightly announces: "Ladies and gentlemen, if you look out to the left, you can get a glimpse of the sea. And if you look to the right, you can....er....see an old lady being mugged at a bus station."
Our laughter tails off abruptly as we realise that he's not being humorous but accurately describing the scene.

7th August 2002
God this place is bleak. The crowd, mainly teenage girls, is the roughest we have yet encountered, and when Sugarbabes take to the stage, bottles are thrown in

their direction. 3SL, a cheesy boy band, do rather better. Their music is awful, but as they are local boys that is overlooked, and when the lead singer hitches up his T-shirt to give a flash of his well-honed abs, the screaming sends the sound department into a conniption.

During transmission, there is another kind of commotion and afterwards I discover from a local policeman that a 14-year-old in the audience had gone into labour but fought off all attempts to get her to hospital, as she didn't want to miss the show.

Which is a compliment, I suppose.

21st August 2002

Arrive at Bodney Camp in Norfolk, for the first day of shooting on a special I'm calling *Horses' Holiday*. I've discovered that every summer the Household Cavalry take several hundred of their horses away from London and the entire regiment bases itself here, close to the sea, for a month of training and relaxation. Matt is going to be given the opportunity to join in various riding exercises and challenges.

As we are a fair way from the nearest hotel, the army have kindly agreed that, as well as Matt, the entire crew can stay on camp. I've been warned that facilities will be pretty basic and naturally I've briefed the crew to this effect. The Nissen huts we are shown to date from the Second World War and are simply furnished with iron cot beds. They have sinks but the bathroom facilities are a short walk away. The intention is that we will share two to a room and, it is explained, several men have gone under canvas to make room for us, as these huts are at a premium on camp, and reserved for officers. I am less than pleased when the crew take one look at all this and refuse point blank to stay in them. Matt, too, is plainly embarrassed by their lapse of manners. A tense exchange follows between myself and the cameraman. I tell him that, if they must, he and his sound recordist can check into the nearest hotel, which is a good half-hour's drive away, but, as per the schedule, we will be starting at the crack of dawn each day and working late, so he must absolutely ensure they are never late. They agree and depart, the atmosphere between us several degrees below freezing.

Matt and I dump our bags in our hut and the officer takes us to tea in the mess. I'd expected this to be a relaxed, serve yourself and have a chat arrangement. Not a bit of it. It is more formal than Fortnum and Mason. Our host introduces us to a small group of fellow officers, all of them talking like Prince Charles, and we are ushered to sit around a mahogany table covered with a gleaming white cloth. Matt's eyes widen as he clocks that we are going to be served by ordinary troopers hovering by our elbows and brandishing china and silver.

"Would you like China or Indian, sir?"
Everyone's uniform is immaculate, so that we feel at a distinct disadvantage in our jeans and T-shirts.
"We'll get you into some proper kit before you meet the C.O. - round here he's, well, how do I put this? – *le grand fromage...*"
One sideways glance and I can recognise the tell-tale signs of incipient hysteria in Matt's expression. He is conspicuously failing to hold his tea cup as the officers do, with little fingers extended.
"So have you ridden much before?"
"Aye, I've had a go here and there," says Matt, cautiously.
Glances are exchanged. This is not a place for novice riders and I look at Matt, trying to signal caution as I may have over-exaggerated his equestrian skills when we were setting up the shoot.
"Well, whatever you do, don't bloody fall orf, will you?" one of them barks. "That'd be a prep schoolboy error!"
A barrage of braying laughter greets this, under the cover of which Matt whispers to me: "What's a prep school?"

22nd August 2002

An extraordinary morning. Matt passed his riding assessment with flying colours and has joined a group of troopers taking their horses for a ride along the vast wide expanse of the nearby Holkham beach. It is a perfect English summer day, with golden sand and cobalt blue skies. But it is more than a scenic gallop. As the troop get closer to our cameras, they turn and ride their horses into the sea. It is a surreal sight, watching these magnificent animals swimming, with the riders on their backs occasionally getting ducked under the waves. It is a wonderful sequence.
But despite the idyllic weather, and the pleasure of watching Matt's confidence and ability blossom under the intense and expert tuition he is receiving, there is no disguising the tension which still lingers between us and the crew. It is the first time this divide has ever happened to me and it is extremely uncomfortable. It is my fault for booking the wrong kind of crew; these guys, with whom I've worked before, are fine in a controlled and scripted environment, with plenty of back-up and facilities. They are not, however, prepared to rough it, or to improvise much, and this situation requires both.
Their attitude has not gone unnoticed by Matt, either. Later, when we are filming him having a jumping lesson, he completes a particularly demanding round of the course and asks to watch the footage back. The cameraman looks shifty but moves aside to let Matt press his eye to the viewfinder. Playback starts and after a few moments, Matt pulls away, in equal measure incredulous and furious.

"What the fuck did you cut for? You missed the key moment, you fucking idiot!" The cameraman admits that he had cut, thinking that Matt had cleared the last jump and realised his mistake too late to run up again.
Matt is livid and so am I. We have to restage the whole sequence, and, from this point on, I no longer trust the crew and check every last take, which is time-consuming and doesn't help the atmosphere. I won't be booking him again. I can accept that he is working out of his comfort zone, and take responsibility for getting the casting wrong, but that does not excuse basic incompetence and the poor attitude.

23rd August 2002
This is a very civilised branch of the army; everyone we meet has perfect manners and they respond immediately to Matt's desire to achieve and work hard. Because of his natural skill, they keep suggesting he try new and ever more ambitious equestrian feats, to which we are only too happy to agree. ("But it's not on the schedule," whines the cameraman).
The socialising is fun too. Over lunch, we are introduced to a Captain Blount, who, we are told "is a bit of a muso. But, whatever you do, don't show any signs of interest or he'll get out his guitar and you'll have to hear him sing."
The Captain is smiling from ear to ear and accepts the piss-taking as par for the course. He explains that he is pretty serious about his music and, having already had some serious interest, is planning to give it a go as a career when he leaves the army. I ask if I can take his photo.
"Just in case I make it big, eh?" he smiles.
"Yeah. Then we'll put it in the *Blue Peter* annual," I promise him.
Matt, meanwhile, is suffering, because, unused to constant hours in the saddle, his whole body has been battered and his muscles are protesting. He has developed a kind of weird bow-legged walking gait, a bit like he's shat his pants. This morning, he is so sore he is barely able to clamber out of bed. But he never complains about any of the physical discomfort. His attention is entirely focused on what we are doing, and in bonding with the lads around us. Some of these are initially wary of "the man off the telly" but he has them laughing, joking and on side within minutes.
Tonight, and until the small hours, we film him taking part in a navigation exercise in the countryside surrounding the camp. We are both exhausted by the time we stumble back to our hut but it's a while before we get to sleep because we can't stop going through the events of the day, swapping impressions of the various characters we've met ("Look like you want to slice his head off, man"), and pissing ourselves laughing.

Captain Blount delivered on his promise and became an internationally successful recording artist as James Blunt.

24th August 2002

The culmination of the film is the full regimental riding competition. In the original plan, we were just to be spectators. So well has Matt done that now he is taking part. He does well enough to be awarded a certificate and we leave the camp on a high, for the long drive back to London. The only downside is that Matt's body is in pieces; he's been riding pretty much non-stop for the past few days and he's really feeling it. Luckily for him, his girlfriend is a physiotherapist, and he calls her to warn her that he will need her to prevent him from seizing up completely.

On the way back, we pass the village of Soham, where two young girls were recently murdered. The roadside is a sea of flowers, stretching for hundreds of metres. In that moment, real life intrudes shockingly into the perfect bubble in which we've spent the last few days.

26th August 2002

Myself, Liz and Paul, our cameraman, fly to New York on Concorde, all in the name of making a film. This is very far from being a hardship, although there is a dicey moment right at the start when I want to film Liz reacting to the supersonic take-off. She says, "It feels just like you're taking off..." and I have to stop her in her tracks and point out that she's stating the bleeding obvious! Liz being Liz, she doesn't take umbrage and just bursts out laughing, before thinking of something more pertinent.

In between the filming, we are treated ridiculously well; a constant flow of first-class food and champagne. I'm surprised at how cramped and noisy it all is. When we arrive at JFK, the pilot invites us to have a look at the cockpit, and we dole out *Blue Peter* badges and have our photo taken.

Meanwhile, Matt and the rest of the crew, flying standard economy to join us for the main shoot, have a nightmare. Their flight is badly delayed and they only reach the hotel in the small hours, absolutely exhausted. Liz and I have agreed to say nothing about our fabulous hassle-free trip cocooned in the lap of luxury. At breakfast the next morning, Matt asks pugnaciously, "So how was Concorde then?"

"Oh fine, you know," I mumble.

"Yeah, all good," adds Liz, equally vague.

He looks suspicious but neither of us meet his eye and the moment passes.

27th August-4th September 2002

Flying back from a manic week in New York. It's been a really happy and successful shoot and I think one of the main reasons is that I agreed that both Matt and Liz could bring their partners (they paid for themselves, of course). Various wise heads in the office counselled against this. "You're setting yourself up for a 'them and us' situation," said one experienced producer.

"Won't they get distracted and just want to piss about and go sight-seeing?" queried another.

Sometimes the lack of trust between production and presenters is a real problem, and one which can go round in circles. Treat them in the old-school way, like rather spoilt children, and that's what they become and how they behave. I prefer to treat them as trusted colleagues, and good friends.

We were in New York long enough for everyone to have enough time apart, as well as evenings where we socialised together. Both Matt's Nicola and Liz's Toddy (his actual name is Michael Todd, but he is always known as Toddy) volunteer to come on most of the shoots, and they don't just stand about gawping or taking pictures, they really help.

Filming in New York is a strange mix of the *laissez-faire*, set up and do what you like, and the permit-heavy, more than my job's worth set of restrictions. Back in London, I got our regular musical director Dave Cooke to record Matt singing a version of the corny old song, *New York, New York*. The plan was to use this as the finale to the film, picking up the various sequences in all the famous landmarks of the city as we shoot. The drawback is that this means we have to lug an old-school ghetto blaster wherever we go for playback, as it needs to be something with enough volume for him to hear over traffic and so on. Depending on where we happen to be in the city, sometimes we have to knock off a shot covertly, with the fixer, Kate, biting her nails and hoping we won't be arrested. This is especially tricky when we attempt the sequences with Matt in costume as a New York cop. It is apparently a federal offence to impersonate a police officer without permission, which we have been denied. But we've brought the costume with us all the way from London and it seems a shame not to use it. We decide it will be safer to shoot the 'Matt as cop' sequences at night, and once he has put on the costume, he keeps it covered with a jacket until we are ready for a take. I decide it will be funny to stage a fracas in the street for 'Matt the cop' to break up, so I rope in Nicola, Toddy and our PA, Shireen to act the part.

Ironically, we have managed to set up some filming with the real NYPD. Matt joins a group of recruits for their fitness training. When he claps eyes on them, he can barely hide his disbelief at their general and painful lack of fitness. We've been given a big pep talk about how "your guy" might struggle with the exercises but in fact Matt breezes through them almost without breaking a sweat. Then we film a sequence in which he learns how to arrest and handcuff a potentially dangerous suspect. Which is where I come in, playing the suspect. Having paid close attention to the officer's technique, when it is his turn, Matt throws himself into role and I find myself slammed into the side of the police car, with the cuffs snapped on at double-quick speed.

"I've always wanted to arrest one of the bad guys," beams Matt. "Now where's the key?"

Since the horror of last year's 9/11, there are inevitably heightened tensions in the city. Filming has been restricted in many of the great landmarks. We can no longer take our cameras to the summit of the Statue of Liberty, for instance. But we do film at the sight of the Twin Towers, and here there are people openly weeping, or wandering around with dazed expressions or standing in little groups, some with their arms round each other or just holding hands. Being here allows a greater sense of the sheer scale of the tragedy and the terror it brought to New York and the whole of America.

The film is supposed to be the classic mix of light and shade, and for the crowning glory in our feel-good ending, we hire a vintage soft top, cram the crew in the front and film Matt perched on the back seat, miming away to *New York, New York* as the driver crawls through the city streets. I've pinched the idea from a promo film Irene Cara shot for *Top of the Pops* when she hit number one with *Fame* back in the 80s.

For the very closing shot of the programme, right in front of the Statue of Liberty, I come up with an idea to change the final credit. This is usually a full-frame graphic with Steve's name on it. For our alternative one-off version, I carefully ink 'Steve Hocking' across Matt's knuckles and, on the last beat of the music, he punches his hand as close as possible to the lens and keeps it there long enough for us to hold the final shot.

9th September 2002

We've booked the newly re-launched Basil Brush as a guest in the studio to plug his new series. I used to love Basil as a kid and I'm surprised at how much Mike Winsor, the new actor playing him, has managed to keep faith with the original. He is very funny (though a few of the production team comment critically that he is "too posh") and introduces some enjoyable anarchy to the studio. I wonder if it might be an idea to give him a regular slot of some kind, almost like having one of our pets talk.

11th September 2002

Studio recording for the Ludwig of Bavaria story. When I was doing the research, I was jubilant to discover that, as a boy, Ludwig had a pet tortoise to which he was devoted. In one of those random acts of child cruelty so common among the royal households of Europe, it was decided that this attachment should be terminated, and the tortoise was abruptly removed. To recreate this moment, I've pressed George, the programme's own tortoise, into service. Given that a tortoise makes a pretty useless TV pet – we basically get two items a year out of him (taking him out of hibernation and putting him back into it again) – this feels like a breakthrough. "One more magic moment for the obituary," I tell the team.

24th September 2002

Filming the story of Madame Tussaud in Baker Street. It is a late call because, as so often with places open to the public, we have to film 'after hours'. This means starting about seven and filming until about two in the morning. To help hold the audience's attention, films like this, with a lot of talking, need to look as sumptuous as possible. "Every shot a Rembrandt", as I put it. Often this means using a dolly and track so that the camera can glide and the shots develop and flow. But inevitably this takes more time to set up, rehearse and record than a simple static shot. Then there is the time it takes to light. Simon is on top of his game these days, but the wordier, fact-filled scripts are always more of a challenge than a quick ad-lib, so they take longer to get absolutely right too.

The shoot starts with us being accompanied by a friendly but rather bored PR woman. Who can blame her? Most filming is very tedious to watch. After a while, when I think she senses we can be trusted, she leaves us to it and nips back to her office. I have adopted a 'leapfrogging' approach to the daunting amount of material I hope to get. I explain each sequence to the crew and as they set up, I move on to check exactly what I want from the next, so I won't hold them up. This works beautifully until we reach the bowels of the building and the infamous Chamber of Horrors.

We are all too focused on the work to be distracted by the creepy atmosphere. At least, until I leave the crew setting up in one part of the Chamber and walk ahead to the next. Because we are recording sound, all of Tussauds' audio/visual circuits have been switched off. This has the unfortunate side-effect of taking out most of the electrical circuits, so that we can only have the emergency lighting on. This is fine wherever we are actually working because of our own lights. If you wander ahead, however, as I am doing, you can barely see a metre ahead in the all-pervading murk.

I march on confidently enough at first but then I have to turn a corner and then another to get to our next set-up. Here, the gloom is almost total and the reassuring sound of the crew working cheerfully away is completely cut-off. I am absolutely on my own now. This part of the Chamber of Horrors is an authentic recreation of a Victorian 'death row', with a grisly parade of the most notorious serial killers and lunatics standing by the prison bars. All the clichés about waxworks are true. It does feel exactly as if their eyes are following you and that at any moment, one of the figures might move, ever so slightly, or even speak. I catch my breath. I will not give in to this ridiculous, irrational fear. I try to focus on why I am here. But it is no good. The silence and the shadows vanquish my reason and although I attempt to walk back to the others calmly and slowly, I end up running like mad and nearly knock myself senseless on a wall which seems to loom out of the darkness.

30th September 2002

A big chunk of today's show devoted to a talented young escapologist who calls himself Tom Lyon. His real name, like mine, is Richard. The booking came about in an odd way. I was sitting at my desk when the phone rang. This very personable and confident person started to tell me about his interest in and skill with escapology and how much he would like the chance to demonstrate this on *Blue Peter.* Assuming he was an adult, I asked him if he had an agent. But then the voice faltered a little and he admitted that he was 15 and still at school.

"Ah, you sound much older," I tell him.

"Yes, I'm often told that," he says.

I ask him to send in a tape and give me his contact details. There is a long pause.

"Are you still there?"

"Yes, yes, I'm here," he responds. "I can send you a tape. But I'd rather not give you my details. Could I not just phone you back same time tomorrow?"

I say I must insist on a contact, if he is serious about appearing on the show.

"Do your parents know you're calling? Is there any reason why you don't want to give me a contact?"

Hesitantly, he reassures me that there will be no issue with his parents, but that he is at boarding school, so making contact isn't straightforward. Then he says, "I thought you might not want to feature kids who go to boarding school."

I say that I'm interested in what a contributor can bring to the programme, not what school they went to.

"Which boarding school is it then?"

Another long pause. I throw in a guess. "Is it Eton?"

"How did you know?"

"I didn't. I just assumed it might be one of the more famous ones and that's the most famous, isn't it?"

From this point, he seemed to relax and we made progress. He sent me his tape, and it was an impressive act. I agreed to book him. But he explained that both

the school and his family would prefer that he perform under a pseudonym, hence Tom Lyon.
During rehearsals, I ask him, "All that palaver over you being at boarding school; what was going on there?"
And he told me, "I just thought you might not want anyone from Eton. It's not exactly fashionable being posh these days, and I didn't want to ruin my chances because of where I happen to go to school."
An interesting perspective.

25th October 2002

Very pleased with today's show, the first of our new run of entertainment-based Fridays. When we were looking for a weekly game to include in the shows, there were various brainstorms and I remembered Double or Drop, which used to be a mainstay of *Crackerjack*. As I recall, the main draw of this was the moment at the end when the winner got to pick their prize from a mouth-watering display of possibilities in the studio. You could vicariously join in this at home, feeling for the contestant's agonising choice, and urging him or her to select the toy or game which you would have gone for in their place. One of our researchers looked into it, and reported that the rights to Double or Drop were available for a very modest fee. As there was nothing better on the table, I went for it and today seems to have vindicated the decision.
It was also the first time we have dispensed with Portapromt (our version of autocue) for an entire show. It is interesting to see how this has sharpened the wits of the presenters and collectively raised their game. I think it will really benefit Matt (who wasn't in today) because he struggles with reading at the best of times and I think he will find doing without the prompt more of a liberation than a chore.
The highlight of the show, though, was the start of our sumptuous thriller serial, *The Quest*, with the characters played by the presenters working for Miss Singleton's Detective Agency. This is shot like *Charlie's Angels*, with Val's voice heard, but only her hands or the back of her head actually seen in shot. Dermot, easily our cleverest and most creative film director, is also a bit of an anorak. The villain in *The Quest* is called the Visage, and he's got Gerald Harper to play him – a neat double in-joke for anyone who remembers *Adam Adamant Lives!*

4th November 2002

Morning recording with all the presenters looking exceptionally glamorous in their costumes for the Bond special we are making. It's rare to have them all in the studio on the same day, so I've taken advantage of the fact and scheduled a read-through of the panto over lunchtime. For some reason, both Simon and

Konnie seem to be in a bit of a mood, which is tiresome. Konnie puts absolutely no effort into reading her lines, so I snap, "Carry on like that and I'll cut your part to ribbons" after which she changes her tune a little and turns on the charm.

Most surreal moment of the day comes later in the studio, where I am supervising Liz having her photo taken for the annual, holding George the tortoise. As the photographer snaps away and I give direction, in the background I can hear Marina, the animal handler, chatting to one of the cameramen, who also happens to be a tortoise owner.

"My one's penis is like a feather," he confides, "very pointy and a bit curved."

"Really?" replies Marina, utterly deadpan. "George's is *very* impressive. Almost donkey-like."

This fact will not be going into the annual.

6th November 2002

Left the house at 5am, and dozed in the cab on the way to the first day of shooting on *Christmas at the Club Blue Peter*. This is the apex of my career so far, not just on *Blue Peter*. A handsomely budgeted hour-long special for the BBC, which I've written and will direct. So many talented people working to realise my script and bring my ideas to life. It is probably the closest I am ever going to get to making my own *Moulin Rouge*.

It's a proper drama shoot, with costume and make-up buses, catering and generators. The location, an Art Deco dance hall called the Rivoli, has been further transformed by the design team and looks superb.

It's the first time I've ever had my own First Assistant Director and to begin with, this is an odd feeling, as he does all the yelling and chivvying, so that I am free to concentrate on performance, shots, and saying "Action!" when everyone is ready for a take. I was also meant to say "Cut!" but so often found myself caught up in the moment that I'd forget and Adrian, the director of photography (much grander than mere cameraman), would do it for me.

The only long face on set belongs to Simon. He absolutely loathes his wig, which he says makes him look like Stephen Fry. I have to agree it is not brilliant, and certainly not what I'd envisaged when I asked Karen, the make-up designer, to base it on Ewan McGregor's in *Moulin Rouge*. I go and have a quick word with her and point this out.

"Yes, yes," she says, tolerantly, "but his wig was hand-made to order and probably cost about £5,000. This one came off a shelf from the BBC wig store. I'll have another go at re-dressing it."

After we wrap, share a cab back with Matt. Our driver has an appalling wig of his own. Matt texts Simon to tell him and Simon texts back, suggesting that we borrow it from him to try tomorrow, as it can't be any worse than the one he's got. Oh dear.

7th November 2002

Today we shoot Liz's first big number, *Venus*. The other presenters have all recorded their own vocals, but not Liz. Her character has a nails-down-the-blackboard screechy speaking voice and when she sings, although she is supposed to sound sensational, her voice is actually being 'ghosted' by Konnie's downtrodden character, Minnie (this is all a steal from the plot of *Singin' in the Rain*).

Liz will actually be miming to a combination of M.D. Dave Cooke's daughter Gemma, and a top backing singer Miriam Stockley, who, between them, have recorded the vocals.

As soon as I arrive, there is a costume kerfuffle; the backing dancers all appear to be wearing black PVC knickerbockers. They look ridiculous. Debbie, the costume designer, is apologetic and explains that the choreographer Gary had told her that because of the nature of the routine, the boys would have to wear kneepads. She lengthened what were supposed to be shorts to hide the kneepads from view. I tell her I hate how they look. Despite the frowns of my First AD, who dreads any delays, I insist that they will have to be altered.

"Are you happy with Liz's outfit?"

Liz is wearing a bright red skin-tight latex devil costume, complete with a tail and little ears. Just what I had requested for her first appearance as the vampish villainess, Venus Chartreuse. She looks sensational and I compliment Debbie.

"Oh, I didn't design it, or make it," she now confesses. "I found it in a sex shop in Soho."

I immediately swear her to secrecy. That's the last thing we need in the press release.

When the boys appear on set, the ghastly knickerbockers have been cut down into shorts, albeit rather skimpier than I'd anticipated. Other than their shorts and boots, the costume consists of white collar and cuffs. I clock Simon watching a nearby monitor and ask him what he thinks.

"Gay porn," he says, raising one eyebrow to reinforce the point.

It's a dull day for him. Most of the time he is just required to sit at a table in the foreground, watching, while the number is performed. But it's a demanding schedule for Liz and the dancers, as we have to shoot multiple passes to get all the coverage we need. We've reached the dance break section of the song when disaster strikes. One of the dancers, Arthur, slips and falls, badly hurting himself. Everything grinds to a halt. It is every dancer's nightmare and he is carted off to hospital while calls are made about liability and insurance. We are missing a key shot where the boys lift Liz up to the camera. Then I have an idea. We have supplemented some of the simpler routines with students from the Pineapple School of Dance. I have a look at them and ask one of the boys if he is up to having a go and subbing for Arthur. He agrees and is whipped into make-up to have his hair dyed black and some colour applied to his pale and interesting torso. Gary runs through the relevant moves and we are good to go. Our student saves the day, the number is in the can, and we finish only 45 minutes over schedule, which feels like a triumph.

13th November 2002

Liz is extraordinary. Today we've been shooting another of her big numbers, *That Don't Impress Me Much.* I've given this a sassy Western theme, with Liz as a take-no-prisoners saloon girl, backed by four of the boy dancers, dressed as cowboys. A couple of weeks ago, when we first rehearsed with Gary, the choreographer, it was a car crash. Liz looked hesitant, reluctant, embarrassed. We talked about it and she told me, "Rich, I just feel really stupid, surrounded by these gorgeous boys who can really dance, moving round me like I'm supposed to be sexy. I hate it."

I told her that she needed to put herself on hold, and transition into the Venus mindset and attitude; it wasn't her up there at all, but the character, and this is a character with the confidence and personality to own the stage. Without this transformation, I knew we would be sunk. Now here we are actually shooting the show and Liz has more than taken to heart the advice. She is brilliant, nailing all the moves and delivering an utterly convincing performance. Better still, she is actually enjoying the process, finding a freedom in surrendering to a character so unlike herself. And that's one of the things I love about Liz. Because she sort of stumbled into the job, she is unlike any other presenter. She doesn't seek attention or compete for it. Often, she has to *think* her way into being able to deliver the goods. She is sustained by her boundless good humour. I've never met anyone more willing to laugh in almost any situation. Given that most of the situations which come the way of a *Blue Peter* presenter are inherently strange, scary or ridiculous, this is a definite asset. I wish Simon could see the funny side of his hated wig. No matter what we do to it, it doesn't flatter him at all. We are too far in to turn back, and knowing that he is not looking his best, in what is, after all, the romantic lead, has been disastrous for his confidence. He's too professional to let it affect his performance, but he's hating the filming, and that is really sad.

By contrast, Matt, playing two parts, fresh-faced juvenile lead 'Junior', and the fat-suited Big Daddy, is wallowing in the opportunity. His attention to detail, adding instinctive little bits of business here and there, all proclaim that he is a natural-born performer. Konnie, too, is showing her ability to sparkle when the work interests her. She can be really funny. They are a talented quartet.

14th November 2002

Today I turned choreographer. Despite the healthy budget, I just couldn't afford to hire Gary, who is in charge of the big showcase numbers, to work on them all, so I have to work out the moves for a couple of the simpler ones myself. I've painstakingly plotted Liz's every move through her husky version of *Santa Baby*, and she can barely see for laughing as I demonstrate the various 'slinky' poses I want her to adopt, dragging a chair across the stage and then straddling it like Christine Keeler. But it all seems to pay off and I'm chuffed.

21st November 2002

Shooting the lavish closing number, a Bollywood version of the old Christmas standard, Slade's *Merry Christmas Everybody*. This is taking the term 'fusion' up a notch and when I first suggested the idea to the MD, he was very far from convinced. It went through several arrangements before we reached the one I was happy with. Alison, the designer, has filled the set with garishly decorated trees, gaudy baubles and garlands of lights. She asks me what I think.

"Like Christmas at Woolworths," I tell her, and then have to rapidly reassure her that I mean this as a compliment rather than a criticism.

It takes a while to get going as Konnie hasn't bothered to learn the words, as per. As the first few takes are obviously going to be hijacked while she gets the lyric in her head, I tell the dancers to mark their moves, rather than really go for it, or they will peak.

Originally, I'd wanted to end this number by firing off 'flutterfetti', brightly-coloured squares of paper which fill the air (and the frame) with a ticker-tape effect of colour and motion. But when the initial budget was calculated, and we were inevitably well over, this was one of the extravagances I had to forgo.

Reluctant to completely surrender the idea, I remembered a tip I'd been given years ago by a choreographer on another show. Each of the dancers is given a handful of confetti, and, at precisely the same moment in the song, they hurl these above their heads. It works superbly and the effect is almost the same as the 'flutterfetti' machines. The only downside is the frantic hoovering which has to go on before we can set up for another take.

Yet more costume issues. The CBBC girls in the chorus of this number are all wearing suitably exotic and glittery outfits, with tops which, from some angles, unmistakably (magnificently, some might say) showcase their breasts. The crew find this delightful, but I'm conscious that this will affect some of our choices in the edit.

27th November 2002

Today we shoot *Eat It*, the spoof Michael Jackson song I've hijacked to provide Matt's very funny star routine as Big Daddy. Planning this number has been a major headache, because every stage involves Matt using (mostly) real food as action props. Food is difficult to work with on just about every level. It is messy, tricky to reset, challenging for continuity, and needs to be handled with absolute precision if the comedy is going to register. The First Assistant Director and AFM pleaded more than once for me to think again, because of the complexity of what we are trying to shoot in one short day. But, though I am sympathetic to their worries, sometimes as a director it is moments like this where you have to dig in your heels and insist that a compromise isn't appropriate. Occasionally it is only your faith in the idea, and your conviction that it can be done, which gives everyone else the energy and drive to deliver.

Practical issues aren't the only concerns. There's also an editorial debate to be had, because *Blue Peter* has a long and pious tradition of never wasting food on screen. Throughout this number, it will be chucked, thrown, smeared and generally trashed with absolute abandon. But the comedy depends on it and, as I point out to Steve, Big Daddy is the arch villain, so *of course* he wastes food.

It's also a fiercely energetic dance, which includes a moonwalk in the middle eight. For Matt, embedded in a thick layer of latex, this makes the day a punishing one. He constantly drinks water through a straw (so as not to disturb his facial prosthetics) but can't rehydrate fast enough and is clearly suffering through much of the filming. A couple of times he loses his temper and gets snappy, especially when he detects anyone around him not fully paying attention or working hard enough to clear up the mess between takes, but on each take, his performance never flags.

28th November 2002

Filming the final number, *Evergreen*, in the grounds and some of the reception rooms of this grand Victorian hotel. It is only when I arrive that I realise that this was also the location for the classic *Doctor Who* story *The Evil of the Daleks*, a fact of significance only to myself.

We've been allocated a kind of small library as a green room, and, as per filming etiquette, everyone leaves their mobiles on a table here. There are some complicated set-ups to achieve, including a 360 tracking shot, and the lighting of hundreds of candles, so Konnie and Simon are cocooned in the green room longer than most. When I go to fetch them for a take, they are both paralytic with laughter. Hearing a text alert, Simon picked up what he assumed was his mobile, only to read an incredibly lewd and descriptive sex message from one member of the production team to another.

"I didn't know what to do," he says, "as if I'd left it, it would have been obvious it had been read. So I deleted it."
It is going to be hard for any of us to see the subject of this text in quite the same way again.

30th November 2002
Night shoot at Three Mills Studios in the East End. This was probably the biggest headache when it came to finding locations, as *Club Blue Peter* is supposed to be set in New York in the 1930s, and finding anywhere even vaguely suitable in modern London is a tall order. In fact, after she'd first read the script and met with me to discuss locations, our designer Alison just laughed and said: "Good luck with that!"
The exterior of these studios gives us the street and alleyways around the entrance to the club, and doing everything at night helps, too. For some of the scenes, I wanted a 'wet down' – i.e. a rain machine – but as these are ferociously expensive, Alison has come up with an ingenious substitute. She has hired a fire engine, with a powerful hose, set to spray, and, like a kid with a toy on Christmas morning, can be seen proudly brandishing this appendage at intervals throughout the evening.
She's not the only one enjoying herself tonight. I'm directing in costume, as I've scheduled my own cameo. I am 'Cop on Street Corner'. "Walk on one," as they used to say ("walk on ones" being extras who got paid a little extra for having been given a specific direction). My cop is definitely more Village People than *Serpico*, and I camp about in front of the camera, drawling Liberace-style, "you wanna see my rings?"
But the night stick turns out to be a handy accoutrement for a director and I quickly get a bit Cecil B. De Mille, waving it about for extra emphasis, while everyone rolls their eyes, unsurprised.

2nd December 2002
Further revelations in the papers about John Leslie, with various women now making a variety of different allegations. Very much the topic of conversation in the office's soft-seating area over lunch. Annie Dixon, nose deep in the *Daily Mail*, reads out: "He smacked my bottom till it was black and blue..."
She snaps the paper shut and announces: "Lucky girl!"
This afternoon, Val Singleton is one of the guests in our studio bring-and-buy sale. I've suggested she helps make the jazzed-up Advent Crown.
"No pressure, Rich!" says Simon. "It'll be like sharing a make with the Queen."
"Well, you managed the real Queen OK, so the *Blue Peter* version shouldn't pose too many problems," I retort.

Actually, Val is surprisingly nervous about the whole thing, and anxious not to take over. We have an interesting conversation in make-up. She tells me, "I'm one of those people who need to go into myself when I'm working" and then recalls a day spent filming in a hospital. Afterwards someone wrote in to complain that she was snooty and stand-offish. When Val next popped into the office, all was quiet, with hardly anyone there. She went off to lunch and when she returned it was much busier. Biddy chose this moment to pick up the letter of complaint and say, "Oh, look at this..." before reading it out loud.

"I could just have died," says Val. "You always had the feeling of being a naughty schoolgirl. John would sometimes say, 'Fuck off, Biddy' but Pete and I never did. It was always, 'You were late' – not 'Why were you late?' – there was an absolute and immediate assumption that you were guilty and there were constant comments like, 'You'd be nothing without us.'"

Val spent more than a decade on the programme, but this was never part of any plan. In fact, the whole job came about in a very casual fashion. She'd been acting and doing a bit of presenting on the side when a friend suggested she audition for a continuity announcer's job at the BBC.

"'Why not?' I thought. I think I got it because I didn't really care if I did or I didn't. I'd meant to prepare a script using that week's *Radio Times*. But I hadn't managed to get a copy the night before, so I just ad-libbed from the copy in front of me."

Once she had started as an announcer, Val found she enjoyed the work, and especially the social culture of the BBC Club. Here she met Chris Trace, who one day mentioned "We're looking for a new girl" and encouraged her to audition. But she didn't get the job.

"The producer, Leonard Chase, sent me a very nice letter saying that they thought I was marvellous but 'you've already got a job and we'd like to give Anita (West) a chance.' It was a very elegant way of saying that she'd done better than me."

When Anita dropped out just a few months later, they asked her to take over. Even then, she didn't really regard it as a career, juggling the one weekly edition with her various continuity commitments. It was only when the show went twice-a-week that she had to choose between them. "My parents were very worried," she recalls. "They said, 'You're giving up this prestigious job for a programme which nobody has ever heard of!'"

She continued to enjoy the BBC club scene and makes me laugh when she remarks that, "Diana Dors in hot pants was a sight to behold."

3rd December 2002

Lots of scenes with Janet Ellis, playing Venus's ultra pushy stage-school mother, Enchilada. I wanted to cast Janet not only because I thought she would do a great job with a fun part (sample line: "If you've got nothing nice to say about anyone, come sit next to me...") but as a small nod to the fact that my ambition to work on the programme was all triggered by watching a film going behind-the-scenes on her first day on *Blue Peter* back in 1983.

I had a fight on my hands to retain Janet's first line: "They call me Enchilada because I'm hot..." but I get away with it by promising that it will be played for laughs, rather than sleaze. Janet scarcely needs a note; she totally gets it. She's embraced the look of the part; too much hair, too much cleavage, too much everything.

I tell her the character was partly based on my memory of once meeting and observing Bonnie Langford's mum. It was during my time on *Going Live!* Every time Bonnie (who was adorable) was on set involved in an item, her mother would be watching intently from the sidelines, muttering "Shine, Bonnie, shine!" When I asked her if she'd like a cup of tea, Bonnie's mum hissed "Sssh!" without switching her gaze from the monitor. I was fascinated and I've nicked "Shine, Bonnie, shine!" and given it to Enchilada. When I tell Janet all this, she roars with laughter and reminisces about one of the first films she made for *Blue Peter*, joining Bonnie in rehearsals for *The Hot Shoe Show*.

"All the dancers were tiny, of course," she says, "and I felt very self-conscious standing next to them in my tights and tap shoes. But Bonnie was just great, such a pro and really supportive."

We also shoot a quick interview with Matt 'in character' as the actor playing Junior, for a fake 'DVD extras' I'm planning to put together for the end of series tape. He is hilarious at this, effortlessly affecting the sing-song patter of an incredibly camp American thesp. "Stacey...would you just hover with those eye drops....?" he shouts in passive aggressive fashion to someone just off camera, before turning to the lens, switching on a great beaming fake smile and launching into, "Every day we all come onto the set, and it's just like a game of tennis...20, 40, *deuce*! Oh, I'm *so* tired...."

4th December 2002

We've taken over the Round Chapel in Hackney, to film a fantasy number with Simon and Liz; a 1920s tennis party flappers and fops version of *I Should Be So Lucky*. It's also the occasion of a royal visit from our nominal executive producer and the head of department, Nigel Pickard. Such is the scale of this operation that Adrian, my editor, is cutting the show as we shoot, and today I've arranged to show Nigel (and everyone else) the Bollywood number we shot the other week. This seems to go down pretty well. Nigel, who has been a fan and ally for *Blue Peter* ever since he arrived, is leaving to go to ITV as director of programmes. This appointment is widely regarded as something of a poisoned chalice; rather like the Tory party, ITV is ruthless in rapidly discarding those chiefs it feels have failed to deliver. But, as Nigel puts it to me, "even if I only last a couple of years, the package is so good, I'll be able to retire or do something else, which I want to do, without having to worry too much about what it pays me."

Other than this visit, and reading the script before we began shooting, Nigel has been the classic old-school exec; hands-off. It is incredibly empowering to feel such trust and it's another spur to deliver.

5th December 2002

We're in the gym of a disused school. It has the perfect retro look; wall bars, ropes and vaulting horses but the downside is that it hasn't been heated in years and is absolutely freezing. This is all right for myself and the crew as we can wear as many layers as we like, but this isn't an option for Simon or the dancers, who are clad in boxing trunks and boots, and who have to be sprayed with glycerine and water to give them the required sweaty sheen. For the first time in this epic shoot, Simon, however, is not complaining. I've told him that as this is a 'fantasy' number, he can wear a beanie which means the hated wig isn't required.

6th December 2002

Watch today's episode of *The Quest* with a sense of relief tinged with a degree of guilt. Dermot, the director, had hired the brilliant magician Paul Kieve to play the part of the creepy Mephisto. Paul certainly looks the part and is a genuine master of illusion, but, alas, when he opens his mouth to say the lines, his voice, slightly estuary and rather camp, ruins the whole effect. If I had allowed it to stay as it is, the episode would have been sunk. Instead, I told Dermot he would have to hire a voice artist and redub Paul's entire performance. It has worked seamlessly but Paul is a lovely man, and I'm sorry we have had to hurt his feelings.

9th December 2002

The final day of work on *Club Blue Peter,* and the only studio recording, for the Bob Fosse inspired music number *These Boots Are Made For Walking.* Gary, the choreographer, has really gone to town and I am thrilled. Liz, whose number this is, and the girls, many of them well-known CBBC faces, are scantily clad in black satin, with bowler hats, kinky boots, and suspenders. As we block through the shots, I notice that the studio is more than usually full. There seem to be a lot of scene shifters, riggers, sparks and geezers in general milling about and enjoying an eyeful. I ask the floor manager to clear the set of anyone who is not supposed to be here. They shuffle off in little groups.

"Oooh, suddenly it's got rather lonely in here," says Liz, perched on her podium.

16th December 2002

Viewing of *Christmas at the Club Blue Peter* with Steve and Nigel. They are very complimentary, but they're also concerned.

"The production values are amazing," says Nigel, "it looks incredible and you've coaxed some fantastic performances from the cast. But we are going to get complaints about some of the music numbers."

The most contentious are *Venus*, with Liz in the devil cat-suit and the dancers in their black latex shorts, and the Fosse pastiche of *Those Boots are Made For Walking*, with Liz and all the girls in black silk hot pants and suspenders. I make the point that the costumes for *Those Boots* are all based on a design submitted by a 12-year old boy as part of our 'design-a-panto-dress for Liz' competition.

"Really?" says Nigel, with a sigh of relief. "Well, that helps."

My other defence is that there are plenty of vintage Hollywood musicals shown without complaint on a Saturday afternoon which have sassier or more suggestive music numbers.

In the end, a compromise is reached. Adrian, the editor, will re-cut both numbers to tone down or remove certain shots. Both of us are disappointed, because the changes are making each sequence worse, and I think that anyone with a mind to complain is still going to do so, whatever we alter. However, it must be said that we have got off pretty lightly. When you view such a scripted piece, in theory there should be no surprises, but the actual realisation makes every difference. I'm incredibly proud of what we have achieved. All the money is on the screen and, with the exception of one or two of the cameos from CBBC stars, the performances are fabulous.

20th December 2002

Directing the Christmas show again, though not live this year. As it has a slot on Christmas Eve, we've agreed to pre-record, rather than eat into everyone's holiday.

2003

6th January 2003

Good news. *Christmas at the Club Blue Peter* had the third highest children's audience to any show in 2002. Consequently, those upstairs are more than satisfied. I hope there will be no more muttering about latex shorts and suspenders. Today, *Ludwig of Bavaria* goes out. Like Ludwig himself, it has soared extravagantly over the top and runs at 17 and a half minutes. This makes today's live show very simple and allows us to pre-record Wednesday's show, too. Proving that what I take with one hand, I give with the other.

10th January 2003

From the moment I arrived, today was one of those days when you are chasing the clock and never quite seem to catch up with yourself. Nothing feels as if it has truly been resolved. I am very nearly late for run-through, and arrive in the gallery out of breath and out of sorts.

"Baby, you're going to love it," says Julian, the director, who has been working on me for months to give the green light to an 1980s special, chiefly so that he can book his favourite childhood group, Five Star. Self-indulgence part one.

For the film, I commissioned one of our directors to tell the story of Stock/Aitken/Waterman and she has done a remarkable job of gathering many of the key talent to contribute. Inevitably, however, it's a talky, interview-heavy film, and I've allowed it a hefty running time of ten minutes. Self-indulgence part two.

Given the emphasis on S/A/W, I felt we should have one of their acts to play us out, and we've settled on Dead or Alive, who are re-releasing their classic number one, *You Spin Me Round*. Self-indulgence part three.

The show just doesn't work. For a start, there are only two presenters, Simon and Konnie, and I never think a double act works as well as a trio. There is no clear narrative; if this had been a Victorian special, we would have isolated all the quirky little facts about the era which might draw a child's interest and spark their curiosity. There is a desultory rattle through 'what the 80s were like', mainly focused on gadgets and technology but the bloated running time of the film, and having two performances, leaves little space for any context or content. It is all a casualty of my insane schedule in the run-up to Christmas, when this show was booked and planned. I didn't have the time to really think about it or apply the usual rigour and now it is too late. Contrary to Julian's expectations, I don't love it, but I'm basically stuck with it. Julian can sense my disappointment and concern, and he's hurt because he's worked hard to pull it together and make it look good.

There is the issue of Dead or Alive's lead singer, Pete Burns, and his quite extraordinary appearance. Since his 80s heyday, he has clearly had truck-loads of plastic surgery, and his lips, in particular, have sex doll proportions. "You wouldn't need a hoover with those beauties," says Simon, during notes.

I ask Julian to cut some of the close-ups.

For some time now, Steve has worked from home on a Friday. When I get back to the office, I find a series of messages asking me urgently to call him. He picks up almost at once, and, without drawing breath, launches into a shouting rant of a kind I have never heard from him before.

"I am just so incredibly angry," he yells in my ear. "What can you have been thinking of? That show was terrible, terrible, awful. It wasn't made for children at all. The film had absolutely no shape or structure, and just went on and on. It was incredibly boring. And how could you have thought it was OK to have that Pete Burns on, looking like he does? Parents are going to have to explain that this is a man, or whatever he is, who has had extreme cosmetic surgery. I do not want the show repeated, so I want you to arrange that please."

During this tirade, I experience a rapid succession of emotions. Embarrassment and guilt, because I cannot disagree with some of what he says, and then, just as powerful, frustration, resentment and anger. It's my turn to explode.

"I'm sorry you hated the show so much, and I agree it was a failure. But aren't we allowed to fail sometimes? You know me. You know the team. Nobody set out to deliberately make a terrible, boring programme. Everyone feels shit about it. As for Pete Burns, well, the world is full of different types of people and some of them have plastic surgery. Parents can use it to warn their kids off, if they want to. But I don't think we should be banning guests on the basis of whether we approve of their faces or not. Anyway, I didn't see what he looked like until run-through."

Steve relents slightly and acknowledges all this. "But ultimately I am the Editor," he says, "and that was a truly awful programme with my name on it."

"Yes, you are the Editor but what does that actually *mean* any more? You've left me to run the actual content of the shows for months now. This is the first time you've hated what I've done. That's not a bad record. But you never see a running order or script, you hardly ever come to an edit or studio, and you're sitting at home and judging what we are doing like a viewer, because that's what you've become. An onlooker instead of an Editor."

As these recriminations come pouring out, I wonder if we can come back from this. Should I resign? Will he get rid of me? Is it the end?

"I don't think we should say any more now," says Steve, once I am done. He no longer sounds angry. "Let's think about it over the weekend and talk again on Monday, when everything has calmed down a bit."

I can't tell what he's thinking now but it's clear he wants to get off the phone. I tell him I'll sort a replacement for the repeat and ring off.

I've never been disloyal to Steve, appreciating that his lack of interest in the content has been my great opportunity. Neither have I joined in or encouraged the frequent bitching about our 'the absentee landlord" but perhaps this call has pushed me to saying things I should have voiced earlier. I feel like shit, though, and drive home depressed beyond belief.

13th January 2003

Steve calls me in to discuss Friday. I didn't know what to expect, and have spent the weekend tormenting myself with a range of dire possibilities, but he is the voice of reason and calm consideration. He starts by saying some extremely complimentary things to me, acknowledging my workload ("about which you never complain") and the routinely high quality of the shows. He apologises for having handled the situation when he was so angry, without having taken the time to consider. He agrees with many of the points and takes me into his confidence; he has decided that, as he can no longer guarantee that he knows the content of the shows inside out, it is time to begin the process of moving on.

"There's no time frame yet," he says, "but I have discussed it with Gina (his wife) and I will keep you in the loop about what I decide."

14th January 2003

The final overspend on *Club Blue Peter* has been calculated. £17,032 (making a total final budget of £353,266). This doesn't feel disastrous to me, considering the moments when I worried it was going to be far, far worse. Letters and emails of praise continue to come in, and to outweigh the fusspots and moaners. Steve tells me that he and his family watched it five times over the holiday.

17th January 2003

We've had a lot of press coverage over my decision to bring Basil Brush onto the show as a Friday regular. We've contracted him for 13 shows and will see how well he works. Also on today's show, Craig David. Or as Liz refers to him on air, "David Craig"!

After transmission, I ask her about this and she pulls a face.

"The drummer was looking at me funny," she says. "And it put me off."

27th January 2003

Dot Prior has been announced as the new head of department. No one is surprised, and no one is excited. Dot is the classic 'number two', good at organisation and with a thorough background in production finance. But she is not a creative or inspiring figure. Nigel Pickard has apparently been fighting her corner, which should have made Alan Yentob (in whose gift is the appointment) suspicious; Nigel, on his way to ITV, knows damn well that Dot won't provide much in the way of competition. Steve, typically, is making the best of it, and says that Dot trusts us to get on with it.

This afternoon, we launch our competition for kids to come up with a storyline for *Grange Hill*. This is not a popular show within the department and today, in the tea bar, a colleague from drama comments: "A ten-year-old can't do any worse than the writers they've got now."

30th January 2003

Snow starts to fall this afternoon, and several people in the office take this as a cue to sidle off sharpish. Unfortunately, I can't follow their example as there is just too much to do. I can't remember snow falling this quickly or this thickly before. The views of West London from our East Tower perch are both magical (snow always has that effect) and worrying (every road as far as the eye could see jammed with traffic). I decide to work as late as possible and at least give the rush hour a miss. But when I eventually start for home around eight, vehicles are queuing, engines off, just to get out of the multi-storey car park. I'm not parked that high up, but still it takes me the best part of an hour to creep down to join the traffic clogging Wood Lane. And so it went on, the occasional inch forward interspersed with minutes at a standstill. I've never seen jams like this before. I call home to explain that I'm not likely to get back until very late and discover that the chaos extends beyond the capital (I subsequently discover that it's taken my mother, who was babysitting the kids, four hours to drive back home from our house, a journey which normally takes 20 minutes). I keep wondering where all these extra cars have come from. Every single road seems to be jammed, and, several hours after the first snowfall, ice has formed so that even when creeping forward, there is the risk of a sudden skid. I spend well over an hour marooned in one street in Harlesden, finally turning off the engine, getting out of the car to stretch my legs and joining other drivers exchanging desultory conversation. No sign of any 'Blitz' spirit; everyone is cold, tired and bewildered by the intensity of the gridlock. Eventually, I negotiate the North Circular and arrive at the start of the M1. Here an apocalyptic scene meets my eyes; abandoned cars either side of the carriageway. It is only possible to drive down the very centre of the road, and then at the slowest of speeds, because the ice has made the entire motorway treacherously slippy. It is like being on some kind of surreal theme park ride, driving in an incredibly slow moving procession of cars, all of them swaying slightly from side to side. With luck (and extreme caution), I manage to avoid the fate which befalls several other drivers, sliding into the hard shoulder or coming to a stop beside the central reservation. Around four in the morning, I finally reach home, some eight hours after I set off from Television Centre.

31st January 2003

An unexpected problem. We've embarked on yet another series of films about a presenter learning to parachute, this time Simon. These have been an occasional staple of the programme since the days of Noakes. Alex Leger, our most experienced director, has been doing them for years and, ever ambitious, has devised a timeline for Simon to progress from beginner to advanced and beyond.

At the start, Simon was almost as keen as Alex to take his aerial achievements further than we have ever managed before. But fear has set in. For some reason, Simon's brain has started to process what he is undertaking and his usual calm, steely professional approach has proved no defence against the terror which his imagination is causing him. Alex is worried that the audience will think Simon is a big wuss and it will damage his popularity. I don't agree.

"Whatever happens," I tell Alex, "we need to be completely up front about what he is going through. Even if he has to give up, there is value in showing the audience that this isn't an activity for everyone and he knew when to stop. It will have even more impact coming from Simon, who is so cool and in control, and so physically capable."

6th February 2003

All day spent in the basement photo studio at TV Centre, shooting the cover and any special photos we need for the annual. Annie Dixon, who has been organising the annual for years, has scheduled everything with incredible precision. It is Annie who works out exactly which shots are needed to go with the various makes and cooks we are including. She bosses the presenters like a Sergeant Major and, although they grumble and mutter, they generally do as they're told.

I've chosen what each of the presenters is wearing for the cover shot; Konnie in her Hawaiian garb from the film she shot there, Simon in his parachuting suit (though this may prove somewhat premature), Matt as a farmer, complete with faithful Meg and handy crock, and Liz in one of the winning designs from our panto dress competition. It is, in fact, slightly different from the drawing submitted by the 15-year-old winner. The child's original concept was very low cut and so I asked our costume designer to add a discreet sequin section which keeps faith with the design but is slightly less revealing.

The main problem with the annual is that the BBC are so fucking half-hearted about it. This is my second year of pulling it all together, and they have no energy or aspiration. The designs they submit always have to be sent back at least once. It is incredibly frustrating. Because they want to print cheaply in the Far East, the lead time for publication in August (to capture the key run up to Christmas market) is a whopping six months; hence our looming deadline to complete the content for this year's edition. It is ludicrously early in terms of reflecting the show's output.

I make the choices for what goes in and I try to get a good mix, though ultimately the deciding factor is which stories have decent photos. There is no budget for professional photographers. The presenters are all used to me whipping out my camera on location and in studio and insisting on "one for the annual", or, as Simon always calls it, "the spaniel".

24th February 2003

My son Rupert is in the show today, to talk about the latest playground craze, Beyblades. This is not mere nepotism. Rupert is currently obsessed with the things, and can tell you anything there is to know about each and every variety. Also in the studio today is Stephen Gately, ex-of Boyzone, here to promote his starring role in the musical *Joseph*. When I pop down to the studio for run-through, Karen, our make-up designer, tells me that while Gately was having his make-up done, Rupert happened to be there too. Being a naturally chatty and curious boy, he asked Gately a few questions. Gately, apparently, soon tired of this and became rather precious and snubbed him, saying, "Who are you anyway?"

Rupert, offended, left the room and returned to the friendlier surroundings of the studio. Karen then told Gately: "He's the boss's son, so perhaps you should watch your manners in future?"

Karen is the kindest woman, but isn't shy about speaking her mind. A bit of an earth-mother, she dispenses far more than mere slap, both on location or in the studio. The make-up chair is always something of a confessional, and she is usually the first to hear what the presenters are thinking and feeling. She will often tip me the wink when one of them is unhappy about something or needing special attention. From time to time, and without being asked, she'll also quietly steer me into the make-up chair, and carefully trim the hair from my ears or nostrils (!), tidy up my eyebrows or put some calming lotion on a shaving rash. A tough job but I'm glad someone does it.

28th February 2003

Jacqueline Wilson is in the studio to meet some of her fans. I'm fascinated by the effect she has on these children. She is a tiny, grey-haired, pixie-faced, quietly spoken woman. There is nothing in the least starry or 'look at me' about her and yet the kids are absolutely mesmerised. It's all because this is the woman who has created the stories they adore. It is *much* more meaningful than meeting a pop star. I make a note to mention this at our next team meeting. So often production teams are full of young people with no children of their own. They invariably think that pop stars must have the greatest currency among the audience and they are invariably wrong. As a rule, pop music is teenage stuff, and very polarising at that. Boys, for instance, are utterly horrified at the prospect of a girl band gyrating about in "silly" clothes. For them, it is a complete turn-off. The real heroes for our audience are writers like Jacqueline Wilson and J K Rowling, sports stars such as David Beckham or Wayne Rooney and a few actors and comedians.

17th March 2003

The launch of the design-a-Fabergé egg competition. I've put up with a lot of good-natured piss-taking over this one, but I reckon that, as competitions go, it doesn't get much better than this. It all started a couple of years ago when I was wandering through the Burlington Arcade in Piccadilly and spotted that there was a shop devoted to Russian-looking boxes, frames and trinkets. There were also a series of eggs in opulent designs. I went in and discovered that the eggs were the work of Carl Fabergé's descendants, Theo and Sarah. I promptly arranged a studio item to display some of their work and so the connection was established.

The next spur was the fact that this year is the 300th anniversary of the city of St

Petersburg. A peg! Or rather, a reason for me to cook up an excuse to return to this alluring city. I suggested the idea of a competition for a viewer to design an egg. The prize would be that the winner would get to keep their own copy of the egg. This alone was going to be worth several thousand pounds. But even better was round the corner. When I started to explore the filming possibilities via our fixer Valery Katsuba, it became obvious that Fabergé's name still has enormous cachet over there too. To cut a long story short, the prize is now much more significant and long-lasting. The winner will still get to keep their egg design, but will also travel to St Petersburg, with two members of their family, all-expenses paid, where they will present the original egg to the Mayor of the city. This will then become part of the permanent collection at the Peterhof Palace. Quite apart from the fabulous prize, I think that the basic concept – asking the audience to come up with a design for an Easter egg – is so child-friendly and accessible across all the ages for which we must cater, that it is almost textbook-perfect.

27th March 2003

Filming in the Cabinet War Rooms under Whitehall. Amazing the difference a few tracking shots make. Such equipment used to be beyond our means, but, like so much technology, lightweight and cheaper versions of the dolly and track have become available and are invaluable for lending atmosphere and a touch of class to narrative films like this. You have to allow the extra time for the kit to be set up, and to light the more complex shots, but this can also be helpful for the presenter, giving them a chance to go over their words. These historical films are an intense short-term memory test. Simon is the undisputed master of them. His sense of humour is very different from the others. He has a sharper wit, tinged with cynicism. We set up a shot in Churchill's lavatory, which was actually a telephone booth in which he could make top secret phone calls to the American president.

On the action, Simon picks up the receiver and says, "Hello. Can you put me through to that twat Bush?"

28th March 2003

Much teasing from the team about my latest cameo, in today's episode of *The Quest*. We shot this last autumn in a library just off Piccadilly. I'm playing a policeman (just for a change) and when the lunch break was called, I took Simon, Liz, and the two guest stars, Brian Cant and Janet Ellis, to a little Italian restaurant over the road. I hadn't bothered to change out of the uniform and I was fascinated by the reaction of the restaurant staff. They were positively fawning over us, ushering us to the best table and offering us drinks on the house.

"I never drink on duty," I said, sternly.
"Of course, of course..." replied the patron, in a flap, whipping away the wine menu.
"I'm pretty sure it's illegal to impersonate a police officer," hissed Janet, across the table.
My turn to feel uncomfortable.

12th April 2003
We are filming the first stage of what might be termed a kind of Eurotrash *Blue Peter*. Inspired by the now oft-repeated clip of the studio doors jamming while Simon and Matt were wearing lederhosen, I've decided to make a film in which they explore the history of these comedy central garments, and take part in an authentic bottom-slapping yee-hawing Austrian folk dancing group.
For the first half of the film, however, we are in Munich. Good old Juergen has managed to locate a bizarre shop which specialises in antique lederhosen, run by a Herbert Lipah, an eccentric character who calls himself the King of Lederhosen. Lipah is apt to wear a gold crown and purple cape over his ubiquitous lederhosen, to reinforce the self-referencing. Simon, suitably garbed himself, is treating the interview as though it's an item on *Panorama*, not giving away by the slightest twinkle of the eye that he's dying to take the piss. Watching from the sidelines, Juergen has what can best be described as a jaundiced look. He despises Germans and rarely makes much of an effort to conceal the fact.
When we have done in the shop, we take several pairs of vintage lederhosen with us, so that we can shoot a sequence with Simon modelling them around this picturesque and historic city. We set up the camera on the balcony of a building to give us an impressive wide shot of Simon walking alone among the crowds in his distinctive garb. We are half-way through the first take when Simon is stopped in his tracks by a man with an extraordinary waxed moustache, who seems to want to talk to him. I can hear Simon over the cans, protesting that he is English and doesn't understand a word of what moustache man is saying.
Juergen, who is also listening in on a set of cans, translates.
"The man is congratulating Simon on being a true National, and showing how a young German should be dressed. He is a fan of the Nazis, I think. This is not surprising to me."

13th April 2003
Matt has joined us in the pretty village of Soell in the Austrian Tirol, where the boys are to join the dance group. They have insisted that they will only do so if I also wear lederhosen during the shoot. They still don't seem to have learned that any kind of dressing up is never a hardship from my point of view, but I am

determined not to let them sneak any photos on this occasion. It would be all I need with the Editorship on the horizon for some "funny" photos to sink my chances. I remind everyone that I decide what goes in the annual, so my revenge could be terrible. Of course, they manage to sneak a couple but nothing full-length or too ridiculous, so I think I'm safe.

14th April 2003

Long drive to what was once a part of East Germany, where the infamous Second World War prison camp Colditz is located. We are all tired and very hungry when we finally arrive, but, even though it is still only early evening, every café and restaurant seems to be shut. Eventually, we are told about one place which might still give us dinner. It doesn't look very promising. With its barred and shuttered windows, and heavy studded door, from the outside, it looks more like a prison than a place to eat. We bang on the door for some time before it is opened, with ill-concealed reluctance, by a stout matron with a splendid growth of facial hair.

Juergen gabbles away and we end up around a long table covered with a sticky plastic tablecloth. There is no menu; dinner is what the meaty-armed matron and her sidekick (husband?), a sullen man with mutton chops, feel like providing. A heavily salted, probably tinned, soup to start, which is served with some nasty stale bread. This is followed by some kind of fried grey meat, with a small selection of pickled vegetables on the side.

"Plated up yesterday," comments our cameraman, Adrian, despondently.

My neck and shoulder are killing me, the legacy of my foolish filming bravado in the Mexican theme park. Matt offers to give me a massage, using skills picked up during his time as a gymnast. Soon, the others are all begging him to have a go on them too and Matt good-naturedly works his way round the table, while mocking everyone's whining for attention.

"Oh do me, please do me, it *really* aches..."

15th April 2003

They take things seriously at Colditz. No question of our usual approach; turn up and start shooting. First we have to be given a solemn tour of the areas in which we will be filming. Our guide is a very tall, very dour man with a lugubrious expression and a sonorous voice. I can't look in the direction of either Simon or Matt, as he intones: "This is the hole (pronounced: hoe-whirl) through which Airey Neave made his escape..."

"Over here is the hoe-whirl in which another attempt was made..."

And so on.

Simon's biggest challenge is a lengthy piece-to-camera about the glider built in secret by some of the POWs, which they planned to launch from the attics as

their means of escape. Unfortunately, they christened it 'The Colditz Cock'.
We have got here in the nick of time, because there is a programme of works underway to turn the Castle into a youth hostel, in the process eradicating both its unhappy history as a POW camp, and its more recent, and equally unhappy, spell as an asylum. Workers are painting over the graffiti left by the soldiers interned here, and filling in and disguising the many escape routes which still exist. I have some sympathy for this. As our guide put it to me: "This is not history of which we are proud. We want to look forwards not back. And this was just six years out of a six hundred-year history."
Nevertheless, I am glad that we are able to capture some of the history before it is destroyed forever.

16th April 2003
A day of dressing up for recreations. I am playing a Nazi guard, and despite the obvious jokes, it is not typecasting. I find it very difficult to look stern and Teutonic, and when I am supposed to be roughly inspecting the mouths of the POWs (played by Simon and our camera assistant, Ross) for hidden contraband, the slightest twitch on their part sets me off, and in seconds we are all crying with laughter.

17th April 2003
Our final day and we are filming out in the countryside, recreating various escape attempts. Dressing up as a woman was one of the successful disguises used by escapees from the castle, so we drag up Sam Diamond, the sound recordist, and rechristen him Samantha Diamanté, a nickname he tolerates for the rest of the shoot. Simon, meanwhile, is disguised as a Hitler Youth, a uniform in which he looks disturbingly to the manner born.
"Lucky we are not in Munich now, eh, Juergen?" I remark. "We might start a riot."
In fact, the wearing of Nazi era uniforms in public is a criminal offence to this day, and we carry with us official written permission to do so. But we still take the precaution of rehearsing with Simon wearing a coat over his costume, only removing this when I am ready for a take.

29th April 2003
Dreadful mess of a pre-record, and thank God for that because it means we can do some damage limitation in the edit. It's partly my fault for agreeing to an item from a new stage show about Tommy Cooper about which I was dubious from the start. It was sold on the basis that the star, Jerome Flynn, has apparently mastered Cooper's fine blend of comedy and crap magic. Flynn is a lovely man, but very serious, actor-y and intense, so that trying to extract some child-

friendly answers during the chat is painfully hard stop and start work. And judging by the extract we feature, the show is not destined for a long life. In this kind of situation, it's hardly helpful to crow "Told you so" – you have to let producers have some autonomy over their content and not try to twist them into spending their working life second guessing what you think would be good. The other main item, promoting a new exhibition called Torture at the Tower, ought to have been a piece of cake but the coverage, especially of close-ups, is inadequate. Not entirely the director's fault either, as, to save money, we have been experimenting with using four rather than five cameras, and it is clearly a false economy.

1st May 2003
Filming the story of Bath Spa, and I am rushing to get Simon's piece to camera outside Number One Royal Crescent in the can before the museum gift shop closes. Those that film with me often know that a cup of tea and some cake, and maybe a little light souvenir shopping, are all part of the filming experience. In my book, anyhow. Simon is deliberately winding me up and taking his time.
"Don't worry, Rich," he says, beaming. "I'm sure they've heard you're coming and will have put some lavender soap on the side for you."
We are filming inside this perfectly preserved Georgian house once it has closed to the public. Karen, our make-up designer, has transformed Liz into a passable facsimile of Jane Austen, and we set up a shot with Liz sitting in front of an elegant tea table, pulling off her long white gloves. The only problem is that the gloves are such a tight fit, she can only tug them off with a face-gurning effort which totally destroys the ladylike illusion.

12th May 2003
In return for allowing Girls Aloud to perform their new single, I've persuaded the record company to agree to them taking part in an item – modelling nurses' uniforms through the ages. There are no problems with the girls who are assigned the sexier versions of the uniforms but red-haired Nicola has been give the less-than-flattering Victorian frock. In consequence she has a face like a smacked arse, which is not helping the item. The plugger takes me to one side and suggests we get one of the presenters to ask her a question. "It's always the same," she confides. "TV companies love Cheryl, Kimberly and Sarah, but Nicola is always left out. Chuck her a question and then I can liven her up for you..."

14th May 2003
We've cooked up an excuse to do a whole show from the garden; it is 25 years since the sunken part was designed and built. A thin anniversary but self-

referencing is part of the language of *Blue Peter*. Our star guest is the children's laureate, Michael Morpurgo, whose books I admire, but to whom I don't take as a person. He makes no secret of the fact that he thinks the content of the show is trivial – we are celebrating George the tortoise's birthday and making a tortoise-shaped chocolate cake in his honour. Morpurgo moans on about the use of slang, the 'sloppy' way the presenters speak and especially lack of time devoted to him. Miserable old sod.

15th-16th May 2003

A couple of days in the picturesque Derbyshire village of Eyam, filming the dramatic story of how the plague was brought here in a bundle of cloth from London during the 17th century.

Death scenes are notoriously difficult to shoot without everyone getting the giggles, not least the corpse, in this case Liz. I've teamed her with Simon, and they work very well together. She remains tolerant of his constant 'annoying brother' piss-taking, and he enjoys himself more than when he is making this kind of film solo. As usual, everyone on the crew is pressed into service for cameos. Gordon, the young camera-assistant, is soon haplessly attired like an extra from *Witchfinder General*, and I clamber into a costume and shoulder-length wig to play a village elder. We've taken over one of the rooms in the hotel to act as a make-up room, and Karen, the designer, scrutinises me intensely when I've shot my scene and it is time for her to remove the wig.

"Long hair really doesn't suit you," she remarks.

A persistent tug and she removes the syrup from my head. Over my shoulder in the mirror, I can see she is still scrutinising me.

"Short hair doesn't suit you either," she concludes.

19th May 2003

Get the results of my 360-degree feedback. This is a trial programme and, so concerned are management by the potentially negative impact on those taking part that we are given our results in the presence of a trainer, equipped, I'm told, to offer us appropriate support should a glimpse of the naked truth be too much to bear. Actually, they are at pains to say that this is not a collection of facts, merely impressions. The colleagues who have contributed (anonymously) have been selected from a range of different grades and responsibilities, the idea being that their feedback will give me some idea of the impact I'm having across the board. So, the results. On the plus side, I'm not too displeased to read comments like "incredible creativity and endless energy – comes up with ideas ALL the time" or "Highly creative programme maker who strives for and demands perfection from his presentation and production teams."

On the other hand, I clearly need to think about remarks like "Could work on being calm, at times he can be explosive" and "Richard is great at tackling things head on but sometimes is inappropriate in terms of where and when."
I tell the trainer that I think it's an invaluable process and much more effective than the moribund appraisal process.

2nd June 2003
Results of the British Museum design-a-poster competition. Glad to see the back of this one. The judging was a nightmare as we hadn't specified that the poster designs should be portrait and not landscape. Turns out the Museum really only want a portrait-sized poster. When Neil McGregor, director of the British Museum, and our head judge, arrived, he was all for dismissing out of hand all the landscape designs. I had to dig in my heels and insist that, as this wasn't a condition we had given to the audience, we must consider all the shortlisted entries. McGregor was very lofty and dismissive about the whole process. Huge ego and a crashing bore.

10th June 2003
Blue Peter summer garden party. Steve makes his farewell speech to the assembled guests and says something on the lines of: "It was time to move on when I realised that I often had no idea what was going to be in a programme..." Afterwards, Sarah Greene sidles up to me. "Very odd that, didn't you think?" she remarks. "I'm not sure I would have basically admitted to not having had a clue what was going on in the programme I was supposed to be editing!"

11th June 2003
Morning recording to tape the cottage interior sequence for my story about the plague at Eyam. Design have done their usual fantastic job. To play the wife of one of the stricken peasants, I've chosen one of our junior researchers, Katie. She has a wonderfully 17th-century face, and, like a total natural, assumes the necessary anxious expression. Afterwards I compliment her on her performance and ask whether she found it difficult.
"No," she replies. "I just thought about how I feel five minutes before we go on air."
Liz is making a father's day card on today's show. Unknown to her, I'd had the idea of inviting her actual dad to make a surprise appearance during live transmission. Given how easily she can sometimes be thrown, I was worried this might completely sabotage the item, but in fact it works like a treat and lifts the item from the mundane to the must-watch.

20th June 2003

Encouraging letter from Biddy Baxter *à propos* of the looming Editor boards: "I can't think of anyone approaching your talent," she writes. "Your track record is superb and I know all the production team are behind you."

Later, I'm on the phone to someone and I sign off by saying, "Cheers!"

Annie, who is sitting within earshot, looks up and says: "Don't say 'Cheers' – it's common. Bad enough for a series producer, but out of the question for an Editor..."

I am suitably chastened.

24th June 2003

Very touched that Rosy, my daughter, has made me a special good luck card for tomorrow. "As you should know, you are the only real person for the job!" she writes. "You can do it, Dad," she says, as she hands this over. I hope I can. Don't think I can bear to disappoint the kids, who have so much faith in me.

25th June 2003

The big day. 0930am and I'm first in the boards for Editor. The interview is conducted by Dot, Steve, Loretta, who is charge of the department's money and a woman from HR called Clare.

Truth is, I don't feel nervous. It's a ravishingly beautiful summer morning and light is streaming through the office in which we are sitting. It is now or never. I've done my homework (I'm clutching it in a plastic folder in my hands). I know these people and they know me. There is no need to act or pretend. This isn't to say that the process isn't taxing. Much of the time we are playing the 'what if' game. A good example: what would happen if you got a call from location to say that a presenter had been seriously injured or killed? My response? Seriously injured: find out more, have standby programmes in place, refer to senior management and press office.

Killed: programme cancelled.

"Seriously?" says Dot

"I can't see any argument you could form for continuing a programme if someone's death is the consequence of making it."

"OK," she nods, and scribbles something on her pad. I wonder if I've committed my first blunder. But this is not a time to second guess anyone.

The other 'what if?' feels less contentious. What is my take on the programme and where it is going over the next five years?

I produce my plastic folder with a flourish and hand out the documents I've prepared to illustrate my proposals. I know that Dot is determined that *Blue Peter* should transform itself into a five-times a week digital proposition. I don't really agree with the thinking; I'm worried that we will be spreading the jam too thin and that the show will lose its special status. But this is what she wants and what she will have, whether I provide the means or some other bugger does. And if it is going to happen, I want to be the one in charge, to ring-fence what matters and preserve the core identity of the programme amid the endless sea of change.

This is the basis on which I've formed my plan, and I've put huge effort in the detail; producing a draft schedule for the first year to show them what my five-times a week *Blue Peter* would look like, a breakdown of how we would actually make the shows, and a detailed budget (much of the sums for this calculated by my 'work wife', our dedicated production executive, Caroline).

The basic premise is that we will be in studio every Monday and Tuesday. Monday will be live on BBC1, repeated on the CBBC channel. Tuesday will be live on the CBBC channel, repeated on BBC1 on Wednesday. The Wednesday CBBC show will be pre-recorded on Tuesday morning. Thursday on CBBC will be a re-versioned repeat or compilation and Fridays will be a special, shot entirely on location.

These proposals inspire a volley of questions from all sides but as I have interrogated every aspect of my plans for weeks, nothing leaves me feeling, "Shit, why didn't I think of that?" and I'm able to respond quickly and with confidence.

At the end of the interview, they all thank me and Steve gives me his Cheshire cat smile, which I know means he is pleased with how it went.

"Well done," he says, "that was really impressive."

27th June 2003

My appointment is announced to the department and the wider BBC. "Richard demonstrated a real passion for *Blue Peter,*" says the email from Dot, "and presented some ambitious ideas and a clear strategy for developing the series on the CBBC channel."

A stream of congratulatory emails and messages follow from friends and colleagues.

I am not quite sure I can really believe it.

3rd July 2003

An interesting mail from Edward Barnes, who writes: "I hear from Biddy that you are now Editor of BP. I must say I am delighted to know that someone who really understands about *Blue Peter* is in charge. Margaret Thatcher used always to ask about a new person, "Is he one of us?" And, in the same way, Biddy, Rose and I would ask, "Does he understand about *Blue Peter*?" – because not everybody did. In fact, some people worked quite well on the programme without really understanding what it was there for. But those who really understood were those who produced the greatest work. It would be disastrous to have someone in charge who was not. And I long ago clocked you as one who understood. I hope you enjoy it – remember that you are in a very powerful position so don't take any shit from above or below."

31st July 2003

Appraisal with Steve. A lot of very complimentary remarks are made, but I think I am most pleased to have in writing the recognition for the success of *Christmas at the Club Blue Peter*. "It provoked a reaction and raised a brief storm," he acknowledges. "It was, above all though, a creative triumph on a scale not seen for some time in CBBC."

Or probably again, given how much it cost.

1st August 2003

A return to St Petersburg, where Valery will once again act as our fixer. I've encouraged him to put together an even more ambitious schedule this time. We are making a complete special and a couple of films, and this is also the pinnacle of the Fabergé competition. Our winner, Natalie Learmouth, and her family fly out to join us for the grand presentation ceremony tomorrow.

4th August 2003

I've asked the crew to bring suits to wear for the presentation and it is odd to see them in such smart attire, rather than the usual jeans and fleeces. I'm grateful that Natalie, the winner of the competition, is 15 – she is nervous but not totally overawed. I didn't expect the ceremony to be quite so grand; it is taking place in the ballroom of the splendid Peterhof Palace, and there are rows of little gilt chairs on which the various dignitaries and guests will sit. Even Valery is impressed.

"All this for a children's television programme," he remarks.

"Not *a* children's television programme," I correct him haughtily, "*the* children's television programme."

The *Blue Peter* egg is formally accepted by the Mayor of St Petersburg, who explains that it will become part of the permanent collection of treasures here. There is much posing for photographs and stilted interviews with Russian TV crews before we leave for another official reception, at the British consulate. Here the wine flows liberally, and one of the patrician but glassy-eyed staff confides to me: "You've no idea what a bore it can be. We're very grateful – your vulgar little *bibelot* has enlivened an otherwise pedestrian week."

5th August 2003

A long day filming at the Catherine and Alexander Palaces. We avoid the crowds by doling out bribes to the officials, who then close off wherever we choose to film.

"You can do anything you want," drawls Valery, laconically, "for dollars."

This could be his catchphrase. The only fuss comes when we film in the recently completed reconstruction of the world-famous Amber Room. This was looted by the Nazis in the Second War, the precious amber stripped from the walls and ceiling, never to be seen again. Over many years, it has been painstakingly restored. But there is concern that the constant footfall of thousands of tourists, as well as the carbon monoxide from their breathing, will rapidly damage what has been achieved. As a result, everyone entering the room must slip on soft plastic overshoes and wear a paper mask. This makes us all look and feel idiotic.

When we break for lunch, Valery takes us to a restaurant crammed into a kind of wooden hut. Service seems to take forever and I get more and more irritable as time which could be spent so much more productively ebbs away in this drab little shack. Hoping for something straightforward and quick, I order chicken soup. This does not turn out to be good for the soul. It arrives and at first I am impressed at the sheer size of the bowl. Then, like Loch Ness in miniature, it reveals the reason for its size. The entire wizened carcass of a long-deceased bird slowly emerges from the liquid – beak first.

6th August 2003

Valery has arranged for Matt to take part in rehearsals in a St Petersburg theatre for a Russian folk dancing show, chiefly performed for tourists. We arrive to an indifferent reception. Matt is inspected dispassionately and it is evident from the body language of the dancers that they do not find him promising. Valery, invariably sleepy-eyed and gentle in approach, suddenly switches into fierce volubility and exchanges heated words with the dance master at the side of the stage. I've impressed on him the importance of this story, as the film needs some fun visual action to off-set all the history and culture.

Some kind of agreement is reached and Matt is beckoned into the circle of dancers, all of them tough, wiry young men. Once they are warmed up, they show him some basic moves, and Matt masters these almost at once. He is in his element in this kind of situation, improvising, showing off, getting people on side with his enthusiasm and ability to precisely follow instructions. And all this without a word of English between them. It is not long before Matt is being pushed to new and more vigorous and ambitious steps. His athleticism is a match for theirs and he is kicking his legs back and forth like a natural-born Cossack. By the time the dance master calls what I think is a wrap, we have got more than enough material. But I'm wrong. He is offering Matt the chance to actually perform in tonight's show, and not merely as a background member of the chorus, either. Instead, Matt will play the wolf in a dance based on a classic Russian fairy story about a village which is terrorised by the creature. If he agrees, there is no time to waste as he will need to learn the moves fast. Matt, of course, is up for it.

As he starts the last-minute rehearsals, I consult with the crew about how best we can cover this performance, given we will only get one go at it. Everyone has a key part to play, as we divide our cameras between the team and the key shots needed between each position. By the time the theatre starts to fill, mainly with American and Japanese tourists, we are all ready to go and thoroughly keyed-up. Matt's eyes are ablaze with adrenalin. He can sense a triumph is his for the taking. I watch from the wings with renewed respect for his determination, charisma and sheer talent.

Afterwards, we are all on a high, though now the endorphins are wearing off, Matt's muscles are clearly feeling the effects of hours of punishing non-stop action. We are having a slightly later start in the morning so I ask Valery if we can book a masseur first thing, to visit Matt in his hotel room.

"Of course, it will be just a few dollars," Valery smiles. "I can get you the best. He works on our Olympic team, very good, very powerful. You want him to massage Matt first and then come to your room?"

I think "Why not?" and agree that, as there is time, he should do just that.

7th August 2003

I'm waiting in my underpants, a towel modestly wrapped on top, when there is a sharp knock on the door. When I open it, standing on the threshold is a short, squat man with eye-catchingly enormous biceps and quads. In fact, his body looks like an anatomical map of the human musculature. He is wearing a kind of P.E. teacher's attire; plimsolls and white socks, tight blue shorts and a white polo shirt, and he is carrying a small sports bag. Unsmiling, he merely nods curtly at me and walks straight in, throwing his bag to one side. As he does not speak a word of English, nor I a word of Russian, all our communication takes the form of gestures and grunts. Not that there is much of this, as it turns out. He tugs the towel from my waist and indicates that I am also to remove my underpants. I hesitate and this seems to annoy him, as there is a stream of voluble Russian and a renewed mime to stop wasting time and lose the boxers. "When in St Petersburg..." I think, and drop 'em.

This spurs him into action. Turning me round so that I've got my back towards him, he grabs my wrists and hoists me up onto his shoulders. I hang there like a side of beef, feet several inches off the floor, my genitals dangling sadly between my legs. He begins to jerk me back and forth, and I can feel my vertebrae responding with a series of clicks and pops. After this unexpected start, for the next 45 minutes or so, there is no let-up. I am hoisted this way and that, sometimes on the bed, sometimes draped across his rock-like form, while he prods, and jabs, stretches and extends. He uses his knuckles, his elbows and his knees with extraordinary precision, strength and flexibility. From the bag, he produces a series of small domed glasses. I am on my hands and knees for this stage of the operation, and I hear a match strike and then a hissing sound, just before he clamps each glass to my back either side of my spine. The skin is somehow drawn up inside the glass, which is an odd and alarming feeling. When he pulls them off, I am left with a serried row of what look like purple bruises.

Much of the time, such is the pain he is dispensing, that I am fighting to breathe and keep my unmanly whimpering to a low level. When he is finally done, he lifts me in one smooth movement from prone on the bed to standing like a guardsman. There is a vigorous inspection of my posture, before he claps me on the shoulders, shakes me by the hand and indicates that he is done.

I get dressed slowly. When I join the others downstairs, I recognise a certain sheepish look in Matt's eyes.

"That masseur..." I say, tentatively.

"Aye."

"I don't know about you, but I feel a bit violated."

Matt nods.

"Tell you what, though, Rich. I couldn't walk this morning, could barely get out of me bed. Now I feel like I could climb a mountain."

"And all this for only ten dollars," pipes up Valery crisply, from the sidelines.

8th August 2003

We spend our final filming day on board the naval ship Aurora. Valery tells me of his own time in the Navy, during the Soviet era, when every young man was required to undergo national service. He was conscripted into the navy, and, perhaps surprisingly, he has nothing but praise for the experience. "These boys sometimes come from villages hundreds of miles away. This can be the making of them, the chance to open their eyes to a world beyond their homes. It made me realise that I had to live in a great city, where there is history, and art, and every kind of person."

Fixers come in all forms; most are pleasant, professional and a little detached. They work with an ever-changing sea of faces from TV companies all over the world. But Valery has been very different, and, on both occasions I have filmed with him, has felt one of us. He is clearly curious about us, and our way of thinking, and his conversation is never limited to the practical and necessary.

Above: 8th December 2001 - *A Rock 'n' Roll Christmas (L to R)* Liz, Matt, Tina Heath, Jenny and Beccy Smith

Left: 29th November 2001 - *Uptown Girl (L to R)* Joe Inglis, Matt, Konnie, *Blue Peter* astronomer Anton Vamplew, Simon

Above: 26th August 2002 - Visiting the Concorde cockpit with Liz

Above: August 2002 - with Matt in New York City

Above: 26th February 2002 - In the trenches - the smile didn't last

Above: 28th March 2003 - PC Editor studying the script of *The Quest*

Above: 24th June 2001 - Muddy Marines - but revenge was imminent

Right: 23rd August 2002 - Captain James Blount - "a bit of a muso"

Above: 13th July 2004 - Albert (RM) and Victoria (Liz) - trying not to laugh in a royal picnic at Balmoral

Above: 17th January 2003 - Basil Brush joins the team to run B.U.M.S. (Basil's Ultimate Mail Service)

Above: 13th April 2003 - Lederhosen madness in Austria. I'll wear them if you will

Above: 13th April 2003 - *Eurotrash* meets *Blue Peter*

Above: 3rd May 2001 - A couple again - Beatrix Potter (LIz) and fiancé (RM)

Above: 21st November 2002 - Cast and crew of *Christmas at the Club Blue Peter*, the most lavish production we ever made

Above: 7th November 2002 - with Liz as Venus in her sex shop catsuit

Above: 30th November 2002 - Another cameo, another cop

Above: 14th November 2002 - Janet Ellis playing Liz's mother, Enchilada

Above: 13th November 2002 - directing Liz in *That Don't Impress Me Much*

Above: 4th December 2003 - Double BAFTA winners - the team celebrate in the studio with series producer Kez Margrie and RM

6th December 2004 - The Magic of Christmas and the arrival of new girl Zöe Salmon

1st September 2003

I'm worried about *The Quest.* Dermot, who wrote and directed the first three series with such imagination and skill, has moved on, and, reluctant to see *The Quest* leave with him, I've committed to carrying on with another director in charge. She is ambitious and hard-working, and her concept, which has a Sixties setting and a time-travel theme, is appealing. But the scripts have come in and they are awful. The plotting is confused and there are sequences I know at first glance will be impossible to achieve, even on the fairly generous budget that *The Quest* is allocated. The dialogue is risible, indeed un-performable.

I've stayed late several nights in a row doing a total rewrite. Unfortunately, as the director sees no flaw in her original work, the temperature between us is several degrees below zero. I am losing patience with her on other levels too. For all her merits, she has never been popular on the team. The presenters find her fake and condescending and I've had various complaints from her peers, too. In this industry, you have to take some of the bitching with a pinch of salt, but there is no doubt that this woman has a 'steamroller' quality to the way she goes about getting her way.

I'm not very happy that she has booked her cameraman husband for all the shoots, despite his lack of drama experience. And then there is the casting issue. Before I went away on holiday, we discussed casting for the main villain, Stryker. This is obviously going to be important. Although conceived as a male character, I felt strongly that we should have a woman in the lead. We argued a little about this but, as I left for my summer break, it was left unresolved. To return to the news that this director had gone ahead and given the part to an unknown actor of her own acquaintance was more than just infuriating. I could tell that she thought she had out-flanked me, and that, with this actor contracted, I would simply have to acquiesce and make the best of it. I thought about this situation long and hard. I've only just taken over as Editor – what kind of message does her action and my response send to the whole team?

I called John Holland, our beautifully spoken contact in Artists Contracts, the department which does all the deals with presenters and actors on our behalf. He explained that, should I feel strongly that a serious artistic mistake had been made, I could pay off the actor and start again. So this is what we have done. To replace him, I've cast Jean Marsh, who I know will absolutely deliver what I'm looking for in a strong and devious villain. Her only proviso is that she doesn't have to wear a wig.

"I can do something sinister with my own hair," she assures me.

Tonight, Channel 5 transmit their very watchable but predictably tacky documentary, *The Curse of Blue Peter*, the premise of which is that there is a kind of *Final Destination* 'black spot' which inexorably claims most of those who

have presented the programme. My 12-year-old daughter Rosy stays up to watch and she gets very cross about how selfish and "ungrateful" some of the old presenters seem to be. They have clearly spent more money on their promotion of the show than the production, which is tattsville.
Within the BBC there is much outrage about the unashamed use of pirated archive (indeed, not a frame of the archive in this doc has been properly cleared or paid for) under the dubious banner of 'fair dealing', a clause which is actually meant to allow news and current affairs programmes to bypass the normal clearance process. I'm more bothered that they have somehow managed to gain access to do some covert filming in the *Blue Peter* garden. Not a great advert for BBC security. But, as I put it in my interview with BBC Radio, it's my belief that it's a compliment for a rival broadcaster to devote an hour of their peak-time schedule to chewing over the gossip around the BBC's flagship children's programme.

8th September 2003
My very first show as Editor, and not a bad way to start. In the morning, we pre-recorded an interview with this young adventurer, Bear Grylls, who really couldn't have been more charming. He is like someone from another time, a kind of classic Edwardian adventurer; a muscular Christian to rival Simon.
And from the sublime to S Club 8, as the juniors have now been rechristened. Actually, not a bad song this. One thing that's always been true of the S Club 'brand' – Simon Fuller stumps up for top quality pop songs. This one – *Sundown* – plays out over the credits, and I sit in the gallery, absurdly nervous and anxious lest my very first Editor credit somehow go AWOL or otherwise fall off the perch. But, no, there it is – and then we are off air. It's hard to explain how it makes me feel, seeing that credit, given the number of years I have wanted the job, and worked for it. It sounds trite and inadequate to use a word like 'happy', but that is what I feel and certainly I am conscious that, even if the show is cancelled next week (!), no one can take this moment from me. It will always exist, always be a fact, and always a source of pride and achievement.

10th September 2003
Random moments in a *Blue Peter* studio day. Liz tells me that when Westlife (or Pondlife, as the production team refer to them) arrived for rehearsals this afternoon, she happened to be passing and said "Hello!" to them, only for one of the band to mutter "Fuck off" under his breath, but loud enough for Liz to hear. She isn't especially bothered, just thinks they are a bunch of knobs. It is true that they never seem to be enjoying themselves, and there is no camaraderie between them. They are as fake as fuck and we shan't have them back.

Then, a minor flap when I watch today's film during run-through. This follows Simon learning to be the conductor of an orchestra. At the critical moment, when he mounts the podium in front of all the musicians, and the audience, I notice that he has his flies undone. They are positively gaping. We have to do some rapid zooming in and re-arranging of shots to cut round this wardrobe malfunction, which would certainly have spoilt the moment and fatally distracted from his impressive achievement. So to speak.

16th September 2003

The first day of filming on *The Quest*. I've done what I can with the scripts but thank God for Jean Marsh, who elevates the whole enterprise with her ability to breathe life into such sheer hokum. As a great favour to me, she has accepted a much lower fee than she could normally command, but then she is a pragmatist about work. "These are the jobs people remember you for," she tells me, "no matter how much you'd sooner it was for your Juliet or your Lear. There's no point being a snob about it. And it's these jobs that give you the currency to do the stage jobs you like."

A very friendly and supportive email from ex-Editor Lewis Bronze: "I've been hearing that you are now in charge of the galleon, and all who sail in her," he writes. "I trust you have a great time and take the programme on to new successes, in the best traditions of the show."

I reply and suggest lunch.

24th September 2003

Mulling over the findings of the audience research which was conducted during August. None of it is hugely surprising; children value the variety, the presenters, the challenges and the way it provides a window on the world. Younger kids find it a harder watch, as it is so information-heavy, and so it can seem dull.

The report concludes that we provide a mix of "edge of seat" and "itch to switch", which I guess is what you'd expect from a magazine programme, with such a broad audience and remit. Some of the specific comments from the children surveyed are priceless, though. On the subject of pop music in the show, one 12-year-old boy comments "It would need to include R & B for me, but that's too dark for *Blue Peter*."

My favourite of all comes in a section of the report titled, 'How does it compare with *Xchange*?' A 12-year-old girl from London says: "I bet if they make a mistake on *Xchange*, they just laugh. On *Blue Peter* they probably get fired."

9th October 2003

Lunch with my predecessor, Lewis Bronze, at the Rotisserie in Shepherd's Bush. He is an interesting man, very bright, pugnacious, admirably entrepreneurial.

Having taken redundancy in 1996, he set up his own company, first to make TV shows for the newly-launched Channel 5, and then to hitch his wagon to the inter-active educational possibilities of the internet. He evidently takes a fairly dim view of the BBC, feeling that they simply let him go after all his years of solid service on *Blue Peter.*

"I went for the Editorship of *Tomorrow's World,*" he told me. "Didn't get it. There was no interest. I was a *children's* television person and that just doesn't have any value outside the East Tower (the TVC tower block where children's programmes are based). I was very bitter about it."

All this is clearly intended as a cautionary tale – don't build your part or have any expectations from a fickle BBC. But he is also warmly encouraging about the current state of the programme.

"Far from there being a curse," he smiles, "it seems to me to be in rude health."

15th October 2003

Ever seeking new twists on fresh ways to celebrate the programme's heritage, I've cooked up a 'presenter for a day' competition to mark today's 45th anniversary programme. The winner is a 12-year-old boy called Ryan Gilpin. We chose him because he has an appealing confidence without a hint of stage school precociousness. Last week Simon shot a film with him, trying out a new rollercoaster, and in the studio, he has a go on the trampoline and helps to put George the tortoise into hibernation; all classic *Blue Peter* items. It makes a change from wheeling out the old turns and time-honoured clips.

It's a pity that the end is a mess, with Simon losing it, forgetting a question and leaving us under. Classic case of run-through going so smoothly that everyone relaxes, loses concentration and, as a result, transmission suffers. The show falls off air instead of finishing in style.

29th October 2003

Fucking BBC Worldwide have been dithering about committing to the next annual for weeks, and now they have finally decided that they are pulling out. Apparently, they are shutting down most of their children's publishing and also I am told that chidingly that "your standards are too high", especially in terms of our design expectations. In other words, we weren't prepared to accept the 'it'll do', thrown-together first go approach of the last couple of years.

While I shan't miss working with this lacklustre bunch, they have left us completely in the lurch, as it is already late to be planning next year's releases. I am absolutely determined not to let it go without a fight and compile a list of publishers who specialise in annuals. I shall contact them all and see if there is any hope of finding a new home for us.

3rd November 2003
Katie, one of our researchers (the one with the 17th-century face) has managed to find and book a Colditz veteran for Simon to interview in the studio off the back of our film. Kenneth Lockwood spent most of the war locked up in that grim castle, and it was a genuine privilege to hear him recount some of his stories. Simon handles the interview brilliantly and the entire studio, from the gallery to the floor, is spellbound throughout. I decide that we will award Mr Lockwood with a gold badge on transmission, the least we can do to show our respect and admiration for his experience and for sharing his testimony.

10th November 2003
The launch of our *Get Together* appeal. We're working with Mencap, and although the subject matter is incredibly strong, this is more than can be said for the actual mechanism for raising the money. This is the fourth year in a row that we have asked viewers to arrange bring-and-buy sales, and the whole mechanism feels stale and unexciting. To some extent, we are the victim of our own success. When bring-and-buys were first introduced in the late 70s, they were a relative novelty. Not so any more. Schools and youth groups regularly organise their own, so the sense of being involved in something unique and special has been lost. For many years, too, the programme alternated the bring-and-buys with recycling appeals, where kids had to collect old clothes or scrap metal or whatever. As a child, I always thought these were much the most fun, and I'm keen to reinvent them. But there is no getting away from the fact that many items suitable for recycling need collecting in huge numbers simply to make a modest sum. Some just aren't suitable or easy enough for kids to access. But you know you're in trouble when everyone on the programme is groaning at the prospect of yet more bring-and-buys. I'm worried about it before we even begin.

14th November 2003
An unfortunate studio day. I've brought back a director who used to work on the show a few years ago, when I was on the studio floor. I always thought he was perfectly competent and likeable, so I had no doubts about hiring him for a short stint as a freelancer. This started and ended today. For some reason, the presenters just hated him. It's the first time I've witnessed mutiny like it; they all felt he was rude, patronising and not on top of the schedule, or using their earpieces to keep them in the loop, which is essential on a live show. I have a post-mortem with the director himself, who says he is surprised at such virulent feedback; he thought the day had gone quite well. But, even though I feel awful for him, I explain that I just can't have the presenters in such a state – it really is unprecedented. We will honour his contract but I tell him he can't direct again.

21st November 2003

Marking 40 years of *Doctor Who* today with a monster parade and a quiz. I suppose it is slightly self-indulgent, but I remain convinced that there are many kids out there more interested in *Doctor Who* than in some of the esoteric material we routinely cover. We've booked the last regular TV Doctor, Sylvester McCoy, to pep things up, and he arrives full of beans and delighted to be involved. "*Doctor Who* never stops surprising me," he says. "Just when you think you've heard the last of it, the phone rings..."

Speaking of surprises, we've also stitched Liz up in today's show, which includes a film about her attempts to learn to sing. This came about as a result of *Christmas at the Club Blue Peter.* Because she was forced to mime throughout, someone on the team posed the question, "Is it actually possible to learn how to sing, if you can't to begin with?" and I promptly commissioned the film to find out.

The answer is inconclusive – well, perhaps cautiously positive might be fairer. Anyway, we are following it up with a surprise live challenge in which Liz must sing a duet with Lemar, a talented performer from the *Fame Academy* series (BBC's slightly lame answer to *X Factor*). The song I've chosen, *I Got You Babe,* has been arranged by our usual MD, Dave Cooke, and it has been quite an operation to rehearse the show without letting on to Liz that anything is afoot. Her reaction on transmission is priceless. There is just a moment when I wonder if, overwhelmed, she is going to wobble and refuse, but, no, she goes for it, and instead of a cringe, finishes the show on a high.

27th November 2003

I'm in reception when David Beckham strolls in. He's been to Buckingham Palace to receive his OBE, and he's wearing full morning suit. Interesting to see the effect he has on everyone around him, including myself. You can't help but stare – he is that charismatic and striking to look at, tall, ridiculously handsome and exuding friendliness and charm. Nature or nurture? Who knows, but it is rare to witness such genuine star quality, even at a place like Television Centre.

1st December 2003

Today marks Konnie's sixth year on the programme, and in honour of the occasion, I've arranged a surprise item on the live show; a quiz we call *A Question of Konnie.* She is flattered by all the fuss and attention, but after transmission she takes me to one side and says, "you're not going to get rid of me, are you?"

"What makes you say that?" I ask, bemused. "We've just spent ten minutes bigging you up."

"Yes, but I thought it might be a bit of a hint. You know, you've been here ages, here are your best bits, now piss off."
Such insecurity.
Meanwhile, very pleasing news from the film team. The designer of the brand new Queen Mary liner has been quoted in the press as saying that he was first inspired to become a ship designer when watching *Blue Peter*. The story checks out. The programme did indeed run a story about the original Queen Mary and the commentary said something on the lines of "There will never again be a ship on the scale of the Queen Mary".
This little boy, watching at home, thought, "Oh yes, there will, because when I grow up, I'm going to build one."
The fact that he has actually done just that is the stuff of fairy stories and what's more, it's got our name all over it. We made contact pronto and now we have had the go-ahead to make a film with the designer and his majestic new ship. I'm sending Konnie, which should please her, as she loves the 'cult' aspects of *Blue Peter*. I'm glad she shows no signs of tiring of the show. She is really popular with children and for all her sometimes exasperating qualities, she is endlessly charming and funny and content to be one of the team, rather than needing to be its star.

3rd December 2003
A night at the BAFTAs. There are four of us in the *Blue Peter* party; myself, Steve, my series producer Kez and Matt. We have been nominated for Best Children's factual, for last year's *Water Aid* appeal. For the second year running, Matt has also been nominated as Best Children's Presenter.
You are given no clues about whether you have won or not. Steve reminds us that it is very rare for a long-running show like ours to win anything; we are expected to have a certain standard, and it is human nature to be more excited in the stuff that's new and innovative. So I think we have all resigned ourselves to just enjoying the evening. It's all a bit like an impersonal wedding reception, with hordes of smartly dressed media types milling about and shamelessly networking. I'm gassing away to a good friend when a man in full Highland rig swaggers past. My friend whispers in my ear: "There's always a cunt in a kilt, isn't there?"
Eventually, everyone is dragooned to sit at their tables and the awards begin. These take place before dinner is served, so most of the audience is fairly drunk and rowdy. Everyone is keen to rattle through the proceedings. When a winner overstays their welcome on the podium, eyes are rolled and looks exchanged between tables.
When it gets to our categories, we win both. Suddenly there is a glare of lights

and a rush of applause and we are all smiling slightly foolishly and being led up to the stage. There is a delay because Kez is a wheelchair-user and access hasn't been taken into consideration. People rally round, and look embarrassed, as well they might. It is poor on their part. When we finally make it, Steve makes a short but pithy speech. We've all been presented with the iconic BAFTA gold-faced statue, which is surprisingly heavy.
"Make a good murder weapon," I remark to Matt, who is beaming from ear to ear and thrilled to have the double win.
"Rich, this is just incredible," he says, sounding like he's doing a piece-to-camera. "I cannot believe it."
We are ushered from the stage (further wheelchair hoo-ha) to have our photographs taken with the man who presented the award, BBC journalist Rageh Omar. Winning certainly transforms the evening. Everyone wants to be our friend and I lose count of the number of hands we shake, all the while smiling and nodding. I suppose we should all be smug with triumph but I can't suppress the uneasy feeling that here we are, dressed in our finery in a grand London hotel, accepting an award simply for the coverage we gave to communities dying for lack of clean water.

4th December 2003
Email from Biddy, congratulating the team for the BAFTAs: "Pretty good for a programme in its 46th year," she writes. "I do hope Dot has been showering all of you with champagne."
Not bloody likely, think I. But there is a letter of warm congratulation from Lorraine, the Controller of BBC1.
It's a good day. We've secured a new deal for the annual. A Devon-based outfit called Pedigree have agreed to take it on for a two-year deal. They are small family company and it was obvious from our first meeting that they were excited by the possibilities and keen to do a decent job. They are going to double the page count and increase the size of the book. They brought in mock-ups of last year's pages, re-designed as they would have done them, and it was a revelation. Much bolder use of colour, imaginative layouts and pictures used much more effectively. We will also be able to go to print later, which will make the content feel fresher. I am so delighted. Worldwide may have done us a favour after all.

8th December 2003
Pre-recording our lavish *Christmas Songbook*, the musical extravaganza which will form the main entertainment in this year's Christmas show. I've chosen a set of classic Christmas songs and asked for each to be interpreted in a very specific fashion. So, we start with *Mary Boy's Child*, with the presenters (and dancers) in

outrageous 70s hippy gear, as a homage to the dance group The Young Generation. Then we have a glam rock tribute in the form of *I Wish It Could Be Christmas Every Day,* shot in the style of a 70s *Top of the Pops.*

I've sent one of our film directors, Cath, to Norway (guaranteed real snow) to shoot a precise recreation of the 1980s Wham! video for *Last Christmas* (with Simon as George Michael) and we have all the presenters performing *Happy Christmas (War is Over)* in a set which is supposed to represent the kind of cool apartment in which I think the audience would like the team to live. The dogs are there, and so is the BAFTA, prominently placed on the coffee table. The presenters seem to enjoy themselves heartily. It only comes a bit unstuck with the closing number.

As a nod to this year's summer trip to Brazil, I've decided on a Latin American version of *White Christmas,* with Konnie, Simon, Matt and Liz bedecked in outrageous carnival costumes. I'm summoned to wardrobe as there is a crisis; Liz is refusing to wear her costume, which has an enormous number of ostrich feathers and an extravagant head dress. I'm surprised as I thought she would love this.

"What's the matter with it?" I ask her.

"I look like Big Bird," she wails.

Liz, always conscious of her height, stands up and demonstrates what she means. You can't ignore artist psychology at moments like these. If she doesn't feel fabulous, it is going to sink the number. I ask Debbie, the designer, to fetch some scissors, and together we prune off the worst excesses of the feathers. We are vandalising the frock, which will cost us, but Liz calms down and even begins to laugh.

"I know I'm such a drama queen."

"You're actually not," I tell her, and share an anecdote or two from my *Top of the Pops* to prove my point. She is especially taken with the tale of Cher and the separate dressing for her selection of wigs, and the fact that, because she didn't know the lyrics to her own song, autocue had to be discreetly embedded at the front of the stage.

Liz, happy with our makeshift modifications, sashays on to the studio floor to shimmy her heart out.

17th December 2003

Live OB from Hampton Court, where we have set up our unit next to the temporary ice rink in front of the palace. We've got Robin Cousins and the cast of his *Holiday on Ice* to perform, a celebrity bring-and-buy sale, a last-minute recipe for mince pies (using bread rather than pastry) and the story of Thomas Wolsey (written by yours truly). This is about the most effective OB we have managed in months, because the producer, Annie, is so experienced and organised, and the location is perfect for the content, all of which is achievable within the technical limits of these tiny trucks and their crews. The consequence is that everyone is enjoying themselves, and this confidence and sense of fun seep through the screen. It's a wonderful feeling to follow transmission with genuine congratulations rather than invigilating a post-mortem about what went wrong.

23rd December 2003

Directing my fourth Christmas show, which must, I think, be my last. I am reluctant to step completely away from the creativity and fun of the coal face; of actually making stuff. During the two years I was series producer, it was a source of low-level, but constant tension between Steve and myself. He kept expecting me to step away from directing, I kept finding sneaky ways to schedule a filming trip here and there. Often, it was my home life which suffered. I spent my last two summer holidays writing the script for the pantos. This year, I didn't have this problem as Dot gave the commission to CBBC entertainment. Ironically, she green-lit the very same proposal which Nigel had turned down in favour of *Christmas at the Club Blue Peter.* She's an odd woman, more Brown Owl than TV-exec. She makes creative decisions like this based on what she thinks is "fair", rather than which is the better proposition. "It's their turn," seems to be her over-riding view.

2004

22nd January 2004

The return of Britney Spears, this time to perform her single, *Toxic.* Quite coincidentally, my daughter Rosy has accompanied me to the studio today; she rapidly gets fed up with the assumption that she's a Britney fan and here to have a gawp at her idol.

As before, we have agreed to pre-record the number. As before, there is the usual retinue of dancers, stylists, make-up, record company hangers-on, and security guys who seem to have been sent from central casting; enormous, black-suited muscle men with wraparound shades. They are also a total pain, and I am summoned to the studio floor because they keep trying to kick various key members of our team out of the studio.

"The deal is essential crew only," jabbers the plugger when I make clear my displeasure at their heavy-handed behaviour.

"I don't need reminding what we agreed, thank you," I snap. "But your staff have no jurisdiction here and if they persist with their rudeness and obstruction, the recording will not go ahead. What are you so worried about? This is a BBC studio in Shepherd's Bush, not a crack den in the Bronx."

The plugger gives me a wintry look. She'd love to storm out, but we both know that's not going to happen. "We have to protect our artist. People might take photos. It happens a lot."

"OK, but you must let my team handle it."
I summon the floor manager and floor assistant and explain that we must politely ask anyone who isn't directly involved in the recording to leave.
"What's she doin' here?" asks one of the ludicrous heavies. He points to Leonie, a lady of a certain age, who is sitting on a chair near the fire lane, reading *The People's Friend.* Leonie has been looking after the *Blue Peter* dogs for the last two decades. I can't imagine anyone less likely to have any interest in Britney Spears and say so.
Finally, we are ready to record. Britney is wearing a crop top and has a very slight pot belly. As the floor manager gives the count down, "10, 9, 8, 7…", I am fascinated to watch how Britney sucks in her stomach, and keeps it that way throughout the three-minute performance. The moment she hears, "And stop recording," she relaxes it again, and the little pot reappears.
In complete contrast, the rest of the show is our annual celebration of Burns Night. One of the APs, herself a Scot, is what you might call the voluble type. She doesn't so much persuade you into an item, as keep talking and talking until you'll either agree or you're driven to reject her idea far more brutally than usual, just to shut her up. She has proudly sponsored the making a traditional Scots pudding called Crannachan, and, during run-through, as I normally do with anything we are cooking on the show, I try a taste. It is utterly nauseating, a kind of slimy sweet porridge. I turn to see the AP beaming at me. "What do you think?" she asks proudly. "Pretty good huh?"

26th January 2004
We've booked the world-famous White Helmets motorcycle display team. This is what we refer to as a 'studio spectacular'. These are invariably expensive, complex from a health and safety point of view, and they eat up rehearsal time too. But they are also an essential part of the mix; they validate the fact that we are live, and that we routinely have access to the big studios here at Television Centre. Not much point in having all that space if you don't use it, and there are always mutterings from the money bods that we could save so much money if we downsized to a smaller studio. Today we manage a double whammy. The White Helmets work like a dream on run-through, and are superb, but on transmission one of their engines stalls, and the whole display falls apart live on air; desperately, they try to get the engine going again, but we are out of time and off air before it will respond. The White Helmets are naturally deeply upset; I am less so. Viewers love the drama of a live disaster and they give the presenters and the show an unmistakable adrenalin and excitement.

6th February 2004

I'm staying late tonight as we're making a film in which Konnie will be the live gallery PA (production assistant) on tonight's edition of *Top of the Pops*. These kind of films, a combination of behind-the-scenes and internal cross-promotion, are always useful not least because they are relatively cheap. I cooked up the idea for this when we were brainstorming potential challenges for Konnie. In some ways, she is the hardest presenter for whom to find the right material. Her strengths are her quirky sense of humour and ability to connect with contributors she finds interesting. Another plus is that she's not hungry for fame (one of her worst forms of condemnation is to label someone "try hard") For Konnie, the challenges need to be more cerebral than physical (I never think it's a good idea to force presenters to do things at which they have no skill or interest).

I was thinking back to the two-and-a-half years I worked on *Top of the Pops* and how I was always fascinated by the skill of the gallery PA. In those days, it was invariably the extremely talented Hilary Bennett whose voice dominated proceedings and quite literally kept the show on the road. Could Konnie manage the same job for one night only?

The PA on any studio programme calls all the numbered shots from the script; this is vital for the camera crew, as it is how they judge where they are and how long they have got between one shot and another. In a music number, it's even more critical, because as well as calling the shots, the PA counts the bars (all music being broken down into beats and bars) which allows the cameraman to know exactly how long they have 'on shot', enabling them to time their move or zoom to fit. On a show like *Top of the Pops*, with music number after music number, as well as VTs to run, astons to super (text graphics to put up on screen) and timings to be kept precise, it is a colossal feat of brain power and dexterity. Right up Konnie's street, I think.

These days, *Top of the Pops* is run by flamboyant ex-presenter Andi Peters, whom I know from way back. We had a meeting in his very swanky office to discuss the idea. Andi is what I call 'telly-stocracy'; he is so marinated in the industry, he cottons on halfway through my first sentence and just says, "Yes, that would be brilliant." I do stress that, in the interests of it being a genuine challenge, she will really have to do the job and Andi readily agrees, with the proviso that the regular PA will be on hand in case of disasters.

Returning to the *Pops* studio tonight is odd. It's been 12 years since I regularly worked on it, and yet it feels so completely familiar; many of the faces in the crew are the same, albeit older. It even has the same smell, a mix of paint, electricity, dry ice and smoke. I used to help warm up the crowd and then push them out of the way of the moving cameras. I always felt sorry for the audience;

all dressed up in their finery, waiting for months for the big night to come, then turning up to be herded around (a lucky few picked out to stand next to the presenter) and the whole show usually done and dusted within 45 minutes. It follows precisely the same pattern tonight. The crowd are shown the door while Konnie emerges from the gallery exhilarated. She has loved every minute.

9th February 2004

There are 600 girl guides in TC1, singing and dancing along to *Reach* by S Club 7. It's absolute mayhem. I decide it will provide the perfect puzzle for the next annual competition; guess how many girl guides are in the studio? This is not a job for an amateur, so we frantically scrabble around to book a photographer who can cope with the assignment and has the head for heights to mount a ladder high enough to get all the kids in shot.

11th February 2004

Frantic calls from location. Liz is supposed to be filming a challenge in which she becomes a circus tightrope-walker. This means engaging with her vertigo again. The director is one of our trainees, a sweet-faced, ginger-haired, slightly nervous type. He's on the phone, stammering out the unwelcome news that Liz has stormed out of the shoot and gone AWOL. She is not answering calls and he has no idea what to do. I tell him to keep the circus people sweet and hold tight. Then I call Liz myself. It goes straight to voicemail, so I leave a message and a few moments later, she calls me back. She is sitting in her car in a lay-by and has just had what sounds like a panic attack. She's spoken to Toddy, her partner, and she feels stupid, but also frightened. We talk it through. I tell her that she doesn't have to go ahead. But if she does decide to return, she can progress at her pace. Nothing needs to happen if she isn't OK with it. Slowly, the fear and panic recede and the old, familiar Liz is back. She even has a laugh about her predicament.

"Rich, you'll never guess what I'm wearing. I'm all in yellow. I look like a banana."

She decides that she will return to the filming and try to see it through. I call the director to let him know and a few hours later he reports back that all has gone really well, after all.

20th February 2004

Yet another record company debacle. I booked the Sugarbabes on condition that they sing live. We all know that, unlike many of the other bands out there, they can at least actually sing. So I am less than pleased when they turn up to be told that they've "got colds" and will have to mime after all. Nobody believes a word of it and I'm pissed off. They won't be asked back.

1st March 2004

Interesting but misconceived item on the science behind the millions of bugs that humans live alongside; we've called it 'how clean is your bedroom?' and it's full of yukky statistics about the state of the average pillow and the allergies which can be caused by dust mites and the like. We've banked on the fact that many kids love these kind of gross facts, which have a kind of playground currency.

Unfortunately, the item has clearly completely freaked a lot of the less robust kids in the audience and I stay late answering emails of complaint from parents who are incensed that their offspring are refusing to go to bed for fear of being "eaten alive" in the night.

Suspect that this one will run and run, and it is all our fault for not being clearer and more reassuring.

8th March 2004

We've booked Manju Mahli, an expert in Indian cuisine, to put to the test Simon's frequent boast that he's yet to encounter a curry that's too hot for him. She has promised that she will be able to provide the curry to break his infamously iron-clad taste buds.

Alas, despite her best efforts, Simon is not thrown by any of the contenders and is still able to speak by the end of the item. This was not what we had in mind so the show ends with a disappointing sense of anticlimax.

11th March 2004

Attend a business lunch on the theme of Corporate Social Responsibility, at which I have to deliver a speech (mainly focused on the work of our appeals). This goes well and there is evidently a lot of love in the room for the programme and its ability to harness the emerging philanthropic feelings of young people. Among the guests is my ultimate boss, Dot, and afterwards we share a cab back to Television Centre. This is a rare opportunity to get her to myself and try to bend her ear about various programme issues.

She's a strange woman, Dot, outwardly bright, friendly, with a seemingly inexhaustible fund of inconsequential small talk (she is especially animated on the subject of shoes, of which she is inordinately fond) but she is notoriously hard to pin down to specifics, or to offer a precise opinion of what she thinks or wants in terms of content. This makes her very frustrating to deal with. She also parries many of my attempts to engage with *Blue Peter*'s various issues by mentioning instead the woes of other shows on her slate, especially *Xchange*. "Oh they work so hard," she says, apropos of nothing. "And they have so little money compared to you."

I don't care for the inference either that they work any harder than our team (they don't) or that because we have a respectable budget, we should somehow feel guilty about it. Generally, *Blue Peter* delivers, whether it's in terms of winning awards, delivering audiences, or, like today, engaging useful and influential opinion formers. *Xchange*, by contrast, is consistently a fairly terrible programme, about which no one much seems to care. This should worry the head of department, of course, but not blind them to our quite separate issues and needs.

Dot is much preoccupied with finding the considerable funds required to redevelop the restaurant block which overlooks the *Blue Peter* garden; the idea is to turn this into a purpose-built studio for the CBBC channel, which all the main shows – from presentation to *Newsround*, *Xchange*, *SMart*, and so on, will share. We have ruled ourselves out (more accusations of elitism and snobbery from the rest of the department) on the grounds that *Blue Peter* has its own distinct identity and the large studio space is a crucial aspect of this.

Several times, I've also registered my concern about the impact on the garden, which would supposedly form the backdrop of the shared CBBC studio. During the consultation period and the various working parties, I've consistently been one of the sceptics. All very well for the shows to use the garden as a backdrop when the weather is fine, but it will look pretty miserable in winter. I keep suggesting they check out *Pebble Mill* and how awful that looked when it rained. Bright sun as a backdrop isn't very camera-friendly either. Then there are the sound issues. Apparently, it would cost too much to soundproof the building, and no one seems to want to answer the awkward questions about how one show rehearses in the shared studio space while another show is actually on the air. It all sounds like a nightmare waiting to happen, but Dot is devoted to the project, and dismisses the critics as negative and short-sighted.

When I started in this job, and asked Dot what she thought about something or what she wanted from us, she would invariably reply, "Oh, I don't know; that's what I've got you for!"

I suppose this should feel liberating, an affirmation that we are working on the right lines. But actually it just feels as if she hasn't a clue what she wants, doesn't often see what we are doing anyway, and generally has other fish to fry. Sometimes, just when you feel you may finally have her attention on some key issue, she will suddenly interrupt with an irrelevant aside or to offer me the second hand, and, alas, invariably uninspiring opinions of her daughter, who is of CBBC age and therefore quoted ad nauseam.

Both her predecessors, Lorraine and Nigel, were very good at 'walking the floor' and making clear the value of *Blue Peter* both to the department and the BBC. By comparison, Dot is woefully deficient, and the team naturally mind this very

much and are always grumbling about her. I come up with excuses, of course, and toe the party line, but she is a problem. I know that I'm far from alone in feeling these frustrations, either.
We arrive back at East Tower and I am none the wiser on any of the points I attempted to raise with her.

22nd March 2004

Bring my daughter Rosy, and her friend Aimée, to TV Centre today, as they have agreed to help model 1950s fashions in a studio item this afternoon. Rosy normally shuns the limelight, so this is a turn-up for the books. The other children are all from stage schools and, during a break in rehearsals, Rosy regales me with how affected and full of themselves they are.
"They kept wanting to know who my agent is," she grimaces, "and whether I've had any head shots done. Dad, what are head shots?"
Meanwhile, Simon is feeling disgruntled. Alex, our longest serving producer, has been filming both Simon and Matt undergoing one of the army's toughest and most gruelling forms of training, 'P company'. Both the boys are physically capable and determined, and they are both competitive, too. In this case, however, I'm not sure that the competition is altogether healthy. They've just completed another section of the shoot, and Simon is suspicious that the cold from which Matt announced that he was suffering was really a way of avoiding the worst of the beasting which followed. "It meant that, however hard I tried, whatever effort I put in, Matt was always going to come out looking like the hero, for battling through it with his cold. The instructors all pulled back from pushing him so hard and obviously thought they could go to town on me instead. The thing is, Rich, I don't give a shit about passing 'P company' – I'm a TV presenter. I'm just trying to make a decent film."
I have a chat with Alex. His theory is that Matt copes better in these situations because of his years as a gymnast. "He is used to people shouting at him," says Alex. "It doesn't bother him in the slightest, it motivates him. But Simon hates it."
I'm sure there is truth in this, but the last thing I want is for genuine rifts to emerge in the otherwise highly effective on-screen partnership between Matt and Simon. It all reminds me how fragile presenters can be. It's an unusual job in the way it involves the psyche and the ego, and it doesn't help that the presenters are so young. I think about how Matt has always been self-conscious about his looks, comparing himself unfavourably to Simon.
"He's such a good-looking lad," says Matt, "and when I sit next to him, I just think, 'Oh aye, here's the ugly one."
"Handsome ugly," I tell him. "A face with character."
"Thanks, Rich, that makes me feel so much better!"

2nd April 2004

We've got Dick and Dom in the studio. They are presenters turned entertainers, their childish routines popular mostly with little boys. During rehearsals, I don't endear myself to either Dick or Dom by remarking that, if they are lucky, they might turn out to be the next Chuckle Brothers. From their vinegary reactions, clearly they'd sooner be the next Ant and Dec. But actually I meant my comment as a compliment; the Chuckle Brothers are enormously and enduringly popular. Their live shows sell-out, and they make a handsome living from their act. Dick and Dom pride themselves on their ability to generate a degree of anarchy, and now they are on *Blue Peter*, they feel obliged to push their luck beyond what's been agreed and rehearsed. During the live show, they decide to hijack the demonstration of a 'no-cook chocolate rabbit'. It livens up proceedings, and there is plenty of laughter, as they mess about with the food and improvise their usual puerile gags, but I sit in the gallery with sinking heart knowing that there will be a slew of complaints about the wasting of ingredients, food hygiene and inappropriate jokes. Sure enough, the log (in which all viewer complaints are carefully recorded) is full of just such complaints and, long before I leave the office, the emails have started to pile up too, demanding attention from a posse of outraged parents across middle England.

7th April 2004

The Pain of P Company transmits. It's not, I think, a very successful programme. Simon and Matt go through a fair amount of physical hell throughout, it's brilliantly covered, but somehow the point of it all is missing. It seems almost suffering for the sake of it. There are no 'magic' contributors, the quirky and funny types you need to bring the humour and humanity to these kind of films. Worst, and a clear reflection of what was going on during the production, the boys don't really seem to be in the experience together; it's more as if they are undergoing it side by side, isolated in their own personal hell, rather than combining forces and sharing everything as you'd hope and expect from a *Blue Peter* duo. Whenever we make a film with the services, we face (sometimes justified) criticism that we are just acting as a recruitment exercise. But on this occasion, I doubt that anyone will watch this film and think, 'Oh, that's for me.'

14th April 2004

Caron Keating has died, succumbing to the cancer with which she was diagnosed a few years ago. It's deeply tragic that someone so young, beautiful and talented has lost their life to this bastard disease; worse still that she's left two small boys behind, who will now have to grow up without their mother. I clear the last section of today's running order to include a tribute, which I write

and set about cutting myself. It's a frantic process to meet the deadline for run-through and transmission. I'm surprised to get a call from Dot, who asks me if we are going to mention her death on the programme. I explain that we are doing more than this, we are running a tribute.
"Are you sure that's a good idea?" she replies. "I mean, kids won't know who she is, will they?"
"Well, a lot of them don't know who Queen Victoria is, but that doesn't stop us banging on about her when it suits us. We'll explain exactly who Caron was – a very popular *Blue Peter* presenter when their mums and dads were watching."
"OK, if you say so," she says, unconvinced. "So long as it isn't self-indulgent."
I'm genuinely puzzled by this take on it and that this is literally the first and only time Dot has taken interest in such a detail. I wonder if she has been nudged by someone. No matter. I think it would be weird to bypass the story. Such has been the scale of the coverage, children can scarcely have missed the news. Caron was one of the more famous and successful presenters, too, so I have no doubts. The crucial concern is to get the tone right – sad, respectful, but celebratory – a case of 'look what she did' and 'wasn't she amazing?' not sad music and sombre voices. To this end, I finish the package with *A Million Kinds of Coffee in Brazil*, one of the many effervescent music numbers in which Caron took part during her time on the show.

4th May 2004
Meeting with Russell T Davies and Phil Collinson to discuss ways in which *Blue Peter* might promote next year's return of *Doctor Who*. Russell is very tall, very friendly and very enthusiastic, gesticulating and laughing loudly. Next to him, Phil is, perhaps inevitably, somewhat quieter, but equally charming, with a lovely smile that off sets his occasionally dry remarks. They are accompanied by a fairly clueless woman from publicity, who, poor thing, is quickly left bemused and out of things as the three of us gabble on and on about both programmes, which, it is quickly obvious, are dear to all our hearts. They share memories of BP and the excitement and ambition of their plans for *Doctor Who*, which are evidently conceived on a huge scale. Russell tells me that he still watches *Blue Peter*, often taking a break in his writing to watch. He loves Matt. I say how much I've admired and enjoyed Russell's work over the years and he hoots when I tell him about watching the first episode of *Queer as Folk* in a hotel room in Portsmouth when I was down there to shoot the HMS Victory story. Just a few minutes in and my phone rang. It was Stuart. "Are you watching this?" he asked me. "Absolutely," I replied. "It's bloody amazing, isn't it?"
"Yeah, get off the line, I don't want to miss anything!"
Then there's *Bob and Rose*. My daughter Rosy has commandeered the DVD, she loves it so much.

It's a wonderfully happy, easy meeting. Of course I am going to do anything I can to support what they are trying to achieve. Russell is very clear that he wants to get the family audience, and that children really matter to him. We agree on a behind-the-scenes film and studio appearances from the cast, with lots of props, and we talk, too, about the possibility of a big competition. Russell remembers the 'design-a-monster' competition back in the late 60s and wonders about something on those lines. I love the idea, though I have one crucial proviso. In the 60s competition, the winning monster wasn't actually used in *Doctor Who.* This seems to me to have been a bit of a cheat. Would Russell be up for our winner actually being seen on screen, even if only in the background? I can see the publicity woman shifting uneasily in her chair, but it might just be because it's not very comfortable. Russell doesn't seem to see a problem so long as he writes the episode.

"And how much better would it be if it was the proper monster, not just an extra?" he ponders aloud.

When they have left, my PA, Sarah, comments: "That seemed to go very well. Pretty much from beginning to end, all I could hear was laughter...."

10th May 2004

George the tortoise, a blink-and-you'll-miss-him member of our pet menagerie for the past 22 years, died last week, and so we kick off today's show with a lengthy and loving obituary. This fact does not escape Simon.

"Why is it that the dead tortoise gets more air time than the recently deceased presenter?" he asks me.

"Fur and feather, love," say I.

This is a phrase beloved of *Blue Peter* and guaranteed to raise the hackles of any presenter. It is short for "fur and feather is more popular than flesh..."

This may be true for the audience, but naturally I prefer the humans. I call in Liz today for a meeting to discuss her future on the show. I tell her how much I rate her and offer a new two-year contract to pick up when her current one expires at the end of the run. She says she'd love to accept. "But..." and her voice tails off.

"But?" I query, my heart sinking.

"The thing is, I'm pregnant, I'm going to have a baby."

And then she is smiling and laughing, and I am too, jumping up to give her a hug. I am so delighted for her. I ask her if she wants to leave and I'm surprised when she replies that she doesn't, but just thought it wouldn't be an option to continue with a baby.

I have a rapid think about this. Why not? I know that in the past when a presenter got pregnant, it was as good as a resignation letter. The thinking was that you couldn't commit to being a mum and a *Blue Peter* presenter at the same

time. But surely times have changed? This is the 21st century, after all.
"If you want to stay, why don't you stay? Be the first presenter to have a baby and remain on the show. The offer stands, if you're interested."
She is. More laughter and delight, at the double dose of good news.

17th May 2004
It's the first day for our new gardener, Chris Collins. I've been thinking for a while that we could do with someone in this role; looking ahead to five-times-a-week, it will be handy to have another regular on the books to handle some of the material we are obviously going to devour. I put it out there that I was looking and one of CBBC's regular presenters, a lovely guy called Jez Edwards, popped into see me to tell me about this bloke he'd worked with on a kids' radio show.
"He's called Chris Collins," he told me. "He's really keen and knows his stuff, and he's a bit of a geezer, dirt behind the fingernails, all that bit."
I take to Chris as soon as I meet him. He's obviously passionate about all things green and growing, and excited by the prospect of the role and what he could bring to it. He does have one major worry; his tattoos.
"I didn't think they'd be in *Blue Peter*'s line," he said.
I reassure him that as long as they're not obscene, they'll be fine. People have tattoos. It's a real world thing and nothing to do with his ability to communicate a love of gardening.

18th May 2004
Pre-recording a show for the summer and today, an item dear to my heart – our homage to Pan's People. This explains that, in the days before videos, *Top of the Pops* had its own in-house dance group. The wafer-thin premise of our item is what would it be like if that were still the case today. Choreographer Kevin Adams has created a routine for what we've called Peter's People; made up of Konnie, Liz and a host of CBBC girls; Dani Harmer, Summer Matthews, Anne Foy, and Lizzie Greenwood. They are dancing to the new track from McFly – but what they don't know is that, during the recording, McFly themselves will be making a surprise appearance. It's a great twist and helps to give a genuine sense of 'live' which is usually very difficult with the pre-recorded shows.

19th May 2004
Pre-recording two shows today. One features an extremely talented and good-looking young gymnast called Louis Smith, displaying his skill on the pommel horse. I introduce myself during rehearsals and he explains that he would love to be a presenter on *Blue Peter.* I like the un-self-conscious way he puts this, as though there is nothing more natural in the world.

"What about all this?" I ask him, indicating the pommel horse.
"I'd give it up tomorrow," he smiles.
I tell him that very few people get to his level in gymnastics; that he should concentrate on this for the time being, but that professional sport is a great grounding for presenting. It requires talent, confidence, stamina and self-discipline, being able to take notes, do the same thing over and over again and to articulate how you are thinking and feeling. I suggest that he practises talking out loud when he is training, to get him used to explaining what he's doing as he's doing it.
"And keep in touch," I conclude. "You've definitely got potential."
Also today, a long and complex item all about the history of home video and recording of TV shows.
I've had a long and sometimes fractious relationship with the Film and VT library here. Last year, when attempting to call up the master tape of my first St Petersburg special, I was less than delighted to be informed that it had gone missing (no reason given for this) and that therefore there were no holdings. Happily, I tend to keep copies of most of my films on Digibeta tape, so it was possible to arrange a replacement copy.
From the moment I joined the programme, I made no bones about the fact that I have an archival interest in its history and preservation. Oliver, the then-Editor, was more than delighted to hive off a particular chore which, for some time, he had been postponing. The library had sent through an enormous glue-bound print out of all the programme's videotape holdings on the now-defunct 2" and 1" formats. Though the plan was to transfer and preserve the actual programme tapes, they wanted his authorisation to junk literally hundreds of others; inserts, studio recordings and some which were merely unidentified. "We can keep some of them," he said, "so long as we can give a reason why. But we can't just keep everything."
So I took this tome away with me and squinted my way through it, marking those tapes which I thought might prove useful in the future – examples of past presenters rehearsing and recording, for instance, might well be of use in a future documentary. The digital preservation project is clearly a colossal undertaking, and mistakes and oversights were always going to be inevitable. Many of the 1970s programmes were recorded from an 'off-air' feed, which meant that they also captured trailers, idents, and the ends of certain, now lost, shows like *Jackanory*. These recordings ran on to include that day's *Newsround*, too. These were consequently very rare survivals, on broadcast quality tape, of the ephemera of transmission and of regular news output. So I was annoyed to discover that some of the transfers slapped an ident over the start of these recordings, covering up the unique material pre the actual programme, and

sometimes cutting off just a few seconds into the *Newsround* which followed it. More recently, I discovered that an entire edition from 1980 had somehow gone astray and been junked "in error". I knew that we had a VHS copy of this episode in the office, and also that a black and white film recording existed. So I contacted the library and explained that I'd like them to use these to create a new version, at their expense, using the restoration techniques devised to bring back to life various vintage *Doctor Who* episodes. What's more, we would film the process and show this as part of a studio item about the history of video recorders and home taping. The design team have created a set which we've filled with antique machines and old tapes.
When I was a child I can remember assuming that everything ever seen on TV would somehow exist somewhere. A view probably reinforced by the frequent recycling of clips on *Blue Peter*, as well as plenty of repeats of other popular mainstream programmes. My view is that this item will educate today's children of a digital era that holding onto TV's past is a complex business.
"It's fucking boring, this, Rich," says Matt, with feeling.

24th May 2004
We break the news that Liz is expecting a baby on air. I've been teasing her that we are going to run a competition to name her baby. "It's in the contract, darling, didn't you read the small print?"

25th May 2004
An evening in Gibraltar, before tomorrow's live OB. A long and involved conversation over drinks with Simon. He has been thinking about his future for some time and, although he knows I don't want to lose him, he's coming close to the end of the year he guaranteed he would do if I got the job, and he wants to set a leaving date in place. It's not that he no longer loves the job; in many ways, he says, it has got better and more satisfying over time. He is part of a team which really works. But he turned 30 last year and is beginning to feel a bit out of step with children's programmes. His great love is sport and he would love to move into this arena permanently. To this end, we give him as many of the sporting items and interviews as we can, and I've had conversations with various execs in sport about him. The problem is that they are extremely snobby about any presenter who doesn't come from a professional sports background; for example, they would rather train a former football player into the job, than just hire a presenter who happens to like the game. It is going to be a difficult leap to make, but Simon is admirably determined. I really am in no hurry to see him depart, and suggest that he does one more complete season, which means he would be there for the launch of our five-times-a-week schedule. He agrees

and we shake hands on it, jokingly rather than formally, but with real mutual affection and respect.

6th June 2004

To Broadcasting House to accompany all four presenters as they appear on Steve Wright's afternoon show on Radio 2. Wright is apparently a genuine fan, who watches on a regular basis with his daughter. It has taken an age to arrange this, as Wright insisted on having all four presenters together.

Since the initial request and during the subsequent weeks of negotiation, it's been a struggle to explain just what a tall order this is; the presenter schedules are so complex, and worked out so far in advance, the chances of them all being free on the same day are negligible. In programme terms, it pretty much only happens a few times a year; on the first and last show of a season, the appeal launch, the Christmas show and the review of the year. Wright's producer was equally adamant that the appearance must be live. Anyway, we managed it eventually, so here we are.

People are often taken aback at the sheer grottiness of Television Centre. Once you've left the fabulously Art Deco reception area, Broadcasting House is even worse, a jumble of dingy corridors peppered with heavy doors leading to studios, everything somewhat seedy. Wright and his 'gang' transmit from a poky, and it must be said, somewhat pongy, little studio. He's clapped on a lot of weight to which he almost immediately and cheerfully refers ("you can eat what you like on radio") and he's effusively friendly to everyone, proving his fan credentials by referring to various recent programmes in affectionate detail. To me, he remarks, "So you're Biddy Baxter then?" to which I reply, "But without the heels," which seems to throw him.

Once on air, it all goes like the clappers and all four of the turns get their chance to shine (they'd been justifiably sceptical about going to so much trouble for potentially a blink and miss it moment), especially Konnie who waxes lyrical about the joys of making a dolls' gym from a cardboard box and other assorted household rubbish ("this is the nearest Konnie's been to a gym in her life," remarks Simon, dryly). Wright also brings up the subject of the show a while back in which we celebrated her six year anniversary, which proved a match to the flame of Konnie's paranoia. This obviously hadn't escaped Wright who laughs, "You kept saying 'I'm not leaving yet...' and this starts Konnie off anew, as she explains how she thought she was about to launch into the classic Blue Peter standby, 'washing the dogs', when she was hijacked into a mini *Mastermind*-style instead, answering questions about her time on the programme and feeling as if she'd been fast forwarded into her own leaving programme. Much laughter from all sides. Once it's over, and as we say our goodbyes, Steve Wright tells Kon, "Take it from me, stay as long as you can." But he's preaching to the converted.

18th June 2004

A heartfelt letter from Gloria Hunniford, who writes: "What a wonderful and sensitive tribute you produced in memory of our gorgeous and beautiful Caron. It evoked every emotion possible from joy to poignant recollection to huge tears. Great memories for all of us but in particular for Charlie and Gabriel in years to come."

Think how strange it will be for those boys, to have access to such an archive charting several years of their mother's life, when she was at her most beautiful, vibrant and animated. Will they gain any comfort from it or will it be a torment? Or will it just seem like watching a stranger who merely resembles the real person they remember? I suppose the same is true for Prince William and Harry. Left with so many visible traces of their mother's life, which, perhaps, in the final analysis, are not much use to them.

26th June 2004

The whole team is back safe and sound from the month of filming in India for the summer expedition and great is the relief. When I took over as Editor, I was absolutely determined that India would be the first summer I would commission. It is a continent fabulously rich with stories and with so many obvious connections with the UK. But it is not an easy place in which to film. I was warned about the potential pitfalls; especially the rampant corruption, so that, at any point, our camera kit might be impounded, or our team arrested, or 'just' hassled until we came up with the right bribe. Happily, our films producer, Matt Gyves, is tough, determined and shares my ambition to make this a truly epic project.

For the first time since 1990, I've committed all the presenters to filming for the entire trip. This was contentious, too, mainly because of Liz's pregnancy. Liz herself had no concerns and was keen to take part, but others within the team clearly thought I was mad to "risk" it. We did seek medical advice and reassurance from two doctors and they both agreed that, given Liz's robust health, and her own willingness to travel, there should be no problems. We did agree that if, for whatever reason, Liz changed her mind or circumstances changed, she would fly back immediately. So it feels wonderful to get this point, with everyone safe, everything shot, and a universal chorus of how successful and rewarding the filming has been. It's odd that we'll be announcing the expedition on the last live show of the series when it's already all in the can. The magic of telly.

28th June 2004

Our last live show of the series. Part of the deal I've put forward for running the programme five-times-a-week is that we return to having a summer break. This means we can still shoot the expedition, and the presenters get a decent holiday too. It's going to be a busy summer for me, with a new set to commission, new music and titles, and the finalising of all our plans for next season. We are also looking for not one but two presenters; someone to replace Simon, and, before that, a fifth presenter to work in tandem with the others. I'm not entirely sure about this rapid expansion of the talent but Liz will need maternity leave of at least three months during our busiest time of the year, and it is foolish to assume that when she returns, she will be able to cope with the same pace of work that she has so far been used to. I've convinced myself that there is something about 'five presenters for five-times-a-week' which works, but it's a major change and I am anxious about it.

This morning I meet a young hopeful; a Welsh guy called Gethin (?) Jones.

"Gethin – I've never met anyone with that name," I say, fatuously, as if I should. He laughs easily.

"It's pretty common where I come from. There were two Gethin Jones' in my class at school, and a Gethin Jenkins. But you can call me Geth."

Our meeting has been arranged by his agent, which is standard enough. Although word hasn't yet leaked that we are actively looking for new talent, *Blue Peter* is always a magnet for wannabes. We get sent hundreds of show reels and begging letters every year. I'm strict about the need to watch all the tapes; no matter how dire most of them turn out to be, they represent someone's dreams, and also, you never know when you might strike gold. I always send a proper letter back rather than a standard rejection. It's small consolation but better than silence or some stock letter. I can still remember how it felt to send out a letter and CV, full of hope, only to receive a printed rejection, or, more often, no reply at all.

As well as the unsolicited submissions, there are those sent to me by their agents or by other producers within the BBC (dread words: "I've just met someone I think would be perfect for *Blue Peter*").

We also have our own talent executive, and she sporadically pushes a hopeful in my direction. Recently she arranged for me to meet Myleene Klass's little sister, Jessie. Alas, although obviously a very sweet person, she didn't seem to have a clue about what the job might entail (Standard question number one: "What do you think you would bring to *Blue Peter*?" Her answer: "I'm young and I'm fun and I love pop music"). Then there was the outfit she had chosen for our chat; a clingy, low-cut number that was more Stringfellows than sticky-backed plastic. Sometimes the talent is there, but other issues or worries get in the way. Lately

I've been lobbied by a young lad called Matt Edmonson, who you can't fault for energy and sense of purpose.

"Hello," he says, when he comes to see me. "I'm your next presenter."

I asked him how he felt so sure, and this was all the cue he needed to launch into an effusive catalogue of skills; magician, comedian, writer, great with animals, great with kids ("I *am* a kid," he laughs) and so on. He talks non-stop and knows all about the programme. The combined effect of all this enthusiasm and energy is a bit insufferable and my first thought is that the audience might find him very annoying. But it is his age which worries me most. He's just 18. The last presenter to be taken on so young was Yvette Fielding. I still remember being a floor assistant during her first year, and witnessing some of her massive struggles with the pressure and expectation. I explain that this is an exceptionally tough job, and that I think it really helps for the presenters to have had some life experience before they take it on. Young Edmonson is tenacious and fights his corner.

"I've got more life experience than most 18-year-olds," he insists. "I may act stupid, but I'm actually really mature."

We're out of time. I tell him to come back in a few years if he still wants the job, which is obviously not want he wants to hear. The effervescent charm slips a little and he becomes sulky, not quite saying "it's your loss", but certainly implying it. With so much self-confidence and fierce ambition, I have no doubt he will do well. I'm still not sure I really believe that presenting *Blue Peter* is his dream job though.

This Gethin is a very different proposition. He's confident and charming, but much calmer and there is evidence of the life experience I'm after; University, where he played rugby to a high level, undergoing trials for Sale until an injury ended all that. He is mad about sport, plays the piano and violin, says he can fly a plane. Parents are teachers. Welsh is his first language and he's currently fronting an S4C kids show not unlike *Blue Peter* (or so he says – probably more like *Xchange*). I stress that there isn't a job going; and might not be for some time.

This doesn't seem to throw him. He's very polite, a little too submissive for my liking, but he's undoubtedly personable and strikingly good-looking (turning heads in the office when he arrives). On a whim, I suggest that I take him down to the studio to have a look at rehearsals and meet the presenters, who are all in today. Once there, I am inevitably distracted and drawn into conversation elsewhere and when I look for him, as if on cue, his head emerges from round the doors into make-up. He smiles but looks bashful, like a schoolboy caught out of bounds.

"What do you think?" I ask him, indicating the bustle of the studio floor.

"It's amazing....brilliant....thanks so much...," he gibbers.
"That's all right," and I reiterate, "Remember, there isn't actually a job going yet."
When he has left, I ask the other presenters what they thought.
"He's gorgeous...." says Liz, and bursts out laughing. "I couldn't work with him, I'd be lookin' at him all at the time!"
Matt rolls his eyes and comments that "he seems like a good bloke, alright."
"Yeah, he wasn't creepy or try hard," says Konnie.
Simon tells me I'm a bastard for dropping Gethin in it like that.
"A pretty good test, though," I retort, "having to meet you fuckers."

13-14th July 2004
Two days of filming in and around Balmoral, with Liz presenting, and playing Queen Victoria (again), with me, mutton chops and moustache glued in place, as her beloved Prince Albert. I enjoy myself mincing about in full Highland dress, hitching up my kilt and announcing: "Not bad legs" to anyone unlucky enough to be in my eye line.
True to the perversity of any filming schedule, we start with my death scene, in the bed of one of our hotel rooms. Trying to rustle up a death rattle without laughing proves tough going.
I've dragooned our feisty Australian PA, Mignon, into playing a village wench, whose key 'moment' is a little scene in which she comes across the royal couple, out for a stroll in the country, and automatically drops a deep curtsey. This kind of servility is utterly alien to the Aussie psyche. Let's just say that Mignon's first attempts are scarcely convincing. Stung by our gales of laughter, she turns on us.
"You Brits and your fucking royals. You need to grow up and get with the 21st century!"
"Ah, but we're in the 19th century," I point out, and mime the respectful action I have in mind.
Later, we film a picnic scene, and there are issues with the camera angle in relation to my kilt. I don't trust our cameraman not to offend my modesty and film a 'funny' version for the end of series tape. I shift about and tug the hemline down as far as I can.
"Are you wearing pants?" asks Liz, suspiciously.
"What a common Queen," I announce, and then hitch up my kilt to prove that I am.
"Oh, put it away," she groans.
"I'm HRH love machine," I tell her, unabashed.
Somehow we manage to keep straight enough faces to get through the various takes, and the taking of a series of stills, too.
"It's all going in the annual," I announce. "We'll be centre spread...."

16th July 2004

Matt's wedding; a very happy day. He is a lucky boy; he's marrying his childhood sweetheart, Nicola, who is beautiful, intelligent and intensely loyal. Partners of *Blue Peter* presenters have a lot to put up with; they have to accept frequent and sometimes prolonged absences. I think, discounting the longer foreign trips, Matt's record (so far) is something like 17 days in a row without a day off. I know, too, from my own experience, that it doesn't help a relationship to return from a filming trip, full of the exciting things you've done and amazing people you've met, when your other half has been stuck in their usual routine, doing the washing and putting out the rubbish. Nicola already has the slightly long-suffering aspect of one who is used to this disconnect. But she knows the deal and believes in him utterly; and she has become essential to him. Together with his parents, Mike and Janice, she is part of the bedrock of Matt's life. He certainly owes much of his precocious self-confidence to their combined loyalty and support, and their shared belief in remaining 'down to earth'. The wedding reflects their values; charmingly traditional, centred around family and close friends. About the most 'showbiz' part of it is the talented young magician who has been hired to entertain the guests. I promptly book him to appear on the first show of the next season. Always on, that's me.

19th August 2004

In the search for our new presenter, we've cast the net as wide as we can afford; carefully worded adverts in *The Guardian, The Stage* and *Disability Now*. These ads don't give away the name of the show, but anyone with half a brain should be able to read between the lines of description and take an educated guess. We are also doing the usual trawl of agents, *Spotlight* (focusing on new talent) and word of mouth within the business. The first stage is an interview in my office. I do these either with my deputy, Kez, or Annie, our most experienced producer. So far it's felt very much like panning for gold; the occasional interesting contender among the obvious duds. One person I really like is a stunning half-English, half-Japanese girl called Eleanor Matsuura, recently graduated from the Central School of Speech and Drama. But she is unsure about being a presenter; not unnaturally, she feels that having spent three years studying, she wants to give acting a go before deviating from the path. I'm disappointed but not surprised when she calls after the interview and withdraws her candidacy. The ad in *Disability Now* has brought forward some interesting contenders. The most promising is Cerrie, a woman born with half a right arm. She is delightful, warm and funny. But I'm concerned that she isn't enough of a contrast to Liz. This is always a major consideration; they can't just be talented, interesting and everything else we're looking, they have to bring something different to the overall mix. I would hate to cast someone 'just' because they had a disability; it's got to be talent first. Likewise with skin colour or background. But equally you can't hide behind that argument; you have to go looking and try to be proactive. There is a very awkward interview with a little person who doesn't seem pleased to be here.

"Why do you want to see me?" she asks, bluntly.

"We are looking for the next *Blue Peter* presenter," I explain. "And that means considering people from every different background."

"Ticking a box, you mean."

"Yes, I guess so," I admit. "If you mean making sure we don't just interview one type of person."

I don't blame her for feeling suspicious but it doesn't help the interview. She makes it clear that she does not want to be helped physically in any way. A fairly excruciating five minutes follows as she attempts to scale the awkward dimensions of the sofa in my office.

I ask her to tell me about the kind of parts she has been playing.

"Mainly monsters," she says. "And dwarfs."

Her stories about the disrespectful way people of her size are treated within the industry make glum listening. But, as we talk, it is interesting that, despite my efforts to open things out to questions about her interests, personality and skills, everything returns remorselessly to size. Take the standard question:

"So what do you think you would bring to *Blue Peter*?"

"I'd be the first presenter who is the same height as one of the dogs."

Then, at last, a glimmer of a sense of humour. "I suppose at least they'd feel at home with me."

She's not right for us, in any way, but it has nothing to do with her size. But afterwards, I reflect at length and I feel uneasy. We weren't prepared; the interview space was difficult for her to negotiate without help. Her understandable cynicism; the fact that the BBC has a bad reputation for making the right noises about disability, but doing little in practice.

It's a topic I discuss further with Kez, who, as a wheelchair-user, inevitably has strong views of her own. We agree that it is a pity that she wasn't free to be involved in the interview. But most of all, we agree that there is only a point in seeing disabled candidates who offer some genuine potential as a *Blue Peter* presenter. Otherwise it is just ticking a box and salving our conscience.

25th August 2004

A blazing hot day in the *Blue Peter* garden, and the first round of serious auditions. I've given a lot of thought to these. Conventionally, the process has been to interview any likely contenders and then, assuming they impress, put them straight through to the studio audition, a complete programme in miniature, in which they make a Christmas card, demonstrate a new toy, talk about the appeal and (famously) have a go on the trampoline.

The studio audition is a pretty rigorous and exacting test, and it's also an expensive one. So it's surprising how many obvious duds have made it through to this stage. I've decided to introduce a much cheaper interim level. Given that whoever we find may potentially be around for the next five years, it doesn't seem too much trouble to go to. I've devised a two-stage process. The candidates are split into boy/girl pairs, so that they will have someone to work alongside and interact with. It strikes me that many *Blue Peter* activities demand a high level of determination, physical skill and co-ordination, as well as the ability to talk engagingly about the experience as it happens. It seems a good idea to put this to the test, so I've hired my own personal trainer, a no-nonsense Aussie called Sam, to put each pair through a gruelling set of circuits. A couple of film team bods will be there with cameras to record reactions and ad-libs. Then, having had a chance to shower and change, each pair will be filmed in an East Tower office doing some simple presenting tasks, principally interviewing. They'll also have to deliver a short extract from one of our history items, which they'll have had to memorise. All this should give me a much clearer sense of whether they have the potential to merit a full studio audition.

There are some interesting possibilities today. The quirkiest, and by far the youngest, pair are Anne Foy and Kenny Skelton. Anne has already had some presenting and acting experience. She's proud of her Northern working-class roots, and has a very likeable zany manner. She reminds me a little of Yvette Fielding and I think kids would either love her or find her insufferable. But better this than bland. I spotted Kenny a couple of years ago when he took part in Channel 4's historical docu-soap, *The Edwardian Country House.* He was the most junior servant, and so endlessly put-upon. I thought he had something of the John Noakes/Matt Baker charm about him, and the ability to comment on his predicament in a funny rather than whiny way.

The other strong contenders are the 'regionals', as one less-than PC member of the team refers to them – Gethin Jones, the Welsh S4C presenter who first came to see me back in June, and Zöe Salmon, from Belfast. Rachel, the production secretary who has brought them round to the garden, offers the view that they would have beautiful children. "Fuck, we're not auditioning them for that," I say. Zöe has an interesting CV; a fully qualified lawyer who also happens to be a former Miss Northern Ireland. She is one of those who applied as a result of the anonymous ad I placed in *The Guardian* and *The Stage.* She arrives today in various shades of blue, shoes, bag, eye make-up, all perfectly co-ordinated. She looks more like a wannabe air-hostess than a prospective children's presenter,

and her accent is fairly strong. I wonder whether the audience would find this a barrier?
Given his credentials, and confident manner, I have high expectations of Gethin, whereas I am prepared for Zöe to struggle. By her own admission, she has never done anything like this before. It doesn't play out like this. Verbally at least, she is quicker off the mark. Her presence seems to nonplus Gethin; his attempts to flirt with her and connect are cheesy and she swats him down, lightly but firmly, obviously used to boys talking gibberish when she's around. They both breeze through the physical tests. He has great natural co-ordination and plenty of stamina and she keeps talking.
"She's a honey," offers Sam from the sidelines.
They do rather less well with the straightforward presenting stuff. Both seem to be acting rather than being themselves, and there is too much of that harsh, fake laughing that all crap presenters use to fill the space. The last thing I want to do is import any of that into *Blue Peter*. But maybe it's just nerves.
I ask CBBC's talent exec, Gabby, what she thinks.
"Like him, hate her," she says. "He's a sweetheart, but she's a madam. That voice. Like nails down a black board. There's just something very cold about her, Rich. I just don't believe she would give a child the time of day."

26th August 2004
Day two of the auditions. All a disaster, really. One of the auditionees starts to hyper-ventilate halfway through the fitness test. We pull her out, give her water and plenty of time to recover but, even then, she can't find the words to articulate the experience, so that's her out.
At least she gave it a go. Another candidate, an actor just out of drama school, who was relatively charming and persuasive in interview, is now referring to himself, somewhat bizarrely, in the third person. He doesn't want to undertake the fitness test at all, saying that he "needs to be true to his brand" and asking, "would Charli do this?" (as in get hot and sweaty) I think we are wasting our time and politely suggest that perhaps this isn't the job for him after all. He shrugs and saunters off, as if it is our loss.
"What a wanker," says Sam the trainer, succinctly.

1st September 2004
Another huge sigh of relief; Simon and our films producer, Matt, are safely back from an 11-day trip climbing Mont Blanc in the Alps. It was a hugely risky exercise, this, especially as Matt not only had to complete the climb alongside Simon, but he had to film it all too. Carrying the extra kit was no joke either.
The origin of the project was when Simon first started to talk to me about having

some kind of exit strategy. Nobody's fool, he had spotted how most presenters going into their final year found their filming schedules downgraded to a procession of non-repeatable domestic stories like animal shows and appeal updates. I agreed that this needed looking at. Apart from anything else, it demoralises the departing presenter at the very moment they have theoretically reached their peak of skill and popularity.

We began to brainstorm some major 'finale' projects for Simon. My first thought was that he could be the first *Blue Peter* presenter to climb Everest. After all, Brian Blessed had done it; Simon has to be fitter than him. Matt Gyves, the films producer, was equally keen.

Matt has a fine track record in children's factual; he is young, personable, intelligent and tough. He didn't, however, want to join the programme. Sometimes this is actually an asset, bringing a freshness of attitude and approach. I eventually persuaded him to join us last year, using the lure of our budget and ability to plan ambitious material long term. He's been flying since day one, and the team admire and respect him.

Amid much excitement, meetings were duly arranged to discuss Everest with a team of experts. Reluctantly, we had to agree that the time-frame for training, the colossal expense, and, most of all, the serious risk that Simon and Matt G might die in the attempt, made it impossible. But a really ambitious climbing story was surely still possible. This is how we ended up with the Mont Blanc project, which was still rife with risk and both costly and time-consuming. To know it has been successfully achieved is a thrilling feeling.

3rd September 2004

Some truly terrible, crushing news. One of our brightest young directors, Steve Vickerstaff, has died. He was only 28. A terrifically popular and genuinely talented guy, I loved working with him. He was always creative and imaginative. It was his idea to tell the story of Dan Dare in the form of a 'living' cartoon strip. It hadn't quite worked, but only because we ran out of time. He made some superb films, and the presenters adored him. Not long ago, he left the BBC; we all thought he'd do well. "Remember me when you're running a channel," I told him.

He was working for MTV over in the States. None of us knew that he was a diabetic; apparently, he hated being labelled with the condition, kept it secret and didn't always look after himself as well as he should. He went into a coma and died in his hotel room. It is so awful to contemplate, because it needn't have happened. Everyone is deeply shocked. One of the APs who knew him really well has asked if he can collect together some of the appearances Steve made on camera during his time here (he was the DJ in my *Rock 'n' Roll Christmas*, for

instance). As we keep all our rushes, I suggest he makes copies of some of these, too, for the family. I also decide to dedicate Monday's show to his memory.
"Won't children wonder who it is?" queries someone on the team.
"Do you think they wonder who the vision mixer is?" I snap. "They don't read credits. It's a gesture. And it's all we can do."

5th September 2004
Pre-recording of our OB at Braemar Highland gathering. It's the usual Scottish heritage biscuit tin nonsense; kilted dancers, tossing the caber, tugs of war and everywhere and all the time, the ceaseless maddening drone of the bagpipes. The people, though, are wonderfully friendly; we have the complete run of the place and we're lucky with the weather. Scots squaddies keep us well supplied with cans of beer and there is a proper carnival atmosphere to proceedings. As well as Simon and Matt, all the boys on the production team (including yours truly) are wearing kilts. Only Liz is contrarily swathed in Burberry, as if to wave the flag for the English somewhere in the mix.
It should be a wonderful day but it is marred by Simon's temper, which steadily worsens. It is extremely unlike him. He snaps at the slightest provocation and gets seriously sweary when he and Matt are being filmed having a go at some of the games.
"It's fucking ridiculous," he growls, having tossed his caber, ineffectually for him. "We could really hurt ourselves."
I take him to the tent we've been allocated as a production office and ask him what's really wrong. It's not just his mood. He looks awful, too, drawn and gaunt, make-up only partially disguising this. He seems suddenly a bit tearful and confesses that he doesn't feel at all well, that he is worried about his health and why he has lost so much weight over the summer, which can't just be down to the rigours of climbing Mont Blanc. I tell him that we will get him checked out as soon as possible.

It turned out that, during his filming in the Solomon Islands, Simon had picked up some kind of intestinal parasite. This was the cause of his rapid weight loss and energy drain. Once treated, he was soon back to full strength and his usual good temper.

6th September 2004
First show in the new season and launch day for the new set, the new music and the new graphics. All involved a time-consuming competitive process. In the end, the arrangement of the theme that I felt most effective was by one of our most talented film editors, Niall Brown, a softly-spoken and self-effacing Scot.

It's incredibly hard to make Barnacle Bill (the nautical name for the actual tune) sound in any way contemporary, but I think he has managed it, using a kind of rising guitar riff. He was also able to incorporate my request to include the sound of the 'ship's whistle' (blown just before the Captain comes on board) right at the start. I thought this might add a distinctive layer to the traditional drumroll.

Naturally, I'm very familiar with the set model, but still this doesn't prepare me for the experience of actually walking into the studio and seeing the full-size version for the first time. I feel like I've been handed the keys to my dream home; it is classy, clean, contemporary and full of visual interest and potential. All the ship logos are the classic design, rather than Kevin Hill's more recent 'bubble' version. Though I loved that, I felt it was diluting the power of our principle and most widely recognised logo, so reluctantly I've retired it.

Within the set itself, I've brought back the option of a hanging perspex ship (not seen since the 70s), but in a striking red, rather than blue. Like all our sets, it's a massive kit of parts, which directors can assemble in all kinds of different ways. It has a catwalk, seating areas, different levels, and truckable 'sail' sections to add background interest, depth and texture. I hope the audience like it because we'll be paying for it over the next three years.

9th September 2004

Interviews with *Broadcast* and *The Bookseller* to promote the launch of our regular book club. The latter is keen as mustard, the former jaded as fuck. "Oh, you mean like Richard and Judy," suggests the blatantly bored journalist on the end of the phone.

"Not like that at all, actually," I counter, before outlining what we have in mind.

"Do kids these days like books, though?"

14th September 2004

Having taken the decision to retire our moribund moggies Kari and Oke, today is the day we introduce our new kitten. I selected him over the summer from a litter rescued by our cat handler, Marina Cragg. The kittens' mother, a pretty tortoiseshell called Topsy, was being kept in a farmer's barn, as a kind of makeshift breeding factory. As fast as she produced one litter, the kittens would be whisked off and sold, and then she'd be pregnant again. With the help of a friend, Marina rescued Topsy and her latest litter from the barn. Now she had to find homes for them all. The programme was going to have one, and I also persuaded my wife Mandy that we should let our kids have another. We travel down to Marina's place near Crawley to take our pick. Rosy and Rupert choose the friendliest and most confident of the bunch, a little white kitten. Cleverly,

Marina tugs Mandy's heart strings by telling her how the mother cats are always nearly impossible to re-house, and so they are often abandoned. Mandy falls for this spiel and so we return home with both the kitten and its mother.
Back in the studio, there is a photocall to introduce our kitten's sibling to the world of *Blue Peter*. All the presenters are called, too, and it is interesting to see them jostling for position to get in the shots; they all know the value of 'fur and feather' and association with a cute pet. The winner is Simon, who proves surprisingly patient and gentle with the poor creature, who squeaks piteously as the cameras click away.

20th September 2004

Our first set of studio auditions. I've recalled four of the contenders from last month – two men and two women. The boys are both Welsh; Alun Williams (another S4C lad) and Gethin Jones. Then there is Zöe, who, at my request has arrived looking much more natural and less 'dressed up' and Ashleigh, a black girl, who is young and sporty but easily the most nervous of the quartet. This sinks her audition. The others are all pretty good, at least technically, but then both the boys have plenty of studio experience. Zöe is the revelation; she is cool, calm and in control, takes direction with aplomb and seems to really enjoy the trampoline stage. Matt, in particular, is impressed. "She's incredible, Rich," he says. "I really think she's got something."
Gabby, CBBC's talent exec, is also impressed. "Where did you find her?" she asks me. It's plain that she doesn't remember Zöe from the first round, so I remind her that in fact she's already seen her and that she'd written her off in no uncertain terms. Realisation dawns and Gabby visibly adjusts. "Oh...yes. Goodness, she does look different. So much better, Rich. Not so hard."
Of the boys, I prefer Gethin. He's got a very likeable manner, and his warmth and enthusiasm will appeal to kids, I think. But his Achilles heel is the make. I always think this is more of a personality test than the trampoline, because it's effectively five minutes of monologue. Skilled presenters turn this into an intimate conversation between them and the viewer, using it to showcase their own style and humour. During his make, Gethin flat-lines, droning on and boring the arse off me.
Matt has other concerns. "I've had five years of hating every two-shot with Simon," he says. "I'm sick of being the ugly one. He's too good-looking, Rich. We want a real person, not a model who just wants to be on TV."

27th September 2004

Zöe Salmon flies over from Belfast so that I can break the news that I'd like her to be our next presenter.

"Oh my goodness!," she exclaims. Brownie points for not swearing.
"You must have guessed," say I, but she is adamant that she had no preconceptions and thought it might just be another round in the process. Given that this has been fairly protracted, I believe her. She doesn't strike me as the disingenuous type. In fact, her directness is one of the qualities I like about her. I open a bottle of champagne to toast her success; she really has done incredibly well, given that she has no television experience at all. None of the arduous audition process seemed to faze her at all.
I suggest that she should phone her parents but stress how important it is to keep the news strictly confidential until we make the announcement. This will have to happen soon as it could so easily leak and, besides, my plan is for Zöe to get a good three-month run- up before we actually introduce her on screen. This has never happened before, but I think it makes total sense. Apart from getting her head round the many demands of the job, she is going to have to move to London, and that will be a massive adjustment in itself. I'm haunted by the memory of Matt's first few weeks on the programme. He was fine if we were filming or in the studio, but when 'home time' came round, he was like a lost soul. He knew no one in London, felt a total fish out of water, yearning for the open spaces and dreading going back to his characterless little flat in West London.
I get the impression that Zöe, however, is actively excited at the imminent prospect of the move and all the opportunities which the job will bring her. It's so odd to think that, at the moment, we scarcely know her, but that over the next few months, and years, her personality will become inextricably bound up with the programme and all of us who make it. Steve Hocking happens to pop into the office and catches a glimpse of her.
"She really is extraordinarily pretty," he tells me.
She's flying back home this afternoon and I've told her that we want her to start with us on 18th October; so that gives her a little time to sort things out. I imagine she'll have a lot to think about on the flight back.
On today's show, the launch of our competition for a viewer to design the BBC1 Christmas ident. This is what comes of having friends in high places; or rather, a Controller of BBC1 who used to be our head of department!
Meanwhile, Biddy emails to offer her congratulations on an "absolutely magnificent" annual. And indeed I couldn't be more delighted myself. Pedigree have really delivered on their promise to increase not just the page-count, but the quality of design and paper. It looks lush. As Biddy puts it: "There's such a variety of content, and the design, drawings and photos look immensely colourful and appealing. A real triumph in the face of so many set backs. I bet Worldwide are ruing turning it down."
Though pleasant to contemplate, I find this unlikely.

28th September 2004

Write to Zöe, congratulating her on the job, saying "you are about to join one of the most exclusive clubs in the world" and that I think that she will be an enormous success; "especially if you can hang on to your natural personality and if you give everything we throw at you your best shot."

I include a copy of the exhaustive *Blue Peter* guide, a kind of in-depth booklet running through the history and minutiae of the programme. The weight of all this tradition might be inclined to freak out some people, but I get the impression that with her legal training, Zöe is someone who will value detail. If not she can use it to make firelighters. Which would also be very *Blue Peter.*

4th October 2004

To the Savoy, for the inaugural dinner for the Caron Keating Foundation. It is all beautifully organised and, at times, moving. There are white feathers on all the tables because, as Gloria explains in her speech, Caron had a lifelong conviction that whenever a single white feather appears, it is a sign that your guardian angel is nearby and watching over you. I wonder what Caron's family will make of the fact that our next presenter is going to be another girl from Northern Ireland. There is a kind of pleasing symmetry to it, though I certainly didn't set out with that in mind. I only hope Zöe will be as successful a presenter as Caron. Family, friends and famous faces have turned out in force, everyone dressed in their best. It doesn't feel in the slightest maudlin. The atmosphere is celebratory and fun, and, before the dinner, there is plenty of time to mingle and chat. I bump into Phillip Schofield for the first time since I was his AFM on *Going Live!* and wonder if he will remember me. He has done so much since. But there is instant recognition and I remember how he had a forensic ability to recall the names of everyone on set, from the humblest chippie to the man in charge. I remind him how sometimes, after the post-transmission hospitality, he used to give me a lift home. As I was then living in a flat in the not-very-salubrious Scrubs Lane, it was quite an eyeful for the neighbours to see him roar up in his latest sports car (in which, rather than sitting upright, one would lie almost horizontally) out of which I would then clamber awkwardly and utter my thanks, before he zoomed off somewhere much more glamorous. Come to that, pretty much anywhere is more glamorous than Scrubs Lane.

25th October 2004

To the studio first thing for Zöe's photocall. This has been the source of considerable tension between myself, the press office and picture publicity. Neither of these outfits are ever keen to stretch themselves beyond the bare minimum. What they wanted was the usual path of least resistance; issuing a

short press release with a small selection of photos, taken in-house.
"Are you mad?" is my response. "She's the first new presenter in over four years. She's from Northern Ireland, like Caron. And she's got a look that the tabloids will love. It's an absolute gift of a story."
There's also a dispute about what to offer in terms of picture set-ups. Picture publicity want to play safe with a few shots of Zöe in simple casual clothes, holding the cat. I want her bouncing around on the trampoline, in something with a little more *jouzz.* We compromise and offer both, and, reluctantly, they concede and agree to arrange a proper photocall, to which all the press will be invited.
"But don't build your hopes up," says Helen, from picture publicity, darkly, "I doubt there'll be much of a turn up."
When I lead Zöe from make-up onto the studio floor, the place is absolutely heaving with photographers, all jostling for position to get the best shots. It's a complete circus and takes longer than we'd planned, but it's also hugely exciting. With her modelling experience, Zöe is in her element and looks fantastic.
Later, an email from Lewis Bronze arrives: "Beauty queen AND a law degree...what more could one ask....central casting if ever I heard it. She looks divine. And another Irish girl...couldn't be better. As I learned, there's nothing like having your 'own' presenters."

26th October 2004

I go into make-up, proudly clutching a thick bundle of the press cuttings from yesterday's photocall. Zöe is splashed across every paper, some of them front page. We haven't had press like this in years, I rattle on, happily. Turns out I'm being less than tactful. The presenters are all pretty jaundiced about it, especially Liz.
"I think they're awful, those pictures," she says. "I'd have hated to be all over the papers, looking like that. She's more Page Three than BP."
Oh dear. Noses are clearly out of joint. I suppose I've been naive to assume it would be easy. A lot will be down to how Zöe herself handles the introductory period. I hope the others give her a decent chance. Matt still seems very much in favour, which is good.

1st November 2004

Worrying feedback from Debbie Martin, who has been directing Zöe in one of her first films, trying a sport called street luge. This involves lying on top of what's basically a giant skateboard, and speeding downwards in pursuit of an accident-free adrenaline rush. Debbie is concerned by Zöe's attitude; according to her account, Zöe demonstrated next to no interest in proceedings, and spent much of the time moaning and complaining. This is standard enough when a presenter has been round the blocks and is sent filming on a story in which they have little interest. But it is rare, even unheard of, in someone who has yet to appear on air.

When I speak to Zöe herself, she waxes lyrical about the experience.

"I loved it," she concludes, emphatically.

Ho-hum.

2nd November 2004

Lunch with Zöe at Julie's in Notting Hill. Anne Gilchrist joins us (she's paying) and, as this is really an opportunity for her to get to know Zöe better, I try to steer the conversation so that it focuses on Zöe, her interests, and background. Zöe chatters away quite happily, but, although it is mostly about her, she doesn't once give the impression that she's in love with herself; more, that she's in love with everything with which she's been seriously involved, from beauty and modelling to her law training and now TV. Anne is impressed to discover that Zöe actually funded her legal degree (at the prestigious Queen's University, Belfast) with money she earned doing part-time modelling. I think it's refreshing that Zöe seems to have no hang-ups about her experience in the beauty business. There's been a lot of chuntering about this in the office; mostly of a predictably judgmental nature. To some extent, Zöe can shut this down because she's demonstrably not a bimbo, but I have warned her that the 'beauty queen' label will never leave her (see also, *Blue Peter*'s first presenter, Leila Williams). She is quite serene about this. It's an achievement she's proud of. She loves all things hair, beauty and fashion – and why not? So do millions of other women, and men, come to that. Anne's eyes widen when Zöe explains that, back at her parents' house, she has an entire spare bedroom as a walk-in wardrobe. Here, all her clothes are carefully stored in covers and woe betide her younger sister Naomi if she's caught trespassing.

When Zöe nips to the ladies, Anne is clearly taken with her and comments: "Did you see the reaction she got when we walked in? I think she has genuine star quality."

This afternoon, Rowan Atkinson is in the studio in character as Mr Bean throughout the show. When he first agreed to come on, he asked for a detailed list of the items which might have the potential to involve Bean. It is absolutely fascinating to watch him work. He's a quietly spoken, almost shy man, with the power of complete concentration (something our presenters could do worse than emulate). His perfect manners don't mask his absolute focus on getting the comedy right; he takes a forensic interest in each stage, scrutinising the situation for comedic possibilities and checking every aspect, from how it will be shot to what the presenters are planning to say and do. Simon, in particular, responds very positively to this way of working; he is enough of a perfectionist to value such precision. Their double act, as Simon attempts to make cheesy bread and butter pudding with Mr Bean's 'help', is a master class in rehearsed spontaneity; nothing is left to chance, yet it feels both fresh and real. The whole show is brilliantly funny, in fact, and I drop an item to allow the room we need for Mr Bean to weave through everything like bindweed. When it is over, I am effusive with thanks and praise, but Rowan shrugs all this off, and insists that the pleasure is all his; he loves *Blue Peter*, he says, and is simply delighted that we asked him to take part.

"Please come back," I ask him, and wonder wildly if I should suggest Bean as our new presenter!

4th November 2004

Reports from yesterday's on-set filming with *Doctor Who*. It was all a bit of a trial, apparently. Dermot, the director, had to fight all day for the access he needed. Some of the crew behaved like wankers, being obstructive and high-handed. It didn't help that they were apparently running well behind schedule so we inevitably were a sideshow that they could do without. But it is disappointing after all the high hopes and promises.

I'm also concerned to hear that, despite the various conversations we had with the *Who* office before the shoot, we were not allowed to shoot the stills promised for next year's annual. Instead, just one photo, of Matt standing next to a Dalek, was taken by their official set photographer, which will, I'm told, be released to us "nearer the time".

This is fucking annoying, as a single posed shot won't make a spread, so I suppose I'll have to use screen grabs, which I hate.

8th November 2004

Launch of our *Welcome Home* appeal, to help the Red Cross fund the reunification of families split up by civil war in Africa. The subject matter is incredibly strong, and, importantly and at last, we have been able to revive recycling as a fund-raising device. This was one of my key objectives when I took over. For this appeal, we are asking viewers to collect old clothes, which is simple and accessible for kids of all ages and backgrounds. Konnie is the lead presenter on the films, and I'm delighted with the results so far; she's at her very best in them, connecting with the emotional heart of the stories but not going over the top and building her part.

Also today, a lovely letter from Rowan Atkinson, who writes "I am so grateful for the tolerance and hospitality you accorded to both me and Mr Bean. I just hope that the casual irritant of Bean was not too much of an irritant, and that the show accrued some benefits from his appearance. I think that what you do and the way you do it are very special, so continued good luck with that great institution of yours."

9th November 2004

Liz's last studio before she goes off on maternity leave; the plan is for her to return full time in April next year. I think she is a little overwhelmed by the weight of affection which engulfs her today; she rarely, if ever, demands the limelight, happier to be one of the team, but today it is all hers, and rightly so.

15th November 2004

That Reggie Yates is one of the celebrities in today's studio, donating clothes (we have a stash of these as props for the celebs who invariably 'forget' to bring their own). During rehearsals, he comments that *Blue Peter* wasn't a show that appealed to him as a child because it was "too middle-class".

Since he went to one of London's most high achieving secondary schools and strikes me as about as middle-class as it's possible to be, I find this tiresome, as well as rude. He'd love to be 'street', but the fact is that he's thoroughly safe and totally BBC. And he'll do very well out of it, too.

24th November 2004

Another round of studio auditions. Gethin is still in the mix, but every time I play his tape, the full horror of his make strikes again. I even think about getting him back but, in the event, I've opted for a fresh set of candidates. There are, ironically, two Matts; both of them actors. I've also recalled Kenny Skelton. Despite his shambolic turn in the second round back in August, there is something there. You can teach technique, but you can't manufacture a personality or sense of humour and, even in the chaos of his first audition, Kenny gave us glimpses of a quick-wit and strong personality. The final boy is called Junior Saunders, and he was a recommendation from the CBBC talent exec. Junior is a Londoner, cheeky, funny, full of beans. He also happens to be black, which gives him additional currency. I've made no secret of the fact that I'd like to cast the first black male presenter, but I'm not going to give anyone the job based on their skin colour alone. It kind of horrifies me when Konnie occasionally trots out her tale of how she thinks she got the job "because I'm brown and they thought I'd do". At one level, this is typical of her self-deprecating sense of humour, but, at another, she clearly thinks there is truth in it as well. And there probably is.

I'm willing this latest quartet to come out fighting and do their best. But Kenny is all over the place, his eyes swivelling like a crack addict. Junior is another car crash, and he can't cope with anything scripted at all. The other two are better, though one of them seems to be going through the motions, rather than lighting up the screen. Matt Landers is the best of the bunch. He's a Northern lad, and as well as the acting, he has played rugby league, so he's sporty too. He might just be our man.

18th November 2004

One of my strategies for our frantic new production schedule is to allocate each presenter a major solo project every 'term'. In this first 'term', September to Christmas, Matt is making *Sporting USA*, a series of films in which he travels to the States to try the most popular American college sports. Konnie is going to be the face of the appeal, filming in Angola. Simon's challenge is a complete programme dedicated to boxing. This came out of the filming I did a while back at the boxing gym in the Harrow Road. I hadn't forgotten what the kids who watched us at work said; that we are happy to use the sport for comedy, but that we would never do a serious story about boxing. I gave this a lot of thought, and discussed it with Peter Salmon, the BBC's head of sport. This is the result; a detailed exploration of boxing, with the spine of the story following Simon training for an actual fight. He has thrown himself into the whole process, putting in the hours in the gym after work, and psyching himself up to face an opponent in the ring.

"What if I break my nose?" he asks me.

"You'll be a hero," I tell him, and promise that we wouldn't duck the issue as the show did when Katy broke her nose playing women's rugby. Oliver decided this injury was too upsetting to show or mention; and, much to Katy's annoyance, she had to sit out a couple of shows until her face looked normal again.

Today, though, a total disaster, which no one was expecting. Simon is having his final pre-fight medical, and it is discovered that he has a detached retina, a souvenir from his school rugby-playing days. Under the ABA's rightly strict health and safety rules, a detached retina permanently rules him out from fighting. The show has lost its big finish and Simon is absolutely gutted. He feels that all his hard graft of the last few weeks has been in vain. We will cobble together an ending of some kind, but it is a cruel disappointment for all of us.

30th November 2004

I've sent Matt Landers off to play a part in a film we're making about Dick Whittington. It's another test, but at least he's getting something definite out of it; a paid part.

In the studio today, an item about lederhosen for dogs. Yes, there is apparently such a thing (call the RSPCA). It's an excuse, as if excuse were needed, to repeat the Lederhosen film and to indulge in an Alpine yodelling master class. Sharing the 'fun' are two CBBC stalwarts, Lizo Mzimbo and Barney Harwood. Both clamber into lederhosen to make fools of themselves, which is just as it should be. But then Barney asks to have a word and I wonder if he's not happy after all. I've not forgotten the day we ran an item about 'men in skirts' and one of the CBBC presenters who showed up to help model them suddenly dissolved in floods of tears; tears of sheer embarrassment. Fortunately, this is not why Barney wants to talk to me.

"I'd like the job," he says. "I want to be your next presenter. But would I have to audition?"

This is not something I'd even considered. *Blue Peter* rarely goes for an established presenter, though the advantages are obvious; someone who knows what they are doing from the start, and who may even have an existing fan base. There is something intoxicating about finding a totally fresh face, allowing both the audience and the production team the opportunity of seeing them develop and flourish. This is great when you've found someone with the obvious raw talent of a Katy Hill or a Matt Baker. But I have to admit that we aren't in that happy situation. Also I've never forgotten Matt's sheer bewildered terror when he first started. I really want whoever we choose to have a three-month run-up off-screen, when they can get to know the team, feel more at home in the studio and bank up some filming. We've arranged this for Zöe and I want the same for whoever our new boy happens to be. But we are beginning to run out of time. Barney clearly means what he's saying. What's more, I rate him highly, like him very much and think he could be perfect.

"No, you wouldn't have to audition," I tell him. But aren't you committed to *Smile*?" (This is CBBC's current Sunday morning offering).

He admits that this is the case, but says that if I'm seriously interested, he would ask to be released. I am and suggest that he explores the possibility of this from his end, while I talk to CBBC's head of entertainment, who is in charge of *Smile*.

"Oh, and if it all works out," I tell him, indicating the lederhosen "you'll be doing lots more dressing up."

"Can't wait," he beams. And I believe him.

1st December 2004

Bad news on the Barney front. *Smile*, apparently, has been going through several presenter changes, and Barney, who, unfortunately, has just signed a new contract with them, is relied upon to act as the anchor while these changes bed in. The programme could only be forced to release him if the powers that be were keen to support my wish to cast him and Barney's wish to do the job. The

head of CBBC entertainment is, understandably, adamantly against this ("he's committed, it's just too bad – you'll find someone, don't worry") while Dot just shrugs and says, "It wouldn't be very fair on *Smile*, would it?"
Naturally, I don't give a flying fuck about *Smile*. From what I've seen, it's the usual pile-it-high, make-it-cheap, disposable shite (Barney being the best thing about it) and only wish others could recognise the strategic benefits of parachuting someone of his talent into what is supposed to be the department's flagship show. I'm pissed off and sad for Barney's sake, too.

3rd December 2004
I'm feeling guilty about Gethin Jones, whom I have kept in a limbo of suspense since his unfortunate studio audition. There is something there, a quality which could really work for us. It's not just his audition which has proved a stumbling block. Another presenter doing the rounds, who sometimes works for the department, has been undertaking a minor smear campaign against Gethin. This person calls me to say that he has heard we are considering Gethin but that we shouldn't "as he's not a good person and you'll be making a mistake."
I ask him to elaborate but he talks in spiteful euphemisms and I dismiss his comments as likely to be sour grapes. But it doesn't feel very good. Could it be a case of no smoke without fire?
Then one of our APs (who I happen to know is friendly with this particular presenter) comes to me and asks if I know that Gethin is "gay but in the closet"?
"Who told you that?" I ask him, and suggest that it was this other presenter.
The AP blushes, evidently amazed that I know.
I have no problem with Gethin being gay and phone him to say so.
"So long as anything you do in your private life is legal, that's fine. But you do need to tell me."
"I'm not gay," he replies, emphatically. "Really, I'm not."
I explain that I've been told that he is, but that he wants to keep it secret. Also of the other insinuations which have been made. Gethin admits that he was once friendly with this other presenter, but that they have since fallen out.
"Evidently," I say. "He's going to a lot of trouble to damage your chances."
Today I decide that I must finally make up my mind. Christmas is looming and it's going to be depressing enough if I leave the rejection any longer. I call him and start my 'let him down gently' spiel.
"You did amazingly well. Very few people get this far. It's been so difficult to make a decision."
I talk about the disaster of the make.
And then something unexpected, and rather wonderful, happens. Instead of his usual (and slightly aggravating) humble acceptance of whatever I have to say, he

interrupts and starts to argue his case. Last chance saloon, I guess. He's really pleading for another chance, but not in a pathetic way, instead saying forcefully that I've got it all wrong and that I can't base my decision on that one moment. At last, I hear genuine passion in his voice, some spirit and fight. He says that he can prove that he has the spark I worry is lacking and he will courier me a tape today, if I'm willing to give him one more chance.

So in the end I agree but when I've rung off, I sit there thinking that in this one conversation he's actually done more to convince me that he could be the man than in most of the previous interviews and auditions combined.

4th December 2004

Great news. Liz's baby, a boy, has finally been born, two weeks late! Obviously hasn't got a showbiz gene, as the delay has ruined my hopes of having Liz involved in the Christmas music pre-record. The plan was for her (and baby) to be sitting in a rocking chair in the corner of the room in which the other presenters sing *Have Yourself a Merry Little Christmas*. I thought this would have been gloriously (and suitably) sentimental. Now a photo on the mantelpiece will have to do.

5th December 2004

Some tapes, and a letter, arrive from Gethin. The tapes are in Welsh, so that's a fat lot of good. But it's the effort he's made to get them here, fight his corner and show some spirit that's made all the difference.

"I appreciate the difficult job you have of selecting the right person for this special job," he writes, "and I hope that I'm not causing you too many headaches!"

Casting this show is one permanent fucking migraine.

6th December 2004

Pre-record for *The Magic of Christmas*, the big musical insert in this year's Christmas show. As the new girl, Zöe is naturally very much front and centre. Matt watches her appraisingly and tells me, "she's really got something, like. I reckon she's going to be great."

It's been decided to curtail the season at the end of April. This is because the powers that be have decided that they would like *Blue Peter* to run on the channel during the summer holidays, from mid-July. Our break has consequently been shifted back so that we will go off-air during May and June. Simon is disgruntled by the news, because it means he will now be leaving two months earlier than planned. He will still get paid the full term of his contract, but that isn't the issue. He admits that he is finding the whole process of leaving much more painful and challenging than he ever imagined it would be. For so long the textbook total professional of the team, he was uncharacteristically difficult at the start of the season. He's back on track now, but I know that he is worried about the future and life away from *Blue Peter*. BBC sport, to which he would dearly like to graduate, seem to have no interest, about which he understandably feels some bitterness. I think this is stupid and short-sighted of them, but then I know Simon's worth and what he could bring to them. He remains determined to focus on sport, if not here, then elsewhere, and he's putting all his efforts into this ambition.

"I've no interest in doing any old shit, Rich," he tells me. "I know I'm not entertainment. I hate reality shows. I need to stick to what I'm good at and what I'm interested in."

I wish he wasn't leaving at all, really.

11th December 2004

In a well below freezing Nurenberg to film the Christmas markets with Matt, as well as a bit of gingerbread-making. Every year since 1964, it's been a *Blue Peter* tradition to display a crib, with beautifully carved figures, as part of the Christmas show. One of these figures has gone missing and so part of the premise of our story is that we're on the hunt for a replacement. We've come here because the programme always explains that this is where the crib was originally found by presenters Chris Trace and Val Singleton. But I've had this film transferred, and there is no sequence in which they buy the crib. Puzzled, I phone Edward Barnes, who was the producer at the time. When I explain the dilemma, he chuckles. "Oh, yes, that was Biddy," he says. "You know what she's like when she's made up her mind about something. It made a better story, you see. The crib actually came from Harrods. I asked a very pretty buyer to find me one and that's where she got it."

Needless to say, this does not form part of our story.

We don't hang about, as it is so bitterly cold. But there is a lengthy delay when my phone rings. It's Barney Harwood's agent. He doesn't bother with any of the pleasantries, launching straight into a full-on rant about "fucking CBBC bastards" who are "ruining" Barney's career.

"Do you want him or don't you?" he demands, pugnaciously.

When I can get a word in, I explain that I did want him, but that the situation is out of my control. Barney is on contract to another programme, who are not willing to release him for us.

"But you're all on the same fucking side, aren't you?"

This is not the moment to explain the naivety of this view. I listen to a long and fuck-filled rant, then suggest he talks to the head of CBBC entertainment. "If you can fix it, I'd be more than happy," I tell him, and he rings off abruptly.

A little while later, another interruption and another call, this time from the head of entertainment. To say she is not happy is an understatement. She is incensed. Barney's agent has been onto her, applying the same sweary steam-roller approach he demonstrated over the phone to me.

"When I told him that we weren't going to let Barney do *Blue Peter*, he was *incredibly* rude," she fumes. "I've never heard anything like it. I'd think very carefully about having someone like that as my agent."

I promise that I'll have a word with Barney and feed this back. The agent's aggression and lack of tact haven't helped, but I have a sneaking sympathy for him, too. As he put it: "Barney wants to do *Blue Peter*. You want Barney to do *Blue Peter*. *Smile* can find someone else, easy. I could find someone for them. What's the fucking problem?"

Like most outsiders, he cannot understand why CBBC isn't more joined-up and strategic.

Zöe has been filming in the area, too, and presently she joins us, content to be a tourist for the afternoon. But I decide it will be fun to give her a little cameo, as a shopper at one of the market stalls, so that her first appearance on the show will be this obscure in-joke, rather than the fanfare of the big reveal.

Barney Harwood had a long wait ahead of him but he did finally achieve his goal of becoming a Blue Peter *presenter in January 2011, replacing Joel Defries, whose contract was terminated a few weeks before. Barney has rewarded the programme not only with his talent and charm, but also with his durability; he stayed with the programme until September 2017.*

13th December 2004

Popstars: The Rivals boy band Phixx (they were the runners-up and their name reflects their feelings about the competition) are in the studio to sing a one-off single called Father Christmas. Off the back of the performance, we reveal that this is actually written by Matt and trail the next show, a special (which I've called *Sing a Song of Matt*) which charts his challenge to write and produce a Christmas pop song. I'm inordinately proud of this project; it is the result of trying to think of fresh ways to showcase Matt's phenomenal abilities, of which musicality is a part. This is a creative rather than physical challenge and the pitfall is that the creative process is hard to film, or to make visual. You tend to be stuck with shots of someone chewing a pencil or taking an 'inspirational' walk. I'm keen for it to offer some genuine insights into the record industry and the way a song is promoted, as well as produced.

I suggested that we ask Mike Stock (of Stock/Aitken/Waterman fame) to act as Matt's mentor, and this has worked like a charm. They are both hard-working, plain-speaking self-starters. We have also peppered the show with tips from top pop stars to whom we have had recent access, most notably Madonna (who was actually plugging some kids' book to which she's put her name) who seems to take a little shine to our Matthew, about which I have been teasing him ever since.

The show concludes with Matt directing his own video for the song (which features his Dad, reprising his role as Father Christmas). I think it is a piece of magic, a really interesting, enjoyable, warm-hearted Christmassy show.

17th December 2004

Liz is in the studio, with her baby, Dexter (Dex for short) I talk to her about how much she is willing to film with him; aware that this is a delicate issue. Before he was born, she was much more relaxed about the idea. Now that he is actually here, a real flesh-and-blood human being, all her naturally protective instincts have been triggered, and she is less certain. I remind her that presenters with their own dedicated pets, like Matt and Meg, are generally more popular than those who are unattached.

"And you're going one better," I suggest. "A baby is *much* cuter than anything else. Instant box office. Now Dex is around, it'll be 'Meg who?' and 'Smudge – whatever!'"

"You're awful," she laughs.

"It has been said," I admit.

21st December 2004

Pre-recording the Christmas show. It will go out in a couple of days, but I'm depressed that we've got a terrible early afternoon slot, which will unavoidably reduce the audience figures. Given it will still be daylight, it will also make a nonsense of the magic moment when we open the studio doors and see the procession of lantern-carrying children walking up the hill. I've done battle with scheduling, to no avail. Increasingly, there is little appetite for a half-hour programme like ours; we get in the way of the kind of family movies which guarantee a big audience over a longer period of time. The general inference is that we're lucky to still be there at all. At least *Radio Times* has made us a choice for the day, thanks to the fact that this is Zöe's first appearance on-screen.

For this key moment, I've nicked an idea I remember from my own childhood. At Christmas 1972, when Cherry Gillespie, joined *Top of the Pops* as the new member of dance-troupe Pan's People, she was disguised inside a present, which the other girls unwrapped to reveal her. Their approach was rather tatty, though; just a load of paper and ribbon. Design have made us a proper life-sized Christmas present which falls open on cue, allowing Zöe to emerge in her glittery party frock.

She's excited but not, I suspect, as much as our other new face. I summoned Gethin to Television Centre this morning and, as soon as he arrived in my office, broke the news that I wanted him to be our new presenter.
"Really?" he said, his whole face lighting up with pleasure.
I nod. "Really. You must have had the longest and most torturous wait for the job ever. Well done, you've really earned it."
I suggest he might like to make a few calls, tell the family. The plan is that, like Zöe, he will have a period of a few months to integrate into the team, and do some filming, before joining on screen at the end of the series in April. But, as a little Christmas present, I suggest that he might like a cameo in today's show; playing Father Christmas. It seems only fair since Zöe had her cameo in the Nurenberg film the other day.
I take him for a humble celebratory lunch in the 'stage door' canteen at Television Centre, and while we are chatting, I spy out of the corner of my eye, a familiar figure bearing down on me. It is Liz, who is in today's show as I am keen to have a 'full house' for the Christmas programme. She is carrying a rolled-up copy of *Hello!* This is the latest issue which features a three-page spread about Zöe, running an array of glamorous photos with the magazine's trademark gushingly bland text. Liz arrives at our table, ignores Geth, and starts to hit me about the head and shoulders, using the magazine as a makeshift weapon.
"Er...Liz, can you stop doing that? People are staring."
She relents, and she's sort of half-laughing, half-furious, ripping open the magazine at the relevant pages.
"What's all this?" she demands. "It's horrible. Zöe in her underwear. Yuck. Why would you agree to something like this just for her? *Blue Peter* doesn't need this kind of publicity. I've never been put forward for *Hello!* magazine."
The injustice of this stings me. "You've always said you aren't interested in publicity," I reply. "And I've always respected that. If you wanted to be in *Hello!* you only have to ask. I'm sure they'd love a feature about you and the baby. Liz, I know you say we don't need this but it is *good* publicity and any programme benefits from that. You can rely on *Hello!* to be positive and upbeat, which is why I agreed to it."
She is just about placated, and now apologises for so melodramatically interrupting our lunch. She says she will let us get on with it and see us back in the studio.
Gethin's eyes are like saucers.
"Welcome to *Blue Peter*," I tell him.

Shortly afterwards, it was arranged for Liz, Toddy and baby Dex to feature in Hello! *magazine too.*

2005

5th January 2005

First live show back, with Zöe's first 'proper' appearance as part of the regular line-up and the glad news that we've smashed the appeal target for the second time. In the usual run of things, this would be quite enough for one running order, but viewer response to the appalling Boxing Day tsunami demands otherwise. We run an item suggesting various emergency fund-raising ideas and hold a bring-and-buy in the studio.

The backdrop to this busy day is the presence of our own film crew, shooting a behind-the-scenes on Zöe's debut. I'm involved at several key points. Although I'm more than used to the odd cameo here and there, this is rather different. Ros, the director, is trying to capture a genuine sense of how the live shows come together and, as Editor, that makes me a fairly crucial contributor. It's educative and uncomfortable having to face the cameras without a costume or character to hide behind. I become very aware of my 'plummy' voice and have to be given the classic note to slow down; everyone tends to move and talk faster when they are filmed. I'm also frantic not to be caught swearing or saying anything inappropriate, especially during presenter notes which are usually a pretty robust free-for-all. In fairness, they need to be. There is often only about 10-20 minutes' turnaround between the notes and the live show, so nothing can be sugar-coated.

It helps that today there are no major crises, either with tone, timing or the running order, which sometimes needs a last-minute tweak to achieve the balance of light and shade, and to make sure the 'box office' moment is given the correct prominence. Zöe is quite extraordinarily self-possessed throughout the whole process, and I can't quite decide if this admirable or uncanny.

10th January 2005

Launch of another top notch competition, for viewers to come up with a design which will be painted on the side of a British Airways plane. This came our way as a result of the *Top of the Pops* film we made with Konnie. Andi Peters, who is in charge of *Pops,* also has some kind of ongoing corporate relationship with BA.

"I bet they'd be up to do something really big and ambitious," he said. "Would you like me to investigate?"

Once all the fine details of compliance and editorial policy have been agreed, this is the result. It's going to be a winner and the correspondence unit are already grumbling about the anticipated onslaught of entries.

18th January 2005

Candidate for most pointless item ever today; a so-called reunion of cat siblings Smudge and his brother, to whom we gave a home back in the summer. Despite the fact that he's a boy, my kids have insisted on calling him Kitty. This will sound daft on air, so, for transmission he will be called 'Felix', the name I tried to get the kids to adopt in the first place.

This morning I bundled the poor bewildered animal into his carrying basket and set off as usual for my hour-long commute down the M1 and round the North Circular. Kitty/Felix mewed piteously the entire way, and it dawned on me forcibly that this wasn't likely to be a fun day out for either of us. He is given his own dressing-room, of course, where I deposit him on arrival, and the loving attentions of our cat-crazy animal handler Marina. I disappear with relief to the relative sanctum of the office.

A very positive meeting with Matt to discuss his future. I've offered him a two-year contract from the summer but he only wants to sign for a year.

"Don't get me wrong, Rich," he says, "I'm very happy and I'd like to think I'll be staying longer than that. But I've spoken to my dad, and I just think I should take it one year at a time."

I'm fine with this, and it is good to hear that he's feeling happy and settled. We talk about the way the team is changing, and how I see him and Konnie as 'head boy' and 'head girl'.

"As things move on, you are going to be the rock for the audience," I explain.

He thinks that the show is in great shape, despite the initial reservations he had about us going five-times-a-week. He has high hopes for Zöe, and admits that he not only is going to miss Simon, but still has his doubts about Gethin.

"I'm just not sure how much is there," he says. "I don't know if I really believe his motivation for being on *Blue Peter*. I think he just wants to be on TV and love himself. There are so many presenters like him. This show is about so much more than that."

I recognise that Matt was never in favour of me casting Gethin, but I ask him to keep an open mind, give him a chance, help and support him.

"He's got a lot to learn, and you could be a big part of that. He's eager to please and he wants to be good. We should make use of that."

"You make it sound like training a puppy."

"You always tell me you're going to use the same techniques when you have children," I remind him. "Why not give some of them a go on Gethin?"

Well, it's worth a try.

Cats are not big on reunions; they don't show much in the way of family feeling at the best of times. I know this because Marina persuaded us to take on the kittens' mother, Topsy; and they co-exist without any noticeable signs of affection. Besides, for poor Kitty/Felix, this is definitely not the best of times. Brought into the studio, he is trembling with terror and vocally demonstrating his fear and displeasure. Smudge isn't happy to see him at all. The sound of stereo hissing fills the air. The presenters brave it out.

After transmission, Kitty (thankfully we can drop the Felix now) mews all the way back round the North Circular and up the M1. I arrive home thoroughly chastened and with my head pounding.

Hours later, when I go to bed, I can still hear phantom mewing in my ears.

18th January 2005

Summoned upstairs to meet Anne Gilchrist (head of CBBC entertainment, under which *Blue Peter* is currently grouped) to discuss a complaint from a professor at Strathclye University, in which the press are showing some interest. It stems from a moment in our paint a plane competition when, seeking to inspire the audience, the presenters were giving their own suggestions about the kind of designs which might work on the side of a plane. Zöe's idea was to use the symbol of the Red Hand of Ulster, where she comes from. This is used by both sides of the province on everything from flags to football shirts. It was the producer's suggestion, but Zöe also called her dad to discuss it. Anyway, this professor maintains that the Red Hand has been adopted by certain paramilitary sections in the province, and is as tainted as the swastika. Naturally, the papers are sniffing around. It's my belief that we should issue a clear rebuttal; just because a tiny minority have sought to hijack the symbol, it is still widely used on both sides of the community. Other than this professor, who, it seems to me, is quite clearly a self-publicist, we have had a total of three other complaints. Hardly cause to panic. But Anne insists that we must issue a full apology. She says that the BBC is often seen as arrogant and slow to admit its mistakes, and that this is an opportunity to show that we can and do listen, and have the humility to admit when we are wrong. I accept all this but not in this context; I just don't believe that this is an example where such a total climb-down is warranted. An apology for causing unintentional offence is as far as I would go but Anne feels strongly that this isn't enough. However, given the strength of my feelings, she says that she is happy to put her name to it and this is agreed.

19th January 2005
Anne's apology reads: "We can assure you that the symbol was used in good faith and it certainly wasn't our intention to be provocative or promote sectarianism. The reason we chose to use it was because it is the official symbol of the province of Ulster. Of Ulster's nine counties, three are located in Eire and six in Northern Ireland and we were advised that both communities are equally attached to the red hand as representative of their province. *Blue Peter* never seeks to offend its audience. We take all complaints seriously and after we received yours we did some detailed investigation into it, the result of which is that we realise that the context in which we were referring to the red hand was inappropriate and mistaken. We'd like to apologise for any upset or concern we have caused."

21st January 2005
Predictably, the press, led by *The Guardian*, have gone to town on the Red Hand of Ulster ("Red faces at *Blue Peter*" indeed) and there is a definite sense of brouhaha. But Anne's unequivocal apology is now causing its own problems, as we are getting a flood of complaints from viewers in Northern Ireland offended that we have bowed to such pressure, and expressing anger and irritation that we did so. Zöe is none too impressed, either.

22nd January 2005
The Red Hand backlash continues, with a story in the *Belfast Telegraph* in which UUP Assembly member Michael Copeland describes our apology as "political correctness gone mad", pointing out that "the Red Hand appears in the symbolism of both the unionist and nationalist communities."
In the same piece, former UUP Lord Mayor of Belfast Jim Rodgers is quoted:

"We must not allow the Red Hand to be surrendered to paramilitaries. I understand that this programme, which has millions of viewers, got four complaints."
The newspaper also reports that on a prominent website "which invites comment on Northern Ireland matters, the BBC apology came under fire from a wide range of contributors."
The whole messy business has been a sobering reminder of the sensitivities which simmer around the area. We've decided to invite the BBC's Northern Ireland political editor to discuss some of the potential pitfalls with the whole production team in the hope that we can avoid being so burnt in the future.

24th January 2005
Panic stations today. The press office alert me that a newspaper has got hold of the news that Gethin is to join us as Simon's replacement. Their advice is that we should bring forward his photocall and make the announcement pronto.
"How pronto?" I ask.
"This afternoon, in time for the morning editions."
This decided, it is action stations all round. I bash out some quotes for the press release. Then there are the photos to think about. As well as a standard shot of a casually dressed Geth posing in the studio, I have to think about some kind of visual 'stunt' to offer the papers. I ask Debbie, our costume designer, to improvise a *Blue Peter* rugby kit. She covers any offending logos by carefully sewing a *Blue Peter* badge over the top. I'm a bit disappointed that she's gone for an old-school look; the shirt is too baggy and doesn't do Geth any favours. There is also no time for him to have the hair cut I think he needs. It's all very frustrating. We knock off the shots in the studio, then Geth changes before we troop out into the garden for the rugby pics. Geth's nerves are obvious and he chatters away to fill the silence.
"Last chance to change your mind, Rich," he quips.
As a couple of the presenters are away filming, we can't offer the standard 'new team' shot, so we have to make do with the dogs, Mabel and Lucy, who do not appreciate the conditions. It is filthy weather, wet and dark. My heart sinks. The attendance is poor and the set-ups are unconvincing and unexciting. However, I'm touched to see that throughout, Geth is grinning like mad, giving it his all, seemingly oblivious to getting steadily soaked and freezing cold.
"Are you all right?" I ask him, at one point.
"All right?" he echoes, incredulously. "I'm absolutely *lovin'* it. I've never been more excited in my life."

2nd February 2005
The saga of the Red Hand continues. We have been deluged with complaints

from those up in arms and offended by the craven apology we issued in response to that Strathclyde shit-stirrer. So far ten M.P.s have signed an Early Day Motion, sponsored by Democratic Unionist party M.P. Gregory Campbell on 25th January. This states "that this House notes the events that followed a children's television edition of *Blue Peter* where a suggestion was made by a Northern Ireland-born presenter that the innocent and perfectly legitimate symbol, the Red Hand of Ulster be one of a number of symbols to adorn an aircraft; and repudiates entirely the complaint to the BBC and reported statement from a professor of sociology at Strathclyde University who attempted to portray the Red Hand as a sectarian symbol ignoring the historic and non-contentious nature of the Red Hand which is worn on football, rugby, gaelic football and other sporting tops, is the centrepiece of many flags that have the loyalty of both sections of Northern Ireland Society and is widely recognized as the logo to represent either modern day Northern Ireland or ancient Ulster by people from both main communities."

Not for the first time, I wish that she'd just chosen her favourite flower instead.

7th February 2005

The first of our *Brain of Blue Peter* quiz specials; a response to requests for us to mount some major interactive specials. Technically and creatively, it's an ambitious and complex undertaking, so I've persuaded Bridget to take charge. She is brilliant and it all looks amazing. Unusually for us, we have a studio audience of kids, all of whom are cheerfully rowdy and adding to the atmosphere. The only disaster occurs when some bright spark thinks it's a good idea to try handing Smudge to Liz for one of her links. When the studio is this busy and this noisy, we usually either stand down the pets altogether or hide them away in make-up. Dragged from his peaceful sanctuary to face the crowd, poor Smudge reacts as one might expect. He goes berserk, badly clawing Liz, before making a desperate escape attempt under the audience rostra. It takes his distraught handler, Marina, some time to coax him back. Liz, dripping blood, makes light of her injury and the show goes on.

9th February 2005

A Mrs V Redmond from Plymouth writes: "No offence but that stupid Irish woman with the stupid voice, what's her name? Zöe or something, is really annoying. We don't have a problem with Irish people. My Gran is Irish so this isn't a racist issue. I realise you probably don't care but everyone in the class I teach is continually complaining about it and I said I'd do something as I agree. So please give her some kind of speech therapy. We have no idea what she is saying half the time. I like my students to feel they can express their opinions freely especially about something that is meant for them."

10th February 2005

Find a moment to reply to the Plymouth viewer: "To write 'no offence' next to 'that stupid Irish woman' strikes me as naive, or sarcastic. There is nothing stupid about Zöe. She completed four years' legal training just before she joined *Blue Peter*. And her accent may not be to your liking but it is natural and her own – and can hardly be dismissed as "stupid" in its own right. We are all in favour of people expressing their views freely – but as I hope you will appreciate with hindsight, your remarks simply read as rude and unhelpful. A new presenter always takes some time to get used to – we can only hope your pupils will grow to like Zöe as they get to know her better."

15th February 2005

Smudge is not a happy cat. Ever since the *Brain of Blue Peter* debacle, he is a shadow of his former self. Presumably, the studio is now an environment he associates with extreme trauma, and he is extremely reluctant to be involved in even the most straightforward link. Unless this proves to be a temporary state of affairs, this is going to be a real problem.

25th February 2005

Patrick Moore is in the studio and I've decided it is high time we awarded him a gold badge. He's lost none of his energy, enthusiasm and mental acuity since I last worked with him, over ten years ago, when I directed a live afternoon on CBBC celebrating the 25th anniversary of the moon landing. He is that over-used term, a "true eccentric", brilliantly able to communicate his knowledge and passion. And when we spring our little surprise, he is plainly delighted and beams from ear to ear as though it's his birthday.

28th February 2005

A tricky studio item in which we've herded together all the various contenders hoping to represent the UK in the forthcoming Eurovision Song Contest. They're here to take part in a kind of mini-quiz about the contest (our desperate attempt to jazz up the dullness of talking-head corporate PR) The most famous of the wannabes is glamour model Katie Price (aka: Jordan), who, at several months pregnant, is eye-catching in a shocking pink leather cat-suit. As the old saying goes, this leaves little to the imagination, but that turns out to be the least of our problems. There is clearly some kind of feud festering between Miss Price and another of the contestants, apparent from the mutual sniping which begins as soon as this motley group arrive in the studio. During camera rehearsals, the comments get ruder and more aggressive and, once everyone is mic'd, impossible to ignore. "Tell that fucking cunt that I'll take her any time she

wants," says our Katie. "I'm not fucking 'avin it."
Nor am I. I hurtle down the gallery stairs and head for the *Song for Europe* PR. Strong words are exchanged. His attitude is that I am over-reacting and should lighten up.
"Katie is well-known for having a strong personality and speaking her mind," he bleats. "Anyway, it's only a rehearsal, she'll rein it in on air."
I indicate a small huddle of children, visiting the studio.
"Too late for them," I say, and suggest that he has a word as a matter of urgency. "The very next 'fuck', 'cunt' or 'bastard' that I hear and she is off the show."
Sulkily, he complies, confirming my suspicion that he's rubbish at his job. If it were me, I'd have gone with the walk-out and the inevitable press stories which would have followed. Alas, whatever he says has the desired effect and La Price clams up, sulking her way through a dreary item which I would have welcomed the excuse to ditch.

1st March 2005
Pre-recording for our Bond special. Simon and Matt are immaculate in their DJs and each of the girls is glammed up to the nines as a foxy Bond girl; Liz is performing *Diamonds are Forever*, and Zöe *For Your Eyes Only*, while the boys are having a go at *A View to a Kill*. Actually, they are murdering it, but that doesn't much matter as it's all obviously tongue in cheek. Anyway, I've decided that a group-shot of them in all their Bond clobber will make the perfect shot for the endpapers in this year's annual; the only snag is that, by the time the annual is published, Simon will have left. So Gethin is here, too, similarly clad in his best bib and tucker, hovering on the sidelines and feeling awkward. This awkwardness only increases when we have finished recording and taken a first round of stills. Simon is now asked to clear and Gethin to take his place.
"Don't spare my feelings, will you?" says Simon, as he walks off set. "Not to worry. I know the way out. I'll just leave my badge on the monitor. Good luck, Gethin, and thank you very much everyone."
Everyone is laughing, except Gethin, who looks stricken.

4th March 2005
Lunch with Biddy at Julie's in Notting Hill. Pouring with rain and freezing cold. Have to choke Konnie off the phone; she is obsessing and going round in circles about her eviction from *Fame Academy* in which she has been taking part.
Biddy looks terrifically glamorous, as usual, swathed in a kind of vibrant purple cloak, with a separate fur collar. There's a nasty moment when we are climbing the stairs and she misses a step, nearly taking a stunt-style backwards tumble. The waiter, right behind her, wouldn't have stood a chance.

"Watch out," he says.
"Too late for that," she raps back, sailing forward, her *sang-froid* intact.
Conversation rattles away and there is never a dull moment. I try to explain some of the current politics and the general feeling that Dot, our head, is woefully deficient. In some ways, it doesn't sound as if much has changed: "Children's programmes are wheeled out when they are useful," agrees Biddy, "but other than that nobody is interested. Dot will have to be caught with her hands in the till, or found to be grossly negligent, for anyone to do anything about her."
Inevitably, we talk a lot about appeals and presenters, the two things which she says used to keep her awake at night, and which now do the same for me. She admires Liz very much, approves of both Simon and Matt, and likes the look of Gethin. "He's a taff, isn't he?"
She's not keen on Konnie and so far Zöe leaves her cold, although it's early days.
"Simon Groom started out as a mistake," she continues, "but we persevered with him because he was a real person."
But he wasn't easy to manage. She talks of his moods and tantrums, and occasional outbursts of jealousy about Peter Duncan. He claimed that, in notes, Biddy "picked on every little word" and wouldn't allow him any jokes or ad-libs. Simon once turned up on Biddy's doorstep at three in the morning with some bee in his bonnet.
"I was in bed fast asleep," she says, "but I got up and let him in."
Peter Purves she brands "boring", and mentions that, like Simon Groom with Pete Duncan, Purves was jealous of Noakes. "He hated being the straight man, you see," she says. "But that's who he was; the heavy."
She recalls some time in the late 60s, having to do the programme at Riverside. "Purves had an awful black girlfriend called Gloria," she says, "who came after him with a gun!"
I wonder if I have heard right.
"I got a call in the gallery," she continues, "'Miss Baxter, we have a lady in reception. She's demanding to see Mr Purves and she's waving a gun."
Biddy relates that Edward (Barnes) always says that she should have shown the woman the way to Purves' dressing room!
I asked her what she actually did. "I told them that she couldn't see him of course and stayed put in the gallery."
Amazingly, this seemed to do the trick and there was no further melodrama.
"But I was never so glad when a programme was over and I could go home!" Biddy adds.
She is a good counsellor. "Editors are rarely popular," she tells me, "but you must stick to your guns and do what you think is right."

14th March 2005

Exhilarating, exhausting day in the studio for our 4000th programme. This is all the result of a particular OCD of mine; when I first joined the show, I quickly realised that the numbering system was inconsistent. Over the years, human error had missed a show here, or not counted another there. I decided to clearly define the rules and then, applying these consistently, to get someone reliable to do a thorough and comprehensive count, right from the very beginning. I asked our most experienced PA, Lucy, whose forensic attention to detail and perfectionism form more than her professional pride; they are part of her identity, too. Lucy interrogated the criteria I gave her, and then set to the task with a will. When I realised that the grand totalling up meant that we were fast approaching the milestone number 4000, I knew that we would be missing a trick not to make a song and dance of it.

Quite literally, in fact – one of the first items I booked was the cast of the new production of *Mary Poppins* to sing *Supercallifragilistic*. Those outside the business are always surprised to learn that, despite the promotional aspect of these performances, BBC rules mean that we still have to pay all the performers and musicians from any show or pop group that we feature. With a cast and orchestra the size of this show, it makes the item very expensive indeed. It also has to be pre-recorded in the morning, so that the cast can get back to the theatre for a matinée.

As well as classic clips chosen by the presenters and the audience, we pepper the show with various gold badge awards. One will be to our principal studio guest, film star Ewan McGregor, for his ceaseless charity work. He is outstandingly charming and clearly thrilled to be here, albeit surprisingly nervous. Indeed, just before we go on air, he tells me that he has never been as nervous as this before – "not only because it's live, but because *Blue Peter* matters to me so much." There is nothing starry about him whatsoever. He tells me that he once sent his own recipe for bird cake into the programme and I immediately ask him to repeat this on air. He agrees readily to everything we want him to do, fully involved from the start of the show (with the presenters riding into the studio on a giant-sized shopping trolley) to the inevitable array of publicity shots which follow transmission.

The other 'celebrity' gold badge is going to David Beckham, again for his charity work. Turns out that he, like McGregor, grew up glued to *Blue Peter* and actually credits a football item featured on the programme back in 1985 for getting him into the game in the first place. Sadly, he can't come to the studio, so we agree to film with him this morning and turn it round in time for transmission. As soon as his booking was confirmed, all the presenters started to lobby for the job of interviewing him and whipping out the gold. But I decided that it would mean

the most to Liz. She is delighted, and slightly incredulous, which makes me feel I've made the right choice.
"There's only one condition," I tell her. "You can't lose it and start talking gibberish."
"I can't promise that," she laughs. "Actually, I can. I promise I'll hold it together, until I've given him the badge anyway. Oh Rich, thank you. I'm so excited!"
The show is a total triumph from start to finish.

15th March 2005
In the wake of our big 4000th, predictable silence from above, but a pleasing email from Biddy, congratulating us on a "stunning" programme. "I sat entranced," she writes. "There was such a warm and happy atmosphere. It really was like being part of a family. For me the programme lasted about five minutes and it was a joy throughout."
Before I shared this with the team, I did delete her comments that, in her view, it "couldn't have presented better evidence for BP *not* going to Manchester. How on earth (and at what cost) could you have got the *Mary Poppins* cast up there, or secured Ewan McGregor when he had to attend his premiere in Leicester Square if you were Manchester-based? You wouldn't have had them."

18th March 2005
It doesn't get more showbiz than this. We are in an enormous British Airways hangar at Heathrow for the live OB in which we will announce the winners of our 'paint-a-plane' competition. As usual, the programme starts with the presenters at the seat unit, apparently in our normal studio. But then the camera pulls back and cranes up, to reveal that we have transported the entire set into this enormous hangar, and that looming behind it, is the actual plane on which the winning design will be painted. It's a fabulous piece of theatre and it's costing a fortune, but it is also everything that's best about this show; unique, ambitious, high-quality factual entertainment. On transmission, as the big reveal takes place, I can feel the hairs rising on the back of my neck and my stomach cartwheeling my excitement.

21st March 2005
Chris Eccleston is in the studio today, to promote the return of *Doctor Who.* This booking has not been without pain. Months ago, when I first met with Russell T Davies and Phil Collinson, we came up with a package of ways in which we might promote the show. Top of the list was a live appearance from the new Doctor and his companion.
"Oh, that's easy," said Phil.

Famous last words. Having trailed the fact that both Eccleston and Billie Piper were going to be here, I am less than delighted to discover that Piper can no longer make it.

"She's really ill," says her agent, by way of explanation. "I'm sorry but she's just not up to it."

This is disappointing but then it occurs to me that we filmed an interview with Piper during our behind-the-scenes on the *Doctor Who* set last November. I get the director to hurriedly put together a little package which we can play in, and, on air, we send a 'get well soon' message to poor sick Billie.

Having been warned that Eccleston might be tricky, it is a relief to discover that, from our point of view, he is a complete delight. He is softly spoken, scrupulously polite and affects to be interested in every aspect of the show. He asks detailed questions about everything and, unlike many actors, he's good at listening. The only problem is that he takes our questions very seriously and some of the answers are rather dense and 'grown-up'. After the run-through, I ask him to bear in mind the age of the core audience but he gets it straightaway. He is a pleasure to work with. I am glad, however, that I earlier decided to cut altogether an item about (supposedly) the world's largest whoopie cushion, which he was down to demonstrate. Not very respectful to any guest, I'd say, and this one is Doctor fucking Who!

22nd March 2005

Not best pleased to see that, far from being unwell and confined to her sick bed, Billie Piper, is pictured in the pages of today's tabloids, out and about with her ex-husband, Chris Evans, looking full of the joys of spring. I get on the phone to the agent and have a rant.

But it quickly transpires that there is more to Billie Piper dropping out than mere whim. Nobody wants to upset the agent, as Piper is key to plans for a second series. My complaint has put a few backs up. Somewhat fraught email exchange follows with *Doctor Who* exec Julie Gardner, for whom this is all an additional and unwanted headache. I feel sorry for her; she is such a lovely woman and has been so helpful, and now I wish I'd just mourned it and moved on. As ever, speak in haste, repent at leisure.

23-24th March 2005

Out of the office for a couple of days, filming a story about National Service with Matt and Gethin. We're working with the Khaki Chums, the same group of historians and re-enactors who created the First War trench in which I nearly froze to death a few years ago. This time we are actually using a full-scale disused army base and, together with the Chums' trademark attention to detail with props and costumes, it's going to be a wonderfully authentic-looking film. I got the idea after hearing some of my father's memories of his National Service and I've included one of them in the script; a parade in which the officer in charge scrapes a cigarette paper along their chin to inspect how closely they have shaved.

For me, the shoot is an interesting opportunity to watch the dynamic between Matt and Geth at close quarters. This kind of film is a breeze for Matt (come to that, what film isn't?) and it allows him to indulge his natural ability to deliver a performance infused with humour. Geth isn't bad either, managing to channel his own slightly hapless quality into the somewhat forlorn character he is playing. Geth *longs* for Matt's approval. He works hard, throwing himself into every take. When he feels like it, Matt will crack a joke that includes his co-presenter, and no one is more delighted and receptive than Geth. But it's all very cat-and-mouse. For all the occasional fun and laughter, there are also sudden moments of ridicule or reproof, and these destabilise Geth's always fragile confidence. He assumes a hunted expression and his head goes down until Matt feels inclined to be generous and include him again. Always, Matt is the leader and Geth the follower, and this is, I think, at the heart of what frustrates Matt about Gethin; to thrive and feel happy, he needs the spur of genuine competition. He definitely wants to do better than anyone else, no doubt about that, but to get there he wants a fair fight and not a rollover.

29th March 2005

Hot on the heels of the red flag farrago, a further round of media madness is brewing, all thanks to the latest busybody with a self-publicising agenda. This time it's a "retired teacher" from Somerset, who apparently heard an interview with Zöe in which she explained that she had got the job after responding to an advert we placed in the *Belfast Telegraph*. This man did some digging and was told, correctly, that our adverts had been placed in *The Scotsman*, the *Belfast Telegraph*, *Scotland On Sunday*, the Belfast edition of *Sunday Life*, *Disability Now*, *The Guardian* and *The Stage*. He promptly reported us to the Commission for Racial Equality on the basis that we discriminated against other ethnic groups as we predominantly advertised the job in newspapers in Belfast and Scotland. Not content with this, he has also gone to the press, accusing us of "crackpot political correctness" and bleating that "They specifically set out to recruit from Ulster and Scotland to find people of a Celtic origin and, in my view, that amounts to racial discrimination. Somebody clearly said they wanted someone with an Irish or Scottish accent. What about the other people with regional and rural accents? I am irritated by the hypocrisy of the BBC because they overtly state their equal opportunities credentials, yet they clearly have a

covert ethnic and cultural agenda for the programme."
We've issued a rebuttal, pointing out, perfectly truthfully, that the search was the "widest ever undertaken by Children's BBC," and that, as well as the national ads we took out, we were also seeking to increase potential opportunities among communities currently under-represented on the BBC. What, one asks, is wrong with that? Nothing; as I confidently predict to be the verdict of any independent enquiry. Pity the CRE for having to waste their time with it. What's the betting that the papers won't exactly be rushing to print that the story is all a load of bollocks? This "retired teacher" must be delightedly rubbing his hands at his five minutes of newsprint fame.

And indeed nothing whatever was ever heard of this complaint again, least of all from the CRE.

4th April 2005
We have a new leader. Well, not quite yet, but on the horizon. Dot has been moved sideways to become controller of production resources ("Head of paper clips" as it's been widely referred to within the department).
Her replacement is to be Alison Sharman, who has been a very successful controller of daytime. She's known to be dynamic, ruthless, super-ambitious and not afraid of double denim with rhinestone detailing. Opinion seems to be divided about her merits as far as they might relate to CBBC, but I'm looking forward to working for someone who actually has an opinion.
Liz is off to Vegas to interview Elton John and award him a gold badge. This is a plum job and it's also a sweetener because I've decided it's just not practical for Liz to join the others going to Japan on the summer expedition. She isn't happy about this; her view is that, even if she couldn't manage the whole month-long shoot, she could take part in a week or two, assuming Toddy flew out with her. But even if this were possible, we just can't afford to send five presenters (and one baby and spouse) when the trip doesn't really require them. I've promised that she will still be kept busy during the same period. My idea is to make use of her availability for a series of films about eccentric hobbies and unusual activities taking place across the UK; perfect for her quirky style and our summer schedule.

6th April 2005
Pleased to receive a supportive email from Lewis Bronze over the widely reported press stories that we have been reported to the CRE over our recruitment of Zöe. "I had similar (actually quite sinister) comments when I hired Diane," he writes. "But nothing ever moves forward unless you take some proactive steps. Stick to your guns."

11th April 2005

There's been a serious falling out between Matt and Zöe. For the last few weeks, they've been making a special programme about the tough world of competitive ballroom dancing. I've called this *Blood, Sweat and Sequins,* and it looks as if it has lived up to its hyperbolic title.

Until now, Matt has been one of Zöe's foremost supporters and vocal fans; but the process of making this one show seems to have totally destroyed his faith in her, and really made him dislike her. The director says that he got increasingly frustrated because she found it hard to let him 'lead' during their dance. Matt is the ultra-perfectionist and was apparently harsh with her about her mistakes. When I speak to him, he is critical about more than just her dancing, slating her attitude, what he perceives as her arrogance and questioning her motives for being a presenter. It is worrying because, other than inevitable minor and temporary disputes, I cannot remember a time when there has been any serious falling out between presenters. Matt seems to have made up his mind; he is adamant that he got her all wrong and that she's bad news. When I speak to Zöe, she makes light of it all, admitting that she couldn't stop 'leading' and dismissing the dispute as merely the natural tension of the competition. I hope she's right.

25th April 2005

Simon's last show, and we go to town to try to give him the kind of send-off he deserves. It starts with him abseiling down from the roof of TC1, then taking a motorised sofa into the studio, where the cast of *We Will Rock You* perform (Queen being Simon's all-time favourite band). There are messages from Brian May, Gary Lineker, the RAF Falcons, and his former *Blue Peter* colleagues. We reboot the super-hot curry challenge (Simon still makes this look easy; the man must have an asbestos mouth) and bring in Barney Harwood and Lizo Mzimba for a final burst of lederhosen dancing. It is a riot, and rushes past, until we are at the closing moments and Simon's chance to ad-lib his own goodbye. Being the ultimate pro, Simon has, of course, carefully thought through what he wants to say, but it remains heartfelt and, up in the gallery, I'm not the only one with blurred eyes and a lump in my throat.

After the show, the farewell party and in my speech, I relate the story of how, very early on, I overheard Simon refusing the other presenters' suggestions that, to avoid being cast in them, he should do deliberately badly with his first dressing-up item. Ignoring this peer pressure, he told them, "I'm going to do everything I'm given as well as I can."

He's certainly delivered on that intention. I relate one of the few times he did lose his cool; when I broke it to him that he would be forced to miss a key moment of the 2002 World Cup so that he could take part in yet another

costumed extravaganza. In honour of all the many times he suffered under make-up and costumes, I present him with his hated wig from *Christmas at the Club Blue Peter*, which he unceremoniously drops-kicks across the studio.
He has been a brilliant presenter, funny, reliable, resilient, and versatile – and a good friend, too. I'm going to miss him like mad.
When I go back to the office, I find a card on my desk. The cover shows a photo of the Golden Gate bridge. "It was on this bridge that we filmed one of my most memorable pieces to camera," writes Simon. "I find it hard to believe that it's all over and that the days of wigs and frocks are gone. I want to thank you, not just for being a brilliant Editor, but for being a friend and a director who taught me a lot – most notably what to do with my arms!!
"I know I'm going to miss it enormously. With all this free time ahead, there's only one thing for it – down the gym and let's pump those arms up!"

26th April 2005
Geth finally makes his first appearance on the show, dressed as Batman, during an item about classic superheroes. The skin-tight black rubber costume absolutely reeks – "sponsored by Goodyear" I call him. For Zöe, I think that having a run-up of a few months filming and observing before her on-screen debut was helpful, I'm not sure with Gethin. In some ways, it seems to have stoked his nerves. I'm glad that the honeymoon period is finally over, and he can feel that he's properly one of the team and not some kind of support act forever waiting in the wings.
We break the news that Meg is expecting her first litter. "That bitch is catching you up," I tease Liz. "You'll have to have triplets next time round, or she'll have won. Fur and feather..."

24th May 2005
The times they are a-changin'. Hot on the spiky heels of our new leader, Alison Sharman, is the news of the man she's appointed her second-in-command, or as the ludicrous title would have it 'Chief Operating Officer'. His name is Richard Deverell and he's been working in news interactive. He's supposed to supply the strategic digital knowledge and wherewithal which Sharman feels is lacking in the department. He looks likes the part; an archetypal boffin with a earnestly geeky aura, and he arrives next month.

25th May 2005
The Smudge situation has not improved. If anything, it is getting progressively worse. We will have to retire him if we can't sort it; it is just too cruel to keep dragging such an unhappy cat into the studio. As a last resort, I've suggested we

book an animal psychologist to work with Smudge; filming the process so that the audience are in on the problem. Then, if we have to cut our losses, they will understand why.

2nd June 2005

I've spent much of the break writing the script for this year's Christmas extravaganza. This makes a welcome change from spending most of my summer holiday scribbling away, distracted and absent, while the family enjoy themselves around me.

This time, I've decided to structure my story in two-parts, with a cliffhanger. By spreading it across a couple of shows, it increases the budget I can devote to it. As well as writing it, I'm going to direct too. It will be the first time since *Club Blue Peter* that I've attempted something on this scale; another all-singing, all-dancing affair, this time set in New York, in the era of my youth, the 1980s. I've called it *Christmas on the Cover*, because it's based in the world of glossy magazines (in this universe, *Blue Peter* magazine is not a kids' comic but a top-flight *Vogue*-esque fashion title) and the idea is to parody the style and look of 1980s American TV shows like *Dynasty* and *Charlie's Angels*.

In a case of art (if you can call it that) reflecting life, I've written Zöe as the arch villainess, an ice-maiden Editor, all big hair and glamour, with Liz as her kooky but downtrodden assistant. Geth will play Liz's sweet but dopy friend and love interest, with Matt again in two roles; one as a sharp-suited big businessman, and the other as an ultra-camp Boy George-type stylist called Ricco. I'm thinking that Matt can use his impression of Britney Spears' camp backing dancer, which is bang on and brilliant. Konnie I'm going to make an elderly Jewish café owner, a total shrew with a huge bouffant wig and a line in nasty floral frocks. I know she will seize on the humour of this and play it for all it's worth.

20th June 2005

Liz has asked for a meeting. She cuts to the chase. "Rich, I want to leave," she says.

Though I'm not entirely surprised, I ask for her reasons. She tells me that she hated being left out of the Japan trip. "It felt awful," she explains, "like I was being punished for having a baby."

I don't think this is fair, and say so, but recognise this is more about feelings than facts. We have honoured our promise to keep Liz busy filming during the break, but, unfortunately, she has hated most of these stories. She cites a particularly horrendous experience shooting the ancient Somerset custom of 'cheese rolling'. This was sold to me as a quirky olde-English tradition which would make an unusual and fun item. The reality is that the event is a poorly organised piss-up, attracts hordes of rowdy locals. Liz became a target for constant lewd and unpleasant remarks. She says that the director was out of her depth, and the whole experience was scary and unsafe.

"And it's going to be a shit film," she concludes, "so it wasn't even worth it."

She reserves especial scorn, however, for her four-day filming trip on board the Royal Navy's HMS Illustrious. I chose her for this partly because I'm getting a bit sick of all the services films being fronted by the boys and I thought Liz would bring out the humour and humanity of life as a sailor on a working ship. This time the director was totally in charge; Alex is far and away our most experienced film-maker. But Liz has never liked him. She feels that he doesn't listen to her or respect her point of view. It doesn't help that most of his films are physically tough and often take place in remote locations. Liz shudders when she recalls a few days spent in a Vietnamese village with Alex (who tends to shoot his stories solo) where she felt completely abandoned and misunderstood. From her point of view, HMS Illustrious wasn't much better.

"I was just really homesick," she tells me. "Trapped on that bloody ship, with Alex barking at me all the time. I kept thinking, 'what am I doing here?' That isn't right. If you're a *Blue Peter* presenter you should be loving every minute, not hating the whole thing."

I have to agree with this and, while all this is incredibly sad to hear, I admire her honesty.

She brings up the casting of Zöe; how it felt as if she were being usurped and replaced while she was still on the show. I'm well aware, of course, that Liz dislikes Zöe and finds her fake, but I wonder if she would have been able to accept anyone in her place. I guess the psychology of the situation was all wrong from the start. Hindsight isn't ever much use. I remind her how different things felt a year ago. Despite the fact that she was pregnant, I had extended Liz's contract for a couple of years, showing my absolute commitment to her. But we were about to go five-times-a-week and neither of us could predict how quickly Liz would return to working full-time, or even how she would feel about it once her baby was born. Given the circumstances, a fifth presenter felt essential. Now I do wonder if we could have managed without, and avoided the disruption and angst which has followed in Zöe's wake. Not Zöe's fault for seizing the opportunity; but so far only Konnie seems really at ease with her.

The 'personality' issues aren't the only factor. Liz has inevitably found being a working mother a strain, especially as her job takes place in a spotlight. Initially, she was happy to make a few films featuring Dex. But then she became aware that viewers watched these with a sometimes critical eye, and there were complaints about her bottle feeding. Understandably, these really upset Liz and make her disinclined to let us film Dex any more.

Throughout all this, I'm thinking on the spot, and wondering what to do for the best. There's a school of thought that, once a presenter decides to go, it's wise to hustle them off as soon as possible. The reasoning for this is that their attitude changes and they lose the essential mindset for the work. They can also spread discontent and a bad atmosphere among those who remain. But I don't believe that these will apply to Liz. She's a thoroughly genuine person and I trust her. I suggest that she stays until next Easter, and that we will guarantee her a couple of major projects for her final months so that she can go out on the high she deserves. She agrees to this and seems relieved. We share a hug and later she texts me: "Rich, I'll be sad 2 leave but I'm really happy for decision. Thank you, x."

23rd June 2005

Full house for the *Blue Peter* prom at the Royal Albert Hall. As one might expect, the audience for this event is unmistakably well-heeled and middle-class. As everyone takes their seats and during the interval, the air echoes with cries of "Olivia, do leave Theo alone" and parents grumbling about the quality of the wine in the bar. "This is supposed to be a Merlot, darling, can you believe it?"
My principal contribution to the running order is the inclusion of a full-orchestral version of Ron Grainer's original theme music for *Doctor Who.* It sounds magnificent, really thrilling, as is the reaction of the kids in the audience. The unlikely rebirth of *Doctor Who* couldn't delight me more.

24th June 2005

Alison Sharman is certainly a change from Dot. She's small, blonde and wired, moving around her office constantly, laughing often and delighting in what might be called a free and frank exchange of views. She doesn't hold back. Not for nothing is her nickname 'The Sharminator'.
My first 'official' encounter follows her meeting with Ian Prince, the Editor of *Newsround.* He leaves the room looking pale and slightly shell-shocked. "Good luck," he murmurs, in passing.
"What do you think of him?" demands Alison, as soon as the door is closed. She doesn't wait for my answer. "Seems wet to me. A bit spineless. I want people who are passionate about the content, who have an opinion. He's like a vicar." She is staring at me, searchingly.
"I have plenty of opinions," I tell her, determined to measure up but not trash my colleagues, whatever my views of them.
"Well, the good news is that I rate *Blue Peter.* It's a very important show. I've been watching a bit and it's in pretty good shape. I think the boys are great, especially Matt. But I'm not a fan of the girls. I think you should sack them as soon as possible."

"All of them?" I query.
She nods. "They don't do it for me."
I explain that Liz is leaving anyway ("that's good"), but that Konnie and Zöe are both on long-term contract.
"Look into it. Maybe we can get rid of them earlier."
She is spectacularly indiscreet; wants to know my views on most of her senior team, sharing her own candid remarks as encouragement. Naturally, I am cautious, wary of traps, wondering what she will soon be saying about me. But it's clear that she's very quickly worked out the obvious deadwood in the department. I don't fancy their chances much. Others I have spoken to find her terrifying and I can quite see why. But to me, she is quite fascinating too, with her machine-gun delivery of opinions and personal prejudices. I admire her naked ambition for the output, too. She wants us to get noticed.
"*Blue Peter* can be a massive part of that. I want you to think big; don't worry about what it costs, if the idea is good enough we will find the money. There's been too much cautious thinking for too long."
I give her an overview of the major projects on the horizon and she seems satisfied for the time being.

28th June 2005

I'm in Paris to shoot a special and a couple of additional stories with Zöe and Gethin. This morning, a brutally early call at a bakers to film the making of croissants. 'Process' films, as we call them, which follow baking or making something, are popular with the audience (most kids like to know how something familiar is put together) but they are usually deadly dull to shoot. They take so much time and present endless continuity problems because you have to cover every stage in a useable wide-shot together with brilliant, precise close-ups to bring the process to life. Above all, everything must be crystal clear, because, as soon as you are vague, kids will lose interest and switch off. The conditions often don't help; they may be cramped, boiling hot or freezing cold, or smell to high heaven (contenders for worst stink: Isle of Man kipper processing plant or Cadbury's chocolate factory).
The bakery, however, smells delightful; though I am amazed and horrified by the quantity of butter which goes into each croissant. Gethin does well with the sequence, establishing an easy rapport with the baker, and doing everything he is bidden with precision and skill. Perhaps because of the early start and the demands of several hours of intense concentration, by the time we are filming links around the Champs-Elysées and on top of the Arc de Triomphe, Geth has relapsed into giddier mode, joking around and not paying attention. The sun is particularly hot and I've forgotten to bring a hat (filming essential in any

weather) so I'm extra grumpy anyway. So Gethin gets a bollocking, and bridles at what he sees as the injustice. I'm not having it.
"Just shut up, stand on your mark and say your words."
He retreats like a kicked cat and we go again.
Later, out of the glare of the sun, and feeling more reasonable, I admit that I may have been a bit hard on him.
"You wouldn't talk to Matt like that," he says, sorrowfully.
"I did once," I tell him. "But the difference is that Matt knows what he's doing now so I don't need to any more."
Geth nods and looks serious. He wants to be liked, but he wants to be good, too. Sometimes these ambitions are not mutually compatible.

29th June 2005

Only Zöe would turn up to film in the sewers wearing a white floor-length skirt, trimmed with *broderie anglaise*, teamed with a flimsy pair of flip-flops. She is quite unrepentant and I almost admire her fashion *chutzpah*. I'm the only one.
"That's going to look lovely, splattered with shit," says Adrian the cameraman, cynically.
Gethin is equally incredulous and tries to make fun of Zöe. He doesn't get very far as she simply freezes him out. It's quite a skill she has, proper ice-maiden stuff. Generally, she treats Geth as though he were an annoying younger brother, or, perhaps more precisely, an annoying younger brother's even more annoying friend.
A dank metal stairwell beckons and down we all go. I make sure to take a low-angled cutaway shot of Zöe's flip-flops flapping through the frame, to show that no fucks were given. And, by some strange alchemy, she later emerges from the shoot without any visible signs of muck on her person.

30th June 2005

We have been given permission to film within the palace of Versailles. Thankfully, some of the private apartments are closed to the public, so that makes life easier, but there are a handful of key pieces-to-camera which we must shoot in the grander rooms, in the brief intervals between tour parties. This puts immense pressure on both the cameraman and presenter. Gethin, at least, has worked to learn his words. But his interpretation of them generally needs a fair degree of direction, taking time we don't have. We rehearse an ambitious shot which will take him from Marie Antoinette's bedchamber, through the door in the wall, down the corridor behind, and into the private chambers beyond. We have just enough time for one take before the bedchamber is invaded by hordes of tourists – or 'oompa loompas' as I tend to call them. If we have to wait for

them to clear, we will slip dangerously behind schedule so the pressure is on.
"Camera ready," says Adrian, quietly. I glance over to Gethin, who is in his opening position, looking a little queasy with nerves.
"Whatever you do, don't fuck it up, all right?" I tell him, adding unhelpfully, "It's at times like this I'm glad that I'm on this side of the camera and not yours. Good luck everyone!"
Gethin is word-perfect, and Adrian declares the shot a triumph. We retrace our steps, push past the 'oompa loompas', and move on to our next set up, jubilant with success.

2nd July 2005

A day at Disneyland Paris. I have distinctly mixed feelings about returning, having last filmed here when I was producing *Disney Club*. It was pretty grim. The park police 'arrested' and detained one of our presenters for trying to have a sneaky fag behind a bush. One minute he was there, the next minute these jobsworths had whipped him away, and I had to plead for him to be allowed back to film. Then we were filming on the nauseatingly twee ride *It's a Small World* when it broke and we were stuck inside for a couple of hours, while the chorus of the song went round and round in a perpetual loop. We felt like we were undergoing some kind of ruthless brainwashing technique. Maybe we were.
Disney are the kings of corporate control. Everything within this place is designed to conform to the rigid dictates of one of the world's most powerful brands. As guests of the company, we exist within the very definition of a gilded cage. Luxurious rooms, complimentary meals (no alcohol), accompanied everywhere by staff ("hosts") whose waxen smiles and over-friendly manners don't camouflage their determination to keep us on message. However, I don't anticipate any problems as, when we were setting up the shoot back in London, we discussed and agreed the rides and activities we would film. The main event will be Zöe and Geth taking part in the daily grand parade of floats, dressed as Mary Poppins and Bert.
It is when we are waiting to set up one of the linking sequences that the atmosphere suddenly sours and I discover that we have a problem. The wafer-thin premise for our filming is that Zöe has happy memories of a childhood holiday here. Her only regret was that she didn't get to meet Mickey. I have written this into the script, with a 'moment' where she finally gets a welcome and warm embrace from Mickey. Ah, how cute, or 'pass the sick bag Alice', depending on your age and point of view.
We arrange to meet Mickey (or rather the unfortunate out-of-work actor having to wear the suit today) near the backdrop of Disney's iconic fairy castle. But

before we can begin setting up, one of our minders asks to have a word.
"I'm really, really sorry, but we can't allow this," he says, in tones of 'this is hurting me more than you.'
"But we agreed it with the press office," I insist.
"I am so sorry," continues the minder, placatingly. "*Totally* our bad. There must have been some kind of misunderstanding. You see, we can't imply that kids who come on vacation here won't get a chance to meet Mickey."
"That's what happened to Zöe, though. It's the whole point of the story; why she still wants to meet Mickey now."
"She can meet Mickey. *Absolutely* she can. She just can't say she didn't meet him back when she was a kid."
"So you want us to lie?"
"No!," says the minder, sounding suitably shocked. "We're just asking you to leave out a little detail."
I don't react very well to this. After all, we have been completely upfront and transparent about our script and intentions. I suggest that, in the circumstances, perhaps we should scrap the filming altogether and leave. This causes a panic. The drones want us to comply, not walk out. That would be an epic PR fail. I wonder what the penalty might be? Six months' service screwed into a character mask on the grand parade? Site engineer for *It's a Small World*?
There is a stand-off while one of our minders rushes off to raise someone from the press office. The crew look for a coffee (though the food and drink are free, sadly it's all pretty disgusting) while Zöe and I sit on the grass and gossip. She's always willing to chat, but she never gives very much away. I think how little I still know her or have any sense of her real thoughts, opinions, passions and prejudices.
The minder returns with press office person and they try a tag team approach to get me back on side. I've no real intention of leaving; we've shot too much good stuff and viewers won't care one way or another about the Mickey sequence. It crosses my mind that I could just shoot the encounter and then have Zöe relate the story of her childhood disappointment in commentary. But instead I just drop the entire sequence. The thought police are aghast.
"We really wanna work something out for you guys here," says the press officer. I refrain from saying, "actually, what you want is for us to do what we're told," and simply insist that as we can't lie about Zöe's experience, it is best just to cut it out.
So Mickey is sent packing, and Zöe misses out on her hug all over again.

3rd July 2005
Most of the day devoted to filming Zöe rehearsing and then performing the Can Can in a slightly down-at-heel Paris nightclub, the Moulin Rouge having politely

declined. Zöe knows this is a moment for her to really shine, and she throws herself into the process. It's all encompassing for her, but much duller for the rest of us, as we only need so many shots of the rehearsals. Besides, we are all distracted and worried by the state of our PA, Mignon. Just before we came away on the shoot, she spent a wet weekend at a music festival. Her feet were stuck inside damp wellies the entire time, and one of them has picked up some kind of infection. Could it be trench foot? To begin with, we joked about it and referred to her having the ultimate in middle-class garden accessories, a 'feature' verdigris foot.

But it has been getting steadily worse, and today Mignon is in so much discomfort and distress that, despite her stolid insistence to the contrary, it is obvious she shouldn't be working. We send her off to be checked out by a doctor, and the verdict is that she must return home immediately and go to hospital. So she leaves us, and we are all worried about her, and sad to see her go.

Later that evening, Zöe takes to the stage, made up to the nines, and Can-Cans to perfection.

4th July 2005

Spend much of the morning filming sequences in, around and up the Eiffel Tower. The weather is sunny, but the higher we ascend, the windier and colder it becomes. Yet again, Zöe is not clad for the conditions and she is soon so cold that we resort to wrapping her in the large silver reflector, which is used to boost the light on a close-up. It acts like those silver foil capes they hand out during marathons, so, although her teeth continue to chatter and she looks pretty miserable, we don't lose her to hypothermia.

Taking the piss out of Gethin has become a bad habit. Almost every time he opens his mouth, I'm slating him or sending him up. He has the occasional go back, but most of the time, I'm having the last word. I can't seem to stop myself. It comes to a head during a journey in our van from one location to another. When we pull up at our destination, Geth gets his revenge by pulling me sideways out of the vehicle, in a singularly undignified fashion.

"You big plum!" he says. "You can beat me with words, but I'll always have better guns."

Which is true.

5th July 2005

We swing by the Moulin Rouge. Although they refused us permission for the Can-Can story, I want a piece to camera outside the club for which the dance is most famous. There is nothing particularly complex or onerous in the words, but for some reason, Geth runs aground. Over and over again, we have a go;

over and over again, he forgets where he is, or jumbles up the words, or becomes distracted and has to stop. It is *agony* to watch, not least because he beats himself up badly for it and becomes trapped in his own nightmare, and virtually unreachable to the director. I think about giving the words to Zöe, but this would be an even more disastrous dagger to his morale, so we persevere. But there is no sense of achievement when the piece is finally, at long last, in the can. Instead, we are all weary, cold and defeated, and Gethin's self-disgust is as pungent as cheap perfume.

6th July 2005

Thankfully, we finish our trip with a few hours enjoyable nonsense, filming Gethin modelling so-called 'high fashion' around the Pompidou centre. There are no words to worry about and he is perfectly happy when all he has to do is strike a few poses and try to look mean and moody in his clobber. There is a thin line between boyish and immature, but fortunately Gethin leans further towards the former than the latter. He has a great energy, and sweetness of nature that all the crew love; he doesn't need to be asked to help carry the kit or generally muck in. He prides himself on being a team player and this in itself can prove a problem. Sometimes presenters need to be selfish and just focus on what they are being asked to do; Geth will be 'one of the gang' until suddenly everyone slips into their professional mode and he is left out, unprepared and exposed like the loser in a game of musical chairs.

His desperate keenness to improve can be another handicap. Last night was a textbook example – he wants to do well so badly that, when he doesn't, his frustration with himself is horrible to witness and difficult to help. I'm glad that this is not how our trip ends. Quite apart from the actual work, and the fun of being back at the coal face, for me it has been an illuminating experience to spend the time with our two new presenters. It is a great pity that they don't have any genuine rapport or common ground. As a result, they co-exist and fake some degree of bonhomie, but aren't truly there for each other.

18th July 2005

My 39th birthday and our first show of the new season. Matt comes to see me, in serious mood. He has just made what sounds like an exceptionally arduous film about medieval jousting and he isn't happy about it.

"Rich, it was seriously unsafe," he says. "I could easily have been killed. I'm sitting on this massive horse, wearing a heavy suit of armour. The ground is wet and ridiculously slippy. And then we're charging away at each other. I was actually frightened. I didn't feel in control at any point."

This is not good to hear, and I promise I'll look into it. I've directed enough to know that there is sometimes a disconnect between what is planned, agreed and allowed for on a schedule and hazard assessment form and what actually happens on the day. But you have to presume a level of common sense too. Matt feels that he is being asked to raise the bar with virtually every film and he's worried about how sustainable this, and at what point he will suffer as a result of it. I remind him that he, too, has a responsibility for health and safety; that he doesn't have to, indeed mustn't, film, if he feels at risk or in danger. Of all the presenters, I'd say he is the least afraid of speaking his mind.

Inevitably, the director tells a slightly different story; he agrees that the conditions were a concern but says that Matt, once engaged with the story, was absolutely committed to undertaking the joust. We talk through the various disaster scenarios that might so easily have occurred and it is obvious a wider discussion is needed with the films producer and production manager. Our health and safety is an area in which we must not and cannot afford to make even one mistake.

19th July 2005

Launch of the *Doctor Who* 'design-a-monster' competition. In the morning, we record a creepy pre-titles designed to echo the early section of *Rose*, the story which first brought the Doctor back to life. The studio is dark and deserted. Gethin is looking for the other presenters when his eye is caught by something in one of the equipment stores just off the floor. He goes to take a look. Three mannequins loom in the half-light. As he investigates, suddenly these twitch into life. There is a wheezing, groaning sound and a familiar blue box appears, out of which Zöe emerges, yelling to Geth to jump inside. The Autons (for it is they) are on the rampage now, so Geth needs no second bidding, hurtling into the TARDIS. The doors slam and the box vanishes into thin air. Run titles.

This doesn't sound like much to record but, in an unwelcome reminder of how long shooting a drama can take, it actually eats up a couple of hours of studio time. This is painfully apparent to me because I've volunteered to play one of the Autons.

When it was first suggested, I didn't give it much thought. "Oh yeah, that'll be fun," was about the size of it. The reality is far from it. The Auton mask into which I am sealed is an oppressively tight fit. Tiny holes allow limited vision and restricted oxygen intake. This is disorientating and, even if you don't suffer from claustrophobia, panic-inducing. The secret to avoiding a total loss of control is to slow down your breathing and remain very calm. It sounds ridiculous but it really isn't easy to just stand there while everyone is fannying around sorting out shots, lighting, make-up and all the other delays which slow down the recording process.

Gethin is vastly amused by my predicament and keeps coming up to me with new witticisms to bellow in my ear.
"I've always said you're a monster," he sniggers. "But actually, I like you better like this. You can't talk so much."

20th July 2005
First time that a *Blue Peter* garden party has been held at the start of a season, rather than the end. As usual, I learn my speech so that I don't have to keep looking down at notes or lose my way. I try to strike a hopeful, but realistic note, and only to say what I genuinely believe myself. "We have to meet our audience on their terms," I suggest. "We know that what to adults feels cutting-edge and even revolutionary is simply normal, everyday and logical to children. Their fully on-demand, interactive world is within reach. When I was 9, no matter how much the presenters warned me to get hold of a pencil and a piece of paper, I could never write down make instructions fast or legibly enough. How fantastic just to hit a button and replay the whole thing on your computer, your mobile or TV whenever suits you. How brilliant to have a searchable database of past makes – of action highlights, of the best trips – in short, to have access to an ever-evolving catalogue of great content that is there when you want it and not when we tell you it is.
"As a child of the 70s, if I wanted to talk about stuff I'd seen on *Blue Peter*, I could only do so at school or in my neighbourhood. Not so today – now if you like stuff you've seen on *Blue Peter*, you can go to the website and meet others like you.
"So often, facing the future seems to be interpreted as something to be afraid of. But we are on the verge of fantastic developments for *Blue Peter* – where technology will only empower our audience more and extend that vital sense of community which is and always has been at the heart of *Blue Peter*'s success.
"You are part of that community whether you are presenters, production team, friends, partners and viewers. Together our job is to invest in and to shape this wonderful, inspiring programme so that future generations can own it on their own terms."

22nd July 2005
After the party, an email from Biddy: "I was full of admiration for your message from the front," she writes. "You always make me regret that you don't have your own programme although I dare say you prefer being behind-the-scenes."
Too bloody right.

26th July 2005
Called over to the studio to mediate with Matt. He's not happy with the costumes he and Geth have been given as part of a comedy pre-record to go with today's

make; a mini-wrestling ring.
"I'm fucking sick of looking ridiculous," he says, indicating the admittedly not very dignified wrestler's outfit.
"It's supposed to be funny," I suggest and point to Gethin, who is chatting away to a girl on the studio floor. "He seems happy enough."
"He would be," says Matt, sharply. "Any chance to show off his muscles."
We compromise by giving the boys T-shirts so the overall effect is less revealing. But Matt still isn't happy and, really, I think, this little drama is yet another manifestation of how he feels uncomfortable alongside Geth. If this had been an item shared with Simon, they'd have both gone for it, sent it up and had a proper laugh (see: lederhosen) But there just isn't the same connection and rapport between Matt and Geth, and if anything the gulf seems to be getting worse not better. They're both adept enough to hide it on screen but it worries me.

2nd August 2005
The *Doctor Who* competition entries are pouring in by the sack-load. At first, everyone was thrilled, but the daily mountain of deliveries is threatening to overwhelm us, and I've had to pay for extra help to sort through them.
We are using a Dalek so often in the studio that the team are joking that we're going to make it the next presenter. Sometimes, I think darkly, it might be easier to work with an evil hate-filled metal robot. Flesh and blood is much more complicated.
Cardiff, the production base for *Doctor Who*, have been in touch. They are concerned that the Dalek hasn't always been in character. They have a point. Directors are fond of giving the machine comedy 'business' and, in the process, the Dalek inevitably loses its scariness and impact. I promise to tighten up on this. We also give Nick, who operates the Dalek, an earpiece, so that the director can give him directions as we go, useful for avoiding eggy moments where he ends up in a position which makes it impossible to conceal that there is a human inside the machine.

6th August 2005
A perfect summer day for Simon's wedding. He's had quite a year. The wrench of leaving *Blue Peter*, and the reward of finally landing a job with Sky Sport, after a nerve-racking period in which he had no idea if the phone would ring. Sky's gain is the BBC's loss. Really, I am full of scorn for the way sport repeatedly flirted with Simon during his time with us (letting him report on the London Marathon, and pop up in various other initiatives) only to shrug their shoulders and pass when he became available to them full-time. Today Simon can celebrate his hard-won success, and his marriage, with his head held high and

everything to look forward to. He and his lovely wife, Gemma, have agreed to my request to film some of the proceedings to show on the programme.
At the reception, have a long chat with Richard Bacon. He's here, not as a former presenter (Richard's loss was Simon's gain) but as Konnie's partner. They've been going out for some time now, although the relationship only blossomed after Richard had left the show. They seem pretty well-matched to me; they share an intense, almost geeky interest in the media and an appealingly off-the-wall sense of humour. They're both very good-looking, too, and can flirt and charm at will.
Richard has matured noticeably since I worked with him; much less of the giddy arrogance and desire to provoke with glib arguments for argument's sake. He has not lost his sense of humour, but he is much more considered, thoughtful and reflective. He is well aware that he probably owes much of his subsequent career to the way he handled the scandal around his departure. Kudos to him for taking and following wise counsel; he never whined or bleated to papers or accepted invitations to appear on tacky TV shows. Instead, he took full responsibility for what had happened and held out for proper work rather than taking the first offers which came his way.
He will always feel sad that he was betrayed by someone he thought was a lifelong friend ("I found out what the value of friendship was," he says, wryly. "About £60,000.") He acknowledges that he might feel more bitterness if his career had stalled. He most regrets the impact the saga had on his family, who were bewildered and bitterly disappointed. But they can be proud of how he dealt with the mess, moved on and found a new, and it must be said, extremely promising future.

15th August 2005
Train to Manchester to shoot the judging of the *Doctor Who* competition. Geth and I take a cab to Russell T Davies's house. Russell opens the door, beaming and ushers us both inside. There's a life-size Dalek in the hall.
"Rich, you need a giant *Blue Peter* ship in yours," quips Geth.
"Don't do it," says Russell. "I got that before I started working on the series. Now it's like a constant reminder of work. It might have to go in a corner of the garden."
Russell's insane workload is the reason we are here; the original plan was for him to be in the studio on Wednesday, with David Tennant, to announce the winners. All this was arranged through *Doctor Who*'s long-suffering Exec, Julie Gardner, to whom I was pretty shirty when she first broke the bad news that he was too bogged down to make it.
"It just looks really poor," I complain, "letting down the audience when you've

said that he will be part of it."
"Leave it with me," she sighs, and then came back with the compromise, for which I'm grateful. They are clearly under insane pressure to which, with our schedule, I can well relate.
Russell is as delightful as ever, and Geth flirts shamelessly. He can't help himself. He does it with everyone and I must say it is generally very effective. We begin the process of examining the bag of shortlisted entries we have brought with us, which we spread all over the dining room table. Some have us in tears of laughter. My own favourite is 'Sad Tony', who is so miserable he kills his victims with the sheer despair of his company. I've worked with a few people just like that.
Russell is amused by 'the Babster', an evil baby in a high chair on wheels, rather like an infant Davros. But the main consideration is that, whatever we choose, Russell is committed to using. This leads us to the Abzorbaloff, which is a neat idea and could work as a combination of prosthetics and CGI.
It's a fun day, marred only by a call from Marina to tell me that Smudge has somehow escaped her garden, run into the road at the front of the house, and has been knocked down and killed. She is distraught, and feels responsible, as well as upset. On the train journey back home, I start to draft out the script breaking the bad news and ponder whether we should pre-record the announcement, so worried am I by the prospect of the presenters losing it and laughing during the necessarily solemn bit of script.

16th August 2005

Back in the director's chair for all the drama inserts I need for the Marie Antoinette story. Every presenter is involved; Zöe as Marie, Gethin as Louis XVI, Matt as a revolutionary gaoler, and Liz as a sly and snippy lady-in-waiting. I've put her in this part as a bit of an in-joke because it reflects the general warmth of her feelings towards Zöe; i.e. several degrees below freezing. Fortunately, Liz sees the funny side of this, and plays the scene with the required venomous relish. Marie Antoinette was infamous for the fashion she encouraged in towering hairstyles, ornamented with jewels, feathers and accessories. Make-up have done an extraordinary job in creating just such a wig for Zöe to wear. It is so heavy that she has to inch her way onto the set, and sit with great care, so that she doesn't literally topple over. It looks magnificently over-the-top.
It's a long day's work, with various sets and assorted costume changes. I've cast my son Rupert as Marie's son, the Dauphin. He has several scenes and a certain amount of dialogue, and I'm impressed with how professionally he handles these. There has been no pre-rehearsal, so we block each scene on the floor and then run to record. This requires a combination of spontaneity and

concentration, so that lines and moves are precisely remembered on every take. He works especially well with Matt, whose creativity and enthusiasm really encourages Rupert to go for it during their scenes in a prison cell. I'm so proud of him.

During a break for a costume and make-up change, the lighting director takes me to one side. "That boy of yours is very talented," he says. "When I saw the boss's son was in the cast list, I thought, 'Here we go, we all know how *he* got the job.' But he's really good, and can take direction; he's quick, precise, intelligent." He then tells me that *EastEnders* are looking for a boy of about Rupert's age, and asks if I'd like to be put in touch. I decline politely. I think the occasional piece of work, like today, can be good for a child; developing their confidence and maturity, as well as being (hopefully) a fun experience. But I've seen too many children channelled into a career, and, from what I've witnessed, it is never good for them, indeed frequently damaging.

17th August 2005

The day of the results of our *Doctor Who* competition. The success of this has been quite extraordinary and unprecedented. To have received 43,920 entries for a competition run during the summer months is unheard of, especially in this era of ever-increasing competition. The new Doctor, David Tennant, is in the studio to make the grand announcement, which I suppose is slightly odd, given that he has yet to be seen on screen (other than the regeneration moment). Tennant is very relaxed, and seems quite at home in a live multi-camera situation, effortlessly finding his close-up as though he's been presenting for years. I think it's a pity that he's going to play the Doctor with a kind of 'mockney' accent rather than his own natural light Scots brogue. Like Ewan McGregor, his star-quality is without question. During rehearsals, the studio settles down to an unusual level of quiet concentration and it is because everyone is watching and listening to Tennant. When he first walks on set, Bridget, the director up in the gallery, temporarily loses it. "Camera one give me David Tennant," she cries. "God, he's just gorgeous, isn't he? Camera four, give me David Tennant too – hell, every camera give me David Tennant. Just give me David Tennant!"

5th September 2005

We have been inundated with cards and tributes for Smudge. Quite extraordinary when you consider how little time he had been around. Marina remains devastated. For her, it is a proper, full-on bereavement and naturally, in some way, she also feels responsible. I may not share this depth of feeling, but I do admire her utter sincerity, and I feel sorry for her. Over the last couple of

weeks, I've phoned her a few times during my long commute home. No one could have looked after him more devotedly. Every night Marina cleans her cats' teeth and she tells me that, as soon he heard the buzzing sound of the electric toothbrush, Smudge would come running. Had I but known this, I should have liked to have filmed it, but don't say so now.
Marina says that she is haunted by the sight of his favourite toys.
"It's really hard, Richard," she wails. "I miss him so much...."
I nearly lose control of the car when she adds, plaintively. "Sometimes I just find myself hugging his cheesy wedge."

7th September 2005
An away-day for the whole team, to think about what we have achieved over the past year, to share worries and concerns and to consider the many and various challenges ahead.
Madame Sharman's hot-knife-through-butter reorganisation of the department has led to *Blue Peter* being shifted from entertainment (where it was, frankly, always an odd fit) to a new factual and magazine programmes division. The head of this outfit comes to address us, says royally that she is looking forward to working with us all, and wants us to think big.
As if we do anything else. Silly cow.
The team's worries, predictably, focus on the intensity of our work load and fears about the forced move to Manchester. On the plus side, there seems to be a genuine sense of shared pride, both in our ability to connect with the audience, and that what we do is second to none. As an example, somebody waxes lyrical about the recent special on Hiroshima, which was part of this year's expedition to Japan. "Anywhere else, this would be shouted about and entered for awards. But on *Blue Peter*, it's just accepted as a standard part of what we do."
I've invited the presenters to give their perspective too. Matt and Gethin love not having autocue, whereas the girls all miss it. I suggest it would help if they came in having read the script in the morning. As if. Zöe stresses that she is much thicker-skinned than people give her credit for. She wants feedback and interaction. Gethin beams that he has had a great introduction to the programme and loves working with the team. Konnie worries that the pressure of five-times-a-week sometimes makes her feel she's just churning out the material, rather than crafting it.
Matt raises the issue of challenges. "We keep on raising the bar," he says. "My question is, 'when is it going to stop? What is going too far?'"
He explains that sometimes he feels the risks involved are too great for the rewards, and that we need to think of more projects like his song-writing special, which was very successful but not exhausting or dangerous.

"Failure can be good," adds Matt. "Maybe a presenter *not* achieving a challenge could still be the highlight of the film," at which I mention as a case in point the way we had to salvage Simon's boxing special last year.

Finally, we have another visitor from upstairs; la Sharman's number two, Richard Deverell. "*Blue Peter* is a really important programme," he says, in the earnest tones of a primary school teacher. "It is one of the programmes that defines the BBC. But what is the essence of *Blue Peter*?"

I look around the room and think, "if you don't know that, you shouldn't be working here."

Disappointingly (to me), Deverell sets out as his chief challenge our 'need' to fit in with *Xchange*, which is still floundering round the schedules like an embarrassing albatross. "You must be distinctive," he says, sagely, "yet complement it."

This seems an odd commandment, especially as I know that 'the Sharminator', only too aware of its poor performance and indifferent quality, has every intention of jettisoning *Xchange* in the near future. But that is, as yet, confidential, so I smile and nod, and keep my trap shut.

12th September 2005

Launch of our *Storytellers* competition. The idea is that kids have to finish one of a range of different stories started by famous children's authors. This involved calling in a few favours, but everyone has delivered. We've got opening paragraphs from Jacqueline Wilson, Eoin Colfer, Anthony Horowitz and Malorie Blackman. For those children who prefer the idea of writing a play, David Wood has provided some initial lines with which to inspire them, while for picture stories, we have opening images from Raymond Briggs and Lauren Child. Quite a stellar line-up, I'd say.

The winners will be published in a special BBC book, with all proceeds from sales to go to this year's appeal. All this has taken a huge amount of negotiation and planning, and it's asking a lot from the audience. I'm praying that it doesn't flop after the quite breath-taking success of the *Doctor Who* competition.

13th September 2005

Gillian Shearing comes us with many of our best make ideas, and for months I've been pleading with her to think up something *Doctor Who* related. Today we unveiled her Dalek pen pot, and showed how to make it. I think it is a work of absolute genius. Gillian works in the correspondence unit, so the makes are generally a sideshow for her and have to be slotted in around the day job. I'm beginning to think she is wasted opening letters and answering emails (important though these jobs are) and that we should be getting her full-time focus on makes, which remain among the most popular items we do.

Shortly afterwards, I did just this, and Gillian was able to spend her time more productively, coming up with creative ways of turning junk into toys.

20th September 2005

Neil Mullarkey is a guest today, showing kids how to improvise stories with their friends. He is such a clever performer. Years ago, I used to watch him perform at the Comedy Store and I've often wondered why he hasn't done quite as well as some of his contemporaries. I last bumped into him during my compulsory BBC senior management training at the Ashridge business centre. This is a residential course where you rub shoulders with all kinds of leaders from across the BBC. I went prepared for the usual hot air and box-ticking, but it was actually very useful to compare notes and share horror stories with other execs in different parts of the BBC.

My favourite was being told in deadly seriousness that the Editor of *Timewatch* cribbed his management style from Hitler; a case of divide and rule, making his generals (or rather producers) compete with each other. More 'learning from history' than 'warning from history', I suppose.

One of the 'training modules' was an extended roleplay and improvisation session, designed to address effective ways of managing conflict. Most people trooped in with their hearts in their boots, dreading the embarrassment they felt sure would follow. But the session was run by Neil, and he made it enormous fun, as well as genuinely insightful. When we were planning the *Storytellers* competition, and brainstorming ways we might inspire the audience to take part, I remembered this session and asked him to devise something suitable. He's delivered, and it occurs to me that he would have made a very effective children's presenter himself.

21st September 2005

Arrive in the office to find a message asking me to go over to the studio urgently. This morning we are pre-recording a major item about the war poets. Design have created a detailed trench dug-out set, while wardrobe have kitted out Matt and Gethin as authentic-looking officers of the era. Everything looks marvellous but the atmosphere on the floor is frigid. Geth is looking uncomfortable, while Matt, who always hates incompetence, is venting. The producer has been on the receiving end of all this and looks craven. He forgot to book Portaprompt (our autocue system) suddenly turning an already complicated word-heavy item into a hideous on-the-spot memory test. This isn't a situation where a

certain amount of ad-libbing can be allowed; we are quoting from several of the most famous poems, so have to be word-perfect.
There is nothing for it but to record in sections short enough to give Matt and Gethin a fighting chance of remembering what they have to say. The pauses between takes are silent except for their frantic mutterings as they run over the lines again and again. I stick around to offer support from the floor, and take the heat off the hapless producer. But it is frustrating for everyone, and because of the memory test burden, takes much longer than it should.

23rd September 2005
Today we launch the first in a mini-series of challenges for Zöe, which I've christened *I'll Try Anything Once.* This is what Zöe said during her introductory chat on her first programme, and it stuck in my mind. The more we can play against her looks, and show the absolute steel beneath, the better. To this end, I've encouraged the film team to think of the toughest, grimiest and most testing scenarios they can find for her. We're starting with a film about Zöe helping to clean the sewers (and not in a *broderie-anglaise* skirt). In future slots, she'll be joining a team of bin-men, trying formula one racing and jumping off Bognor pier as part of a man-powered flight competition. Next year, I want her to compete in the London Marathon.
On camera she's all smiles and "bring it on", whereas off camera, while she isn't exactly punching the air, neither does she complain or turn up her nose. I still can't really work her out. She says that she's "loving" the job, yet I rarely get any sense of real joy or passion. Perhaps she just isn't wired that way. The boys are frequently and harshly critical of her but I wonder if that's because they, too, can't understand or relate to her, and that this unnerves them.
Konnie, on the other hand, gets on with Zöe just fine. I ask her if this doesn't sometimes put her in an awkward position, given that Liz is no fan either.
"Not really. You know I love Liz but I've got no problems with Zöe. Anyway, Liz is leaving," she laughs mischievously, "and so it makes sense to get on with Zöe, yeah?"
She's nobody's fool, that Konnie.

26th September 2005
Tomorrow Gethin is having his body painted by an artist who specialises in 'living' works of art. The plan is to cover his torso with a *Blue Peter* ship design against a matching background into which he will then be completely camouflaged.
True to his Celtic origins, Geth is, however, fairly hirsute and the artist requires an utterly smooth surface on which to work. As a result, he's agreed to have his

chest waxed and I've decided that this painful ordeal will make an entertaining studio challenge. What Geth doesn't know is that I thought we should add a surprise twist. To this end, Liz and Konnie have secretly trained in the waxing process, so that, during transmission, the beauty therapist steps to one side, and they take over. This is the idea but, somehow, in the adrenalin of the 'live' show, their technique suffers (or rather evaporates) and they start to rip away at small patches of Geth's copious chest hair. The poor lad is writhing around in genuine agony. It isn't quite the hilarious ending I'd anticipated. As soon as we are off air, I nip downstairs to check on him. His skin is covered in an angry red rash and, though they can't quite help laughing, the girls are mortified at what they've put him through.

28th September 2005

Spend the morning in the studio, directing a remake of the colourful story of Zarafa, the first giraffe to be brought to Paris, whose image inspired all kinds of outrageous fashions. When I first mounted this item, Stuart and Katy had been the presenters; and both had cut up rough about the costumes and wigs, Katy in particular. The fashion for a towering hair do 'a là Giraffe' was very much not to her liking and she belly-ached about it throughout the recording. Six years later and Gethin and Zöe are in the roles. What a contrast; they are both full of beans in the make-up room and buzzing to get on the floor. No moaning and no complaints about damaging their street cred. So I enjoy myself much more.

10th October 2005

Spend the morning recording auditions. There isn't a vacancy but this is my response to pressure from above to try some more disabled talent. One of the auditionees had polio as a boy, and wears braces to support his leg. His arm function is also affected. Given that the audition involves making a Christmas card, and having a go on the trampoline, I'm worried that he is not going to cope. I offer to alter the tests, but he is absolutely determined that we shouldn't. The make starts badly, but then Geth intervenes and, without once upstaging the auditionee, helps him out, turning the item into a double act. This actually works pretty well, but the trampoline is much more demanding and fairly painful to watch. He's not right, but it has nothing to do with his disability and I am so admiring of this boy's guts and spirit.

Someone else facing the cameras is CBBC presenter Gemma Hunt. She has a fresh approach and a lovely, warm character, and I think she has real potential. I know, too, that she'd desperately like the job, not that there is one quite yet. I pop into make-up to wish her luck and I'm taken aback that she seems almost catatonic with nerves. "Try to relax," I tell her. "Don't pressure yourself by thinking of anything else except what you're doing; once you get going, you'll enjoy the experience."

But I'm wrong and the audition is a bit of a disaster. She is competent, which you would expect from her experience, but it is as though all her true personality has been leeched away. There is no trace of the sweetness and spontaneity that I know she possesses. Afterwards, I go down to the floor to commiserate. There is no point pretending that it has gone well. She mumbles a few words about nerves having got the better of her. It is such a pity, but I remind her that, at this stage, the whole exercise is purely speculative in any case. There might be another chance. She nods but doesn't look convinced.

It is a relief to escape into cab and have lunch with Biddy, which is always fun. "Goodness knows how you manage to look so relaxed and carefree," she exclaims when she sees me. "It must be because stress is so exhilarating."

She thinks I am mad for having countenanced the *Storytellers* competition. "I haven't forgotten the nightmare of having to read all the entries in the *Grange Hill* competition," she shudders. "Drawings are so much easier."

I brief her about the imminent launch of the appeal and the pleasing fact that Alison Sharman has secured us a commission for a Christmas Day special. La Sharman also sorted a decent amount of cash with which to make it. When she first asked for ideas, I pitched a feel-good premise based around each of the presenters surprising really deserving kids, each with a heart-warming story, and awarding them with gold badges, as well surprise trips and special celebrities. So far we have secured the likes of David Beckham, Jonny Wilkinson, Girls Aloud and Chris Martin, and it is shaping up to be a magnificent show.

Biddy confesses that she was once asked for a Christmas Day *Blue Peter*, and declined. "But in those days, of course, it would have been live," she explains, "and I just couldn't face ruining the team's Christmas."

Afterwards she sends me a characteristically encouraging thank-you note: "Richard, you are a brilliant Editor – never forget how lucky the BBC is to have you."

Note to self!

16th October 2005

Text from Alison Sharman: "Just watching Friday episode of bp. Very strong. Love puppy make. Zöe, Gethin and Matt very strong line-up."

Given that three months ago, she wanted me to get rid of Zöe, this must count as progress.

17th October 2005

Results of our *Storytellers* competition. We've had 33,000 entries, which far exceeded anything I expected, given what we were asking of the audience. It's yet another validation of our policy of covering the best children's books, despite frequent carping from within the department that these items are "boring". Anything is boring if you do it in a boring way. Our team have lavished a lot of energy on thinking of fresh and creative ways of covering books on TV. This is one of them, and its success is a great satisfaction.

18th October 2005

Absolutely disastrous live show on the CBBC channel. Quite unexpected, too. The show had been fine in rehearsal. I was pleased with the coup of having the cast of *Nanny McPhee*, led by Emma Thompson, together with the donkey who features in the film too. It was a pretty straightforward item; Emma and the kids were friendly and charming, and the donkey was perfectly docile. It should have presented no problems for Liz whatsoever, but, on transmission, she lost it as I have never seen any presenter lose it before. It was excruciating. Her questions made no sense, and she failed to pick up her cues, so that there were awkward pauses littered among the whole faltering nightmare. She almost seemed to forget where she was, as well as what she was supposed to be doing. By the end, you could see Liz's fear and discomfort reflected in the frozen expressions and uncomfortable body language of the guests. Only the donkey was oblivious.

As the horror unfolded, I knew that we couldn't possibly allow the show to be repeated. It was bad enough that this had gone out to the CBBC channel audience, but tomorrow's repeat would be on BBC1, where the figures would be much higher. As soon as we were off-air, I rushed down to the floor and begged the film company people to stay on so that we could re-record the item. Seeing that this would be in their interests, too, they agreed. But time was of the essence as they needed to leave for their premiere in town.

The crew started to set up, while I talked to Liz, who was still in a state of shock from the ghastly TX.

"You need to forget that now," I tell her. "This is our chance to get it right. Just concentrate and focus and you'll be fine."

It is too much to hope for. Liz, her confidence badly knocked, is, if anything, more at sea during the pick-ups. We stagger through them, stopping and starting to cover her hesitancy and fluffs. Emma Thompson is heroically kind and supportive, gently saying to Liz at one point: "Don't worry, we've all been there at some time. You're fine, it'll be fine."

Somehow we get to the end, long having overrun our agreed slot. *Nanny McPhee* and entourage flee the studio, Liz looks near to collapse, and the director glumly makes for the edit, to start the painstaking rescue job for tomorrow's repeat.

Slightly cheered up by a text from Zöe, who is filming with Matt in Egypt: "Seriously lovin' it here," she writes. "Happy anniversary 2 me! I started *Blue*

Peter a yr ago today! It's been the best year of my life! Thanks 4 believing in me and 4 all ur support and encouragement. PS – get me a latte!"

21st October 2005

Special Trafalgar programme to mark the 200th anniversary of Nelson's death. I handed responsibility for this to Alex Leger, who is our most experienced producer/director.

But when I watch the section devoted to the story of HMS Victory and the 'powder monkeys' (the young boys who kept the guns loaded and ran messages from deck to deck during battle) I am struck with a powerful sense of *déjà vu*. It is word for word, shot for shot, precisely the same film that I made with Stuart Miles a few years ago. When I quiz Alex about this, he cheerfully admits the plagiarism.

"I thought, no point trying to outdo the boss, so I just copied the whole thing."

Imitation might be the sincerest form of flattery, but it didn't impress Gethin, who tells me: "Rich, Alex actually had a copy of your old film with him. Before each take, he would check the tape, and he wouldn't allow any changes at all. Not one. I basically spent a day having to copy Stuart Miles. Mad!"

31st October 2005

"Have you got any fears or phobias?" is one of the standard questions we always ask new presenters. When Gethin told me that he has always been scared of the dark, it got me thinking. So many kids are scared of the dark, perhaps we could find a constructive way of harnessing Geth's night terrors? The result is the centre-piece of today's Halloween show; a film in which Geth is challenged to sleep overnight in a dark and deserted London Dungeon. He is allowed to take his favourite toy or comforter with him, and wears an ear-piece which connects him throughout to a psychotherapist, who is there to support him and talk him through the experience. For someone with such a genuine fear, it is a major feat of bravery. The film is a triumph; imaginative, well-executed, and one of Geth's finest achievements so far. I think kids will love him for it, especially those who share his fear.

When I go over to the studio for run-through, and pop into make-up, it turns out that alpha male Matt has a very different view of the film. He is utterly scornful of both idea and Geth himself.

"What a complete Jessie," he says. "Being scared of the dark at his age! You're going to make him look ridiculous!"

I strongly disagree and seek to persuade Matt that he's taking an antediluvian attitude. But he's quite made up his mind. I go up to the gallery, and run-through begins. The show opens with the presenters grouped around a large and

bubbling cauldron, from which they extract various clues about today's show. When it is Matt's turn, he fishes out a voluminous garment of some kind. "Oh look," he cries, "It's a big girl's blouse! This must belong to you, Gethin..."
This raises laughs from the crew, but has a disastrous effect on Geth, who looks persecuted and proceeds to fluff his way through the rest of the show. I am annoyed.
"It was just a joke," says Matt, defensively, when I challenge him about it during notes.
"It was unnecessary," I reply. "And unkind. A fear of the dark is a genuine phobia, you know. Just because you can't imagine it, doesn't mean it isn't real."
It's damaging because Gethin obviously feels some real sense of shame about his fear, into which Matt's 'joke' has expertly tapped. I urge him to focus and not to drop the ball during transmission, but his head is down, the damage is done and the show, which should have been a breeze, is peppered with fluffs and mistakes, about which I know he will afterwards spend hours beating himself up.

2nd November 2005
First day of shooting on *Totally Blue Peter*, as I've rechristened this year's Christmas special, and the usual before dawn start. I'm wise to this game now and take my pillow with me. When the cab picks me up, I bury my head in this and catch a little extra sleep during the long drive from St Albans to south London.
Our first location is a very swanky loft-style apartment, and we're here for the next couple of days. The script has been quite a challenge for the design department, as it's supposed to be set in 1980s New York. But judging by this location, they are measuring up. It's all white wood and windows, and it's the base for one of Matt's two characters, the super-camp stylist Ricco. As per my instructions, make-up have invested Matt with Boy George-style dreads and wardrobe have remade one of the iconic 80s 'Choose Life' T-shirts for him. He is in his absolute element and (not for the first time) I wonder if perhaps I've gone too far when Ricco catches his first glimpse of Gethin as Joey, the cute but dim hero, and drawls, "So unspoilt....it's almost a pity to polish you up...."

3rd November 2005
Shooting Ricco's big music number, *Be Young, Be Foolish, Be Happy*. Matt is so inventive, always thinking of extra bits of business and little flourishes to make the comedy work harder. We egg each other on. It's been a while since we've collaborated like this. Over the last few months, as his boss, rather than his director or his friend, sometimes there has undeniably been tension and

frustration. I've occasionally found him dogmatic, argumentative and closed-minded, especially about Gethin, about whom I think he is often unreasonable. But I suspect he's found me just as belligerent and equally determined to have my own way. We are both, in different ways, alpha males and we care way too much about the programme, too, which affects everything. So it is wonderful to go back to what we both love the most, collaborating on something we believe in, which we can embellish and bring to life together.

4th November 2005

We take over the hair salon at Television Centre for a comedy cutaway of three old dears all glued to their copies of *Blue Peter* magazine. The dears are being played by the two longest-serving ladies from our correspondence unit, Cilla and Sheila, and sandwiched in the middle is a bewigged Konnie.

Design have painstakingly mocked up some convincing dummy copies of the mag, using a black and white shot of yours truly on the back cover. This was taken by a photographer when I was working on *Top of the Pops* in the late 80s and it couldn't be more reflective of the era; enormous shoulder pads ahoy. Konnie is most amused by it and keeps saying it's "cult".

At least, I *think* that's the word she's using.

6th November 2005

We've taken over the Starbucks at the nearby White City complex, and design have transformed it into an American-style coffee bar. As Geth's character, Joey, is supposed to be a barista, he's been sent ahead of filming to get fully trained in the dark art of making frothy coffees. As Geth frequently seems to have the mental age of an 8-year-old, this means that he keeps wanting to show off his newly-acquired skill, making an annoying racket and producing large amounts of steam at all-too regular intervals.

Back in the summer, when I wrote this epic, I got a quick sense of how well the presenters would cope with the need to adopt an American accent. Matt, Liz and Konnie had no problems. I'd already decided that, in true-*Dynasty* style, Zöe would play the villainess, Cassie, as a snooty English woman, and I was delighted by how easily this accent came to her. Which left Geth as the only stumbling block. He did his best, but every time he tried a line, we'd both end up virtually crying with laughter at how terrible it sounded.

"He's not Caribbean," I'd gasp. "Or Pakistani."

Then I had an idea. We had been given the chance to make a film at the animation studios Pixar, based in the States. I decided to send Gethin, and to ask the director to make another film while he was out there; in which Geth would try to acquire an authentic American accent. They have returned with a fresh and funny story, in which Geth is at his most likeable. Alas, however, the accent can't truly be said to have improved much. But at least we gave it our best shot. "Keep practising!" I tell him at intervals, to which he invariably responds by putting on his 'in character' face and reciting one of the lines from the script, "I won't let you!" so that this quickly becomes a catchphrase.

7th November 2005

Morning recording with rugby royalty Jonny Wilkinson, who, as heroes go, is about as unassuming as it is possible to be. He seems slightly overwhelmed to be here at all, as though it's all a case of mistaken identity. We take the inevitable shots for the annual, first with Matt and Gethin, and then just with Gethin.

"Why?" he asks, beadily.

"Just in case Matt leaves before the next annual," I hiss. "Now shut up and smile."

"Devious fucker," he mutters, doing as he's told.

This afternoon, the launch of our *Treasure Trail* appeal, the aim of which is to raise money to substantially increase the number of calls which the charity ChildLine can answer.

Appeals are always demanding and stressful, but this one presents particular challenges. The nature of much of ChildLine's business is hearing from children with terrible tales of domestic cruelty, abuse and bullying. There are definite limits to what we can show at teatime, but equally we mustn't be too squeamish. Given the subject matter, I've decided to break with the usual film-making tradition and frame most of our appeal stories as little dramas which carefully relate some of the scenarios to which ChildLine respond. They are all based on actual cases but this approach maximises the impact of the drama while protecting the identities of the real people involved. The downside is that drama is much more time-consuming and expensive to shoot. None the less, I could see no more effective way of getting across the crucial messages.

Both Liz, and my deputy Kez, who is overseeing the films, have undergone the training to be ChildLine counsellors; and yet again we have managed to avoid a return to the tired old bring-and-buy. This time we are collecting old phones and used currency (hence the child-friendly title I've given the appeal).

ChildLine have been facing serious financial difficulties, and, within the BBC, there was some doubt about their robustness as a potential partner. But the cause couldn't be more relevant to the audience, and if we can mobilise them to make a genuine difference, it will be our best work of the year.

After today's launch, a text from Simon Thomas: "Thought the appeal film was brilliant," he writes. "Also one of the clearest appeals I've seen in a while. Great stuff."

9th November 2005

Someone up there is smiling on this filming because, against all predictions, we have bright sun. I'm on duty as more than director today as I've lined up my customary in-joke cameo as a New York cop. As well as my cameo, we've got *Blue Peter* gardener Chris Collins, wearing an appalling curly wig, as an unlikely news vendor.

I'm still worrying about how convincing it's going to be; asking the wilds of West London to stand-in for the Big Apple. Adrian, my brilliant editor, has various ideas to help; as well as using some of the GV's (general views) I shot during my New York filming trip, he's going to key in a few skyscraper backgrounds where he can. He's also made the point that the sound mix will help give an authentic background vibe.

The advantage of filming at this time of year is that I don't have to schedule a super-expensive night shoot; it is dark by around 4 and then we set up the shots of our red carpet premiere. The TV anchor woman is our third cameo of the day, and this time it's my long-serving (some would say long-suffering) PA, Sarah Courtice.

Sarah is Australian and, true to the archetype of the nation, she's a "no worries" person. Her natural warmth and friendliness work like a charm, whether she is dealing with a testy BBC executive or an eccentric member of the public. She's kind but tough; a good gate-keeper, and incredibly discreet.

On several occasions, for my sake, she has gone above and beyond the call of duty. Once, I was bringing my son Rupert, and his best friend Jason, to TV Centre for the day. Halfway down the motorway, Rupert succumbed to violent travel sickness and vomited copiously all over the car, and his unfortunate friend. I called Sarah and she was there to meet us in the multi-storey car park, armed with a bucket of water, cloths, cleaning spray and plenty of kitchen roll. What's more, she didn't leave us to it, she joined in and helped to clean up.

But her best rescue job was one morning when I'd gone to the gym. I finished my session and started to change, only to discover that my trousers were missing. I'd carried my suit from the car park on a hanger, so, with a sinking feeling, it occurred to me that, somewhere en route, the trousers must have fallen off. I phoned Sarah to tell her what had happened. She could barely talk for laughing but promised to have a look. Ten minutes later she put her head round the changing room door, and again fell about laughing, this time at the unlovely sight of me standing there trouser-less, in my socks, pants, shirt, tie and jacket. The good news was that she had found my trousers languishing on the pavement near the Wood Lane tube.

"Maybe it's time for a new suit," she said, as she handed them over. "Since even a tramp wasn't tempted to steal these!"

11th November 2005

We've commandeered the Hammersmith Palais to shoot all the scenes around the *Blue Peter* magazine party.

Most of our extras have been corralled from the production office, so there is a slightly carnival atmosphere. Tina Heath is here, playing Matt's frustrated spinster PA, Veronica. I really enjoy working with Tina. She's such a thoughtful person and approaches the work as though she's in a *Play for Today* rather than a glorified panto. A good example is an issue she raised with me the other day about a line that she's uncomfortable with. As part of the story, Liz's character goes undercover as a Mexican maid, and uses this guise to parry Veronica's questions. "Me no speak Engleesh," she says, to which Veronica is scripted to respond: "Your sort never do."

Tina is worried about the inherent racism of this, but I'm reluctant to cut it, as it illustrates precisely the kind of woman Veronica is supposed to be. Tina concedes but I'm glad she's taking it this seriously. She's being wonderfully vinegary in the part. Of course, when I relate this to Matt, he immediately starts spouting the in-joke of my David Garrick script from a couple of years ago; "When I was at drama school, I was taught that most important aspect of acting is to be truthful..."

13th November 2005

Another day in Starbucks, this time to shoot one of Geth's big music numbers, *It Must Be Love.* All the tracks I've selected are 80s classics, with the exception of the closing song (hence the introductory line: "this is *totally* next decade")

Geth doesn't actually have a bad voice. It's slightly strange watching him in this part, though, as almost all his 'costume' has actually come from my own wardrobe; genuine 1980s stuff that I couldn't bear to throw away. Unfortunately, because he generally looks good in pretty much anything he wears, this reduces the comedy impact of the clothes.

15th November 2005

All day in TC4 to record the studio material for *Totally Blue Peter*. We have until ten o'clock, which gives us a couple of hours for each number. This isn't much at all once you have factored in rehearsals and retakes. The edit chews up shots for the dance sequences; it really is a case of the more, the merrier. A couple of them are relatively straightforward vocal passes of songs for which we've already shot sequences on location.

Liz steps in front of the camera to record *A Little More Love,* for which her vocal has been provided by Gemma, our MD's daughter, who has ghosted Liz's voice throughout her time on the show. It's a sultry, sassy number and at first, Liz just can't get into it; she looks self-conscious and out of sync. We take a short break and have a chat.

"It's OK now, Rich," she tells me. "I've got it. I'm going to own it. Don't worry."

We run playback again and Liz suddenly transforms into vamp mode, to such an electrifying extent that there is a guffaw of laughter from Adrian, the Lighting Cameraman. Liz never does things by halves. Once we've got the laughs out of the way, we run up again and Liz nails the song in one take.

The rest of the day goes equally well until we are left with only one major number to shoot, *Ready or Not*, which features Geth on lead vocals, with Matt (as his Ricco character), Liz and Konnie as his band (Konnie on drums).

Just as we break for supper, I hear the news that Alison Sharman has quit and will be leaving to join ITV. There is considerable anger within the East Tower, apparently, and among the higher echelons of the BBC. Her job in children's was seen as a kind of stepping-stone to greater things within the corporation (see also: Lorraine Heggessy) but it transpires that, true to form, 'the Sharminator' has simply used it as a chip to bargain her way into a bigger job with the other side. She's the shortest-lived of any children's head, but in her brief reign, she certainly shook things up. I think she rated me; she put up my salary and suggested she should be my mentor. It might have been better for me if she stayed around. But all the presenters are delighted; especially the girls, in whom it was obvious that Sharman had no interest. Only Matt expresses a slight regret, because Madame (rightly) thought he was key talent and recently offered him a kind of 'write your own' contract extension. This wasn't especially helpful for morale, as Matt promptly announced it to the others, leaving all noses well out of joint. But he hasn't actually signed anything, and we have yet to seriously discuss any kind of deal, so perhaps now it is academic.

After the gossip, and supper, we crack on with the number. I don't know what it is; whether the dramatic news of Alison's departure, or the 'end of term' feeling that we have shot so much great stuff today, but the evening is uninhibited and joyful. All the presenters are on a high and it shows in their performances.

During one break, Liz comes over to me, eyes shining, and just says, simply, "Oh Rich, this has been such a happy day."

17th November 2005

Today we film what must be a contender for one of my favourite shots of all-time; a cutaway of Konnie, as café-owning Jewish momma shrew Maria, sitting on her sofa, sharing a TV dinner with her dogs (played, of course, by Lucy and Mabel)

This one shot takes forever to set up, as both the dogs prove to be shit actors, but when we finally get the 'moment', it is perfect, and hilariously funny.

25th November 2005

Our revamped Book Awards was the most watched of any children's programme last week. I go to town with this delightful statistic, knowing that there are still those who doubt the validity of us covering children's books. It's also a great reward for the sheer amount of effort and creativity which went into making it so much more than another routine awards show.

28th November 2005

An unusual evening at the Notting Hill Brasserie – an official dinner for all the former Editors of the programme – Biddy, Lewis Bronze, Oliver Macfarlane and Steve Hocking, and myself. Edward Barnes is also there, as one of the programme's founding fathers. Between us, the assembled company have run *Blue Peter* since 1962. The most senior figure is Edward Barnes, who joined the programme a few weeks before Biddy and later rose to become head of department. As Edward puts it, "Biddy and I got off to a pretty dusty start" – because she was much less experienced and had won the top job against all the odds and the obvious competition, which included Edward. In an act of typical BBC corporate sensitivity, Edward had nonetheless been assigned to the series to give expert support to the fledgling new arrival, which he understandably resented. But the tension didn't last long. Edward and Biddy soon discovered that they shared the same ambition to raise the game on this little weekly children's show; they were both tenacious, flamboyant and extremely opinionated when it came what and who they thought worked best.

Edward and Biddy's incredibly close working relationship is the secret of so much of what became *Blue Peter* – not just the style of the programme and the choice of presenters but key ingredients like the summer expeditions, the appeals and the badges. Biddy became Editor in 1965, when the show went twice a week. Edward, meanwhile, moved onwards and upwards in the summer of 1970, when he became first deputy head of department and then, in 1978, head. But he always retained close links with *Blue Peter* and gave Biddy unstinting support.

It was Edward who spotted the talent of the young Lewis Bronze, who was a producer on *John Craven's Newsround*, before Edward moved him over to become first a producer on BP and then, from 1983, Biddy's deputy. By the time Lewis took over from Biddy five years later, he was thoroughly marinated in the programme and full of his own ideas about how to develop and enhance it.

So there we all are around the table – Edward, Biddy, Lewis, Oliver, Steve, myself – and, a wide-eyed outsider in the form of Richard Deverell, who stands blinking behind his glasses and taking it all in. There's no such thing as a free lunch or, in this case, a free dinner; tonight is at Deverell's behest; he wants to get the *Blue*

Peter old guard on side with the proposal to move CBBC to Manchester. Good luck with that, I think to myself.
A few minutes of small talk and then Lewis suddenly calls for silence as he stands and proposes a toast – to the programme and to me. There is noisy applause and I am genuinely touched. Conversation begins to flow more freely. We are a small enough group for everyone to be included so that there is none of the frustration of only being able to talk to those seated nearest you.
Edward tells everyone that, in his opinion, there are three shows which should run forever on children's BBC – *Blue Peter, Record Breakers* and *Grange Hill* – the latter as school will always be an essential part of every child's life and formative experiences. He is in various ways, responsible for all three (as well as *Newsround* and the Saturday morning shows), which is a remarkable achievement.
Lewis raises a toast to Edward for taking a gamble on him and making him a producer on *Newsround* when he was only 22.
"And it wasn't just me," he says. "This is a man who has launched so many careers."
Edward acknowledges the tribute gracefully and explains that in Lewis's case there had, in fact, been someone else in the running for the job with much more experience. Lewis was a rank outsider. But he did well in the board and when the favoured candidate began to play hard to get and demand various conditions which Edward felt disinclined to grant, he decided to take a chance and offer the job to Lewis instead.
"I'm nearly 50," says Lewis, "a time when you inevitably take stock of your life. Edward changed everything for me."
Biddy makes the point that *Blue Peter* always had a strong tradition of spotting production talent early and giving it an opportunity to thrive. "But," she adds, "there are the disasters too..."
Biddy's mention of the "disasters" (including one "who started on Monday and was sacked on Thursday") prompts Lewis to remind her about a hapless trainee assistant producer who was on attachment from the World Service. This AP was put in charge of a complicated studio item about giant chess pieces being used to demonstrate a particular move called Fool's Mate. Everything had been set up correctly for the run-through but when it came to resetting for the live transmission, the AP got mixed up so that the pieces were all in the wrong position. The item was a disaster.
"Biddy got her own back in a characteristic way," observes Lewis, dryly. "Back then, during the appeal, we always had a big map of the UK in the studio into which the production team would place a pin to mark every reported *Blue Peter* bring-and-buy sale. This particular year, for some reason, the design

department had made the map from exceptionally strong wood so that hammering in each pin was a real chore. For the rest of his short time on the programme, it became the *special* responsibility of this poor AP."

Not getting on the wrong side of Biddy is the theme of several further anecdotes. "Having to look after the fucking parrot was one very effective punishment," says Edward, to gales of laughter from the table. Another anecdote concerned Peter Salmon, who, until the summer, was the BBC's head of sport. He started his career as a nervous general trainee on *Blue Peter*. Salmon apparently dines out on the tale of how, on his first day, Biddy thrust a pile of newspapers at him and left him to his own devices, returning some hours later to ask how he was getting on. "Not badly; I've found some good items in some of them," he replied. "You're not supposed to be looking for items," came the withering response. "You're supposed to be making a dog's bed..."

I mention that, these days, Peter Salmon always maintains that he was one of the few members of the production team in the early 80s to raise disquiet about the middle-class 'Brownie Britain' tone of the programme.

"No he didn't," Biddy protests vehemently. "Too much of a creep!"

Biddy left in the summer of 1988. She was always going to be a tough act to follow. Edward admits that finding her successor had been a genuine headache – she was such a towering figure and the programme so associated with her and her standards. In Lewis, he felt there was someone who understood the show, its values and heritage but who wouldn't be scared to do his own thing and follow his own instincts and hunches.

The subject of presenters now dominates the conversation for a while. I ask if it was true that Michael Sundin had really learned that his contract wasn't being renewed on the very last show of the season? I've been told that he only found out when told he needn't bother planning his wardrobe for the summer expedition to Australia as he wasn't going.

Lewis sighs and says this was indeed true – or something like it.

"We were trying to make the trip as economically as possible," he explains. "Every cost was being scrutinised and when it came to buying factor 35 for the presenters, I simply told wardrobe not to get any for Michael. That's how the information leaked – through the wardrobe department. Information often leaked through the wardrobe department."

A meeting was hurriedly called with Edward, Biddy and Lewis to discuss the situation. The deputy head of children's, a dour figure called Roy Thompson, happened to be passing and they told him that they were discussing the Sundin situation.

"What shall we do?" they asked.

"Sack him," came the reply.

So they called Sundin and his agent in to break the bad news which Sundin seemed to take well at first.

"A few moments after they'd left," Lewis continues, "Sundin's agent came back and popped his head round the door and mentioned that he had several other artists they should consider now that they'd be looking for a replacement. This was my introduction to the ways of agents!"

Sundin then called Edward in the early hours of the morning to complain about his dismissal.

"At that time of the morning, I was pretty short with him," says Edward.

Biddy would never admit openly that a presenter had been sacked. She preferred the euphemism of saying that "their contract was not renewed" as she felt this was more generous to the departing artist. By anyone's standards, poor Michael Sundin had been a grievous casting mistake and that's why Biddy and Edward brought Peter Duncan back to replace him, feeling that the programme had taken a severe knock and that Duncan's familiarity and star quality would help restore the equilibrium.

I say that I believe that nowadays there is far less room for error with a new presenter. Everyone – from management upstairs to the audience as a whole – expects them to arrive fully trained and ready to shine – and there is less tolerance for them to develop on the job. The whole table agrees. Biddy points out that it had taken more than two years for Simon Groom to settle in and find his feet and Edward says that John Noakes had been an utter disaster during his first few months on the programme. Lewis recalls how, after persevering for two years with Diane-Louise Jordan, he and Oliver had eventually decided to admit defeat and talked to her about ending her contract. Then, unexpectedly, Yvette Fielding decided to leave and was replaced with Anthea Turner. The new combination of John, Diane and Anthea worked brilliantly and Diane was saved and, after that, just got better and better.

At this point, Lewis pays tribute to John Leslie and says how much he had enjoyed working with him. He reminisces about the special programme they had made in Edinburgh – "It was just a massive ego massage for John, really," he admits – and said how, during rehearsals, John had taken him to one side to tell him that he was going out with Catherine Zeta Jones, then Britain's hottest TV star in *The Darling Buds of May*. We discuss John's fall from grace. There is considerable sympathy for the fact that, although tried and acquitted, his career in television has effectively been ruined.

There follows an involved debate about whom each of us would choose as the defining *Blue Peter* presenter. The consensus is that John Noakes towers over them all, not simply because of his longevity, but because of the real love audiences had for him, in response to his apparently unrehearsed, natural style on-camera. The reality was much more complex. Noakes, an ex-actor like so many former presenters, was effectively playing a part and the relationship eventually went sour in a very public fashion over the BBC's ownership of Shep, John's Border Collie and on-screen sidekick.

Lewis vividly recalls the occasion of the show's 35th birthday, walking in to a studio full of past presenters to see this overweight old man shambling in the fire lane and being shocked to realise it was the great Noakes. Steve Hocking asks Edward if he would have done anything differently had he known how bitter the row over Shep was going to turn out.

"Yes," Edward replies at once. "I would have made damn sure that the clause about him not using the dog for adverts was already in place when we first talked about Noakes having him."

Edward thinks that the dispute all boiled down to typical Yorkshire stubbornness and a too-rigid adherence to the idea of 'a man's word should be his bond'. Noakes never misses a chance to badmouth Biddy and I wonder how she feels about this. She shrugs. "Well, we didn't force them to sign a contract year after year and he signed 12 of them. If the job, and me, were such hell, why on earth did he stay? It's sad but it's the viewers I feel sorry for, because it tarnishes their memories."

Despite the feud, everyone agrees that Noakes had been a truly great presenter and that *Blue Peter* probably wouldn't have been the success it was without him. Steve ponders what John would think if he could hear us all discussing him in these terms.

There are a few runner-ups in the 'best presenter' stakes. Biddy nominates Sarah Greene ('Greeno') for her intelligence and sensitivity, her understanding of the programme and the audience, and for being such a pleasure to work with. I recall when I was a floor assistant on *Going Live!* being mesmerised by Sarah's professionalism and charm; she took such a genuine interest in the people she worked with and met. She also had a fabulously filthy sense of humour.

I mention that Lesley Judd had been my favourite presenter as a viewer, and both Biddy and Edward agree that she had been very popular with many skills but that she was not always easy to manage. When Biddy first booked her, she came up against opposition from both the artists bookings and variety department, who were unhappy about Lesley being offered another BBC contract. This all stemmed from an incident when Lesley had been working as a dancer in The Young Generation. Apparently, she had dropped out of a series without notice to stay with a man she'd met on holiday in France.

"Lesley was a 'bolter' by nature," explains Biddy. "She went where her heart took her."

During her first few months on the programme, Lesley met and married the actor and presenter Derek Fowlds, who was then famous for fronting *The Basil Brush Show.* But just a few months later, in the summer of 1974, she left him abruptly. Biddy was on holiday in Cornwall when she took a call from a distraught Fowlds telling her of the break and how much it had upset him and threatening to tell his story to the press. Realising that this would be distressing for everyone involved (Fowlds had two sons who adored Lesley) and disastrous for both Lesley and the programme, Biddy told him that if he did so, she would use her influence with Bill Cotton (then the powerful Controller of BBC1) to make sure that Fowlds never worked for the BBC again.

"It was a total bluff," she confesses. "But I had to do something and I banked on an actor's natural sense of insecurity."

It worked – Fowlds kept his counsel and Lesley kept her job, though Biddy warned her that if the story broke she would probably have to go. A reminder of how much the moral climate has changed.

I tell everyone how I had queued up to get Lesley's autograph at the National Cat Club show in 1972 and how that signed photo now has a special place in my office at Television Centre. Lewis recalls how, years after leaving, Lesley had visited the studio for some reason and they had been introduced.

"Hello, I'm Lesley Judd," she had smiled and he says that, such was her beauty and charisma, in that moment he knew he would have done anything for her.

Another presenter for whom there is high regard is Peter Duncan, even though it is agreed that he could be a nightmare to work with. I relate the story of how I had cast Peter as Father Christmas in the 40th anniversary Christmas special. While we were rehearsing, Peter kept badgering me to play the part as a "modern" Father Christmas. "What does that mean?," I asked him, genuinely mystified. "Well, without any beard or the long white hair; so you can see my face. You do want to see it's me, don't you?" I told him he was being ridiculous and that was the end of that – but he was another presenter who really cared about the show and the audience, although, like many of them, he absolutely hated the chore of having to sit in the office or make-up and sign his publicity cards.

"In the end, I had to have them forged," says Biddy, "Or we would never have had enough to send out."

I'm surprised that no one has mentioned Valerie Singleton. Edward believes that she is a good example of someone who worked well on the programme without really understanding it. He also feels that she had some surprising limitations.

"I made the *Blue Peter Royal Safari* with her and I always felt that, if during the interview with Princess Anne, the Princess had announced that she was a lesbian, Val would just have nodded and moved onto the next question on her list."

He also recalls how, during the filming of the *Blue Peter Special Assignment* to Rome, how odd he thought it was that between takes Val was glued to a book about the Six Wives of Henry VIII.

"It was typical of a certain kind of perversity she had," he comments.

As his alternative to Noakes, Lewis chooses Diane, stressing how significant it was that she was the programme's first black presenter and how she had to deal with all the pressure and expectation that came from that. Oliver seconds this and adds that it was not dissimilar when he cast Konnie Huq as the first Asian presenter. Biddy is not a fan of Konnie's and finds her irritating. I instantly leap to her defence and say that while it is true that many adults find Konnie resistible, she is enormously popular with children, precisely because she is herself childlike – unskilled in some of what she does on the programme but always friendly and enthusiastic. She is also someone who definitely understands *Blue Peter* and is secure enough about herself never to compete with her fellow presenters, which is so often a problem.

I also say how different I find Konnie off-screen and one-to-one; she is very sexy and flirty, enormous fun, well-informed and extremely intelligent. Her frequent laziness drives me crazy but she is a good judge of character and the bedrock of the presenting team, like an indulged older sister.

Biddy remains unconvinced. Neither does she much care for the look of Zöe, feeling that she comes over as a bit fake. A slight tension as I again bridle at this criticism and defend Zöe, thinking that this is all a bit rich coming from Biddy, who was after all responsible for some less-than-successful presenters.

"As we all know," I remark, "casting presenters is about the most inexact science there is."

I add that Matt is a worthy successor to Noakes – truly down to earth, with an incredible versatility – and the gifts to take on almost any challenge and master it with extraordinary rapidity. Unlike Noakes, Matt is not acting – what you see is what you get, though his own perfectionism and high standards mean that he doesn't suffer fools gladly and can be difficult with anyone he feels isn't up to their job. I explain that this is his seventh season on the show and that he is currently trying to decide whether to stay on for an eighth. He is very tired and hasn't entirely settled with the new team of Gethin and Zöe, which, considering how closely he worked with Simon Thomas and Liz Barker, isn't, perhaps, surprising.

In the light of Matt's marathon run – and whether or not he will continue – we talk about the optimum time for presenters to stay. Aware that children hate change, Edward says that he knows that he has been guilty of persuading presenters to stay too long. Peter Purves is a good example – he should have left a few years earlier than he did. Lewis feels strongly that five years is about the most you could expect before repetition sets in and everything in the relationship starts to get a bit difficult.

I mention how I'd recently seen Katy Hill – who left after five years – and how she'd said she could no longer really remember what had driven her to leave her dream job. She felt slightly jealous of the current team who were all outstripping her and seemed very secure and content. "Why didn't you persuade me to stay?" she asked me, only half-joking. Lewis says that not attempting to persuade presenters to stay was something that he had learnt from Biddy. He remembers that when Mark Curry came to see him and said that he wanted to leave, he simply echoed what Biddy used to say; "Oh, well, we'll give you a jolly good send-off."

Oliver was the Editor who had to deal with Richard Bacon; the most challenging presenter departure of them all. It was very sad and depressing but he still believes that there was no other option. I recall one of the hundreds of letters which flooded in after Richard's sacking. It was from a small boy who said that his teacher had told him that even though Coke was bad for you, it was OK as an occasional treat.

Gradually, the conversation shifts to tales of the most disastrous live programmes. Steve shudders at the memory of a nearly-calamitous celebrity bring-and-buy sale which came in seven minutes under and had to be ruthlessly padded to fit the time slot. There was the reverse problem with a special programme themed around Japan. This included a complicated eight-minute item explaining the intricacies of the traditional Japanese tea ceremony. The designer built a beautifully detailed set and the contributor had gone to endless trouble to brief the presenters. In the event, the programme was so badly over-length, the decision was taken to cut the tea ceremony down to a one-line mention – something to the effect of – "And the Japanese are famous for their elaborate tea ceremonies...." as the presenter simply walked through the set, which, as a result, was glimpsed only for a matter of seconds.

Lewis mentions an item which came from a stock of standbys which Biddy kept handy to fill any sudden holes in a running order. Most of these she culled from her local newspaper, the *Leicester Mercury* (Biddy had a cottage there to which she often returned at weekends).

This particular item was about an old man whose hobby was spending hours and hours painstakingly making bird mobiles from string, paper and pots of glue. Biddy finally placed this in a running order and the old man duly made his way to the studio and rehearsed. Alas, the programme was running over so the whole thing was cut.

"The standard response in this situation," explains Lewis, "was to say, 'Can you come back another week?'"

The old man agreed to this and returned – only for the item to be dropped again. Lewis also recalls a live OB from an RNLI boat station the climax of which was to be the launch of a new lifeboat which had been paid for by *Blue Peter* viewers. The weather was extremely rough and as the afternoon went on and transmission grew close, an RNLI official took Lewis to one side to say, 'The weather is just too unpredictable to launch the boat'. Lewis told him that there was no debate to be had; the boat must be launched, no matter what.

"Quite right, ducky," interjects Biddy.

The RNLI did as they were told and the boat launched into incredibly rough seas. "The boat was virtually standing up in the water," recalls Lewis "The presenter was absolutely terrified – but the item went ahead."

Edward comments on how amazing it is that the programme has got away with filming so much high risk action and adventure over the years without killing anybody. He explains how the action films began back in the early days. He made a film with Chris Trace, who was a very good driver, operating all kinds of construction vehicles on a building site in central London. Edward spotted a tower crane and suggested that Trace climb it as the climax of the film. "Not on your life," came the reply, as Trace was scared of heights. Driving home through the city, Edward saw more and more tower cranes and thought again what a good film they would make. Noakes had just joined and so he suggested it to him instead. The item was a great success and that was the beginning of a whole genre of gravity-defying *Blue Peter* films.

As the evening draws to a close, talk turns from the past to the future and the prospect of the wholesale shift of children's programmes to Manchester. Biddy is adamant that this will "kill the programme."

She knows that this is her opportunity to fight the decision in front of Deverell, a senior member of the current BBC administration. She talks in detail about the recent 4000th edition of the show, arguing that this ambitious and star-studded event "wouldn't have been possible" from Manchester – that getting the top guests and the topical items demanded that the programme be based in London. Lewis wades in against her. "But that's no use to Richard or to anyone working on the programme now," he reasons. "Whatever any of us feel is largely academic in any case, as the people who will make the ultimate decision are above our level. It will be imposed and it will be up to whoever is there to deal with it. If it had happened during my first two years, I would have gone – the programme would undoubtedly have been different – but why not?"

Biddy counters that surely a move on such a scale would be seen "rightly" by the public as a colossal waste of licence fee money. It offers next to no benefits to the majority of viewers and is purely an exercise in pleasing politicians. I feel that if it does happen, it will have to be seen as an opportunity. It wouldn't be

possible to lead the programme into such uncharted territory without a clear strategy and a sense of excitement for the future. I worry that the move might represent an opportunity to 'downsize' the programme. Every year the argument about the scale of the resources commanded by *Blue Peter* intensifies.
"This is the department's flagship programme," I stress. "It is the BBC's flagship children's programme. It really matters. It is surely right that we have the budget to allow us to remain ambitious and experimental, to offer programmes with a real sense of scale and the highest possible production values."
I feel we need to know much more about the facilities which might be on offer in Manchester; the size of the studio for one thing. I also point out that the press are already asking what would happen to the *Blue Peter* garden and that it occurs to me that moving it lock, stock and barrel, like those rich Americans who buy British mansions and ship them over to the States, might actually make a great *Blue Peter* film. "There are always different ways of doing things," I reason. "But my question is whether Manchester offers a bright new opportunity or a poisoned chalice."
The evening ends late but in a cheerful atmosphere of great good humour and mutual regard. As a parting gift, I give everyone a copy of the brand new *Blue Peter* annual and the *Blue Peter Storytellers* book, both of which have just been published. I step from the warmth of the restaurant into a foggy London street to begin the long journey home. It is one of the rare moments when you actually stop to consider how lucky you are. When you give years of your life to this programme, you become part of a unique and closely connected family.

29th November 2005
Bump into Gabby, now a senior executive in the department, who tells me that she's just been chatting to Richard Deverell. He's told her about last night and how well it had gone and how surprised he had been at just how complimentary and supportive the former Editors had been towards me. Don't know whether to be flattered or insulted.

5th December 2005
Geth is in Cardiff, playing a Cyberman in *Doctor Who*. He owes this 'fun' experience to all the taunting he dished out to me in the summer when I was screwed inside the Auton costume and couldn't answer back. It occurred to me then that playing a monster, with all the claustrophobia this entails, would actually make a great behind-the-scenes film and a proper challenge for a presenter. It took a little persuading to get the *Doctor Who* brigade to agree; they worried about giving away too much of the magic. It never hurts to use Geth as a carrot; they can't get enough of him in Cardiff.
I wonder why?

14th December 2005

Lunch at the Bluebird café in the King's Road, and another gathering of the *Blue Peter* family; the occasion is a celebration of two of the longest-serving members of the team, Annie Dixon and Alex Leger. They've both been with the programme for 30 years and I felt strongly that this achievement should be marked in some way. We often give presents and throw parties for departing members of the team, some who have only been with us for a few months. It seems to me that long, loyal and excellent service should equally be recognised and rewarded. Both are eminently deserving of a gold badge, which I'll hand over during the lunch.

It's taken several weeks to organise, not least because I wanted it to be a surprise, and not much gets past either of these two. I was warned that Annie, in particular, wouldn't want any fuss or attention drawing to her longevity; people might interpret it as a sign of imminent retirement. It's one reason why I thought we should hold the party away from Television Centre. Co-ordinating the guest list was a challenge, too. Annie started as Biddy's secretary, and Alex as a trainee assistant producer; they owe their *Blue Peter* breaks to Biddy and Edward, who are both here. Likewise Lewis Bronze, who made Annie a producer and gave Alex many opportunities to film all over the world. From the current team, I invited Bridget Caldwell and my deputy, Kez Margrie.

Which presenters to include? This was tricky. They had to be liked and respected by both Alex and Annie. The final list was John Leslie, Katy Hill, Simon Thomas and, from the existing line-up, Gethin.

One of the qualities which I most respect about Annie is that she doesn't hand out her friendship with a pound of butter; she takes her time to work out whether she trusts you, and what you're about. We had a slow burn. She was, I think, naturally suspicious of my keenness and ambition. She's seen so many young thrusters come and go, and her bullshit monitor is set on permanently high alert. A typical response to someone pitching a lame idea: "Fuck-a-duck, love, don't hold me back! We don't want to bore them to death."

She is an old-school producer, by which I mean she is hard-working, incredibly thorough and both bossy with and protective towards her team. I once referred to her as being a bit of a 'mother hen' and, although I meant it entirely as a compliment, she shrieked with horror. "Christ on a bike, Richard, that's horrible," she said. "You're *not* to call me that."

When she's talking through a running order, she'll often sell an item and the duration she's given it with a breezy "bit of fun – three minutes" and, if you're close enough, a sudden hard slap of her hand for emphasis. Her eagle eye misses nothing in the office, and she's a great one for quietly reminding you of someone who is feeling a bit miserable or left out, or identifying anyone who has the potential to be given more responsibility. She is hugely kind and patient with those she rates but has an extremely low tolerance for anyone idle or too full of themselves and if you've pissed her off, she makes no secret of the fact.

Having been here so long, and always working closely with whichever Editor is in charge, Annie, more than anyone else, knows where all the bodies are buried – and I don't mean the pets in the *Blue Peter* garden. She has a pithy anecdote about almost everyone in the world of *Blue Peter*, past and present, and can be wonderfully cynical. Only the other day she was regaling me with the story of Michael Sundin's first appearance in the office.

"He was wearing a skin-tight leather jump suit, with a zip down the front, left undone to show off his chest, which was obviously shaved." A roll of the eyes. "After he'd been in, I said to Biddy, 'Bender!' but she wasn't having it, 'Oh no, darling, that's just what young people are wearing. Anyway, I asked him and he says he's got a girlfriend!"

Before joining the BBC, Alex had a brief spell in the army, and has retained a slightly military manner; the clipped patrician tones, the occasional brusqueness and, thankfully, once he has fought his corner, the ability to take orders. He came to *Blue Peter* on attachment and, apart from a brief spell in studios, quickly became one of the most tenacious and adaptable film-makers the programme has ever had. An early triumph, about which he modestly says, "I didn't really have to do anything, it just sort of happened in front of me", was the oft-repeated spectacle of John Noakes climbing Nelson's column. His two main areas of specialism are shooting in the remotest parts of the world and masterminding the toughest and most exciting action films. He is a genuine eccentric, quite incapable of affecting a pose or playing any political game. All he wants to do is make films and he can be very territorial if he thinks a young Turk is trying to encroach on his patch. Many of his stories are made with the services. When I first joined and had some success with Richard Bacon undergoing officer cadet training at Sandhurst , he was the lone critical voice. "I couldn't see the point," he said, dismissively.

Similarly, when he found out that I was taking Matt to film the Royal Marines potential recruits' course, he was incandescent. Alex lives in Topsham in Devon, very close to the Marines' base, and he actually complained to Steve Hocking that "everyone here will think I've been sacked if they don't see my name on the credits after a Marines film."

But left to his own devices, Alex is supremely happy behind the lens and quite uninterested in status or power. When I got this job, he told me: "Well, good luck, old boy, but rather you than me. I worked out a long time ago that once you get to the top, there's nowhere to go but down – and probably out!"

Which made a sobering change from the usual bland congratulations.

He is incapable of being disingenuous and, if asked, will always tell you what he thinks. This sometimes, and inevitably, gets him into trouble. At a production meeting to discuss the role of PAs on filming, Alex caused uproar among their number when he announced, "Oh I never take a PA on location. It's one less bed to pay for, and, besides, I can make my own tea."

But those who dismiss him as a kind of Colonel Blimp character are missing the point; he is one of that breed of true British adventurers, and he does his exploration on our behalf. I find it an absolute pleasure to encourage his natural ambition to roam. His occasional gaffes and tactless remarks are just a side effect of his utter honesty, a quality I find useful in a senior producer. He can take blunt speaking himself too.

Most recently, I commissioned him to make a special show following Geth's attempts to undertake the famously gruelling Royal Marines Commando Yomp. This is a timed 30-mile march across bleak moorland carrying full kit, and must be accomplished within 8 hours. Geth made a valiant effort and only failed by a matter of minutes; frustratingly, much of the delay is caused by our own requirement to get overhead shots from a helicopter, which was hampered by the weather conditions. It is still an extraordinary and unusual achievement for a civilian with minimal training. When he reached the finishing line, Geth cried from a combination of exhaustion and emotion. I knew this because he told me all about it. But when I saw Alex's first cut, there were no tears.

"Oh we don't want to see him blubbing, surely?" said Alex.

"Absolutely we do," I tell him. "The tears are what makes him human and why we care about him."

"OK," shrugs Alex, "If you insist."

Over the years, there have been various attempts to oust him. He came very close when Oliver was Editor and there was a cost-cutting drive. Then again when I took over, attempts were made to persuade me that we should dispense with his services.

"Personally, I don't think it's appropriate that a producer is paid more than his Editor," said our HR woman, slyly.

"Then give me a pay rise," I responded.

Alex is worth his salary. He was the first to adapt to the new self-shooting technology, and this has given us access to all kinds of stories we would never have been able to afford if we had shot them with conventional crews. The downside of him shooting most of his own stories is that he tends to film way too much. This makes him difficult in the edit, as he is so close to the material. He hates being told to cut anything. He once shot what was supposed to be an eight-minute film with Katy at the Household Cavalry. The first edit was 26 minutes long and he resisted every cut.

Most of the presenters clamour to work with him. Because he rarely works from a script (thankfully; he is no writer and his scripts are basic, to say the least), his films create an experience in which the presenter is immersed. It's up to them to communicate what they are seeing and feeling. It's a wonderful showcase, and the clever ones seize the opportunity and relish the freedom.
Both Alex and Annie are towering figures in the story of *Blue Peter*, and, though neither has ever complained about a lack of recognition, today is about ensuring that they have some idea of the respect and affection they've generated over the years, quite apart from the enormous worth of their work.

19th December 2005
Tonight's the night of the Christmas party. Under the headline, 'But where do you put your *Blue Peter* badge, Zöe?', the *Mail* has also run a story about the "Christmas special you'd never have caught Val Singleton in'. This is accompanied by a couple of photos of Zöe in the *Material Girl* number from the panto, or, as the paper puts it, "frolicking in a bikini that leaves precious little space for her *Blue Peter* badge."
Breathlessly, the piece informs its readers that "Miss Salmon struts through a dance routine with hunky lifeguards" and that "BBC insiders have dubbed the former Miss Northern Ireland's performance '*Blue Peter*'s new Christmas appeal.'"
This typical tabloid nonsense is, however, enough to trigger another outburst from Liz, with whom I have a somewhat fraught meeting which starts with her telling me that she'd like to leave immediately and that she's sick of being "public property."
But it's actually about more than her distaste for the latest publicity around Zöe. A couple of weeks ago, we celebrated Dex's first birthday in the studio and since then, we've had some nasty letters from a handful of viewers complaining about Liz setting a poor example as a mother. This happens every time we feature Dexter and I've instructed the correspondence unit to show me any of these kind of complaints first so that I can decide whether or not it is a good idea to pass them onto Liz. Most of them are plainly from nutters. One even accuses her of setting a bad example as a "single mum", despite the fact that Liz is happily married. Someone has shown her the latest of these crank notes, and maybe that's helped tip her over the edge today.
We have a long chat. I think perhaps we have over-extended her departure. She resigned in the summer, it's six months later and she's still got four months to go. This is not really the kind of job which you can do with one foot in the door and one foot out. I remind her of what we agreed; that her final months wouldn't be a damp squib. She calms down and agrees that we've kept our side of the bargain

and that she's really enjoyed her work on the panto and the appeal. We are friends again.

Later, come back to my office to find a note on my desk: "I think it's all good," writes Liz. "U can go to party safe from abuse. I'm happy and will end my days on a high, love it, have no complaints and here's to a great New Year."

25th December 2005

The Christmas Day show is just wonderful. Alas, it is buried away in a morning slot, so it's unlikely to get the audience it deserves. But, still, it's a supremely confident way to end the year.

2006

4th January 2006

The first appearance of our new kitten. After the protracted Smudge debacle, I thought long and hard before deciding to have another cat on the programme. Only the very first, Jason, seems to have been relatively unflappable and at ease during his time on the show. Since then, every cat combination has been complicated and unsatisfying. Jack and Jill were known, with good reason, as the 'disappearing' cats. Willow had to be retired early as her behaviour became too eccentric and aggressive. Kari and Oke were infrequently seen and without much in the way of personality.

In any case, is the whole idea cruel?

Over the years, the show has become noisier and more dynamic, and therefore less cat-friendly. I have to bear in mind, too, that, although looked after by a dedicated handler, these animals are the property and responsibility of the BBC; Willow was retired in 1991, but we still had to pay for her upkeep until her death last year. The same will be true for Kari and Oke.

Before committing to another, I did some research. I wanted to know if there was any breed which might be better suited to the demands of a busy studio environment. Jason was a pedigree cat; did that make a difference? This is what has led to me choosing a breed called a rag doll. I'm assured that these cats are, by nature, placid and easy-going, and are happiest when allowed to flump

around doing nothing (now I come to think of it, there are a few people in this department who share exactly the same characteristics).
I've waited to introduce the kitten until today, in the cynical hope that the age-old magic of fur and feather will give our audiences a start of year boost.

9th January 2006
More schedule-tweaking. We are now 'simulcasting' shows between BBC1 and the CBBC channel, except that the latter requires an extra four minutes. So we have a somewhat clunky moment of on-air crossover between the two, and then the headache of filling the final few minutes of the channel-only broadcast with something that doesn't feel like an add-on or an also-ran. It's going to have an unsettling effect on the rhythm of the running orders, over which we spend much time and energy. The aim is always to create something with a genuine arc of light and shade. It's heretical to say so, but so much of the time the channel seems to be about filling airspace, rather than doing anything especially worthwhile or watchable.

11th January 2006
Today we launch our *Music Makers* competition. This is a partnership with BBC Talent, whose chief exec, Angela Wallis, is an old pal of mine. Years ago, we laboured under the iron hand of Esther Rantzen during a long series of *That's Life!* Angela was a researcher, I was the AFM, and we hit it off over the overloaded props table at the back of the Television Theatre. Esther was a great one for production team parties at which everyone was expected to do a turn, with Esther herself 'treating' us all to her once-heard quickly forgotten impersonation of Edith Piaf.
Angela and I joined forces with producer Richard Woolfe (who has just been made Controller of Sky). None of us could be described as shy and we rehearsed our performance for days; an outrageous dance routine to *Better the Devil You Know.* Clad in lycra and sequins, we called ourselves 'Kylie and her Two Dicks'. Esther seemed to love it (but then she enjoyed seeing anyone humiliate themselves in the name of entertainment).
Angela was then, and remains, brassy, bossy and loud. She's also great fun and she gets things done. So when she came to me and suggested some kind of shared project, I was only too keen to help spend her substantial budget. The idea we developed is to re-record the *Blue Peter* theme, using an arrangement by composer Murray Gold, who has cred with our audience because he scores *Doctor Who.* The competition will hunt for an orchestra of kids, not necessarily with any musical training, who will come together in a residential programme to work together and eventually play on the final version. This will become our

Above: 21st September 2005 - Tension in the trenches of Television Centre

Above: 3rd April 2006 - the changing team *(L to R)* Gethin, Konnie, RM, Zöe and Matt

Above: 13th November 2005 - shooting *Totally Blue Peter* with a little help from my son, Rupert

Above: 2nd July 2005 - stand off at Disneyland Paris

Above: 15th November 2005 - The talent in *Totally Blue Peter*

Above: 15th November 2005 - recording the finale of *Totally Blue Peter* - "such a happy day"

Above: 16th August 2005 - Wigs all round - the story of Marie Antoinette with Rupert as the Dauphin

Above: 19th June 2006 - In the gallery, all eyes on the monitors

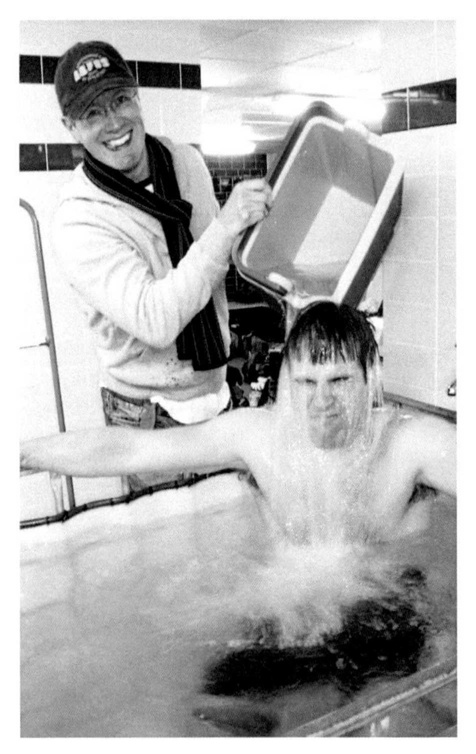

Above: 17th October 2006 - Edinburgh ice bath

Above: 4th July 2005 - Geth's revenge in Paris

Above: 19th June 2006 - Giving notes before Andy's final audition

Above: 28th June 2007 - messing about with the boys during my last studio day

Above: 15th May 2007 - Socks not Cookie - the claws are out and the ships are black

Above: 21st December 2004 - with the famous Christmas crib (supplied by Harrods)

Above: 2nd May 2007 - Editor as Emperor and Gladiator Geth

Above: 13th June 2007 - A swansong shoot aboard the Orient Express

Above: 28th June 2007 - making my farewell speech as Editor

Left: 17th October 2008 - with Biddy at the 50th anniversary exhibition, wearing the gold badge which she presented to me

Right: 16th October 2008 - A kiss from Lesley Judd at the 50th party

Above: 16th July 2016 - 50th birthday reunion with my dream team

new sig tune from this autumn. It's exactly the kind of creative, ambitious, and potentially life-changing stuff which defines the competitions I think we do best.
Today we also named our new kitten. He's going to be called Socks, which is a very suitable name considering the markings on each of his paws. But he is nearly called Cookie instead.
At run-through, there is a dust-up between myself and the producer, because I'm very far from happy to learn that the name suggestions (from a shortlist I chose) have been set up on the website as a 'one click, one vote' straw poll. This system allows kids to vote multiple times, which I don't think is robust or fair and, besides, I believe that the programme must have the casting vote for such a long-term decision. I thought this was clearly understood, but it appears not and now I have to decide whether to go with Cookie, which is overwhelmingly, and, I think, suspiciously, in the lead, or the runner-up, which is Socks. I decide that, from the show's point of view, Socks is much the better name so Socks it is.

13th January 2006
First of the films from our 'Winter Safari to Namibia'. I commissioned these to provide some warmth and colour during the cold winter months, and to provide what I hoped would be a make-or-break opportunity for Matt and Gethin to finally bond. It's always on the truly immersive foreign trips that the best and strongest connections are made. Geth has loved it. When I ask him how he got on with Matt, he tells me, "He's fucking funny, Rich. I haven't laughed like that for ages."
But when I ask Matt the same question, he says, "I'm a good actor," and my heart sinks.

16th January 2006
A show to celebrate the fantastic success of the appeal. We start by exploding the Totaliser, and then, throughout the show, Catherine Tate appears in character as her famously sulky teenage creation, Lauren (catchphrase: "Am I bovvered?").
Catherine is a delight, and keen to take direction, which is very necessary as, though popular with kids, Lauren is very much a 'post-watershed' creation. This means we have to plan the various moments really carefully so that it's funny and true to the character, but not going to inspire an avalanche of outraged complaints either. When we occasionally try this approach, it works only when the presenter understands that they are the 'straight' man or woman. They can't start trying to get the laughs themselves or, even more disastrously, neither can they try to get the upper hand in any way. It's a particular skill to steer the item

whilst apparently being the passive party. Simon managed it brilliantly when Rowan Atkinson brought Mr Bean to the studio. Gethin, too, has the knack and his various interactions with the ever-stroppy Lauren work like a dream. When I compliment him on this, he indicates Zöe and says, "It's because I'm used to sulky girls with loads of attitude."

20th January 2006

Press office alert me to a major piece in today's *Guardian* by the writer Kate Figes. Under the headline, 'Hello Boys!', with a photograph of Zöe from the *Material Girl* number in *Totally Blue Peter*, it details at some length Ms Figes's objections to Zöe. She calls her "a full-size Barbie doll", brands her "insincere and fatuous" and suggests that "she rarely seems comfortable around children, talking to them in slow, patronising tones".

It is Figes's theory that Zöe has been cast in a deliberate attempt to "sex up" and "dumb down" the programme. I think it's a pretty spiteful piece, and it comes complete with trademark *Guardian* howlers, stating that Zöe was 'Miss Ireland 1999' rather than Miss *Northern* Ireland, which is rather a significant difference, and suggesting that Zöe's "semi-naked" body has "adorned" the tabloids, whereas in fact some of the tabs have simply run a few inoffensive shots from Zöe's modelling work (none of it "semi-naked"); work which funded her law degree.

I give Zöe a ring to warn her and discuss it, and tell her that I will be replying to *The Guardian* in due course. She sounds bewildered and says, "Why single me out? Is it so bad to have been a beauty queen?" I explain that, as far as *The Guardian* women's pages go, it probably ranks as a category A crime.

But it's not just an attack on Zöe, it's an attack on the editorial of the programme (i.e. me) and the narrow injustice of this is infuriating. *Of course* we make mistakes. *Inevitably,* not everything we feature works or can be popular with all the audience (this goes for presenters as well as the actual items). Zöe is never going to be everyone's cup of tea, any more than the other presenters. But there is no balance whatsoever in this piece; not a mention of some of the brilliant, and, one would think, *Guardian*-pleasing aspects of our recent output; the Childline appeal, the range of films celebrating different cultures, the coverage of arts, history and the environment. Just an outpouring of snide bitchery and cheap digs.

I'm equally dismayed by the total absence of support or interest from upstairs; perhaps they haven't seen it? (unlikely). Perhaps they think the writer is on to something? (possible). Or perhaps they just don't give a shit and think it will just blow over? (more likely). Whatever, nice to know they have our backs.

23rd January 2006

The sale of *Blue Peter* badges on eBay is getting out of hand. I've been aware of it for some time. At first, I was slightly mystified by the prices these little triangles of plastic were fetching. Then I started to get calls from some of the attractions on our badge list, among them Edinburgh Zoo and Madame Tussaud. They've spotted a surge in the numbers of kids presenting badges for free entry, and it hasn't escaped them that some of the badges are not the current design. It seems that some parents are buying badges on eBay and using them to take their kids on trips to which they aren't entitled. Not unnaturally, the attractions are now comparing notes and threatening to withdraw from the scheme altogether. I'm holding them at bay but something must be done. I've been trying to get the BBC to engage with the issue for several months, but it is complicated. We can't exactly prevent people from selling their own property. With eBay's co-operation, the BBC Investigations Unit have closed down some of the sales which look dodgy; multiple badges from one account.

Some of these accounts have subsequently been traced and one in particular turns out to belong to an Assistant Producer in the department, who worked on the show a couple of years ago. A grim disciplinary process followed. This AP had apparently held on to a bag of badges, which they have been slowly disposing of via ebay, making some tidy sums in the process. HR believed that this was gross misconduct, and insisted that the person was sacked, if only to send a clear message to the rest of the department. I was very uncomfortable about this draconian verdict. The person in question was clearly full of remorse and had an otherwise good record. The whole experience counts as one of my absolute lows on the programme.

24th January 2006

The Guardian print part of my response to the 'Hello Boys!' article, in which I do my best to redress the balance: "I don't think *Blue Peter*'s audience of children would recognise Kate Figes' character assassination of Zöe Salmon," I write. "In her year on the programme, Zöe has established her bravery, skill and versatility in true *Blue Peter* tradition. She has tackled everything from formula one racing, RNLI sea survival training, rubbish collecting, potholing and singing at the last night of the Proms. She is about to become the first female *Blue Peter* presenter to run the London Marathon.

"Ms Figes complains that Zöe appeared "stripped down to a skimpy bra and knickers" in the *Blue Peter* panto, but she fails to note that all the other female presenters in recent years have also taken part in glamorous dance routines in our Christmas entertainments. On the usual editions, Zöe, like her predecessors and contemporaries, dresses fashionably and not to look overtly sexy.

"*Blue Peter* is not being sexed up or dumbed down. We have just concluded our highly successful *Treasure Trail* Appeal for ChildLine and launched a UK-wide music-making initiative aimed at children from all backgrounds. The 2005 *Blue Peter* Book Awards was the top-rated children's show in its week of transmission and more than 32,000 children entered our *Storytellers* competition, finishing stories started by famous writers. The best entries were published in a special book. Your readers may be interested to know that we have had no complaints about Zöe from our target audience."

1st February 2006

Live OB from Buckingham Palace. No royals involved, though we are plugging the 'Party at the Palace' and how kids can get a ticket. There's also a lavish film telling the story of Buckingham Palace. Once upon a time, not so very long ago, I would have seized the opportunity to direct this myself, but I'm just too busy. Instead, I've asked Bridget to take charge, knowing what a fabulous job she'll do. I've made poor Gethin present. I say 'poor' because he's forever banging on about how he's a republican and not a royalist. I tease him, saying "It's in your contract to love the Queen and show humble respect to the Prince of Wales," to which he responds with a robust "Fuck that!"

He's discovered that my middle name is Kingsley, which he finds hilarious, and abbreviates to "Kings". So when I summon him to my office, he breezes in with a cheeky, "Alright, Kings! What am I in trouble for today?"

"On the contrary, you're being given a great honour," I smirk, before breaking the news that he is going to front the Buckingham Palace film.

"Wear a suit, have a shave and try not to sound too common," I tell him.

Someone in no danger of this is today's star guest, top children's author Anthony Horowitz. He's a fascinating man. As well as his very popular and skilfully crafted kids' adventure stories, he has a lucrative line in TV drama, too, the latest of which is ITV's *Foyle's War*. The success of this is marred only by the vagaries of ITV commissioning, who characteristically blow hot and cold about whether or not they want another series, and the hazards of working with the demanding and eccentric leading man (in TV drama, it was ever thus). Horowitz isn't just a clever wordsmith. He's an absolute charmer, too. He had a particularly unhappy childhood (we compare notes about the miseries of boys' boarding schools) but there is no trace of dysfunction or bitterness. We reminisce about the success of the competition we ran with him during my first season as Editor; this was for viewers to design a spy gadget which Horowitz would write into his story. He's hustling for another slice of the action, perhaps on the same lines. I demur, as, though I'm more than happy to work with him again, it needs to be something fresh and even more ambitious. What about a storyline for his next major TV drama? We kick around ideas and brainstorm the possibilities. Being able to think big is one of the keenest pleasures of the job.

3rd February 2006

Zöe comes to my office to discuss the poisonous *Guardian* article. She's seen my response, of course, but wants to have her own say, too. She's made of stern stuff but she's upset and rattled, and I don't blame her. It comes on top of a rough few months she's had in terms of hostile media. There was all the circus of the Red Hand business and then the entirely specious accusations around the recruitment process which led to her appointment. She's not exactly been welcomed with open arms by everyone on the programme, either, though, thankfully, as well as her critics, she does have her fans and champions too.

She brings a hefty document with her; she's used her legal training to work her way through the article, carefully and thoroughly rebutting all the half-truths and insinuations it contains. I read through it, laughing at some of the points she makes. In answer to a dig Figes makes about men "ooh-ahing" over her "tastiness" on websites, Zöe has written: "Me and hundreds of other female and male presenters, In fact, I would be flattered if I was getting anything near the number of internet hits of the likes of Cat Deeley."

Figes inevitably dredged up the Red Hand farrago, and the attempt to follow it up by blaming Zöe for holding up a child's competition entry in which the whole of the UK was covered with the Union flag. "Was this stupid or deliberate?" she asked. This invites the following response: "I did not pre-select it. It was handed to me a few minutes before live transmission. When discussing it live on air, I did not make reference to the fact that one of our viewers did not know the correct geography of the UK and the republic of Ireland but instead I focused on the Olympic logo which the viewer had also drawn and I chatted about London's Olympic bid. Was I stupid? No. That would be the viewer. Was it deliberate? The entry ended up in my hands, it is as simple as that."

And so it goes on, all the way through the article. When I've finished reading it, I say, "I'm glad I'm never going to have to face you in a court room. But sounds like writing it was pretty cathartic?"

Zöe agrees but she is frustrated at the lack of any genuine right of reply. Presenters are public figures and must take the rough with the smooth. It is a compliment that *Blue Peter* still matters enough to raise passions and inspire debate, although this is usually a side effect of some other agenda. She must mourn it and move on, and hope that there isn't a sequel.

6th February 2006

More management musical chairs; Richard Deverell has been made controller of children's (evidently plain old 'head' no longer fit for purpose) and Anne

Gilchrist is creative director. What this actually means is that we effectively have two bosses (though not, alas, for the price of one) – Richard will be the 'outward face' of the department, and in charge of strategy and spearheading the move to Manchester. Anne will be the commissioner, in charge of the creative side of the department. I have my doubts about this arrangement; it's hard enough trying to please one boss, never mind two. Richard seems to be a fan of *Blue Peter*; certainly, he speaks glowingly of Gethin. He was, however, utterly bemused by the panto; he clearly just didn't get it on any level. Not a song and dance man.

Anne is very much from an entertainment background, though her somewhat dour manner seems to belie this. She doesn't find it easy to chat freely to those she doesn't know, and she can seem stern and stand-offish. We've been friends for years, though this isn't necessarily an advantage in a professional sense. Our views on *Blue Peter* only meet in places; she would happily jettison more of the heavyweight content. We clashed fairly head on over her handling of the Red Hand business; she rushed headlong into an apology which caused more harm than good. But in other ways she has been supportive, and she at least says what she thinks.

13th February 2006

Morning pre-recording for an item about the extraordinarily gruelling Atlantic rowing race in which the terribly posh and utterly charming Ben Fogle has just taken part. To make it more interesting than a straightforward interview, Ben agrees to a mini-rowing challenge with Gethin, to see who can row the fastest/hardest over a minute. Geth is determined to beat our guest, his face undergoing several changes of colour as he pours absolutely everything he's got into the task. He is declared the winner, and is clearly delighted, but such is his extreme exertion that he cannot articulate his triumph. Ben congratulates him warmly and I don't want to be the one who points out that he has clearly been holding back, his perfect manners allowing Geth the upper hand. The unfortunate side-effect of this feat is that Geth is pretty much fucked for the rest of the day and, as ever when he is tired, his concentration slips and his presenting suffers.

It's a busy day because, as well as the morning pre-record, we have a live show in the afternoon. The centrepiece of this is a stunt we've been planning for a while in response to requests for us to fit in with a CBBC themed week called 'Ha Ha Half Term'. I wanted to 'prank' the presenters and my idea was to feature a ludicrous mime artist, of a type not perhaps a million miles from the kind we might actually book, revealing part way through the 'performance' that the artist was in fact a familiar face. I thought that Simon Thomas might be up for the

joke. I called him and he agreed immediately, assuming he could get the go-ahead from his new bosses at Sky. Happily, they seem to have a sense of humour so we were in business. It's been quite an operation to plan but as 'Alphonse – Theatre of the Body' camera rehearse, it's plain that the presenters haven't a clue.
"It's fucking shite, this, Rich," says Matt, watching critically from the sidelines. "I don't get it."
"I know, he's weird isn't he?" I agree. "But I'm told his shows are selling out in Europe."
On transmission, it delivers precisely the sucker-punch surprise I wanted; the presenters' reactions are textbook; shocked, amused, delighted. Afterwards, I race down to the floor and join the huddle of Matt, Liz and Simon, all talking nineteen to the dozen. There is so much affection in the air, and such an immediate shorthand between us all. And then the poignancy of this strikes me forcibly; that this is all illusory. Simon is just here for this fleeting moment, and this is a merely a momentary flashback to what we all once had, and which has gone for good.

14th February 2006
The press office are on the phone. They've taken a call from *The Sun* enquiring after Geth, who, they say, has collapsed during filming with the young boxer Kevin Mitchell and has been taken to hospital. Would we like to comment?
I'd like to know what's happened first. I get on to the director pronto. Gethin is fine, and recovering fast, he says, but, yes, it is true that paramedics had to be called. The story is supposed to focus on the extraordinary fitness demanded of a professional boxer. Mitchell and his trainer (central casting: a mean-faced bald geezer) put Geth through a relentless series of circuits. Just as he was with Ben Fogle, Geth is determined to shine and put everything he's got into the exercises. But this trainer is equally determined to break him and show the poof off the telly what it's like in a man's world. It's obvious that the call to *The Sun* came from Mitchell's people, too; after all, it's a gift of a story – this guy's usual training regime breaks a *Blue Peter* presenter.
I'm not very pleased with the director, because it sounds as if he ceased to be in control and became more a spectator in a kind of televised bullying session. I dish out a lecture. Geth is young and fit, but, I spell out, it's not impossible for young and fit people to suffer cardiac arrests or other calamities. When I speak to Geth himself, he's more embarrassed than anything else, blaming his lack of sleep and a decent breakfast for his humiliating collapse. He sets himself such a high bar that I'm sure his perpetual anxiety to do his best didn't help either. Anyway, the most important thing is that he is OK. Later, I take a call from the

photographer I'd sent to capture the story for the annual.
"I got a marvellous shot of Gethin being sick in a bucket," he enthuses. "Hmm," I reply. "Well, I suppose you never got that from Valerie Singleton."

5th March 2006
A difficult meeting with one of our new producers. She's annoyed with me and I'm annoyed with her. The reason for our antipathy; the script for her next programme. The usual routine is that every producer submits his or her draft script to me for any tweaks and changes. With a competent producer, these should be minor and perfunctory. But every script I've had so far from this woman has pretty much required a top-to-toe rewrite. The grammar is non-existent and the spelling a disgrace (and no, she's not dyslexic – I checked). When I first challenged her about the standard of what she is submitting, she just laughed.
"Why do you care so much?" she said. "I mean, it's not as if the scripts are going up on screen. It's just an outline – a guide for the presenters."
I disagree. Ceefax use our scripts as the basis for their subtitling, and a poorly written, badly spelt script throws the presenters and puts the pressure to fix it on them. In my book, it's basic professionalism – why get it wrong if you can get it right? If she were a rubbish producer, I might understand it but in every other respect I like her and think she's great. Bright, funny, enthusiastic, good with her team, full of ideas and plainly (other than in our script meetings) pleased to be here. I consider whether I should allow these qualities to offset the consistently appalling scripts, which demand so much work to put right. But this is not all I have to consider. There is the message tolerating this situation sends to the rest of the team; if it's OK for her to get away with such an attitude, why not for everyone else?
I try to explain this to her in our meeting, but, for the first time, she visibly shuts down on me and just won't have it.
"If you want to spend your time slaving over a script no one reads, that's your decision," she says. "It's not Shakespeare, it's a kids' TV programme."
There is nowhere to go after this and we both know it, I think. As soon as she leaves my office, I call HR to explain that it isn't working and I'd like to let her go as soon as practically possible. Then I get back to fixing the deficiencies of the script in front of me.

10th March 2006
Matt directed the film in today's show, following a day-in-the-life of a talented young gymnast. This is the second time this season a presenter has directed a film (Konnie shot one of the appeal films). It's empowering for the presenter,

and helps them to understand the demands of making the show, as well as fronting it. They invariably do an excellent job, as they understand so thoroughly both the technical and the artistic requirements. I wish I could make this happen more often, but such are the demands of their schedules, it's just not possible; directing even a simple film requires at least a couple of days' prep, perhaps a recce, a day on location and then two or three days in the edit, with the dub and final mix to finish it off. Matt, of course, went one stage better when he directed and shot the little films we ran last year about Meg's puppies; but then he always does go one better.

11th March 2006

Our team have had a trying day on the set of the Will Young video. This has a vintage *Blue Peter* theme; the concept is that Young is a presenter during the 70s and 80s, and, to this end, I've agreed with the record company that they can have access to the archive, into which the singer will be 'painted'. It's a pity the actual song, *Who Am I?*, is a bit of a dreary dirge, but he's a popular artist so maybe it will do OK. The record company's side of the bargain is granting full access for us to make a behind-the-scenes film covering the process (green screen, mainly), and a small cameo role for Konnie, who is presenting the report. She tells me that Young is a diva; filming with us only reluctantly, and after extended persuasion from various parties, that he complains constantly of being "tired" and wanting to be left in peace. All the usual tedious pop star twattishness. She thinks we should have sent Gethin – "a bit of eye-candy might have done the trick," she theorises. "He sure as hell wasn't interested in me!"

13th March 2006

Not the best start to the day as Konnie turns up so under the weather that there is no option other than to send her home. Really, it is a miracle that this doesn't happen more often; the presenters have extraordinary stamina, considering their relentless schedules. Back in Biddy's era, she had a tough rule of "no show, no dough"; so that if a presenter missed a studio, their pay was duly docked. A slightly draconian incentive.

Fortunately, our main guest for the day is Mark Speight, from CBBC's very popular and long-running art show, *SMart*. He's a very capable presenter, so he happily fills the void. He's in the studio with a bunch of kids to undertake a large-scale painting in the style of Jackson Pollock. Speight is a great enthusiast; he genuinely loves what he does and he is brilliant with the kids, pushing them on, making them laugh, firing out suggestions. He's got an amazing face, too; the cheekbones are ridiculous, and this is topped with a shock of peroxided hair.

I've agreed to some guests of my own, today. Three students from my old school,

Felsted, who are here to watch proceedings, interview me and, in due course, produce a report for the school magazine. I meet them on the studio floor, where they are hovering in a huddle. When I introduce myself, they have the surface self-assurance that public schools instil in you, though their eyes tell a different story – these are swivelling furtively this way and that, trying to take everything in. On the drive to work, I've been racking my brains trying to think what I can and can't say in answer to their questions. I don't want to be too bitter or rude about my experiences at school (which I'm sure is very different today) but neither do I want to completely perjure myself and paint some kind of Enid Blyton fairy story. I give them all the positives I can think of; how boarding schools develop your self-confidence and independence, that they often have characters you remember for life (though I don't always specify why), but that I think the idea that your school days are the best years of your life is a profoundly depressing notion.

14th March 2006

This morning I met with Matt to discuss the offer we have made him; another year on the programme, with a respectable pay rise. It isn't quite what Alison Sharman promised him last year. Though this was never a formal offer, she promised him a longer deal with a series of sweeteners (spin-off shows etc). "Basically, she told me that I could write my own contract," he told me at the time.

Neither have I accommodated some of the wilder suggestions Matt has come up with over the last few weeks. Because he has now moved into the Hertfordshire countryside (not that far from me, in fact) he is struggling with the demands of the commute, and requests a guarantee that he will always have a later call time for studios. As well as this consideration, he'd like approval of his key filming projects, input into our choice of directors, and more time off in the summer. I've explained why all these conditions aren't acceptable; that they would create a 'one rule for Matt' resentment among the other presenters.

He is exhausted, that is obvious. Matt works ridiculously hard, and often his are the most physical stories. He is literally a victim of his own success. But then he has been doing this job for nearly seven years. That's a long time to be a *Blue Peter* presenter, especially such a high-functioning one.

He tells me that he's decided to leave. I feel a strange combination of emotions; relief and sadness in equal measure. It has been increasingly difficult to manage him lately; his customary positivity and cheerfulness, his enjoyment of the work and sense of fun, all have slowly evaporated among the continuing workload and the alienation he feels from the new presenters. But, for all this, I struggle to imagine the show without him. He is so brilliant and so committed, and we

share a basic philosophy of what makes *Blue Peter* special.
"I just think I need to stop," he says. "It's not that I'm unhappy about the offer; you've been generous and I appreciate it. But you know I've been thinking about this for ages, trying to make up my mind. And I think it's time to do something different."
We talk about what the "something different" might be; he needs to find an agent for starters (he's never seen the point of one during his commitment to *Blue Peter*). He suggests that he wants to become "the Alan Titchmarsh of the dog world" (rather him than me). Meg, of course, will leave with him.
I ask him if he's happy for us to keep the news under wraps for the time being. Given that Liz's departure is imminent, I'm keen to avoid stories in the press about 'sinking ships' and all that bollocks.
"I'll do whatever it needs, Rich," he says. "I want to go out on a high, if I possibly can."

15th March 2006
Matt is off sick today. I wonder if he needs to process yesterday's decision?
Much of the morning spent recording an item about 'fashion disasters' through the decades. I only hope this is as much fun to watch as it is to record. Konnie is in her element, and even the habitual sniping between Zöe and Gethin seems to be temporarily on hold. At lunch, I send him and one of the film team to Shepherd's Bush Green. Geth is clad in a copy of David Beckham's infamous sarong, a fashion disaster only Becks could get away with. The mission is to shoot the (hopefully startled) reactions of passers-by, as Geth casually strolls around, although this being London there's a good chance no one will turn a hair. Anyway, the two of them set off in high spirits.
I think how differently this would have been if Matt hadn't been unwell, as this was supposed to be his part of the item. He'd have done it, no doubt about that, but probably only after having a good moan about it. The truth is that he's lost the fun of the job and that's a major reason why I think he's made the right decision both for him and the programme.

27th March 2006
Having finally managed to persuade the powers that be that, thanks to the eBay situation, the entire badge system is on the verge of imminent collapse, I've got the go-ahead to announce that we are suspending the scheme with immediate effect. All of our partners at the various attractions have been incredibly supportive and patient. They don't want to see it founder, but neither can they continue to tolerate the wholesale fraud, which has steadily increased over the last few months. This is an act of faith; we will put the entire scheme on ice until

we can devise and agree a practical method to protect both the attractions and the children who have genuinely won their badges. So far the suggestions haven't been practical or would be too expensive; and there are the usual issues around data protection, too.

28th March 2006

Spend the morning recording *You're the Top*, a musical performance to insert into Liz's last show. This is a last hurrah, not just for Liz and Matt, who have shared so many singing and dancing moments over the last six years, but for Gary (Lloyd), our usual choreographer, and Dave (Cooke) as MD. By the end, I've actually got a lump in my throat at the thought that this is the last time we'll be able to have this much fun working together.

Back to reality with a bump in the afternoon, and what should be a straightforward item about owls. The first problem is Zöe's pronunciation of the word 'owl' ("oiyall"). I worry that it is so distracting that it will derail the item. I discuss it in notes and Zöe is distinctly cool about it. I can't blame her as it is only her natural accent and I'd be the first to defend her against anyone criticising her for speaking the way she does. Never the less, I decide to make the item a two-hander with Matt. While this helps the clarity, I still feel a bit shitty about the way I've handled it.

During the recording, one of the "oiyalls" decides to abandon its perch and fly up to the lighting grid, from where it observes us all impassively. It's a great moment, and very funny, but as soon as we have stopped recording we are faced with a problem. The owl won't come down.

"He might stay up there for hours," the handler informs us.

"Oh no, he won't," says the floor manager. "There's another show due in here tomorrow and the set and strike is starting now."

Sure enough, there is a crashing and banging around us as the setting crew get stuck in, loading a teddy truck with bits of the set. The Studio Resources Manager now appears, looking harassed.

"If the owl won't come down of its own accord, it'll have to be shot down," he says. I wonder if I've heard correctly.

"What! You can't possibly shoot it!" I protest.

"It wouldn't kill it," says the SRM, patiently. "It would be a tranquilliser gun. But it can't be allowed to stay up there."

"How long have we got?"

"About half an hour," he tells me. "I'll need to make some phone calls."

I swear that owl could understand every word. For the next half an hour, it remained oblivious to the scores of human beings scurrying about beneath it, and impervious to the various entreaties of its hapless handler. Then, with under a minute to go before drastic action, it flapped its wings self-importantly and swept down from its vertiginous vantage point. Crisis over.

29th March 2006

I'm putting together two 'goodbye Liz' compilations and today we filmed the links for these in the garden. Last summer, when Liz decided to leave, I spoke to the powers that be about some kind of exit strategy. It struck me as shameful that after six years' fine service on their flagship magazine programme, the BBC had shown absolutely no interest in Simon Thomas. He is now working for Sky, so that they, instead of us, are reaping the benefits of his skill and reputation. I suggest that we should learn from this and not repeat the same mistake with Liz. Anne Gilchrist is not a fan, and doesn't really rate Liz, but Richard Deverell agrees with me and so it has been decided that Liz will move straight into presenting CBBC's *Totally Doctor Who*. This is the latest of the various spin-offs designed to tap into the revival's phenomenal success. Liz isn't exactly a fan of *Doctor Who* – in fact, I think she is completely bewildered by it, but she should be able to mask this, and she won't be alone. Her co-presenter will be our 'nearly man', Barney Harwood. They'll make a great team. Liz would really like to do some more acting, but recognises that this is unlikely, as she's not willing to fight for it. Her perpetually laid-back manner is not a pose, but a reflection of how she ticks.

31st March 2006

Today I appear on various news programmes to discuss the suspension of the badge scheme. News 24 is quite an operation; it's like landing on a fast running conveyor belt. You turn up to news reception and get buzzed through thick glass security doors where a floor manager-type greets you in hushed tones and asks you to wait in a kind of ante-area just off the studio. I say studio, but it's more of a 'transmission space' carved out of the huge open-plan news offices. When it's your turn, you are smuggled in, seated and mic'd up while the presenters are talking on a close-up. Over a piece of VT, one of them, Matthew Amroliwala, briefly leans over to say "Hello, Richard" and then we are on, and rattle through the questions. As quickly and seamlessly as I arrive, I am de-mic'd and gently ejected back onto the other side of the security glass.

PM is rather less clinical. For this, I report to another outpost area within the maze of TV Centre, and I'm led into a studio where the presenter, Eddie Mair, greets me affably and indicates a chair to one side of him. I'm handed a head set to wear and sit as a spectator for about ten minutes until we are on. I stress the point that we are not saying people can't sell their badges; they are free to do what they like with their own property. Our only concern is to protect the badge

scheme for the children who've earned the right to access its privileges, and for the attractions which are currently being defrauded.
Eddie Mair comments on how "youthful" I am. Hmm, I think. Perfect face for radio, more like.

3rd April 2006
The first of two live programmes devoted to our interactive Four Nations challenge quiz. These are ambitious and intelligent, but still I am uneasy about them. It just feels as if our true identity is being hijacked to tick boxes for CBBC and the endless ambition for more interactive content. I can't see the point of this unless it is authentically linked to the core values and genuine characteristics of the show itself. I have to pick my battles, and I've batted off some of the dafter or more cynical proposals, but sometimes you have to play ball and show willing.

7th April 2006
Thank God the awful experiment of the simulcast is over; no more clunky junctions switching from BBC1 to the channel, and dodging the more-often-than-not lame fillers which make up the final 3 minutes of the channel TX. We're also at the end of five-times-a-week. From next week, we lose the Friday slot.
"I think you've been asked to do too much," explains Richard Deverell, when he breaks the news.
I must say I am relieved. The whole 'stripped' schedule was a condition of the job when I took over. I did my best with it, because it was that or watch someone else fuck around with the show I love. I'm fairly proud of what we've achieved, but it has been exhausting for all of us, and especially the presenters. I think it has contributed to Matt's malaise, in particular. Five presenters always felt too many, as well; so that when Liz departs in a couple of weeks, we'll be back to a quartet.
"You're irreplaceable," I tell her, in gushing tones.
"What are you after?" she laughs, suspiciously.

8th April 2006
At Stonyhurst in Lancashire (posh Catholic boarding school; alma mater of the DG Mark Thompson) for the *Music Makers* residential camp. This has been organised by Annie Dixon, and she's done a magnificent job. Quite apart from the work which needs to be accomplished to get to a standard good enough for the recording on Monday, and the fact that we need to film enough to fill two special shows along the way, there is the sheer responsibility of keeping such a disparate group of kids fed, watered, entertained and happy for the duration.

She, and the team, have accomplished this, not only with an imaginative and thoroughly well-organised programme of activities but with their warmth, kindness and clear leadership. The kids are all smiles and seem to have bonded incredibly well, with all kinds of friendships being forged in the various workshops, rehearsals and bouts of organised fun. As well as Annie, I'm incredibly impressed with Ben Foster, who is Murray's musical number two. Ben's enthusiasm and charm inspire everyone.
"I think I've got a bit of a crush on you," I tell him.
"Join the queue, love," says Annie, quick as a flash.

9th April 2006

We decamp to BBC Manchester (a run-down dump which makes me long for TV Centre) for the final recording of Murray Gold's arrangement of the sig tune. All our Music Maker kids are carefully positioned alongside the BBC Philharmonic. There's a wonderful sense of excitement in the air, and so much pride in the expressions of these kids. It's been an experience which I suspect will live with them for the rest of their lives. It's emotional for all of us; the presenters, the kids' families, even the more hard-bitten members of the production team. Unlike the 'Four Nations' shows, it feels very much a natural extension of what *Blue Peter* can achieve on a grand scale; inspiring, encouraging and rewarding its audience's aspiration .
"This is so wonderful," says Angela Wallis, the BBC Talent head whose investment made the competition possible. "We need to follow it up with something just as big next year."
I don't need persuading. I sit with the stirring music filling the air and begin to daydream about the possibilities.

10th April 2006

Liz's last show. We devote the show to a kind of *This is Your Blue Peter Life*, with a parade of guests including Simon Thomas, Toddy and baby Dex, bobsleigh athlete Michelle Coy, with whom Liz competed in the world championships, and Kitty Hart, who provided a heart-breaking eyewitness account in Liz's film about Auschwitz.
"Isn't this going to be a real downer?" asks the producer, during the planning. "Not to mention the fact that we are coming to Auschwitz straight off the back of Basil Brush?"
"It's *Blue Peter,*" I shrug. "We are masters of the gear change. This show is all about celebrating every aspect of it, and what Liz has achieved. It'll be fine."
We've given Liz one of the ground floor star dressing rooms to share with her family, and, after run-through, and presenter notes, it's here that I head for.

Liz is a true chameleon. How she looks is so often a barometer of her feelings. When she comes in clad in something shapeless in a drab colour, I know that trouble is a foot and she's feeling anxious, worried or depressed. When she's in a positive and happy frame of mind, she embraces vivid colours and will look quirky, stylish and unique. Today she looks her very best, radiantly beautiful. She's not been in rehearsals, so I talk her through the running order.
"It's all about you," I remind her. "The audience who love you, the production team, everyone around you. Don't resist it. Go on and enjoy the love!"
We show a montage of moments in which Liz has awarded various badges, and out of this, we have a child present her with her own gold badge. This continues a tradition I started with Simon. It is not to everyone's taste, with some on the team arguing that it "devalues" the currency of the gold. But I think this is bollocks. Our presenters are the absolute heart of the show. When they have stayed as long, and been as successful, as Simon or Liz, I think the audience, to whom they have often been heroes, will absolutely applaud the moment when they get their gold. It might, I suppose, present a problem if the departing presenter is a Chris Wenner or Michael Sundin, but I'm sure there are ways round that. I only hope I never have to wrestle with that problem.
Later, when I'm back home, Liz texts me. "Thank u for a lovely last day," she says. It's only what she deserved and I'm glad she enjoyed it. But now it is finally over, I feel horribly flat.

11th April 2006
Spend the morning pre-recording *Summer Nights* from the latest production of *Grease*, with Gethin stepping in as Danny, and Zöe as Sandy. Their vocals may not quite be West End standard, but they both certainly look the part and absolutely go for it. As is par for the course, though, when I nip down during camera rehearsals to give them a bit of love, Geth is quick to put himself down.
"Do you think Matt will be pissed off that I'm doing this?" he asks me. "Because he would do it brilliantly, wouldn't he?"
"Don't worry about Matt," I tell him firmly. "He's done more than his share of singing and dancing. Just focus on your own performance."
Later, a text from Simon Thomas: "Good 2 cu yesterday," he writes. "Enjoyed seein u all again, brought back lots of good memories. Just watched Liz's first highlights prog. V. good. What was she wearin 4 links? Only Liz! Was Geth OK? He didn't seem v happy. I told him 2 hang in there. I think once Matt goes he has 2 really grasp the moment."
This is sound advice.

19th April 2006

Pre-record an interview with Lis Sladen to promote her imminent return to *Doctor Who.* This isn't the half of it, though, as CBBC are also planning a spin-off series based around her character, which is one reason why we want to get in there early and establish a connection. It must seem extraordinary to this sixty-something actress that the idea of such a show has resurfaced a quarter of a century after it was last tried, in 1981's *K9 and Company.*

Sladen is absolutely tiny and much younger-looking than her years. She is also patently nervous, which I find surprising. I mention that she must have done countless interviews and promotions over the years.

"Mmm," she nods. "But this is *Blue Peter.* I mean, c'mon. *Blue Peter.*"

I briefly wonder if she's putting it on, applying a little flattery, but, no, I think she is quite sincere. Neither do I suspect her of faking her wide-eyed reaction to the fact that we are in one of the studios frequently used during her time in *Doctor Who.*

"It's like a goose walking over your grave. Extraordinary. Really powerful."

My old mate (and rampant *Who* fan) Patrick has brought along a friend's 12-year-old son to meet this reborn icon of the show. Sladen happily poses for photographs and I think the boy's presence helps her to relax. She's charming with him. Geth, who is doing the interview and wanders onto the floor while all this is going on, watches for a moment and then comments to me: "What a pro, eh?"

I introduce them, and they have a quick chat, in which Sladen talks about her own brief brush with presenting, for a BBC schools programme. "It was really odd," she says. "They chose me but it was like they had second thoughts somewhere along the line and it was a really unhappy experience. We flew out to this oil rig to film, so we really were in the middle of nowhere, and I was just left to my own devices, to work it out for myself. If you're used to direction, that's hard."

"Oh, you get plenty of direction round here," laughs Geth, with feeling.

"You need it," say I.

I've taken pains to brief Geth on possibly the most important principle of any interview – namely, "get the bugger's name right".

This turns out to be a mistake as it obviously somewhere in Geth's brain, it plants the idea of getting it wrong, so that when Sladen emerges from the TARDIS on take one, he refers to her as "Jo". She is immediately frosty and I am exasperated. Fortunately, Geth has the charm to smooth over the awkward moment and we go again. I've persuaded the actress to hold Socks, despite her nervous protests.

"I'm not very good with cats," she says. "He won't bite, will he?"

"Absolutely not," I reply, reassuringly. "He's virtually stuffed."

24th April 2006

And so the auditions for Matt's successor begin. This morning, we put four possibles through the process. These include Sid Sloane, who is one of the regular presenters on CBeebies. Sid had a key part in *Christmas at the Club Blue Peter*, was a joy to work with, and was quite superb. But the audition doesn't do him justice. I think he's finding it hard to 'age up' the presenting, despite this forming part of our first discussions. Anyway, I'm disappointed.

I've also invited back Matthew Landers, who did so well the last time round, and was certainly in with a chance. He's kept himself busy since and has written a well-received play, which is impressive. When I called him to ask if he'd like another shot at it, I mentioned that, as this would be to replace Matt, how would he feel about adopting a stage name in the event he gets the job?

"I just worry that replacing Matt with another Matt might be misinterpreted by the audience," I explain. "It might go against you, if you see what I mean."

He does, and suggests that he could adopt his grandad's name, Joe. So this time round he auditions as Joe Landers.

"Don't I recognise him?" asks Konnie, and I explain. She is vastly amused at the way he has been rechristened.

"Maybe we should have a competition to name the new presenter?" she suggests.

"I've had enough of that kind of competition," I remark.

Matt/Joe does well. He's certainly a contender, though as a white, sporty Northerner, with a background in acting, I suppose he wouldn't be that much of a contrast to either Matt or Geth. Matt/Joe has played rugby league at a high level and this inevitably interests the rugby-obsessed Geth.

"We could make a film together," he offers. "I could play on one side and he could be on the other."

"You're brave," I respond. "He's obviously *much* tougher than you. You'd be in pieces."

Jokes like this are always risky with the thin-skinned Geth, who now assumes a look of hurt feelings.

"Well, I'm tougher than you, anyway," he says, punching me hard on the arm.

Our final contender is a slightly geeky-looking guy who, as a kind of audition party-piece, has written his own *Blue Peter* song, and brought his own guitar, on which to accompany himself. Konnie is nearly beside herself at the prospect of having to sit next to him on camera, listening to this.

"I can't," she pleads with me. "I just can't. I know it's going to be hyper-cringey. I'll lose it, and that would be so mean. Please don't make me."

But it's not the song that turns out to be a cringe. He actually manages to pull this off with an engaging quirky charm, and, once he's past the first verse, everyone visibly relaxes. The problem emerges with the trampoline stage of the audition. Like everyone who endures the process, he's obviously nervous. This affects people in different ways. Some find their mouth so dry that the words almost literally get stuck there. For many, the intense adrenaline speeds everything up and so they talk much too quickly. For this auditionee, it's his intestines which let him down.

He's diligently following the expert's instructions, bouncing up and down, when he suddenly lets rip with an explosive fart. Up in the gallery, the noise is so violent that at first I think that there must be a problem with the sound. As it dawns on me what has actually happened, gales of laughter erupt from every corner. Down on the floor, Konnie and Gethin are cued to join by the side of the trampoline, and Konnie's face is weirdly contorted with the effort of not giving into hysterics. It is unavoidably hilarious, but it is crushingly awful for the poor bloke himself. Somehow he manages to keep going to the end. I compose myself, and go down to the studio, deciding only to mention it if he does. He doesn't.

During this afternoon's live show, the focus is on Zöe, who yesterday ran the London Marathon, and seems remarkably unaffected by her ordeal. I notice a small pile of chocolate bars in make-up and have stern words with Carmella, the floor manager. She's always doing this; bribing Zöe with a selection of her favourite sweets.

"You're like her feeder," I say, accusingly.

Carmella is not a bit sorry. "It keeps her happy," she shrugs. "If you've got a couple of Mars bars and a Snickers handy, you never have any trouble with Zöe."

Carmella knows every trick in the book. She and I go back a long way; she was the first floor manager for whom I regularly worked as a floor assistant when I first joined the BBC. She achieved this highly responsible and important job when she was still in her 20s, an incredible feat at the time, and for a woman. Small, blonde and stylish, she never seems to age. There is more than a touch of *AbFab* about her. One of her favourite tricks is to arrange lunch with some girl friends, at which she merrily works her way through champagne and three courses. Naturally, they are all amazed. What they don't know is that she hasn't eaten for the previous 24 hours and won't for the following 24 hours either. She will have been working extra hard at the gym, too, where she regularly demonstrates her ruthless self-discipline. "It's worth it, just to see their faces," she confides.

Carmella has show business in her veins – her mother is the pioneering BBC announcer Sylvia Peters, and her father was a distinguished director and producer. I worked for Carmella many times during the early years of my career, usually on *Going Live!* and *Top of the Pops*, and quickly discovered that, as well as being one of the best floor managers in the business, she is a fount of gossip, endlessly amusing and tenaciously loyal.

When I started directing, I booked her as often as I can, even when I was doing *The Big Breakfast*. On that occasion, she seemed to be late and I was getting worried. I'd had to negotiate to get the go-ahead to bring her in, so I needed her to impress. I wandered down to the house, and eventually found Carmella in make-up. She'd arrived in plenty of time, but, such is her aura of glamour and confidence, it had been assumed that she was a guest, and she had been rushed into make-up. "Darling," she exclaimed, "I'm so sorry. I just thought this was how you got treated on the other side!"

When I took over, *Blue Peter* often had rather 'mumsy' and pedestrian floor managers. One of these even had pronounced BO, which wasn't a great asset given the nature of the job. Carmella is much more in tune with the presenters (even when that means bribing them with a stash of chocs) and the A-list artists that thankfully we often attract. She also keeps me well informed of anything she thinks I should be aware of, which I suppose has a sneaky touch of the Iron Curtain about it, but is useful all the same.

25th April 2006

Today the BBC proudly unveils the findings of its Creative Futures project, months of internal debate about the future of the corporation and ways in which it needs to reshape itself to be fit for the fight.

For CBBC, the key recommendation is a lowering of the target age group, making it 8-12, rather than the current 8-15. This really concerns me; it would mean shutting off our competitions to a huge group of kids. Surely in an era of intense competition, it is madness to effectively turn away 'customers' who want to engage with our output. Then there is the thorny question of what's going to be provided instead for this newly disenfranchised group of children. There is some vague talk about online services, but nothing which sounds either exciting or properly funded. I know that in some ways it will suit Richard Deverell, who is uncomfortable with some of the drama, especially *Byker Grove* and *Grange Hill*, both of which he feels engage with issues which are too 'teenage' for the CBBC channel. But this ignores the fact that children perpetually 'reach up' and aspire to content that's aimed slightly above their head. It seems to me the height of arrogance to dismiss this, and the many years of important and pioneering work these core dramas have achieved. There are obvious implications for the factual output, too.

I seek to discuss all this with Anne Gilchrist, but she's not in the mood for a debate, says that it's all a done deal and that I will simply need to adjust *Blue Peter* accordingly.

"But how are we going to explain this to the audience?" I ask her. "Do we just tell them, 'Sorry, fuck off, you're not welcome at the party anymore?' What about the parents? You know how some of them will kick off. In this case, I can't blame them."

She looks at me coldly. "Are you questioning the findings of Creative Futures?"

"Yes," I reply simply. "What's wrong with that? I didn't realise we weren't allowed to question these findings."

"You went to some of the consultations, didn't you?" she asks, and I nod.

"That was the chance to debate everything. You can't fight this and you mustn't. As a senior executive, it's your responsibility to support your team through the process of change and adjustment."

It is a total stand-off. It's perfectly plain that she'd like me to just shut up, fuck off and get on with it. But I feel I'm being forced to take part in some ridiculous Emperor's New Clothes exercise which benefits no one, least of all the audience.

2nd May 2006

Frustrating fall-out from the Will Young video. Peter Purves and Val Singleton are up in arms because they've been offered no money for the use of their clips. They seem to think that the fault lies with us. I explain that it was the record company's responsibility to negotiate all the necessary clearances, given that it was their project and nothing intrinsically to do with the BBC. But they've tried the record company and been given the bum's rush.

I do understand their annoyance and I promise to look into it. According to artists' contracts, much depends on the nature of the original contracts. These appear to have been on a 'buy-out' basis, with no clause for royalties or repeat payments. This is why the record company are playing hard ball. They don't seem to be under any obligations to pay a cent. But I am annoyed. It is damaging to the goodwill that exists between the programme and its past presenters – goodwill I feel I've done much personally to nurture, especially given their fairly jaundiced view of the past. This situation has reignited all that 'them and us' distrust. What would it have cost the record company to offer all the presenters involved a one-off 'good will' payment? If I had thought there would be this kind of dispute, I would have made just such a payment a condition of our co-operation. So now I feel aggrieved on all counts; our good will taken advantage of by the record company, and unjustly accused of ripping off presenters I've never done anything other than admire and support.

3rd May 2006

Dismal day in the studio. The morning is given over to another round of auditions, all of them a total waste of time. Then, during the run-through, I'm confronted with a garden item that's so perfunctory and badly directed that I feel I've got no choice but to drop it altogether. It's replaced with a repeat of one of Matt's American college sports films, but it should never have happened. Producing garden items is difficult precisely because it takes a lot of effort, imagination and skill to make them entertaining and worthy of inclusion in the mix. This was so obviously a case of going through the motions that I find it insulting. Various bollockings ensue, and, as I bump into her, I mention it to Anne Gilchrist too.

"Why bother with the garden any more?" she says. "I think we've got to accept a time is fast coming when *Blue Peter* can't still be expected to do the worthy stuff. The audience won't tolerate it, they'll just switch off. We should focus on doing what they like most in the brand."

While I agree that, as never before, we need to raise our game, I don't see that this means restricting our content to the obvious box-office. Assuming the treatment *is* box-office, there's got to be ways of introducing kids to new experiences and interests, and that's got to be part of our responsibility. I don't like being told to take the path of least resistance. The whole exchange depresses me profoundly.

16th May 2006

A superb programme today. We hijack the highways and byways of TV Centre to mount a mini-version of the Knaresborough bed race. This surreal spectacle is great fun, and gives the start of the show a fantastic energy. Our studio guest is the charismatic John Lasseter, the genius who runs Pixar studios. Awarding him a gold badge is a no-brainer.

"This is like your version of the Oscars, right?" he asks me.

22nd May 2006

Excellent film in today's show in which Zöe masters barefoot waterskiing. This was directed by Tim Fransham, one of the 'young thrusters' on the film team, who makes no secret of his ambition. What fascinates me is that Zöe seems always to work best with the toughest directors. She responds much better to clear, direct instruction than to people who fanny about trying to schmooze her and bribe her into co-operation with a latte or a few of her favourite chocolate bars. Alex Leger, who has been here longer than anyone, has a theory (but then he always has a theory). He thinks that the minute Zöe gets the sense that someone is intimidated by her, the game is over, and she will act up, and be awkward.

"I've never had the slightest problem with her," he says. "Because she knows I'm the boss and so she can get on with her job."

Whatever the psychology, it is clear that Zöe does her best work under duress, whether that's physical or mental.

23rd May 2006

I finally schedule *The Mechanical Turk*, the very last caption story. These are a long *Blue Peter* tradition dating back to the early 60s, in which historical stories are part-illustrated by one artist, Bob Broomfield. As a child I used to love them, and they very much helped to inspire my love of history. From 1963 to 1988, when they were dropped by Lewis Bronze, these items were almost always written by Dorothy Smith, who was billed as the programme's historian. She was always a freelance and was married to Edward Barnes, who rose from being a *Blue Peter* producer to head of the department.

"We used to think that was shameful," Valerie Singleton once told me. "Employing your wife like that. I thought the BBC were supposed to have rules against that kind of thing."

I dismissed this as part of Val's unquenchable resentment towards Edward and Biddy. After all, even if there was a degree of nepotism involved, Dorothy did actually do the work, didn't she?

Dorothy died in 1990, but I brought Bob back into the fold in 1998. Over the decades, he has painted literally thousands of pictures for the programme (he probably holds some kind of world record). He has done some lovely work for me (a few framed examples are displayed in my downstairs loo). But he is in his 70s now, and, the last couple of times I've called him to commission some paintings, it was clear that he was slightly dreading the prospect.

"It takes me much longer these days," he explains, regretfully.

There can't be many people whose names have appeared regularly on the end credits of a programme from 1963 to 2006.

25th May 2006

During the producers' meeting, a request comes in from the *One O'Clock News*, who want to run a report on our forthcoming *Bark in the Park* charity dog walk events. Naturally, they want to chat to a presenter. The only possibility is Matt, who is in today to cut his show reel (at our expense) with one of our editors. But there is no need to disrupt this as the news piece shouldn't take long. I call Matt into my office to chat through the logistics with some of the team involved and explain that we need him to do this interview for the programme. He is immediately angry and aggressive.

"I don't give a shit about the programme," he shouts. "It's had enough of me."

He continues on the same lines, getting steadily more and more worked up, until I interrupt, and say that he needs to calm down and stop shouting.

"Fine," he replies. "Fuck off then."

At which he storms out of the room, with Meg at his heels, banging the door so hard that the wall rattles.

I am shaking with shock and wondering if he's just walked out for good. I think about calling the press office for advice in case he has. But then I text him and just ask him to come back and talk to me one-to-one.

Within minutes, he reappears, walks into my office, shuts the door, and apologises. Then he collapses onto the sofa. He says that he doesn't want to go, that this programme is all he'd ever wanted to do and that he is really unhappy. It's very emotional.

"Sometimes I go home and I'm shattered. I sit in the bath, and I start crying, because I don't know how much harder I can work or what else I can do to make it right again."

My heart breaks for him and I feel tears stinging my own eyes. I tell him how sad and awful it has been to witness his anger, frustration and unhappiness over the last few months. I feel as if I've lost connection with him. He tells me that he thinks he has cared too much and worried too much and it has been making him ill.

"Do you really think that you're making a mistake leaving?" I ask him.

He thinks for a while, head down, and then, quietly indicates no.

"I've had my time," he says. "We had something so special, our gang of four. It's not the same. Zöe and Gethin – they don't want the job for the same reasons that I did."

He reminds me of what I always used to say to the presenters; that no matter what you have to give, *Blue Peter* will take it and still want more. Calm restored, we have a hug. Truth is, I love the boy and can't bear to see him so genuinely miserable, confused and distressed.

"It's just a TV show," I mutter.

Except that we both know that it isn't.

26th May 2006

This morning, Matt did the *One O'Clock News* report and then we have lunch. He tells me that he'd actually enjoyed himself and we talk with real affection and honesty about yesterday's explosion and all the complex and conflicting emotions which led up to it. I remind him about something Simon said; that leaving *Blue Peter* is like divorcing someone you love; you have to almost make yourself hate it before it is possible to walk out of the door. This was his reasoning for his own sometimes (and uncharacteristically) difficult behaviour before he left. Matt nods in agreement. This show isn't easy to leave.

5th June 2006

Another morning of studio auditions. Two strong contenders emerge. The first is a guy called Joe Crowley, who seems to have a kind of textbook CV for a potential *Blue Peter* presenter. He's a Norfolk boy, who loves the countryside, he's sporty, musical and has trained as an actor. I liked him the minute I met him. There's an immediate warmth and sincerity there. He auditions well, too, and it wouldn't be in any way difficult to imagine him doing the job. And yet. All through this process, I've made it clear that I'd like to cast a black guy. It's been ten years since Diane left the show, and we have never had a male black presenter. It's all very well to say that the job must go to the best candidate, but, if you want to make a positive change in the casting mix, you've also got to go looking, and be proactive. This has led to some dismal interviews. But this morning there is at last a glimmer of potential. Last week, Catherine, one of our directors, put her head round my door and said that there was a runner in the department whom she'd recently met and who might be worth talking to.

"He was with a group of us in the bar," she explains, "and he was the centre of attention, in a good way. Really funny and charming. I think he's got something. I don't know how much he wants to be a presenter, though."

This guy's name is Andy Akinwolere. I arranged to meet him with my deputy Jack, at the end of the day. It was baking hot and neither of us was really in the mood to chat with yet another wide-eyed wannabe. But when Andy turned up, he was, as Catherine had suggested, immensely engaging. He talked non-stop and although some of this was probably down to nerves, he seems a confident and self-aware type of person. His ambition is to make documentaries, rather than present kids' TV shows. In my book, this is helpful. There is no pose. He's thoroughly down-to-earth, with a slight Brummie accent the legacy of where he grew up, although his family are much travelled.

His audition is technically inept and full of the trademark pitfalls of the totally inexperienced presenter; he talks way too fast, stumbles over his words, loses his way, looks at the wrong camera and makes a hash of the make. But he is likeable and watchable, and, despite the procession of mistakes, both these qualities remain uppermost. I don't think I could give him the job on the basis of this audition alone, but he might be worth a recall.

We are fast running out of time. At the end of today's live show, Matt announces he is to leave, his voice breaking with emotion. Emerging from the sidelines Konnie starts to plead, "Don't go!", which is only going to confuse the audience who will no doubt think if he's so upset at the thought of going and she's begging with him not to, why is he actually leaving? It is all a bit of mess.

11th June 2006

Amusing story in the *Daily Star* headlined, 'Konnie will be hostess with the mostest', which claims that "worried *Blue Peter* chiefs have promised Konnie Huq a 'job for life' after an exodus of presenters." Apparently, "she'll also get a big pay-rise."

Not a line of truth in it, of course, but full marks to Konnie's agent for trying.

19th June 2006

Final recalls for our three strongest hopefuls: Matt/Joe Landers, Joe Crowley and Andy Akinwolere. Given that this is the second time around each of them (the third for Matt/Joe), I've varied the content so that, among other delights, they will each demonstrate a toy Dalek and have a go at belly dancing. Konnie, Gethin and Zöe are there to share the sofa and give us a chance to road-test the feel of what will be our new team.

For Matt/Joe, it is game over. He just looks uncomfortable throughout, and the belly-dancing, which should be a chance to show off his sense of humour, is leaden and laugh-free. Perhaps he just over-thought it.

Andy Akinwolere isn't technically much of an improvement on his first go, but he is more relaxed and he strikes up an immediate rapport with the presenters, especially Geth. I lodge this very much at the forefront of my brain; after all the tension and dissent between the old and the new team, I so want the chemistry to work.

Joe Crowley is brilliant. He sails through the entire process as if he's been born to it. The warmth and likeability I first noticed about him is present and correct on camera, and, when he's playing for laughs with the belly-dancing, there's almost a Stan Laurel quality to him. The biggest problem he's got is nothing he can do anything about. It's that, curiously, he is almost a morph of Matt and Gethin; not just physically, where he reminds me of what a court room artist might produce if I described either Matt, Geth or Joe; but in terms of his skill-set and personality. I pick up that Geth is unsure, too.

"I don't want to ruin his chances," he says, when I quiz him about what he thinks. "I'm sure he'd be great."

"Stop trying to be Mr Nice Guy, and tell me what you think. It's important."

"I worry that we would want to do exactly the same films," he admits. "I mean, we're very different, really, but we've got similar skills and stuff that we like."

I'm sending the tapes out to a few primary schools, to see what groups of kids in the core audience think. This, amazingly, has never been tried before, and I really can't think why. But then it never occurred to me before, either.

A patchy show this afternoon. Geth flounders about with the make, which has never been his strong point and nearly sank his chances in the first place.

Admittedly, this one is more than usually complicated; build your very own 'Black Pearl' ship from *Pirates of the Caribbean.*
"How are we going to improve it?" I ask him in notes.
"Give it to Konnie?" he quips.
Meanwhile, we can at last announce the welcome news that the badge system is up and running again. We are introducing a 'badge card' to go with each badge, which will feature the child's photo and the date of their eligibility for free access to the attractions on the list. We think this will actually add something to the cachet of winning a badge, rather like their own mini-passport. A few critics have moaned that it's a foretaste of ID cards for the adult population, and might be seen as an infringement of a child's civil rights but I think this is so specious as to be beyond comment. It's taken a while to devise the most efficient way of processing these cards, as we have to address the huge existing database of badge winners, not just the (substantial) numbers given out each week. There were the expected tiresome wrangles to get the extra cash, too. I've managed to dodge the Creative Futures age restriction bullet, on the basis that it is hardly fair (and would cause a furore) to retrospectively expel those between 13 and 15 from the scheme. It's all been a colossal headache, and has eaten up a huge amount of time and energy, but I do feel that we've come up with a fair and robust solution. I was particularly keen to find a viewer who might have made a similar suggestion, so that we could give them the credit rather than claiming it for ourselves. This has been rather like the famous search for the golden ticket in *Willy Wonka*, but, marvellously, we eventually found one Helen Jennings, who not only suggested a card, but even drew her own prototype.

20th June 2006

Spend the morning back in the director's chair to rattle through the links we need from Matt for *Baker's Dozen*, a selection of his finest *Blue Peter* specials from the last seven years. A few weeks ago, I tentatively suggested that these might make a great mini-season on CBBC, and, rather to my surprise, they bit my hand off and said "yes, please" PDQ. More, I suspect, because it will fill a decent number of slots, rather than because it will give Matt a celebratory send-off, but, whatever our individual motives, everyone's a winner. As we record each link, Matt and I cannot help being occasionally side-tracked down memory lane. It's the experiences of a lifetime in bite-sized chunks.
A characteristically buoyant email from Biddy: "How absolutely brilliant of you to have got the ID cards up and running in such double quick time," she writes. "And even more brilliant to have found Helen Jennings, who, quite rightly, has taken the credit! And so she should. Three cheers for *Blue Peter* viewers!"

21st June 2006

The verdicts have returned from the primary schools to which we sent the audition tapes. It's a landslide. The kids seem to love Andy, and there isn't a critical comment among the sample. It's the final validation we need and I only hope the wider audience take to him so immediately. I don't think he quite knows what's hit him. It's hardly surprising. In the space of a few short days, he has gone from working as a runner, the most lowly-paid and junior members of the department, to being signed up as one of the stars of its flagship programme. I've had the usual checks and balances conversations with him ("Have you ever taken drugs? Have you ever been involved in any criminal activity? Is there anything that's ever happened to you or your family which might make a tabloid headline?") and he is confident and bright-eyed. The plan is that we will tease his introduction on the last show of the season (with him standing in silhouette behind a screen) but that the audience won't get to properly meet him until the new series. In the meantime, he'll join the others on the summer expedition to the Southern States of the USA. This was intended to be our destination last year, until CBBC suddenly commissioned *Only in America*, a USA road trip for the egregious Fearne Cotton and Reggie Yates. The prospect of this rained thoroughly on our parade, so I decided we should switch our attentions elsewhere, at least until we knew what form *Only in America* would take, and how well it would do. Given that it was a self-indulgent mess, which didn't do well enough to win a second series, I felt we were on safe ground to revive our plans to thoroughly explore a part of the States we haven't covered in detail before.

22nd June 2006

Can't stop thinking about the conversation I had with Joe Crowley, to break the news that he hasn't got the job. It's wonderful when you can give someone a literally life-changing opportunity, but these moments are outweighed by the crushing nature of having to let down those who get close but don't quite make it. I was driving home when I called Joe, so I pulled over into a lay-by. I cut to the chase and then sat there in the sun, listening to him struggle to process his disappointment. I told him how well he had done. Not empty words or platitudes.

"You could be a brilliant *Blue Peter* presenter," I tell him, immediately realising that he must be thinking, 'So why aren't you making me one?', though of course he doesn't say this.

"It's just not the right time," I continue, hating myself for using such a cliché. I remind myself that however difficult I'm finding this, it's much worse for him. I want him to understand the situation. I explain my genuine concern at the similarities between Geth and him, and the need for contrast. I explain, too, that the audience might have thought we were trying to replace Matt with a bit of a clone. "Not that you are, in any way, but you're trying to anticipate the audience, and it's just another of the factors."

Joe does not conceal that he's upset and bitterly disappointed, but he says that the experience has convinced him that this is what he wants to do. "I won't give up," he tells me, fervently. "I know I could be really good."

I can only agree with him and admire his courage and focus.

"I really hope that you do get there, and that we might work together in the future."

No doubt he thinks these are empty words, but I mean them. I wish him luck, and say goodbye.

The whole conversation has churned me up, so I don't set off straight away, but sit there, mulling it over. I think I'm partly mourning the fact that I was never in the slightest doubt about how much Joe wanted the job, or how well he would do it. Andy was thrust into the audition; he didn't come looking for it and *Blue Peter* wasn't part of his childhood, so doesn't carry the same resonance for him as it evidently did for Joe.

I think I've made the right decision for the show but, for Andy, it's a brilliant career opportunity rather than the realisation of a childhood dream. I keep thinking about the nature of chance and fate; if Catherine hadn't met Andy in the bar, if he hadn't wanted to give the audition a go, then Joe would have walked it. Equally, if Joe had come along when we were auditioning for Simon's replacement, he would almost certainly have got the job then. Not that I'm wishing away Gethin, as I'm certainly not – but the odds were stacked against him, in a way they weren't for Joe, so that in some ways it's incredible that it eventually went Geth's way.

The workings of chance and fate again.

Joe Crowley became a successful presenter in his own right; most recently, as one of the regular reporters on The One Show.

26th June 2006

Matt's last show is curiously anti-climactic. I think we have all been through so much to get to this point, it's almost as if there's not much emotional energy left to spare. Most of us are exhausted. We're reaching the end of the longest continuous run of *Blue Peter* in 40 years. I've been told that, from September, we will be dropping back to three-shows-a-week, which will return me full circle to how I began on the show.

The weather is indifferent so I make the decision to move the garden party, and

Matt's farewell, into the studio. During my speech, I pay heartfelt tribute to him. "Seven years and over 700 programmes is an extraordinary achievement even by *Blue Peter* standards, but then Matt is an extraordinary person. We were always trying to find something he couldn't do well and we only ever really succeeded with one thing – and that was reading an autocue. Matt is so utterly natural and warm. His courage and sense of humour shine through the screen and not surprisingly audiences love him."

I share some of my favourite memories of working with him; our times with the Royal Marines ("they're gonna shave off my eyebrows!"), the Russian ballet and the NYPD.

"Oh, how I'm going to miss doing my Matt impression," I say.

As he basks in the collective affection and respect of everyone here, I catch sight of Andy standing on the sidelines, looking more than a little overwhelmed by the prospect of what he's taking on.

28th June 2006

Run-through disaster. We are about five minutes under. This kind of discrepancy in the timings is unusual, but today I have a ready-made solution to the crisis. We've stuck to the plan of teasing Andy's introduction, with him concealed behind a screen and only seen in silhouette.

"But now viewers are going to meet you sooner than they think," I tell him. "You're on..."

Quickly, we block out a new end to the show in which Andy will be revealed, introduced, given his badge and interviewed by the rest of the team. There is no time to prevaricate and it's a classic example of the *Blue Peter* studio machine swinging into action. Lighting readjust, sound dig out an additional mic, the director talks through the additional shots, and I agree the questions with the presenters. Make-up and wardrobe rapidly turn their attentions to Andy, who, poor lad, clearly doesn't quite know what's about to hit him. And then we are on air, and 20 minutes in, he's sitting on the sofa, beaming and being welcomed to the show, as if this was always the plan.

"That was quite an introduction, bud," says Geth, as soon as we go off air.

"Is it always like this?" asks Andy, visibly reeling from the sudden adrenalin rush. The other presenters just laugh.

2nd July 2006

Filming in sweaty temperatures in Volendam for my Amsterdam special. I could have lived without setting off on an extended shoot immediately after the end of the run, but this is my opportunity to spend some uninterrupted time with Andy, to get to know him better, and to give him some undivided attention. Geth is along for the ride, too, and today we are filming the boys taking part in traditional Dutch folk dancing. Accordingly, they are both clad in a fetching baggy black costume, with ridiculous clogs on their feet. The trousers are so wide that Andy is inspired to start dancing like MC Hammer and, as we are filming in a kind of street market, his free-styling quickly attracts a small crowd, who think he is busking.

Once we move inside to film with a dance group, everything gets rather more serious. Mostly middle-aged couples, these people take their dancing seriously, and expect Andy and Geth to do the same. They are each assigned partners, and it amuses me to see a subtle little contretemps play out between two of the ladies in the group, both of whom evidently fancy the chance to show Geth a move or two. He flirts disgustingly with all the women.

In the evening, an interesting discussion with Andy about what it feels like to be the only black person in the place. Throughout the day, I spotted the occasional point or stare; curious rather than hostile. But if I were Andy it would certainly irritate me. So far I've seen no sign of either irritation or anger in him. Much of the time, as you'd expect from a young man, he is laughing and joking and messing around. But when he talks about this, he becomes suddenly very serious and articulate. "It's about visibility, Rich," he says, and he considers it a great responsibility to represent black kids just by being on screen every week.

3rd July 2006

Film an interview with an old lady called Jacqueline van Maarsen (cue the inevitable surname jokes from the boys) who, as a girl, was one of Anne Frank's best friends. Like Anne, Jacqueline and her family were forced into hiding by the arrival of the Nazis. It was their luck to survive, and there is something slightly unreal about the knowledge that this polite, friendly, well-groomed woman, was a participant in so such a terrifying piece of history. She is a brilliant interviewee, and understands the need to frame her answers in a way to which children might relate.

"We were ordinary people," she says, "Ordinary children. But to survive, we had to hide ourselves away, and hope that we wouldn't be betrayed or discovered."

Later, we shoot a canal trip, pretty much obligatory if you're making a film about Amsterdam, and the gentle pace of this allows us all a chance to try to process what we have heard this morning. I'm dreading tomorrow's filming at the Anne Frank house. For the same reason that I declined the opportunity to make the Auschwitz film; I know enough about the obscenity of the Nazi horror, and I've no wish to revisit it myself. But having met Jacqueline, I feel inspired to leave my ego out of it and just make the best and most moving film I can.

4th July 2006

An edge-of-the-seat day because one of our stories collapses round our ears. Via our fixer, we'd arranged to follow a day-in-the-life of a young Dutch girl, following her at school and on the famous flower market, where her family have a stall. Alas, while perfectly sweet, the girl the fixer has found us is deadly dull and painfully shy. She keeps stealing uncomfortable sideways glances at the lens. Andy tries his best to put her at her ease, but is hampered by the language barrier, overcompensates and ends up gabbling garbage, until I tell him to put a sock in it. It's just a waste of time trying to make this work, so, having already wasted half the day, I cut our losses and we have a rapid council of war to think of a replacement.

The fixer, aware that his casting has been found wanting, is keen to salvage his reputation. He suggests that he could hire a couple of Segways, these gimmicky new motorised scooters, on which the rider stands upright and whizzes along. As this seems the best in a limited range of options, I go for it. Geth and Andy have a brief burst of training and then they set off, with cameras attached to the Segways, for a scenic rattle round the city.

On a Segway, Andy turns out to be enthusiastic rather than skilled. "Fuck me," says Geth, when they park up. "He's a maniac on that thing."

I have nasty flashbacks to Simon's scooter incident in Rome, and it is a great relief when we have shot enough material to wrap.

"What are you thinkin', boss?" asks Geth as we head back to the hotel. He is always sensitive to moods and I've been unusually silent for the past few minutes.

"Put it this way," I tell him, "I somehow doubt that we'll be entering this one for a BAFTA."

6th July 2006

No trip to Amsterdam is complete, or so I'm told, without a stroll through the red-light district. Geth, Andy and the crew are keen, so after dinner, off we set. The main spectacle seems to be a series of shop windows in which the 'girls' display themselves. Should they receive a customer, these windows are fitted with shutters for the sake of privacy and anonymity. I become increasingly glum at the sleazy sights around me.

"What's the matter with you, Grandad?" asks Geth, noticing my long face.

"I hate this shit-hole," I tell him. "All these poor women are somebody's daughter. It makes me think about my daughter and how I'd hate it if this is what her life came to."

"Shit, Rich. Downer."

7th July 2006

Very early call, so that we can film everything we need inside the Anne Frank house before it opens to the public. I've no idea how on earth they preserve this cramped and fragile space from the daily onslaught of thousands of tourists, but I am grateful that we have it to ourselves for the shoot. I read Anne Frank's diary as a child, and I've never forgotten the moment that it dawned on me that this chatty, companionable, observant girl, who, through her writing seemed so alive, was doomed to be wrenched from her hiding-place to be transported to a death camp.

Geth has really done his homework and learnt the script inside out. The challenge for him is to get the tone right. "You don't want to sound like you're at a funeral," I tell him. "Make it as matter-of-fact as you can. Leave the emotion for the audience."

This is harder than it sounds, and especially when you are surrounded by all the poignant, pathetic reminders that, as Jacqueline said, these were just "ordinary" people, trying to survive an apocalyptic situation out of their control.

8th July 2006

When you're planning a half-hour special, you need some action in the mix. Finding this in Amsterdam has been a challenge. Everything here is so laid-back and relaxed. We jump in a hired bus and drive out of the city, so that the boys can take part in a ditch-jumping competition. This sport requires each competitor to use a very long wooden pole, rather like a punt, to propel themselves high up into the air, and over one of the ditches which criss-cross the boggy Dutch countryside. When we arrive, we stand watching some of the competitors having a go. It all seems rather monotonous and, indeed, pointless to me.

"What's wrong with a game of football?" says Andy, and it is hard to disagree.

Nevertheless, as Annie might say, it should stretch to "a bit of fun – five minutes" so we get down to constructing a logical sequence. Turns out that both of the boys are pretty good at the action. Some of the other participants misjudge their jump and, to a chorus of jeers and laughter from the spectators, inevitably end up sliding into the watery ditch. For the sake of a bit of much-needed comedy, I want one of the boys to do the same.

"I suppose it had better be me," says Geth, with a slight whiff of the martyr. "Andy's the new boy, let's give him the moment to shine."

I'm pleased to see that Geth and Andy seem to have struck up an immediate and easy rapport. They can blether (boringly, in my opinion) about football for hours, and, on the surface at least, they seem to share an easy sense of humour. If this early promise settles into a genuine friendship, it will hugely benefit both them and the show. The only real fault I can find with Andy is that he has a marked tendency not to listen. Socially, this is irritating. Professionally, it could be a serious flaw. You start to give him a note and he immediately cuts in with, "Yeah, yeah Rich, I hear you..." before you've finished what you're saying or made your point. I'll need to watch this tendency and alert the directors to it. I think it stems from an anxiety to please rather than an innate reluctance to pay attention, but it already feels like it could become an unfortunate habit.

14th July 2006

Various frantic calls from Alex, who is making a film with Andy abseiling down the Humber Bridge with a party of Royal Marines. Alex isn't at all happy with the safety arrangements, and it is touch and go whether the film will actually happen or not.

"I don't want to kill the poor bugger off before he begins," barks Alex. I ask him how Andy is coping with the prospect of making the descent. I've commissioned the film as a dry run for an epic helicopter bungee-jump which will be the first major film from the Southern States expedition. Not that this has anything to do with the States, per se, it's just that it's the only place in the world where we can safely film such a terrifyingly ambitious stunt. It's going to cost an absolute fortune. Given that Andy has a fear of heights, I thought we should rigorously test his limits before sending him on the bungee jump and potentially writing off thousands of pounds should he decide he can't go through it.

15th July 2006

The Humber Bridge abseil is accomplished; though Alex isn't happy with the coverage. But Andy managed the feat without a meltdown so this is encouraging given what he's about to face in the States.

My 40th birthday party. I knew this was happening (although I don't actually reach the dreaded figure until Tuesday) but none of the details, which have all been organised and kept as a surprise by my amazing wife. It's a wonderful celebration with guests from every stage of my life. Adrian Gooch, one of the very best of our film editors, has cut a special film celebrating my life to show after the meal. It starts with 1960s cine film of me toddling about and, later, there is inevitably, much emphasis on *Blue Peter* and particularly some of the extraordinary life experiences it has given me. This is partly dictated by the fact that there is a lot of good, funny, action-packed material to use. But it's also a reflection of how much it has totally dominated my life over the years. It makes me confront the price that must be paid for such an incredible job; the ceaseless demands on time, energy, passion and head space. Everything else comes second. I know that this must be the case with all kinds of comparably important and responsible jobs. But watching this film has made me consider not only everything I have gained from the programme, but also what I've sacrificed on its behalf and lost because of it.

29th August 2006

Today, Geth heads off to Malawi to make the first of this year's appeal films. It's significant on several counts. We are going to be working with UNICEF to raise money for African communities decimated by the HIV/AIDS virus. It has required a considerable amount of persuasion on my part to convince the powers that be that it's an appropriate subject for a children's programme. Because HIV/AIDS is spread principally through sexual intercourse, this immediately makes middle England (and senior management) jumpy. But I've argued forcibly that there are ways of navigating the key information we give out, and that our audience should be aware of what's going on in much of the developing world, where it is children of their own age who are left behind to cope without parents or older siblings.

As the appeal is necessarily going to be so child-centric, rather than just sending a presenter to front the films, I've decided to send two kids as representatives of the audience. This has been quite a process in itself, not only to find an articulate boy and a girl with the right sensitivity and yet also robust enough to cope with the rigours of such a trip. To make the films, I've recruited a freelance films director called Simon Morris. When he first came to see me, Simon was blunt about the prospect of working on *Blue Peter.*

"I never watched it as a kid," he explains. "It seemed to me to exist in a kind of never-never land. It just didn't speak to me or kids like me."

This is not an unfamiliar confession, but I urge him to look at some of the more recent content, and explain that I'm not looking for someone to join the team long-term, just to seize this particular mission and craft the very best possible films. Everything relies on the strength and clarity of our narrative. Given the acute sensitivities of filming with such vulnerable people, there is much more than just the TV to consider. No decent film-maker could resist such a lure, and Simon rapidly commits, in every possible sense. There is so much resting on the work he and his crew, Gethin, and the kids, Charlie and Mica, deliver. I've brought them all together but now I can only sit here and wait and hope it all takes light.

1st September 2006

We've moved into a vast new office space just off the first floor of the East Tower. I don't much like it. The main part of the work space has been laid out like a call centre, and the office I've been given sits apart on the corner of this. It's very spacious, with its own seating area, and the windows overlook the tube line, so there's a regular and comforting rattle of trains thundering past. I've quickly filled it with all my clutter, and covered the walls with a collage of production and publicity photos. When Anne Gilchrist sees it, her first comment is, "It's bigger than Richard (Deverell)'s or mine..." and it occurs to me that perhaps she doesn't think this appropriate. Which is annoying, as I don't have any other options and I'd be perfectly happy in a more modest space. In fact, the geography of the entire office, slightly set apart from the rest of East Tower, with its own access to the ring road behind, isn't going to help the notion within the department that *Blue Peter* is stand-offish with its own empire set apart from the rest of CBBC.

11th September 2006

Murray Gold's finished version of the *Music Makers* sig tune has come in and it's awful. Everyone I've played it to hates it, and it just doesn't seem to have anything contemporary or fresh about it. It's not just a bitter disappointment, it's a serious worry, given that the end result is supposed to be our new theme, and the resolution of the *Music Makers* prize. I take it up to Anne Gilchrist, and she hates it, too.

"We can't use it, can we?" I say.

She shakes her head. "It's very disappointing."

The only saving grace is that, as part of the package, Murray has also supplied a closing music bed, and this is much better and works well. I suggest that we use this for the time being, and see if perhaps there is a way of salvaging the main sig further down the line. It's less than satisfactory, but we agree that it's the best decision for the programme and for the audience, if not the *Music Makers*, whose disappointment will have to be carefully managed.

"It's not as if they haven't had some pretty amazing rewards already," says Anne, which is true. I point out that they are playing on the bed, at least, which is some consolation.

But nonetheless, it's all a major downer.

14th September 2006

Pleasing email from ex-Editor Lewis Bronze, praising the "fantastic annual" which he calls an "absolute *tour de force*."

Couldn't be more of a contrast to the reaction when I take new copies upstairs to Anne Gilchrist, who shows no interest whatsoever, except to remind me that it can't be plugged on the programme.

19th September 2006

I've introduced a new routine for the presenters; after each studio, they come back to my office to watch back the show. Konnie grumbles about it, but the others seem keen, and it is particularly beneficial for Andy. He finds it very difficult to slow down and shut up, and to actually consider a range of possibilities, rather than just going where instinct takes him. He has a fantastic energy and spontaneity, but he has a long way to go before he masters the technique of live multi-camera TV or the essential ability to judge a gear change. A case in point today is an item in which Geth is supposed to be showing Andy how to cook his beloved Auntie Jean's Welsh cakes. To make a double-handed item like this flow and seem natural actually requires a lot of discipline and the ability to listen to each other. Rehearsal is crucial, and Geth is painstaking over this, but Andy finds it hard to do the same thing twice without making it seem stale and laboured. It is a problem. He's bright enough to get there eventually, but it will take time, and audiences are not hugely forgiving of ineptitude on the part of a new presenter. They already slightly resent them for having taken the place of an old favourite. So these programme reviews are a useful way of going over both mistakes, as well as reinforcing what's gone well, while the show is still fresh in the presenters' minds. It's also a good chance for them to air any general worries or grievances, and for me to keep them in the loop of future plans or concerns.

What I don't share with them are the terrible figures we've so far been getting this season. I've long since learnt that figures are an imprecise art, and don't often reflect the actual content; the weather is a major factor (a sunny afternoon = kids go outside), and so is the competition. We are busting a gut to try to make every show as box office as possible, so it's dismaying to see both the ratings and the share dip as low as it has.

21st September 2006

Biddy pays a royal visit to our new domain, and is obviously surprised at the scale of the office ("Darling, it's sumptuous!"), the neatness of my part of it ("I've never, ever seen anywhere so tidy!") and the size of the team. "But what do they all *do*?" she exclaims, sounding like Lady Bracknell. In fact, we don't have more people, it's just that the old offices took up an entire floor and so everyone was more spread out. I take Biddy to lunch, and then, at her request, she watches a tape of the first show of the season. She watches intently, and comments favourably about both Geth – "so much more confident than the last time I saw him", and feels that "there's every chance Andy will become a popular success."

Geth pops in to see me, which gives Biddy the chance to give him a grilling. "The great thing is to just *keep going*...until they find out you're crap..." she tells him, conspiratorially.

Both Geth and I are vastly amused.

22nd September 2006
Email from Biddy, to thank me for lunch and the tour of inspection. "Now I must try to remember that BP is transmitted on consecutive days," she concludes. "I wish I had more faith in those programme consultants who seem to know all the answers. I wonder whether they do?"

2nd October 2006
This afternoon we introduce the programme's new guide dog puppy, our first since Honey in 1992. When Matt left, he took Meg with him and, as well as this vacancy, it occurred to me that the old *Blue Peter* theory of "love my dog, love me" might help the audience bond with Andy. The advantage of a guide dog is that we get a lot of ready-made content from the training, and Andy isn't permanently saddled with the responsibility of a pet.

10th October 2006
I'm struggling with an inept new producer. It's not really her fault; she was forced on me by a tag team of Anne and HR. Both are on a mission to move on what they see as the 'old guard' (Annie, Alex, Bridget, and, in due course, me) and bring in a flood of what they call 'fresh talent'. Would that it was. I first met this particular producer back in the summer, and, though she was friendly and likeable, I was profoundly underwhelmed by her obvious lack of experience and lack of ideas and opinions. I reported back my scepticism and was asked to meet her again.
"She's so lovely," said the HR woman. "And really keen to do the job."
I wasn't disputing either fact, but it was a three-line whip so agreed to another meeting. Although I was still left lukewarm, I was eventually told that taking her on was a *fait accompli,* and given an infuriatingly unfair lecture about my responsibilities to nurture new talent. So here she is and, as I feared, it's not working. Her running orders are dire, and when I reject an item, which is often, she looks utterly crestfallen and on the verge of tears. Her team have rapidly lost confidence in her too.
It's a hideous situation because she knows I was ambivalent about her at best, and whatever I say now, it probably looks to her as if I'm willing her to fail. This is deeply frustrating as no one would be more delighted than me if she suddenly turned a corner and started to deliver. I do wonder about her common sense, though. She recently pitched a show which would have involved her team shooting an item on location.
"You're the *studio* team," I remind her. "Every show gets a film allocated to it, and we can't afford to start shooting extras just because you've found an item you like which won't work in the studio."

"But we'd do all the work," she says. "The film team wouldn't need to get involved."
"So how are you going to cover the costs of the crew and the edit?"
Her face falls, as she evidently hasn't considered these factors.
When I raise my doubts upstairs, it's implied that I'm rushing her and that perhaps I'm being too harsh and need to give her more support.
"Other than basically coming up with her running orders and writing her scripts for her, you mean?"
It doesn't help that many of the junior members of the team are new, too, and, in their way, equally inexperienced. They all *want* to do a great job, they all *want* to be here. But whether they can and whether they should is a different matter. Today's show is a case in point. The Wednesday team (of which this woman is in charge) have again fallen for a story which involves making a film in order to justify its inclusion in the running order. It's about a family who also happen to make up a band which plays music that's a cross between R & B and swing. The idea is that one of the APs will shoot a profile of the family, showing how they tick and run the band alongside family life, and that off the back of this, they will perform in the studio.
Aware that the constant knock-backs are demoralising this team, and thinking that at least the story for once has some potential, I give it the go-ahead. Then it transpires that the family are precious beyond belief, hampering the filming with their demands and presenting difficulties to such an extent that the end result is dreadful. The studio performance is equally lacklustre. It's all been a total waste of time and money, and, unless something is done, the show will sink under the weight of this disaster. For the first time ever, I resort to pulling the whole show apart in the edit to restructure it. I drop the film altogether and insert another, shifting the performance to the very end of the show, where it can do least damage. It's a salvage job, and, though a little clunky in places, it just about works.
But with this producer 'in charge', and her floundering team, their every show is a crisis, and it can't go on indefinitely.

16th October 2006

In Edinburgh for a week with Geth to shoot a special and a couple of films. Today I'm revisiting Howie Nicholsby, a personable young kilt-designer I filmed with a few years back when I shot the story of kilts with Simon. Howie runs a company called 21st Century Kilts, and he specialises in updated, funky, contemporary kilt designs, using every kind of fabric, from denim and linen, to leather and PVC. Some of his kilts have been worn by celebrities like Robbie Williams and Vin Diesel, and today it's Geth's turn. We borrow a variety of the more eye-catching and outrageous styles and head into the city to shoot the modelling sequences of the story. One of the kilts is made from see-through plastic (Geth is wearing boxer shorts underneath) and I want a shot of Geth strolling along wearing this without a care in the world, while the Edinburgh crowds mill around him. He makes token sounds of resistance to this plan until I stop him abruptly in his tracks.

"Don't give me all that shit," I tell him. "You know damn well that you're in your element whenever everyone's looking at you. You'll love every minute of it."

Geth laughs loudly at this.

"Just thought I shouldn't look too keen," he smiles.

17th October 2006

Devote the day to filming behind-the-scenes at Murrayfield, the home of Edinburgh rugby club. As a laugh, I've put Geth in full Welsh kit, which isn't just a cheap joke, but means that when we film him taking part in some team drills, he clearly stands out from the other players.

Geth is a massive rugby fan, and, given the slightest encouragement, can recite a seemingly endless stream of rugby-related stats and facts. Despite the slight issue of competing nationalities, round here he's got eyes like saucers, and when he interacts with the players he's more 10-year-old-boy than TV presenter. His enthusiasm and keenness are positive assets; the club PR respond by offering us more than we had negotiated for when we set up the shoot. Geth gets to train in the gym alongside some of the players and, at the suggestion of Chris Paterson, the captain, we end the sequence with Geth taking an ice bath. This is standard procedure in modern rugby, to combat inflammation and promote healing. But, to the outsider, it just looks like a refined form of torture. Paterson takes me to one side and suggests that he surprise Geth by creeping up from behind and tipping an extra load of ice over his head. Naturally I agree and this gives us a neat comedy 'end'. Because we have to shoot various angles and takes, it all takes quite a long time, and not once does Geth moan or complain. Only when I produce the stills camera and start to take shots for the annual does he ask how much longer I think it will be.

"Shut up and sort out your nipples. They'll have someone's eye out."

That evening, we have a brilliant meal in a posh Edinburgh restaurant. Conversation turns to our respective backgrounds, and the democratic nature of TV; how our careers have given us all a gateway to so many amazing experiences, no matter where we all came from in the first place. Geth keeps banging on about his humble origins and making out that I'm some kind of Lord Snooty. I decide to embrace the charge and play the part.

"Let's face it, we are only sharing a table because of a twist of fate," I tell him. "I'm

used to all this, but you scarcely know how to use a knife and fork."
"Say what you think, eh, plums?" he says, laughing. "I can't believe you. You're such a snob."
"I'm just telling it like it is."
"What do you mean?" he goads me.
I look down my nose at him and proclaim snootily.
"You were born to *carry* the coal, not watch it burn."

18th October 2006
We report to the Army School of Bagpipe Music and Highland Drumming. Here we are given a warm greeting, and, while the crew set up, and Geth is led off to change into the uniform they're providing, I'm taken to a little office used by the NCOs and offered a mug of typical army tea; strong but disgustingly sweet. It always amuses me that the services instinctively treat a director as an officer. The NCOs are all very friendly, but I'm hampered by the embarrassing fact that I can scarcely understand a word that any of them are saying. So much so that I wonder if they're taking the piss. Gradually my ears adjust and I get my head round the accent, though the frequent use of army or musical jargon doesn't help. Over the years, *Blue Peter* has had various attempts at getting presenters to have a go at the bagpipes. They are a notoriously difficult instrument to master, not least because of the amount of air you have to generate and the control you need to exercise over your breathing. The NCO in charge takes me to one side and, grinning, makes a suggestion.
"You should motivate him the way we do with recruits," he suggests. I ask him to explain and, once he has, I pass this threat on to Geth.
"If you can't manage a decent tune, there's a standard penalty," I tell him.
His eyes narrow and he looks suspicious. "What's that then?"
"You have to drink all the spit that's collected in the water trap at the bottom of the pipes."
"Aye," adds the NCO. "And this one has'nae been emptied in a while."
Geth visibly gags at the thought (and so do I). But he has musicality on his side, a quality we've already put to good use elsewhere on the programme. Geth doesn't just produce a noise from the bagpipes, he actually manages a discernible tune. It's a source of great satisfaction to see the complacent looks on the faces of the army musicians replaced first by genuine amazement and then a grudging admiration.
Of course, they immediately raise the bar to see if they can identify Geth's breaking-point, but he has done very much better than anyone expected and I feel a kind of smug parental pride in his achievement.

19th October 2006

To Edinburgh Zoo, to film the penguin parade. When I was last here for the recce, I shoved my mobile in my back pocket and managed to bum call my cameraman (whose name happened to be first in my address book) several dozen times. This cost him a small fortune, as he was abroad filming somewhere which charged per call received. When I eventually retrieved my phone, I found a procession of increasingly frantic messages begging me to stop. So I owe him one and have booked him for this week. Actually, I would have done anyway, as he's brilliant but at least I don't feel quite as guilty for the crimes committed by my arse.

20th October 2006

We're at Mary Erskine and Stewart's Melville, a very posh Edinburgh school, to film a story about education in the olden days here. Geth has been kitted out as one of the pupils in full school uniform. It's break time and the playground is heaving with excited kids all dressed the same. While I discuss the sequences I need with the crew, Geth wanders off to talk to some of them. By the time we are ready for him, he's in the thick of the crowd, his tie askew, socks down, laughing and jostling to get a kick at the football. It's pretty much only his superior height which marks him out as one of us and not one of them.

21st October 2006

Today we have the run of the royal yacht Britannia. It's a fascinating ship and we poke our noses in everywhere. Geth is dressed in the smart white uniform of a sailor in the royal service, which meets with the obvious approval of the very friendly trio of women who are looking after us. Geth blossoms under their admiring gaze, and gets a little giddy, so that I keep having to bring him to heel to focus on what we are doing. I'm giving him one of my lectures when he whips out a camera and takes a photo of me.

"What did you do that for?" I ask him.

"I wanted to capture that special look you have for me when you're giving me a bollocking," he grins. "So you can see what it's like."

You can't be cross with Geth for long. He is so genuinely good-natured and loving what he does. We set up a shot in the bridge. On the action, Geth is to walk in, cross over and take a seat on the captain's chair. We block this slowly, but when we go for the actual take, Geth misjudges the height of the ceiling and, when he hops up into the chair, he bangs his head hard into the metal roof. He's obviously in a fair amount of pain but still manages to quip, "Lucky there's not much in there, isn't it?"

His trio of new fans titter from the sidelines.

6th November 2006

Launch of the *ShoeBiz* appeal. It's been a long journey to get to this point, but it's exciting to witness the motivation of the team, which I can only hope will translate to the audience. I'm also delighted with the human quality of the films; moving without being mawkish.

As the name suggests, we are asking kids to collect shoes, thereby keeping faith with my intention to keep our appeals focused on raising money through recycling. This, it must be said, is not especially popular with the charities themselves, who would far rather we asked for cold hard cash (or return to the well-worn bring-and-buys). Any recycling initiative involves working with secondary partners and a slower turnaround in releasing the funds. But in my view it adds enormously to a child's level of engagement and their sense of being able to actively help. It's part of the USP of the show. Many of the shoes we collect will end up being sent to Africa, which feels neatly connected (those in too poor condition will be turned into material for building roads).

In the House of Commons, six MPs' have sponsored an Early Day Motion, congratulating us on the launch of the appeal, and urging MPs to take part. I'm told this is gathering momentum, with cross-party support, and, apart from anything else, it should please them upstairs.

7th November 2006

A lavish pre-record for the Victorian Christmas insert which I've written. Design have gone to town and created a series of splendid sets showing upstairs and down in a typical late-19th-century town house. All four presenters are in full costume and make-up, with Gethin and Zöe as the master and mistress of the house, Konnie and Andy as the maid and footman, and Chris the gardener as a blue-suited Father Christmas (blue was the colour before the now traditional red took its place).

Konnie is grumbling about having to play the maid.

"Is it because I'm brown?" she asks, when I breeze into make-up.

"No, it's because you're common as muck," I tell her. "Anyway, just think how much sexier you look as a maid."

"Andy – do you think I look sexy?" she pouts, checking her reflection in the mirror.

"You're hot. Always," he says without pausing to think about it.

It's the right answer. She is mollified.

Andy is more interested in the script for once.

"I can't believe some of this shit, Rich," he tells me.

He can't get his head round the fact that, in some posh houses, a footman had to stand on duty next to the Christmas tree, which was laden with real candles, in the not unlikely event that it caught fire.

We rehearse/record our way through the various scenes, and, as ever with anything approaching drama, it is a time-consuming business demanding serious attention to detail.

During the afternoon, there is a VIP visit, hosted by CBBC's Creative Director, Anne Gilchrist. These are not infrequent, and I'm used to swooping in, fielding questions and giving the guests the spiel about *Blue Peter*, its eclectic range of content, and its continual pursuit of excellence. They watch entranced as we prepare to record an elaborate scene with child carol singers, and all the pets.

"How much did all this cost?" Anne asks me, *sotto voce.*

"Well, it wasn't cheap," I admit, "but the money's all on screen. It's part of our special Christmas content."

"Well, enjoy it while you can," she says, lightly.

"What do you mean?" I reply.

"I'm afraid financially there are tough times coming, and *Blue Peter* won't be immune, you know."

"That doesn't sound very optimistic."

"We're going to have to make choices, and there is never enough to fund everything we'd like. When you look at what we spend on *Blue Peter*, in terms of what it delivers, and how often we can show it, it's hard to argue that we shouldn't be redistributing the money to make it go further across the department."

"So you're the ghost of Christmas future?" I reply, trying to sound calm and not overreact. After all, it's a mantra I've heard before, especially during Dot's time at the top. Anne and her guests depart and leave us to it. But, for me at least, her words of warning have altogether managed to snuff out any festive spirit.

14th November 2006

A day of director problems, this time in the form of yet another graduate from the CBBC school of 'want to direct *Blue Peter*, can't direct *Blue Peter*.' Two of today's items (the first about a bunch of goats in the garden, the other a make) which should both have been straightforward, are a total dog's dinner. Neither has the quality of close-ups needed for the viewer to be drawn in and care. Instead, they seem thrown together, without any discernible style.

The director responsible came to us with the direct recommendation of Anne Gilchrist, who credits him with establishing the tone and style of *Dick and Dom in da Bungalow*. This manic slice of entertainment anarchy has been a big hit for CBBC, especially among boys, and her view was that this director might import some of his own energy and verve into *Blue Peter*. While I'm up for any injection of energy or freshness of approach, the problem is that the shows are utterly different in terms of what they are trying to achieve. The whole point of *Dick and Dom* is that it feels slightly subversive and almost thrown-together. *Blue Peter* is about the craft, and showing the detail, then stylishly navigating the change from one item to another. This requires a colossal amount of effort, planning and homework from the director. Someone like Bridget (dismissed as 'old-school') makes it look deceptively simple.

This guy has come in, full of swagger, and basically tried to blag it. He's out of the door before anyone else, and his camera scripts are usually a sea of scarcely scripted pages. It's perfectly fine for some sequences to be "as directed", as it's called (in other words, the shots are decided on the day, once the item is in front of the cameras) but "directed" is the longer of the two words, and just as much of a skill as scripting everything out. This guy is shining in neither department and doesn't seem to be much bothered by the criticism he's getting, not only from me, but the producers and presenters too. I'm forced to the conclusion that he is just lazy, not to mention right up himself. In which case, I do wish he would fuck off.

20th November 2006

Another woeful transmission, attributable in the main to the shockingly poor direction. After the Somme of notes, the gallery was hideously tense. The presenters are in uproar, because they feel under-rehearsed and confused by this director's lackadaisical approach. They have all asked how much longer we have to put up with him and I explain I'm making as much noise as I can with HR, who don't really want to know.

"He's supposed to be a catch," I tell them, grimly.

"He's a clown," says Konnie.

26th November 2006

To the Hilton in Park Lane, for the Children's BAFTA awards. We've been nominated in the Best Factual category for last year's Book Awards, and naturally I'm praying that we win. Despite the obvious bias (!), I really believe that we deserve it and I know that we could do with the boost.

The brief I gave the team was that it should be a show which was just as entertaining for the non-readers as for the avid bookworm. It was a major creative challenge to craft such a special show; densely packed with content, but also full of humour, pace, energy, great performances and fabulous visuals. It also empowered the child judges, so that the narrative was driven by them as the representatives of the audience. At our team meeting at the start of the series, I was asked which one programme had stood out for me during the last season. This was my choice. It had delivered on every possible level, and was the highest-rated children's programme during the week of transmission, which was the best validation of all. Until now, that is.

A win would be so well-timed, because not only would it give the team (who have had a rocky start to the season) a much-needed morale boost, but also it would be a public thumbs-up which the powers that be wouldn't be able to ignore.

I'm encouraged to feel hopeful by the competition; *Serious Amazon, The Really Wild Show* and *Michaela's Wild Challenge.* These are all quality offerings, of course, but the first two are not really doing anything especially different to their well-established formats and *Michaela's Wild Challenge* is simply a variation on a well-worn theme, which, as the title implies, relies heavily on the star power of its presenter. But when the award is read out, it is this which wins, and, along with Ros and Hugh (the director and producer of the Book Awards), I'm left with a fatuous bland smile on my face, when really I want to kick my heels and revert to the tantrum cry of "It's not fair!". I'm actually surprised at how bitterly disappointed I feel. I'm aware of the essentially arbitrary nature of these awards; I've sat on enough judging committees to realise how partisan some of the decision-making is ("they've won before..." or "they had a bigger budget"..."I've never really 'got' that presenter") and yet...and yet. It feels *hurtful.* I mind it so much for the team; enormous talent and hard labour was poured into that show and such a high-profile reward for its success would really have helped us to continue to fight the good fight. Now all we are left with is our runner-up certificates and a goody bag to remember a night I'd sooner forget.

27th November 2006

A dismal day. At various points tempted to cry, "Is there a director in the house?" such is the anarchy which derives from having someone in the gallery with such a poor grip on proceedings. My constant complaints have at least meant that today will be his last chance to royally fuck things up. We're supposed to be launching the first of a short series of phone-in competitions, to raise money for the appeal. Called *Whose Shoes?* the plan is to show a close-up of a celebrity's feet, and then get the audience to call in and guess to whom the shoes belong. The idea was pitched in our last producers' meeting by Melissa, who is in charge of forward planning, not so much to raise actual funds, as to have an excuse to add a bit of *jouzz* to the appeal. I was dubious, mainly because I was concerned about whether 25 minutes is enough time to set up the competition and resolve it by the time we go off-air. The company running the tech assure us that, although it is tight, it is achievable.

Our first mystery 'celeb' is a pleasant young lad from *EastEnders.* I don't blame him for feeling bemused by the barely restrained sense of chaos in which he finds himself. But however ill-prepared and under-rehearsed, there is no arguing with live transmission and we stagger on air. It is all a mess. For a moment, it looks as if the phone lines aren't going to work or give us a caller, but then we hear an uncertain voice, the item continues and we waffle through to the end of the show.

Only then am I informed that the phone lines did, in fact, fail and that the caller we heard was actually a 'substitute' pulled from a team of kids visiting the studio. This turns out to be a back-up plan devised by Nat, the AP, and Emma, the researcher, who both had concerns about the technology. Why on earth they decided to hatch this plan without consulting their producer, or Jack (the Deputy Editor) or myself, is anyone's guess. Standing on the studio floor, I can feel myself at screaming pitch. But bollockings are pointless. All this chaos comes from having a totally ill-suited, inexperienced team. They are mostly good people with the best intentions, but many are totally out of their depth. I think about the show as it was when I first joined. Yes, there were people who had been there a long time; in some cases, too long. Yes, there was invariably a *Blue Peter* way of doing things, which could suffocate fresh thinking. But it feels as if, in the name of 'freshness' and 'new talent' we have been forced to open the gates to any fucker who fancies a go. This is the result. A hideous day for everyone involved, and, for the audience, a bloody awful programme.

"Tell the phone company they can fuck off for a start," I snarl. "That was the first and last time we are doing that bollocks."

With all the recriminations and post-mortems, I don't leave the office until gone 9. I feel so shattered that I drive home with the windows wide open. Better to freeze than meet my maker on the M1.

28th November 2006

In TC1 to record the second of this year's big Christmas entertainments. This is the all-singing (well, all-miming), all-dancing *Strictly Blue Peter*, with the presenters playing both the contestants and the judges. Zöe is treating us all to a singular attempt at Tess's Northern accent. Geth is several shades more orange than usual as a dyspeptic Craig Revel Horwood, Konnie has donned a black wig to impersonate Arlene, and Andy is having a brave but doomed attempt at camping things up as Bruno. It's all highly entertaining and a welcome antidote to yesterday's horrors, not least to the pleasure of witnessing such a master class in brilliant direction (Bridget again).

29th November 2006

Spent most of the day at the Globe Theatre, as one of the judges in our 'win-a-part in *Doctor Who*' competition. My fellow judges are casting director Andy

Pryor and actress Annette Badland, who recently played a flatulent monster called a Slitheen. Both are charm itself, and better qualified than I to judge the individual performances on show. The shortlisted kids have all brought their mums and dads (with the occasional grandad or grandma) and the green room is a sea of happy faces. I speak to the assembled company, reminding them how brilliantly they have all done to get to this stage, and hoping that they are enjoying the process.

"The difficult bit is that there can only be one winner," I conclude. "That's going to be tough for the rest of you, but your mums and dads will be there to remind you just how well you've done and that you're still going to be on TV, as the stars of a special *Blue Peter* all about *Doctor Who*, which we'll be showing next year." Everyone is nodding and looking perfectly happy, and then it dawns on me that this is because they are all assuming that they are going to win. Losing is for the other kids. I feel slightly sick at heart and make my way round the room, speaking to each set of families, to reinforce the fact that they'll need to help us manage the inevitable disappointments.

The standard is superb, and it is agony to start going through the list to narrow down our choices. But this is nothing to the process of breaking the news, one by one, on camera. I think it ranks as one of the most unpleasant and distasteful experiences of my life. Not one of the runner-ups can handle the rejection, no matter how gently we express it. Hopeful smiles fade away, lips quiver and tears well. That's just the initial reaction, too. Within half an hour, the green room is full of heartbroken children and mutinous parents. Our Andy, who is presenting, does his best to console and reassure.

I speak to Russell T Davies on the phone to explain the fall-out, and he is immediately sympathetic. "God, it sounds awful," he says. "Would it help if we found non-speaking parts for a couple of the runner-ups?"

I seize on the offer. Anything to soften the blows. I speak again to all the families one-to-one. They are accepting and dignified, but sullen and sad, too. One by one, they leave us and head for their homes, in different parts of the UK.

I clamber into a cab bound for Television Centre, which I share for part of the journey with Annette Badland. We post-mortem the experience.

"The thing is," she says, "they were all so good, it was easy to think of them as professionals. But, of course, they are still just kids."

It's been a cautionary experience for me. We know kids love watching shows like *Big Brother, The X Factor* and *Britain's Got Talent.* But their enjoyment of TV's 'theatre of cruelty' doesn't mean that they are mature enough to experience it themselves. We can't possibly show the awful intensity of the reactions we've just witnessed. Kids dealing with sudden rejection does not make comfortable viewing.

Of course, in time I hope that their disappointment will fade a little, and that, as I tried to explain to them, they'll still be proud and excited to be part of the show we eventually transmit. But for me, we got it wrong today, and it's taught me a lesson I'll never forget.

11th December 2006

Oh the joy of having Chris Biggins in the studio. It's nearly panto season and I've booked him to teach Andy how to be a dame. Andy, it must be said, isn't hugely enthusiastic at the prospect but Biggins's ebullient won't-take-no-for-an-answer personality, and his glorious laugh, win him over. Just.

"Mate, you're a bloody ugly woman," says Geth.

"That's good, because you're not my type," raps back Andy, which Biggins overhears. He claps his hands and exclaims delightedly, "He's learning, he's learning. We'll make a lady of you yet!"

Matt was back this morning, taking part in our Christmas pudding panto race, and when Biggins told him what was afoot for Andy, he grinned and said, "I'm surprised it's taken Rich that long to get him in a frock...."

18th December 2006

Anne Gilchrist wants me to leave *Blue Peter* and work for her as an 'indie' exec. This would mean that I'd become the CBBC contact for companies making factual shows for the department, and, as well as nurturing the relationship, I'd have the sign-off on whatever they produced for us. She breaks this to me during our routine and is very complimentary both about my personality and my skills, which she thinks would be put to great use in this new role. But I am not enthusiastic. I'm not so cynical that I disbelieve her praise, but I do suspect the motives. She's made no secret of the fact that she thinks it is time I move on from the programme, and that she finds tiresome my objections to some of the changes she'd like me to embrace. "You can be like a Rottweiler at the door," is how she put it recently. "I think there's a danger that you're standing in the way of the show's evolution."

This rather depends on what you regard as evolution. I like to think that I'm not a snob about a good idea; and that I embrace change enthusiastically where I feel it is creatively or practically beneficial. But though I've always liked her, I've never believed that Anne 'gets' *Blue Peter*, and I think that it frustrates her to have someone in the way of what she'd really like to do, which is cut it back, dumb it down and play around with it. As she said to me not very long ago, "I'd like to see how far we can stretch the elastic before it snaps."

Which sounds needlessly reckless to me. I see my job as the curator of something precious, which needs careful handling, not rough-housing.

However, I do recognise that I need to think about a future away from the programme. Next year I will have been here a decade. It's only over the last few weeks, which one way and another have been pretty grim, that for the first time I've found myself thinking that it's not sustainable and, 'what next?'. Perhaps she is picking up on this. But I don't want to be hustled out of the door yet either, and, arrogantly or not, I fear for the show in my absence. I'd like to hand it over to someone who shares at least a few of my values and has a genuine belief in the programme. At the moment, to my mind, there is no obvious successor.

Anne wants to know what I think about her suggestion. I say that I'm flattered and realise that I need to start thinking about the next move, but that I'm not sure about the timing.

"When would you want me to start?" I ask, cautiously. She gives one of her rare, sweet smiles and I realise that she thinks she's on the verge of a breakthrough.

"We could announce that you were moving on just before Christmas," she suggests. "Then there could be a handover period in the New Year, while we hold boards for someone to take over."

Suddenly, I know with absolute and violent certainty that I don't want this at all.

"I'm not sure," I hedge. "Won't it look a bit abrupt, like I'm leaving everyone in the lurch? We haven't had the best start to the season..."

"I don't think you should worry about that," she says. "Sometimes you have to put yourself first. No one can say you haven't done your bit for *Blue Peter*."

I think 'fuck it' and lay my cards on the table.

"The thing is, I really want to be here for the 50th anniversary."

The smile evaporates and her face hardens. Not what she wants to hear. I gabble on.

"I was thinking I'd do one more season, which would take me to the summer of 2008, by which point there could be a successor ready to take over. Then I'd stick around until the anniversary in October, taking charge of everything to do with that, and being on hand to make sure the cross-over went smoothly."

"I don't think you can plan that far ahead," she replies, coolly. "The landscape is changing too rapidly. These days, in a year everything can get turned on its head."

A pause, a stand-off. Then she continues.

"I know that leaving is going to be difficult for you. But it's going to have to happen and probably sooner than later. It would be so much better if you took ownership of it."

She suggests that I think about it over Christmas. When I leave her office, I feel as if the decision is already made and she is simply waiting for me to catch up. An intense melancholy ensues.

20th December 2006

It's our Christmas show and in the gallery to cut it, at my request, is one of the BBC's best vision mixers, Priscilla Hoadley. Priscilla is vastly experienced, especially with live music. She is also, and always, terrifically elegant. A couple of days ago, she called me and asked, "I wonder if I might wear my fur tippet in the gallery?"

I said that of course she could but was curious as to why she felt the need to get my permission. Her voice dropped an octave.

"There was a nasty incident on *Songs of Praise*," she says, darkly. "*Somebody* took exception to me wearing real fur, so I had to leave the scanner halfway through the hymn."

I assure her that there is no danger of this happening on *Blue Peter*, and we sail through *O Come All Ye Faithful* and reach the closing glitter ship without incident.

21st December 2006

Touched by a Christmas card of understated design from Andy. "To one who seeks perfection in educating the adults of tomorrow," he writes inside. "Merry Christmas Richard and thanks for the opportunity of a lifetime."

2007

9th January 2007

Feeling optimistic about the changes to the team. Thankfully, I've been allowed to jettison some of the so-called 'fresh' faces who should never have been here in the first place. I've finally been allowed to hire Crispin Clover, a producer I first interviewed last year but was dissuaded from hiring on the basis that he was too posh. This despite the fact that he was demonstrably the strongest and most credible candidate. It's my good fortune that he's just become available again. He's young, bright, personable and extremely organised. He has to be as he has a daily commute of two hours each way, the price for living deep in the country. Earlier in his career, Cris was a BBC continuity announcer and he has a lovely voice to go with his perfect manners.

Our new director is Peter Leslie, who, once upon a time, was a producer/director in children's entertainment. When I first started studio directing on a big LE show called *Hangar 17,* Peter was my producer. I poured many hours of sweat and effort into that first camera script, but when I came to show it to him, Peter just waved it away and said, "Oh, I don't want to read that. We'll find out if you can do it tomorrow, in studio. And don't worry, if you can't, I'll just push you out of the chair and do it myself."

It sounds harsher than it was; actually, it helped steady my nerves because I got the sense that he had absolute faith. Peter was and is old-school; he knows what

he wants and he doesn't mess around. He's had a bit of a rough time in recent years, personally and professionally, so I'm glad this has worked out.
Centre piece of Peter's first show is the launch of our latest partnership with BBC Talent; *Can You Cook It?* – a culinary competition to find a child capable of being our resident chef for a series. Annie Dixon, who did such a magnificent job with *Music Makers*, is again producing and she's booked top TV chef Heston Blumenthal to be the 'expert' face of the competition. Heston doesn't seem very pleased to be here. In fact, he is generally solemn and sullen, and I'm worried that this is going to cause problems, especially at the point where he will have to interact with the kids.

10th January 2007

Heston Blumenthal has dropped out of *Can You Cook It?* This doesn't come as a huge surprise and it certainly clears up my worries about his suitability, but it also leaves us scrabbling about for a replacement.
Meanwhile, an amusing morning recording which presents a potted history of famous TV cooks through the years; clips interspersed with little sketches with the presenters dressed up. Zöe appears on the floor as the reincarnation of the terrifying Fanny Cradock (stuffing a turkey), with Geth ever-so-slightly typecast as her craven, gibbering assistant. When I tease him about this, he's immediately indignant.
"Can't believe you're slating me again," he pouts. "I just try to make it work, that's all."
"I think it's about time you spoke your mind. Instead of complaining to anyone who'll listen."
"She does me head in."
"That's obvious. The thing is, though, you're the one with the problem, not her."
"I don't get you..."
"Zöe obviously really bothers you. But I have to say she just gets on with it; she's never once complained to me about you, or about anything, come to that."
I can see this has momentarily stumped him.
"You're not a child. If you've got a problem with her, I think you should sort it out between you."
This is a potentially risky strategy but I am sick of being asked to mediate, which is, in any case, made pretty much impossible by Zöe's denial that there is an issue.

17th January 2007

When we first interviewed Andy last summer, I was surprised to discover that he can't drive. I've decided that he should learn on the programme, on the basis that children often love to play at driving cars and it will be another way for them to bond with our new presenter. From a practical point of view, it's a nightmare to have a non-driving presenter on the books, so at the very least it will sort that problem too.

Over the next few months, the whole process should provide plenty of opportunities for his personality to shine, which is what I'm looking for in all the major projects we assign him; it is really important that we give him the chance to develop his own style like this. Andy is weakest when he's placed in a generic presenter capacity, or asked to deliver information parrot fashion. It's partly that he hasn't yet developed the technique to conceal the bits he's less interested in; it's also that he is just wired differently. He has a very appealing natural giddiness and spirit. I'm sure it's this quality to which children responded in those test screenings after his audition. We need to harness this and not obliterate it in our customary search for perfection. His likeability is not in question; the team have all taken to him and there are encouraging signs from the audience too, borne out in the emails and cards which flood in every week.

19th January 2007

Yesterday we transmitted the first special from our *Journey to Oman* film series. This trip is the result of my strong feeling that we need to feature more coverage of countries in the Middle East. We spent a lot of time and effort hoping to negotiate the access to film a summer expedition to Iran, but, after a hopeful start, these plans foundered amid a plethora of complications and risks. Oman is the back-up and I'm really pleased with the mix of stories that our talented producer/director Debbie Martin has achieved. A key sequence follows the preparations for a traditional Shuwa feast, including the purchase of a goat from the market, which is then slaughtered in the Halal custom before being slow-roasted in a fire-pit in the ground. Debbie painstakingly filmed every stage in this process; before she set off, we had long discussions about how we might use the story to clearly explain what Halal (a sign now seen in many UK butchers) actually means. Debbie shot the moment of slaughter with particular care, with the animal out of focus in the background; but none the less showing a few seconds of its death throes. Back in the edit, the inclusion of this shot was debated at length between Debbie and the film editor, the series producer, my deputy and myself. Although it would inevitably upset some children and parents, I took the view that it accurately reflected that, in many ways, the people of Oman have a more honest relationship with the food that they eat than we do back home. We've all seen the research which indicates how few children in the UK associate the meat on their plates with the animal from which it derives.

Sure enough, after the special went out, there were a number of the expected complaints. I apologised for any offence that we caused, but carefully explained the thinking behind the decision. But I hadn't reckoned with the strength of feeling of my own head of department, Richard Deverell, who is tight-lipped and disapproving.

"Do you really feel that it was appropriate?"

This is clearly a rhetorical question.

I give my explanation; of the intention behind including this particular shot, the importance of context, and the amount of discussion which took place beforehand.

"You could have shown the story without it, though," he frowns.

"We could," I admit. "But I felt this was an opportunity to grasp the nettle about an issue which is so often swept under the carpet. Children should have some understanding of where food comes from. It wasn't overtly horrific; we weren't showing battery farming or slaughter houses. Part of the point was to credit that culture for a more natural approach to the food they eat."

"Well, I think that should be a decision for parents, or schools, rather than us," he says, and asks me to issue an unequivocal apology to the dozen or so complainants.

It all reminds me of the fuss which greeted the gamekeeper film I made a few years ago; this shared a very similar aspiration, and the complaints were on much the same lines. The difference is that back then I had the absolute support of my bosses.

23rd January 2007

Have to have words with Alex Leger. He may be our most experienced producer/director, but he is still apt to show a degree of scorn for the burgeoning paperwork which has been a by-product of the drive for improved health and safety in TV. As he tends to specialise in films which contain a higher than average degree of risk, this can be an issue. A properly written detailed hazard assessment for one of these kind of films can (indeed, should) run to many pages.

Alex has been here so long that a substantial number of his films are remakes of material he has shot, sometimes several times before with different presenters. He is now revisiting the Royal Navy submarine escape story, last shot with Simon, now recast with Geth. This is an extremely risky operation and there is a real possibility that, if Geth panics during the escape, things could go badly wrong. Or as Alex puts it; "Hazard identified: Gethin could die."

24th January 2007

Bit of welcome praise from upstairs for the Anne Frank film, together with the interview with her school friend which I shot in Amsterdam last summer. "Fantastic," writes Richard Deverell. "Really engaging, superb editing and well judged. Very moving."

25th January 2007

Take a call from Geth, who, among other things, wants to chat about the Edinburgh special which went out today. Something about the acoustic gives away his location.

"Are you on the toilet?" I ask him, crossly. He has a revolting tendency to call me whenever he has just settled down for a poo ("I've got the time to talk then, see?") and I'm trying to break him of the habit. He giggles into the receiver.

"I was dying for a shit, and whenever I need a shit, I think of you."

This is what they call 'banter'. Or at least I hope it is.

30th January 2007

Ewan McGregor makes a welcome return to the studio, this time in his capacity as an ambassador for UNICEF, the charity with whom we are working on this year's appeal. He's lost none of his charm, and his genuine interest in the appeal and what we hope to achieve with it is borne out by the intelligence of his questions. I manage to tell him without too much of a cringe how much my wife and I loved *Moulin Rouge*. "I'll always remember how we went to the cinema in the pouring rain, not really knowing anything about it, and this jewel of a film exploded around us; not, like a lot of so-called movies, just an overblown TV play, but a genuinely thrilling piece of cinema."

Of course, he must have heard this kind of hyperbole countless times before, but he has the grace to conceal the fact and laughs long and hard when I relate the saga of Simon's wig in *Christmas at the Club Blue Peter*. "It was supposed to look just like yours," I explain, "only we had rather less money to spare. He said he looked more like Stephen Fry than you."

The show also includes a 'reversion' of my 2001 Beatrix Potter film, for which I book Tina Heath to provide the voice of Beatrix. I love this aspect of the *Blue Peter* 'family' – that you can literally pick up the phone and bring someone in who will do a brilliant job, and whose involvement also adds a vicarious pleasure for at least some of the audience.

2nd February 2007

A note from Biddy to thank me for last week's lunch. I shared some of the anxieties which are currently keeping me awake at night.

"I know you will win the short-term battles," she writes. "The long term is anyone's guess. As you so rightly said, four years is a long time in television terms. The department has always been jealous of BP because it is successful, popular and such a hugely powerful and respected brand. Last Wednesday's was a great programme. I only wish the same could be said for the so-called *Newsround.* Tragic to see a once great programme sink so low. A disgrace to the department and a betrayal of the audience."

14th February 2007

I'm not the only self-confessed *Blue Peter* fan to work on the team. I was first introduced to Richard Turley, one of our most imaginative film directors, by a producer who told me, 'He's almost as much of an anorak about it as you'. This series Richard has been joined by another bright young guy, called Jamie Wilson, who is rather more junior in terms of the production team, but just as much of a fan. Today is a proud moment for Jamie; a while ago, he came to me to pitch the idea for a make. At the time, my heart sank slightly, because makes are notoriously hard to get right; obviously the basic idea needs to be appealing to children and the ingredients have to be easily accessible and inexpensive. It also has to be possible to demonstrate the whole making process in several clear stages which all add up to no more than seven minutes of screen time. It is a tough brief for which many are called, but few are chosen. But I didn't want to disillusion him and so I suggested that he seek out Gill (who does the makes full time), enlist her advice and give it a go. He's come up with a beauty; a bird feeder in the shape of the TARDIS. Attractive, practical, easy to make; a winner. I'm so pleased for him.

20th February 2007

It's the 100th anniversary of the Scouts and Chief Scout Peter Duncan is here with a hundred scouts to try a pancake flipping challenge. Pete is an inspired choice for this role; he'd be the first to admit that part of him has never really grown up, and he has always sought adventure and taken chances throughout his life. I've decided that, for all his work to inspire and help children, he is well deserving of our highest award, a gold badge, and this we present to him today. He is utterly and genuinely thrilled. There is not the slightest trace of cynicism about the sheer enthusiasm of his reaction. This lack of cynicism is one of the qualities I most like about him.

22nd February 2007

Out of the blue, an encouraging email from Richard Deverell who writes to praise the quality of the films. "For example, all that I saw from Oman and

Malawi v strong with many of the latter being deeply moving."

This at least makes a change from Anne Gilchrist's terse observation about the appeal which she threw at me recently; "Do you really need a Totaliser in the studio? It's a very expensive prop; couldn't you achieve it in a cheaper way? Maybe an on-screen graphic?"

The sting in the tail of Deverell's email is his comment that while "it seems to me at times the studio is used very effectively – e.g. scouts and pancakes – other editions do not make full use of the size of the studio."

Groans. I've tried to explain that we always use the studio to capacity; even when there aren't the big spectaculars (which, after all, cost more money) like the scouts or the latest Cirque du Soleil, we are often recording more than one show in a day, or pre-recording complex items for future shows. But this idea that we are somehow squandering the size of the studios at our disposal is getting like a stuck record.

27th February 2007

Shining example of the brilliant use of a studio today. Back in the director's chair, Bridget masterminds an exceptionally ambitious day (in fact, we only just make transmission) with the presenters cleverly embedded in a kind of bespoke mini-adventure with the talented cast of a touring production of *Scooby Doo*. We've written the script – *The Mystery of the Missing Badges* – and given Zöe two parts, as herself, and as Zelda, her evil twin sister. ("And I would have gotten away with too...") The whole show concludes with the team leaving the studio in the authentic replica of the Mystery Mobile. It won't be to everyone's taste, but there is no arguing that it's creative, ambitious, cleverly realised and different. And if you love *Scooby Doo*, it's an absolute riot.

28th February 2007

Pre-recording tomorrow's show, which I've devoted to the man I call "everyone's favourite Welshman – Gethin Jones".

Geth puts up with endless piss-taking about his unaffected patriotism and his ripe pronunciation of certain words (video = *vidgeyo*, toothpaste = *tuthpaste*, January = *jannaUary*, and so on) Just as I used to tease Matt Baker that I'd build a dry-stone wall when he wrote a history script, so I tease Geth that I'll do a speech in Welsh (it's his first language) the day he manages a show without a single fluff. Actually, I've long since lost this particular bet, but every time he tries to coach me in the language he loves so much, he's so exacting that it's a hopeless task and I know I'd never pull it off to his satisfaction. He has a friend called Rhydian and just trying to pronounce this name to his satisfaction is like the world's worst parlour game.

"Rhyd-i-yan," I try.
"No!" barks Geth. "You're rubbish! It's easy. Come on. Just say it after me. Rhydyjan" (or something like that).
I haven't managed it once yet. So as tomorrow is St. David's Day, I've decided we should indulge his proud sense of nationality. He will speak Welsh throughout the show, go head-to-head in a leek-eating challenge with Andy, and sing *Bread of Heaven* backed by the London Male Welsh Choir. No prizes for originality.

1st March 2007
We are yet again standing on shifting sands. Ominously, I've been asked to consider moving the programme to a standing set in TC2, which until last year was the home of the benighted *Xchange.* "There's a missile coming your way," purrs Tamara Howe, CBBC's new Head of Operations, "and there's nothing you can do to stop it."
It sounds like a line from a bad soap, but it is delivered with absolute sincerity. I remember this woman well from my time at LWT, where she rapidly made a name for herself with ruthlessly adept financial management. Such was her reputation that programme makers used to chant, "The sun won't come out Tamara..."
Now she's arrived in CBBC, a distinctive figure in killer heels, with a mission to make a difference in a hurry, and she's quickly targeted the size of our budget. During our few brief exchanges, her questions are invariably combative and abrupt, as though we've somehow laundered the money we've been allocated, rather than used it to make the most ambitious and best possible content. Her suggestions are all wearingly predictable; get rid of the big studios, cut back on the overseas filming, and ditch the craft of crews in favour of the production team shooting (and preferably editing) everything themselves. Standard asset-stripping of contemporary TV.
If Tamara is comfortable as bad cop, Richard Deverell clearly prefers to be seen as good cop. When I go to him with my concerns about selling the programme short, he is quick to reassure me that this isn't what anyone has in mind. "We have got serious financial challenges," he says, patiently, "and *Blue Peter* must be expected to play its part in dealing with these. But I don't want you to feel that we've lost confidence in the show. Not at all. *Blue Peter* is very important to us."
I raise the issue of studios. "You absolutely should have access to the larger studios," he agrees, fervently. "*When* the content requires it," he adds. "But there are shows where you could just as well be in a smaller space, and paying less money for it."

The trouble is that it's the thin edge of the wedge. I take a depressing tour of the poky TC2 and try to imagine the show reduced to its narrow confines. Perhaps design might be able to help. I remember how *Going Live!,* which used the equally diminutive TC7, always looked much bigger on camera. Part of this was due to clever configuration; a stage area which could be set and struck during the show, and a raised area which gave height and depth. But would we be able to pull off the same trick, and would we be allowed to spend the money to achieve it? Tamara is amazed to discover we have our own in-house design team.

"But what for?" she demands.

I'm tempted to suggest she tries watching some of the fucking output, but even for one as bad at politics and game-playing as I am, I recognise that this would be unhelpful, so launch instead into what I hope is a patient and reasonable explanation of their value.

5th March 2007

Absolutely gutting news for Geth. We've been in the process of reviving the boxing special we first attempted with Simon. That was undermined by the last-minute discovery that Simon had a detached retina, and so, under ABA rules, couldn't fight, depriving us of a decent ending and him of the pay-off for all the weeks of hard training. Unbelievably, it has happened again with Geth; the detached retina is an unwelcome side-effect of his extreme myopia. No point in recriminations about why this wasn't checked earlier; but I'm determined that we must come up with a better solution than last time. It's Geth who comes up with the best suggestion.

"I've got this mate," he says, "wants to be a presenter. Gagging to get on TV. He's done a bit of boxing."

This mate is a young lad called Matt Johnson. He is, indeed, keen to do whatever we ask. The idea is that we film Geth training alongside him and that Matt takes part in the actual fight. Marginally better than last time, but it's still a disappointment. Maybe we should have put Zöe in the ring instead? She'd take no prisoners.

7th March 2007

Routine with Anne Gilchrist, who has a face like thunder. "I want to talk to you about music," she says.

"Oh yes," I reply, rapidly scanning my brain to think of recent musical guests with whom she may have a problem.

"That film about the Royal Yacht Britannia. I was so angry when I watched it and heard Rod Stewart's *Sailing*. We have to use *contemporary* pop music which kids will know, not something ancient and irrelevant. It really made me angry." She's not the only one; as I made the film (a fact I'm not sure she was aware of) I'm now bridling too. I just don't agree that we should take such a narrow view with our music choices; every edition of *Blue Peter* generally contains a mix of different types and styles, but these days, contemporary pop music is pretty much always part of the mix. I point out that the Britannia film also used Take That's latest single. I also argue that today's kids often grow up in households where their parents will be playing a wide range of pop and rock music which has stood the test of time; and also that they will come across a much richer range of musical references thanks to the proliferation of availability and choice (YouTube, digital radio etc). Also, if you confine your choices to current pop (of the suitable non-sweary, non-overtly sexy variety), not only are your options limited, every film on which you use these date rapidly. I work my way through all these points of view, but I can see they are falling on deaf ears, so retreat, bruised and fuming.

9th March 2007

At the fag-end of the afternoon, take a call from a BBC journalist querying a comment she has found on one of the *Have Your Say* message boards. This is from the mother of one of the kids who were visiting the studio during the grisly *Whose Shoes?* debacle. In the wake of the current, and ongoing, media storm over phone-ins and competitions, this woman has related what she witnessed in the studio; one of the kids (not hers) being plucked from the group to be the voice on the phone during the live show. I prevaricate and stall. Obviously the story is going to break, and before I start getting embroiled in making any comment, I need to raise the alarm with the relevant people. A lengthy call to editorial policy ensues, by the end of which it is clear that all hell is going to be let loose. Drive home sick to the stomach, and pondering the various implications.

13th March 2007

A day of intense activity as plans come together for the press release about the phone-in disaster, what remedial action was and is being taken, and the various discussions about how we should handle it on the programme itself. I'm asked to draft a script which the presenters will deliver on tomorrow's show. I do my best to keep this as clear and simple as possible, aware of the danger of confusing the audience. The script is read by everyone on high, as well as various interested parties like editorial policy and the BBC's legal team. At all times, I'm conscious of the need to remain as calm and focused as I can, and not to give into any of the emotional turmoil this situation is inducing. I can't sleep and food makes me nauseous, so I'm lightheaded a lot of the time, which is a curious and unwelcome feeling. It adds a sense of unreality to an already surreal situation. I've been asked the same questions so many times now, my answers feel automatic where once they were heartfelt and spontaneous.

"Why didn't you refer the situation up?" is the one which comes back again and again. Here I feel hobbled by the fact that the management now is the same as the management then; anything I say which shows a lack of confidence in their ability to support and help me at the time will surely go against me now, just at the point I need them to stand by me. But the unpalatable fact is that, back in November, I felt (and have felt for most of my editorship, except for the brief Alison Sharman era) that no one above me was much interested, either in my own issues or the problems and challenges of *Blue Peter* itself. Lip service was paid, but most of the time, the programme seems to me to be regarded by children's management as 'the enemy within', responsible for devouring vast resources, disliked for having a quite separate and more stellar identity than the rest of the output. The pressure I always felt was to change; bring in a new relevance and modernity, interactivity is all; and as many new faces as possible to deliver this nirvana.

The problems I took to management were the ones I felt couldn't be otherwise be resolved from within; issues with the appeal, for instance, or with staffing, where I wasn't actually empowered to make independent decisions.

The other major factor was that I felt that Emma, the hapless researcher, had suffered enough. She was so certain she was going to lose her job. And indeed, one senior figure remarked to me yesterday, "You should have thrown her to the dogs. It's the first rule of survival. If you'd have done that, all of this would have been avoided."

Perhaps this is true. Do I really believe that, had I referred up, much would have been done about it? No, not really. But my own lack of confidence in the hierarchy is hardly helpful now.

I am dismayed to have discovered that the telephone company retains all the caller information; we have resolved to run the competition again (off-screen) to identify a genuine winner. It's been a bitter pill to discover that, had we been told back in November, we could easily have done this at the time. Perhaps I should have asked more searching questions then; but it strikes me as deeply negligent that those in the know didn't make us aware until now.

Every minute of the day, I feel as if I am on borrowed time. At my first meeting with Richard Deverell, I raised the question of whether I should resign, and was told that this wouldn't be necessary. But I also know that, as far as the higher echelons of the BBC are concerned, *Blue Peter*'s job is to bring glory to the corporation and not shame and embarrassment.

14th March 2007

Anyone who works on *Blue Peter* is familiar with the need to deftly navigate from one utterly disparate item to another. Today, an extreme example, as we career from the joyful results of our immensely popular design-a-character for *The Beano* competition (winner: 'Wayne's in Pain', a boy who is forever injuring himself) into wholesale sackcloth and ashes for the horror of *Whose Shoes?*

During camera rehearsals, we have agreed a brief period of access for news crews to shoot some GVs (general views) in the studio. I leave the gallery and am about to nip down the South Hall stairs when I hear raised voices from outside the studio doors. An aggressive BBC journalist, with camera operator in tow, is angrily venting at this controlled access. She is demanding the chance to interview me and the presenters. Her way is barred by our press officer, who is patiently explaining that neither of these requests are possible.

"But this is ridiculous," she storms. "We're the BBC. This programme has defrauded viewers and we have a legitimate right to investigate. Why are our requests for an interview with the Editor being blocked? What did the presenters know? Why can't we talk to them?"

Actually, none of us are stonewalling but the powers that be have decided that Richard Deverell will handle all the media interviews. For this I am profoundly grateful.

I take the other route to the studio floor. Various crews are taking shots of the presenters rehearsing the drive-in at the top of the show. They are joined by the grumpy BBC double act. I am chatting to our floor manager when I become aware that the Channel 4 crew have twigged who I am and are framing up on me. The press officer stands in their way and indicates that I should make myself scarce. I skedaddle upstairs. I'm only here because I've decided that not only should the presenter apology be pre-recorded, but that I should direct it, ensuring I've taken full responsibility for the entire message. Inevitably, despite the pains I have taken with them, to me the words sound mealy-mouthed and laboured. It doesn't help that I know that this clip will probably resurface for years to come, joining other clunky programme lowlights like the news of the vandalising of the *Blue Peter* garden, and Lorraine's sub-royal directive about the dismissal of Richard Bacon.

15th March 2007

There is the expected feeding frenzy in the press. The story is splashed everywhere, and there has plainly been much enjoyment among hacks only too delighted to score a point against the 'goody-goody' perception of *Blue Peter*. Not surprisingly, no one seems in a rush to make clear that unlike *Richard and Judy* et al, we didn't deliberately set out to defraud our audience and take their

money for our own gain.
Richard Deverell emails me and the presenters to thank us for yesterday's programme ("you did it brilliantly") and to say that the DG, Mark Thompson, feels that "you got the tone exactly right". He adds, "I'm sorry you had to do this – but it was the right thing to do."
There's a call from the office of a senior member of management, who wants to visit the studio and show the presenters some support. I suggest that I meet this person by the South Hall lifts. "Actually, can you come up to the Sixth Floor?" asks the imperious voice of the PA on the end of the line. It transpires that this grandee has no idea how to find the studios.
In the spirit of 'there but for the grace of God', there seems to be a considerable degree of sympathy for me as well as the turns. "You're not on your own," texts Joe Godwin, the head of CBBC entertainment, which is also under scrutiny for various apparent audience misdemeanours. I also receive texts from Alison Sharman, urging me not to lose faith in myself and my judgement.
Chris Bellinger, the Editor of *Going Live!* when I was the AFM, pops his head round my office door. "I just wanted to offer you a word of encouragement," he says. "Editors have to make tough decisions and you're obviously a bloody good Editor. Don't lose sight of that."

16th March 2007
Cheering to read a supportive editorial in today's *Guardian*: "Last week's justified outrage over rip-off TV phone-ins has given way to a witch hunt," it reads, "and the children's show is now in its sights. 'Here's one I made earlier' may be the catchphrase' but there's nothing pre-cooked about this stalwart of live broadcasting, so occasional slip-ups are inevitable. Indeed they have been part of the draw since Lulu the elephant displayed her lack of toilet training in 1969. The phone-in debacle is no more than another mishap in the same tradition. The carping must stop, and the show must go on."
If only.

20th March 2007
Pre-record a slightly spurious item charting the history of famous duets. This features Konnie and Andy impersonating Sonny and Cher performing *I Got You Babe*, and Konnie and Geth, looking rather too mature as the supposedly teenage stars of *High School Musical*. As an in-joke, I've also shoe-horned in a cover of Trevor Horn's pop classic *Mirror, Mirror*, with Gethin and Zöe dragged up as 80s dizzy-blonde frothsters Dollar. There may have been an element of 'fiddling while Rome burns' behind this. Or perhaps it's more a case of 'making hay while the sun shines'?

But, for all my guilt about a sudden dose of self-indulgence, it's an entertaining package, some welcome light relief and the presenters perform it with gusto.

21st March 2007

Geth has been complaining about the relentless physical pressure of his *Have a Go Geth* film series (nicknamed *Have a Go at Geth* in the office). While he's been making these miniature epics over the last few months, he's sustained various minor injuries and feels constantly tired (although managing constant exhaustion is a basic requirement for most *Blue Peter* presenters). But there is a limit to what we can do about all this. The machine needs feeding and the more interesting and ambitious films come at a physical and mental cost. At times, too, Geth does have a tendency to whine and demand sympathy in return for doing what, after all, he's been desperate to do for years. I support him as best we can; he's working with experts and has access to great medical care should it be needed. But today, tired myself and sensing another marathon whinge in the offing, I shut him down with the simple suggestion: "How about we ditch *Have a Go Geth* and replace it with *Action Andy*?"

He takes my point.

24th March 2007

Worried about the Matt Johnson fight which forms the finale in Geth's boxing film. It's gritty and blood-spattered and, because the audience won't really know who they're rooting for, I'm concerned that the bloodshed seems too random and gratuitous. Having said that, I'll bet there will be fewer complaints about spilling human blood than there were about goat's blood. My solution is to ape in-vision DVD commentaries; we'll put Geth and Matt together in a booth, and they can talk viewers through the fight sequence. Putting them in a box in the top right corner of the screen will distract from the bloodbath, and the fact that Matt will be there with Geth, un-battered and full of beans, will also offset the savagery and hopefully reassure the audience.

27th March 2007

Freema Agyeman, who is playing the new companion in *Doctor Who*, is a guest on today's show. She's no trouble at all, happily going along with some time-consuming CSO work to bring life to a gag in which we accidentally send her back to a 1981 *Blue Peter* before dragging her back to answer a whole load of viewers' questions. One of these asks how she feels about being the first black companion on *Doctor Who*. Freema is perfectly happy to answer this, but there is a slight interlude with the *Doctor Who* PR, who ponders whether this line of questioning might be too "sensitive". Fortunately, I don't have to get involved, as both Freema and Andy start to discuss the importance of mainstream BBC shows like *Doctor Who* and *Blue Peter* routinely embracing people of colour. The question is approved. Noel Clarke, another black actor who starred in the series and is doing fabulously well for himself, pops into the studio to say hello and to wish Freema good luck. This is very reminiscent of TV Centre as it used to be in the old days, with actors and presenters all popping in and out of each other's studios to touch base, and show an interest in what was going on around them. While Freema's interview would fit comfortably into TC2, the main studio item most certainly wouldn't. This features Zöe, for one performance only, joining the cast of the Irish dancing spectacular *River Dance*. The show has retained its superlative energy and expression, and Zöe masters her part brilliantly; you absolutely wouldn't be able to pick her out as the amateur.

28th March 2007
At long last during the post-transmission presenter playback in my office, Geth finds his voice and, when he doesn't agree with something Zöe says, actually articulates it, instead of sulking and complaining later. I am so delighted. It sounds like such a small thing, but, really, it's quite significant, because it can only give Geth some sense of empowerment, and whatever he says hardly rattles Zöe, who possesses a daunting resilience. I genuinely don't think she much cares what he thinks; she simply isn't bothered by the need to be liked or approved of. This is unusual in any presenter, and people find it unnerving.

6th April 2007
Geth Gloves Up, the boxing special, went out last night, so far without any backlash or complaints to speak of. Either we've got it right or no one was watching. I know it's not the latter, if only from the cheering text which Matt Johnson sent to me: "A great response from what seems like the whole of Wales," he writes. "Family really proud! I couldn't ask for more. The whole experience has been amazing, it's given me the self-respect I needed. Gutted it's all over!"

Matt Johnson later went on to have his own career as a successful TV presenter on shows like This Morning *and* Surprise Surprise.

9th-14th April 2007
A long, exhausting and complicated week, filming an ambitious joint project between us and BBC Four; *TV Timeslip*. The idea is to take a group of typical 21st-century children and each day take them back in time, in a specially designed living space, to every decade from the 1950s onwards. Each afternoon, they are given a supper which reflects the relevant era, have access to the books,

comics, and toys of the time, and sample a typical afternoon children's TV schedule. The results, and their reactions, will form the basis of two *Blue Peter* specials, and then an hour-long adult version for BBC Four. Having devised much of this format, I've also spent hours carefully compiling the schedules, basing them around the most representative possible reflection of each era's children's programmes. We've put these together as complete packages with continuity and trails, so that when the kids switch on, the schedule keeps running all the way through, just as it would have done at the time. As continuity was so rarely archived, for the sections from the 1950s to the 1970s, this has given me the opportunity to fulfil a minor lifetime's ambition; to provide the reassuring (if slightly pompous) voice which announces, "This is BBC1....and now..." (link to programme). We stockpile these in one dubbing session, and I enjoy myself hugely, though it is harder than I'd expected, as every word must be so precisely enunciated to sound authentic.

13th April 2007

So apparently the programme, and me in particular, are now the subject of a *Panorama* investigation. I was first alerted to this by a phone call from a former member of the production team who had left the programme in slightly acrimonious circumstances a year or so ago.

"This guy from *Panorama* turned up on my doorstep," he tells me. "says that he knows that we fell out, and that this is my chance to get my own back. Then he asks me to give him any dirt that I might have on you. I think you should know, mate, they're obviously out to get you..."

Subsequently, I discover that *Panorama* have somehow obtained the home addresses of various child contributors, and have been door-stepping them as part of the same investigation. They can only have got these details from someone within the programme, which is not a pleasant feeling. Meanwhile, one of my senior team has a good friend on *Panorama* and she reports back that the Editor has apparently issued the instruction that I should be targeted and "taken down".

I report all this upstairs, and Richard Deverell promises to look into it. My understanding is that their 'investigation' has been triggered by finding out that, at a team meeting three days after the phone-in debacle, I supposedly "congratulated" the researcher for "keeping the show on the road". This is partly true. But only partly. Team morale was at rock bottom, and, in the days afterwards, two of the producers came to see me about the impact on Emma in particular. She was understandably mortified and scared that her career was in jeopardy. But, although she had fucked up royally, for which she had been bollocked, her *intentions* had been entirely honourable. This is what I stressed to the team; essentially that she was a decent person, that what she did was an attempt to "keep the show on the road" and that, in a stressful, live situation, this was what you would expect. As ever, the devil is in the detail.

"Can't believe all this *Panorama* bollocks," texts my series producer Audrey. "Hope you're OK and just wanted to remind you (in case you forget) that you're a bloody good boss who makes bloody good programmes and you bring out the best in your team."

This may be true but it's not such a good story.

23rd April 2007

Panorama went out tonight. It was, I thought, rather badly made; even the title, 'TV's Dirtiest Secrets' was tacky. (The critics roar: but then he would say that). It was absolutely surreal to see myself presented as a 'shady character' with the reporter filmed furtively fumbling through my BBC publicity shots. Ultimately, the accusations didn't amount to more than this hoary charge that I "congratulated" the researcher responsible. In fact, thankfully the entire *Blue Peter* section was a bit blink-and-you'll-miss-it and felt as if it was there to give some balance to the much more serious allegations about ITV output.

After transmission, a flurry of texts. "Total lack of revelation," wrote our series producer, Audrey. "Can't believe the wider BBC let prog get dragged through it again. No news! Don't let it grind you down and let's do our own exposé on the working practices of so-called current affairs flagship."

"Pitiful," sends Bridget. "I'd be investigating them for their claims of being a serious news programme."

"Pfff," texts Geth. "Will remember other stories more than ours. Ours was one-off. Sleep easy. Still feelin sick after the movin camera style of shooting!"

In 2011, it was Panorama*'s turn to be in the news for deceiving its audience. The BBC Trust ruled that a 2008 edition had included undercover footage purporting to show children working on clothing intended for retail giant Primark which was "more likely than not" faked. The Trust stated that this was "a serious error" and an RTS award won by this edition had to be handed back. But, happily, no jobs were lost over the debacle.*

24th April 2007

The start of our *Can You Cook It?* specials. The judges are James Martin, who stepped in at the very last minute to replace Heston Blumenthal, and the winner of last year's *Celebrity Masterchef*, Hardeep Kholi. Hardeep and I go way back; at one time, before his media career took off, he was an AP in the children's department, and I always enjoyed his calculatedly provocative contributions to departmental meetings. He was absolutely comfortable making jaws drop with the occasionally outrageous observation. It was perfectly apparent then that he was never going to toe the party line. We gossip about the way things have gone in TV general; and the curious fact that as there is ever more apparent attention paid to courting the opinions of staff, inviting everyone to get stuck into feedback, think tanks, brainstorms and creative sessions of all kinds, there is actually much more fear about stating an honest opinion if it is likely to upset the party line. People fear for their jobs and their promotions, so you get a kind of collective mush.

Only the other day, I took part in a review of the recent output in children's factual. There we sat, a group of execs, all nodding and smiling, and when it was everyone's turn to speak about *Do Something Different*, the latest attempt at an interactive magazine show, a fly-on-the-wall might have been confused. The show has so far absolutely tanked with audiences, and it has all the same try-hard, wannabe cool tattiness which sank *Xchange*. Yet the various observations range from "the team have worked really hard" to "it's very ambitious, isn't it?" When it is my turn, I suggest that no one in the audience much cares if the team have worked hard (anyway, surely that's a given?) or if they are trying to be ambitious; they just want to watch a good show. And this isn't a very good show. I've put my foot right in it.

"That's easy for you to say," snipes one of my colleagues. "You've got a budget the rest of us would kill for, and you're not trying to launch an unknown quantity; everyone knows exactly what *Blue Peter* is."

This is the same old bullshit I used to hear from Dot; the idea that we should be *ashamed* of having a budget, and that it is somehow easier to make *Blue Peter* because it's been running so long. In my view, both its longevity and its reputation can be a burden; you need to innovate, evolve, keep fresh, but not upset people's expectations and cosy assumptions.

After the meeting, the head of factual quietly takes me to task for being "unnecessarily" confrontational. "Everyone is trying to be positive and encouraging," she says, in the soothing tones of a nurse with a difficult patient. I despair. What's the point of being positive about a show that's dead from the neck up? But this only underlines just how pointless these kind of gatherings have become. No one wants to speak their mind for fear of upsetting colleagues and losing allies who might prove useful in the next round of corporate musical chairs.

1st May 2007

A really strong programme today. One highlight is a return appearance from the brilliant young gymnast Louis Smith, whose first appearance I recall vividly because he sounded me out about his presenting ambitions. He's doing well and seems to have lost interest in switching careers just yet, which is a good thing in my view. Another champion, Jake, the winner of our *Can You Cook It?* competition, rustles up a pasta bake, and Andy finishes the show starring in a spectacular studio recreation of the famous *Thriller* video. The only pity is that there are a couple of technical errors during the live transmission, but it's an extraordinarily confident performance from Andy and a textbook use of a big studio. You couldn't pull off this kind of spectacle in the cramped confines of TC2.

2nd May 2007

An email apropos *Panorama* from Richard Deverell, who has returned from a holiday in the Alps. "I'm sorry you had to endure this," he writes. "I thought it was thin and shoddy. Their approach to BP throughout was pretty peculiar and does not fit with my understanding of impartial journalism."

Blue Peter life goes on. This morning, a lengthy and time-consuming pre-record designed to plug a new CBBC drama, *The Roman Mysteries*. I'm told that this has turned out to be something of a disaster. The company who won the commission had no previous drama experience, and nearly went under during its troubled production. Artistically, the euphemism being bandied around is that it is "disappointing". Anyway, we've been asked to do our bit to talk it up, hence the item, which, following a brief clip from the show, seeks to illustrate the various similarities between us and our Roman ancestors. Design, costume and make-up have gone to town, and I've bagged the cameo role of a snooty Roman Emperor (typecasting, so I'm told). This means clambering into a toga, with a garland of gilded laurel leaves jammed in what's left of my hair. Geth finds the sight of me in this get-up especially amusing, though he looks equally ridiculous with his torso oiled and glistening as a good-to-go gladiator. It's an amusing and diverting morning, and makes a refreshing change from recent real life.

This afternoon, further promotion, this time for the latest attempt to find a winning song to represent the UK in the Eurovision Song Contest. It's a superbly catchy effort called *Flying the Flag*, fronted by an outfit called Scooch, who make Steps look and sound like U2. I insisted that we couldn't simply book this dodgy lot to perform; there needed to be some extra *Blue Peter* element to it. I had a look at the video for the song, which, in keeping with the theme of the ditty, featured the band dressed as dancing trolley-dollies.

"If they are willing for Zöe and Geth to dress up and join in, we'll book them," I say.

It's a deal, so Scooch, plus two, take to our set and strut their stuff. It's probably one of the campest items we've ever transmitted; and impossible to spot the

join between the genuine super-cheesy pop monkeys and the fake-tanned duo of gyrating presenters.
"Can you imagine what Matt Baker would say if he could see us now?" Geth asks during notes.
"He'd set the dog on you," I tell him.

9th May 2007
A pre-dawn call time for the first day of shooting with the Household Cavalry at their Knightsbridge barracks. It has taken weeks of delicate negotiation to set this story up, in which Geth will be trained to ride as a state trooper in a ceremonial procession. The man in charge rejoices in the marvellous moniker Dicky Waygood, a name which delights Geth. He keeps repeating it over and over again, rolling the words around with his own fruity accent. "Now *he* is proper posh," I tell him, as Waygood addresses us both as though we're a pair of house prefects being given special privileges. We are both charmed by the man's suave personality and his touching faith in Geth's ability to attain the necessary standard.
"So long as you're not afraid of falling orf a few times, we'll get you to the required standard," he says in man-to-man tones.
But the purpose of this morning is purely scene-setting; to ride out with the regiment during one of their periodic early morning rehearsals. It is a deeply impressive, precisely organised machine, redolent of the heyday of Victorian Empire. We are given seats on one of the state carriages. At various points, the cameraman and I have to duck out of sight to enable the other crew, filming from street level, to shoot the various passing shots that we need. At this hour, central London is more or less deserted, and it is exhilarating to experience it like this. Everyone is in great good humour.
"Rich," says Geth, his eyes shining like a kid on Christmas morning, "I just can't believe how awesome this job is!"
One of the better days at the office in recent weeks.

10th May 2007
Team meeting. Richard Deverell appeared to address the team, speaking carefully from a bundle of notes. He said that he was aware that someone within the programme had acted as a 'mole' for *Panorama* and that this person had "let down the BBC and *Blue Peter*, as well as themselves." He concludes by stating baldly that if he ever finds out who it was, he'll fire them.
Upstairs to his office for my routine. We spend a few minutes chatting about Konnie and her new agent, and then he sort of swallows hard and blurts out, "Look, there isn't any nice way of saying this but I really don't think you can continue to be Editor, *Blue Peter*."

It sounds stupid to say that I was expecting this, when, in so many ways, I have been counting the days to be given my marching orders ever since the middle of March. It's just that, from the start of this nightmare, Richard has constantly stressed his belief in me and that I should continue in the job. I've probably been spectacularly naive, and not for the first time. I am so completely rubbish at politics and this is a man who has made his fortune from the adroit navigation of the ebb and flow of corporate currents. He now admits that there has been "huge" pressure on him from above, against the context that the BBC was facing the prospect of an unprecedented fine of £50-100,000. He explains that my departure might take "the wind out of the sails" and that it was about protecting me too. He stresses that he believes that, throughout, I have behaved with integrity and that this was not in question.

I have gone very numb and I'm sitting perched on the edge of his sofa, feeling ridiculous and humiliated. I don't want to hear his awkward compliments or to be patronised about my various abilities, but this is what follows, along with the news that, once I've finished this season (so: two months to go), I'm to be transferred to work for Anne Gilchrist as an executive in charge of independent programmes. "CBBC can ill afford to lose somebody of your creativity and dedication," he tells me. At least he isn't reading from notes. But I'm not asked for my opinion about whether this new job is something I want to do, or to which I feel suited. It carries the same rank, salary and perks, and I suppose my reaction should be one of relief and gratitude. I find I can't say anything just yet, the numbness is still too complete. I'm aware that this is one of life's turning points, a significant moment, and yet I'm struggling to marshal any truly coherent thoughts. I must look like I've lost the power of speech. This forces him to talk more, I suspect, than he'd liked or (probably) rehearsed beforehand with HR. He offers his view that, at times, he felt that I had pushed *Blue Peter* "to its limits" to express my creativity. I'm unsure to what this refers; possibly the panto, which I know wasn't to his reserved Anglo-Saxon tastes. He seems to think better of this line of address, and switches to something more brusque and fact-based; the timing of the announcement. Fearful of leaks, he wants to get this decision out there as soon as possible. He tells me to take some time to think. As if I'll be doing anything else, once the numbness wears off. We shake hands, which reminds me of all the times I got into trouble with my housemaster at school, when he would follow a lecture by offering me his hand.

Just minutes after leaving, I receive text messages from Richard ("I will give you every possible support"), HR ("thinking of you" – fucking hell, like I've died!), and Anne Gilchrist, who offers to "go 4 a walk, whatever".

All neatly choreographed, this.

11th May 2007

Reasons to be sad about leaving:
1. It was my dream job. Will anything else measure up?
2. I'll miss some of the people a lot.
3. It's not on my terms.
4. I won't be there for the 50th anniversary.
5. Less range and possibilities in other jobs.
6. Will mean moving right away from creative production.

Reasons to go and be cheerful:
1. I've done ten series – a quarter of my life.
2. I'm knackered and it's not good for me.
3. I won't have the worry of the budget cuts and all the managing of decline. Don't want to be forced into a small studio and have to make films on sellotape.
4. I need to see what else I can do.
5. I've got too much of a *Blue Peter* OCD.
6. I'm sick of the hypocrisy and the shit management.
7. I've had the best of it; so many incredible, unforgettable experiences.
8. I won't have to worry about when will it all end any more?

On balance, the reasons to go and be cheerful outweigh the reasons to be sad. So why do I feel so sad?

14th May 2007

Talking to Geth. He is bending my ear about various issues, most of which will now be out of my hands. He can pick up that something is not right; perhaps my uncharacteristically vague answers are a clue. Decide to confide the news that I'm leaving. He goldfishes like crazy and, at first, refuses to believe I'm not just trying to wind him up. Eventually, it sinks in that I'm serious and then he's visibly dismayed, which is flattering but twists the knife a little deeper.

Later, he texts me. "I'm really touched that you u told me 2day," he writes. "Ure a legend. Now get down the gym you old git."

15th May 2007

This morning starts in the 'doughnut' (the central circle of Television Centre) where we are pre-recording an item with this extraordinary South African paralympian Oscar Pistorius. He runs with the help of prosthetic lower legs which look like something from *Doctor Who*; a true Cyberman in fact. Like so many elite athletes, there is a definite reserve; he's not naturally chatty and takes himself utterly seriously. I pair him with Zöe, who runs alongside him as they chat, and she is the cause of the one glimpse of personality he reveals, although it is off-camera. During a pause, he turns to me, smiles and comments on how lucky British kids are to have a show like this, and, indicating Zöe, one presented by someone so attractive. Then we are ready to record and the smile vanishes and is replaced with a look of concentration.

When we have finished outside, and are back in the studio rehearsing an item about football fashion through the years, a text arrives to warn me that the email announcing my departure will be sent out at lunch time. The presenters are all in high spirits and I watch distractedly from the sidelines, knowing what I know, and that this will change everything for them too. I tell the floor manager that I need a few minutes to speak to them off the studio floor, and a basement dressing room is made available. Here we gather and, as simply as I can, I let them know that I'm going to be leaving at the end of the season. There is a babble of reaction and a barrage of questions, except from Geth, who, of course, already knows. It's intensely emotional. For a few moments, there is a shared embrace, and I'm touched by the sight of tears in Konnie's eyes.

Having broken the news to the presenters, there is a team meeting. Everybody crowds round the seating area, scores of them as we are a big team, and all their familiar faces are a blur, as my eyes are already blurring with the sting of tears. Fiercely, I blink them back. I have been dreading this moment, because I am so scared that I will completely lose it and start sobbing my heart out. I'm not ashamed of the emotion but it occurs to me that perhaps there will be those present who might find this spectacle rather enjoyable. I force myself to sound calm and field the inevitable questions as best I can, parrying those about which it would be imprudent to be frank. "Everyone here knows how much I love *Blue Peter,*" I conclude, "and how it was always my dream job to be Editor (voice breaks a little at this). I think it is the best children's programme in the world and I hope that you will all continue to cherish it, protect it and do your best for its audience. I'll miss it – and you – more than I can say."

I expect them all to trickle away and get back to whatever they are doing, but instead, one by one, everyone in the room stands up and applauds me, and in the face of this spontaneous outpouring of warmth and feeling, I can no longer hold back my tears.

The word is out and the email confirming it follows. As well as breaking the news, it informs the world that Tim Levell (currently Editor of *Newsround*) will be appointed acting Editor after my exit until a new appointment is made. "I would like to thank Richard for his great contribution to *Blue Peter* over the past ten years," writes Deverell. "He is a hugely talented, committed and creative person."

I call Biddy to let her know, and she is clearly astounded that it has come to this. "Obviously life is very, very difficult and frantic for you," she says, "but Edward and I would like to take you out to say an enormous thank you for everything you've done for *Blue Peter* which has been absolutely priceless. So when you have a moment..."

It's a mark of how dazed I'm feeling that it has to be pointed out to me during transmission that design have spontaneously painted black all the ship logos on the set and that the presenters are wearing their badges upside down.

All afternoon and into the evening, emails and texts pour in. "I thought everyone's reaction on the team was very moving," writes Hugh Lawton, one of the producers. "I think that says a lot about how much they rely on you and trust you."

"You have a led a team who are inspired by your love of the show," says Ros Sewell, a film director. "Our conscientiousness stems from your belief that *Blue Peter* will endeavour to deliver the best possible output and that constraints of time and money should be seen as a challenge rather than a hindrance. You strive for originality, never mediocrity."

"So sorry to hear you are leaving the ship," texts Nick Harris, who was one of our studio directors. "I do hope it wasn't because of that phone nonsense. Bloody idiots. The whole place is going to rack and ruin. BP simply won't be the same without you."

And from Anne Gilchrist, this text: "Every1 I've spoken 2 thinks it's a good move 4 u."

I've got to believe that too, haven't I?

16th May 2007

A text from Geth makes me smile. "I've been talking about you 4 the past 24 hours and I'm exhausted," he writes. "Goodness knows how you feel."

The truth is I feel absolutely shattered and brain-dead, but as we are in the studio, it's eyes and teeth and get on with the job while I still have it.

17th May 2007

To the Barbican Centre with Konnie for the RNLI Awards. We are here to collect a 'lifetime achievement' award on behalf of the programme. This is going to be presented to us by the Duke of Kent, so, as usual when royalty are involved, there are the careful preliminaries about protocol. When these are done with, we are shown to a pair of hard chairs back stage, where we wait our turn to be called up. Here, Kon and I have an interesting conversation about the prospect of leaving. She has a new agent, who is keen for her to cut her ties with *Blue Peter*. We both joined at pretty much the same time, so, over the years, we've shared in all the ups and downs together.

"I know it's the sensible thing to do," she confesses, "but I don't want to go. I just love it so much. And I can't really see why I should; I mean, I'm still enjoying it, I know what I'm doing and I don't look too old…"

I can't disagree with any of this. "It's just the way things are now," I suggest. "If you stay longer than a couple of years in any TV job, people are suspicious. You've always got to be moving on to the next big thing."

"I still think this is the best job on TV," she admits, before asking, "what about you? Do you really want to leave?"

I admit that I don't, though I've got no choice in the matter. "At least I won't have to spend most of my time and energy battling to keep it going any more. I won't miss any of that."

"Why do they hate it so much, do you think?" she ponders.

"I don't know if they do hate it. They just don't understand it or why it matters. They think it's just a programme that's a bit too big for its boots. It's always been like that, I think, years before we were here. My biggest sadness over all the phone-in shit is that it's basically like handing them the keys to the safe. They'll do whatever they want now, and no one will challenge them."

Konnie sighs. "If the public only knew…"

22nd May 2007

These days we rarely book pop acts, but today I've made an exception for a new American singer called Rihanna, who is clearly a cut above the usual tribe. It's cost a fortune because of the size of her band, and a number of backing dancers, and it would have cost more if we had given in to the record company's demands for 'practical' rain effects (the single is called *Umbrella*; the choreography reflects the title). Even without real water, it is an impressive performance.

When I get home, my son, Rupert, who these days is fast growing out of children's programmes, is grudgingly admiring and tells me that Rihanna is pretty cool. High praise.

Speaking of sons, today we also carry the good news that Matt Baker and his wife have had their first child, a boy called Luke.

23rd May 2007

Back to the Household Cavalry and a busy day filming Geth trying out their elaborate kit ("if it's comfortable, it doesn't fit right") and training to get his equestrian skills up to scratch. It's *Blue Peter* filming at its best – great access, strong contributors (though I have to tell one of the instructors that they can't call Geth a "mong" on camera whenever he gets things wrong) and the camaraderie of an excellent crew. I struggle not to feel too sentimental about it. The plan that's been agreed is that Geth will continue his training in the autumn, and take part in a major state ceremonial procession before the end of the year, possibly around Christmas. I explain that, as I am leaving the show, I will have to pass on responsibility for continuing the story. The obvious candidate to take it on is Alex, for whom these kind of 'special event' films are second nature. When I mention this plan to Tim Levell, though he nods and makes the right noises, I can see him glassing over so I have my doubts about whether anything will actually happen. This gives me an idea. There's still one page of the annual to be filled. We've got some good photos from the shoots so far, so I decide to use these and write some text which makes it clear this is supposed to be an ongoing story. It's the best that I can do to keep faith with the Household Cavalry, who have given us such great access and perhaps it will encourage Tim to do the right thing. But I wouldn't be at all surprised if the whole venture simply dies with my departure.

It did. Gethin never had the chance to deliver on the promise of his initial training and that page of the 2007 annual is a tiny echo of what might have been.

24th May 2007
The *Daily Mirror* has leaked the news that the BBC plan to cut the show back from three shows to two. In response, the press office have issued a studiously snide statement: "Editors change, presenters change, and sometimes the show changes. Any changes made will not affect the quality."
We'll see about that.

29th May 2007
All of the presenter links in today's special *Green Peter* programme are animated. It's not quite Cosgrove Hall, but it's an effective and fresh way of communicating the environmental messages which sometimes sink shows like this under the weight of their own worthiness.

31st May 2007
After months of angst, Konnie has come to the decision that she'll leave at the end of her current contract. This takes her to January next year. The decision was made a little easier once I pointed out that this will just be enough to make Konnie the programme's longest running female presenter, nudging Val Singleton into second place. This very much appeals to Konnie, and by leaving just four months into the next season, the other benefit is that she won't have to commit to an entirely new regime.
Unfortunately, news that she will be going has somehow leaked online and both we and the press office are being inundated with emails and calls. We've left it a

couple of days to see if the questions and speculation die down, but as there is no sign of this, we must obviously do something about it. I consult with Konnie, her agent, and the press office. The agent is, in any case, only too keen to get the news out there, as it will telegraph that his client is becoming available. So we agree to announce it at the end of today's programme, taking the hopefully reassuring line that there is still six months to go, so viewers have plenty of time to get used to the idea. I write the script and run through it with Konnie. She is terrified of losing it on transmission, and her voice shakes even reading through the lines in make-up.

"Oh Rich," she says, "I never thought it would feel like this."

I don't need say anything; unspoken empathy flows between us.

Geth watches all of this and comments, "I hope I feel as strongly when it's my turn to go."

"Why shouldn't you?" I ask.

"I'm worried about what's going to happen to the show," he admits. He tells me that he has even quizzed Richard Deverell himself, asking about the cut-backs, only to be told "we think you're doing too much, and you should do less, but better."

Which is fucking insulting when you consider the amazing standard of so much of this season, and how much harder it's going to be to deliver the goods when they hive off half the budget.

2nd June 2007

Recording the TARDIS make for the forthcoming *Doctor Who* special (*Who Peter*) with John Barrowman here to give Geth a helping hand. It'll be a miracle if anything transmittable emerges from the edit; John is on his worst behaviour, by which I mean he misses no opportunity for filthy innuendos and suggestive remarks. I'm not surprised; I once directed John in a series of *The Movie Game* for CBBC, and he was hilariously inappropriate for much of the time. Every week, I'd devise games which indulged John's rampant love of dressing up; one week he was a mountie, next week a US cop, and so on. He wasn't quite so happy when I dressed him as a yokel farmer, until he clocked that the game involved the contestants herding inflatable sheep into a pen. The prop buyer had bought these sheep from a sex shop; they had pouting red lips and a convenient hole at the back. Shooting the game was a nightmare, as I tried to avoid focusing on either of these 'features', and John kept losing it and falling about laughing. He's a total pro, but once he gets going, he's a law unto himself.

Poor Geth is totally out of his depth. "Put the sticky stuff back..." starts John, innocently, before amending it to a husky "put my sticky stuff on your back."

Then Geth produces five little cardboard circles, which, glued together, will make up the time rotor.

"I've got five rings altogether.." he announces. "I'm the Lord of the Rings."
"You don't know how happy that makes me," leers John.
"Behave!"
"Listen I know how to put things into a hole...I know what goes in first...I'm good at fitting big things into small spaces."
Geth flounders under the combined assault of the double entendres and the very fiddly demands of this particular make. "You're actually shit at this, aren't you?" John suggests.
"You noticed!" says Geth, amused despite himself. "That's why I never get to do them!"
They actually have great chemistry, these two, though it all takes longer than it should. When it is finally done and dusted, Geth and John pose for the annual, and, from the corner of his gleaming showbiz smile, John hisses like a camp ventriloquist, "It's like I always say, if you've never had a blow job from a gay man, you don't know what you're missing..."

5th June 2007
One of the more irksome aspects of these final days is having to engage in the pantomime of the succession. The 'acting Editor', Tim (already nicknamed 'Nice but Tim') turns up from time to time to trail around after me in oleaginous fashion, smarmy to a fault but beady for everything he's about to get his hands on. I say this because it's utterly apparent that, whatever 'process' is undergone, this is the man who is going to be given the job. He knows it too, so that an unappealing smugness can be added to the irritation of the daft questions he asks. Sample: "Why do you bother having a script?"
He also asks me why I spend so much time in the studio. "Because that's where the show is made."
"Oh, I'd leave that to other people," he says. "I'll have better things to do with my time."
He doesn't specify what but corporate arse-licking springs to mind. Today he quizzes "What's the point of changing things after run-through?"
"To make the show better?" I respond.
The other day he piped up, "do let me know what I need to do for this year's annual. I'm looking forward to that."
"Nothing," I tell him. "It's all been done and delivered."
He can enjoy his honeymoon period because all the big decisions have been made. I've commissioned the summer trip to Bolivia, and this year's appeal (in aid of young carers) which will again focus on recycling (of CDs, DVDs and computer games) to raise funds. I've even bequeathed him the perfect name; the Disc Drive appeal.

But I shudder to think what is going to happen to the show under his limp direction; he seems to me to have made a bloody mess of *Newsround*. Once he's got his feet under the table here, it's perfectly clear that nothing will be decided without back-seat driving from above.

I am trying to be tough with myself. None of this will be my concern. I feel sorry for the team who will depend on this clown and have to deal with him on a daily basis.

"I've got *Blue Peter* in my DNA," he tells them.

"And bullshit in my every breath," remarks one of our wittier producers.

10th June 2007

On the flight to Venice with Gethin and my favourite crew, Adrian and Sam, for my very last *Blue Peter* filming trip. When the shit hit the fan, we were in the process of setting up a trip to Turkey, which I would have shot in August. That's now been postponed (I guess it may never happen now, but all the research has been done) but I was determined to have one last jaunt before jumping off the end of the cliff. It's been made possible because we've got a couple of weeks of specials coming up, which means I can get away from the office. The plan is to make a couple of films (which I can't resist calling *Geth in Venice*), at which point Konnie will join us and we will then return to the UK on the legendary Orient Express, shooting a story about this as we go.

11th June 2007

A beautiful morning filming Geth as a gondolier. Paulo, the genuine article, is there to act as Geth's mentor. He bosses Geth around as if he were his own son, good-natured, but constantly admonishing him for his lack of skill at the surprisingly difficult art of controlling a gondola. As Geth always responds best to a 'tough love' approach, the approach is very successful.

"Do you want me to fall in, Rich?" asks Geth, as we wobble about in the middle of the Grand Canal. We all agree it would make the perfect ending. As it's a one-take situation, we talk it through carefully, so that everyone knows precisely what will happen. But, although everyone does exactly what's been discussed, Geth slightly over-eggs it, so that it doesn't look quite as natural as I'd have liked. He's drenched so I have to live with it. As Adrian, the cameraman, always says, "Spontaneity is always better on the second take..."

12th June 2007

Filming in a Venetian mask shop with a very sweet lady contributor. At one point, I have to speak sternly to Geth as his attempts to flirt are making me queasy.

"Face it, she's not into you," I tell him. "It's coming over as creepy."
The familiar hurt look.
After we wrap, and before dinner there is the chance for me to wander off on my own. Away from the crew and the need to be 'eyes and teeth', I can give in to the crushing sadness I feel whenever I surface from the task in hand and remember that my time is fast running out. Venice is a consolation; it has remained the constant in centuries of change. I am just one of the millions of insignificant humans who have passed this way and witnessed its glories. I can feel this staggeringly beautiful place gently giving me back a sense of scale and proportion. I spend a few moments in the shadows of a little church, which reeks of incense and candle wax. I seem to be quite on my own in silence and shadows. Others might find this oppressive or even sinister, but I am moved, as I am by all ancient places of worship. I light two candles; one to celebrate the past, another to show hope for the future. I leave the darkness and return to the warmth of the early evening sun. I feel unusually calm, restored perhaps by the act of acquainting myself with my own transience and mortality.

13th June 2007
Morning call on the platform by the utterly splendid Orient Express, which so far has absolutely lived up to the hype; a gleaming beacon of elegance from another age. Geth is in the smart blue uniform of the well-trained staff, while Konnie is in an eccentric ensemble of 1920s satin and lace, complete with be-feathered cloche hat and beads. This is because I want to start the film in homage to my favourite movie, *Some Like It Hot*, with Konnie making her entrance exactly like Marilyn Monroe. This involves focusing the camera on her heels, but it soon becomes obvious that Konnie doesn't have quite have Marilyn's elegance of tread or natural bounce (as they say in the film: "it's like Jell-O on springs!"). "You're walking like some slapper off *EastEnders*," I tell her, at which she immediately gets the giggles and then we all become a little frantic as the train needs to leave.
Once we are all on board, the pace relaxes and, because it is going to take us two days to make the journey, the filming can be stretched out between long intervals of eating, drinking, chatting and sleeping. We have one entire corridor of the train to ourselves, which given the prices per cabin must have cost the company dear. We are sharing a cabin each; Adrian and Sam (camera and sound) in one, Konnie and the PA in another, and Geth and myself in a third. Claiming age before beauty, I bag the top bunk and he is vastly amused that I'm slightly too long for this and can easily poke my feet out of the window.
It's all a bit like making an ultra-posh road movie. Konnie is very funny slipping in and out of character as a super-demanding customer, forever summoning

Geth on the flimsiest pretext. Once we wrap for the night, we make up a party for dinner in the softly lit dining carriage. It's an evening heavy with nostalgia. We've all worked together so closely and for so long, and each of us knows this is our final fling. The cocktails flow and the gossip intensifies.

A few hours later, we stagger to bed. Cocooned in our cabin, Geth and I whisper in the dark, and periodically he torments me with his chronic flatulence, until at last tiredness dulls my senses and I give in to the soothing rhythm of the passing rail tracks.

14th June 2007

It can't be said to be the most comfortable night's sleep I've ever had, but when you wake up to fabulous scenery outside your window and a breakfast tray of fresh fruit, warm croissants and coffee from an elegant silver pot, who's complaining?

For the final leg of the journey, we leave the Orient Express and transfer to a vintage Pullman, which brings us to London. On the way, a champagne afternoon tea is served but alas, by this point, we have all eaten so extravagantly that we scarcely make inroads into the magnificent display. We sip our champagne as if it's homework.

"We're all suffering from a bad case of affluenza," says Sam, the sound recordist.

As we near the end of the trip, Adrian and Sam present me with a special gift; one of the very *luxe* Orient Express photo frames. Suddenly, I'm choked.

"We wanted to thank you for all the amazing trips we've shared over the years," says Adrian. "It's been so much more than just a job."

18th June 2007

Very pleasing email from Russell T Davies, who writes that he watched *Who Peter* over the weekend and thought "it was MARVELLOUS. Lovely, lovely bit of telly. It really did us proud."

26th June 2007

My daughter Rosy accompanies me to Television Centre for the day. We go to the studio and she chats with Gethin and Andy, while I'm talking to Carmella, the floor manager, who has handed me a welcome coffee. When Rosy comes back over to me, she says, "Dad, Gethin gave me a hug, and he was really hard."

I nearly spit out my coffee on the spot, and then twig that she's referring to his muscles and not his manhood. This doesn't mean I miss the chance to tease him about it.

"Er...Geth, I'd like a word with you."

"What?"

"So, Rosy tells me you gave her a hug. And that you were *hard*."
A look of horror. "No, no, Rich, it wasn't like that. Honestly, that isn't what she meant..."
And then he sees that I've dropped the poker face and am grinning at his discomfort.
"You fucker," he says. "That's really not what you want to hear when you're a kids' TV presenter."

28th June 2007
The last live show of the season. There's a great flap on as the powers that be speak sternly to the presenters and warn them that they are absolutely not to say anything about me live on air. Touchingly, they all ignore this dictate and bid me a fond farewell as they finish the show by driving a convertible out of the studio. I only discover this afterwards, when I thank them for their words. Konnie says, "they can all fuck off."
The weather is too miserable to hold the traditional 'al fresco' end of series party, so I have it relocated to the studio instead. But I've spent a chilly half hour or so out in the garden by myself, memorising my last speech as Editor. Needless to say, I've given this a lot of thought. I start by paying tribute to our track record of quality and innovation over the last year. I name-check major projects like *Can You Cook It?, Me and My Movie* and *TV Timeslip* and the staggering success of the Shoebiz Appeal, in which we found effective ways of talking to our audience about the HIV/AIDS pandemic, inspiring them to collect nearly one and a half million pairs of shoes to help communities in Malawi. I praise the definitive film-making "covering everything from bar mitzvahs to bereavement" and applaud a team which has "worked hard to keep the traditional material fresh, relevant and exciting. Video blogs, podcasts and uploads to YouTube have become part of the furniture but are underpinned by the same skill and attention to detail which defines the best of our content. Is that content too broad-ranging in a multi-channel era? Perhaps. But this year the rich mix has never been richer. And that's all down to the talent and hard work of our production team and presenters."
From this I segue into addressing the 'elephant in the room': "The fact that *Blue Peter* is still seen as the gold standard of children's TV means of course that when things go wrong, everyone notices and everyone cares. The phone-in controversy brought with it a storm of hysteria and hypocrisy. I would like to reiterate one key point – that the mindset of the *Blue Peter* team isn't and wasn't a cynical or exploitative one. The mistakes that were made were not made because of any disrespect for our audience."
I bring the speech to a close on an inevitably personal level, paying tribute to

presenters and production teams past and present. "I'm so grateful for the opportunities I've had on this eccentric, unique and special programme."
I conclude by saying that "next year will undoubtedly be another challenging year for *Blue Peter*. That much never changes. Talent and confidence are what it's all about and I'll be rooting for you."
At this point, I'm expecting to run a brilliant end of season VT which Duncan Bragg, one of our best editors, has cut to the aptly-chosen Keane track, *Somewhere Only We Know*. But before I can give the cue, Biddy steps forward from the crowd of onlookers, wrests the mic from my hands and launches into a speech of generous tribute and praise, which touches me deeply. Then she produces a gold badge with the words, "You'd better pin this on yourself, darling!" and I just about manage not to drop the thing and fix it proudly to my lapel.

5th July 2007
My last day in the studio (TC1), recording our Harry Potter special, which will transmit on the 20th, my final day as Editor.
There isn't much time to feel sentimental as it's a big show, with J.K. Rowling herself here to field questions from a group of kids and (though she doesn't know it beforehand, of course) to receive a gold badge. It's a mutual admiration society as Jo, although a naturally reticent person, has always been a great supporter of *Blue Peter*. She's on top form, charming everyone, and overriding the fussing of the small posse of attendant sidekicks from her publishers. Because it is all rehearse/record (with Bridget in the director's chair, sailing through it with customary panache), it doesn't feel like a typical studio day at all. The fact that the presenters are all smartly dressed adds to the sense of slight unreality too. And then we reach the final link of all, and I perch on a bit of the set next to the *Blue Peter* ship neon and think, "This is it. The end. Whatever comes next, there will be no more of this."
The lights come up, and the scene crew swing into action, crashing and banging, and getting on with it. Because that's what happens. As the saying goes, no one is indispensable. In just a few weeks' time, this process will start happening all over again, but without me. I walk into the sunlight which streams beyond the vast studio doors, creasing up my eyes against the glare. Don't look back.
I'd like just to go home now, but instead I must summon the energy to embrace my farewell; a leaving party which has been organised by some of my closest colleagues. They seem excited, and giggly, in the mood perhaps to eradicate some of the tension and sadness they've had to endure for the last few months. They clearly want me to be excited too, to embrace the moment, and show that I am on the receiving end of their affection and respect. A small group of us

clamber in a cab and set off for the venue, hampered by the various gift-wrapped presents which I'm to be given in due course. Traffic takes its toll and the journey drags on, stop, start, stop, start though the worst of London traffic. I feel familiar waves of car sickness well up, though as I haven't eaten anything very much all day, the nausea doesn't have much to work with. I wrench open the window and reel from the petrol-fumed air.

Finally, we arrive at this little wine bar in God-knows-where. It is already crowded with a sea of familiar faces, and, as soon as I am spotted, I'm crowded by them, seeking kisses and hugs and a line to show that I'm still the same person with my sense of humour and resilience intact. "That's showbiz!" is what I always tell them in moments of crisis. Don't complain because you're lucky to have what you've got. In the spirit of this, I give myself to the moment but stay away from alcohol, because I am determined to stay in control.

Tonight's guests span my whole *Blue Peter* era; John Comerford, who encouraged me to apply in the first place. The presenters; Konnie, Simon, Liz, Geth, Zöe, Andy and Peter Duncan repping the old school. There are scores of brilliant people from across the production team past and present; everyone from researchers and APs, to directors, producers and editors.

Opening my presents is a bit of a nightmare. It's like a public version of that self-conscious birthday and Christmas moment familiar from childhood when you're required to unwrap a gift under the gaze of beadily expectant relatives. I start with one whose shape indicates what it contains; a framed copy of my credit. It's standard practice for someone departing the team to be given one of these, and I'm pleased to have it. It can go in the downstairs loo.

The next offering is something else in a frame, though much larger. I rip off the wrapping to reveal a strange sight which makes immediate sense of why Jack, my deputy, recently asked me to name my all-time favourite presenters. It's a painting by Bob Broomfield, for so many years our illustrator for historical caption stories, with me in the centre of a group of presenters past and present. It is not, it has to be said, one of Bob's finest efforts. My head appears to be too big for my body (is he trying to say something?) and he's painted me with what looks suspiciously like a pronounced pot belly. Worse, it's not just a painting of me and the various presenters; we have been placed in period dress, as the last of the Romanovs, the Russian Imperial family who were all murdered during the Revolution. It's obviously supposed to be a little in-joke, reflecting my love of this era and my fascination for its dramatic tragedies. But it all strikes me as rather odd and unsettling, not only because of the inevitable suggestion that I'm at the centre of some kind of parallel misfortune, but also because it means that several of the presenters in the picture appear to be dressed as children. I do my best to make the right noises. It's the thought that counts (quite).

I don't fool Bridget who sidles up afterwards and says, "I don't know what they were thinking of. I think it's hideous. If it had just been a picture of you and the presenters, fine, but that's just weird."
This makes me laugh. It is weird, but funny too and I'm touched by the effort that's involved. I'm moved, too, by some of the small and personal presents which are pressed on me throughout the evening; silver Tiffany cuff links from Konnie and Zöe, an electronic photo frame from Geth, and a wallet from Andy, among others.
A tape is played crammed with tributes from those who aren't here in person, and the accumulation of all the funniest and most outrageous out-takes. It finishes with the team singing along to Take That's *Never Forget*, the lyrics of which couldn't be more appropriate:
We've come so far and we've reached so high
And we've looked each day and night in the eye
And we're still so young and we hope for more
Never forget where you've come from
Never forget that it's not real
Someday soon this will all be someone else's dream

13th July 2007
A lovely card from Konnie: "By the time you read this, I will be in Bolivia on my last summer trip," she writes. "But I just wanted you to know that over our 9 plus years together, you have been so much more to me than just a boss, such that we could shout at each other and cry together. We've been through so much together...highs, lows, laughter, tears. You've taught me loads and have been such a brilliant leader on our show. I fear for it in your absence. Your integrity and judgement calls have been superb always and don't let certain recent events ever cloud that. Thank you so much for everything from the bottom of my heart, all you've done for both me and the show. I'll miss you heaps....."
And the post brings a similarly touching card from Liz, too: "There has never been an Editor like you," she says, "and the programmes you have made have been amazing (especially the ones with me in them haha!) You are a genius and long may you continue to enrich TV."

20th July 2007
My last day as Editor. The office is a bit of a graveyard, as so many people have already departed on leave. My office has been reduced to a shell, as I've spent the last couple of weeks painstakingly sorting through the vast accumulation of the past ten years. I don't especially want to transform my home into a *Blue Peter* museum, so I've been selective about what I keep, what I bin, and what I try to

find a secure home for. As I feel a duty to posterity, and have a strong suspicion that the programme is about to enter a kind of 'year zero', I've enlisted the excellent staff of the BBC Written Archive Centre in Caversham to find a home for many of the old production files. These include all of those which relate to the appeals, and the master copies of the Editors' scripts going back to the 1970s. Caversham have also taken a mountain of photographs and negatives. I've also sent them files of my own correspondence as I routinely keep hard copies of emails. My Caversham contact exclaims over these, as it is unusual for them to be offered much in the way of contemporary paperwork, and no one has yet devised an effective system for archiving electronic material. As well as all this activity, I've invited BBC Heritage to audit the various artefacts which should be worthy of preservation; the awards, some of the pictures and so on. The database (listing every show and its content) is up to date; I wonder if anyone will continue this after my time. It is all academic and out of my control. I've got the next two months off; although for much of that time, I'll be writing the 50th anniversary book, which the BBC have licensed out to Hamlyn. The team behind this seem incredibly keen and they've enthusiastically embraced the proposal I've devised for a coffee table book with content, and not just pictures. It's been agreed that this will be billed as a "personal account" so that I can invest the text with some personality and opinion. As a fully authorised publication, it will still have to be read and vetted by the powers that be, but I can't see this presenting any major problems. It's intended as a celebration so I shan't focus too much on the various traumas which have beset the show.
I feel calm. Grateful that I've had these last few weeks to adjust to the idea of leaving my dream job forever. I will always hate how it ended and deeply regret my failure to be more prudent and act in a way which protected both myself and the programme which I love. The thought of what will happen to it in the hands of the vandals makes me shudder and cringe. But I know I somehow have to walk away and let go. I wonder how easy that will be.

As I set off on my long summer break, I was told that the BBC had decided to widen their trawl through perceived offences involving the deception of audiences, and that this had brought up the issue of the naming of the Blue Peter *cat nearly 18 months earlier. I wrote a brief account of what I recalled and, during my holiday, took a call from Anne Gilchrist who told me, "I thought you'd like to know that it's been decided not to take this any further."*
In the middle of August, BBC1 broadcast an edition of You Can't Fire Me, I'm Famous, *in which Richard Bacon revisited the saga of his departure from the programme. I'd given an interview for this during my final weeks on the show,*

and it was odd to see myself back in the Blue Peter *office, as the spokesperson for the programme. It was strange to think that I wouldn't be returning. As Simon Thomas once put it, "You leave* Blue Peter, *but it doesn't leave you."*
Towards the end of the month, I was deep in writing the 50th anniversary book when I was tipped off that the decision not to take the cat-naming any further had been reversed and that there was now a full-scale investigation under way. I wasn't invited to contribute to this process. When I returned to work at the start of September, I was finally interviewed for my perspective, though by then it all felt very much like a done deal.
The following week I was summoned to a meeting on the sixth floor of Television Centre where Richard Deverell told me that the BBC were going to publicly apologise for the incident, and that they had no choice but to terminate my employment with immediate effect. My wife had come to meet me that afternoon; she was waiting in main reception and she drove us home through driving rain. I was utterly dazed.
Reaction in the outside world wasn't perhaps entirely what the BBC expected. The Guardian*'s respected media journalist Peter Preston wrote that it was "an absurdly small deception. When does a stinky scandal slither into bathos? When long-serving, obviously talented employees get sacked as a result of an 'internal enquiry' that seems something between open season for snitchers and an inquisition...for Richard Marson, what kind of 'justice' attends his sacking?"*
Even the Daily Mail, *which might have been expected to lambast the BBC for another 'betrayal' of its audience, instead ran a piece which started "has there ever been anything dafter than the* Blue Peter *cat-naming scandal? The whole fiasco would be a bad joke, except for the fact that the first-class Editor, Richard Marson, has been sacked."*
Interviewed in The New Statesman, *Russell T Davies was even more blunt. "Don't even get me started on that shit," he says. "I was appalled. That man was utterly dedicated to* Blue Peter. *So they changed the name of a cat in a poll. Who gives a fuck?"*
I was deluged with emails, letters and cards of expressing support and dismay. "I hope that the kitten nonsense will be seen for the sheer daftness that it is," wrote Edward Barnes, a distinguished former head of children's. "I think my old department is losing its mind."
A Kafka-esque situation then ensued; months of negotiation with the BBC before a final settlement, and all the time I was not only writing the book celebrating the programme's forthcoming half century; I was also, at the BBC's suggestion, acting as the consultant on the official 50th anniversary exhibition at the National Museum of Media in Bradford.
I kept closely in touch with the programme, too, which, with hindsight, wasn't the best idea. It returned to the screen, reduced to a couple of editions a week, and

confined to a particularly nasty little set in TC2, cluttered and babyish. Much of the craft of the programme seemed to have been discarded; the overall style was now as shouty and try-hard as so many other lame CBBC offerings. I found it desperately squirmy to watch. Every week I'd hear the latest woes of the presenters and several key members of the production team. Very often, they'd seek my advice, which I would give, although, with hindsight, I should have kept my distance. When Peter Salmon, a senior member of BBC management, attended a team meeting and was openly critical of the new approach, morale took a further knock. The team were only doing what they had been told to do. It was clearly a miserable and confusing time for many people. Certainly it was for me. And, as my diary entries from 2008 show, I was not quite yet done with Blue Peter, *nor it with me.*

2008

20th May 2008
Geth calls, very worked up indeed. He tells me that Zöe had come into this morning's dub very breezily to announce that she was leaving the programme too. "We can leave together," she said.
He is furious and feels cheated and lied to. He had wanted to go back in January, but had been persuaded to remain until the end of the season next month. His only condition was that he would leave solo, and that therefore the focus would be on him and him alone. This assurance was given.
"You know me, Rich," he says, "I'm a good boy, once it's all clear, I do as I'm told. But they were just playing me."
He's told Tim (Levell) how angry he feels and said that he's not going into work tomorrow; he's done his last show for "those fuckers". I advise him to think carefully about this. He is so close to the end of his time, better to negotiate for the kind of departure which might work better for him. Apparently, Tim is not a fan of departing presenters having their own special compilation shows. I suggest that this could be a bargaining chip for Geth. He could see out the remaining weeks in return for his own special, which he wouldn't have to share with anyone. Geth likes this idea. I call Jack, the deputy, to let him know this is the way to keep Geth relatively on side.
Later, I have dinner with Zöe at Albertine's, just off Shepherd's Bush Green. She

is very bright and talkative. She tells me the sorry saga of her own imminent departure. A fortnight ago, she was told that Anne Gilchrist wanted to see her and Tim. Zöe was in the office that day, and as the appointed time of 4 o'clock came close, she just assumed she would go up with him. But when she put her head round his door, he'd already left. She thought, 'That's nice of you' and went up to find him already sitting in Anne's office.

"I thought, 'This isn't good'," she tells me. "Tim did all the talking and told me that my contract wasn't being renewed. Anne just sat there, looking miserable." Zöe asked why they didn't want her to continue and was told that she no longer demonstrated any passion in what she did. She asked for an example. Tim mentioned an item about a recycled dress. This infuriated her because "I actually felt incredibly passionate about this. I carried on working on it in the office, when I could have been at home with my feet up."

Tim then said she hadn't engaged with the camera while she had been making the dress, to which she pointed out that she couldn't be looking down the lens as she was busy sewing.

It was a pointless debate, in any case, as their minds were already made up. She was told to own the decision. Afterwards, Tim asked her, "Are you OK? Do you want to go out for a coffee?" This is an-all-too familiar scenario; people don't want you to hate them, even when they are wielding the knife. The irony is that he's since written a press release in which he says Zöe always gave 110%.

While we are dining, her phone rings twice. Both times it is Tim. The second time Zöe answers and tells him that she is having dinner with me.

On the train back home, another call from Geth. He still feels furious and betrayed but he's been promised his special and so he's going in. "I'll be the better person," he says. "Not that it's hard with those cunts."

My son Rupert died on 8th June 2008. It was sudden and shocking; for a long, long time, it felt like the end of everything. We struggled to survive, mainly for the sake of our daughter, Rosy. And, although it was frequently tempting to hibernate and hide away, with the love, help and support of others, we made efforts to engage with the real world. This included Blue Peter, *which was about to celebrate its 50th anniversary.*

11th September 2008

About to set off to London to be interviewed for the BBC2 documentary, *Blue Peter at 50.* I've dithered for a long time about whether I should take part, but I like and respect Lucy Bowden, who is producing it. She first approached me asking for help with clips and suggestions for unusual and provocative archive, and then, after a while, floated the idea of an interview. I'm wary of the way my

answers might be cut, but I trust her, so here I am, in my suit, being given a final inspection by Mandy and Rosy.
"What are those weird shoes you're wearing?" asks Rosy.
The 'weird' shoes are actually ankle-length brogues, which won't be on camera. "I could be wearing stilettos," I say. Rosy rolls her eyes. Next she points to my shirt, which she says is too unbuttoned. "You can't have chest hairs poking out." Good point. I do a button up.
"Now you look too nerdy."
Finally, I load the tattered remnants of my self-esteem into the cab which takes me on the long and dreary trek to Twickenham. The interview is being shot at Dave Cooke and Tina Heath's house (Dave has his studio right on the top floor). I've been here countless times to record the presenters' vocals for lots of shows and musical items. The last time I was here I actually did some singing myself, so I could mime my part in an elaborate spoof in the 2007 end of series tape. We had been heavily cross-promoting the BBC talent show *Any Dream Will Do.* For the party tape, I was filmed in the *Blue Peter* garden (with my deputies on backing vocals) singing a rewritten version of one of the key songs:
Close every door to me
Take back my badge from me
Goodbye Blue Peter
And all of the pets....
It had got a big laugh at the party. But the line which followed, "And the BBC are now looking for a new Editor, in *Any Tim Will Do"* brought the house down.
Anyway, it is kind of Dave and Tina to suggest that I might be more comfortable at their place rather than somewhere more anonymous. I'm far too early, as Tina, who is also being interviewed, has only just finished having her make-up done. So I sit for a while and listen to her answer her questions. An awkward moment when she's asked about the Ethiopia appeal.
"I didn't go there. Do you mean Cambodia?"
"Yes, that's the one."
"I didn't go there either."
Tina relates how she got the part in *Lizzie Dripping* by pretending to be 16 and saying that she came from Preston. "I kept this going all the way through the pilot and halfway through the first series. Then one day on location in the hotel, I decided I was going to come clean and tell them. And then I had to audition all over again for the second series!"
"Quite right too," I piped up, "serves you right for faking it."
Much laughter.
My turn to be made up. The make-up artist reminds me of fleeting 80s pop star Taylor Dayne, with her impressive mane of frizzy blonde hair. As she dabs away

at my face, she chats cheerfully about her work, mainly personal make-up jobs for celebs going to parties and premieres. She just loves rubbing shoulders with the rich and famous. “If there was a book group devoted to *Hello!*, I’d join like a shot,” she trills. She does her best with me, clarting my face with foundation, smoothing my eyebrows, and tweaking at my thinning thatch like she’s putting the finishing touches to a Rembrandt (or perhaps a Picasso would be more accurate).

“I hope I don’t look like a drag queen,” I mutter, as she declares herself done.

“No, you look gorgeous,” she assures me. She’s obviously good at her job as, without prompting, she has spotted the vexing issue of the peeping chest hair and that my shirt doesn’t look good buttoned up. She produces some kind of tape and fiddles about until she’s made me look casually dignified.

We start the interview; Lucy has also agreed to shoot some material for the Bradford Museum of Media exhibition – they want to have stuff playing on interactive video screens as people wander around. So we work through these questions as well as the ones for the doc. It all feels slightly ‘out of body’ but I do my best and it seems to go OK. I’d never be able to tell from Lucy, as like every decent director, she’s too good at enthusing and cheerleading to show what she might really be thinking. The crew are a better barometer and they don’t seem bored, and even smile in the right places. When it’s all done, Dave announces that it’s “pop o’clock” and hands round glasses of champagne. They’ve gone to a lot of trouble to make me feel welcome and loved; everyone is gentle and patient. I just wish this didn’t make me feel a little like an outpatient from a psychiatric unit.

28th September 2008

I’ve just replied to an extraordinary letter from Val Singleton. This starts with congratulations on the “impressive” 50th book, but rapidly turns into a series of gripes and snipes. “You have rather toed the party line,” she suggests. “Perhaps it might have been nice if you had spoken to some of us to get our recollections too. Rather like not speaking to us to check our employment status with the BBC before the Will Young video went ahead!”

She bangs on about how Lulu the Elephant was live and not recorded, as I state in the text, and complains that I’ve misrepresented the reasons for her being dropped from the *Blue Peter Special Assignments*. “I wonder why you felt the need to put this in....making out Peter was wrong about Lulu and I have a faulty memory about the specials. Disparaging us both. Was that deliberate I wonder. Edward’s decision to suddenly find lots of excuses not to use me for the specials was ‘sheer bloody pique’. It is, I’m afraid, how a lot of people at the BBC work.”

I am pissed off and decide by return of post to let her have it with both barrels.

"Thank you for your kind congratulations about the book," I write. "As you will appreciate, it was a labour of love. But not just love. I spent a huge amount of time researching it in great detail, interviewing a long list of people and watching the unexpurgated tapes of all the interviews shot for the 40th (which included yours). Precisely because I am aware that history tends to be written by the 'victors' (though I don't believe that I exactly fit that bracket myself), I attempted throughout to get at least two and sometimes several sides of each story."

I put her right about Lulu the elephant: "I'm not sure why this bothers you and Peter Purves so much. However strongly you feel, you are still mistaken. It was recorded at Lime Grove on 2 July 1969, and transmitted the following day. I mentioned it partly because viewers tend to assume it is THE classic example of live TV, whereas in fact it was recorded. Also because Peter in particular keeps bringing it up in TV interviews as though there is some bizarre conspiracy theory about it. I think this makes him look rather foolish, given the facts."

I also deal with the Will Young saga, saying that "instead of taking issue with the company responsible, I was upset that the artists involved, all of whom in different ways I have employed and supported and been loyal to over the years decided to send me a threatening legal letter instead of approaching me directly for an explanation. The lawyers looked at this letter and just laughed. I was advised not to respond and so didn't. I am left disappointed that people to whom I have only ever shown loyalty and kindness should have jumped to such an utterly unreasonable conclusion."

As for the *Special Assignments*, I explain that as it was contentious, I tried to give both sides of the story. "Edward was absolutely adamant about his point of view. You had indeed told me your version of events at the lunch we had at your club last summer (I keep a diary and referred to this when I wrote the piece – I've just looked at it again with your letter and they pretty much exactly match up). The book states that you met Edward for lunch to discuss plans for the next series and later continues: *Val remains convinced that Edward's decision was actually triggered by a minor dispute during the lunch involving what she was being paid for the use of her photograph in the annual.*"

"This clearly gives your point of view, about which you are as adamant as Edward is about his. I simply reflected the conflict of opinion and memory. Other than this, Edward has only ever spoken about you in glowing terms – to me."

I point out that "there does seem to be an extraordinary amount of bitterness and bad blood between you (and John and Peter) and Biddy and Edward, which I think is sad. It is so many years later and both parties did pretty well out of the mutual association, held in respect and affection by very many people, myself included, for their professional achievements. I had no intention of being disparaging to either you or Peter."

I quote examples from the text and mention that "several times I refer to you, John and Peter as "the dream team". Then I conclude by saying, "in writing the book, I tried hard to be fair and balanced. So I'm sorry that I seem to have touched a nerve – but equally I think much of your letter is itself either inaccurate or unfair."

30th September 2008

Further to my snotty exchange with Val, I've now had an email from Peter Purves pouring oil on troubled waters, which starts by referring to my "splendid" 50th book, and then goes on to raise the thorny subject of whether or not Lulu the Elephant was live. "I remained unconvinced," he writes, "until, in a conversation with Valerie, I asked her to look it up in her diary, and discovered to my horror that my memory has been playing tricks for all these years. I just wanted to put the record straight from my point of view and I attach the paragraph from my upcoming autobiography that I trust will be an acceptable apology. I regret also the situation that arose with the Will Young affair. It was a disappointing time. You have always seemed to be an honest man and a genuine fan of the programme. You have over the years made many flattering comments about me, John and Valerie, for which I can only say thank you. So I am sorry if you feel sullied by our reaction to the production of the video."

Nothing from Val, but it's clear he's speaking for them both. I'm relieved. I've always liked Pete, and I was aggrieved by the ludicrous idea that I somehow have an agenda to do them down or leave them out of pocket.

15th October 2008

The Queen is holding a tea party at Buckingham Palace to celebrate *Blue Peter*'s 50th, and I'm invited. Lucky it's taking place inside, as the weather is miserable, with dark grey skies and constant rain.

I'm wearing a black suit, with Rupert's school tie, and my gold badge on the lapel. Set off around 2.15 and drive there in the KA. It amuses me that my little banger will be allowed to park right in the grand central quadrangle of HMQ's place.

As I arrive early, I'm asked to wait for a few moments right in front of the main gates, and from here I watch other familiar faces turning up by cab or on foot; John Noakes and Valerie Singleton, a demurely dressed Diane-Louise Jordan. Just behind me, on the vast statue of Queen Victoria, I can see Joel and Helen from the current team filming some pieces to camera, with a director I brought into the show. Matt Baker is watching from the sidelines. A glimpse of the old life.

Suddenly, there is a tap at the window, and a producer sticks his head in and asks if I'd mind if Simon Groom waits with me. Naturally, I say that this is fine and Simon clambers in. He's very friendly and excited by the honour of being asked. The presenters on the guest list must all have served five years or longer, I'm told, though that twerpy Tim has fucked up by not inviting Peter Duncan. Pete, who is understandably upset at being excluded, pointed out that over his two stints, he completed five and half years on the show. Tim apparently told him that they'd decided to count each of these separately! Simon doesn't just gossip about all this nonsense; he is sensitive to the horror of our recent months, and I appreciate this. Matt looms at the window, so we get out of the car and a little *Blue Peter* posse starts to form. Katy Hill, Tango orange and wearing a very short skirt, makes an entrance. We're joined by Jay Hunt, the Controller of BBC1, excited as a schoolgirl in her party frock and heels. I introduce Jay to Katy, but, alas, Katy mishears and, clearly not having a clue who the woman is, says distantly, "Oh hi, Jo", as if to a fan. Matt is killing himself laughing. "That'll go down well with *le grand fromage*," he whispers to me, and, indeed, Jay is now looking a mite frosty. She cheers up a bit when Lesley Judd arrives, a tiny figure with a hairdo of elaborate Marie Antoinette curls. "You can blame breakfast telly for these," she laughs, throatily. "They gave me a make-over."

She's very friendly. I tell her how much my daughter Rosy used to love the makes, and that she had a compilation tape with some of the classics, many presented by Lesley. "Her primary school teacher asked her who her favourite presenter was, and she said you, which caused a bit of confusion."

"How sweet!" Lesley laughs. These days, she lives in France and rarely emerges into the limelight.

Lewis Bronze sidles up, also wearing his gold badge. "Snap!" I say.

I notice Anne Gilchrist approaching us. She's wearing black from head to foot with a pair of extremely spiky-toed boots . "Who's *that*?" Lewis asks, in derogatory tones.

"It's Anne Gilchrist," I tell him. "She worked for you for two years, remember?" He is amazed at her transformation and remarks wryly: "Well, I suppose if she's here, at least she won't be able to cancel the show for a bit longer!"

At last we are signalled to make our entrance. Simon jumps back in the car and we drive through the gates, though we have to pause to allow the Changing of the Guard to troop past. It's a surreal sight; the smartly marching soldiers in their scarlet tunics with a plethora of dolled-up past presenters dotted about in the foreground.

Once we are inside the Bow Room, where the party is to take place, the gallery of *Blue Peter*'s great and good expands to include Margaret Parnell, Annie Dixon, Leonie Pocock (the dedicated dog lady) and Cilla Collar (who ran the correspondence unit for decades). Those being specifically presented to Her Majesty are given a special briefing. As I'm to offer her a copy of the 50th book, the choreography of this is carefully discussed. It will be handed to me to show HMQ, but will then be deftly removed by an equerry.

It's an odd kind of tea party. Everyone is on edge, so there aren't many customers for the delicious cakes and finger sandwiches. Placed on a long table covered with an immaculate white cloth, there is a magnificent iced cake with a *Blue Peter* ship emblazoned on it. Earl Grey is served from trays by spotty footmen, and if you want milk you have to add it yourself from a little jug. A fiddly challenge too far for most of those present. I loathe Earl Grey in any case.

"Shall I ask loudly for Lapsang Souchong?" I suggest to a giggly Konnie. I note that although she's wearing very high heels, she's teamed them with pop socks. Typical Kon.

Annie regales me with a staggering tale of Tim's tactlessness with his new presenter, Helen. "He asked her how she feels about taking over from such a glamorous presenter as Zöe," Annie relates. "Helen told him that she feels fine about it, to which he says, 'Oh well, you're doing it for the ugly ones.'"

"Jesus Christ," says Annie, smacking me on the arm, "it doesn't get much better than that, does it?"

Have a quick catch-up with a friendly Peter Purves, still keen to mend fences over the book hoo-ha, but I make only cool eye contact with Val Singleton, who is pretending to be busy with her handbag.

Poor old Noakes has shrunk and looks sour and out of things. None of them look especially pleased to be reunited with each other. So much for the 'dream team.'

Biddy arrives late and flustered, but resplendent in shocking pink and pearls. Shortly afterwards, an equerry asks us to gather into our various groups; past presenters, past production teams, and Editors. I remark that Edward, Lewis, Oliver, Steve and myself will look like Biddy's backing band.

"Too bloody true," remarks Lewis, acidly. "Just the way she likes it."

He asks if I thought that my being asked here today was a sign that I had been forgiven by the BBC. I say that I thought it had more to do with the death of my son in June. "Too high a price to pay, if it's true," he mutters.

Well, quite.

As if on cue, Richard Deverell chooses this moment to come over and shake my hand. He says that he hopes I am feeling proud. "Of what the programme was, not what's it's become," I say blandly, and he looks awkward and retreats.

In marked contrast, the Queen arrives in an explosion of light from all the various cameras. She is smiling radiantly, and is patient and gentle with a small group of overwhelmed children who have all won gold badges. My moment isn't helped by Tim, acting as tour guide, who forgets to introduce me, so that I have

to do this myself and resist a wild impulse to blurt out, "I'm the Editor what got done in for naming a cat, ma'am."
I manage to repress this and, as planned, someone smoothly hands me the book. I hear myself saying, "This is the 50th anniversary book that I wrote, Your Majesty. The problem was what to leave out."
"Oh indeed," she beams. "I should think that there was so much to include with 50 years to choose from."
I say that this is true but that she is in there, and then hand it over, commenting that it is great to see her wearing her gold badge.
"Oh yes," she says, "I believe it came from Windsor Castle."
She glides on and everyone in our little group relaxes. As with all these royal occasions, it is over surprisingly quickly; the meat is in the anticipation and the aftermath. The party thins out quickly. I have a moment to catch up with Yvette Fielding, who was always so kind and friendly another lifetime ago when I was a floor assistant. She tells me that she uses me as an example of how important it is to be nice to people on the way up, as you never know where they'll end up. I'm introduced to Joel, the new boy on the show. He is thin, bright, cocky, trying to be funny. Reminds me a little of Richard Bacon.
I escape as quickly as I decently can, as I feel utterly drained. But, before I leave, I'm again cornered by Richard Deverell, who seems to want to talk to me about the speech he is planning to make at the 50th anniversary party this coming week. "I do the boring speeches, you see," he says, "but I'll try to keep it short." It is bizarre to be talking to him at all, really, but I find myself being pleasant and friendly and think, 'Is this dignity, good karma, or total sell-out?'

16th October 2008

The day of the 50th anniversary and the big BBC party being thrown for the programme at the Science Museum. For so long, this date was my personal beacon; a perfect finishing point at which to aim, the natural conclusion of so many years of hard work and sheer obsession. But life is so very different now, shaped by the maelstrom of events over the last 18 months, and culminating in the shattering death of Rupert.
So I have agonised about whether or not I should attend tonight. Close friends from the programme have been adamant that I should, and the family think so, too. "Dad, if you really hate it, you can just leave," says my daughter Rosy with eminent logic.
I've arranged to meet a small group of mates beforehand, Kez (my former deputy), Bridget and Matt, who have been working together today on a live Olympic parade. Someone asks Matt about his son, Luke, and I watch him talking with shining-eyed pride, just as I used to talk about Rupert.

Thankfully, conversation soon switches to the Palace party, and Matt surprises me by saying that he's been reading a book by the Dalai Llama, and that some of its teachings had stuck in his mind. "When the Queen approached me," he says, "I thought, 'You're just an old woman.'"

"That's what happens when you read books," I can't resist teasing him. "Sometimes it changes your perspective."

We discuss the whole Zöe and Gethin situation, and why it went so wrong between them and Matt. Matt says that he still thinks that Zöe is basically very talented, but that she needed to be forced out of her own particular bubble. "I always wanted to take her up to the farm and say, 'That's a cow, that's a field, that's real bloody life.'"

Whatever I say, he still holds on to his view that Geth wanted the job "for all the wrong reasons." But he also tells me, "Rich, you are a great man, with your passion and enthusiasm and drive and focus. Never forget that." I am momentarily overwhelmed, and confess that I am dreading tonight. He promises to be my 'minder' and make sure that I am protected from anyone I don't want to talk to.

At first, when we arrive at the museum, it is pretty bad; a queue of bright, well-meaning faces, hugs and smiles, kisses here and kisses there, and little sideways looks of appraisal, sad concern and slight embarrassment. Everyone very much dressed up, except for me, a curmudgeon in jeans and a green checked shirt. "I look like I've been dressed by you," I say to Matt, who laughs, and delivers on his promise, expertly fending off exactly the characters with whom he senses I won't wish to engage.

"I've missed you!," one woman gushes effusively.

"Well, I haven't missed you," I think to myself, but before she can get stuck in to whatever it is she wants to say, Matt swoops in, curtails her flow, and says, "Excuse me, I just want a word with Rich," before leading me away and leaving her mid-sentence.

Jack Lundie, whom I had brought into the programme and who was first my deputy and then Tim's, approaches me dressed in the epitome of corporate chic, a sharp grey suit, with button-down polo shirt. "Why are you dressed like John Birt?" I ask him. "Is it fancy dress?" He looks visibly hurt but before he can say much, Matt again swoops in and Jack is gone.

Several times, Matt performs this rescue operation and I am so grateful. People keep asking me to sign their copies of the 50th book and I find it oddly difficult to write legibly (though I've had nothing whatsoever to drink). Someone shows me a copy of the latest annual, and I wish they hadn't. It is appalling, a travesty of what Annie and I worked so hard to develop and embellish.

I wouldn't have lasted five minutes at this party without Matt's shepherding. He allows the genuine to get through, among them Peter Duncan, who gives me a hug and a kiss, Lesley Judd, who praises the book to the rafters, and poses for a couple of photos, and then Stuart Miles and Sarah Greene (wonderfully glam in an off-the-shoulder dress and a stole of floaty little feathers). Stuart and I tell her how we had travelled through Mexico on the summer trip doing endless impressions of her and Phillip.

"Go on then," she says, "show me!"

So we launch into our *Going Live!* early morning trailer ("Coming up, it's more fun and frolics with the bears from the Evergreen Forest!") until she is laughing and laughing. "That's made my evening!" she says.

Katy Hill makes it through the Baker barrier, and is amusingly catty about Zöe's spectacular shiny mini-dress, revealing acres of leg. "Is that appropriate clothing for *Blue Peter* presenters these days?" she ponders, seemingly oblivious to the irony of her own frock; an equally tiny number also leaving little to the imagination. Tina Heath comes over and just tells me that she loves me, as does Konnie, which is nicely simple, obviously heartfelt, and which I appreciate.

I finally meet the new girl, Helen Skelton, who is clearly the stand-out talent in the current line-up. I tell her so and she is equally complimentary to me, saying, "I've heard so much about you, and it's all good." I advise her to keep some kind of record of all the experiences she is having, as they will flash by so fast. Have another chat with skinny, silly Joel, but this time I like him much more than at the Palace. It's obvious, though, that he's the type to need strong production, which I rather doubt he'll be getting.

At some point, we are all herded together for a speech from Richard Deverell. He thanks all the Editors in turn and, at the end, makes a special presentation to Biddy of "Richard Marson's excellent history of *Blue Peter*, signed by all the presenters."

Clearly taken by surprise, Biddy steps out of the crowd like a startled scarecrow, snatches the book and says, *sotto voce*, "Judging by today, I think *Blue Peter* will run for another 50 years," before scarpering sharpish back into the throng. Later, she seeks me out and demands, "Why hadn't it been signed by you?" and adds that she notes that John Noakes has written "with love from"; "so he obviously had no idea who he was signing it for!"

Tim also makes a speech, and again I am name-checked as he introduces a clip from the Malawi HIV/AIDS appeal. He concludes by expressing the hope that "we can hand *Blue Peter* on to the next generation of viewers, who will end up doing our jobs."

"They should start them now," says Gethin, next to me. "Any ten-year-old would do a better job than him."

Once the speeches are done, a bossy-boots from picture publicity herds the

Editors and presenters up a long corridor to a stairwell in which various photographs are taken. These all took a long time. Steve Hocking tells me that he thinks Joel is in danger of getting himself into trouble, indicating to where Joel is slouching near the back, swigging from a bottle of beer. "If it was you or me in charge, we'd be over like a shot to talk to him," says Steve, with a frown. I turn to talk to Peter Purves, who chats about the process of writing his autobiography, and the dilemma of what to put in and what to leave out. I advise him against following Val's recent example, in which she gave a ghastly interview to the *Mail on Sunday*, confessing to having had an abortion during her time on the programme. Pete agrees, though I'm not sure we are quite on the same wavelength when he remarks, "the thing is, the abortion would have been a great selling point for a book, but it will be old news now."

Anthea Turner produces her copy of the book for me to sign. We reminisce about when she was on *Blue Peter*, and I was the AFM on *Wogan*, how she often used to pop in just to watch Terry at work. "You can learn so much just studying how the greats do it," she used to say. Anthea has had a terrible time of it in recent years, and for a while she was a kind of tame punchbag for the press. But she seems happy enough with her husband, the slightly creepy Grant, who is hovering about in the sidelines.

The photo session takes so long that the evening is almost over; I need to leave, not only because I have had enough but also Mandy and Rosy (wearing her pyjamas) have driven into town to collect me. For the last time, Matt takes charge and acts as bodyguard, steering me past scores of familiar faces, all nodding and waving, and trying to catch my eye, while I collect my things. He leads me out into the freezing night and over to our car, where he hugs Mandy, and says a warm hello and goodbye to her and Rosy. Then, standing on the pavement, he gives me a last loving hug and watches as I climb in and we drive off.

17th October 2008

To King's Cross, to accompany Biddy, Edward and Rosemary Gill to the National Media Museum in Bradford, for the opening of the 50th exhibition. Biddy has us all moved to first class, where we are dismayed to be told that as the boiler has broken, there will be no tea or coffee. "Cranberry juice makes rather a poor substitute," says Biddy, fiercely, to a woebegone guard. "Do you think I might also ask for an apple, *if* that's not too much trouble?"

But the journey speeds by, as this trio are not only very old friends, with all the short hand this brings, they are also excellent raconteurs. One anecdote follows another in quick succession.

At Leeds, we are joined by the very first presenter, Leila Williams, who pre-dates even this trio. She is dressed up to the nines, the picture of old-school elegance, with shiny co-respondent shoes which make her look as if she's about to break out into a tap routine. We all clamber into a people carrier booked to take us to Bradford. Biddy and Leila are soon comparing notes about Clive Parkhurst, the producer who gave Leila her marching orders. "He was a terrible drunk," says Biddy, "who ended his days as the commissionaire of the Shepherd's Bush cinema."

"*Manager*," corrects Rosemary, patiently. "Typical Biddy – she's demoted him!"

We are staying in the Midland Hotel, and here we are met by Tim Levell, doing his best Uriah Heep impression. The museum have told me that the BBC (via Tim) refused their requests to invite any of the other presenters, claiming it would be a breach of data protection to pass on their contact details. Gawd help us.

The museum space is white and gleaming, and full of familiar artefacts. But after my first favourable impressions, I can feel the old professional pulse kicking into gear, and I begin a list of notes and corrections. Photos too small, one wall looks dull, dates are wrong here, that object makes more sense with this one, and so on. There's a large blow-up of a 1970 photo of John Noakes driving a 'car of the future' in Paris. Edward actually directed this film, and when he sees the shot, he groans. "I don't know what they'd say now, but the bloody thing broke down, so I had to have it towed everywhere. We just pretended that it worked!"

We are gathered by the museum staff for a photocall. While we are waiting for the photographer, Edward takes Tim to task over the dropping of any Christian element to the Christmas show. Tim squirms a bit, and suggests that he'd like to make a film in Nazareth and Bethlehem "but not this year, as we don't have the money."

"Singing a carol in the studio wouldn't cost you a penny," says Edward, shortly.

Tim gulps and returns to waxing lyrical about the Nazareth/Bethelem fantasy. "I don't think it's been done before," he smiles brightly, before I correct him and say that, on the contrary, it's been filmed on several occasions.

The subject of gold badges is raised. I mention how surprised I was to hear that Tim gave one to Jack, our mutual deputy, who worked on the programme for just over a couple of years, and hardly under the most illustrious circumstances. "Oh, I thought it was tradition," he says, lightly. I suggest that it might be a good plan to award one to Gill Shearing, the dedicated creator of makes, whom he has just made redundant. Her work has given countless children hours of fun and enjoyment over the years. He flounders some more and I expect that he's heartily relieved that the photographer is now ready for us. A large and sweaty character, the photographer clicks away, ignoring Biddy's request for a more flattering angle. "You, sir, you're a bit tall," he says to me. "Can you crouch down and keep in?"

After the shoot, we are able to return to the hotel and have a break, because the formal opening reception isn't until this evening. Here I'm reunited with Mandy, Rosy and her boyfriend Kieran, who have travelled up to join me and share in the evening. We dress up and head back to the museum where there are drinks and speeches. Rosy, looking round the various displays, comments, "It's like our attic, really, isn't it Dad?"

Biddy and I sit side by side in the shop and sign books for a healthy crowd. It touches me that they consist of all ages, representatives of the audiences who have loved this programme for five decades. One rather lugubrious man and his trio of silent staring children stand in front of us and monopolise the table for some time. The Dad tells us how desperate he is to get a replacement for his lost badge. "I don't know where it can have gone." He has emailed the programme, he says, but hasn't had a response. I notice that one of his offspring is wearing a badge of her own, stuck to her jumper with several layers of Sellotape.

"Is that a security measure?" I ask her, brightly.

"No, pin fell off t'back," she replies, flatly and without blinking.

None of them look like making a move and I can sense that, beside me, Biddy is getting restless. Others in the line are starting to sigh, too. I have a sudden brainwave. "I know just the person who might be able to help you with your badge problem," I tell the Dad, and finally his face lights up. "He's standing over there, talking to the Mayor," and I indicate Tim Levell pressing the flesh in a corner. The man needs no second bidding and off he sets with his monosyllabic family. Some time later, I'm gratified to note that they are still circling Tim and showing no signs of moving on.

Eventually, duty done, we return to the hotel. Up in our room before dinner, my mobile rings. It is Anne Gilchrist calling with "what I think is good news"; OFCOM are not going to pursue their own investigation into the cat-naming saga. There will be no fine, and no further judgements. I suppose that is good news, relatively speaking.

At dinner, I sit between Mandy and Claire, the enthusiastic and hard-working exhibition curator, and just opposite Tim. My old studio management 'split-hearing' (a skill developed by having to listen to talkback in one ear, and whatever is being said on the studio floor with the other) comes in handy as I hear him boasting to the museum director that he'd been instructed to use this party as a way of keeping the "old brigade on message."

But despite the irritation of having to tolerate these and other artless gaffes, I'm glad that I was given the chance to work on this exhibition; it was another way of doing my bit to celebrate a programme which was so significant, not only to me, but to millions of others too.

I eventually returned to the BBC in 2011, to make the feature-length documentary Tales of Television Centre. *This was an enormous privilege, as it gave me the chance to take a long and loving farewell to a building which had meant so much to me (and countless others) over the years. Inevitably, I included some* Blue Peter *moments and the enormous guest list (everyone kept saying yes) included Biddy Baxter, Edward Barnes, Sarah Greene and Matt Baker, the latter lamenting the destruction of the* Blue Peter *garden. It was poignant to be working here during its final few months as a production base; as the weeks went past, more and more sections would close and there were fewer and fewer people to be seen in the labyrinthine corridors. Ironically, one of these diehards turned out to be my former boss, Richard Deverell. No longer the Controller of Children's Programmes (despite his cheerleading for the move, he himself declined to locate to Manchester), he had moved to some kind of role helping to manage the dispersal of the BBC's W12 property portfolio. The first time I saw him, he was visibly aghast. I was on the phone so he was spared the need to talk and beat a hasty retreat. The next time, he must have seen me first, because he was hiding. I only spotted him out of the corner of my eye, his lanky form uncomfortably wedged behind a vending machine just round the corner from the Stage Door lifts.*

POSTSCRIPT

16th July 2016

A perfect English summer day, and a good thing too, because my 'surprise' 50th birthday party is held *al fresco* in the grounds of the Earthworks charity in St Albans. It is a beautiful venue, and everywhere there are thoughtful and imaginative touches; from the balloons tied to the trees on the lane outside, to the room in which tea and cake are served, whose walls are covered in photos from every stage of my life.

God knows how I ever got so old. I suppose everyone feels that way; time accelerates and there you are, the sum of your experiences, with aspects of the inner you untouched and unchanged beneath the visible and invisible scars of so much life.

I've no precise idea of the guest list; my wife Mandy has been in charge of that and all other arrangements. My daughter Rosy has made me a magnificent birthday cake. It is a day to share with those I love the most; family and close friends, and those who blur the lines between the two. Liz Barker appears, smiling (of course), with her husband Toddy and their four beautiful children. Konnie is here, too, looking exceptionally slim and as animated as I always think of her. She is accompanied by her two boys and her husband, Charlie. When Simon and Matt join the party, they are both wearing lederhosen T-shirts, laughing at their own joke, which I naturally appreciate. They've brought their families, too, and Matt's son Luke is soon helping some of the younger kids to have a go on the coconut shy, one of the various entertainments provided for the children. Gethin has driven all the way from Wales to be here, and he's quickly charming everyone in sight. Bridget, the best director we ever had, is looking pretty and vivacious. There's Kez, my one-time series producer, and her partner Ali, who designed *Christmas at the Club Blue Peter*. Audrey Neil, who ran the film team for me, and Duncan Bragg, one of our best film editors, are here with their families, as are cameraman Adrian Homeshaw and director Julian Smith. Melissa Hardinge and Anne Gilchrist have travelled solo, but they, too, are part of the fabric of my life and the many intense experiences we all shared. There is a lot of reminiscing and laughter. Mandy tells me later that all this ceaseless chatter meets with the disapproval of the young daughter of one of our friends, who says of me: "He talks so much. What's wrong with just saying, 'Hello'?"

I give a short speech, and the theme is survival; how reaching such a landmark age inevitably makes you think about those who are no longer here to share your life. Matthew Jackson, my best friend at boarding school, who died suddenly last year. Peter Cochran, the English master without whom I would undoubtedly have messed up my A-levels and perhaps my future. Beverley Ives, my fellow floor assistant and AFM at the BBC, brutally struck down by cancer when she was only in her early 30s. Steve Vickerstaff, the talented young assistant producer on *Blue Peter*, and another who died way before his time. Then those members of your family who you would so dearly love to be able to see again, if only for one last conversation in which to ask all the questions which must remain unanswered in their wake. For me, this means my grandparents and, especially, my witty and always insightful Uncle Geoff. More than anyone, it means my son Rupert, whose absence never diminishes. Our vicar got it just right when he said that Rupert had a short life, but not a small one.

Loss is part of life; and you cannot live in any meaningful way without it. My speech seeks to honour those who have left their mark on my heart, and who live on there and in my memory. It also allows me to thank those I'm lucky still to have in my life, of whom a sizeable number are here today. It occurs to me how many share a deep bond through the extraordinary power of *Blue Peter*, which, for most of us, was never just a job or a programme, but a way of life with its own distinct language, characters, stories and secrets, and one which has given us all a lasting legacy of rich rewards.

ABOUT THE AUTHOR

Richard Marson graduated from the University of Durham in 1987 and joined the BBC, progressing rapidly from floor assistant to producer/director. His credits include *The Movie Game, Disney Adventures* and *Disney Club, The Big Breakfast, Record Breakers* and *Tomorrow's World.* In 1997 he joined *Blue Peter,* where he remained for a decade, with four years as the programme's Editor. During this time, he won a BAFTA, and was nominated for another BAFTA and an RTS award. In 2007, he was Executive Producer of BBC FOUR's *Children's TV On Trial* and in 2009 wrote the script for the BBC's Darwin anniversary Prom. He also produced and directed the 90-minute *Tales of Television Centre* for BBC FOUR.

Since 2013, he has been an Executive Producer at TwoFour, where his credits include *The Holiday Makers* (Sky One), *I Know What You Weighed Last Summer* (BBC THREE), and four series of the CBBC documentary series *Our School.*

He is the author of several books, including six of the famous *Blue Peter* annuals, *Inside Updown: The Story of Upstairs, Downstairs, Blue Peter 50th Anniversary, Totally Tasteless: The Life of John Nathan-Turner* and *Drama and Delight: The Life of Verity Lambert.*

Richard has contributed to many TV and radio programmes, including *Newsround* (BBC ONE), *You Can't Fire Me, I'm Famous* (BBC ONE), *Blue Peter at 50* (BBC TWO), *Newsnight* (BBC TWO), *The Culture Show* (BBC TWO), *Doctor Who Confidential* (BBC THREE), *Archive on Four* (BBC Radio Four), *PM* (BBC Radio Four), *The Media Show* (BBC Radio Four) and *The Richard Bacon Show* (BBC Five Live).

FROM THE SAME AUTHOR

DRAMA AND DELIGHT

THE LIFE AND LEGACY OF VERITY LAMBERT

by Richard Marson

For five decades, the name Verity Lambert appeared on the end credits of many of Britain's most celebrated and talked about television dramas. She was the very first producer of **Doctor Who**, which she nurtured through its formative years at a time when there were few women in positions of power in the television industry. Later, she worked within the troubled British film business and became a pioneering independent producer, founding her own highly-successful company, Cinema Verity.

Within her profession, she was hugely respected as an intensely driven, sometimes formidable but always stylish exponent of her craft, with the stamina and ability to combine quantity with quality. Many of her productions have had a lasting cultural and emotional impact on their audiences and continue to be enjoyed to this day.

But who was the woman behind all these television triumphs and what was the price she paid to achieve them?

Combining months of painstaking research and interviews with many of Lambert's closest friends and colleagues, *Drama and Delight* will capture the energy and spirit of this remarkable woman and explore her phenomenal and lasting legacy.

ISBN 978-1-908630-33-9

FROM THE SAME AUTHOR

TOTALLY TASTELESS

THE LIFE OF JOHN NATHAN-TURNER

by Richard Marson

Totally Tasteless: The Life of John Nathan-Turner tells the story of the most controversial figure in the history of **Doctor Who**.

For more than a decade, John Nathan-Turner, or 'JN-T' as he was often known, was in charge of every major artistic and practical decision affecting the world's longest-running science fiction programme.

Richard Marson brings his dramatic, farcical, sometimes scandalous, often moving story to life with the benefit of his own inside knowledge and the fruits of over 100 revealing interviews with key friends and colleagues, those John loved to those from whom he became estranged. The author has also had access to all of Nathan-Turner's surviving archive of paperwork and photos, many of which appear here for the very first time.

This new edition includes a new chapter covering the period from the book's inception to its release and beyond, as well as a number of previously unpublished photographs.

ISBN 978-1-908630-65-0

publishing